Lucretia

Webster's French
Thesaurus Edition

for ESL, EFL, ELP, TOEFL®, TOEIC®, and AP® Test Preparation

Edward Bulwer-Lytton

TOEFL®, TOEIC®, AP® and Advanced Placement® are trademarks of the Educational Testing Service which has neither reviewed nor endorsed this book. All rights reserved.

ICON CLASSICS

Published by ICON Group International, Inc.
7404 Trade Street
San Diego, CA 92121 USA

www.icongrouponline.com

Lucretia: Webster's French Thesaurus Edition for ESL, EFL, ELP, TOFEL®, TOEIC®, and AP®
Test Preparation

This edition published by ICON Classics in 2008
Printed in the United States of America.

Copyright ©2008 by ICON Group International, Inc.
Edited by Philip M. Parker, Ph.D. (INSEAD); Copyright ©2008, all rights reserved.

All rights reserved. This book is protected by copyright. No part of it may be reproduced, stored in a retrieval system, or transmitted in any form or by any means, electronic, mechanical, photocopying, recording, or otherwise, without written permission from the publisher.

Copying our publications in whole or in part, for whatever reason, is a violation of copyright laws and can lead to penalties and fines. Should you want to copy tables, graphs, or other materials, please contact us to request permission (E-mail: orders@icongroupbooks.com). ICON Group often grants permission for very limited reproduction of our publications for internal use, press releases, and academic research. Such reproduction requires confirmed permission from ICON Group International, Inc.

TOEFL®, TOEIC®, AP® and Advanced Placement® are trademarks of the Educational Testing Service which has neither reviewed nor endorsed this book. All rights reserved.

ISBN 0-497-96357-4

Contents

PREFACE FROM THE EDITOR 1

PREFACE TO THE EDITION OF 1853 2

PREFACE TO THE FIRST EDITION 4

PART THE FIRST. 8
    PROLOGUE TO PART THE FIRST. 9
    CHAPTER I A FAMILY GROUP 15
    CHAPTER II LUCRETIA 49
    CHAPTER III CONFERENCES 77
    CHAPTER IV GUY'S OAK 92
    CHAPTER V HOUSEHOLD TREASON 104
    CHAPTER VI THE WILL 114
    CHAPTER VII THE ENGAGEMENT 122
    CHAPTER VIII THE DISCOVERY 143
    CHAPTER IX A SOUL WITHOUT HOPE 151
    CHAPTER X 160
    EPILOGUE TO PART THE FIRST. 170

PART THE SECOND. 214
    PROLOGUE TO PART THE SECOND. 215
    CHAPTER I THE CORONATION 229
    CHAPTER II LOVE AT FIRST SIGHT 245
    CHAPTER III 259
    CHAPTER IV JOHN ARDWORTH 266
    CHAPTER V THE WEAVERS AND THE WOOF 287
    CHAPTER VI THE LAWYER AND THE BODY-SNATCHER 293
    CHAPTER VII THE RAPE OF THE MATTRESS 305
    CHAPTER VIII PERCIVAL VISITS LUCRETIA 313
    CHAPTER IX THE ROSE BENEATH THE UPAS 319
    CHAPTER X THE RATTLE OF THE SNAKE 331

CHAPTER XI LOVE AND INNOCENCE	337
CHAPTER XII SUDDEN CELEBRITY AND PATIENT HOPE	342
CHAPTER XIII THE LOSS OF THE CROSSING	354
CHAPTER XIV NEWS FROM GRABMAN	360
CHAPTER XV VARIETIES	367
CHAPTER XVI THE INVITATION TO LAUGHTON	379
CHAPTER XVII THE WAKING OF THE SERPENT	386
CHAPTER XVIII RETROSPECT	393
CHAPTER XIX MR. GRABMAN'S ADVENTURES	413
CHAPTER XX MORE OF MRS. JOPLIN	421
CHAPTER XXI BECK'S DISCOVERY	426
CHAPTER XXII THE TAPESTRY CHAMBER	436
CHAPTER XXIII THE SHADES ON THE DIAL	440
CHAPTER XXIV	454
CHAPTER XXV THE MESSENGER SPEEDS	457
CHAPTER XXVI THE SPY FLIES	462
CHAPTER XXVII LUCRETIA REGAINS HER SON	470
CHAPTER XXVIII THE LOTS VANISH WITHIN THE URN	475
EPILOGUE TO PART THE SECOND.	479
GLOSSARY	490

PREFACE FROM THE EDITOR

Webster's paperbacks take advantage of the fact that classics are frequently assigned readings in English courses. By using a running English-to-French thesaurus at the bottom of each page, this edition of *Lucretia* by Edward Bulwer-Lytton was edited for three audiences. The first includes French-speaking students enrolled in an English Language Program (ELP), an English as a Foreign Language (EFL) program, an English as a Second Language Program (ESL), or in a TOEFL® or TOEIC® preparation program. The second audience includes English-speaking students enrolled in bilingual education programs or French speakers enrolled in English-speaking schools. The third audience consists of students who are actively building their vocabularies in French in order to take foreign service, translation certification, Advanced Placement® (AP®) or similar examinations.

Webster's edition of this classic is organized to expose the reader to a maximum number of difficult and potentially ambiguous English words. Rare or idiosyncratic words and expressions are given lower priority compared to "difficult, yet commonly used" words. Rather than supply a single translation, many words are translated for a variety of meanings in French, allowing readers to better grasp the ambiguity of English, and avoid them using the notes as a pure translation crutch. Having the reader decipher a word's meaning within context serves to improve vocabulary retention and understanding. Each page covers words not already highlighted on previous pages. If a difficult word is not translated on a page, chances are that it has been translated on a previous page. A more complete glossary of translations is supplied at the end of the book; translations are extracted from Webster's Online Dictionary.

Definitions of remaining terms as well as translations can be found at www.websters-online-dictionary.org. Please send suggestions to websters@icongroupbooks.com

The Editor
Webster's Online Dictionary
www.websters-online-dictionary.org

PREFACE TO THE EDITION OF 1853

"Lucretia; or, The Children of Night," was begun **simultaneously** with "The Caxtons: a Family Picture." The two fictions were intended as **pendants**; both serving, amongst other **collateral** aims and objects, to show the influence of home education, of early **circumstance** and example, upon after character and conduct. "Lucretia" was completed and published before "The Caxtons." The moral design of the first was **misunderstood** and **assailed**; that of the last was generally **acknowledged** and approved: the moral design in both was nevertheless precisely the same. But in one it was sought through the darker side of human nature; in the other through the more **sunny** and **cheerful**: one shows the **evil**, the other the **salutary** influences, of early circumstance and training. Necessarily, therefore, the first resorts to the **tragic** elements of **awe** and distress,—the second to the **comic** elements of humour and **agreeable emotion**. These differences serve to explain the different reception that **awaited** the two, and may teach us how little the real **conception** of an author is known, and how little it is cared for; we judge, not by the purpose he **conceives**, but **according** as the impressions he effects are **pleasurable** or painful. But while I cannot **acquiesce** in much of the **hostile** criticism this fiction produced at its first appearance, I readily allow that as a mere question of art the story might have been improved in itself, and **rendered** more acceptable to the reader, by **diminishing** the **gloom** of the **catastrophe**. In this edition I have endeavoured to do so; and

French

according: selon, s'accorder.
acknowledged: reconnus.
acquiesce: se résigner, acquiescer.
agreeable: agréable, aimable.
assailed: assaillis.
awaited: attendîmes.
awe: crainte.
catastrophe: catastrophe, désastre.
cheerful: gai, joyeux.
circumstance: circonstance, état de fait.
collateral: collatéral, nantissement, garantie.
comic: comique, drôle.
conceives: conçoit.
conception: conception, élaboration.
diminishing: diminuant, décroissant.
emotion: émotion, attendrissement, sentiment.
evil: mal, mauvais.
gloom: mélancolie, obscurité.
hostile: ennemi, hostile.
misunderstood: mal compris, incompris.
pendant: pendentif, pantoire.
pleasurable: très agréable.
rendered: rendis, plâtras, crépi.
salutary: salutaire.
simultaneously: de façon simultanée, de manière simultanée.
sunny: ensoleillé, exposé au soleil.
tragic: tragique, dramatique.

the victim whose **fate** in the former cast of the work most **revolted** the reader, as a **violation** of the **trite** but **amiable** law of Poetical Justice, is **saved** from the hands of the Children of Night. Perhaps, whatever the faults of this work, it equals most of its **companions** in the sustainment of interest, and in that **coincidence** between the **gradual** development of **motive** or **passion**, and the sequences of external events **constituting plot**, which mainly **distinguish** the physical awe of **tragedy** from the **coarse horrors** of **melodrama**. I trust at least that I shall now find few readers who will not **readily acknowledge** that the **delineation** of crime has only been employed for the **grave** and impressive purpose which brings it within the due **province** of the poet, — as an element of **terror** and a warning to the heart.

London, December 7.

French

acknowledge: reconnaître, croire, avouer, confesser.
amiable: aimable.
coarse: grossier, vulgaire, rude, rustique, brut.
coincidence: coïncidence.
companion: compagnon, camarade, accompagnateur.
constituting: constituant.
delineation: tracé, délimitation, profil.
distinguish: distinguer, dégager, identifier, reconnaître.
fate: sort, destinée, fatalité, fortune.
gradual: graduel, progressif.
grave: tombe, grave, sérieux.
horror: horreur, aversion, dégoût, répulsion, abomination, atrocité.
melodrama: mélodrame.
motive: motif, lieu, occasion, mobile.
passion: passion, ardeur.
plot: intrigue, parcelle, tracer, terrain, conspiration, comploter, position visualisée.
province: province, domaine, région.
readily: aisément, de façon prête, de manière prête, facilement.
revolted: révolté.
saved: épargna, sauvé, économisâmes, enregistrèrent.
terror: terreur, effroi.
tragedy: tragédie.
trite: banal.
violation: violation, infraction.

PREFACE TO THE FIRST EDITION

It is somewhere about four years since I appeared before the public as the writer of a fiction, which I then intimated would probably be my last; but bad habits are stronger than good intentions. When Fabricio, in his hospital, **resolved** upon **abjuring** the **vocation** of the Poet, he was, in truth, **recommencing** his desperate career by a **Farewell** to the Muses,—I need not apply the **allusion**.

I must own, however, that there had long been a desire in my mind to trace, in some work or other, the strange and secret ways through which that Arch-ruler of Civilization, **familiarly** called "Money," **insinuates** itself into our thoughts and motives, our hearts and actions; **affecting** those who undervalue as those who **overestimate** its importance; **ruining** virtues in the **spendthrift** no less than **engendering** vices in the **miser**. But when I half **implied** my farewell to the character of a **novelist**, I had **imagined** that this conception might be best worked out upon the stage. After some **unpublished** and **imperfect** attempts towards so **realizing** my design, I found either that the subject was too wide for the limits of the Drama, or that I wanted that **faculty** of concentration which alone enables the **dramatist** to **compress multiform** varieties into a very limited compass. With this design, I **desired** to **unite** some exhibition of what seems to me a principal **vice** in the hot and emulous **chase** for **happiness** or **fame**, fortune or knowledge, which

---

French

abjuring: abjurant.
affecting: affectant, attendrissant, émouvant, influant.
allusion: allusion.
chase: chasser, pourchasser, pousser, faire avancer.
compress: comprimer, condenser.
desired: désiré.
dramatist: dramaturge.
engendering: engendrant.
faculty: faculté, corps professoral.
fame: renommée, gloire, réputation, célébrité.
familiarly: familièrement, de façon familière, de manière familière.
farewell: adieu.
happiness: bonheur, félicité.
imagined: imagina.
imperfect: imparfait.
implied: impliquâtes, tacite.
insinuates: insinue.
miser: avare, ladre.
multiform: multiforme.
novelist: romancier, nouvelliste.
overestimate: surestimer, majorer.
realizing: réalisant.
recommencing: recommençant.
resolved: résolu.
ruining: ruinant.
spendthrift: dépensier, gaspilleur, prodigue.
unite: unir, unissez, joindre, accoupler, apparier, unifier.
unpublished: inédit.
vice: vice, étau, vertu.
vocation: vocation.

is almost **synonymous** with the **cant** phrase of "the March of Intellect," in that crisis of society to which we have arrived. The vice I **allude** to is Impatience. That eager desire to press forward, not so much to **conquer** obstacles as to **elude** them; that **gambling** with the **solemn** destinies of life, seeking ever to set success upon the chance of a die; that **hastening** from the wish conceived to the end accomplished; that **thirst** after quick returns to **ingenious toil**, and **breathless** spurrings along short cuts to the goal, which we see everywhere around us, from the Mechanics' Institute to the Stock Market,—beginning in education with the **primers** of **infancy**, deluging us with "Philosophies for the Million" and "Sciences made Easy;" **characterizing** the books of our writers, the speeches of our statesmen, no less than the dealings of our speculators,—seem, I confess, to me to constitute a very **diseased** and very general symptom of the times. I hold that the greatest friend to man is labour; that knowledge without toil, if possible, were **worthless**; that toil in pursuit of knowledge is the best knowledge we can **attain**; that the continuous effort for fame is nobler than fame itself; that it is not wealth suddenly acquired which is **deserving** of **homage**, but the virtues which a man exercises in the slow pursuit of wealth,—the abilities so called forth, the self-denials so imposed; in a word, that Labour and Patience are the true **schoolmasters** on earth. While occupied with these ideas and this belief, whether right or wrong, and slowly convinced that it was only in that **species** of composition with which I was most familiar that I could work out some portion of the plan that I began to contemplate, I became **acquainted** with the histories of two criminals existing in our own age,—so remarkable, whether from the extent and darkness of the guilt committed, whether from the **glittering accomplishments** and lively temper of the one, the profound knowledge and intellectual capacities of the other, that the examination and analysis of characters so **perverted** became a study full of intense, if gloomy, interest.

In these persons there appear to have been as few **redeemable** points as can be found in Human Nature, so far as such points may be traced in the kindly instincts and generous passions which do sometimes accompany the

French

accomplishment: accomplissement, réalisation, ouvrage.
acquainted: renseignai, informé.
allude: faire allusion, insinuer.
attain: atteindre, parvenir, acquérir, remporter, aboutir.
breathless: essoufflé, hors d'haleine, haletant.
cant: incliner, équarri, moulure biseautée, flache, canter, biseauter, tors, bille dédossée, argot, dévers.
characterizing: caractérisant.
conquer: conquérir, vaincre.
deserving: méritant.
diseased: malade.
elude: éluder, éviter, déjouent.
gambling: jeu de hasard, pari.
glittering: scintillant, éclat.
hastening: hâtant, s'empressant, accourant, empressant.
homage: hommage.
infancy: enfance, minorité, petite enfance.
ingenious: ingénieux, astucieux.
perverted: pervers.
primer: amorce, apprêt, couche primaire.
redeemable: rachetable, remboursable, amortissable.
schoolmaster: instituteur, maître.
solemn: solennel, sérieux, grave.
specie: monnaie, numéraire.
synonymous: synonyme.
thirst: soif, avoir soif.
toil: labeur, travailler dur.
worthless: nul, sans valeur.

perpetration of great crimes, and, without **excusing** the individual, **vindicate** the species. Yet, on the other hand, their **sanguinary wickedness** was not the dull **ferocity** of **brutes**; it was accompanied with instruction and culture,—nay, it seemed to me, on studying their lives and **pondering** over their own letters, that through their cultivation itself we could arrive at the secret of the ruthless and **atrocious** pre-eminence in evil these Children of Night had attained; that here the monster vanished into the mortal, and the phenomena that seemed **aberrations** from Nature were explained.

I could not resist the temptation of reducing to a tale the materials which had so **engrossed** my interest and tasked my inquiries. And in this attempt, various incidental opportunities have occurred, if not of completely carrying out, still of incidentally **illustrating**, my earlier design,—of showing the influence of Mammon upon our most secret selves, of **reproving** the impatience which is **engendered** by a civilization that, with much of the good, brings all the evils of competition, and of **tracing** throughout, all the influences of early household life upon our subsequent conduct and career. In such incidental bearings the moral may doubtless be more obvious than in the delineation of the darker and rarer crime which forms the **staple** of my narrative. For in extraordinary guilt we are slow to recognize ordinary warnings,—we say to the peaceful conscience, "This concerns thee not!" whereas at each instance of familiar fault and commonplace error we own a direct and sensible **admonition**. Yet in the portraiture of gigantic crime, poets have rightly found their sphere and fulfilled their destiny of teachers. Those terrible truths which **appall** us in the guilt of Macbeth or the villany of Iago, have their moral uses not less than the popular **infirmities** of Tom Jones, or the every-day **hypocrisy** of Blifil. Incredible as it may seem, the crimes **herein** related took place within the last seventeen years. There has been no **exaggeration** as to their extent, no great departure from their details; the means employed, even that which seems most far-fetched,—the instrument of the **poisoned** ring,—have their foundation in literal facts. Nor have I much altered the social position of the criminals, nor in the least **overrated** their attainments and intelligence. In those more **salient** essentials

---

French

aberration: aberration, erreur.
admonition: sommation, avertissement, admonestation, observation, recommandation, remontrance.
appall: consterner, épouvanter.
atrocious: atroce, horrible, affreux.
brute: brute, ébruter, gros projecteur, sauvage.
engendered: engendras.
engrossed: grossoyâmes.
exaggeration: exagération.
excusing: excusant.
ferocity: férocité.
herein: en ceci.
hypocrisy: hypocrisie.
illustrating: illustrant.
infirmity: infirmité.
overrated: surtaxèrent, surfis, surévaluas.
perpetration: perpétration.
poisoned: empoisonné, arseniqué.
pondering: réfléchissant, considérant, pesant.
reproving: réprimandant, reprochant, grondant, sermonnant.
salient: saillant.
sanguinary: sanguinaire.
staple: agrafe, parenthèse, crampon, fibre, cavalier de jonction.
tracing: recherche, calquage, tracé.
vindicate: justifier, défendre.
wickedness: méchanceté, atrocité, cruauté.

which will most, perhaps, **provoke** the Reader's **incredulous wonder**, I **narrate** a history, not **invent** a **fiction** [These criminals were not, however, in actual life, as in the **novel**, **intimates** and **accomplices**. Their crimes were of similar character, effected by similar agencies, and **committed** at dates which **embrace** their several careers of **guilt** within the same period; but I have no authority to suppose that the one was known to the other.]. All that **Romance** which our own time **affords** is not more the romance than the **philosophy** of the time. Tragedy never **quits** the world,—it **surrounds** us **everywhere**. We have but to look, **wakeful** and **vigilant**, **abroad**, and from the age of Pelops to that of Borgia, the same crimes, though under different garbs, will **stalk** on our paths. Each age **comprehends** in itself **specimens** of every **virtue** and every vice which has ever **inspired** our love or **mowed** our horror.

London, November 1, 1846.

French

abroad: à l'étranger, dehors.
accomplice: complice.
affords: produit.
committed: commîtes, engagé.
comprehend: comprendre.
embrace: embrasser, prendre dans les bras, étreinte.
everywhere: partout, en tous lieux.
fiction: fiction, œuvre d'imagination.
guilt: culpabilité.
incredulous: incrédule.
inspired: inspirâtes, s'enthousiasmé, vous enthousiasmâtes, nous enthousiasmâmes, m'enthousiasmai, t'enthousiasmas.
intimate: intime, pulsion intime.
invent: inventer.
mowed: fauchas, tondîtes.
narrate: raconter, conter.
novel: roman, nouveau.
philosophy: philosophie.
provoke: provoquer, irriter, agacer.
quits: quitte.
romance: romance, fabuler.
specimen: spécimen, échantillon.
stalk: tige, queue, chaume, faire les cent pas, rafle, pédoncule.
surround: entourer, encercler.
vigilant: vigilant, diligent.
virtue: vertu.
wakeful: éveillé.
wonder: s'étonner, merveille, miracle, se demander.

PART THE FIRST.

PROLOGUE TO PART THE FIRST.

In an apartment at Paris, one morning during the Reign of Terror, a man, whose age might be somewhat under thirty, sat before a table covered with papers, arranged and labelled with the **methodical** precision of a mind fond of order and **habituated** to business. Behind him rose a tall **bookcase surmounted** with a **bust** of Robespierre, and the **shelves** were filled chiefly with works of a scientific character, amongst which the greater number were on chemistry and medicine. There were to be seen also many rare books on **alchemy**, the great Italian historians, some English philosophical **treatises**, and a few manuscripts in Arabic. The absence from this collection of the **stormy** literature of the day seemed to **denote** that the owner was a quiet student, living apart from the **strife** and passions of the Revolution. This **supposition** was, however, **disproved** by certain papers on the table, which were formally and **laconically** labelled "Reports on Lyons," and by packets of letters in the **handwritings** of Robespierre and Couthon. At one of the windows a young boy was **earnestly** engaged in some occupation which appeared to **excite** the curiosity of the person just described; for this last, after examining the child's movements for a few moments with a silent scrutiny that **betrayed** but little of the half-complacent, half-melancholy affection with which busy man is **apt** to regard childhood, rose **noiselessly** from his seat, approached the boy, and looked over his shoulder unobserved.

French

alchemy: alchimie.
apt: doué, juste, apte, enclin, intelligent.
betrayed: trahîtes.
bookcase: bibliothèque.
bust: buste.
denote: indiquer, dénoter.
disproved: réfuta.
earnestly: sérieusement, de façon sérieuse, de manière sérieuse.
excite: exciter, irriter, agacer, hérisser.
habituated: te 'habituas, vous 'habituâtes, se 'habituèrent, nous 'habituâmes, me 'habituai.
handwriting: écriture, manuscrit.
laconically: de façon laconique, de manière laconique, laconiquement.
methodical: méthodique, systématique.
noiselessly: de façon silencieuse, de manière silencieuse, silencieusement.
shelve: enterrer, garnissez, ajourner.
stormy: orageux, tempétueux, démonté, houleux.
strife: conflit.
supposition: hypothèse, supposition.
surmounted: surmontai.
treatise: traité.

Lucretia

In a **crevice** of the wood by the window, a huge black spider had formed his web; the child had just discovered another spider, and placed it in the **meshes**: he was watching the result of his operations. The **intrusive** spider stood motionless in the midst of the web, as if fascinated. The **rightful possessor** was also **quiescent**; but a very fine ear might have caught a low, **humming** sound, which probably augured no **hospitable** intentions to the **invader**. Anon, the stranger insect seemed suddenly to awake from its **amaze**; it **evinced** alarm, and turned to fly; the huge spider darted forward; the boy uttered a **chuckle** of delight. The man's pale lip curled into a sinister sneer, and he **glided** back to his seat. There, leaning his face on his hand, he continued to contemplate the child. That child might have furnished to an artist a fitting subject for fair and **blooming** infancy. His light hair, **tinged** deeply, it is true, with red, hung in **sleek** and glittering abundance down his neck and shoulders. His features, seen in profile, were delicately and almost **femininely** proportioned; health glowed on his cheek, and his form, slight though it was, gave promise of **singular** activity and vigour. His dress was fantastic, and betrayed the taste of some **fondly** foolish mother; but the fine linen, **trimmed** with lace, was rumpled and stained, the velvet jacket unbrushed, the shoes **soiled** with dust,—slight tokens these of neglect, but serving to show that the foolish **fondness** which had invented the dress had not of late presided over the toilet.

"Child," said the man, first in French; and observing that the boy heeded him not,—"child," he repeated in English, which he spoke well, though with a foreign accent, "child!"

The boy turned quickly.

"Has the great spider **devoured** the small one?"

"No, sir," said the boy, colouring; "the small one has had the best of it."

The tone and heightened **complexion** of the child seemed to give meaning to his words,—at least, so the man thought, for a slight frown passed over his high, thoughtful brow.

French

amaze: étonner, stupéfier, abasourdis.
blooming: en fleur.
chuckle: glousser.
complexion: teint, complexion.
crevice: crevasse, fente, fissure.
devoured: dévoré, engloutîmes.
evinced: montré.
femininely: de façon féminine, de manière féminine.
fondly: de manière tendre, de façon tendre, tendrement.

fondness: affection, penchant, prédilection, tendresse.
glided: glissa.
hospitable: hospitalier.
humming: bourdonnement, vrombissement.
intrusive: intrusif, importun.
invader: envahisseur.
mesh: maille, engrener, treillis, s'engrener, prendre au filet, mesh, grillage.
possessor: propriétaire, possesseur,

détenteur.
quiescent: quiescent, tranquille, passif, calme, repos.
rightful: légitime.
singular: singulier.
sleek: lisse, onctueux, filandre, film d'huile, ligne de ferrasse.
sneer: ricaner, tourner en ridicule, remarque moqueuse.
soiled: sale, souillé, sali.
tinged: teinté.
trimmed: taillé, paré, rogné.

"Spiders, then," he said, after a short pause, "are different from men; with us, the small do not get the better of the great. **Hum**! do you still miss your mother?"

"Oh, yes!" and the boy advanced **eagerly** to the table.

"Well, you will see her once again."

"When?"

The man looked towards a clock on the mantelpiece,—"Before that clock strikes. Now, go back to your spiders." The child looked **irresolute** and **disinclined** to **obey**; but a **stern** and terrible expression gathered slowly over the man's face, and the boy, growing pale as he remarked it, **crept** back to the window.

The father—for such was the relation the owner of the room bore to the child—drew paper and **ink** towards him, and wrote for some minutes rapidly. Then starting up, he glanced at the clock, took his hat and **cloak**, which lay on a chair beside, drew up the collar of the **mantle** till it almost **concealed** his **countenance**, and said, "Now, boy, come with me; I have promised to show you an execution: I am going to keep my promise. Come!"

The boy **clapped** his hands with joy; and you might see then, child as he was, that those fair features were capable of a cruel and **ferocious** expression. The character of the whole face changed. He caught up his gay cap and **plume**, and followed his father into the streets.

Silently the two took their way towards the Barriere du Trone. At a distance they saw the crowd growing thick and **dense** as **throng** after throng **hurried** past them, and the dreadful **guillotine** rose high in the light blue air. As they came into the **skirts** of the **mob**, the father, for the first time, took his child's hand. "I must get you a good place for the show," he said, with a quiet smile.

There was something in the grave, **staid**, **courteous**, yet **haughty** bearing of the man that made the crowd give way as he passed. They got near the

---

French

clapped: claqua.
cloak: manteau.
concealed: cachas, dissimulèrent.
countenance: encourager, figure, mine, visage.
courteous: courtois, poli.
crept: rampé, cheminâmes, traîna, glissé.
dense: dense, compact.
disinclined: peu disposé.
eagerly: de façon avide, de manière avide.
ferocious: féroce, sauvage.
guillotine: guillotine, massicot.
haughty: hautain, arrogant.
hum: bourdonner, ronronner, ronflement, chantonner.
hurried: hâtif, pressé, dépêché.
ink: encre, couleur à semelles, pâte, tracé, colorer.
irresolute: indécis, hésitant, irrésolu.
mantle: manteau, pèlerine.
mob: foule, assaillir, bande.
obey: obéir, obtempérons.
plume: panache, traînée, souffle, plumet, faisceau de fumée, gaz d'échappement.
silently: silencieusement, de façon silencieuse, de manière silencieuse.
skirt: jupe, embase de blindage.
staid: sérieux, sobre.
stern: poupe, arrière, sévère.
throng: affluer, cohue, foule, multitude, se presser.

dismal scene, and obtained entrance into a **wagon** already crowded with eager **spectators**.

And now they heard at a distance the harsh and **lumbering** roll of the **tumbril** that bore the victims, and the **tramp** of the horses which **guarded** the procession of death. The boy's whole attention was absorbed in expectation of the **spectacle**, and his ear was perhaps less **accustomed** to French, though born and reared in France, than to the language of his mother's lips,—and she was English; thus he did not hear or **heed** certain observations of the **bystanders**, which made his father's pale cheek grow paler.

"What is the batch to-day?" quoth a butcher in the wagon. "**Scarce** worth the baking,—only two; but one, they say, is an aristocrat,—a ci-devant **marquis**," answered a **carpenter**. "Ah, a marquis! Bon! And the other?"

"Only a **dancer**, but a pretty one, it is true; I could pity her, but she is English." And as he pronounced the last word, with a tone of **inexpressible** contempt, the butcher **spat**, as if in **nausea**.

"Mort diable! a **spy** of Pitt's, no doubt. What did they discover?"

A man, better dressed than the rest, turned round with a smile, and answered: "Nothing worse than a lover, I believe; but that lover was a proscrit. The ci-devant marquis was caught **disguised** in her apartment. She betrayed for him a good, easy friend of the people who had long loved her, and revenge is sweet."

The man whom we have accompanied, nervously twitched up the collar of his cloak, and his **compressed** lips told that he felt the **anguish** of the laugh that circled round him.

"They are coming! There they are!" cried the boy, in **ecstatic** excitement.

"That's the way to bring up citizens," said the butcher, patting the child's shoulder, and opening a still better view for him at the edge of the wagon.

The crowd now abruptly gave way. The tumbril was in sight. A man, young and handsome, standing **erect** and with folded arms in the fatal vehicle, looked along the mob with an eye of **careless scorn**. Though he wore

---

French

accustomed: accoutumé, se 'habitua, nous 'habituâmes, me 'habituai, te 'habituas, vous 'habituâtes, habituel.
anguish: angoisse.
bystander: spectateur.
careless: négligent, distrait, étourdi, insouciant.
carpenter: charpentier, menuisier.
compressed: comprimé.
dancer: danseur.
disguised: déguisé.

dismal: sombre, triste, morne, banal, désagréable, misérable, repoussant, pénible, pauvre, maussade, malheureux.
ecstatic: extatique.
erect: fonder, ériger, droit, bâtir, construire, édifier.
guarded: protégé, gardé.
heed: attention.
inexpressible: inexprimable, indicible.
lumbering: lourd.

marquis: marquis.
nausea: nausée, écœurement, la nausée.
scarce: insuffisant, rare.
scorn: dédain, mépris.
spat: naissain.
spectacle: spectacle.
spectator: spectateur.
spy: espion, épier.
tramp: clochard, tramp, vagabond.
tumbril: tombereau.
wagon: chariot, wagon.

CHAPTER I

A FAMILY GROUP

One July evening, at the **commencement** of the present century, several persons were somewhat **picturesquely** grouped along an old-fashioned terrace which skirted the garden-side of a manor-house that had considerable **pretensions** to **baronial** dignity. The architecture was of the most **enriched** and elaborate style belonging to the reign of James the First: the porch, opening on the terrace, with its **mullion** window above, was **encased** with **pilasters** and reliefs at once **ornamental** and massive; and the large square tower in which it was placed was surmounted by a stone **falcon**, whose **talons** griped fiercely a scutcheon **blazoned** with the five-pointed stars which heralds recognize as the arms of St. John. On either side this tower extended long wings, the dark **brickwork** of which was relieved with noble stone **casements** and carved **pediments**; the high roof was partially concealed by a **balustrade perforated** not **inelegantly** into **arabesque** designs; and what architects call "the sky line" was broken with imposing effect by tall chimney-shafts of various form and fashion. These wings **terminated** in **angular** towers similar to the centre, though kept duly subordinate to it both in size and decoration, and **crowned** with stone **cupolas**. A low balustrade, of later date than that which **adorned** the roof,

---

French

adorned: ornas, ornâmes, ornèrent, orné, para, parèrent, paré, parâtes.
angular: anguleux, osseux.
arabesque: arabesque.
balustrade: balustrade, rampe, accoudoir.
baronial: baronnial.
blazoned: blasonna.
brickwork: briquetage, maçonnerie.
casement: croisée, châssis, vantail.
commencement: début, commencement, inauguration.
crowned: couronné.
cupola: coupole, cubilot, dôme.
encased: enferma, emboîté, enrobé.
enriched: enrichit, étoffé.
falcon: faucon.
inelegantly: de manière inélégante, de façon inélégante.
mullion: meneau, montant central, cloison.
ornamental: décoratif, ornemental.
pediment: fronton, pédiment, glacis d'ablation.
perforated: perforâtes, poinçonnai, dentela, trouèrent, piqué.
picturesquely: de manière pittoresque, pittoresquement, de façon pittoresque.
pilaster: pilastre.
pretension: prétention, tension préalable.
talon: talon, griffe, serre.
terminated: terminèrent, résilias.

relieved by vases and statues, **bordered** the terrace, from which a double flight of steps descended to a smooth lawn, **intersected** by broad gravel-walks, shadowed by vast and stately **cedars**, and gently and gradually **mingling** with the wilder scenery of the park, from which it was only divided by a ha-ha.

Upon the terrace, and under cover of a temporary **awning**, sat the owner, Sir Miles St. John of Laughton, a **comely** old man, dressed with faithful precision to the costume which he had been taught to consider appropriate to his rank of gentleman, and which was not yet wholly obsolete and eccentric. His hair, still thick and **luxuriant**, was carefully **powdered**, and collected into a club behind; his nether man **attired** in gray **breeches** and pearl-coloured silk stockings; his vest of silk, opening wide at the breast, and showing a **profusion** of **frill**, slightly sprinkled with the pulvilio of his favourite Martinique; his three-cornered hat, placed on a stool at his side, with a gold-headed crutch-cane (hat made rather to be carried in the hand than worn on the head), the diamond in his shirt-breast, the diamond on his finger, the **ruffles** at his wrist,—all **bespoke** the gallant who had chatted with Lord Chesterfield and supped with Mrs. Clive. On a table before him were placed two or three **decanters** of wine, the fruits of the season, an **enamelled** snuff-box in which was set the portrait of a female (perhaps the Chloe or Phyllis of his early love-ditties), a **lighted taper**, a small china jar containing tobacco, and three or four pipes of homely clay,—for cherry-sticks and meerschaums were not then in fashion, and Sir Miles St. John, once a gay and sparkling **beau**, now a popular country gentleman, great at county meetings and sheep-shearing festivals, had taken to smoking, as in harmony with his **bucolic** transformation. An old **setter** lay **dozing** at his feet; a small spaniel—old, too—was **sauntering lazily** in the immediate neighbourhood, looking gravely out for such stray bits of biscuit as had been thrown forth to provoke him to exercise, and which hitherto had escaped his attention. Half seated, half **reclined** on the balustrade, apart from the **baronet**, but within reach of his conversation, **lolled** a man in the prime of life, with an air of unmistakable and sovereign elegance and distinction. Mr. Vernon was a

---

French

attired: vêtis.
awning: tente, auvent, marquise, bâche.
baronet: baronnet.
beau: dandy, galant.
bespoke: fait sur mesure.
bordered: bordé.
breech: culasse, fesse.
bucolic: bucolique, pastoral.
cedar: cèdre.
comely: beau, avenant.
decanter: carafe, décanteuse, bassin décanteur.
dozing: sommeillant.
enamelled: émaillé.
frill: volant, froncer.
intersected: entrecoupâtes, intersecta, croisas.
lazily: de façon paresseuse, de manière paresseuse, paresseusement.
lighted: allumé, éclairé, enflammé.
lolled: pendîmes.
luxuriant: luxuriant, exubérant.
mingling: mêlant, mélangeant.
powdered: pulvérisé.
profusion: profusion.
reclined: reposé.
ruffle: hérisser, troubler, rider, ébouriffer, ruche.
sauntering: flânant.
setter: piqueteur, setter, sertisseur, incubateur, gravure de cambrage, support d'enfournement, passeur.
taper: cône, effiler, dépouille, conicité.

guest from London; and the London man,—the man of clubs and dinners and **routs**, of noon loungings through Bond Street, and nights spent with the Prince of Wales,—seemed stamped not more upon the careful **carelessness** of his dress, and upon the worn expression of his delicate features, than upon the **listless ennui**, which, characterizing both his face and attitude, appeared to take pity on himself for having been entrapped into the country.

Yet we should convey an **erroneous** impression of Mr. Vernon if we designed, by the words "listless ennui," to **depict** the slumberous **insipidity** of more modern **affectation**; it was not the ennui of a man to whom ennui is **habitual**, it was rather the **indolent prostration** that fills up the intervals of excitement. At that day the word blast was unknown; men had not enough sentiment for **satiety**. There was a kind of Bacchanalian fury in the life led by those leaders of fashion, among whom Mr. Vernon was not the least distinguished; it was a day of deep drinking, of high play, of **jovial**, reckless **dissipation**, of strong appetite for fun and riot, of four-in-hand coachmanship, of prize-fighting, of a strange sort of **barbarous manliness** that strained every nerve of the constitution,—a race of life in which three fourths of the competitors died half-way in the **hippodrome**. What is now the Dandy was then the Buck; and something of the Buck, though **subdued** by a chaster taste than fell to the ordinary members of his class, was apparent in Mr. Vernon's costume as well as air. Intricate folds of **muslin**, arranged in **prodigious** bows and ends, formed the **cravat**, which Brummell had not yet arisen to reform; his hat, of a very peculiar shape, low at the crown and broad at the **brim**, was worn with an air of devil-me-care defiance; his watch-chain, **garnished** with a profusion of rings and seals, hung low from his white **waistcoat**; and the adaptation of his **nankeen** inexpressibles to his well-shaped limbs was a **masterpiece** of art. His whole dress and air was not what could properly be called **foppish**, it was rather what at that time was called "rakish." Few could so closely approach **vulgarity** without being **vulgar**: of that privileged few, Mr. Vernon was one of the elect.

Farther on, and near the steps descending into the garden, stood a man in an attitude of profound abstraction, his arms folded, his eyes bent on the

French

affectation: affectation, minauderie, afféterie.
barbarous: barbare.
brim: bord, lisière.
carelessness: négligence, imprudence, insouciance.
cravat: foulard, cravate.
depict: peindre, dépeindre, représenter, peignons.
dissipation: dissipation, noce.
ennui: ennui.
erroneous: erroné, abusif.
foppish: dandy.
garnished: garni.
habitual: habituel.
hippodrome: hippodrome.
indolent: indolent, peu évolutif.
insipidity: insipidité.
jovial: enjoué.
listless: apathique, indifférent.
manliness: virilité.
masterpiece: réussite exceptionnelle.
muslin: mousseline, toile écrue.
nankeen: nankin.
prodigious: prodigieux.
prostration: prostration.
rout: fraiser, mettre en déroute, détourer, déroute, débâcle, creuser les blancs d'un cliché.
satiety: satiété.
subdued: soumîmes, subjugua.
vulgar: vulgaire, trivial.
vulgarity: vulgarité.
waistcoat: gilet.

ground, his brows slightly **contracted**; his dress was a plain black surtout, and **pantaloons** of the same colour. Something both in the fashion of the dress, and still more in the face of the man, bespoke the **foreigner**.

Sir Miles St. John was an accomplished person for that time of day. He had made the grand tour; he had bought pictures and statues; he spoke and wrote well in the modern languages; and being rich, hospitable, social, and not **averse** from the reputation of a patron, he had opened his house freely to the host of **emigrants** whom the French Revolution had driven to our coasts. Olivier Dalibard, a man of considerable learning and rare scientific attainments, had been tutor in the house of the Marquis de G—, a French **nobleman** known many years before to the old baronet. The marquis and his family had been among the first emigres at the outbreak of the Revolution. The tutor had remained behind; for at that time no danger appeared to threaten those who **pretended** to no other **aristocracy** than that of letters. **Contrary**, as he said, with repentant **modesty**, to his own **inclinations**, he had been **compelled**, not only for his own safety, but for that of his friends, to take some part in the subsequent events of the Revolution,—a part far from **sincere**, though so well had he **simulated** the **patriot** that he had won the personal favour and protection of Robespierre; nor till the fall of that **virtuous exterminator** had he withdrawn from the game of **politics** and effected in **disguise** his escape to England. As, whether from kindly or other motives, he had employed the power of his position in the **esteem** of Robespierre to save certain noble heads from the guillotine,—amongst others, the two brothers of the Marquis de G—, he was received with grateful welcome by his former patrons, who readily **pardoned** his career of Jacobinism from their belief in his excuses and their obligations to the services which that very career had enabled him to **render** to their **kindred**. Olivier Dalibard had accompanied the marquis and his family in one of the frequent visits they paid to Laughton; and when the marquis finally **quitted** England, and fixed his refuge at Vienna, with some connections of his wife's, he felt a lively satisfaction at the thought of leaving his friend **honourably**, if **unambitiously**, provided for as secretary and librarian to Sir Miles St. John.

French

aristocracy: aristocratie.
averse: opposé.
compelled: obligeas, astreintes.
contracted: contracté.
contrary: opposé, contraire.
disguise: déguisement, travestir.
emigrant: émigrant.
esteem: estime, apprécier, considérer.
exterminator: exterminateur, désinsectiser, destructeur de nuisibles.

foreigner: étranger, inconnu.
honourably: de façon honorable, de manière honorable.
inclination: inclinaison, propension, pendage, penchant, tendance, dévers, déclivité.
kindred: parenté, famille.
modesty: modestie, pudeur.
nobleman: noble, seigneur.
pantaloon: pantalon.
pardoned: pardonné.
patriot: patriote.

politic: politique.
pretended: feint, feignit, prétendu.
quitted: quittèrent.
render: rendre, plâtrez, reproduction, renformis, crépis, enduire, interpréter.
simulated: simulèrent.
sincere: sincère, honnête.
unambitiously: de manière sans ambition.
virtuous: vertueux.

In fact, the **scholar**, who **possessed** considerable powers of **fascination**, had won no less favour with the English baronet than he had with the French **dictator**. He played well both at chess and **backgammon**; he was an extraordinary **accountant**; he had a variety of information upon all points that rendered him more convenient than any cyclopaedia in Sir Miles's library; and as he spoke both English and Italian with a **correctness** and **fluency** extremely rare in a Frenchman, he was of considerable service in teaching languages to, as well as **directing** the general literary education of, Sir Miles's favourite **niece**, whom we shall take an early opportunity to describe at length.

Nevertheless, there had been one serious **obstacle** to Dalibard's acceptance of the appointment offered to him by Sir Miles. Dalibard had under his charge a young **orphan** boy of some ten or twelve years old,—a boy whom Sir Miles was not long in **suspecting** to be the scholar's son. This child had come from France with Dalibard, and while the marquis's family were in London, remained under the eye and care of his guardian or father, **whichever** was the true connection between the two. But this **superintendence** became impossible if Dalibard settled in Hampshire with Sir Miles St. John, and the boy remained in London; nor, though the generous old gentleman offered to pay for the child's **schooling**, would Dalibard consent to part with him. At last the matter was arranged: the boy was invited to Laughton on a visit, and was so lively, yet so well **mannered**, that he became a favourite, and was now fairly **quartered** in the house with his **reputed** father; and not to make an unnecessary mystery of this connection, such was in truth the relationship between Olivier Dalibard and Honore Gabriel Varney,—a name significant of the double and **illegitimate** origin: a French father, an English mother. **Dropping**, however, the purely French **appellation** of Honore, he went familiarly by that of Gabriel. Halfway down the steps stood the lad, **pencil** and **tablet** in hand, **sketching**. Let us look over his shoulder: it is his father's likeness,—a countenance in itself not very remarkable at the first glance, for the features were small; but when examined, it was one that most persons, women especially, would have

---

French

accountant: comptable, agent comptable, expert comptable.
appellation: nom, surnom.
backgammon: trictrac, jacquet.
correctness: exactitude, rectitude.
dictator: dictateur.
directing: direct, diriger.
dropping: largage, chute, déjections, dépôt de jeunes plants, dérivation des voies, goutte, rejet de la levure, touche en feinte.
fascination: fascination.
fluency: maîtrise, aisance, facilité.
illegitimate: illégitime, bâtard, illogique.
mannered: maniéré, affecté.
niece: nièce.
obstacle: obstacle, empêchement.
orphan: orphelin, bout de ligne.
pencil: crayon, le crayon.
possessed: possédâtes.
quartered: quartier, en quartier.
reputed: réputé.
scholar: savant, écolier, érudit.
schooling: scolarisation, rassemblement en bancs, instruction, dressage.
sketching: traçage, esquisser.
superintendence: surveillance, contrôle, direction, personnel chargé de la conduite des travaux.
suspecting: soupçonnant.
tablet: comprimé, tableau, liste.
whichever: celui que, n'importe quel.

pronounced handsome, and to which none could deny the higher praise of thought and **intellect**. A native of Provence, with some Italian blood in his veins,—for his grandfather, a merchant of Marseilles, had married into a Florentine family settled at Leghorn,—the dark complexion common with those in the South had been subdued, probably by the habits of the student, into a bronze and **steadfast paleness** which seemed almost fair by the contrast of the dark hair which he wore unpowdered, and the still darker brows which hung thick and prominent over clear gray eyes. Compared with the features, the skull was **disproportionally** large, both behind and before; and a physiognomist would have drawn conclusions more favourable to the power than the **tenderness** of the Provencal's character from the compact **closeness** of the lips and the breadth and **massiveness** of the iron jaw. But the son's sketch exaggerated every feature, and gave to the expression a **malignant** and terrible irony not now, at least, apparent in the quiet and **meditative** aspect. Gabriel himself, as be stood, would have been a more tempting study to many an artist. It is true that he was small for his years; but his frame had a **vigour** in its light proportions which came from a premature and almost **adolescent** symmetry of shape and muscular development. The countenance, however, had much of **effeminate** beauty: the long hair reached the shoulders, but did not curl,—straight, fine, and glossy as a girl's, and in colour of the pale **auburn**, tinged with red, which rarely alters in **hue** as childhood matures to man; the complexion was **dazzlingly** clear and fair. Nevertheless, there was something so hard in the lip, so bold, though not open, in the brow, that the girlishness of complexion, and even of outline, could not leave, on the whole, an impression of effeminacy. All the **hereditary keenness** and intelligence were stamped upon his face at that moment; but the expression had also a large share of the very irony and **malice** which he had conveyed to his **caricature**. The drawing itself was wonderfully vigorous and distinct; showing great artistic promise, and done with the **rapidity** and ease which betrayed practice. Suddenly his father turned, and with as sudden a **quickness** the boy concealed his tablet in his **vest**; and the sinister expression of his face **smoothed** into a **timorous**

French

adolescent: adolescent.
auburn: châtain roux.
caricature: caricature.
closeness: proximité, efficacité dans l'estimation, compacité.
dazzlingly: de façon éclatante, de manière éclatante.
disproportionally: de façon disproportionnée, de manière disproportionnée.
effeminate: efféminé.
hereditary: héréditaire.

hue: teinte, nuance, tonalité chromatique.
intellect: intellect, esprit, raison.
keenness: finesse.
malice: méchanceté, malice, malveillance.
malignant: malin, grave.
massiveness: massiveté.
meditative: méditatif.
paleness: pâleur.
quickness: rapidité, vitesse.
rapidity: rapidité.

smoothed: bords lisses.
steadfast: ferme, inébranlable, constant.
tenderness: tendresse, sensibilité à la palpation, câlinerie, endolorissement.
timorous: craintif, timoré.
vest: gilet, maillot de corps.
vigour: force, vigueur, activité, énergie.

smile as his eye encountered Dalibard's. The father beckoned to the boy, who approached with **alacrity**. "Gabriel," whispered the Frenchman, in his own tongue, "where are they at this moment?"

The boy pointed silently towards one of the cedars. Dalibard mused an instant, and then, slowly **descending** the steps, took his **noiseless** way over the smooth **turf** towards the tree. Its **boughs** drooped low and spread wide; and not till he was within a few paces of the spot could his eye perceive two forms seated on a bench under the dark green **canopy**. He then paused and **contemplated** them.

The one was a young man whose simple dress and subdued air strongly **contrasted** the artificial graces and the modish **languor** of Mr. Vernon; but though wholly without that **nameless** distinction which sometimes **characterizes** those conscious of pure race and habituated to the atmosphere of courts, he had at least Nature's stamp of aristocracy in a form **eminently** noble, and features of **manly**, but **surpassing** beauty, which were not rendered less **engaging** by an expression of modest **timidity**. He seemed to be listening with thoughtful respect to his companion, a young female by his side, who was speaking to him with an **earnestness** visible in her gestures and her **animated** countenance. And though there was much to notice in the various persons scattered over the scene, not one, perhaps,—not the **graceful** Vernon, not the thoughtful scholar, nor his fair-haired, hard-lipped son, not even the handsome **listener** she addressed,—no, not one there would so have arrested the eye, whether of a physiognomist or a casual observer, as that young girl, Sir Miles St. John's favourite niece and **presumptive** heiress.

But as at that moment the expression of her face **differed** from that habitual to it, we **defer** its description.

"Do not," such were her words to her companion,—"do not alarm yourself by **exaggerating** the difficulties; do not even contemplate them: those be my care. Mainwaring, when I loved you; when, seeing that your diffidence or your pride **forbade** you to be the first to speak, I **overstepped** the modesty or the **dissimulation** of my sex; when I said, 'Forget that I am

---

French

alacrity: enthousiasme, avidité, empressement.
animated: animé.
bough: branche, rameau.
canopy: baldaquin, dais, verrière, couvert.
characterizes: caractérise.
contemplated: contemplâtes.
contrasted: contrasté.
defer: différer, reporter.
descending: descendant, décroissant.
differed: différâtes.
dissimulation: dissimulation.
earnestness: sérieux, gravité.
eminently: de façon éminente, de manière éminente, éminemment.
engaging: engageant, accrochant, engrenant, enclenchant, attirant, embrayage.
exaggerating: exagérant, outrant.
forbade: interdit.
graceful: gracieux, élégant, mignon.
languor: langueur.
listener: auditeur, écouteur.
manly: viril, mâle.
nameless: anonyme, inconnu.
noiseless: silencieux, antisouffle.
overstepped: dépassâtes.
presumptive: présomptif.
surpassing: surpassant, dépassant, maîtrisant.
timidity: timidité.
turf: gazon, engazonner, pelouse, turf.

the reputed heiress of Laughton, see in me but the faults and **merits** of the human being, of the wild unregulated girl, see in me but Lucretia Clavering'" (here her cheeks **blushed**, and her voice sank into a lower and more **tremulous whisper**) "'and love her if you can!'—when I went thus far, do not think I had not measured all the difficulties in the way of our union, and felt that I could **surmount** them."

"But," answered Mainwaring, **hesitatingly**, "can you **conceive** it possible that your uncle ever will consent? Is not pride—the pride of family—almost the leading **attribute** of his character? Did he not **discard** your mother—his own sister—from his house and heart for no other offence but a second marriage which he **deemed** beneath her? Has he ever even **consented** to see, much less to receive, your half-sister, the child of that marriage? Is not his very **affection** for you **interwoven** with his pride in you, with his belief in your **ambition**? Has he not **summoned** your cousin, Mr. Vernon, for the obvious purpose of favouring a suit which he **considers** worthy of you, and which, if successful, will unite the two branches of his ancient house? How is it possible that he can ever hear without a scorn and indignation which would be **fatal** to your fortunes that your heart has **presumed** to choose, in William Mainwaring, a man without **ancestry** or career?"

"Not without career," **interrupted** Lucretia, **proudly**. "Do you think if you were master of Laughton that your career would not be more brilliant than that of **yon** indolent, **luxurious** coxcomb? Do you think that I could have been poor-hearted enough to love you if I had not recognized in you energies and talents that **correspond** with my own ambition? For I am ambitious, as you know, and therefore my mind, as well as my heart, went with my love for you."

"Ah, Lucretia, but can Sir Miles St. John see my future rise in my present obscurity?"

"I do not say that he can, or will; but if you love me, we can wait. Do not fear the **rivalry** of Mr. Vernon. I shall know how to free myself from so **tame** a **peril**. We can wait,—my uncle is old; his habits **preclude** the chance of a

---

French

affection: affection, amour.
ambition: ambition, souhait, aspiration.
ancestry: ascendance.
attribute: attribut, imputer, privilège, propriété, caractère qualitatif.
blushed: rougi.
conceive: concevoir, conçois.
consented: consenti, acquiesçâmes.
considers: considère, envisage.
correspond: correspondre.
deemed: crurent, crûtes, crus, crûmes, cru, crut, réputé.
discard: écarter, jeter.
fatal: fatal, mortel.
hesitatingly: de façon hésitante, de manière hésitante.
interrupted: interrompit.
interwoven: entremêlé.
luxurious: luxueux, somptueux.
merit: mérite, gloire.
peril: danger, péril.
preclude: empêchons, exclus.
presumed: présumas.
proudly: fièrement, de façon fire, de manière fire.
rivalry: rivalité, concurrence, antagonisme binoculaire.
summoned: convoqués, appelé.
surmount: surmonter.
tame: apprivoisé, dresser, dompter, docile.
tremulous: timide, tremblotant.
whisper: chuchoter, murmurer.
yon: y, là.

much longer life; he has already had severe attacks. We are young, dear Mainwaring: what is a year or two to those who hope?" Mainwaring's face fell, and a **displeasing chill** passed through his **veins**. Could this young creature, her uncle's petted and trusted darling, she who should be the soother of his infirmities, the **prop** of his age, the sincerest **mourner** at his grave, **weigh coldly** thus the chances of his death, and point at once to the **altar** and the **tomb**?

He was saved from the embarrassment of reply by Dalibard's approach.

"More than half an hour absent," said the scholar, in his own language, with a smile; and drawing out his watch, he placed it before their eyes. "Do you not think that all will miss you? Do you suppose, Miss Clavering, that your uncle has not **ere** this asked for his fair niece? Come, and **forestall** him." He offered his arm to Lucretia as he spoke. She hesitated a moment, and then, turning to Mainwaring, held out her hand. He pressed it, though scarcely with a lover's warmth; and as she walked back to the terrace with Dalibard, the young man struck slowly into the opposite direction, and passing by a gate over a **foot-bridge** that led from the ha-ha into the park, bent his way towards a lake which **gleamed** below at some distance, half-concealed by **groves** of **venerable** trees rich with the **prodigal** boughs of summer. Meanwhile, as they passed towards the house, Dalibard, still using his native tongue, thus **accosted** his pupil:—

"You must pardon me if I think more of your interests than you do; and pardon me no less if I **encroach** on your secrets and alarm your pride. This young man,—can you be guilty of the folly of more than a passing **caprice** for his society, of more than the **amusement** of playing with his **vanity**? Even if that be all, **beware** of **entangling** yourself in your own meshes."

"You do in truth **offend** me," said Lucretia, with calm **haughtiness**, "and you have not the right thus to speak to me."

"Not the right," repeated the Provencal, **mournfully**, "not the right! Then, indeed, I am mistaken in my pupil. Do you consider that I would have lowered my pride to remain here as a dependent; that, conscious of

---

French

accosted: accosta, abordé.
altar: autel.
amusement: distraction, amusement, détente, récréation, divertissement.
beware: attention, prendre garde, se méfier.
caprice: caprice.
chill: froid, trempe, refroidir.
coldly: froidement, de façon froide, de manière froide.
displeasing: déplaisant, mécontentant.
encroach: empiéter, usurper.
entangling: empêtrant, entortillant.
ere: avant.
foot-bridge: passerelle.
forestall: anticiper, devancer, empêcher, prévenir.
gleamed: luie, luis.
grove: bosquet, bois, ouvrage souterrain.
haughtiness: arrogance, hauteur.
mourner: pleureuse, personne en deuil.
mournfully: de façon sombre, de manière sombre.
offend: offenser, insulter, pécher.
prodigal: prodigue.
prop: support, étai, appui, étançon, étayer.
tomb: tombe.
vanity: vanité, futilité.
vein: veine, filon, nervure.
venerable: vénérable.
weigh: peser, pèses, pesons.

attainments, and perhaps of abilities, that should win their way, even in **exile**, to distinction, I would have frittered away my life in these **rustic** shades,—if I had not formed in you a deep and **absorbing** interest? In that interest I ground my right to **warn** and **counsel** you. I saw, or **fancied** I saw, in you a mind **congenial** to my own; a mind above the **frivolities** of your sex,—a mind, in short, with the grasp and energy of a man's. You were then but a child, you are scarcely yet a woman; yet have I not given to your intellect the strong food on which the statesmen of Florence fed their pupil-princes, or the noble Jesuits the noble men who were **destined** to extend the secret empire of the **imperishable** Loyola?"

"You gave me the taste for a knowledge rare in my sex, I own," answered Lucretia, with a slight tone of regret in her voice: "and in the knowledge you have **communicated** I felt a charm that at times seems to me to be only fatal. You have **confounded** in my mind evil and good, or rather, you have left both good and evil as dead **ashes**, as the dust and **cinder** of a **crucible**. You have made intellect the only conscience. Of late, I wish that my **tutor** had been a village priest!"

"Of late, since you have listened to the **pastorals** of that **meek** Corydon!"

"Dare you **despise** him? And for what? That he is good and honest?"

"I despise him, not because he is good and honest, but because he is of the common **herd** of men, without aim or character. And it is for this youth that you will sacrifice your fortunes, your ambition, the station you were born to fill and have been reared to improve,—this youth in whom there is nothing but the lap-dog's merit, sleekness and beauty! Ay, **frown**,—the frown betrays you; you love him!"

"And if I do?" said Lucretia, raising her tall form to its **utmost** height, and **haughtily** facing her inquisitor,—"and, if I do, what then? Is he **unworthy** of me? **Converse** with him, and you will find that the noble form **conceals** as high a spirit. He wants but wealth: I can give it to him. If his

French

absorbing: absorbant, passionnant, captivant.
ash: cendre, frêne.
attainment: réalisation, acquisition.
cinder: cendre, escarbille, scories.
communicated: communiquâtes.
conceals: cache, dissimule.
confounded: confondu, déconcertâmes.
congenial: convenable, sympathique.
converse: converser, intervenir.
counsel: conseil, avis, avocat, défenseur.
crucible: creuset.
despise: mépriser, dédaigner.
destined: destinas.
exile: exiler, bannir.
fancied: imaginaire.
frivolity: frivolité.
frown: froncement de sourcils, se renfrogner, sourciller.
haughtily: de façon hautaine, de manière hautaine.
herd: troupeau, bande, collection, ensemble, harde, are.
imperishable: impérissable.
meek: humble, doux.
pastoral: pastoral.
rustic: rustique, villageois, paysan, campagnard, champêtre.
tutor: tuteur, précepteur.
unworthy: indigne.
utmost: extrême, le plus éloigné, maximum.
warn: avertir, alerter.

temper is gentle, I can **prompt** and guide it to fame and power. He at least has education and **eloquence** and mind. What has Mr. Vernon?"

"Mr. Vernon? I did not speak of him!"

Lucretia gazed hard upon the Provencal's countenance,—gazed with that unpitying air of triumph with which a woman who **detects** a power over the heart she **does** not desire to conquer **exults** in **defeating** the reasons that heart appears to her to prompt. "No," she said in a calm voice, to which the **venom** of secret **irony** gave **stinging** significance,—"no, you spoke not of Mr. Vernon; you thought that if I looked round, if I looked nearer, I might have a fairer choice."

"You are cruel, you are unjust," said Dalibard, **falteringly**. If I once presumed for a moment, have I repeated my offence? But," he added **hurriedly**, "in me,—much as you appear to despise me,—in me, at least, you would have **risked** none of the dangers that **beset** you if you seriously set your heart on Mainwaring."

"You think my uncle would be proud to give my hand to M. Olivier Dalibard?"

"I think and I know," answered the Provencal, **gravely**, and disregarding the **taunt**, "that if you had **deigned** to render me—poor exile that I am!—the most **enviable** of men, you had still been the heiress of Laughton."

"So you have said and urged," said Lucretia, with evident curiosity in her voice; "yet how, and by what art,—wise and subtle as you are,—could you have won my uncle's consent?"

"That is my secret," returned Dalibard, **gloomily**; "and since the madness I **indulged** is forever over; since I have so schooled my heart that nothing, despite your **sarcasm**, save an **affectionate** interest which I may call **paternal** rests there,—let us pass from this painful subject. Oh, my dear pupil, be warned in time; know love for what it really is, in the dark and complicated history of actual life,—a brief **enchantment**, not to be disdained, but not to be considered the all-in all. Look round the world; **contemplate** all those who have married from passion: ten years **afterwards**, **whither** has the passion

---

French

affectionate: affectueux, tendre, attaché, dévoué, amoureux.
afterward: après, plus tard.
beset: assaillir.
contemplate: contempler, envisager, méditer.
defeating: vainquant.
deigned: daigné, condescendu.
detects: détecte, dépiste.
doe: biche, hase, lapine, daine.
eloquence: éloquence.
enchantment: enchantement,

ensorcellement.
enviable: enviable.
exult: exulter.
falteringly: de manière hésitante, de façon hésitante.
gloomily: de façon sombre, de manière sombre.
gravely: gravement, de façon tombe, de manière tombe.
hurriedly: à la hâte, de façon hâtive, de manière hâtive, précipitamment.

indulged: gâtas, gâtâtes, gâté, gâtèrent.
irony: ironie.
paternal: paternel.
prompt: invite, ponctuel, prompt, mobile, sollicitation, souffler.
risked: risqué.
sarcasm: sarcasme.
stinging: piquant, piqûre, cuisant.
taunt: sarcasme, railler.
venom: venin.
whither: où.

flown? With a few, indeed, where there is community of object and character, new excitements, new aims and hopes, spring up; and having first taken root in passion, the passion continues to shoot out in their fresh stems and fibres. But **deceive** yourself not; there is no such community between you and Mainwaring. What you call his goodness, you will learn **hereafter** to despise as **feeble**; and what in reality is your mental power he soon, too soon, will shudder at as **unwomanly** and hateful."

"Hold!" cried Lucretia, **tremulously**. "Hold! and if he does, I shall owe his hate to you, — to your lessons; to your **deadly** influence!"

"Lucretia, no; the seeds were in you. Can **cultivation** force from the soil that which it is against the nature of the soil to bear?"

"I will **pluck** out the **weeds**! I will **transform** myself!"

"Child, I **defy** you!" said the scholar, with a smile that gave to his face the expression his son had **conveyed** to it. "I have warned you, and my task is done." With that he **bowed**, and leaving her, was soon by the side of Sir Miles St. John; and the baronet and his **librarian**, a few moments after, entered the house and sat down to chess.

But during the dialogues we have sketched, we must not suppose that Sir Miles himself had been so wholly absorbed in the **sensual gratification bestowed** upon Europe by the **immortal** Raleigh as to neglect his guest and **kinsman**.

"And so, Charley Vernon, it is not the fashion to smoke in Lunnon." Thus Sir Miles pronounced the word, according to the Euphuism of his youth, and which, even at that day, still **lingered** in **courtly jargon**."

"No, sir. However, to **console** us, we have most other vices in full force."

"I don't doubt it; they say the prince's set **exhaust** life pretty quickly."

"It certainly requires the fortune of an earl and the constitution of a prize-fighter to live with him."

"Yet methinks, Master Charley, you have neither the one nor the other."

French

bestowed: accordas, me octroyai, nous octroyâmes, se octroya, te octroyas, vous octroyâtes.
bowed: incliné, courbé, arqué.
console: consoler, pupitre de commande.
conveyed: transmîtes, véhicula, acheminai.
courtly: courtois.
cultivation: culture, façons culturales, fidélisation.
deadly: mortel, meurtrier, de façon morte, de manière morte.
deceive: tromper, tricher, décevoir.
defy: défier, provoquer.
exhaust: échappement, épuiser, gaz d'échappement.
feeble: faible, débile.
gratification: satisfaction, plaisir.
hereafter: après, désormais, dorénavant.
immortal: immortel.
jargon: jargon, charabia.
kinsman: parent.
librarian: bibliothécaire.
lingered: traîné.
pluck: cueillir, ramasser, plumer, fressure, courage.
sensual: sensuel, voluptueux.
transform: transformer, résoudre.
tremulously: de façon tremblante, de manière tremblotante.
unwomanly: peu féminin.
weed: sarcler, mauvaise herbe, désherber.

"And therefore I see before me, and at no very great distance, the Bench and—a consumption!" answered Vernon, **suppressing** a slight **yawn**.

"'T is a **pity**, for you had a fine estate, properly managed; and in **spite** of your faults, you have the heart of a true gentleman. Come, come!" and the old man spoke with tenderness, "you are young enough yet to reform. A **prudent** marriage and a good wife will save both your health and your acres."

"If you think so highly of marriage, my dear Sir Miles, it is a wonder you did not add to your **precepts** the value of your example."

"Jackanapes! I had not your infirmities: I never was a spendthrift, and I have a constitution of iron!" There was a **pause**. "Charles," continued Sir Miles, **musingly**, "there is many an **earl** with a less **fortune** than the conjoined estates of Vernon Grange and Laughton Hall. You must already have understood me: it is my intention to leave my estates to Lucretia; it is my wish, nevertheless, to think you will not be the worse for my will. **Frankly**, if you can like my niece, win her; settle here while I live, put the Grange to nurse, and **recruit** yourself by fresh air and field-sports. Zounds, Charles, I love you, and that's the truth! Give me your hand!"

"And a grateful heart with it, sir," said Vernon, **warmly**, **evidently** affected, as he started from his indolent position and took the hand extended to him. "Believe me, I do not **covet** your wealth, nor do I **envy** my **cousin** anything so much as the first place in your regard."

"Prettily said, my boy, and I don't **suspect** you of **insincerity**. What think you, then, of my plan?"

Mr. Vernon seemed **embarrassed**; but **recovering** himself with his usual ease, he replied archly: "Perhaps, sir, it will be of little use to know what I think of your plan; my fair cousin may have **upset** it already."

"Ha, sir! let me look at you. So, so! you are not **jesting**. What the **deuce** do you mean? 'Gad, man, speak out!"

French

cousin: cousin.
covet: convoites.
deuce: égalité, deux.
earl: comte.
embarrassed: embarrassé, gêné.
envy: envie, jalousie.
evidently: évidemment, de façon évidente, de manière évidente.
fortune: fortune, sort, destin.
frankly: franchement, de façon franche, de manière franche.
insincerity: hypocrisie, manque de sincérité.
jesting: plaisantant.
musingly: de façon rêveuse, de manière rêveuse.
pause: pause, repos, trêve.
pity: pitié, plaindre, compassion, apitoiement, avoir pitié, mal, s'apitoyer.
precept: précepte.
prudent: prudent, raisonnable.
recovering: récupérant, recouvrant.
recruit: recruter, enrôler, gagner, s'adjoindre des aides.
spite: rancune, dépit.
suppressing: étouffant, réprimant, supprimant.
suspect: suspecter, soupçonner, se méfier.
upset: renverser, stupéfait, vexé, bouleverser.
warmly: chaudement, de façon chaude, de manière chaude.
yawn: bâillement.

"Do you not think that Mr. Monderling—Mandolin—what's his name, eh?—do you not think that he is a very handsome young fellow?" said Mr. Vernon, drawing out his **snuffbox** and offering it to his kinsman.

"Damn your snuff," quoth Sir Miles, in great choler, as he rejected the proffered **courtesy** with a **vehemence** that sent half the contents of the box upon the joint eyes and noses of the two **canine** favourites dozing at his feet. The setter started up in an **agony**; the **spaniel** wheezed and sniffled and ran off, **stopping** every moment to take his head between his **paws**. The old gentleman continued without heeding the sufferings of his **dumb** friends,—a **symptom** of rare discomposure on his part.

"Do you mean to **insinuate**, Mr. Vernon, that my niece—my **elder** niece, Lucretia Clavering—condescends to notice the looks, good or bad, of Mr. Mainwaring? 'Sdeath, sir, he is the son of a land-agent! Sir, he is intended for trade! Sir, his highest ambition is to be partner in some fifth-rate **mercantile** house!"

"My dear Sir Miles," replied Mr. Vernon, as he continued to brush away, with his **scented handkerchief**, such **portions** of the prince's mixture as his nankeen inexpressibles had **diverted** from the sensual **organs** of Dash and Ponto—"my dear Sir Miles, ca n'empeche pas le sentiment!"

"Empeche the fiddlestick! You don't know Lucretia. There are many girls, indeed, who might not be trusted near any handsome flute-playing **spark**, with black eyes and white teeth; but Lucretia is not one of those; she has spirit and ambition that would never **stoop** to a mesalliance; she has the mind and will of a queen,—old Queen Bess, I believe."

"That is saying much for her talent, sir; but if so, Heaven help her intended! I am **duly** grateful for the **blessings** you propose me!"

Despite his anger, the old gentleman could not help smiling.

"Why, to **confess** the truth, she is hard to manage; but we men of the world know how to **govern** women, I hope,—much more how to break in a girl scarce out of her **teens**. As for this fancy of yours, it is sheer **folly**: Lucretia knows my mind. She has seen her mother's fate; she has seen her

French

agony: agonie, angoisse, abois.
blessing: bénissant, bénédiction.
canine: canin.
confess: confesser, avouer, reconnaître.
courtesy: courtoisie, affabilité, politesse.
diverted: distrait, détournai.
duly: dûment.
dumb: muet.
elder: sureau, aîné, ancien.
folly: folie, sottise.
govern: gouverner, régner, règne, surveiller, régir.
handkerchief: mouchoir, foulard.
insinuate: insinuer.
mercantile: mercantile, commercial.
organ: organe, orgue.
paw: patte, pied, jambe.
portion: partie, portion.
scented: parfumé.
snuffbox: tabatière.
spaniel: épagneul.
spark: étincelle, jaillir, trottinette des neiges, flammèche, ligne de feu, lueur.
stoop: s'incliner, pencher.
stopping: arrêtant, cessant, interrompant, stoppant, plombage, obturation.
symptom: symptôme, signe fonctionnel.
teen: adolescent.
vehemence: véhémence, ardeur.

sister an exile from my house. Why? For no fault of hers, poor thing, but because she is the child of **disgrace**, and the mother's sin is visited on her daughter's head. I am a good-natured man, I fancy, as men go; but I am old-fashioned enough to care for my race. If Lucretia demeaned herself to love, to encourage, that lad, why, I would strike her from my will, and put your name where I have placed hers."

"Sir," said Vernon, gravely, and throwing aside all affectation of manner, "this becomes serious; and I have no right even to whisper a doubt by which it now seems I might benefit. I think it **imprudent**, if you wish Miss Clavering to regard me **impartially** as a **suitor** to her hand, to throw her, at her age, in the way of a man far superior to myself, and to most men, in personal advantages,—a man more of her own years, well educated, well mannered, with no evidence of his inferior birth in his appearance or his breeding. I have not the least ground for **supposing** that he has made the slightest impression on Miss Clavering, and if he has, it would be, perhaps, but a girl's innocent and **thoughtless** fancy, easily shaken off by time and **worldly** reflection; but pardon me if I say **bluntly** that should that be so, you would be wholly **unjustified** in **punishing**, even in **blaming**, her,—it is yourself you must blame for your own carelessness and that **forgetful** blindness to human nature and **youthful** emotions which, I must say, is the less **pardonable** in one who has known the world so intimately."

"Charles Vernon," said the old baronet, "give me your hand again! I was right, at least, when I said you had the heart of a true gentleman. Drop this subject for the present. Who has just left Lucretia yonder?"

"Your protege, the Frenchman."

"Ah, he, at least, is not blind; go and join Lucretia!"

Vernon bowed, **emptied** the remains of the Madeira into a **tumbler**, drank the contents at a **draught**, and **sauntered** towards Lucretia; but she, **perceiving** his approach, crossed abruptly into one of the **alleys** that led to the other side of the house, and he was either too **indifferent** or too well-bred to force upon her the **companionship** which she so evidently **shunned**.

French

alley: allée, ruelle.
blaming: blâmant.
bluntly: de façon émoussée, de manière émoussée.
companionship: compagnie, équipe, camaraderie.
disgrace: disgrâce, honte, déshonneur.
draught: tirant d'eau, prise, profondeur d'enfoncement, esquisse, épure, dépouille, courant d'air, coup, appel d'air, plan, projet.
emptied: vidé, vidâmes, vidèrent.
forgetful: distrait, oublieux.
impartially: impartialement, de façon neutre, de manière neutre.
imprudent: imprudent.
indifferent: indifférent, impartial.
pardonable: excusable, pardonnable.
perceiving: apercevant, percevant, discernant.
punishing: punissant.
sauntered: flânas.
shunned: évitèrent, fui, fuîtes, fuit, fuis, fuirent, fuîmes.
suitor: prétendant, soupirant.
supposing: supposant.
thoughtless: irréfléchi, étourdi, inconsidéré.
tumbler: culbuteur, verre.
unjustified: injustifié.
worldly: mondain, terrestre.
youthful: jeune, juvénile.

He threw himself at length upon one of the benches on the lawn, and leaning his head upon his hand, fell into reflections which, had he spoken, would have shaped themselves somewhat thus into words: —

"If I must take that girl as the price of this fair heritage, shall I gain or lose? I grant that she has the finest neck and shoulders I ever saw out of marble; but far from being in love with her, she gives me a feeling like fear and **aversion**. Add to this that she has evidently no kinder **sentiment** for me than I for her; and if she once had a heart, that young gentleman has long since **coaxed** it away. Pleasant auspices, these, for **matrimony** to a poor **invalid** who wishes at least to decline and to die in peace! Moreover, if I were rich enough to marry as I pleased; if I were what, perhaps, I ought to be, heir to Laughton,—why, there is a certain sweet Mary in the world, whose eyes are **softer** than Lucretia Clavering's. But that is a dream! On the other hand, if I do not win this girl, and my poor kinsman give her all, or nearly all, his possessions, Vernon Grange goes to the **usurers**, and the king will find a **lodging** for myself. What does it matter? I cannot live above two or three years at the most, and can only hope, therefore, that dear **stout** old Sir Miles may outlive me. At thirty-three I have worn out fortune and life; little pleasure could Laughton give me,—brief pain the Bench. '**Fore** Gad, the philosophy of the thing is on the whole against **sour** looks and the noose!"

Thus deciding in the progress of his revery, he smiled, and changed his position. The sun had set, the **twilight** was over, the moon rose in **splendour** from amidst a thick **copse** of **mingled beech** and oak; the beams fell full on the face of the muser, and the face seemed yet paler and the **exhaustion** of premature decay yet more evident, by that still and **melancholy** light: all ruins gain dignity by the moon. This was a **ruin** nobler than that which painters place on their canvas,—the ruin, not of stone and brick, but of humanity and spirit; the **wreck** of man **prematurely** old, not **stricken** by great **sorrow**, not bowed by great toil, but fretted and mined away by small pleasures and poor excitements,—small and poor, but daily, **hourly**, momently at their gnome-like work. Something of the gravity and the true

French

aversion: aversion, antipathie.
beech: hêtre, bois de hêtre.
coaxed: cajolai.
copse: taillis.
exhaustion: épuisement, éreintement, essorage, procédé exhaustif, abattement.
fore: avant, à l'avant.
hourly: horaire, constant.
invalid: invalide, non valable, périmé.
lodging: hébergement, logement,
verse.
matrimony: mariage.
melancholy: mélancolie, sombre, abattement.
mingled: mélangeâtes, mêlé, mêlâtes, mêlas, mêlèrent.
prematurely: de façon prématurée, de manière prématurée.
ruin: ruine, abîmer, abaisser, ravager.
sentiment: sentiment.
softer: plus doux.
sorrow: abattement, chagrin.
sour: aigre, acide, acerbe, s'aigrir, maussade, s'acidifier.
splendour: splendeur, éclat, magnificence, pompe.
stout: corpulent, fort, gros, stout.
stricken: accablé, affligé, blessé.
twilight: crépuscule, pénombre, aube, scotopique.
usurer: usurier.
wreck: épave, naufrage, accident, détruire.

lesson of the hour and scene, perhaps, forced itself upon a mind little given to sentiment, for Vernon rose **languidly** and muttered,—

"My poor mother hoped better things from me. It is well, after all, that it is broken off with Mary. Why should there be any one to **weep** for me? I can the better die smiling, as I have lived."

Meanwhile, as it is necessary we should follow each of the principal characters we have introduced through the course of an evening more or less **eventful** in the destiny of all, we return to Mainwaring and accompany him to the lake at the bottom of the park, which he reached as its smooth surface **glistened** in the last beams of the sun. He saw, as he neared the water, the fish sporting in the **pellucid** tide; the **dragonfly** darted and **hovered** in the air; the tedded grass beneath his feet gave forth the **fragrance** of crushed **thyme** and **clover**; the swan paused, as if slumbering on the wave; the **linnet** and **finch** sang still from the neighbouring copses; and the heavy bees were **winging** their way home with a **drowsy** murmur. All around were images of that **unspeakable** peace which Nature whispers to those **attuned** to her music; all fitted to **lull**, but not to deject, the spirit,—images dear to the holiday of the world-worn man, to the **contemplation** of **serene** and retired age, to the **boyhood** of poets, to the youth of lovers. But Mainwaring's step was heavy, and his brow clouded, and Nature that evening was dumb to him. At the margin of the lake stood a solitary **angler** who now, his evening's task done, was employed in **leisurely disjointing** his rod and **whistling** with much **sweetness** an air from one of Izaak Walton's songs. Mainwaring reached the angler and laid his hand on his shoulder.

"What sport, Ardworth?"

"A few large **roach** with the fly, and one pike with a gudgeon,—a noble fellow! Look at him! He was lying under the reeds **yonder**; I saw his green back, and teased him into biting. A heavenly evening! I wonder you did not follow my example, and escape from a set where neither you nor I can feel very much at home, to this green **banquet** of Nature, in which at least no

---

French

angler: pêcheur à la ligne.
attuned: accordâmes, adapté.
banquet: banquet, festin.
boyhood: enfance, adolescence.
clover: trèfle.
contemplation: contemplation, méditation, recueillement.
disjointing: disjoignant.
dragonfly: libellule.
drowsy: somnolent, assoupi, ensommeillé.
eventful: mouvementé.
finch: pinson.
fragrance: parfum, fragrance.
glistened: scintillé.
hovered: planas, voltigeai, flotté.
languidly: de façon languissante, de manière languissante.
leisurely: paisiblement, lentement, calme.
linnet: linotte.
lull: bercer, accalmie.
pellucid: transparent.
roach: gardon, rousse, dévers, cafard.
serene: serein, tranquille.
sweetness: douceur, gentillesse, sucrosité, teneur en sucre.
thyme: thym.
unspeakable: indicible, indescriptible, innommable.
weep: pleurer, sourdons, suinter, larmoyez.
whistling: sifflement.
winging: arrimage en abord.
yonder: là, y.

man sits below the salt-cellar. The birds are an older family than the St. Johns, but they don't throw their **pedigree** in our teeth, Mainwaring."

"**Nay**, nay, my good friend, you wrong old Sir Miles; proud he is, no doubt, but neither you nor I have had to complain of his **insolence**."

"Of his insolence, certainly not; of his **condescension**, yes! Hang it, William, it is his very **politeness** that **galls** me. Don't you observe that with Vernon, or Lord A—, or Lord B—, or Mr. C—, he is easy and off-hand; calls them by their names, pats them on the shoulder, rates them, and **swears** at them if they **vex** him. But with you and me and his French **parasite**, it is all **stately decorum** and **punctilious** courtesy: 'Mr. Mainwaring, I am delighted to see you;' 'Mr. Ardworth, as you are so near, dare I ask you to ring the bell?' 'Monsieur Dalibard, with the utmost **deference**, I venture to **disagree** with you.' However, don't let my **foolish susceptibility** ruffle your pride. And you, too, have a worthy object in view, which might well **detain** you from roach and jack-fish. Have you stolen your interview with the superb Lucretia?"

"Yes, stolen, as you say; and, like all **thieves** not thoroughly **hardened**, I am **ashamed** of my gains."

"Sit down, my boy,—this is a bank in ten thousand; there, that old root to **lean** your **elbow** on, this soft moss for your **cushion**: sit down and confess. You have something on your mind that preys on you; we are old college friends,—out with it!"

"There is no **resisting** you, Ardworth," said Mainwaring, smiling, and drawn from his reserve and his gloom by the frank good-humour of his companion. "I should like, I own, to make a clean breast of it; and perhaps I may profit by your advice. You know, in the first place, that after I left college, my father, seeing me **indisposed** for the Church, to which he had always destined me in his own heart, and for which, indeed, he had gone out of his way to maintain me at the University, gave me the choice of his own business as a **surveyor** and land-agent, or of entering into the mercantile profession. I chose the latter, and went to Southampton, where we have a

French

ashamed: honteux.
condescension: condescendance.
cushion: coussin, gomme de liaison, amortir, matelas de vapeur dans un cylindre, élément d'émission élastique, carreau.
decorum: décorum, bienséance.
deference: déférence, ajournement.
detain: détenir, retenir, détiens, retiens, réprimer.
disagree: être en désaccord.
elbow: coude, le coude.

foolish: sot, idiot, stupide, abracadabrant, insensé.
gall: bile, fiel, galle, amer.
hardened: durci, trempé, endurci.
indisposed: indisposé, souffrant.
insolence: effronterie, insolence.
lean: maigre, appuyer, accoter, s'adosser, s'accoter, mince, adosser.
nay: non.
parasite: parasite.
pedigree: pedigree, ascendance.

politeness: politesse, galanterie.
punctilious: pointilleux.
resisting: résistant, réimplantation.
stately: imposant, majestueux.
surveyor: arpenteur, géomètre.
susceptibility: susceptibilité, recevabilité, prédisposition, sensibilité.
swear: jurer, jurons, blasphémer, prêter serment.
thieve: vole, volons.
vex: chagriner, vexer, vexons.

relation in business, to be **initiated** into the **elementary** mysteries. There I became acquainted with a good **clergyman** and his wife, and in that house I passed a great part of my time."

"With the hope, I trust, on better consideration, of **gratifying** your father's ambition and learning how to **starve** with **gentility** on a cure."

"Not much of that, I fear."

"Then the clergyman had a daughter?"

"You are nearer the mark now," said Mainwaring, colouring,—"though it was not his daughter. A young lady lived in his family, not even related to him; she was placed there with a certain **allowance** by a rich relation. In a word, I **admired**, perhaps I loved, this young person; but she was without an independence, and I not yet provided even with the **substitute** of money,—a profession. I fancied (do not laugh at my vanity) that my feelings might be returned. I was in **alarm** for her as well as myself; I sounded the clergyman as to the chance of **obtaining** the consent of her rich relation, and was informed that he thought it **hopeless**. I felt I had no right to **invite** her to poverty and ruin, and still less to **entangle** further (if I had chanced to touch at all) her affection. I made an excuse to my father to leave the town, and returned home."

"Prudent and **honourable** enough, so far; unlike me,—I should have run off with the girl, if she loved me, and old Plutus, the **rascal**, might have done his worst against Cupid. But I **interrupt** you."

"I came back when the county was greatly agitated,—public meetings, speeches, mobs; a sharp election going on. My father had always taken keen interest in politics; he was of the same party as Sir Miles, who, you know, is red-hot upon politics. I was easily led—partly by ambition, partly by the effect of example, partly by the hope to give a new turn to my thoughts—to make an appearance in public."

"And a **devilish creditable** one too! Why, man, your speeches have been **quoted** with **rapture** by the London papers. **Horribly aristocratic** and Pittish, it is true,—I think **differently**; but every man to his taste. Well—"

French

admired: admirâtes.
alarm: alarme, alerte, sirène, timbre, réveil, stupéfaction, préoccuper, consterner, avertisseur, terreur, abattement.
allowance: allocation, indemnité, tolérance, bonification, prestation, majoration.
aristocratic: aristocratique.
clergyman: prêtre, abbé, curé, ecclésiastique, pasteur.
creditable: honorable, estimable.
devilish: diabolique, satané.
differently: autrement, différemment, de façon différente, de manière différente.
elementary: élémentaire, primaire.
entangle: empêtrer, entortiller.
gentility: distinction.
gratifying: contentant, satisfaisant, gratifiant.
honourable: honorable, vénérable.
hopeless: impossible, sans espoir, désespéré.
horribly: de façon affreuse, de manière affreuse.
initiated: initié.
interrupt: interrompre.
invite: inviter, conviez.
obtaining: obtenant.
quoted: cité, citèrent, citâmes, citai.
rapture: ravissement.
rascal: fripon, coquin, vaurien.
starve: affamer, mourir de faim.
substitute: substituer, remplacer, succédané, mettre en place de.

"My attempts, such as they were, **procured** me the **favour** of Sir Miles. He had long been acquainted with my father, who had helped him in his own elections years ago. He seemed **cordially delighted** to **patronize** the son; he **invited** me to visit him at Laughton, and hinted to my father that I was **formed** for something better than a counting-house: my poor father was **intoxicated**. In a word, here I am; here, often for days, almost weeks, together, have I been a **guest**, always welcomed."

"You pause. This is the primordium,—now comes the **confession**, eh?"

"Why, one half the confession is over. It was my most **unmerited** fortune to **attract** the notice of Miss Clavering. Do not **fancy** me so self-conceited as to imagine that I should ever have presumed so high, but for—"

"But for encouragement,—I understand! Well, she is a **magnificent creature**, in her way, and I do not wonder that she **drove** the poor little girl at Southampton out of your thoughts."

"Ah! but there is the sore,—I am not sure that she has done so. Ardworth, I may trust you?"

"With everything but half-a-guinea. I would not **promise** to be rock against so great a temptation!" and Ardworth turned his empty **pockets** inside out.

"Tush! be serious, or I go."

"Serious! With pockets like these, the devil's in it if I am not serious. Perge, precor."

"Ardworth, then," said Mainwaring, with great emotion, "I **confide** to you the **secret** trouble of my heart. This girl at Southampton is Lucretia's sister,—her half-sister; the rich **relation** on whose allowance she lives is Sir Miles St. John."

"Whew! my own poor dear little cousin, by the father's side! Mainwaring, I trust you have not **deceived** me; you have not **amused** yourself with **breaking** Susan's heart? For a heart, and an **honest**, simple, English girl's heart she has."

French

amused: amusèrent.
attract: attirer, allécher, allèches, solliciter, appâter.
breaking: rupture, floculation, brisement, broyage, fracture.
confession: confession, aveu.
confide: confier.
cordially: cordialement, de manière cordiale, de façon cordiale.
creature: créature.
deceived: trompâtes, déçu, trichâmes.
delighted: enchanté, ravi.
drove: conduisis, poussâmes, pourchassèrent, actionna, pilotèrent.
fancy: imaginer, fantaisie, songer, rêver éveillé, aimer.
favour: faveur, service, grâce, complaisance, favoriser.
formed: formé.
guest: hôte, invité, convive, client.
honest: honnête, intègre, loyal, sincère.
intoxicated: ivre, enivras, intoxiqué.
invited: invitèrent, conviâtes.
magnificent: magnifique, grandiose.
patronize: patronner, protéger.
pocket: poche, empocher, case.
procured: procuras.
promise: promettre, assurer.
relation: relation, abord, rapport.
secret: secret, arcane.
unmerited: immérité.

"Heaven **forbid**! I tell you I have never even declared my love; and if love it were, I trust it is over. But when Sir Miles was first kind to me, first invited me, I own I had the hope to win his esteem; and since he had always made so strong and cruel a distinction between Lucretia and Susan, I thought it not impossible that he might consent at last to my union with the niece he had refused to receive and acknowledge. But even while the hope was in me, I was drawn on, I was **entangled**, I was spell-bound, I know not how or why; but, to close my confidence, while still doubtful whether my own heart is free from the **remembrance** of the one sister, I am pledged to the other."

Ardworth looked down gravely and remained silent. He was a **joyous**, careless, reckless youth, with **unsteady** character and pursuits, and with something of vague poetry, much of unaccommodating pride about his nature,—one of those youths little likely to do what is called well in the world; not **persevering** enough for an independent career, too **blunt** and honest for a **servile** one. But it was in the very **disposition** of such a person to judge somewhat **harshly** of Mainwaring's disclosure, and not easily to comprehend what, after all, was very natural,—how a young man, new to life, **timid** by character, and of an extreme susceptibility to the fear of giving pain, had, in the surprise, the gratitude, the emotion, of an **avowed attachment** from a girl far above him in worldly position, been forced, by receiving, to seem, at least, to return her affection. And, indeed, though not wholly insensible to the brilliant prospects opened to him in such a connection, yet, to do him justice, Mainwaring would have been equally entangled by a similar **avowal** from a girl more his equal in the world. It was rather from an **amiability bordering** upon weakness, than from any more **degrading** moral **imperfections**, that he had been betrayed into a position which neither **contented** his heart nor satisfied his conscience.

With far less ability than his friend, Ardworth had more force and **steadiness** in his nature, and was wholly free from that **morbid delicacy** of **temperament** to which **susceptible** and shy persons owe much of their errors and **misfortunes**. He said, therefore, after a long pause: "My good

---

French

amiability: amabilité, gentillesse.
attachment: attachement, saisie, annexe, accessoire.
avowal: aveu, confession.
avowed: déclaré, avouâmes.
blunt: émoussé, épointer.
bordering: aboutissant, bordant, bourrage, garnissage.
contented: content, satisfait.
degrading: dégradant, avilissant.
delicacy: friandise, délicatesse, finesse.

disposition: disposition, don, talent, aptitude.
entangled: empêtra, entortillé.
forbid: interdire, défendre, prohiber.
harshly: rudement, de façon vulgaire, de manière vulgaire.
imperfection: imperfection, défectuosité.
joyous: joyeux, heureux.
misfortune: malheur, infortune, malchance.

morbid: morbide.
persevering: persévérant.
remembrance: souvenir, mémoire.
servile: aplaventriste, servile.
steadiness: fermeté, régularité, stabilité.
susceptible: sensible, susceptible.
temperament: tempérament, nature.
timid: timide, peureux, craintif.
unsteady: instable, chancelant, inconstant.

fellow, to be plain with you, I cannot say that your confession has improved you in my **estimation**; but that is perhaps because of the **bluntness** of my understanding. I could quite comprehend your **forgetting** Susan (and, after all, I am left in doubt as to the extent of her **conquest** over you) for the very different charms of her sister. On the other hand, I could still better understand that, having once fancied Susan, you could not be commanded into love for Lucretia. But I do not comprehend your feeling love for one, and making love to the other,—which is the long and short of the business."

"That is not exactly the true statement," answered Mainwaring, with a powerful effort at **composure**. "There are moments when, listening to Lucretia, when, **charmed** by that **softness** which, contrasting the rest of her character, she **exhibits** to none but me, struck by her great mental powers, proud of an unsought triumph over such a being, I feel as if I could love none but her; then suddenly her mood changes,—she utters sentiments that chill and **revolt** me; the very beauty seems vanished from her face. I recall with a sigh the simple sweetness of Susan, and I feel as if I deceived both my mistress and myself. Perhaps, however, all the circumstances of this connection tend to increase my doubts. It is **humiliating** to me to know that I **woo clandestinely** and upon **sufferance**; that I am **stealing**, as it were, into a fortune; that I am eating Sir Miles's bread, and yet **counting** upon his death; and this shame in myself may make me **unconsciously unjust** to Lucretia. But it is useless to **reprove** me for what is past; and though I at first imagined you could advise me for the future, I now see, too clearly, that no advice could avail."

"I grant that too; for all you require is to make up your mind to be fairly off with the old love, or fairly on with the new. However, now you have stated your case thus frankly, if you permit me, I will take advantage of the strange chance of finding myself here, and watch, **ponder**, and counsel, if I can. This Lucretia, I own it, **puzzles** and **perplexes** me; but though no Oedipus, I will not take **fright** at the **sphinx**. I suppose now it is time to

---

French

bluntness: état émoussé, manque de tranchant.
charmed: charmé.
clandestinely: de façon clandestine, de manière clandestine.
composure: repos, calme, impassibilité.
conquest: conquête.
counting: comptage, dénombrement.
estimation: estimation, évaluation, jugement.
exhibit: exposer, exhiber, montrer, objet exposé.
forgetting: oubliant, désapprenant.
fright: peur, effroi, anxiété, frayeur, terreur.
humiliating: humiliant.
perplex: embarrasse.
ponder: peser, réfléchissent, pesons, pèses, considérons.
puzzle: énigme, confondre, consterner, puzzle, stupéfier, troubler, abasourdir.
reprove: réprimander, reprocher, gronder, sermonner.
revolt: révolte, se révolter.
softness: douceur, mollesse.
sphinx: sphinx.
stealing: vol, volant, voler.
sufferance: tolérance, attente.
unconsciously: de façon inconsciente, de manière inconsciente, inconsciemment.
unjust: injuste, prévaricateur.
woo: faire la cour, courtisez.

return. They expect some of the **neighbours** to drink tea, and I must **doff** my fishing-jacket. Come!"

As they strolled towards the house, Ardworth broke a silence which had **lasted** for some moments.

"And how is that dear good Fielden? I ought to have **guessed** him at once, when you spoke of your clergyman and his young charge; but I did not know he was at Southampton."

"He has **exchanged** his living for a year, on account of his wife's health, and rather, I think also, with the wish to bring poor Susan nearer to Laughton, in the chance of her uncle seeing her. But you are, then, acquainted with Fielden?"

"Acquainted!—my best friend. He was my tutor, and prepared me for Caius College. I **owe** him, not only the little learning I have, but the little good that is left in me. I owe to him apparently, also, whatever chance of **bettering** my prospects may arise from my visit to Laughton."

"Notwithstanding our **intimacy**, we have, like most young men not related, spoken so little of our family matters that I do not now understand how you are cousin to Susan, nor what, to my surprise and **delight**, brought you **hither** three days ago."

"Faith, my story is easier to explain than your own, William. Here goes!"

But as Ardworth's **recital partially** involves references to family matters not yet **sufficiently** known to the reader, we must be pardoned if we assume to ourselves his task of **narrator**, and necessarily **enlarge** on his details.

The branch of the **illustrious** family of St. John represented by Sir Miles, **diverged** from the parent **stem** of the Lords of Bletshoe. With them it placed at the **summit** of its pedigree the name of William de St. John, the Conqueror's **favourite** and trusted **warrior**, and Oliva de Filgiers. With them it blazoned the latter alliance, which gave to Sir Oliver St. John the lands of Bletshoe by the hand of Margaret Beauchamp (by her second marriage with the Duke of Somerset), **grandmother** to Henry VII. In the following

---

French

bettering: renforcement.
delight: délice, enchanter, ravir, plaisir.
diverged: divergèrent.
doff: enlever, levée, lever.
enlarge: agrandir, accroître, augmenter, étendre, amplifier.
exchanged: échangées.
favourite: favori, préféré.
grandmother: aïeule, mémé.
guessed: deviné.
hither: ici.

illustrious: illustre, célèbre, fameux.
intimacy: intimité.
lasted: duré, durèrent, dura, durâmes.
narrator: narrateur, récitant.
neighbour: voisin, semblable.
owe: devoir, doivent, dois, devez, avoir une dette.
partially: en partie, partiellement, de façon partielle, de manière partielle.

recital: récital, considérant.
stem: tige, tronc, queue, étrave, racine, fût, jambe, rafle, radical, pied.
sufficiently: suffisamment, assez, passablement, plutôt, de façon suffisante, de manière suffisante.
summit: sommet, cime, faîte, pointe, comble, summon, bout, haut.
warrior: guerrier, militaire.

generation, the younger son of a younger son had founded, partly by offices of state, partly by marriage with a wealthy heiress, a house of his own; and in the reign of James the First, the St. Johns of Laughton ranked amongst the chief gentlemen of Hampshire. From that time till the **accession** of George III the family, though it remained **untitled**, had added to its consequence by **intermarriages** of considerable dignity,—chosen, indeed, with a **disregard** for money **uncommon** amongst the English aristocracy; so that the estate was but little **enlarged** since the reign of James, though **profiting**, of course, by improved cultivation and the different value of money. On the other hand, perhaps there were scarcely ten families in the country who could **boast** of a similar **directness** of descent on all sides from the proudest and noblest aristocracy of the soil; and Sir Miles St. John, by blood, was, almost at the distance of eight centuries, as pure a Norman as his **ancestral** William. His grandfather, nevertheless, had **deviated** from the usual **disinterested** practice of the family, and had married an heiress who brought the **quarterings** of Vernon to the crowded **escutcheon**, and with these quarterings an estate of some 4,000 pounds a year **popularly** known by the name of Vernon Grange. This rare occurrence did not add to the domestic happiness of the **contracting** parties, nor did it lead to the ultimate increase of the Laughton possessions. Two sons were born. To the elder was destined the father's inheritance,—to the younger the **maternal** property. One house is not large enough for two **heirs**. Nothing could exceed the pride of the father as a St. John, except the pride of the mother as a Vernon. **Jealousies** between the two sons began early and rankled deep; nor was there peace at Laughton till the younger had carried away from its **rental** the lands of Vernon Grange; and the elder remained just where his **predecessors** stood in point of possessions,—sole lord of Laughton sole. The elder son, Sir Miles's father, had been, indeed, so chafed by the rivalry with his brother that in **disgust** he had run away and thrown himself, at the age of fourteen, into the navy. By accident or by merit he rose high in that profession, acquired name and fame, and lost an eye and an arm,—for which he was gazetted, at the same time, an **admiral** and a baronet.

French

accession: adhésion, accession, présentation, inscription, acquisition.
admiral: amiral.
ancestral: ancestral.
boast: fanfaronner, vanter, se vanter, faire le malin.
contracting: contractant, conclusion de marché, passage de contrat.
deviated: dévié, s'affolé, m'affolai, vous affolâtes, t'affolas, nous affolâmes.

directness: franchise.
disgust: dégoût, écoeurer.
disinterested: désintéressé, indifférent.
disregard: négliger, méconnaissance, mépris.
enlarged: agrandi, prorogeâmes.
escutcheon: écusson, entrée de serrure.
heir: héritier, légataire.
intermarriage: mariage consanguin, intermariage.

jealousy: jalousie, envie.
maternal: maternel.
popularly: populairement, de façon populaire, de manière populaire.
predecessor: prédécesseur.
profiting: bénéficiant.
quartering: casernement, division par quartiers, inquartation, quartage.
rental: location, loyer.
uncommon: rare.
untitled: sans titre.

Thus **mutilated** and **dignified**, Sir George St. John retired from the profession; and finding himself unmarried, and **haunted** by the apprehension that if he died **childless**, Laughton would pass to his brother's heirs, he resolved upon **consigning** his remains to the nuptial **couch**, previous to the surer peace of the family **vault**. At the age of fifty-nine, the grim veteran succeeded in finding a young lady of **unblemished** descent and much marked with the small-pox, who consented to accept the only hand which Sir George had to offer. From this marriage sprang a numerous family; but all died in early childhood, frightened to death, said the neighbours, by their tender parents (considered the **ugliest** couple in the county), except one boy (the present Sir Miles) and one daughter, many years younger, destined to become Lucretia's mother. Sir Miles came early into his property; and although the **softening** advance of civilization, with the liberal effects of travel and a long residence in cities, took from him that provincial **austerity** of pride which is only seen in stanch perfection amongst the lords of a village, he was yet little less susceptible to the duties of maintaining his **lineage** pure as its representation had descended to him than the most superb of his predecessors. But **owing**, it was said, to an early disappointment, he led, during youth and **manhood**, a **roving** and **desultory** life, and so put off from year to year the grand experiment **matrimonial**, until he arrived at old age, with the philosophical determination to select from the other branches of his house the successor to the heritage of St. John. In thus **arrogating** to himself a right to neglect his proper duties as head of a family, he found his excuse in adopting his niece Lucretia. His sister had chosen for her first husband a friend and neighbour of his own, a younger son, of unexceptionable birth and of very agreeable manners in society. But this gentleman **contrived** to render her life so miserable that, though he died fifteen months after their marriage, his widow could scarcely be expected to **mourn** long for him. A year after Mr. Clavering's death, Mrs. Clavering married again, under the mistaken notion that she had the right to choose for herself. She married Dr. Mivers, the provincial **physician** who had attended her husband in his last illness,—a gentleman by education, manners, and

---

French

arrogating: usurpant.
austerity: austérité.
childless: sans enfant.
consigning: consignant.
contrived: inventâmes.
couch: canapé, divan, presse coucheuse.
desultory: décousu.
dignified: digne.
haunted: hanté, égaré.
lineage: lignage, descendance, souche.

manhood: virilité, âge d'homme.
matrimonial: conjugal, matrimonial.
mourn: regretter, vous lamentez, s'affliger, te lamentes, lamentez-vous, se lamentent, pleurer, me lamente, nous lamentons, être en deuil, porter le deuil.
mutilated: mutilé, détérioré, tronqué.
owing: devant, dû.
physician: médecin, docteur.

roving: mèche, boudinage, rôdant, vagabondant, roving, rôder, affinage des mèches, bambrochage, itinérant.
softening: ramollissement, adoucissement, amollissant, attendrissant, assouplissement, se ramollissant.
ugliest: le plus laid.
unblemished: sans tache.
vault: voûte, chambre forte.

profession, but **unhappily** the son of a silk-mercer. Sir Miles never **forgave** this connection. By her first marriage, Sir Miles's sister had one daughter, Lucretia; by her second marriage, another daughter, named Susan. She survived somewhat more than a year the birth of the latter. On her death, Sir Miles formally (through his agent) applied to Dr. Mivers for his **eldest** niece, Lucretia Clavering, and the physician did not think himself **justified** in **withholding** from her the **probable** advantages of a transfer from his own roof to that of her **wealthy** uncle. He himself had been no worldly **gainer** by his connection; his practice had suffered **materially** from the sympathy which was felt by the county families for the supposed wrongs of Sir Miles St. John, who was personally not only popular, but **esteemed**, nor less so on account of his pride,—too dignified to refer even to his domestic **annoyances**, except to his most familiar **associates**; to them, indeed, Sir Miles had said, briefly, that he considered a physician who **abused** his entrance into a **noble** family by stealing into its alliance was a character in whose punishment all society had an interest. The words were repeated; they were thought just. Those who **ventured** to suggest that Mrs. Clavering, as a **widow**, was a free agent, were regarded with suspicion. It was the time when French principles were just beginning to be held in horror, especially in the provinces, and when everything that **encroached** upon the rights and **prejudices** of the high born was called "a French principle." Dr. Mivers was as much scouted as if he had been a sans-culotte. **Obliged** to **quit** the county, he settled at a distance; but he had a career to **commence** again; his wife's death **enfeebled** his spirits and damped his **exertions**. He did little more than earn a bare **subsistence**, and died at last, when his only daughter was fourteen, poor and embarrassed On his death-bed he wrote a letter to Sir Miles **reminding** him that, after all, Susan was his sister's child, gently **vindicating** himself from the unmerited charge of **treachery**, which had **blasted** his fortunes and left his orphan penniless, and closing with a **touching** yet a manly appeal to the sole relative left to befriend her. The clergyman who had attended him in his dying moments took charge of this letter; he brought it in person to Laughton, and delivered it to Sir Miles.

French

abused: abusa.
annoyance: contrariété, peine, ennui, désolation.
associate: associé, s'accoupler.
blasted: désolé, foudroyé, grenaille.
commence: commencer, débuter, aborder.
eldest: aîné.
encroached: empiétas.
enfeebled: débilita.
esteemed: estimé.
exertion: effort.
forgave: pardonnâtes, excusâtes.
gainer: gagnant.
justified: justifié, dressé, cadrèrent.
materially: matériellement.
noble: noble, élevé.
obliged: obligea.
prejudice: préjugé, léser.
probable: probable, vraisemblable.
quit: quitter, abandonner, démissionner, délaisser, re retirer, livrer.
reminding: rappelant.
subsistence: subsistance.
touching: attendrissant, touchant, émouvant.
treachery: traîtrise, déloyauté.
unhappily: de façon malheureuse, de manière malheureuse.
ventured: osé.
vindicating: justifiant.
wealthy: riche.
widow: veuve.
withholding: retenant, rétention, refus.

Whatever his errors, the old baronet was no common man. He was not **vindictive**, though he could not be called **forgiving**. He had considered his conduct to his sister a duty **owed** to his name and **ancestors**; she had placed herself and her **youngest** child out of the pale of his family. He would not receive as his niece the grand-daughter of a silk-mercer. The relationship was **extinct**, as, in certain countries, **nobility** is **forfeited** by a union with an **inferior** class. But, niece or not, here was a claim to **humanity** and **benevolence**, and never yet had appeal been made by suffering to his heart and **purse** in **vain**.

He bowed his head over the letter as his eye came to the last line, and remained silent so long that the clergyman at last, moved and **hopeful**, approached and took his hand. It was the **impulse** of a good man and a good priest. Sir Miles looked up in surprise; but the calm, **pitying** face **bent** on him **repelled** all return of pride.

"Sir," he said tremulously, and he pressed the hand that grasped his own, "I thank you. I am not fit at this moment to decide what to do; tomorrow you shall know. And the man died poor,—not in want, not in want?"

"Comfort yourself, **worthy** sir; he had at the last all that **sickness** and death require, except one **assurance**, which I ventured to whisper to him,—I trust not too rashly,—that his daughter would not be left **unprotected**. And I **pray** you to reflect, my dear sir, that—"

Sir Miles did not wait for the conclusion of the sentence; he rose **abruptly**, and left the room. Mr. Fielden (so the good priest was named) felt confident of the success of his mission; but to win it the more support, he sought Lucretia. She was then seventeen: it is an age when the heart is **peculiarly** open to the household ties,—to the memory of a mother, to the sweet name of sister. He sought this girl, he told his **tale**, and pleaded the sister's cause. Lucretia heard in silence: neither eye nor **lip** betrayed emotion; but her colour went and came. This was the only sign that she was moved: moved, but how? Fielden's experience in the human heart could not guess.

French

abruptly: brusquement, abruptement, sèchement, de façon abrupte, de manière abrupte.
ancestor: ancêtre, ascendant.
assurance: assurance, garantie.
benevolence: bienveillance.
bent: courbé, cambrai, penché, disposition.
extinct: éteint, disparu.
forfeited: forfaits, perdu.
forgiving: pardonnant, excusant, indulgent.
hopeful: optimiste, plein d'espoir.
humanity: humanité.
impulse: impulsion, incitation, pulsion.
inferior: inférieur, de second ordre, en indice inférieur, subordonné.
lip: lèvre, bord.
nobility: noblesse.
owed: dûtes, dû, dûmes, durent, dus, dut.
peculiarly: de façon étrange, de manière étrange.
pitying: compatissant.
pray: prier, prions.
purse: sacoche, bourse, sac à main.
repelled: repoussas, refusé.
sickness: maladie.
tale: conte, récit, relation.
unprotected: non protégé.
vain: vain, vaniteux, abortif, frivole.
vindictive: vindicatif.
worthy: digne.
youngest: le plus jeune.

When he had done, she went quietly to her desk (it was in her own room that the conference took place), she **unlocked** it with a **deliberate** hand, she took from it a **pocketbook** and a case of **jewels** which Sir Miles had given her on her last **birthday**. "Let my sister have these; while I live she shall not want!"

"My dear young lady, it is not these things that she asks from you,—it is your affection, your **sisterly** heart, your **intercession** with her natural **protector**; these, in her name, I ask for,—'non gemmis, neque **purpura** venale, nec auro!'"

Lucretia then, still without apparent emotion, raised to the good man's face deep, **penetrating**, but unrevealing eyes, and said slowly,—

"Is my sister like my mother, who, they say, was handsome?"

Much **startled** by this question, Fielden **answered**: "I never saw your mother, my dear; but your sister gives promise of more than common comeliness."

Lucretia's **brows** grew slightly compressed. "And her education has been, of course, neglected?"

"Certainly, in some points,—mathematics, for **instance**, and **theology**; but she knows what ladies generally know,—French and Italian, and such like. Dr. Mivers was not unlearned in the **polite** letters. Oh, trust me, my dear young lady, she will not disgrace your family; she will **justify** your **uncle**'s favour. **Plead** for her!" And the good man clasped his hands.

Lucretia's eyes fell musingly on the ground; but she **resumed**, after a short pause,—

"What does my uncle himself say?"

"Only that he will decide to-morrow."

"I will see him;" and Lucretia left the room as for that object. But when she had **gained** the **stairs**, she paused at the large embayed casement, which formed a **niche** in the landing-place, and gazed over the broad **domains** beyond; a stern smile **settled**, then, upon her lips,—the smile seemed to say, "In this **inheritance** I will have no rival."

French

answered: répondis.
birthday: anniversaire.
brow: sourcil, front.
deliberate: délibéré, intentionnel.
domain: ensemble compact, propriété.
gained: gagné.
inheritance: héritage, succession.
instance: exemple, instance.
intercession: intercession.
jewel: bijou, joyau.
justify: justifier, dressez, cadrent, motiver.
niche: niche, microhabitat, lien écologique.
penetrating: pénétrant, transfixiant, dégrippant, mordant.
plead: plaider, implorer.
pocketbook: livre de poche.
polite: poli, courtois.
protector: protecteur, parafoudre, armement, dispositif de protection.
purpura: purpura.
resumed: reprîtes, recommençâtes.
settled: réglé, sédimenté, déposé, tassé, vida, vidâmes, vidé, vidèrent, colonisa, domicilié, arrangé.
sisterly: de soeur.
stair: marche, escalier.
startled: surprîtes, effarouché, effrayé, alarmai.
theology: théologie.
uncle: oncle.
unlocked: ouvrit, ouvert.

Lucretia's influence with Sir Miles was great, but here it was not needed. Before she saw him he had decided on his course. Her **precocious** and apparently **intuitive** knowledge of character **detected** at a glance the safety with which she might **intercede**. She did so, and was chid into silence.

The next morning, Sir Miles took the priest's arm and walked with him into the gardens.

"Mr. Fielden," he said, with the air of a man who has chosen his course, and **deprecates** all attempt to make him **swerve** from it, "if I followed my own **selfish** wishes, I should take home this poor child. Stay, sir, and hear me, — I am no **hypocrite**, and I speak honestly. I like young faces; I have no family of my own. I love Lucretia, and I am proud of her; but a girl brought up in **adversity** might be a better nurse and a more **docile** companion, — let that pass. I have reflected, and I feel that I cannot set to Lucretia — set to children unborn — the example of **indifference** to a name **degraded** and a race **adulterated**; you may call this pride or prejudice, — I view it differently. There are duties due from an individual, duties due from a nation, duties due from a family; as my ancestors thought, so think I. They left me the charge of their name, as the fief-rent by which I hold their lands. 'Sdeath, sir! — Pardon me the **expletive**; I was about to say that if I am now a childless old man, it is because I have myself known **temptation** and **resisted**. I loved, and denied myself what I believed my best chance of happiness, because the object of my attachment was not my equal. That was a bitter struggle, — I triumphed, and I **rejoice** at it, though the result was to leave all thoughts of **wedlock** elsewhere **odious** and **repugnant**. These principles of action have made a part of my **creed** as gentleman, if not as Christian. Now to the point. I **beseech** you to find a **fitting** and **reputable** home for Miss — Miss Mivers," the lip slightly **curled** as the name was said; "I shall provide **suitably** for her maintenance. When she marries, I will **dower** her, provided only and always that her choice fall upon one who will not still further **degrade** her lineage on her mother's side, — in a word, if she select a gentleman. Mr. Fielden, on this subject I have no more to say."

French

adulterated: falsifié, adultérai.
adversity: adversité, abaissement.
beseech: implorer, solliciter, supplier, adjurer.
creed: credo, foi.
curled: bouclé, frisé.
degrade: dégrader, avilir.
degraded: dégrada, avilit.
deprecates: désapprouve.
detected: détectâmes, dépisté.
docile: docile.
dower: douaire.
expletive: explétif.
fitting: convenable, ajustage, conforme, raccord, essayage, montage, posage, liquidation, ferrure, adaptation.
hypocrite: hypocrite.
indifference: indifférence.
intercede: intercéder.
intuitive: intuitif.
odious: odieux.
precocious: précoce.
rejoice: réjouir, être joyeux.
repugnant: répugnant, inconciliable.
reputable: honorable.
resisted: résistai.
selfish: égoïste.
suitably: de façon convenable, de manière convenable.
swerve: écart, zigzaguer, embardée.
temptation: tentation, séduction.
wedlock: mariage.

In vain the good clergyman, whose very conscience, as well as reason, was shocked by the deliberate and **argumentative** manner with which the baronet had treated the **abandonment** of his sister's child as an absolutely moral, almost religious, duty,—in vain he **exerted** himself to **repel** such **sophisms** and put the matter in its true light. It was easy for him to move Sir Miles's heart,—that was ever gentle; that was moved already: but the **crotchet** in his head was **impregnable**. The more **touchingly** he painted poor Susan's unfriended youth, her sweet character, and promising virtues, the more Sir Miles St. John considered himself a **martyr** to his principles, and the more **obstinate** in the **martyrdom** he became. "Poor thing! poor child!" he said often, and **brushed** a tear from his eyes; "a thousand pities! Well, well, I hope she will be happy! Mind, money shall never stand in the way if she have a suitable offer!"

This was all the worthy clergyman, after an hour's eloquence, could extract from him. Out of breath and out of patience, he gave in at last; and the baronet, still holding his reluctant arm, led him back towards the house. After a prolonged pause, Sir Miles said abruptly: "I have been thinking that I may have **unwittingly** injured this man,—this Mivers,—while I deemed only that he injured me. As to **reparation** to his daughter, that is settled; and after all, though I do not publicly acknowledge her, she is half my own niece."

"Half?"

"Half,—the father's side doesn't count, of course; and, **rigidly** speaking, the relationship is perhaps forfeited on the other. However, that half of it I grant. Zooks, sir, I say I grant it! I **beg** you ten thousand pardons for my vehemence. To return,—perhaps I can show at least that I bear no malice to this poor doctor. He has relations of his own,—silk mercers; trade has reverses. How are they off?"

Perfectly **perplexed** by this very **contradictory** and **paradoxical**, yet, to one better acquainted with Sir Miles, very characteristic, benevolence, Fielden was some time before he answered. "Those members of Dr. Mivers's

French

abandonment: abandon, délaissement, abdication.
argumentative: chamailleur, chicanier, argumentatif, raisonneur.
beg: mendier, demander, prier, solliciter, implorer, quémander, supplier.
brushed: brossa.
contradictory: contradictoire, opposé.
crotchet: noire.

exerted: pratiquas, t'efforças, s'efforça, nous efforçâmes, exerças, m'efforçai, vous efforçâtes, efforcés.
impregnable: imprenable.
martyr: martyr.
martyrdom: martyre, supplice.
obstinate: obstiné, têtu, tenace, entêté.
paradoxical: paradoxal.
perplexed: embarrassâtes, perplexe.

reparation: réparation.
repel: repousser, refusons, refoulent.
rigidly: rigidement, de façon rigide, de manière rigide.
sophism: sophisme.
touchingly: de façon attendrissante, de manière attendrissante.
unwittingly: involontairement, de façon involontaire, de manière involontaire.

family who are in trade are sufficiently **prosperous**; they have paid his debts,—they, Sir Miles, will receive his daughter."

"By no means!" **cried** Sir Miles, quickly; then, recovering himself, he added, "or, if you think that **advisable**, of course all **interference** on my part is withdrawn."

"Festina lente!—not so **quick**, Sir Miles. I do not yet say that it is advisable,—not because they are silk-mercers, the which, I **humbly** conceive, is no **sin** to **exclude** them from **gratitude** for their proffered **kindness**, but because Susan, poor child, having been brought up in different **habits**, may feel a little strange, at least at first, with—"

"Strange, yes; I should hope so!" interrupted Sir Miles, taking **snuff** with much energy. "And, by the way, I am thinking that it would be well if you and Mrs. Fielden—you are married, sir? That is right; **clergymen** all marry!—if you and Mrs. Fielden would take charge of her yourselves, it would be a great **comfort** to me to think her so well placed. We **differ**, sir, but I respect you. Think of this. Well, then, the doctor has left no relations that I can aid in any way?"

"Strange man!" **muttered** Fielden. "Yes; I must not let one poor **youth** lose the opportunity offered by your—your—"

"Never mind what; **proceed**. One poor youth,—in the shop, of course?"

"No; and by his father's side (since you so esteem such vanities) of an **ancient** family,—a sister of Dr. Mivers married Captain Ardworth."

"Ardworth,—a goodish name; Ardworth of Yorkshire?"

"Yes, of that family. It was, of course, an imprudent marriage, contracted while he was only an **ensign**. His family did not **reject** him, Sir Miles."

"Sir, Ardworth is a good squire's family, but the name is Saxon; there is no difference in race between the head of the Ardworths, if he were a **duke**, and my **gardener**, John Hodge,—Saxon and Saxon, both. His family did not reject him; go on."

French

advisable: recommandé, judicieux, à propos.
ancient: antique, ancien.
clergymen: ecclésiastique.
comfort: confort, consoler, réconfort.
cried: pleuré.
differ: différer, être différent.
duke: duc.
ensign: pavillon, enseigne, aspirant.
exclude: exclure, excepter, exempter, dispenser.
gardener: jardinier, ouvrier jardinier.
gratitude: gratitude, reconnaissance, remerciement.
habit: habitude, coutume, port, usage.
humbly: humblement, de manière humble, de façon humble.
interference: interférence, brouillage, ingérence, perturbation, immixtion, serrage.
kindness: amabilité, gentillesse, bonté, aménité.
muttered: barbotée.
proceed: procéder, avancer.
prosperous: prospère.
quick: rapide, prompt, vite.
reject: rejeter, refuser, repousser, rebuter.
sin: péché, commettre une faute.
snuff: tabac à priser, effleurer, moucher.
youth: jeunesse, ado.

"But he was a younger son in a large family; both himself and his wife have known all the distresses common, they tell me, to the **poverty** of a **soldier** who has no **resource** but his pay. They have a son. Dr. Mivers, though so poor himself, took this boy, for he loved his sister **dearly**, and meant to bring him up to his own **profession**. Death **frustrated** this intention. The boy is high-spirited and deserving."

"Let his education be completed; send him to the University; and I will see that he is put into some career of which his father's family would **approve**. You need not mention to any one my intentions in this respect, not even to the **lad**. And now, Mr. Fielden, I have done my duty,—at least, I think so. The longer you **honour** my house, the more I shall be **pleased** and **grateful**; but this **topic**, allow me most **respectfully** to say, needs and bears no further comment. Have you seen the last news from the army?"

"The army! Oh, fie, Sir Miles, I must speak one word more. May not my poor Susan have at least the comfort to embrace her sister?"

Sir Miles paused a moment, and **struck** his crutch-stick **thrice** firmly on the ground.

"I see no great **objection** to that; but by the address of this letter, the poor girl is too far from Laughton to send Lucretia to her."

"I can **obviate** that objection, Sir Miles. It is my wish to continue to Susan her present home amongst my own children. My wife loves her dearly; and had you consented to give her the **shelter** of your own roof, I am sure I should not have seen a smile in the house for a month after. If you **permit** this plan, as indeed you honoured me by **suggesting** it, I can pass through Southampton on my way to my own living in Devonshire, and Miss Clavering can visit her sister there."

"Let it be so," said Sir Miles, briefly; and so the conversation closed.

Some weeks afterwards, Lucretia went in her uncle's **carriage**, with four post-horses, with her **maid** and her footman,—went in the state and **pomp** of heiress to Laughton,—to the small lodging-house in which the kind **pastor crowded** his children and his young guest. She stayed there some days. She

---

French

approve: approuver, donner son accord.
carriage: wagon, chariot, voiture, affût.
crowded: bondé, encombré.
dearly: de manière chère, de façon chère.
frustrated: frustré, déjoua, déçu.
grateful: reconnaissant.
honour: honneur, honorer.
lad: garçon, gosse.
maid: femme de chambre, servante, domestique, bonne.
objection: objection, opposition, réclamation.
obviate: obvions.
pastor: pasteur, prêtre, curé, abbé.
permit: permis, autoriser.
pleased: content, satisfait, plu.
pomp: pompe, splendeur.
poverty: pauvreté, misère.
profession: profession.
resource: ressource.
respectfully: de manière respectueuse, de façon respectueuse.
shelter: abri, refuge, s'abriter, garantir, gîte, se mettre à l'abri, se retrancher, héberger.
soldier: soldat, militaire.
struck: frappé, assénée, raclé, démontage.
suggesting: suggérant.
thrice: trois fois.
topic: sujet, thème, topique, actualité, composition.

did not weep when she **embraced** Susan, she did not weep when she took leave of her; but she showed no want of actual kindness, though the kindness was formal and stately. On her return, Sir Miles forbore to question; but he looked as if he expected, and would **willingly** permit, her to speak on what might naturally be **uppermost** at her heart. Lucretia, however, remained silent, till at last the baronet, **colouring**, as if ashamed of his **curiosity**, said,—

"Is your sister like your mother?"

"You forget, sir, I can have no **recollection** of my mother."

"Your mother had a strong family **likeness** to myself."

"She is not like you; they say she is like Dr. Mivers."

"Oh!" said the baronet, and he asked no more.

The sisters did not meet again; a few letters passed between them, but the **correspondence** gradually **ceased**.

Young Ardworth went to college, prepared by Mr. Fielden, who was no ordinary scholar, and an **accurate** and **profound** mathematician,—a more important **requisite** than **classical** learning in a tutor for Cambridge. But Ardworth was **idle**, and perhaps even **dissipated**. He took a common degree, and made some debts, which were paid by Sir Miles without a murmur. A few letters then passed between the baronet and the clergyman as to Ardworth's future **destiny**; the latter **owned** that his **pupil** was not persevering enough for the Bar, nor **steady** enough for the Church. These were no great **faults** in Sir Miles's eyes. He resolved, after an effort, to judge himself of the capacities of the young man, and so came the **invitation** to Laughton. Ardworth was **greatly** surprised when Fielden communicated to him this invitation, for **hitherto** he had not **conceived** the slightest **suspicion** of his **benefactor**; he had rather, and naturally, supposed that some relation of his father's had paid for his maintenance at the University, and he knew enough of the family history to look upon Sir Miles as the proudest of men. How was it, then, that he, who would not receive the daughter of Dr. Mivers, his own niece, would invite the **nephew** of Dr. Mivers, who was no relation

French

accurate: précis, ponctuel, exact.
benefactor: bienfaiteur.
ceased: cessé.
classical: classique.
colouring: coloration, prétannage, teinture, encrage.
conceived: conçurent.
correspondence: correspondance.
curiosity: curiosité.
destiny: destin, sort, fortune.
dissipated: dissipé, dispersai.
embraced: embrassé.

fault: défaut, panne, faute, faille, erreur.
greatly: de façon grande, de manière grande.
hitherto: jusqu'ici.
idle: inactif, tourner au ralenti, ralenti, fainéant, inoccupé, paresseux, au repos.
invitation: invitation.
likeness: ressemblance, similitude, portrait.
nephew: neveu.

owned: possédé.
profound: profond.
pupil: pupille, élève, écolier.
recollection: souvenir, mémoire.
requisite: requis, condition requise.
steady: régulier, stable.
suspicion: soupçon, méfiance, suspicion.
uppermost: le plus haut, suprême, en dessus.
willingly: volontiers, de manière volontaire, de façon volontaire.

to him? However, his curiosity was **excited**, and Fielden was **urgent** that he should go; to Laughton, therefore, had he gone.

We have now **brought** down to the **opening** of our **narrative** the general **records** of the family it **concerns**; we have **reserved** our account of the **rearing** and the **character** of the **personage** most important, perhaps, in the development of its events,—Lucretia Clavering,—in order to place **singly** before the **reader** the **portrait** of her **dark**, misguided, and ill-boding youth.

French

brought: apporta, amenèrent.
character: caractère, personnage, signe, nature, témoignage, tempérament.
concern: souci, concerner, regarder, intéresser, soin, inquiétude, être en relation avec, importance, préoccupation.
dark: foncé, sombre, obscur, noir.
excited: excitèrent, hérissèrent.
narrative: récit, relation, narratif.
opening: ouverture, ouvrant, orifice, début, déclenchement.
personage: personnage.
portrait: portrait, effigie, format vertical.
reader: lecteur, chargé de cours, dispositif de lecture de bande, indicateur, livre de lecture, microlecteur, morceaux choisis, appareil de lecture.
rearing: élevage, éducation, encastage à crémaillère, cabrement.
record: enregistrer, disque, record, rapport, document, relation, article, dossier, acte, compte rendu.
reserved: réservé.
singly: de façon célibataire, de manière célibataire.
urgent: urgent, pressant, impérieux.

CHAPTER II

LUCRETIA

When Lucretia first came to the house of Sir Miles St. John she was an infant about four years old. The baronet then lived **principally** in London, with occasional visits rather to the Continent or a watering-place than to his own family **mansion**. He did not pay any minute attention to his little ward, satisfied that her nurse was **sedulous**, and her nursery airy and **commodious**. When, at the age of seven, she began to interest him, and he himself, **approaching** old age, began seriously to consider whether he should select her as his heiress, for hitherto he had not formed any decided or definite notions on the matter, he was startled by a **temper** so **vehement**, so self-willed and **sternly imperious**, so **obstinately** bent upon **attaining** its object, so **indifferently contemptuous** of warning, **reproof**, **coaxing**, or punishment, that her **governess honestly** came to him in **despair**.

The management of this **unmanageable** child interested Sir Miles. It caused him to think of Lucretia seriously; it caused him to have her much in his society, and always in his thoughts. The result was, that by **amusing** and **occupying** him, she forced a stronger hold on his affections than she might have done had she been more like the ordinary run of **commonplace** children. Of all dogs, there is no dog that so **attaches** a master as a dog that

---

French

amusing: amusant, drôle, plaisant.
approaching: approchant, abordant, rapprochant, s'approcher.
attache: attaché.
attaining: atteignant, parvenant.
coaxing: cajolerie, câlin.
commodious: spacieux.
commonplace: banal, trivial.
contemptuous: dédaigneux, méprisant.
despair: désespoir.
governess: gouvernante.
honestly: honnêtement, de façon honnête, de manière honnête.
imperious: impérieux.
indifferently: de façon indifférente, de manière indifférente, indifféremment.
mansion: immeuble, château, mansion.
obstinately: de façon obstinée, de manière obstinée, obstinément.
occupying: occupant.
principally: principalement, surtout, de façon commettante.
reproof: reproche.
sedulous: assidu.
sternly: de manière poupe, sévèrement.
temper: humeur, tremper, durcir, tempérament, gâcher.
unmanageable: indocile, intraitable.
vehement: véhément, violent, passionné.

snarls at everybody else,—that no other hand can venture to pat with **impunity**; of all horses, there is none which so **flatters** the rider, from Alexander downwards, as a horse that nobody else can ride. Extend this principle to the human species, and you may understand why Lucretia became so dear to Sir Miles St. John,—she got at his heart through his vanity. For though, at times, her brow **darkened** and her eye flashed even at his **remonstrance**, she was yet no sooner in his society than she made a marked distinction between him and the subordinates who had hitherto sought to control her. Was this affection? He thought so. Alas! what parent can trace the workings of a child's mind,—springs moved by an idle word from a nurse; a whispered conference between **hirelings**. Was it possible that Lucretia had not often been **menaced**, as the direst evil that could **befall** her, with her uncle's **displeasure**; that long before she could be sensible of mere worldly loss or profit, she was not impressed with a vague sense of Sir Miles's power over her fate,—nay, when trampling, in **childish wrath** and scorn, upon some menial's **irritable** feelings, was it possible that she had not been told that, but for Sir Miles, she would be little better than a servant herself? Be this as it may, all weakness is prone to **dissimulate**; and rare and happy is the child whose feelings are as pure and transparent as the fond parent **deems** them. There is something in children, too, which seems like an **instinctive** deference to the aristocratic appearances which **sway** the world. Sir Miles's stately person, his imposing dress, the respect with which he was surrounded, all tended to **beget** notions of superiority and power, to which it was no shame to **succumb**, as it was to Miss Black, the governess, whom the maids answered **pertly**, or Martha, the nurse, whom Miss Black **snubbed** if Lucretia tore her **frock**.

Sir Miles's affection once won, his penetration not, perhaps, **blinded** to her more evident faults, but his self-love **soothed** towards regarding them **leniently**, there was much in Lucretia's external gifts which justified the **predilection** of the haughty man. As a child she was beautiful, and, perhaps from her very imperfections of temper, her beauty had that air of distinction which the love of command is apt to **confer**. If Sir Miles was with his friends

---

French

befall: arrives.
beget: engendrer.
blinded: ébloui, aveuglèrent.
childish: enfantin, puéril.
confer: conférer.
darkened: fonça, foncé, assombris.
deem: croire, être d'avis, croyez, penser que, regarder.
displeasure: déplaisir, mécontentement.
dissimulate: dissimuler.
flatters: flatte, adule, amadoue.
frock: robe, froc.
hireling: stipendié, larbin.
impunity: impunité.
instinctive: instinctif.
irritable: irritable, irascible.
leniently: de façon indulgente, de manière indulgente.
menaced: menacé.
pertly: de manière coquine, de façon coquine.
predilection: prédilection.
remonstrance: remontrance, protestation.
snarl: enchevêtrement, grondement.
snubbed: amarré sur bitte.
soothed: rassurèrent, calmé, abattis.
succumb: succomber.
sway: vaciller, balancement, oscillation, se balancer.
wrath: colère, courroux.

when Lucretia swept into the room, he was pleased to hear them call her their little "princess," and was pleased yet more at a certain dignified **tranquillity** with which she received their caresses or their **toys**, and which he regarded as the sign of a superior mind; nor was it long, indeed, before what we call "a superior mind" developed itself in the young Lucretia. All children are quick till they are set **methodically** to study; but Lucretia's quickness **defied** even that **numbing** ordeal, by which half of us are rendered **dunces**. Rapidity and precision in all the tasks set to her, in the comprehension of all the explanations given to her questions, evinced singular powers of readiness and reasoning.

As she grew older, she became more reserved and thoughtful. Seeing but few children of her own age, and mixing **intimately** with none, her mind was **debarred** from the usual objects which **distract** the **vivacity**, the restless and **wondrous** observation, of childhood. She came in and out of Sir Miles's library of a morning, or his drawing-room of an evening, till her hour for rest, with unquestioned and sometimes **unnoticed** freedom; she listened to the conversation around her, and formed her own conclusions **unchecked**. It has a great influence upon a child, whether for good or for evil, to mix early and **habitually** with those grown up,—for good to the mere intellect always; the evil depends upon the character and discretion of those the child sees and **hears**. "Reverence the greatest is due to the children," **exclaims** the wisest of the Romans [Cicero. The sentiment is borrowed by Juvenal.],—that is to say, that we must **revere** the **candour** and **inexperience** and innocence of their minds.

Now, Sir Miles's habitual associates were persons of the world,—well-bred and **decorous**, indeed, before children, as the best of the old school were, avoiding all **anecdotes**; all allusions, for which the prudent **matron** would send her girls out of the room; but with that reserve speaking of the world as the world goes: if talking of young A—, **calculating carelessly** what he would have when old A—, his father, died; naturally giving to wealth and station and ability their fixed importance in life; not over-apt to single out for eulogium some quiet goodness; rather inclined to speak with irony of

---

French

anecdote: anecdote.
calculating: calculant, comptant.
candour: candeur, franchise, sincérité.
carelessly: de façon négligente, négligemment, de manière négligente.
debarred: exclut, interdit.
decorous: bienséant.
defied: provoqué, défié.
distract: distraire.
dunce: cancre.
exclaim: exclamer, s'exclamer.
habitually: de façon habituelle, de manière habituelle, habituellement.
hears: entend, oit.
inexperience: inexpérience, manque d'expérience.
intimately: de façon intime, de manière intime, intimement.
matron: matrone, directrice, mère de famille, surveillante.
methodically: de manière systématique, de façon méthodique.
numbing: engourdissant.
revere: révérer, révères.
reverence: révérence, vénération, respect.
toy: jouet, joujou.
tranquillity: tranquillité.
unchecked: incontrôlé, non vérifié.
unnoticed: inaperçu.
vivacity: vivacité, verve.
wondrous: merveilleux, étonnant.

pretensions to virtue; rarely speaking but with respect of the worldly **seemings** which rule mankind. All these had their inevitable effect upon that keen, quick, yet moody and **reflective** intellect.

Sir Miles removed at last to Laughton. He gave up London,—why, he acknowledged not to himself; but it was because he had outlived his age. Most of his old set were gone; new hours, new habits, had stolen in. He had ceased to be of importance as a **marrying** man, as a personage of fashion; his health was **impaired**; he **shrank** from the fatigues of a **contested** election; he resigned his seat in parliament for his native county; and once settled at Laughton, the life there soothed and **flattered** him,—there all his former claims to distinction were still fresh. He amused himself by collecting, in his old halls and chambers, his statues and pictures, and felt that, without **fatigue** or trouble, he was a greater man at Laughton in his old age than he had been in London during his youth.

Lucretia was then thirteen. Three years afterwards, Olivier Dalibard was established in the house; and from that time a great change became noticeable in her. The **irregular** vehemence of her temper gradually **subsided**, and was replaced by an habitual self-command which rendered the rare **deviations** from it more effective and **imposing**. Her pride changed its character wholly and permanently; no word, no look of scorn to the lowborn and the poor escaped her. The **masculine** studies which her **erudite** tutor opened to a **grasping** and **inquisitive** mind, **elevated** her very errors above the **petty** distinctions of class. She **imbibed** earnestly what Dalibard assumed or felt,—the more dangerous pride of the fallen angel,—and set up the intellect as a **deity**. All belonging to the mere study of mind charmed and enchained her; but active and practical in her very **reveries**, if she brooded, it was to scheme, to plot, to **weave**, **web**, and mesh, and to smile in haughty triumph at her own **ingenuity** and **daring**. The first lesson of mere worldly wisdom teaches us to command temper; it was worldly wisdom that made the once **impetuous** girl calm, **tranquil**, and serene. Sir Miles was pleased by a change that removed from Lucretia's **outward** character its chief blot,—perhaps, as his frame declined, he sighed sometimes to think that with so

French

contested: contesté.
daring: audace, hardi, osant, aventurant.
deity: divinité, déité, dieu.
deviation: déviation, écart, déroutement.
elevated: élevé, relevâtes, dressa, sublime, en élévation.
erudite: érudit, savant.
fatigue: fatigue, épuisement, usure.
flattered: flatté, adulai, amadoua.
grasping: avide, empoignant, étreignant, saisir.
imbibed: absorbèrent, bus, but, bûmes, bu, bûtes, burent.
impaired: endommagèrent, diminuai, abîmèrent, altérèrent.
impetuous: impétueux, fougueux.
imposing: imposant, contraignant.
ingenuity: ingéniosité.
inquisitive: curieux, inquisiteur.
irregular: irrégulier, non réglé.
marrying: se mariant, épousant.
masculine: masculin, mâle.
outward: sortie, vers l'extérieur.
petty: mesquin, petit.
reflective: réfléchissante.
reverie: rêverie.
seeming: semblant, paraissant.
shrank: rétrécies.
subsided: nous affaissâmes, t'affaissas, vous affaissâtes, s'affaissèrent, m'affaissai.
tranquil: tranquille, calme, paisible.
weave: tisser, tramer, armure.
web: toile, web, âme.

much **majesty** there appeared but little tenderness; he took, however, the merits with the faults, and was content upon the whole.

If the Provencal had taken more than common pains with his young pupil, the pains were not solely disinterested. In **plunging** her mind amidst that profound **corruption** which belongs only to intellect **cultivated** in scorn of good and in **suppression** of heart, he had his own views to serve. He watched the age when the passions **ripen**, and he grasped at the fruit which his training sought to mature. In the human heart ill **regulated** there is a dark desire for the **forbidden**. This Lucretia felt; this her studies **cherished**, and her thoughts brooded over. She detected, with the quickness of her sex, the preceptor's **stealthy** aim. She started not at the danger. Proud of her **mastery** over herself, she rather triumphed in luring on into weakness this master-intelligence which had lighted up her own,—to see her **slave** in her teacher; to despise or to pity him whom she had first contemplated with awe. And with this mere pride of the understanding might be connected that of the sex; she had **attained** the years when woman is curious to know and to sound her power. To **inflame** Dalibard's **cupidity** or ambition was easy; but to touch his heart,—that **marble** heart!—this had its **dignity** and its **charm**. Strange to say, she succeeded; the passion, as well as interests, of this dangerous and able man became **enlisted** in his hopes. And now the game played between them had a terror in its **suspense**; for if Dalibard **penetrated** not into the recesses of his pupil's complicated nature, she was far from having yet sounded the hell that lay, black and **devouring**, beneath his own. Not through her affections,—those he scarce hoped for,—but through her inexperience, her vanity, her passions, he contemplated the path to his victory over her soul and her fate. And so **resolute**, so **wily**, so **unscrupulous** was this person, who had played upon all the subtlest keys and **chords** in the scale of **turbulent** life, that, despite the **lofty** smile with which Lucretia at length heard and repelled his suit, he had no fear of the ultimate issue, when all his projects were **traversed**, all his mines and **stratagems** abruptly brought to a close, by an event which he had wholly unforeseen,—the appearance of a rival; the **ardent** and almost **purifying** love, which, **escaping**

French

ardent: ardant, ardent.
attained: atteint, parvîntes.
charm: charme, amulette, ravir, breloque.
cherished: chérîmes.
chord: corde, accord.
corruption: corruption.
cultivated: cultiva.
cupidity: cupidité.
devouring: dévorant, engloutissant.
dignity: dignité.

enlisted: enrôlai.
escaping: échappant, enfuyant.
forbidden: interdit, défendu.
inflame: enflammer, s'enflammer.
lofty: haut, élevé.
majesty: majesté, seigneurie.
marble: marbre, bille.
mastery: maîtrise, prééminence.
penetrated: pénétra.
plunging: plonger, soyage.
purifying: purifiant, épurant.
regulated: réglâtes, régulâmes.

resolute: résolu, déterminé.
ripen: mûrir.
slave: esclave, asservir.
stealthy: furtif.
stratagem: stratagème, ruse.
suppression: répression, suppression.
suspense: suspens, en souffrance.
traversed: traversé.
turbulent: turbulent, agité.
unscrupulous: sans scrupules.
wily: rusé, malin.

a while from all the **demons** he had **evoked**, she had, with a girl's frank heart and impulse, conceived for Mainwaring. And here, indeed, was the great crisis in Lucretia's life and destiny. So interwoven with her nature had become the hard calculations of the understanding; so habitual to her now was the **zest** for **scheming**, which **revels** in the play and vivacity of **intrigue** and plot, and which Shakspeare has perhaps intended chiefly to depict in the villany of Iago,—that it is probable Lucretia could never become a character thoroughly amiable and honest. But with a happy and well-placed love, her ambition might have had legitimate **vents**; her restless energies, the woman's natural field in sympathies for another. The heart, once opened, **softens** by use; gradually and unconsciously the **interchange** of affection, the companionship with an upright and **ingenuous** mind (for virtue is not only beautiful, it is contagious), might have had their **redeeming** and **hallowing** influence. Happier, indeed, had it been, if her choice had fallen upon a more commanding and lofty nature! But perhaps it was the very **meekness** and susceptibility of Mainwaring's temper, relieved from **feebleness** by his talents, which, once in play, were **undeniably** great, that pleased her by contrast with her own hardness of spirit and **despotism** of will.

That Sir Miles should have been blind to the position of the lovers is less **disparaging** to his penetration than it may appear; for the very **imprudence** with which Lucretia abandoned herself to the society of Mainwaring during his visits at Laughton took a resemblance to candour. Sir Miles knew his niece to be more than commonly clever and well informed; that she, like him, should feel that the conversation of a superior young man was a relief to the ordinary **babble** of their country neighbours, was natural enough; and if now and then a doubt, a fear, had crossed his mind and rendered him more touched than he liked to own by Vernon's remarks, it had vanished upon perceiving that Lucretia never seemed a shade more **pensive** in Mainwaring's absence. The **listlessness** and the melancholy which are apt to accompany love, especially where unpropitiously placed, were not visible on the surface of this strong nature. In truth, once assured that Mainwaring returned her affection, Lucretia **reposed** on the future with a calm and

French

babble: murmure confus, babiller, bavarder.
demon: démon.
despotism: despotisme.
disparaging: dénigrant, désobligeant, vilipendant.
evoked: évoquâtes.
feebleness: faiblesse, débilité.
hallowing: sanctifiant.
imprudence: imprudence.
ingenuous: ingénu, candide, naïf.
interchange: échange, rupture de charge, compensation des données de factures, modification interchromosomique, point d'échange, relais.
intrigue: intriguer.
listlessness: indifférence, alanguissement, indolence, langueur.
meekness: douceur de caractère, humilité.
pensive: pensif, songeur.
redeeming: rachetant.
reposed: reposé.
revel: se divertir, s'amuser.
scheming: intrigant, magouille, comploter.
softens: adoucit, amollit, attendrit, se ramollit.
undeniably: de façon indéniable, de manière indéniable, indéniablement.
vent: évent, conduit, décharger, cheminée.
zest: zeste, vigueur, enthousiasme.

resolute confidence; and her **customary** dissimulation closed like an unruffled sea over all the undercurrents that met and played below. Still, Sir Miles's attention once, however slightly, **aroused** to the recollection that Lucretia was at the age when woman naturally **meditates** upon love and marriage, had suggested, **afresh** and more **vividly**, a project which had before been **indistinctly** conceived,—namely, the union of the divided branches of his house, by the marriage of the last male of the Vernons with the heiress of the St. Johns. Sir Miles had seen much of Vernon himself at various intervals; he had been present at his **christening**, though he had refused to be his **godfather**, for fear of raising **undue** expectations; he had visited and munificently "tipped" him at Eton; he had accompanied him to his quarters when he joined the prince's regiment; he had come often in contact with him when, at the death of his father, Vernon retired from the army and blazed in the front ranks of metropolitan fashion; he had given him counsel and had even **lent** him money. Vernon's spendthrift habits and dissipated if not **dissolute** life had certainly confirmed the old baronet in his intentions to trust the lands of Laughton to the lesser risk which property **incurs** in the hands of a female, if tightly settled on her, than in the more **colossal** and multiform luxuries of an expensive man; and to do him justice, during the **flush** of Vernon's **riotous** career he had **shrunk** from the thought of **confiding** the happiness of his niece to so unstable a partner. But of late, whether from his impaired health or his broken fortunes, Vernon's follies had been less **glaring**. He had now arrived at the mature age of thirty-three, when wild **oats** may reasonably be **sown**. The composed and steadfast character of Lucretia might serve to guide and direct him; and Sir Miles was one of those who hold the doctrine that a **reformed rake** makes the best husband. Add to this, there was nothing in Vernon's reputation—once allowing that his thirst for pleasure was slaked—which could excite serious **apprehensions**. Through all his difficulties, he had maintained his honour unblemished; a thousand **traits** of amiability and kindness of heart made him popular and **beloved**. He was nobody's enemy but his own. His very distresses—the prospect of his ruin, if left **unassisted** by Sir Miles's

---

French

afresh: de nouveau, encore.
apprehension: appréhension, arrestation, inquiétude.
aroused: réveillas, éveillé.
beloved: aimé, cher.
christening: baptême.
colossal: énorme, formidable, immense.
confiding: confiant.
customary: habituel, accoutumé, coutumier.
dissolute: dissolu, débauché.
flush: affleurant, rougeur.
glaring: éblouissant, flagrant, éclatant.
godfather: parrain.
incur: encourir, subir, engager une dépense, contracter une dette.
indistinctly: de façon trouble, indistinctement, de manière trouble.
lent: prêta, carême, empruntas.
meditates: médite, songe.
oat: avoine.
rake: râteau, ringard, inclinaison, ratisser.
reformed: réformé, redressées.
riotous: séditieux, tapageur.
shrunk: rétréci, retrait.
sown: ensemencées, semé, emblavé.
trait: trait, caractère.
unassisted: sans aide.
undue: indu.
vividly: de façon vive, de manière vive.

testamentary dispositions—were arguments in his favour. And, after all, though Lucretia was a nearer relation, Vernon was in truth the direct male heir, and according to the usual prejudices of family, therefore, the **fitter** representative of the ancient line. With these feelings and views, he had invited Vernon to his house, and we have seen already that his favourable impressions had been confirmed by the visit.

And here we must say that Vernon himself had been brought up in boyhood and youth to regard himself the presumptive **inheritor** of Laughton. It had been, from time **immemorial**, the custom of the St. Johns to pass by the claims of females in the settlement of the **entails**; from male to male the estate had gone, **furnishing** warriors to the army, and **senators** to the State. And if when Lucretia first came to Sir Miles's house the bright prospect seemed somewhat obscure, still the mesalliance of the mother, and Sir Miles's obstinate **resentment** thereat, seemed to **warrant** the supposition that he would probably only leave to the orphan the usual portion of a daughter of the house, and that the lands would go in their ordinary **destination**. This belief, adopted **passively**, and as a thing of course, had had a very **prejudicial** effect upon Vernon's career. What mattered that he overenjoyed his youth, that the **subordinate** property of the Vernons, a **paltry** four or five thousand pounds a year, went a little too fast,—the splendid estates of Laughton would recover all. From this dream he had only been **awakened**, two or three years before, by an attachment he had formed to the portionless daughter of an earl; and the Grange being too far **encumbered** to allow him the proper settlements which the lady's family required, it became a matter of importance to **ascertain** Sir Miles's intentions. Too delicate himself to sound them, he had **prevailed** upon the earl, who was well acquainted with Sir Miles, to take Laughton in his way to his own seat in Dorsetshire, and, without **betraying** the grounds of his interest in the question, learn carelessly, as it were, the views of the wealthy man. The result had been a severe and terrible disappointment. Sir Miles had then fully determined upon constituting Lucretia his heiress; and with the usual **openness** of his character, he had **plainly** said so upon the very first **covert**

French

ascertain: constater, vérifier.
awakened: réveilla.
betraying: trahissant.
covert: couvert, voilé, caché, implicite, invisible.
destination: destination.
encumbered: encombré, obéra, grevé, être grevé d'un droit.
entail: comporter, entraîner.
fitter: ajusteur, installateur, essayeur.
furnishing: fournissant, meublant, ameublement.
immemorial: immémorial.
inheritor: héritier.
openness: franchise, aspect découvert, degré relatif d'effilochage de la fibre d'amiante, ouverture.
paltry: misérable.
passively: passivement, de façon passive, de manière passive.
plainly: de manière plaine, simplement, clairement.
prejudicial: préjudiciable, nuisible.
prevailed: prévalus.
resentment: ressentiment, rancune, dépit.
senator: sénateur, père conscrit.
subordinate: subordonné, inférieur, subalterne.
testamentary: testamentaire.
warrant: garantir, cautionner, assurer, mandat, warrant, bon de souscription.

and **polished** allusion to the subject which the earl slyly made. This discovery, in breaking off all hopes of a union with Lady Mary Stanville, had crushed more than **mercenary** expectations. It affected, through his heart, Vernon's health and spirits; it rankled deep, and was **resented** at first as a fatal injury. But Vernon's native nobility of disposition gradually **softened** an indignation which his reason convinced him was **groundless** and unjust. Sir Miles had never encouraged the expectations which Vernon's family and himself had **unthinkingly** formed. The baronet was master of his own fortune, and after all, was it not more natural that he should prefer the child he had brought up and reared, to a distant relation, little more than an **acquaintance**, simply because man succeeded to man in the **mouldy** pedigree of the St. Johns? And, Mary fairly lost to him, his constitutional indifference to money, a certain French levity of temper, a **persuasion** that his life was nearing its wasted close, had left him without regret, as without resentment, at his kinsman's decision. His **boyish** affection for the **hearty**, generous old gentleman returned, and though he **abhorred** the country, he had, without a single interested thought or calculation, cordially accepted the baronet's hospitable **overtures**, and deserted, for the wilds of Hampshire, "the sweet **shady** side of Pall-Mall."

We may now enter the drawing-room at Laughton, in which were already assembled several of the families **residing** in the more immediate neighbourhood, and who **sociably** dropped in to chat around the national tea-table, play a rubber at whist, or make up, by the help of two or three children and two or three grandpapas, a **merry** country-dance; for in that happy day people were much more **sociable** than they are now in the houses of our rural Thanes. Our country seats became bustling and animated after the Birthday; many even of the more important families **resided**, indeed, all the year round on their estates. The Continent was closed to us; the **fastidious exclusiveness** which comes from habitual residence in cities had not made that **demarcation**, in **castes** and in talk, between neighbour and neighbour, which exists now. Our **squires** were less educated, less **refined**, but more hospitable and **unassuming**. In a word, there was what does not

---

French

abhorred: abhorrâtes, exécras.
acquaintance: connaissance, relation, personne de connaissance, abord.
boyish: puéril, de garçon, enfantin.
caste: caste.
demarcation: démarcation, bornage.
exclusiveness: exclusivité.
fastidious: difficile.
groundless: sans fondement.
hearty: cordial, chaleureux.

mercenary: mercenaire.
merry: joyeux, gai.
mouldy: moisi, chanci.
overture: ouverture.
persuasion: persuasion, croyance.
polished: poli.
refined: raffina, délicat, tendre, affiné, épuras.
resented: ressenti.
resided: résidâmes, demeurai.
residing: résidant, demeurant.
shady: ombragé, louche, véreux.

sociable: sociable.
sociably: de façon sociable, socialement, de manière sociable.
softened: amollîmes, adoucit, attendrit, se ramollit, me ramollis, nous ramollîmes, vous ramollîtes, te ramollis.
squire: chaperonner, châtelain.
unassuming: prétention, sans prétention.
unthinkingly: de façon irréfléchie, de manière irréfléchie.

exist now, except in some districts remote from London,—a rural society for those who sought it.

The party, as we enter, is **grouped** somewhat thus. But first we must cast a glance at the room itself, which rarely failed to be the first object to attract a stranger's notice. It was a long, and not particularly well-proportioned apartment,—according, at least, to modern notions,—for it had rather the appearance of two rooms thrown into one. At the distance of about thirty-five feet, the walls, before somewhat narrow, were met by an arch, supported by carved pilasters, which opened into a space nearly double the width of the previous part of the room, with a **domed** ceiling and an embayed window of such depth that the **recess** almost formed a chamber in itself. But both these divisions of the apartment **corresponded** exactly in point of decoration,—they had the same small **panelling**, painted a very light green, which seemed almost white by candlelight, each **compartment wrought** with an arabesque; the same enriched **frieze** and **cornice**; they had the same high **mantelpieces**, **ascending** to the ceiling, with the arms of St. John in bold relief. They had, too, the same old-fashioned and venerable furniture, **draperies** of thick **figured** velvet, with immense chairs and sofas to correspond,—interspersed, it is true, with more modern and commodious inventions of the upholsterer's art, in grave **stuffed** leather or lively **chintz**. Two windows, nearly as deep as that in the **farther** division, broke the outline of the former one, and helped to give that irregular and nooky appearance to the apartment which took all **discomfort** from its extent, and **furnished** all convenience for **solitary** study or **detached flirtation**. With little respect for the carved work of the panels, the walls were covered with pictures brought by Sir Miles from Italy; here and there marble busts and statues gave **lightness** to the character of the room, and **harmonized** well with that half-Italian mode of decoration which belongs to the period of James the First. The shape of the chamber, in its divisions, lent itself **admirably** to that friendly and sociable intermixture of amusements which **reconciles** the tastes of young and old. In the first division, near the **fireplace**, Sir Miles, **seated** in his easy-chair, and **sheltered** from the opening

French

admirably: de façon admirable, de manière admirable, admirablement.
ascending: montant, ascendant.
chintz: chintz.
compartment: compartiment, spécialité, case, domaine.
cornice: corniche, bandeau.
corresponded: correspondîmes.
detached: détaché.
discomfort: malaise, gêne.
domed: bombé, calotte.
drapery: draperie.
farther: plus loin.
figured: figuré, chiffrées.
fireplace: cheminée, foyer.
flirtation: flirt.
frieze: frise, ratine, burat.
furnished: fournîtes, meublâtes.
grouped: groupés.
harmonized: harmonisâtes.
lightness: clarté, légèreté, leucie, luminosité.
mantelpiece: chambranle de cheminée, tablette.
panelling: lambris, facettes, panneautage.
recess: pause, alcôve, repos, niche, trêve, vacances.
reconciles: réconcilie, raccommode, rapproche.
seated: assis.
sheltered: abrité, protégé.
solitary: solitaire, seul, pur.
stuffed: bourré, farci.
wrought: forgé, travaillé.

door by a seven-fold **tapestry** screen, was still at chess with his librarian. At a little distance a middle-aged gentleman and three turbaned matrons were cutting in at whist, **shilling** points, with a half-crown bet optional, and not much ventured on. On tables, drawn into the recesses of the windows, were the day's newspapers, Gilray's caricatures, the last new publications, and such other ingenious suggestions to chit-chat. And round these tables grouped those who had not yet found elsewhere their evening's amusement,—two or three shy young clergymen, the parish doctor, four or five squires who felt great interest in politics, but never **dreamed** of the **extravagance** of taking in a daily paper, and who now, **monopolizing** all the journals they could find, began fairly with the **heroic** resolution to **skip** nothing, from the first advertisement to the printer's name. Amidst one of these groups Mainwaring had **bashfully** ensconced himself. In the farther division, the **chandelier**, suspended from the domed ceiling, threw its cheerful light over a large circular table below, on which gleamed the **ponderous** tea-urn of massive silver, with its usual **accompaniments**. Nor were wanting there, in addition to those airy nothings, **sliced infinitesimally**, from a French roll, the more substantial and now **exiled** cheer of cakes,—plum and seed, Yorkshire and saffron,—attesting the light hand of the **housekeeper** and the strong **digestion** of the guests. Round this table were seated, in full gossip, the maids and the matrons, with a slight **sprinkling** of the bolder young gentlemen who had been taught to please the fair. The warmth of the evening allowed the upper casement to be opened and the curtains drawn aside, and the July **moonlight feebly** struggled against the **blaze** of the lights within. At this table it was Miss Clavering's obvious duty to **preside**; but that was a **complaisance** to which she rarely **condescended**. Nevertheless, she had her own way of doing the honour of her uncle's house, which was not without courtesy and grace; to **glide** from one to the other, exchange a few friendly words, see that each set had its well-known amusements, and, finally, sit quietly down to converse with some who, from gravity or age, appeared most to neglect or be neglected by the rest, was her ordinary, and not **unpopular** mode of **welcoming** the

---

French

accompaniment: accompagnement, escorte.
bashfully: de façon timide, de manière timide.
blaze: flamme, feu.
chandelier: lustre.
complaisance: complaisance.
condescended: condescendîmes, daignâmes.
digestion: digestion, lessivage, cuisson, scheidage.
dreamed: rêvé.
exiled: exilé.
extravagance: extravagance.
feebly: de façon faible, de manière faible.
glide: glisser, planer, vol plané, coulé, patin.
heroic: héroïque.
housekeeper: gouvernante, intendant de collectivité.
infinitesimally: de façon infinitésimale, de manière infinitésimale.
monopolizing: monopolisant, accaparant.
moonlight: clair de lune.
ponderous: lourd, pesant.
preside: présider.
shilling: schilling.
skip: saut, skip, capitaine, benne.
sliced: tranché, en tranches.
sprinkling: aspersion, arrosage.
tapestry: tapisserie.
unpopular: impopulaire.
welcoming: accueillant, hospitalier.

guests at Laughton,—not unpopular; for she thus avoided all interference with the flirtations and conquests of humbler **damsels**, whom her station and her **endowments** might otherwise have crossed or humbled, while she insured the good word of the old, to whom the young are seldom so **attentive**. But if a stranger of more than provincial **repute** chanced to be present; if some **stray** member of parliament, or **barrister** on the circuit, or wandering artist, accompanied any of the neighbours,—to him Lucretia gave more **earnest** and **undivided** attention. Him she sought to draw into a conversation deeper than the usual babble, and with her calm, searching eyes, bent on him while he spoke, seemed to **fathom** the intellect she set in play. But as yet, this evening, she had not made her appearance,—a sin against **etiquette** very unusual in her. Perhaps her recent conversation with Dalibard had absorbed her thoughts to **forgetfulness** of the less important demands on her attention. Her absence had not **interfered** with the gayety at the tea-table, which was frank even to **noisiness** as it centred round the laughing face of Ardworth, who, though unknown to most or all of the ladies present, beyond a brief introduction to one or two of the first **comers** from Sir Miles (as the host had risen from his chess to bid them welcome), had already contrived to make himself perfectly at home and **outrageously** popular. Niched between two **bouncing** lasses, he had **commenced** acquaintance with them in a strain of familiar drollery and fun, which had soon **broadened** its circle, and now embraced the whole group in the happy **contagion** of good-humour and young animal spirits. Gabriel, allowed to sit up later than his usual hour, had not, as might have been expected, attached himself to this circle, nor indeed to any; he might be seen moving quietly about,—now **contemplating** the pictures on the wall with a curious eye; now pausing at the whist-table, and noting the game with the interest of an **embryo gamester**; now throwing himself on an **ottoman**, and trying to **coax** towards him Dash or Ponto,—trying in vain, for both the dogs abhorred him; yet still, through all this general movement, had any one taken the pains to observe him closely, it might have been sufficiently apparent that his keen, bright, restless eye, from the corner of its long, sly lids, **roved** chiefly towards

---

French

attentive: attentif.
barrister: avocat, défenseur.
bouncing: rebondissement, bondissant.
broadened: élargi.
coax: cajoler, amadouer.
comer: arrivant.
commenced: commenças.
contagion: contagion.
contemplating: contemplant.
damsel: demoiselle.
earnest: sérieux, sincère, grave.
embryo: embryon, foetus, germe, prégroupement.
endowment: dotation, fondation.
etiquette: étiquette, protocole, convenances.
fathom: brasse, sonder.
forgetfulness: oubli, manque de mémoire.
gamester: joueur.
interfered: interférâtes.
noisiness: bruyance, turbulence.
ottoman: ottoman, pouf.
outrageously: de façon scandaleuse, de manière scandaleuse.
repute: réputation, renommée.
roved: rôdâtes, rôdé, rôdèrent, vagabonda, boudina, rôdai.
stray: errant, écartons, formation géologique imprévue, égarer, champ de dispersion, animal errant, s'égarer.
undivided: indivis, non divisé.

the three persons whom he approached the least,—his father, Mainwaring, and Mr. Vernon. This last had ensconced himself apart from all, in the angle formed by one of the pilasters of the **arch** that divided the room, so that he was in command, as it were, of both sections. Reclined, with the careless grace that seemed **inseparable** from every attitude and motion of his person, in one of the great **velvet** chairs, with a book in his hand, which, to say truth, was turned upside down, but in the lecture of which he seemed **absorbed**, he heard at one hand the mirthful laughter that circled round young Ardworth, or, in its pauses, caught, on the other side, muttered **exclamations** from the grave whist-players: "If you had but trumped that **diamond**, ma'am!" "Bless me, sir, it was the best heart!" And somehow or other, both the laughter and the exclamations affected him **alike** with what then was called "the spleen,"—for the one reminded him of his own young days of joyless, careless **mirth**, of which his mechanical gayety now was but a **mocking** ghost; and the other seemed a **satire**, a **parody**, on the fierce but noiseless rapture of **gaming**, through which his passions had passed, when thousands had slipped away with a **bland** smile, **provoking** not one of those natural ebullitions of emotion which there accompanied the loss of a shilling point. And besides this, Vernon had been so accustomed to the success of the drawing-room, to be a somebody and a something in the company of **wits** and princes, that he felt, for the first time, a sense of **insignificance** in this provincial circle. Those fat squires had heard nothing of Mr. Vernon, except that he would not have Laughton,—he had no **acres**, no vote in their county; he was a nobody to them. Those ruddy **maidens**, though now and then, indeed, one or two might **steal** an **admiring** glance at a figure of **elegance** so unusual, regarded him not with the female interest he had been accustomed to **inspire**. They felt **instinctively** that he could be nothing to them, nor they to him,—a mere London **fop**, and not half so handsome as Squires Bluff and Chuff.

Rousing himself from this little vexation to his vanity with a conscious smile at his own weakness, Vernon turned his looks towards the door, waiting for Lucretia's entrance, and since her uncle's address to him, feeling

---

French

absorbed: absorbèrent, épongèrent, résorbé.
acre: acre.
admiring: admirant.
alike: semblable, pareil.
arch: arc, cintre, voûte, arche, arcade.
bland: doucereux, doux, fade.
diamond: diamant, carreau.
elegance: élégance, chic, galanterie, grâce.
exclamation: exclamation.
fop: dandy.
gaming: jeu.
inseparable: inséparable, indivisible.
insignificance: insignifiance.
inspire: inspirer, dicter, enthousiasmer.
instinctively: instinctivement, de façon instinctive, de manière instinctive.
maiden: brin, vierge.
mirth: gaieté, allégresse.
mocking: bafouant, dérision.
parody: parodie.
provoking: provoquant, chiffonnant.
rousing: stimulant, excitant, irritant.
satire: satire.
steal: voler, dérober, dépouiller, subtiliser, d'acier.
velvet: velours, oodiniase, de velours, profit facile.
wit: esprit, intelligence.

that new and **indescribable** interest in her appearance which is apt to steal into every breast when what was before but an indifferent acquaintance, is suddenly enhaloed with the light of a possible wife. At length the door opened, and Lucretia entered. Mr. Vernon lowered his book, and gazed with an earnestness that **partook** both of doubt and admiration.

Lucretia Clavering was tall,—tall beyond what is admitted to be tall in woman; but in her height there was nothing either awkward or masculine,— a figure more perfect never served for model to a **sculptor**. The dress at that day, **unbecoming** as we now deem it, was not to her—at least, on the whole **disadvantageous**. The short waist gave greater sweep to her **majestic** length of **limb**, while the classic **thinness** of the drapery betrayed the exact proportion and the **exquisite contour**. The arms then were worn bare almost to the shoulder, and Lucretia's arms were not more **faultless** in shape than **dazzling** in their **snowy** colour; the stately neck, the falling shoulders, the firm, slight, yet rounded bust,—all would have charmed equally the artist and the **sensualist**. Fortunately, the sole defect of her form was not apparent at a distance: that defect was in the hand; it had not the usual faults of female youthfulness,—the superfluity of flesh, the too rosy healthfulness of colour,—on the contrary, it was small and thin; but it was, nevertheless, more the hand of a man than a woman: the shape had a man's nervous **distinctness**, the veins swelled like **sinews**, the joints of the fingers were marked and prominent. In that hand it almost seemed as if the iron force of the character betrayed itself. But, as we have said, this slight defect, which few, if seen, would hypercritically notice, could not, of course, be **perceptible** as she moved slowly up the room; and Vernon's eye, glancing over the noble figure, rested upon the face. Was it handsome? Was it **repelling**? Strange that in feature it had pretensions to the highest order of beauty, and yet even that experienced **connoisseur** in female charms was almost as puzzled what sentence to **pronounce**. The hair, as was the fashion of the day, **clustered** in **profuse curls** over the forehead, but could not **conceal** a slight line or **wrinkle** between the brows; and this line, rare in women at any age, rare even in men at hers, gave an expression at once of thought and **sternness** to

French

clustered: en grappe.
conceal: cacher, dissimuler, celer, masquer.
connoisseur: connaisseur.
contour: contour, courbe de niveau.
curl: boucle, friser, rotationnel, coiffer, faire tournoyer, battre, roulage, gode, fourche.
dazzling: éblouir, éclatant.
disadvantageous: désavantageux, défavorable, lésionnaire.
distinctness: différenciation, distinction, netteté.
exquisite: exquis, délicat.
faultless: impeccable, irréprochable, parfait.
indescribable: indescriptible.
limb: membre, limbe, flanc.
majestic: majestueux, imposant.
partook: prîmes, prirent, pris, prit, prîtes.
perceptible: perceptible, apercevable.
profuse: abondant, profus, prodigue.
pronounce: prononcer.
repelling: horrible, affreux, épouvantable, repoussant.
sculptor: sculpteur.
sensualist: voluptueux, sensualiste.
sinew: tendon.
snowy: neigeux, de neige.
sternness: sévérité.
thinness: maigreur, minceur.
unbecoming: inconvenant.
wrinkle: ride, sillon, pli, plisser.

the whole face. The **eyebrows** themselves were straight, and not strongly marked, a shade or two perhaps too light, — a fault still more apparent in the **lashes**; the eyes were large, full, and though bright, **astonishingly** calm and deep, — at least in ordinary moments; yet withal they wanted the charm of that steadfast and open look which goes at once to the heart and invites its trust, — their expression was rather vague and **abstracted**. She usually looked **aslant** while she spoke, and this, which with some appears but **shyness**, in one so self-collected had an air of **falsehood**. But when, at times, if earnest, and bent rather on examining those she addressed than **guarding** herself from penetration, she fixed those eyes upon you with sudden and direct scrutiny, the gaze impressed you **powerfully**, and haunted you with a strange spell. The eye itself was of a peculiar and displeasing colour, — not blue, nor gray, nor black, nor hazel, but rather of that cat-like green which is drowsy in the light, and vivid in the shade. The profile was purely Greek, and so seen, Lucretia's beauty seemed **incontestable**; but in front face, and still more when inclined between the two, all the features took a **sharpness** that, however regular, had something **chilling** and severe: the mouth was small, but the lips were thin and pale, and had an expression of effort and contraction which added to the **distrust** that her **sidelong** glance was calculated to inspire. The teeth were dazzlingly white, but sharp and thin, and the eye-teeth were much longer than the rest. The complexion was pale, but without much delicacy, — the paleness seemed not natural to it, but rather that hue which study and late **vigils** give to men; so that she wanted the **freshness** and bloom of youth, and looked older than she was, — an effect confirmed by an absence of **roundness** in the cheek not noticeable in the profile, but **rendering** the front face somewhat harsh as well as sharp. In a word, the face and the figure were not in harmony: the figure prevented you from **pronouncing** her to be masculine; the face took from the figure the charm of feminacy. It was the head of the young Augustus upon the form of Agrippina. One touch more, and we close a description which already perhaps the reader may consider **frivolously** minute. If you had placed before the mouth and lower part of the face a mask or **bandage**, the whole

French

abstracted: distrait, abstraits, abrégé.
aslant: obliquement.
astonishingly: de façon étonnante, de manière étonnante.
bandage: bandage, pansement, emmailloter.
chilling: refroidissement brusque, chilling, trempe, givrage, réfrigération.
distrust: méfiance, se méfier, défiance.
eyebrow: sourcil.
falsehood: mensonge, supercherie.
freshness: fraîcheur.
frivolously: de manière frivole, de façon frivole.
guarding: garde, placement des onglets, montage sur onglet, défense musculaire, dispositif de protection.
incontestable: incontestable.
lash: fouetter, aiguilleter, dard, mèche, attacher.
powerfully: de façon puissante, de manière puissante.
pronouncing: prononçant.
rendering: interprétation, enduit, rendu, crépi.
roundness: rondeur, arrondi.
sharpness: acuité, netteté, finesse.
shyness: timidité, embarras, réserve, sauvagerie.
sidelong: de côté, oblique.
vigil: veille, vigile.

character of the upper face would have changed at once,—the eye lost its glittering **falseness**, the brow its **sinister contraction**; you would have **pronounced** the face not only beautiful, but sweet and womanly. Take that bandage suddenly away and the change would have startled you, and startled you the more because you could **detect** no sufficient **defect** or disproportion in the lower part of the countenance to explain it. It was as if the mouth was the key to the whole: the key nothing without the text, the text uncomprehended without the key.

Such, then, was Lucretia Clavering in outward appearance at the age of twenty,—striking to the most careless eye; interesting and **perplexing** the student in that dark language never yet deciphered,—the human countenance. The reader must have observed that the effect every face that he **remarks** for the first time produces is different from the impression it leaves upon him when habitually seen. Perhaps no two persons differ more from each other than does the same countenance in our earliest recollection of it from the countenance regarded in the **familiarity** of repeated **intercourse**. And this was especially the case with Lucretia Clavering's: the first impulse of nearly all who **beheld** it was distrust that partook of fear; it almost inspired you with a sense of danger. The judgment rose up against it; the heart set itself on its guard. But this **uneasy** sentiment soon died away, with most **observers**, in **admiration** at the chiselled outline, which, like the Grecian **sculpture**, gained the more the more it was examined, in respect for the intellectual power of the expression, and in **fascinated** pleasure at the charm of a smile, rarely employed, it is true, but the more attractive both for that reason and for its sudden effect in giving **brightness** and persuasion to an aspect that needed them so much. It was literally like the **abrupt** breaking out of a **sunbeam**; and the **repellent** impression of the face thus **familiarized** away, the **matchless** form took its natural influence; so that while one who but saw Lucretia for a moment might have pronounced her almost plain, and certainly not **prepossessing** in appearance, those with whom she lived, those whom she sought to please, those who saw her daily, united in

French

abrupt: abrupt, brusque, raide, subit, soudain, escarpé, inattendu, à pic.
admiration: admiration.
beheld: vit, remarquâtes, vu, vîmes, vis, vîtes, virent, aperçûtes.
brightness: luminosité, éclat, brillant.
contraction: contraction, retrait, endognathie, striction, étranglement, raccours, resserrement.
defect: défaut, malfaçon, tare, imperfection, anomalie.
detect: détecter, dépister.
falseness: fausseté.
familiarity: familiarité.
familiarized: familiarisâtes.
fascinated: fascinai, passionnâmes, captivé.
intercourse: rapport sexuel, relations.
matchless: incomparable, sans égal.
observer: observateur, spectateur.
perplexing: embarrassant.
prepossessing: avenant.
pronounced: prononcé.
remark: remarque, observation, commentaire.
repellent: épouvantable, horrible, affreux, répulsif.
sculpture: sculpture, statuaire.
sinister: sinistre.
sunbeam: rayon de soleil.
uneasy: agité, gêné, inquiet.

acknowledgment of her beauty; and if they still felt awe, **attributed** it only to the force of her understanding.

As she now came midway up the room, Gabriel started from his seat and ran to her **caressingly**. Lucretia bent down, and placed her hand upon his fair **locks**. As she did so, he whispered,—

"Mr. Vernon has been watching for you."

"Hush! Where is your father?"

"Behind the screen, at chess with Sir Miles."

"With Sir Miles!" and Lucretia's eye fell, with the direct **gaze** we have before referred to, upon the boy's face.

"I have been looking over them pretty often," said he, meaningly: "they have talked of nothing but the game." Lucretia **lifted** her head, and glanced round with her **furtive** eye; the boy divined the search, and with a scarce perceptible **gesture** pointed her attention to Mainwaring's **retreat**. Her **vivid** smile passed over her lips as she bowed slightly to her **lover**, and then, **withdrawing** the hand which Gabriel had taken in his own, she moved on, passed Vernon with a commonplace word or two, and was soon **exchanging greetings** with the **gay** merry-makers in the farther part of the room. A few minutes afterwards, the **servants** entered, the tea-table was removed, chairs were **thrust** back, a single lady of a certain age volunteered her services at the **piano**, and **dancing** began within the **ample** space which the arch **fenced** off from the whist-players. Vernon had watched his opportunity, and at the first sound of the piano had gained Lucretia's side, and with grave politeness pre-engaged her hand for the opening dance.

At that day, though it is not so very long ago, **gentlemen** were not ashamed to dance, and to dance well; it was no **languid saunter** through a **quadrille**; it was fair, deliberate, **skilful** dancing amongst the courtly,—free, bounding movement amongst the gay.

Vernon, as might be expected, was the most admired **performer** of the evening; but he was thinking very little of the notice he at last excited, he was

French

acknowledgment: accusé de réception, reconnaissance.
ample: ample, large, étendu.
attributed: attribué.
caressingly: de façon tendre, de manière tendre.
dancing: dansant, bouillement.
exchanging: échangeant.
fenced: clôturé.
furtive: furtif, sournois.
gay: gai, joyeux, homosexuel, enjoué.
gaze: regard.
gentlemen: messieurs.
gesture: geste, signe.
greeting: salutation, accueillant.
languid: langoureux, traînant, biseau, indolent.
lifted: élevai, soulevé.
lock: serrure, écluse, verrou, fermer.
lover: amant, amoureux, maîtresse.
performer: interprète, exécutant, artiste.
piano: piano.
quadrille: quadrille.
retreat: retraite, se retirer, décéder, recul, refuge.
saunter: flâner, se balader.
servant: serviteur, domestique.
skilful: habile.
thrust: poussée, force de propulsion, chevauchement, botte, réaction de la planche, butée.
vivid: vif, éclatant.
withdrawing: retirant.

employing such ingenuity as his experience of life **supplied** to the **deficiencies** of a very imperfect education, limited to the little **flogged** into him at Eton, in **deciphering** the character and getting at the heart of his fair **partner**.

"I wonder you do not make Sir Miles take you to London, my cousin, if you will allow me to call you so. You ought to have been presented."

"I have no wish to go to London yet."

"Yet!" said Mr. Vernon, with the **somewhat fade gallantry** of his day; "beauty even like **yours** has little time to spare."

"Hands across, hands across!" cried Mr. Ardworth.

"And," continued Mr. Vernon, as soon as a pause was **permitted** to him, "there is a **song** which the **prince sings**, written by some **sensible** old-fashioned **fellow**, which says,—

"'Gather your **rosebuds** while you may,
For time is still a flying.'"

"You have **obeyed** the **moral** of the song yourself, I believe, Mr. Vernon."

"Call me cousin, or Charles,—Charley, if you like, as most of my friends do; nobody ever calls me Mr. Vernon,—I don't know myself by that name."

"Down the middle; we are all waiting for you," **shouted** Ardworth.

And down the middle, with wondrous **grace**, glided the exquisite nankeens of Charley Vernon.

The **dance** now, thanks to Ardworth, became too animated and riotous to allow more than a few broken **monosyllables till** Vernon and his partner gained the end of the set, and then, **flirting** his partner's **fan**, he recommenced,—

"Seriously, my cousin, you must sometimes feel very much **moped** here."

French

dance: danse, bal.
deciphering: déchiffrant, décryptant.
deficiency: déficience, carence, insuffisance, manque, défaut.
employing: employant.
fade: se faner, pâlir, déteindre, décolorer, fondu, flétrir, s'affaiblir.
fan: ventilateur, souffler sur, éventail.
fellow: homme, individu, camarade, ensemble, mâle.
flirting: flirt.
flogged: fustigé, flagellé.
gallantry: vaillance, galanterie, bravoure.
grace: grâce, charme.
monosyllable: monosyllabe.
moped: vélomoteur, cyclomoteur, mobylette, pétrolette.
moral: moral.
obeyed: obéis, obéîtes.
partner: associé, partenaire.
permitted: permis.
prince: prince.
rosebud: débutante.
sensible: raisonnable, sensé, prudent.
shouted: crié, criai, criâmes.
sings: chante.
somewhat: une certaine quantité, quelque peu, un peu.
song: chanson.
supplied: fourni.
till: caisse, jusqu'à ce que, à.
yours: vôtre, tien, votre, vous.

"Never!" answered Lucretia. Not once yet had her eye **rested** on Mr. Vernon. She felt that she was **sounded**.

"Yet I am sure you have a **taste** for the pomps and vanities. **Aha**! there is ambition under those careless curls," said Mr. Vernon, with his easy, **adorable impertinence**.

Lucretia winced.

"But if I were **ambitious**, what field for ambition could I find in London?"

"The same as Alexander,—**empire**, my cousin."

"You forget that I am not a man. Man, indeed, may hope for an empire. It is something to be a Pitt, or even a Warren Hastings."

Mr. Vernon stared. Was this **stupidity**, or what?

"A woman has an empire more **undisputed** than Mr. Pitt's, and more **pitiless** than that of Governor Hastings."

"Oh, **pardon** me, Mr. Vernon—"

"Charles, if you please."

Lucretia's brow darkened.

"Pardon me," she **repeated**; "but these **compliments**, if such they are meant to be, meet a very **ungrateful** return. A woman's empire over **gauzes** and **ribbons**, over tea-tables and drums, over fops and **coquettes**, is not worth a journey from Laughton to London."

"You think you can despise admiration?"

"What you mean by admiration,—yes."

"And love too?" said Vernon, in a whisper.

Now Lucretia at once and abruptly raised her eyes to her partner. Was he **aiming** at her secret? Was he **hinting** at **intentions** of his own? The look **chilled** Vernon, and he turned away his head.

Suddenly, then, in **pursuance** of a new train of ideas, Lucretia **altered** her manner to him. She had detected what before she had **surmised**. This

French

adorable: adorable, séduisant.
aha: ah.
aiming: visant, pointage, peinant, visée.
altered: altérai, retoucha, modifié.
ambitious: ambitieux.
chilled: frappé, refroidi.
compliment: compliment, féliciter, flatterie.
coquette: coquette.
empire: empire.
gauze: gaze, mousseline, toile

métallique, tamis.
hinting: optimisation.
impertinence: impertinence, insolence.
intention: intention, dessein, propos.
pardon: pardon, excuser, grâce.
pitiless: impitoyable.
pursuance: exécution.
repeated: répéta, redirent, redîtes.
rested: reposé.
ribbon: ruban, feuille.

sounded: sonna.
stupidity: stupidité, ânerie, bêtise, connerie.
surmised: conjecturé.
taste: goût, saveur, déguster.
undisputed: incontesté.
ungrateful: ingrat, disgracieux.

sudden familiarity on his part arose from notions her uncle had instilled,—the visitor had been **incited** to become the suitor. Her **penetration** into character, which from childhood had been her passionate study, told her that on that light, polished, **fearless** nature scorn would have slight effect; to meet the familiarity would be the best means to secure a friend, to **disarm** a **wooer**. She changed then her manner; she summoned up her extraordinary craft; she accepted the intimacy held out to her, not to unguard herself, but to lay open her opponent. It became necessary to her to know this man, to have such power as the knowledge might give her. **Insensibly** and gradually she led her companion away from his design of approaching her own secrets or character, into frank talk about himself. All unconsciously he began to lay bare to his listener the infirmities of his **erring**, open heart. Silently she looked down, and plumbed them all,—the frivolity, the **recklessness**, the half gay, half **mournful** sense of waste and ruin. There, blooming amongst the wrecks, she saw the fairest flowers of noble manhood profuse and **fragrant** still,—generosity and courage and disregard for self. Spendthrift and **gambler** on one side the medal; gentleman and soldier on the other. Beside this maimed and imperfect nature she measured her own prepared and profound intellect, and as she listened, her smile became more bland and frequent. She could afford to be **gracious**; she felt **superiority**, scorn, and safety.

As this seeming intimacy had **matured**, Vernon and his partner had quitted the dance, and were **conversing** apart in the recess of one of the windows, which the newspaper readers had deserted, in the part of the room where Sir Miles and Dalibard, still seated, were about to commence their third game at chess. The baronet's hand ceased from the task of **arranging** his **pawns**; his eye was upon the pair; and then, after a long and **complacent** gaze, it looked round without **discovering** the object it sought.

"I am about to task your kindness most **improperly**, Monsieur Dalibard," said Sir Miles, with that politeness so displeasing to Ardworth, "but will you do me the favour to move aside that fold of the screen? I wish for a better view of our young people. Thank you very much."

French

arranging: arrangeant, disposant, rangeant, ordonnant, agençant, accommodant.
complacent: complaisant.
conversing: conversant.
disarm: désarmer.
discovering: découvrant, dépouillant.
erring: errant, aberrant.
fearless: intrépide, courageux.
fragrant: parfumé, aromatique, odorant.
gambler: joueur, parieur, spéculateur.
gracious: gracieux, courtois, gentil.
improperly: de manière incorrecte, incorrectement, de façon incorrecte.
incited: incitai, émûtes, émut, émus, ému, émurent, émûmes.
insensibly: de façon insensible, de manière insensible.
matured: mûrîtes, fit, fîtes, mûri, fis, fait, fîmes, firent.
mournful: morne, sombre, mélancolique, triste.
pawn: pion, soldat, emprunter sur gages, gage, mettre en gage.
penetration: pénétration, densité téléphonique, saillie, croisement, collage noir, attaque de rupture, avancement.
recklessness: imprudence, témérité, insouciance.
superiority: supériorité.
wooer: prétendant.

Sir Miles now discovered Mainwaring, and observed that, far from regarding with self-betraying jealousy the apparent flirtation going on between Lucretia and her kinsman, he was engaged in animated conversation with the chairman of the quarter sessions. Sir Miles was satisfied, and **ranged** his pawns. All this time, and indeed ever since they had sat down to play, the Provencal had been waiting, with the **patience** that **belonged** to his character, for some observation from Sir Miles on the subject which, his **sagacity** perceived, was **engrossing** his thoughts. There had been about the old gentleman a **fidgety restlessness** which showed that something was on his mind. His eyes had been frequently turned towards his niece since her entrance; once or twice he had cleared his throat and hemmed,—his usual **prelude** to some more important communication; and Dalibard had heard him **muttering** to himself, and fancied he caught the name of "Mainwaring." And indeed the baronet had been **repeatedly** on the **verge** of **sounding** his secretary, and as often had been checked both by pride in himself and pride for Lucretia. It seemed to him beneath his own dignity and hers even to **hint** to an inferior a fear, a doubt, of the heiress of Laughton. Olivier Dalibard could easily have led on his **patron**, he could easily, if he pleased it, have dropped words to **instil** suspicion and prompt question; but that was not his object,—he rather shunned than **courted** any reference to himself upon the matter; for he knew that Lucretia, if she could suppose that he, however **indirectly**, had betrayed her to her uncle, would at once **declare** his own suit to her, and so **procure** his immediate dismissal; while, aware of her powers of dissimulation and her influence over her uncle, he feared that a single word from her would **suffice** to remove all suspicion in Sir Miles, however **ingeniously implanted**, and however **truthfully grounded**. But all the while, under his apparent calm, his mind was busy and his passions burning.

"Pshaw! your old play,—the bishop again," said Sir Miles, laughing, as he moved a **knight** to **frustrate** his adversary's supposed plan; and then, turning back, he once more contemplated the growing familiarity between Vernon and his niece. This time he could not contain his pleasure. "Dalibard,

French

belonged: appartenu.
courted: briguées.
declare: déclarer, proclamer.
engrossing: grossoyant, absorbant.
fidgety: agité, remuant.
frustrate: frustrer, déjoue, décevoir.
grounded: mis à la terre, interdit de vol.
hint: insinuer, faire allusion, allusion, conseil.
implanted: implantâmes.
indirectly: indirectement, de façon indirecte, de manière indirecte.
ingeniously: de façon ingénieuse, de manière ingénieuse, ingénieusement.
instil: instiller.
knight: chevalier, cavalier.
muttering: barbotant.
patience: patience, impatiens, balsamine.
patron: protecteur, mécène, client.
prelude: prélude.
procure: procurer, se procurer.
ranged: étendu.
repeatedly: plusieurs fois, à plusieurs reprises, de façon répétée, de manière répétée.
restlessness: agitation, instabilité psychomotrice.
sagacity: sagacité.
sounding: sondage, sonore.
suffice: suffire.
truthfully: véridiquement, de façon véridique, de manière véridique.
verge: accotement, bord.

my dear sir," he said, **rubbing** his hands, "look yonder: they would make a **handsome** couple!"

"Who, sir?" said the Provencal, looking another way, with **dogged** stupidity.

"Who? **Damn** it, man! Nay, pray **forgive** my **ill** manners, but I felt **glad**, sir, and **proud**, sir. Who? Charley Vernon and Lucretia Clavering."

"Assuredly, yes. Do you think that there is a chance of so happy an event?"

"Why, it **depends** only on Lucretia; I shall never force her." Here Sir Miles stopped, for Gabriel, **unperceived** before, picked up his patron's pocket-handkerchief.

Olivier Dalibard's **gray** eyes rested coldly on his son. "You are not dancing to-night, my boy. Go; I like to see you amused."

The boy obeyed at once, as he always did, the paternal **commands**. He found a partner, and joined a dance just begun; and in the **midst** of the dance, Honore Gabriel Varney seemed a new being, — not Ardworth himself so **thoroughly** entered into the **enjoyment** of the exercise, the lights, the music. With **brilliant** eyes and **dilated nostrils**, he seemed prematurely to feel all that is **exciting** and **voluptuous** in that **exhilaration** which to **childhood** is usually so **innocent**. His **glances** followed the fairest form; his **clasp** lingered in the softest hand; his voice **trembled** as the warm breath of his partner came on his **cheeks**.

Meanwhile the conversation between the chess-players continued.

"Yes," said the baronet, "it depends only on Lucretia. And she seems pleased with Vernon: who would not be?"

"Your penetration rarely **deceives** you, sir. I own I think with you. Does Mr. Vernon know that you would permit the alliance?"

"Yes; but—" the baronet stopped short.

"You were saying, but— But what, Sir Miles?"

French

brilliant: brillant, magnifique, luisant, génial, éclatant.
cheek: joue, chape, la joue.
childhood: enfance.
clasp: agrafe, fermoir.
command: commande, ordre, ordonner, enjoindre, sommer, instruction.
damn: damner, condamner.
deceives: trompe, triche.
depend: dépendre, compter sur.
dilated: dilatâtes.
dogged: obstiné.
enjoyment: jouissance, usufruit.
exciting: excitant, passionnant, captivant, palpitant, hérissant.
exhilaration: réjouissance.
forgive: pardonner, excuser.
glad: joyeux, content, heureux.
glance: coup d'œil, jeter un coup d'oeil, regard.
gray: gris, gray.
handsome: beau.
ill: malade, malsain, mal.
innocent: innocent.
midst: milieu, millieux.
nostril: narine, naseau.
proud: fier, altier, orgueilleux.
rubbing: frottement, ponçage du feuil, dépolissage, broyage de minerai, estampe.
thoroughly: de façon minutieuse, de manière minutieuse.
trembled: tremblé.
unperceived: inaperçu.
voluptuous: voluptueux, sensuel.

"Why, the dog affected diffidence; he had some fear **lest** he should not win her affections. But **luckily**, at least, they are disengaged."

Dalibard looked grave, and his eye, as if **involuntarily**, glanced towards Mainwaring. As ill-luck would have it, the young man had then ceased his conversation with the chairman of the quarter sessions, and with arms **folded**, brow contracted, and looks, earnest, **anxious**, and **intent**, was contemplating the **whispered** conference between Lucretia and Vernon.

Sir Miles's eye had followed his secretary's, and his face changed. His hand fell on the chess board and upset half the men; he uttered a very **audible** "Zounds!"

"I think, Sir Miles," said the Provencal, **rising**, as if **conscious** that Sir Miles **wished** to play no more,—"I think that if you spoke soon to Miss Clavering as to your views with **regard** to Mr. Vernon, it might ripen matters; for I have heard it said by French mothers—and our Frenchwomen understand the female heart, sir—that a girl having no other affection is often prepossessed at once in favour of a man whom she knows **beforehand** is prepared to woo and to win her, whereas without that knowledge he would have seemed but an ordinary acquaintance."

"It is **shrewdly** said, my dear Monsieur Dalibard; and for more reasons than one, the sooner I speak to her the better. **Lend** me your arm. It is time for **supper**; I see the dance is over."

Passing by the place where Mainwaring still **leaned**, the baronet looked at him **fixedly**. The young man did not notice the gaze. Sir Miles **touched** him **gently**. He started as from a revery.

"You have not **danced**, Mr. Mainwaring."

"I dance so **seldom**, Sir Miles," said Mainwaring, colouring.

"Ah! you **employ** your head more than your **heels**, young gentleman,—very right; I must speak to you to-morrow. Well, ladies, I hope you have enjoyed yourselves? My dear Mrs. Vesey, you and I are old friends, you know; many a **minuet** we have danced together, eh? We can't dance now,

---

French

anxious: inquiet, soucieux, agité, anxieux, impatient.
audible: audible, appel d'automatique, perceptible.
beforehand: d'avance, au préalable.
conscious: conscient.
danced: dansé.
employ: employer, embaucher, user de, se servir de, appliquer, engager.
fixedly: de façon fixe, de manière fixe.

folded: plié, plissé.
gently: doucement, gentiment, de façon douce, de manière douce.
heel: talon, gîte.
intent: intention, alerte, résolu.
involuntarily: de façon involontaire, involontairement.
leaned: adossés.
lend: prêter, emprunter.
lest: de peur que.
luckily: heureusement, de façon

chanceuse, de manière chanceuse.
minuet: menuet.
regard: considérer, estime, regarder, contempler, égard.
rising: élévation, lever, levée.
seldom: rarement.
shrewdly: de manière sagace, de façon sagace.
supper: souper, dîner.
touched: touché.
whispered: chuchoté.
wished: désira, souhaité.

but we can walk arm-in-arm together still. Honour me. And your little grandson—vaccinated, eh? Wonderful invention! To supper, ladies, to supper!"

The company were gone. The lights were out,—all save the lights of heaven; and they came bright and still through the casements. Moonbeam and Starbeam, they seemed now to have the old house to themselves. In came the rays, **brighter** and longer and bolder, like fairies that march, rank upon rank, into their kingdom of **solitude**. Down the oak stairs, from the casements, blazoned with **heraldry**, moved the rays, creepingly, **fearfully**. On the armour in the hall clustered the rays **boldly** and **brightly**, till the steel shone out like a mirror. In the library, long and low, they just entered, stopped short: it was no place for their play. In the drawing-room, now deserted, they were more curious and **adventurous**. Through the large window, still open, they came in freely and archly, as if to spy what had caused such disorder; the stiff chairs out of place, the smooth floor **despoiled** of its carpet, that flower dropped on the ground, that **scarf** forgotten on the table,—the rays lingered upon them all. Up and down through the house, from the base to the roof, roved the children of the air, and found but two spirits awake amidst the **slumber** of the rest.

In that tower to the east, in the tapestry chamber with the large **gilded** bed in the recess, came the rays, **tamed** and wan, as if scared by the grosser light on the table. By that table sat a girl, her brow leaning on one hand; in the other she held a rose,—it is a love-token: exchanged with its sister rose, by **stealth**, in **mute** sign of **reproach** for doubt excited,—an assurance and a reconciliation. A love-token!—shrink not, ye rays; there is something **akin** to you in love. But see,—the hand closes **convulsively** on the flower; it hides it not in the breast; it lifts it not to the lip: it throws it **passionately** aside. "How long!" muttered the girl, impetuously,—"how long! And to think that will here cannot **shorten** an hour!" Then she rose, and walked to and fro, and each time she gained a certain niche in the chamber she paused, and then **irresolutely** passed on again. What is in that niche? Only books. What can books teach thee, pale girl? The step **treads** firmer; this time it halts more

French

adventurous: aventureux, périlleux.
akin: apparenté.
boldly: de façon grasse, de manière grasse, hardiment.
brighter: plus de lumière.
brightly: de façon claire, de manière claire.
convulsively: de façon convulsive, de manière convulsive.
despoiled: spolié.
fearfully: de manière effrayante, de façon effrayante.
gilded: dorèrent, dora, dorâmes, doré.
heraldry: héraldique, science héraldique.
irresolutely: de façon indécise, de manière indécise.
mute: muet, sourdine, commutateur de sourdine.
passionately: de façon passionnée, de manière passionnée.
reproach: reproche, gronder, réprimander, sermonner.
scarf: foulard, écharpe, fichu.
shorten: raccourcir, abréger, écourter, réduire.
slumber: dormir, sommeil.
solitude: solitude.
stealth: furtif.
tamed: apprivoisé.
tread: piétiner, fouler aux pieds, semelle, marcher sur, giron, bande de roulement, faire les cent pas, chape.

resolved. The hand that clasped the **flower** takes down a volume. The girl sits again before the light. See, O **rays**! what is the volume? **Moon** and Starbeam, ye love what lovers read by the **lamp** in the **loneliness**. No love-ditty this; no yet holier **lesson** to patience, and moral to hope. What hast **thou**, young girl, strong in health and rich in years, with the **lore** of the leech,—with **prognostics** and symptoms and diseases? She is tracing with hard eyes the signs that **precede** the **grim** enemy in his most sudden approach,—the habits that invite him, the warnings that he gives. He whose wealth shall make her free has twice had the **visiting** shock; he starves not, he lives frae! She closes the volume, and, **musing, metes** him out the hours and days he has to live. **Shrink** back, ye rays! The love is disenhallowed; while the hand was on the rose, the thought was on the charnel.

Yonder, in the opposite **tower**, in the small casement near the roof, came the rays. Childhood is **asleep**. Moon and Starbeam, ye love the slumbers of the child! The door opens, a dark figure steals noiselessly in. The father comes to look on the sleep of his son. **Holy** tenderness, if this be all! "Gabriel, wake!" said a low, stern voice, and a rough hand shook the **sleeper**.

The sharpest test of those **nerves** upon which depends the **mere** animal **courage** is to be **roused** suddenly, in the **depth** of night, by a **violent** hand. The impulse of Gabriel, thus startled, was neither of timidity nor surprise. It was that of some Spartan boy not new to danger; with a **slight cry** and a **fierce** spring, the son's hand **clutched** at the father's throat. Dalibard shook him off with an effort, and a smile, half in approval, half in irony, played by the moonlight over his lips.

"Blood will out, young tiger," said he. "**Hush**, and hear me!"

"Is it you, Father?" said Gabriel. "I thought, I dreamed—"

"No matter; think, dream always that man should be prepared for defence from peril!"

"Gabriel," and the pale scholar seated himself on the bed, "turn your face to mine,—nearer; let the moon fall on it; lift your eyes; look at me—so! Are you not playing **false** to me? Are you not Lucretia's spy, while you are

---

French

asleep: endormi.
clutched: agriffa, saisi.
courage: courage, abattage.
cry: pleurer, cri, vagir, crier.
depth: profondeur, intensité, creux.
false: faux, feint, perfide.
fierce: féroce, violent.
flower: fleur, la fleur.
grim: macabre, menaçant, sinistre.
holy: saint, sacré.
hush: silence, faire taire.
lamp: lampe, ampoule.
lesson: leçon, cours.
loneliness: solitude, isolement.
lore: lorum.
mere: pur, seul, simple.
mete: infligez.
moon: lune.
musing: méditer, rêverie.
nerve: nerf, toupet, courage, fortifier.
precede: précéder, avancer.
prognostic: pronostique.
ray: rayon, raie, bande, rayure, radio, rai.
roused: irritâtes, excitèrent, stimulâtes.
shrink: rétrécir, se ratatiner.
sleeper: dormeur, traverse.
slight: léger, affront, insignifiant.
thou: tu, toi, vous.
tower: tour, pylône.
violent: violent, brutal.
visiting: visitant.

pretending to be mine? It is so; your eye betrays you. Now, heed me; you have a mind beyond your years. Do you love best the **miserable garret** in London, the hard **fare** and **squalid** dress, or your lodgment here, the sense of **luxury**, the sight of splendour, the atmosphere of wealth? You have the choice before you."

"I choose, as you would have me, then," said the boy, "the last."

"I believe you. Attend! You do not love me,—that is natural; you are the son of Clara Varney! You have supposed that in **loving** Lucretia Clavering you might vex or **thwart** me, you scarce knew how; and Lucretia Clavering has gold and **gifts** and soft words and promises to **bribe** withal. I now tell you **openly** my plan with regard to this girl: it is my aim to marry her; to be master of this house and these lands. If I **succeed**, you share them with me. By betraying me, word or look, to Lucretia, you frustrate this aim; you plot against our rise and to our ruin. Deem not that you could escape my fall; if I am driven hence,—as you might drive me,—you share my fate; and mark me, you are **delivered** up to my **revenge**! You **cease** to be my son,—you are my foe. Child! you know me."

The boy, **bold** as he was, shuddered; but after a pause so brief that a breath scarce passed between his silence and his words, he replied with emphasis,—

"Father, you have read my heart. I have been **persuaded** by Lucretia (for she **bewitches** me) to watch you,—at least, when you are with Sir Miles. I knew that this was mixed up with Mr. Mainwaring. Now that you have made me understand your own views, I will be true to you,—true without threats."

The father looked hard on him, and seemed **satisfied** with the gaze. "Remember, at least, that your future rests upon your truth; that is no threat,—that is a thought of hope. Now sleep or **muse** on it." He dropped the **curtain** which his hand had drawn aside, and **stole** from the room as noiselessly as he had entered. The boy **slept** no more. **Deceit** and cupidity and **corrupt** ambition were at work in his brain. Shrink back, Moon and

French

bewitches: ensorcelle, charme.
bold: gras, audacieux, épais, gros, hardi, intrépide.
bribe: corrompre, soudoyer.
cease: cesser, s'arrêter.
corrupt: corrompu, pervertissons, altérer.
curtain: rideau, pont fixe, feston, courtine.
deceit: duperie, tromperie.
delivered: livrâtes, rendu destination, délivrai.
fare: aller, se porter, prix du billet.
garret: mansarde, grenier.
gift: cadeau, don.
loving: amoureux, aimant, aimer.
luxury: luxe, richesse.
miserable: malheureux, misérable, pauvre, maussade, mauvais, méchant, vide, pénible, sombre, mal.
muse: muse, songer, méditer, rêver.
openly: ouvertement, franchement, publiquement.
persuaded: persuada.
pretending: feignant, prétendant.
revenge: revanche, vengeance.
satisfied: satisfait, contentâtes, rassasié.
slept: dormîmes, roupillé, pioncé.
squalid: misérable, sordide.
stole: étole, vola.
succeed: réussir, arriver, succéder, parvenir, aboutir.
thwart: contrecarrer, banc de nage.

Starbeam! On that child's brow play the demons who had followed the father's step to his bed of sleep.

Back to his own room, close at hand, crept Olivier Dalibard. The walls were **lined** with books,—many in language and deep in lore. Moon and Starbeam, ye love the midnight solitude of the scholar! The Provencal stole to the casement, and looked forth. All was serene,—breathless trees and **gleaming** sculpture and **whitened** sward, girdled by the mass of shadow. Of what thought the man? Not of the present **loveliness** which the scene gave to his eye, nor of the future mysteries which the stars should whisper to the soul. Gloomily over a stormy and a **hideous** past roved the memory, stored with **fraud** and **foul** with crime,—plan upon plan, **schemed** with **ruthless** wisdom, followed up by **remorseless** daring, and yet all now a ruin and a blank; an intellect at war with good, and the good had **conquered**! But the conviction neither touched the **conscience** nor **enlightened** the reason; he felt, it is true, a moody sense of **impotence**, but it brought **rage**, not **despondency**. It was not that he submitted to Good as too powerful to **oppose**, but that he deemed he had not yet gained all the mastery over the **arsenal** of Evil. And evil he called it not. Good and evil to him were but subordinate genii at the command of Mind; they were the slaves of the lamp. But had he got at the true secret of the lamp itself? "How is it," he thought, as he turned **impatiently** from the casement, "that I am baffled here where my fortunes seemed most assured? Here the mind has been of my own training, and prepared by nature to my hand; here all opportunity has smiled. And suddenly the merest commonplace in the vulgar lives of mortals,—an unlooked-for rival; rival, too, of the **mould** I had taught her to despise; one of the stock gallants of a comedy, no character but youth and fair looks,—yea, the lover of the stage starts up, and the fabric of years is overthrown." As he thus mused, he placed his hand upon a small box on one of the tables. "Yet within this," resumed his **soliloquy**, and he struck the **lid**, that gave back a dull sound,—"within this I hold the keys of life and death! Fool! the power does not reach to the heart, except to still it. **Verily** and indeed were the old **heathens mistaken**? Are there no philters to change the

French

arsenal: arsenal, dépôt.
conquered: conquîtes.
conscience: conscience.
despondency: découragement, abattement.
enlightened: éclairas.
foul: faute, fétide, engagé, salir.
fraud: fraude, escroquerie, tromperie, imposture, dol, filouterie.
gleaming: luisant.
heathen: païen, barbare, sauvage.

hideous: hideux, horrible, abominable, odieux, abject, repoussant, affreux.
impatiently: de façon impatiente, de manière impatiente.
impotence: impuissance, impotence.
lid: couvercle, capot, plaque de regard.
lined: ligné, doublé.
loveliness: beauté.
mistaken: abusif, trompé.

mould: modeler, moule, moisissure, fondre, forme, matrice, façonner.
oppose: opposer, se mettre en travers, rouspéter.
rage: fureur, rage, tempêter, furie.
remorseless: sans remords.
ruthless: impitoyable, cruel.
schemed: comploté.
soliloquy: soliloque, monologue.
verily: en vérité, vraiment.
whitened: blanchîmes.

current of **desire**? But **touch** one **chord** in a girl's **affection**, and all the **rest** is **mine**, all, all, **lands, station**, power, all the rest are in the **opening** of this lid!"

Hide in the **cloud**, O Moon! **shrink** back, ye Stars! **send** not your **holy, pure**, and trouble-lulling **light** to the **countenance blanched** and **livid** with the thoughts of **murder**.

French

affection: affection, amour.
blanched: blanchis, étiolé, mondèrent.
chord: corde, accord.
cloud: nuage, brouiller, rendre trouble.
countenance: encourager, figure, mine, visage.
current: courant, en cours.
desire: désir, souhait, envie.
holy: saint, sacré.
land: terre, atterrir, pays, aborder, contrée, s'abattre.
light: léger, lumière, clair, allumer, feu, faible, enflammer, rayonnement visible, lampe.
livid: livide.
mine: mine, mienne.
murder: assassiner, meurtre, rectifier, crime de meurtre.
opening: ouverture, ouvrant, orifice, début, déclenchement.
pure: pur, blanc, propre.
rest: repos, se reposer, reste, débris, support, trêve, pause, appui, silence.
send: envoyer, adresser, expédier.
shrink: rétrécir, se ratatiner.
station: station, gare, poste.
touch: toucher, contact.

CHAPTER III

CONFERENCES

The next day Sir Miles did not appear at breakfast,—not that he was **unwell**, but that he **meditated** holding certain audiences, and on such occasions the good old gentleman liked to **prepare** himself. He belonged to a school in which, amidst much that was hearty and convivial, there was much also that **nowadays** would seem **stiff** and formal, contrasting the other school immediately **succeeding** him, which Mr. Vernon represented, and of which the Charles Surface of Sheridan is a **faithful** and **admirable** type. The room that Sir Miles **appropriated** to himself was, properly speaking, the state **apartment**, called, in the old **inventories**, "King James's **chamber**;" it was on the first floor, **communicating** with the **picture-gallery**, which at the farther end opened upon a **corridor admitting** to the principal bedrooms. As Sir Miles cared nothing for holiday state, he had **unscrupulously** taken his cubiculum in this chamber, which was really the handsomest in the house, except the banquet-hall, placed his bed in one angle with a huge screen before it, **filled** up the space with his Italian **antiquities** and curiosities; and fixed his favourite pictures on the **faded gilt leather** panelled on the walls. His main motive in this was the communication with the **adjoining** gallery, which, when the weather was **unfavourable**, furnished ample room for his

---

French

adjoining: adjacent, attenant, contigu, aboutissant.
admirable: admirable, excellent.
admitting: admettant.
antiquity: antiquité.
apartment: appartement.
appropriated: approprié.
chamber: chambre, salle, pièce, local.
communicating: communiquant.
corridor: couloir, corridor.
faded: pâlit, fané, pâlîmes, décolora, déteint.
faithful: fidèle, loyal, honnête, droit.
filled: rempli, fourré.
gilt: doré, jeune truie, cochette.
inventory: inventaire, recensement, stocks.
leather: cuir, en cuir, relier en cuir.
meditated: méditâtes, songea.
nowadays: actuellement, de nos jours, aujourd'hui.
picture-gallery: pinacothèque.
prepare: préparer, apprêter.
stiff: rigide, raide.
succeeding: réussissant, succédant, aboutant.
unfavourable: défavorable, désavantageux.
unscrupulously: de manière sans scrupules, de façon sans scrupules.
unwell: indisposé, malade, souffrant.

habitual walk. He knew how many **strides** by the help of his **crutch** made a mile, and this was **convenient**. Moreover, he liked to look, when alone, on those old portraits of his ancestors, which he had **religiously conserved** in their places, **preferring** to thrust his Florentine and Venetian masterpieces into bedrooms and **parlours**, rather than to **dislodge** from the gallery the stiff **ruffs**, **doublets**, and farthingales of his predecessors. It was whispered in the house that the baronet, whenever he had to reprove a tenant or **lecture** a **dependant**, took care to have him brought to his **sanctum**, through the full length of this gallery, so that the victim might be duly prepared and awed by the imposing effect of so stately a journey, and the grave faces of all the generations of St. John, which could not fail to **impress** him with the dignity of the family, and alarm him at the prospect of the **injured** frown of its **representative**. Across this gallery now, following the steps of the powdered **valet**, strode young Ardworth, staring now and then at some portrait more than usually grim, more often wondering why his **boots**, that never **creaked** before, should **creak** on those particular boards, and feeling a quiet curiosity, without the least mixture of fear or awe as to what old Squaretoes intended to say to him. But all feeling of **irreverence** ceased when, shown into the baronet's room, and the door closed, Sir Miles rose with a smile, and cordially **shaking** his hand, said, dropping the punctilious courtesy of Mister: "Ardworth, sir, if I had a little prejudice against you before you came, you have conquered it. You are a fine, manly, **spirited** fellow, sir; and you have an old man's good wishes,—which are no bad beginning to a young man's good fortune."

The colour **rushed** over Ardworth's **forehead**, and a **tear** sprang to his eyes. He felt a rising at his throat as he **stammered** out some not very audible reply.

"I wished to see you, young gentleman, that I might judge myself what you would like best, and what would best fit you. Your father is in the army: what say you to a pair of colours?"

"Oh, Sir Miles, that is my utmost ambition! Anything but law, except the Church; anything but the Church, except the desk and a counter!"

French

boot: botte, coffre, amorcer, tétine.
conserved: préservé.
convenient: commode, convenable, opportun.
creak: grincer, craquer.
creaked: grincé, craquai.
crutch: béquille, fourche, soutien.
dependant: personne à charge.
dislodge: déloger, détacher.
doublet: doublet, objectif dédoublable.
forehead: front, chanfrein.
impress: impressionner, clicher.
injured: blessé, détériorâtes, abîmâs, lésé.
irreverence: irrévérence.
lecture: conférence, exposé, cours magistral.
parlour: salon.
preferring: préférant, privilégiant.
religiously: de façon religieuse, de manière religieuse.
representative: représentant, député, délégué.
ruff: chevalier combattant, combattant varié, fraise.
rushed: précipité.
sanctum: sanctuaire.
shaking: secouant, ébranlant.
spirited: vif, animé, fougueux.
stammered: bégayé.
stride: pas, faire les cent pas, enjambée, foulée.
tear: larme, déchirer, pleur.
valet: valet.

The baronet, much pleased, gave him a **gentle pat** on the **shoulder**. "Ha, ha! we gentlemen, you see (for the Ardworths are very well **born**, very), we gentlemen understand each other! Between you and me, I never **liked** the law, never thought a man of **birth** should **belong** to it. Take money for lying,—shabby, **shocking**! Don't let that go any farther! The Church-Mother Church—I honour her! Church and State go together! But one **ought** to be very good to **preach** to others,—better than you and I are, eh? ha, ha! Well, then, you like the army,—there's a letter for you to the Horse Guards. Go up to town; your business is done. And, as for your outfit,—read this little book at your leisure." And Sir Miles thrust a pocketbook into Ardworth's hand.

"But pardon me," said the young man, much **bewildered**. "What claim have I, Sir Miles, to such **generosity**? I know that my uncle **offended** you."

"Sir, that's the claim!" said Sir Miles, gravely. "I cannot live long," he added, with a touch of melancholy in his voice; "let me **die** in **peace** with all! Perhaps I injured your uncle,—who **knows** but, if so, he hears and pardons me now?"

"Oh, Sir Miles!" **exclaimed** the thoughtless, generous-hearted young man; "and my little playfellow, Susan, your own niece!"

Sir Miles drew back haughtily; but the **burst** that offended him rose so evidently from the heart, was so **excusable** from its motive and the youth's **ignorance** of the world, that his frown soon **vanished** as he said, **calmly** and gravely,—

"No man, my good sir, can allow to others the right to touch on his family **affairs**; I **trust** I shall be just to the poor young lady. And so, if we never meet again, let us think well of each other. Go, my boy; **serve** your king and your country!"

"I will do my best, Sir Miles, if only to merit your kindness."

"Stay a moment: you are intimate, I find, with young Mainwaring?"

"An old college **friendship**, Sir Miles."

"The army will not do for him, eh?"

French

affair: affaire, chose, cas.
belong: appartenir, faire partie de.
bewildered: effarâmes, éperdu.
birth: naissance, accouchement, mise bas.
born: né.
burst: crever, salve, éclater, rafale, explosion, bouffée, choc d'ionisation.
calmly: de façon calme, de manière calme.
die: mourir, meurs, décéder, décède, matrice, crever, puce.
exclaimed: exclamâtes.
excusable: pardonnable, excusable.
friendship: amitié, camaraderie.
generosity: générosité, largesse.
gentle: doux, gentil, suave, sucré.
ignorance: ignorance, méconnaissance.
knows: connaît, sait.
liked: aimé.
offended: offensas, insultèrent.
ought: devoir, doivent, doit, devez, dois.
pat: taper, caresse.
peace: paix, tranquilité.
preach: prêcher.
serve: servir, sers, desservir, être de service.
shocking: choquant, affreux, bouleversant, révoltant.
shoulder: épaule, accotement.
trust: confiance, fiducie, trust, foi, se fier, fidéicommis.
vanished: disparu.

"He is too **clever** for it, sir."

"Ah, he'd make a **lawyer**, I suppose,—glib **tongue** enough, and can talk well; and lie, if he's paid for it?"

"I don't know how lawyers regard those matters, Sir Miles; but if you don't make him a lawyer, I am sure you must leave him an honest man."

"Really and truly—"

"Upon my honour I think so."

"Good-day to you, and good **luck**. You must catch the **coach** at the **lodge**; for I see by the papers that, in spite of all the talk about peace, they are **raising regiments** like wildfire."

With very different feelings from those with which he had entered the room, Ardworth quitted it. He hurried into his own chamber to thrust his **clothes** into his **portmanteau**, and while thus **employed**, Mainwaring entered.

"**Joy**, my dear fellow, wish me joy! I am going to town,—into the army; abroad; to be shot at, thank Heaven! That dear old gentleman! Just **throw** me that coat, will you?"

A very few more words sufficed to explain what had passed to Mainwaring. He sighed when his friend had finished: "I wish I were going with you!"

"Do you? Sir Miles has only got to write another letter to the Horse Guards. But no, you are meant to be something better than food for **powder**; and, besides, your Lucretia! **Hang** it, I am sorry I cannot stay to examine her as I had promised; but I have seen enough to know that she certainly loves you. Ah, when she changed flowers with you, you did not think I saw you,—sly, was not I? Pshaw! She was only playing with Vernon. But still, do you know, Will, now that Sir Miles has spoken to me so, that I could have sobbed, 'God **bless** you, my old boy!' 'pon my life, I could! Now, do you know that I feel **enraged** with you for **abetting** that girl to deceive him?"

"I am enraged with myself; and—"

French

abetting: troublant, secourant, émouvant, agitant, aidant.
bless: bénir.
clever: habile, adroit, astucieux, rusé, malin, intelligent, artificieux.
clothe: vêtir, vêtent, vêts, vêtons, habiller, revêtir.
coach: entraîneur, wagon, coach, autocar, voiture, répétiteur.
employed: employé.
enraged: exaspéra, enragés, fâché.
hang: pendre, suspendre, retomber, faisander, accrocher.
joy: joie, allégresse.
lawyer: avocat, défenseur, juriste, homme de loi.
lodge: loge, héberger, gîte, pavillon, auberge, déposer.
luck: chance, fortune, sort, destinée.
portmanteau: valise.
powder: poudre, pulvériser.
raising: élevage, martelage, soulèvement, relèvement, relevage, percement d'un montage, montage, extraction, arborant, lainage, levant.
regiment: régiment, enrégimenter.
throw: jeter, jet, projeter, lancer, course.
tongue: langue, tenon, timon, plaque de blocage, parole, lame d'aiguillage, la langue, emboîtement mâle, doigt guide, travelling latéral, barre de traction.

Here a servant entered, and **informed** Mainwaring that he had been **searching** for him; Sir Miles **requested** to see him in his room. Mainwaring started like a **culprit**.

"Never fear," whispered Ardworth; "he has no suspicion of you, I'm sure. **Shake** hands. When shall we meet again? Is it not odd, I, who am a **republican** by theory, taking King George's pay to fight against the French? No use stopping now to **moralize** on such **contradictions**. John, Tom,—what's your name?—here, my man, here, throw that portmanteau on your shoulder and come to the lodge." And so, full of health, hope, vivacity, and spirit, John Walter Ardworth **departed** on his career.

Meanwhile Mainwaring slowly took his way to Sir Miles. As he **approached** the gallery, he met Lucretia, who was coming from her own room. "Sir Miles has sent for me," he said meaningly. He had time for no more, for the valet was at the door of the gallery, waiting to **usher** him to his **host**. "Ha! you will say not a word that can betray us; **guard** your looks too!" whispered Lucretia, hurriedly; "afterwards, join me by the cedars." She passed on towards the **staircase**, and glanced at the large **clock** that was placed there. "Past eleven! Vernon is never up before twelve. I must see him before my uncle sends for me, as he will send if he suspects—" She paused, went back to her room, rang for her maid, **dressed** as for walking, and said carelessly, "If Sir Miles wants me, I am gone to the **rectory**, and shall probably return by the village, so that I shall be back about one." Towards the rectory, indeed, Lucretia bent her way; but half-way there, turned back, and passing through the **plantation** at the **rear** of the house, awaited Mainwaring on the **bench** beneath the cedars. He was not long before he joined her. His face was **sad** and **thoughtful**; and when he seated himself by her side, it was with a **weariness** of spirit that **alarmed** her.

"Well," said she, fearfully, and she placed her hand on his.

"Oh, Lucretia," he exclaimed, as he **pressed** that hand with an emotion that came from other passions than love, "we, or rather I, have done great wrong. I have been leading you to betray your uncle's trust, to **convert** your

French

alarmed: alarmé.
approached: approché, rapprocha.
bench: banc, banquette, établi, gradin.
clock: horloge, pendule, générateur de rythme.
contradiction: contradiction.
convert: convertir, transformer.
culprit: coupable.
departed: partîmes.
dressed: habillé, vêtu.
guard: garde, protéger, contrôleur, préserver, dispositif de protection, arrière, chef de train.
host: hôte, amphitryon, aubergiste, hostie, foule.
informed: informas, renseignas.
moralize: moraliser.
plantation: plantation, futaie.
pressed: appuyé, pressés, estampé à la presse.
rear: élever, arrière.
rectory: presbytère.
republican: républicain.
requested: demandé.
sad: triste, affligé, peiné, maussade, désolé, sombre.
searching: recherche, chercher, fouille.
shake: secouer, ébranler, agiter, bardeau.
staircase: escalier, cage d'escalier.
thoughtful: réfléchi, pensif.
usher: placeur, huissier, portier.
weariness: fatigue, lassitude.

gratitude to him into hypocrisy. I have been unworthy of myself. I am poor, I am humbly born, but till I came here, I was rich and proud in honour. I am not so now. Lucretia, pardon me, pardon me! Let the dream be over; we must not sin thus; for it is sin, and the worst of sin,—treachery. We must part: forget me!"

"Forget you! Never, never, never!" cried Lucretia, with **suppressed** but most earnest vehemence, her **breast heaving**, her hands, as he dropped the one he held, clasped together, her eyes full of tears,—transformed at once into softness, meekness, even while racked by passion and despair.

"Oh, William, say anything,—reproach, **chide**, despise me, for mine is all the fault; say anything but that word 'part.' I have chosen you, I have sought you out, I have **wooed** you, if you will; be it so. I **cling** to you, you are my all,—all that saves me from—from myself," she added falteringly, and in a **hollow** voice. "Your love—you know not what it is to me! I scarcely knew it myself before. I feel what it is now, when you say 'part.'"

Agitated and **tortured**, Mainwaring writhed at these burning words, bent his face low, and covered it with his hands.

He felt her clasp **struggling** to **withdraw** them, **yielded**, and saw her **kneeling** at his feet. His manhood and his gratitude and his heart all moved by that sight in one so haughty, he opened his arms, and she fell on his breast. "You will never say 'part' again, William!" she gasped convulsively.

"But what are we to do?"

"Say, first, what has passed between you and my uncle."

"Little to relate; for I can repeat words, not tones and looks. Sir Miles spoke to me, at first **kindly** and **encouragingly**, about my prospects, said it was time that I should **fix** myself, added a few words, with **menacing** emphasis, against what he called 'idle dreams and desultory ambition,' and **observing** that I changed countenance,—for I felt that I did,—his manner became more cold and severe. Lucretia, if he has not detected our secret, he more than suspects my—my **presumption**. Finally, he said **dryly**, that I had better return home, **consult** with my father, and that if I preferred entering

---

French

breast: poitrine, sein, mamelle, front de taille.
chide: réprimander, gronder.
cling: adhérez, vous cramponnez, te cramponnes, se cramponnent, s'accrocher, nous cramponnons, me cramponne, adhères, cramponner.
consult: consulter.
dryly: sèchement.
encouragingly: de façon encourageante, de manière encourageante.
fix: fixer, fixons, attacher, réparer, déterminer, refaire, restaurer, remédier, point, adapter, repère.
heaving: pilonnement, gonflement.
hollow: creux, cavité, caver.
kindly: complaisamment, de façon gentille, de manière gentille.
kneeling: baraquage, à genoux, agenouillé.
menacing: menaçant, sinistre.
observing: observant, respectant, remplissant.
presumption: présomption, supposition.
struggling: luttant.
suppressed: étouffé, réprimâmes.
tortured: torturé.
withdraw: retirer, décéder, prélever.
wooed: courtisâmes.
yielded: cédai, cédèrent, cédé, cédâtes.

into the service of the Government to any mercantile profession, he thought he had sufficient interest to **promote** my views. But, clearly and **distinctly**, he left on my mind one impression,—that my visits here are over."

"Did he allude to me—to Mr. Vernon?"

"Ah, Lucretia! do you know him so little,—his delicacy, his pride?"

Lucretia was **silent**, and Mainwaring continued:—

"I felt that I was **dismissed**. I took my leave of your uncle; I came hither with the intention to say farewell forever."

"Hush! hush! that thought is over. And you return to your father's,—perhaps better so: it is but hope **deferred**; and in your absence I can the more easily **allay** all suspicion, if suspicion **exist**. But I must write to you; we must correspond. William, dear William, write often,—write kindly; tell me, in every letter, that you love me,—that you love only me; that you will be **patient**, and confide."

"Dear Lucretia," said Mainwaring, **tenderly**, and moved by the **pathos** of her earnest and imploring voice, "but you forget: the **bag** is always brought first to Sir **Miles**; he will **recognize** my hand. And to whom can you trust your own letters?"

"True," replied Lucretia, despondingly; and there was a pause. Suddenly she lifted her head, and cried: "But your father's house is not far from this,—not ten miles; we can find a **spot** at the **remote** end of the park, near the path through the great wood: there I can leave my letters; there I can find yours."

"But it must be seldom. If any of Sir Miles's servants see me, if—"

"Oh, William, William, this is not the language of love!"

"Forgive me,—I think of you!"

"Love thinks of nothing but itself; it is **tyrannical**, absorbing,—it **forgets** even the object **loved**; it **feeds** on danger; it **strengthens** by obstacles," said Lucretia, tossing her hair from her forehead, and with an expression of dark and **wild** power on her brow and in her eyes. "Fear not for me; I am sufficient guard upon myself. Even while I speak, I think,—yes, I have

---

French

allay: apaisent.
bag: sac, poche, ensacher.
deferred: différé.
dismissed: licenciai, renvoyèrent, congédiâtes, déboutai.
distinctly: distinctement, de façon nette, de manière nette.
exist: exister, vivre, être.
feed: alimenter, nourrir, manger, faire paître, déjeuner, avance, paître.
forgets: oublie, désapprend.

loved: aimé, chéri, aimèrent, aimai.
mile: mille, lieue.
pathos: pathétique.
patient: patient, malade.
promote: promouvoir, favorisent, encourager, monter en division supérieure, lancer.
recognize: reconnaître, croire, retrouver.
remote: lointain, éloigné, distant, isolé, écarté.
silent: silencieux.

spot: tache, endroit, place, point, salir, lieu, destination, spot, souiller, localité, message publicitaire.
strengthens: fortifie, renforce, affermit.
tenderly: tendrement.
tyrannical: tyrannique.
wild: sauvage, effréné, fin de saison, frimé, irrégulier, violent.

thought of the very spot. You remember that hollow **oak** at the bottom of the **dell**, in which Guy St. John, the Cavalier, is said to have **hid** himself from Fairfax's soldiers? Every Monday I will leave a letter in that hollow; every Tuesday you can search for it, and leave your own. This is but once a week; there is no risk here."

Mainwaring's conscience still **smote** him, but he had not the strength to resist the energy of Lucretia. The force of her character **seized** upon the weak part of his own, — its **gentleness**, its fear of **inflicting** pain, its **reluctance** to say "No," — that simple cause of **misery** to the over-timid. A few sentences more, full of courage, confidence, and passion, on the part of the woman, of **constraint** and yet of soothed and grateful affection on that of the man, and the affianced parted.

Mainwaring had already given orders to have his **trunks** sent to him at his father's; and, a **hardy pedestrian** by habit, he now struck across the park, passed the dell and the hollow tree, commonly called "Guy's Oak," and across **woodland** and fields golden with **ripening corn**, took his way to the town, in the centre of which, square, solid, and imposing, stood the **respectable** residence of his bustling, active, **electioneering** father.

Lucretia's eye followed a form as fair as ever **captivated** maiden's glance, till it was out of sight; and then, as she emerged from the **shade** of the cedars into the more open space of the garden, her usual thoughtful composure was **restored** to her steadfast countenance. On the terrace, she caught sight of Vernon, who had just quitted his own room, where he always breakfasted alone, and who was now languidly **stretched** on a bench, and basking in the sun. Like all who have abused life, Vernon was not the same man in the early part of the day. The spirits that rose to **temperate** heat the third hour after **noon**, and **expanded** into **glow** when the lights shone over gay carousers, at morning were flat and **exhausted**. With hollow eyes and that **weary** fall of the muscles of the cheeks which betrays the votary of Bacchus, — the convivial three-bottle man, — Charley Vernon forced a smile, meant to be airy and **impertinent**, to his pale lips, as he rose with effort, and extended three fingers to his cousin.

French

captivated: captivâtes.
constraint: contrainte, gêne, restriction.
corn: maïs, cor, grain, blé.
dell: vallon.
electioneering: propagande électorale.
exhausted: épuisé, exténué.
expanded: expansé, développâmes.
gentleness: bonté, douceur.
glow: ardeur, incandescence, brûler, lueur, être en feu.
hardy: robuste, courageux.
hid: cachai, masqua.
impertinent: hardi, impertinent.
inflicting: infligeant.
misery: misère, tristesse.
noon: midi.
oak: chêne, écorce.
pedestrian: piéton, pédestre.
reluctance: réluctance, répugnance.
respectable: respectable, convenable.
restored: restaurâmes, rétablit.
ripening: mûrissant, maturation.
seized: saisîtes, agrippâmes.
shade: ombre, nuance, teinte.
smote: frappa.
stretched: tendu.
temperate: sobre, tempéré, modéré.
trunk: tronc, malle, coffre, trompe, torse, jonction, tambour, circuit.
weary: fatigué, las.
woodland: bois, forêt claire, pays boisé, région boisée, terrain boisé, zone boisée.

"Where have you been **hiding**? **Catching bloom** from the roses? You have the **prettiest** shade of colour,—just enough; not a hue too much. And there is Sir Miles's valet gone to the rectory, and the **fat footman** puffing away towards the village, and I, like a faithful **warden**, from my post at the **castle**, all looking out for the truant."

"But who wants me, cousin?" said Lucretia, with the full blaze of her **rare** and **captivating** smile.

"The knight of Laughton **confessedly** wants thee, O damsel! The knight of the Bleeding Heart may want thee more,—dare he own it?"

And with a hand that trembled a little, not with love, at least, it trembled always a little before the Madeira at luncheon,—he lifted hers to his lips.

"Compliments again,—words, idle words!" said Lucretia, looking down bashfully.

"How can I **convince** thee of my **sincerity**, unless thou takest my life as its **pledge**, maid of Laughton?"

And very much **tired** of standing, Charley Vernon drew her gently to the bench and seated himself by her side. Lucretia's eyes were still **downcast**, and she remained silent; Vernon, suppressing a yawn, felt that he was **bound** to continue. There was nothing very **formidable** in Lucretia's manner.

"'Fore Gad!" thought he, "I suppose I must take the heiress after all; the sooner 't is over, the sooner I can get back to Brook Street."

"It is **premature**, my fair cousin," said he, aloud,—"premature, after less than a week's visit, and only some **fourteen** or **fifteen** hours' permitted friendship and intimacy, to say what is uppermost in my thoughts; but we spendthrifts are **provokingly** handsome! Sir Miles, your good uncle, is pleased to forgive all my follies and faults upon one condition,—that you will take on yourself the task to reform me. Will you, my fair cousin? Such as I am, you **behold** me. I am no **sinner** in the disguise of a **saint**. My fortune is spent, my health is not strong; but a young widow's is no mournful position.

French

behold: voici, voilà, apercevoir, voir.
bloom: fleur, efflorescence, bloom, pruine, floraison, bleuissement.
bound: bond, relié, limite, lié.
captivating: captivant, charmer.
castle: château, tour.
catching: attrapant, prenant, capturant, accroche, frappant.
confessedly: de manière confessâmes.
convince: convaincre, persuader.
downcast: abattu, abaissé, baissé.
fat: gras, graisse, gros, épais.
fifteen: quinze.
footman: valet de pied.
formidable: formidable, extraordinaire, singulier, prodigieux, redoutable.
fourteen: quatorze.
hiding: cachant, masquant, dissimulation.
pledge: gage, nantissement, promettre, engagement.
premature: prématuré, anticipé, avant terme, lavé, précoce.
prettiest: le plus joli.
provokingly: de façon provoquante, de manière provoquante.
rare: rare, saignant.
saint: saint.
sincerity: sincérité, bonne foi.
sinner: pécheur.
tired: fatigué, las.
warden: directeur, gardien.

I am gay when I am well, good-tempered when **ailing**. I never betrayed a trust,—can you trust me with yourself?"

This was a long speech, and Charley Vernon felt pleased that it was over. There was much in it that would have touched a heart even closed to him, and a little **genuine** emotion had given light to his eyes, and **color** to his cheek. Amidst all the **ravages** of dissipation, there was something interesting in his countenance, and manly in his **tone** and his gesture. But Lucretia was only sensible to one part of his confession,—her uncle consented to his suit. This was all of which she desired to be **assured**, and against this she now **sought** to screen herself.

"Your candour, Mr. Vernon," she said, **avoiding** his eye, "deserves candour in me; I cannot affect to **misunderstand** you. But you take me by surprise; I was so **unprepared** for this. Give me time,—I must **reflect**."

"Reflection is dull work in the country; you can reflect more **amusingly** in town, my fair cousin."

"I will wait, then, till I find myself in town."

"Ah, you make me the **happiest**, the most grateful of men," cried Mr. Vernon, rising, with a semi-genuflection which seemed to **imply**, "Consider yourself **knelt** to,"—just as a courteous assailer, with a motion of the hand, **implies**, "Consider yourself horsewhipped."

Lucretia, who, with all her intellect, had no capacity for **humour**, **recoiled**, and looked up in positive surprise.

"I do not understand you, Mr. Vernon," she said, with **austere gravity**.

"Allow me the bliss of **flattering** myself that you, at least, are understood," replied Charley Vernon, with **imperturbable** assurance. "You will wait to reflect till you are in town,—that is to say, the day after our **honeymoon**, when you **awake** in Mayfair."

Before Lucretia could **reply**, she saw the **indefatigable** valet **formally** approaching, with the **anticipated** message that Sir Miles requested to see her. She replied hurriedly to this last, that she would be with her uncle

---

French

ailing: souffrant.
amusingly: de manière amusante, de façon amusante.
anticipated: anticipa, prévu.
assured: assura, garantites.
austere: austère, simple.
avoiding: évitant, esquivant.
awake: éveillé, réveillé.
color: couleur, colorer.
flattering: flattant, adulant, amadouant.
formally: de manière formelle,
formellement, de façon formelle.
genuine: véritable, authentique, franc, sincère.
gravity: gravité, pesanteur.
happiest: le plus heureux.
honeymoon: lune de miel, voyage de noces.
humour: humour, humeur.
imperturbable: imperturbable.
implies: implique.
imply: impliquer, signifier, suggérer.
indefatigable: infatigable, inlassable.
knelt: agenouillé.
misunderstand: mal comprendre.
ravage: ravager, dévastation.
recoiled: reculé.
reflect: refléter, réfléchir, renvoyer.
reply: réponse, répliquer.
sought: cherchâtes, raillèrent.
tone: ton, tonalité, timbre, tonicité.
unprepared: improvisé, non préparé.

immediately; and when he had again **disappeared** within the **porch**, she said, with a **constrained** effort at frankness,—

"Mr. Vernon, if I have misunderstood your words, I think I do not mistake your character. You cannot wish to take advantage of my affection for my uncle, and the **passive obedience** I owe to him, to force me into a step of which—of which—I have not yet sufficiently considered the results. If you really desire that my feelings should be **consulted**, that I should not—pardon me—consider myself **sacrificed** to the family **pride** of my **guardian** and the interests of my suitor—"

"Madam!" exclaimed Vernon, **reddening**.

Pleased with the **irritating** effect her words had produced, Lucretia continued calmly, "If, in a word, I am to be a free agent in a choice on which my happiness depends, **forbear** to **urge** Sir Miles further at present; forbear to press your suit upon me. Give me the **delay** of a few months; I shall know how to **appreciate** your delicacy."

"Miss Clavering," answered Vernon, with a touch of the St. John haughtiness, "I am in despair that you should even think so grave an appeal to my honour necessary. I am well aware of your **expectations** and my poverty. And, believe me, I would rather **rot** in a prison than **enrich** myself by **forcing** your inclinations. You have but to say the word, and I will (as becomes me as a man and gentleman) screen you from all chance of Sir Miles's displeasure, by taking it on myself to decline an honour of which I feel, indeed, very undeserving."

"But I have offended you," said Lucretia, **softly**, while she turned **aside** to conceal the glad light of her eyes,—"pardon me; and to prove that you do so, give me your arm to my uncle's room."

Vernon, with rather more of Sir Miles's **antiquated stiffness** than his own rakish **ease**, offered his arm, with a profound reverence, to his cousin, and they took their way to the house. Not till they had passed up the stairs, and were even in the gallery, did further words pass between them. Then Vernon said,—

French

antiquated: vieilli, désuet.
appreciate: apprécier, estimer, aimer, aimons.
aside: aparté, de côté, excepté.
constrained: contraint, forçâtes, gêné, forcé.
consulted: consultai.
delay: retard, délai, différer, ajourner, renvoyer, reculer, suspendre, sursis.
disappeared: disparûmes.
ease: soulager, aise, aisance, facilité.
enrich: enrichir, amender, étoffe, féconder, fertiliser.
expectation: espérance, expectative.
forbear: s'abstenir.
forcing: forçage, forcer, forgeage, intensification de la valeur d'ajustage, pression, chauffage.
guardian: tuteur, gardien, curateur.
irritating: irritant, agaçant.
obedience: obéissance, soumission.
passive: passif, inactif.
porch: porche, portique, véranda.
pride: fierté, orgueil.
reddening: rougissant.
rot: pourrir, se gâter, rouir à l'excès, se pourrir, carie, clavelée, gâter.
sacrificed: sacrifié.
softly: doucement, de façon douce, de manière douce.
stiffness: raideur, inflexibilité, froideur, fermeté.
urge: inciter, presser, être urgent, exhorter, pousser.

"But what is your wish, Miss Clavering? On what **footing** shall I remain here?"

"Will you suffer me to **dictate**?" replied Lucretia, stopping short with well-feigned confusion, as if suddenly aware that the right to dictate gives the right to hope.

"Ah, consider me at least your slave!" whispered Vernon, as, his eye resting on the contour of that matchless neck, partially and **advantageously** turned from him, he began, with his constitutional admiration of the sex, to feel interested in a **pursuit** that now seemed, after piquing, to **flatter** his self-love.

"Then I will use the **privilege** when we meet again," answered Lucretia; and drawing her arm gently from his, she passed on to her uncle, leaving Vernon midway in the gallery.

Those faded portraits looked down on her with that melancholy gloom which the **effigies** of our dead ancestors seem **mysteriously** to acquire. To noble and **aspiring** spirits, no **homily** to truth and honour and fair ambition is more **eloquent** than the mute and melancholy **canvas** from which our fathers, made, by death, our household gods, contemplate us still. They appear to confide to us the charge of their unblemished names. They speak to us from the grave, and heard **aright**, the pride of family is the guardian **angel** of its heirs. But Lucretia, with her hard and **scholastic** mind, **despised** as the **veriest weakness** all the poetry that belongs to the sense of a pure **descent**. It was because she was proud as the proudest in herself that she had nothing but **contempt** for the virtue, the **valour**, or the **wisdom** of those that had gone before. So, with a brain busy with **guile** and stratagem, she trod on, beneath the eyes of the simple and **spotless** Dead.

Vernon, thus left alone, mused a few moments on what had passed between himself and the heiress; and then, slowly **retracing** his steps, his eye roved along the stately series of his line. "Faith!" he muttered, "if my boyhood had been passed in this old gallery, his Royal Highness would have lost a good fellow and hard **drinker**, and his Majesty would have had

---

French

advantageously: de façon avantageuse, de manière avantageuse.
angel: ange.
aright: juste.
aspiring: aspirant, futur.
canvas: canevas, toile.
contempt: mépris, désobéissance, dédain.
descent: descente, origine.
despised: méprisèrent, dédaignâtes.
dictate: dicter, imposer.
drinker: buveur.
effigy: effigie.
eloquent: éloquent.
flatter: flatter, aduler, amadouer.
footing: pied, semelle.
guile: astuce, fourberie.
homily: homélie.
mysteriously: de manière mystérieuse, de façon mystérieuse.
privilege: privilège, prérogative.
pursuit: poursuite, occupation, recherche.
retracing: reconstituer, retraçant.
scholastic: scolastique.
spotless: sans tache, immaculé, impeccable.
valour: valeur, vaillance, courage.
veriest: le plus très.
weakness: faiblesse, débilité, impuissance, mollesse.
wisdom: sagesse, intelligence.

perhaps a more distinguished soldier,—certainly a worthier subject. If I marry this lady, and we are **blessed** with a son, he shall walk through this gallery once a day before he is flogged into Latin!"

Lucretia's interview with her uncle was a masterpiece of art. What pity that such craft and **subtlety** were **wasted** in our little day, and on such petty objects; under the Medici, that spirit had gone far to the **shaping** of history. Sure, from her uncle's openness, that he would **plunge** at once into the subject for which she deemed she was summoned, she evinced no **repugnance** when, tenderly **kissing** her, he asked if Charles Vernon had a chance of winning favour in her eyes. She knew that she was safe in saying "No;" that her uncle would never force her inclinations,—safe so far as Vernon was concerned; but she desired more: she desired thoroughly to **quench** all suspicion that her heart was pre-occupied; entirely to remove from Sir Miles's thoughts the image of Mainwaring; and a **denial** of one suitor might **quicken** the baronet's eyes to the **concealment** of the other. Nor was this all; if Sir Miles was seriously bent upon seeing her settled in marriage before his death, the dismissal of Vernon might only **expose** her to the **importunity** of new candidates more difficult to deal with. Vernon himself she could use as the **shield** against the **arrows** of a host. Therefore, when Sir Miles repeated his question, she answered, with much gentleness and seeming modest sense, that Mr. Vernon had much that must **prepossess** in his favour; that in addition to his own advantages he had one, the highest in her eyes,—her uncle's **sanction** and approval. But—and she **hesitated** with becoming and natural diffidence—were not his habits unfixed and roving? So it was said; she knew not herself,—she would trust her happiness to her uncle. But if so, and if Mr. Vernon were really **disposed** to change, would it not be prudent to try him,—try him where there was temptation, not in the **repose** of Laughton, but amidst his own **haunts** of London? Sir Miles had friends who would honestly inform him of the result. She did but suggest this; she was too ready to leave all to her dear guardian's **acuteness** and experience.

French

acuteness: intensité, acuité.
arrow: flèche, fiche.
blessed: bénirent, bénîmes, bienheureux.
concealment: dissimulation, recel, réticence.
denial: démenti, déni, refus, dénégation.
disposed: disposé.
expose: exposer, montrer, mettre à nu, insoler, affleurer, démasquer, dévoiler.

haunt: hanter, fréquenter.
hesitated: hésita, barguignâmes.
importunity: importunité.
kissing: embrasser, baisant.
plunge: plonger, se jeter, se précipiter, risquer de grosses sommes, piquer du nez, inclinaison, chute, enfoncer.
prepossess: préoccuper.
quench: étouffer, éteindre.
quicken: hâte, accélérez, hâtons.
repose: repos, se reposer, trêve.

repugnance: répugnance, aversion.
sanction: sanction.
shaping: façonnage, taille de formation, profilage, rabotage à l'étau limeur, toupillage, formage, déformation, forçage, galbage.
shield: bouclier, blindage, enseigne, écran de protection, protection, écusson, écu.
subtlety: subtilité.
wasted: gaspilla, prodiguèrent, gâché.

Melted by her **docility**, and in high approval of the **prudence** which **betokened** a more **rational judgment** than he himself had evinced, the good old man clasped her to his breast and **shed** tears as he **praised** and **thanked** her. She had decided, as she always did, for the best; Heaven forbid that she should be wasted on an **incorrigible** man of pleasure! "And," said the frank-hearted gentleman, unable long to keep any thought concealed,—"and to think that I could have wronged you for a moment, my own noble child; that I could have been dolt enough to suppose that the good looks of that boy Mainwaring might have caused you to forget what—But you change colour!"—for, with all her dissimulation, Lucretia loved too **ardently** not to shrink at that name thus suddenly pronounced. "Oh," continued the baronet, drawing her still nearer towards him, while with one hand he put back her face, that he might read its expression the more closely,—"oh, if it had been so,—if it be so, I will pity, not **blame** you, for my **neglect** was the fault: pity you, for I have known a similar struggle; **admire** you in pity, for you have the spirit of your ancestors, and you will conquer the weakness. Speak! have I touched on the truth? Speak without fear, child,—you have no mother; but in age a man sometimes gets a mother's heart."

Startled and alarmed as the **lark** when the step nears its **nest**, Lucretia summoned all the dark **wile** of her nature to **mislead** the **intruder**. "No, uncle, no; I am not so unworthy. You misconceived my emotion."

"Ah, you know that he has had the presumption to love you,—the puppy!—and you feel the **compassion** you women always feel for such **offenders**? Is that it?"

Rapidly Lucretia considered if it would be **wise** to leave that impression on his mind. On one hand, it might account for a moment's **agitation**; and if Mainwaring were detected **hovering** near the domain, in the exchange of their correspondence, it might appear but the idle, if hopeless, romance of youth, which haunts the mere home of its object,—but no; on the other hand, it left his **banishment absolute** and confirmed. Her **resolution** was taken with a promptitude that made her pause not perceptible.

French

absolute: absolu, complet, inéluctable, immense, illimité, pur.
admire: admirer.
agitation: agitation, bagarre, brassage, barouf.
ardently: ardemment, de façon ardante, de manière ardante.
banishment: bannissement, exil.
betokened: présagèrent.
blame: blâme, reprocher, gronder, sermonner, réprimander.
compassion: compassion, pitié, apitoiement.
docility: docilité.
hovering: planant, vol stationnaire, voltigeant, flottant.
incorrigible: incorrigible.
intruder: intrus, importun.
judgment: arrêt, jugement.
lark: alouette, blague.
mislead: égarer, tromper.
neglect: négliger, dédaigner, coups partis avec éléments erronés.
nest: nid, nicher, faire son nid.
offender: offenseur, contrevenant.
praised: loué.
prudence: prudence, précaution.
rational: rationnel, raisonnable.
resolution: résolution, motion, pouvoir de résolution, définition.
shed: hangar, verser, abri, baraque, kiosque, échoppe, stand, remise, foule, cabane.
thanked: remerciâtes.
wile: ruse.
wise: sensé, raisonnable.

"No, my **dear** uncle," she said, so **cheerfully** that it **removed** all **doubt** from the mind of her listener; "but M. Dalibard has **rallied** me on the subject, and I was so **angry** with him that when you touched on it, I thought more of my **quarrel** with him than of poor timid Mr. Mainwaring himself. Come, now, own it, dear sir! M. Dalibard has **instilled** this **strange** fancy into your head?"

"No, 'S life; if he had taken such a **liberty**, I should have lost my librarian. No, I **assure** you, it was rather Vernon; you know true love is jealous."

"Vernon!" thought Lucretia; "he must go, and at once." Sliding from her uncle's **arms** to the **stool** at his feet, she then **led** the **conversation** more familiarly back into the **channel** it had lost; and when at last she **escaped**, it was with the **understanding** that, without promise or **compromise**, Mr. Vernon should return to London at once, and be put upon the **ordeal** through which she felt assured it was little likely he should pass with success.

French

angry: fâché, en colère, irrité, furieux.
arm: bras, armer, branche, accoudoir.
assure: assurer, certifier, garantir.
channel: canal, chenal, tube, voie, tuyau, chaîne, la Manche, conduit, rigole, radiocanal.
cheerfully: de manière gaie, de façon gaie.
compromise: compromis, transiger.
conversation: conversation, discussion, entretien.
dear: cher, coûteux.
doubt: doute.
escaped: échappé, enfuirent.
instilled: inculquas, insufflèrent.
led: menâmes, mena, conduit, mené, menèrent, guidâtes, about it, laissa.
liberty: liberté.
ordeal: désolation, épreuve.
quarrel: querelle, dispute, se disputer, se quereller, noise.
rallied: rallia.
removed: ôta, supprimai, ôtai, ôtâmes, ôtas, ôtâtes, ôté, ôtèrent, enlevâmes.
stool: tabouret, banquette, escabeau, selles.
strange: étrange, singulier, drôle, bizarre.
understanding: comprenant, abord, relation, entendement.

CHAPTER IV

GUY'S OAK

Three weeks afterwards, the life at Laughton seemed restored to the cheerful and somewhat **monotonous** tranquillity of its course, before chafed and **disturbed** by the recent **interruptions** to the **stream**. Vernon had departed, satisfied with the **justice** of the **trial imposed** on him, and far too high-spirited to **seek** to **extort** from niece or uncle any **engagement** beyond that which, to a nice sense of honour, the trial itself imposed. His **memory** and his heart were still faithful to Mary; but his senses, his fancy, his vanity, were a little involved in his success with the heiress. Though so free from all mercenary **meanness**, Mr. Vernon was still enough man of the world to be sensible of the **advantages** of the **alliance** which had first been pressed on him by Sir Miles, and from which Lucretia herself **appeared** not to be averse. The season of London was over, but there was always a set, and that set the one in which Charley Vernon principally moved, who found town **fuller** than the country. **Besides**, he went **occasionally** to Brighton, which was then to England what Baiae was to Rome. The prince was **holding** gay court at the Pavilion, and that was the **atmosphere** which Vernon was habituated to **breathe**. He was no parasite of **royalty**; he had that strong personal affection to the prince which it is often the good fortune of royalty to attract. Nothing

---

French

advantage: avantage, intérêt.
alliance: alliance, coalition.
appeared: apparus, comparus.
atmosphere: atmosphère, ambiance.
beside: près de, chez, tous près de, parmi, sur, au bord de, à côté de, à.
breathe: respirer, aspirer, exhaler, murmurer.
disturbed: dérangeai, gêna, gênèrent, gêné, gênâtes.
engagement: fiançailles, engagement, enclenchement, accordailles.
extort: extorquer, soutire, arracher.
fuller: gravure de roulage.
holding: entretien, tenue, maintien, attente.
imposed: imposa, contraignit.
interruption: interruption, rupture, coupure.
justice: justice, équité.
meanness: mesquinerie, vilenie.
memory: mémoire, souvenir.
monotonous: monotone.
occasionally: occasionnellement, de façon occasionnelle, de manière occasionnelle, de temps en temps.
royalty: royauté, règne.
seek: chercher, railler, recherche.
stream: ruisseau, courant, jet, fleuve, rivière, flot.
trial: jugement, essai, épreuve, procès, désolation.

is less founded than the complaint which poets put into the lips of princes, that they have no friends,—it is, at least, their own **perverse** fault if that be the case; a little amiability, a little of frank kindness, goes so far when it **emanates** from the rays of a crown. But Vernon was stronger than Lucretia deemed him; once contemplating the prospect of a union which was to **consign** to his charge the happiness of another, and feeling all that he should owe in such a marriage to the confidence both of niece and uncle, he evinced steadier principles than he had ever made **manifest** when he had only his own fortune to **mar**, and his own happiness to **trifle** with. He joined his old companions, but he kept **aloof** from their more dissipated pursuits. Beyond what was then thought the **venial** error of too **devout libations** to Bacchus, Charley Vernon seemed reformed.

Ardworth had joined a regiment which had departed for the field of action. Mainwaring was still with his father, and had not yet announced to Sir Miles any wish or project for the future.

Olivier Dalibard, as before, passed his mornings alone in his chamber,—his noons and his evenings with Sir Miles. He avoided all private conferences with Lucretia. She did not provoke them. Young Gabriel amused himself in **copying** Sir Miles's pictures, sketching from Nature, **scribbling** in his room **prose** or **verse**, no matter which (he never showed his lucubrations), **pinching** the dogs when he could catch them alone, **shooting** the cats, if they appeared in the plantation, on **pretence** of love for the young **pheasants**, sauntering into the cottages, where he was a favourite because of his good looks, but where he always contrived to leave the trace of his visits in disorder and **mischief**, **upsetting** the tea-kettle and **scalding** the children, or, what he loved dearly, setting two **gossips** by the ears. But these occupations were over by the hour Lucretia left her apartment. From that time he never left her out of view; and when encouraged to join her at his usual **privileged** times, whether in the gardens at **sunset** or in her evening niche in the drawing-room, he was sleek, **silken**, and **caressing** as Cupid, after plaguing the Nymphs, at the feet of Psyche. These two strange persons had indeed apparently that sort of **sentimental** familiarity which is sometimes seen

---

French

aloof: distant.
caressing: tendre, caressant.
consign: consigner, expédier.
copying: copie, duplication.
devout: dévot, pieux.
emanates: émane.
gossip: cancaner, jaser, commérage, bavard.
libation: libation.
manifest: manifeste, évident.
mar: gâter, gâtons.
mischief: malice, tort, méfait,
dégâts.
perverse: pervers.
pheasant: faisan.
pinching: pincement, croquage, pinçage.
pretence: prétexte, simulacre.
privileged: privilégié.
prose: prose.
scalding: brûlant, échaudage, roussissement, ébouillantage, bouillant.
scribbling: droussage, précardage.
sentimental: sentimental.
shooting: tirant, tir, tournage, fusillade, chasse, prise de vues.
silken: soyeux, de soie.
sunset: coucher du soleil, de temporarisation.
trifle: bagatelle, babiole.
upsetting: bouleversant, déranger, forgeage par refoulement, matage, refoulage, vexant, aplatissement.
venial: véniel.
verse: vers, strophe.

between a fair boy and a girl much older than himself; but the attraction that drew them together was an **indefinable instinct** of their **similarity** in many traits of their several characters,—the **whelp leopard** sported **fearlessly** around the she-panther. Before Olivier's midnight conference with his son, Gabriel had drawn close and closer to Lucretia, as an **ally** against his father; for that father he cherished feelings which, beneath the most docile obedience, concealed horror and hate, and something of the ferocity of revenge. And if young Varney loved any one on earth except himself, it was Lucretia Clavering. She had **administered** to his ruling passions, which were for effect and display; she had devised the dress which set off to the utmost his **exterior**, and gave it that **picturesque** and artistic appearance which he had sighed for in his study of the portraits of Titian and Vandyke. She supplied him (for in money she was generous) with enough to **gratify** and forestall every boyish caprice; and this **liberality** now turned against her, for it had increased into a settled vice his natural taste for extravagance, and made all other considerations subordinate to that of **feeding** his cupidity. She praised his drawings, which, though self-taught, were indeed extraordinary, **predicted** his fame as an artist, lifted him into consequence amongst the guests by her notice and **eulogies**, and what, perhaps, won him more than all, he felt that it was to her—to Dalibard's desire to conceal before her his more **cruel** propensities—that he owed his father's change from the most refined **severity** to the most paternal gentleness.

And thus he had **repaid** her, as she expected, by a **devotion** which she trusted to employ against her tutor himself, should the baffled **aspirant** become the scheming rival and the secret foe. But now,—thoroughly aware of the gravity of his father's objects, seeing before him the chance of a settled establishment at Laughton, a positive and influential connection with Lucretia; and on the other hand a return to the poverty he recalled with disgust, and the terrors of his father's solitary malice and revenge,—he entered fully into Dalibard's **sombre** plans, and without **scruple** or **remorse**, would have **abetted** any harm to his **benefactress**. Thus craft, **doomed** to have accomplices in craft, **resembles** the **spider**, whose web, spread indeed

French

abetted: aidâmes, aidas, ému, aidé, troublâtes.
administered: administrâmes.
ally: allié.
aspirant: aspirant.
benefactress: bienfaitrice.
cruel: cruel, atroce, méchant.
devotion: dévotion, piété.
doomed: condamné.
eulogy: panégyrique, éloge.
exterior: extérieur, aspect, spectacle, vue.
fearlessly: de façon intrépide, de manière intrépide.
feeding: alimentant, nourrissant, épaississement, affouragement.
gratify: satisfaire, gratifient, contentons.
indefinable: indéfinissable.
instinct: instinct, pulsion.
leopard: léopard.
liberality: libéralité, générosité.
picturesque: pittoresque.
predicted: prédirent, prévu.
remorse: remords.
repaid: remboursa.
resemble: ressembler, rejoindre.
scruple: scrupule.
severity: sévérité, austérité, rigueur, gravité.
similarity: similarité, ressemblance.
sombre: sombre.
spider: araignée, croisillon.
whelp: petit, savon de grande longueur, chienner, couteau pour voûte de four.

for the fly, **attracts** the fellow-spider that shall thrust it **forth**, and profit by the meshes it has **woven** for a victim, to **surrender** to a master.

Already young Varney, set quietly and **ceaselessly** to spy every movement of Lucretia's, had reported to his father two visits to the most retired part of the park; but he had not yet ventured near enough to discover the exact spot, and his very watch on Lucretia had **prevented** the **detection** of Mainwaring himself in his stealthy exchange of correspondence. Dalibard bade him continue his watch, without hinting at his **ulterior** intentions, for, indeed, in these he was not decided. Even should he discover any communication between Lucretia and Mainwaring, how reveal it to Sir Miles without forever **precluding** himself from the chance of profiting by the **betrayal**? Could Lucretia ever forgive the injury, and could she fail to detect the hand that **inflicted** it? His only hope was in the removal of Mainwaring from his path by other agencies than his own, and (by an appearance of generosity and self-abandonment, in keeping her secret and **submitting** to his fate) he trusted to **regain** the confidence she now **withheld** from him, and use it to his advantage when the time came to defend himself from Vernon. For he had learned from Sir Miles the passive understanding with respect to that candidate for her hand; and he felt assured that had Mainwaring never **existed**, could he cease to exist for her hopes, Lucretia, despite her dissimulation, would succumb to one she **feared** but **respected**, rather than one she evidently trifled with and despised.

"But the course to be taken must be adopted after the evidence is collected," thought the subtle **schemer**, and he **tranquilly** continued his chess with the baronet.

Before, however, Gabriel could make any further discoveries, an event occurred which excited very different emotions amongst those it more immediately interested.

Sir Miles had, during the last twelve months, been visited by two **seizures**, **seemingly** of an **apoplectic** character. Whether they were **apoplexy**, or the less **alarming** attacks that arise from some more gentle

---

French

alarming: alarmant, consternant.
apoplectic: apoplectique.
apoplexy: apoplexie.
attracts: attire, allèche, appâte.
betrayal: trahison.
ceaselessly: continuellement, de façon incessante, de manière incessante.
detection: détection, dépistage, découverte.
existed: exista.
feared: craint.

forth: en avant.
inflicted: infligé.
precluding: empêchant, excluant.
prevented: empêchâtes, prévins.
regain: regagner, rattraper, recouvrer.
respected: respecté.
schemer: intrigant.
seemingly: apparemment, de manière paraissante, de façon paraissante.
seizure: saisie, prise, capture, apoplexie, confiscation, attaque.
submitting: soumettant.
surrender: abandon, se rendre, reddition.
tranquilly: de façon tranquille, de manière tranquille.
ulterior: ultérieur.
withheld: retint, retîntes, retenu.
woven: tissé.

congestion, occasioned by free living and indolent habits, was matter of doubt with his physician,—not a very skilful, though a very formal, man. Country doctors were not then the same able, educated, and scientific class that they are now rapidly becoming. Sir Miles himself so **stoutly** and so eagerly **repudiated** the least hint of the more unfavourable interpretation that the doctor, if not convinced by his patient, was awed from **expressing** plainly a contrary opinion. There are certain persons who will **dismiss** their physician if he tells them the truth: Sir Miles was one of them.

In his character there was a weakness not uncommon to the proud. He did not fear death, but he shrank from the thought that others should **calculate** on his dying. He was **fond** of his power, though he **exercised** it gently: he knew that the power of wealth and station is enfeebled in proportion as its dependants can **foresee** the date of its transfer. He **dreaded**, too, the comments which are always made on those visited by his **peculiar** disease: "Poor Sir Miles! an apoplectic fit. His intellect must be very much **shaken**; he **revoked** at whist last night,—memory sadly impaired!" This may be a **pitiable foible**; but heroes and statesmen have had it most: pardon it in the proud old man! He **enjoined** the physician to state throughout the house and the **neighbourhood** that the attacks were wholly innocent and **unimportant**. The physician did so, and was generally believed; for Sir Miles seemed as **lively** and as **vigorous** after them as before. Two persons alone were not deceived,—Dalibard and Lucretia. The first, at an earlier part of his life, had studied **pathology** with the profound research and ingenious application which he brought to bear upon all he **undertook**. He whispered from the first to Lucretia,—

"Unless your uncle changes his habits, takes exercise, and forbears wine and the table, his days are numbered."

And when this intelligence was first conveyed to her, before she had become acquainted with Mainwaring, Lucretia felt the shock of a **grief** sudden and sincere. We have seen how these better sentiments changed as human life became an obstacle in her way. In her character, what **phrenologists** call "destructiveness," in the comprehensive sense of the

French

calculate: calculer, compter, estimer, évaluer.
congestion: congestion, encombrement, afflux de sang, embouteillage.
dismiss: renvoyer, licencier, débouter, suspendre, congédier.
dreaded: redouté.
enjoined: enjoignis.
exercised: exercé.
expressing: exprimant, extériorisant.
foible: faible.
fond: tendre, affectueux, indulgent.
foresee: prévoir, présager.
grief: peine, chagrin, désolation, abattement, douleur.
lively: animé, vif, spirituel, fin, mental, de manière vivre, plein d'entrain, de façon vivre.
neighbourhood: voisinage, quartier.
pathology: pathologie.
peculiar: étrange, singulier, drôle, particulier.
phrenologist: phrénologiste.
pitiable: pitoyable.
repudiated: répudias, nié.
revoked: révoquâtes.
shaken: secoué, ébranlé.
stoutly: de manière corpulente, de façon corpulente.
undertook: entreprîmes.
unimportant: mineur, insignifiant, négligeable, sans importance.
vigorous: vigoureux, énergique.

word, was **superlatively** developed. She had not actual **cruelty**; she was not **bloodthirsty**: those vices belong to a different cast of character. She was rather deliberately and **intellectually unsparing**. A goal was before her; she must march to it: all in the way were but hostile **impediments**. At first, however, Sir Miles was not in the way, except to fortune, and for that, as **avarice** was not her leading vice, she could well wait; therefore, at this hint of the Provencal's she ventured to urge her uncle to **abstinence** and exercise. But Sir Miles was **touchy** on the subject; he feared the interpretations which great change of habits might suggest. The memory of the **fearful** warning died away, and he felt as well as before; for, save an old **rheumatic gout** (which had long since left him with no other apparent evil but a **lameness** in the joints that rendered exercise **unwelcome** and painful), he possessed one of those comfortable, and often **treacherous**, constitutions which **evince** no displeasure at **irregularities**, and bear all liberties with **philosophical** composure. Accordingly, he would have his own way; and he contrived to coax or to force his doctor into an authority on his side: wine was necessary to his constitution; much exercise was a dangerous fatigue. The second attack, following four months after the first, was less alarming, and Sir Miles fancied it concealed even from his niece; but three nights after his recovery, the old baronet sat musing alone for some time in his own room before he retired to rest. Then he rose, opened his desk, and read his will **attentively**, locked it up with a slight **sigh**, and took down his Bible. The next morning he despatched the letters which summoned Ardworth and Vernon to his house; and as he quitted his room, his look lingered with melancholy fondness upon the portraits in the gallery. No one was by the old man to interpret these slight signs, in which lay a world of meaning.

A few weeks after Vernon had left the house, and in the midst of the restored tranquillity we have described, it so happened that Sir Miles's physician, after **dining** at the Hall, had been summoned to attend one of the children at the **neighbouring** rectory; and there he spent the night. A little before **daybreak** his slumbers were disturbed; he was recalled in all **haste** to Laughton Hall. For the third time, he found Sir Miles **speechless**. Dalibard

French

abstinence: abstinence, voix refusée.
attentively: attentivement, de façon attentive, de manière attentive.
avarice: avarice, cupidité.
bloodthirsty: sanguinaire, avide de sang.
cruelty: cruauté, sévices.
daybreak: aube, aurore, point du jour.
dining: dînant.
evince: montres.
fearful: effrayant, affreux, craintif.
gout: goutte, bouchon, matière étrangère prise dans le tissage.
haste: hâte, précipitation.
impediment: empêchement, entrave, obstacle.
intellectually: intellectuellement, de façon intellectuelle, de manière intellectuelle.
irregularity: irrégularité, inégalité.
lameness: boiterie, impotence, boîterie ancienne intermittente, claudication, faiblesse.
neighbouring: adjacent, avoisinant.
philosophical: philosophique.
rheumatic: rhumatismal.
sigh: soupir.
speechless: muet, sans voix.
superlatively: de façon superlative, de manière superlative.
touchy: susceptible, délicat.
treacherous: traître, déloyal.
unsparing: prodigue, généreux.
unwelcome: importun, fâcheux.

was by his **bedside**. Lucretia had not been made aware of the seizure; for Sir Miles had previously told his valet (who of late slept in the same room) never to alarm Miss Clavering if he was taken ill. The doctor was about to apply his **usual remedies**; but when he drew forth his **lancet**, Dalibard **placed** his hand on the physician's arm.

"Not this time," he said slowly, and with **emphasis**; "it will be his death."

"Pooh, sir!" said the doctor, **disdainfully**.

"Do so, then; **bleed** him, and take the responsibility. I have **studied medicine**,—I know these symptoms. In this case the apoplexy may spare,—the lancet kills."

The physician drew back **dismayed** and **doubtful**.

"What would you do, then?"

"Wait three **minutes** longer the effect of the cataplasms I have **applied**. If they fail—"

"Ay, then?"

"A chill **bath** and vigorous friction."

"Sir, I will never permit it."

"Then murder your patient your own way."

All this while Sir Miles lay **senseless**, his eyes wide open, his **teeth locked**. The doctor drew near, looked at the lancet, and said irresolutely,—

"Your practice is new to me; but if you have studied medicine, that's another matter. Will you **guarantee** the success of your plan?"

"Yes."

"Mind, I **wash** my hands of it; I take Mr. Jones to witness;" and he appealed to the valet.

"Call up the footman and **lift** your master," said Dalibard; and the doctor, glancing round, saw that a bath, filled some seven or eight **inches** deep with water, stood already prepared in the room. Perplexed and irresolute, he offered no obstacle to Dalibard's movements. The body,

French

applied: appliquèrent, pratiqué.
bath: bain, baignoire, cuvette.
bedside: chevet.
bleed: saigner, purger.
disdainfully: de façon dédaigneuse, de manière dédaigneuse.
dismayed: atterrâmes, consterné.
doubtful: incertain, douteux.
emphasis: emphase, accentuation.
guarantee: garantie, cautionner, assurer, aval.
inch: pouce.
lancet: lancette, ogive.
lift: ascenseur, lever, soulever, élever, portance, se soulever, sustentation.
locked: bloqué, fermé.
medicine: médicament, médecine, remède.
minute: minute, moment, la minute, instant.
placed: placé, plaçai.
remedy: remède, ressource, moyen, assainir, guérir.
senseless: insensé, stupide, sans connaissance, déraisonnable.
studied: étudié, délibéré.
teeth: dents, maillons.
usual: habituel, ordinaire, général, usuel, accoutumé, courant.
wash: laver, lavons, lavage, blanchissage.

seemingly **lifeless**, was placed in the bath; and the servants, under Dalibard's directions, applied vigorous and **incessant friction**. Several minutes **elapsed** before any **favourable** symptom took place. At length Sir Miles heaved a deep sigh, and the eyes moved; a minute or two more, and the teeth chattered; the blood, set in motion, appeared on the surface of the skin; life ebbed back. The danger was passed, the dark foe **driven** from the **citadel**. Sir Miles spoke **audibly**, though **incoherently**, as he was taken back to his bed, warmly covered up, the lights removed, noise forbidden, and Dalibard and the doctor remained in silence by the bedside.

"Rich man," thought Dalibard, "thine hour is not yet come; **thy** wealth must not pass to the boy Mainwaring." Sir Miles's recovery, under the care of Dalibard, who now had his own way, was as rapid and complete as before. Lucretia when she heard, the next morning, of the attack, felt, we **dare** not say a guilty joy, but a terrible and **feverish** agitation. Sir Miles himself, informed by his valet of Dalibard's **wrestle** with the doctor, felt a profound gratitude and **reverent** wonder for the simple means to which he probably owed his **restoration**; and he **listened**, with a docility which Dalibard was not prepared to expect, to his learned secretary's urgent admonitions as to the life he must lead if he desired to live at all. **Convinced**, at last, that wine and good **cheer** had not blockaded out the enemy, and having to do, in Olivier Dalibard, with a very different temper from the doctor's, he **assented** with a **tolerable** grace to the trial of a **strict regimen** and to daily exercise in the open air. Dalibard now became **constantly** with him; the increase of his influence was as natural as it was apparent. Lucretia trembled; she divined a danger in his power, now separate from her own, and which threatened to be independent of it. She became abstracted and uneasy; jealousy of the Provencal possessed her. She began to **meditate** schemes for his **downfall**. At this time, Sir Miles received the following letter from Mr. Fielden:—

Southampton, Aug. 20, 1801.

French

assented: assenties.
audibly: de manière audible, de façon audible.
cheer: acclamation, applaudir.
citadel: citadelle.
constantly: constamment, continuellement, de façon constante, de manière constante.
convinced: convainquîtes.
dare: oser, ose, osez, aventurer, oses, osons, osent, défi.
downfall: chute, débâcle, ruine.

driven: poussé, conduit, pourchassé, actionné, piloté.
elapsed: passé, écoulé.
favourable: favorable, propice.
feverish: fiévreux, fébrile.
friction: frottement, friction, désaccord.
incessant: incessant.
incoherently: de manière incohérente, de façon incohérente.
lifeless: sans vie, inanimé.
listened: écoutâtes.

meditate: méditer, songer, réfléchir.
regimen: régime.
restoration: restauration, rétablissement.
reverent: respectueux, révérend.
strict: sévère, austère, strict, rigoureux.
thy: ton.
tolerable: supportable, tolérable, passable.
wrestle: lutter, catcher, se débattre.

Dear Sir Miles,—You will remember that I informed you when I arrived at Southampton with my dear young charge; and Susan has twice written to her sister, **implying** the request which she **lacked** the courage, seeing that she is timid, **expressly** to urge, that Miss Clavering might again be permitted to visit her. Miss Clavering has answered as might be expected from the **propinquity** of the relationship; but she has perhaps the same fears of **offending** you that **actuate** her sister. But now, since the worthy clergyman who had undertaken my **parochial** duties has found the air **insalubrious**, and **prays** me not to **enforce** the engagement by which we had exchanged our several charges for the space of a **calendar** year, I am **reluctantly** compelled to return home,—my dear wife, thank Heaven, being already restored to health, which is an unspeakable **mercy**; and I am sure I cannot be sufficiently grateful to Providence, which has not only provided me with a liberal independence of more than 200 pounds a year, but the best of wives and the most **dutiful** of children,—possessions that I venture to call "the riches of the heart." Now, I pray you, my dear Sir Miles, to gratify these two deserving young persons, and to suffer Miss Lucretia **incontinently** to visit her sister. Counting on your consent, thus boldly demanded, I have already prepared an apartment for Miss Clavering; and Susan is busy in what, though I do not know much of such **feminine** matters, the whole house declares to be a most beautiful and **fanciful** toilet-cover, with roses and forget-me-nots cut out of muslin, and two large silk **tassels**, which cost her three shillings and fourpence. I cannot **conclude** without **thanking** you from my heart for your noble kindness to young Ardworth. He is so full of **ardour** and spirit that I remember, poor lad, when I left him, as I thought, hard at work on that well-known problem of Euclid **vulgarly** called the Asses' Bridge,—I found him describing a figure of 8 on the village **pond**, which was only just **frozen** over! Poor lad! Heaven will take care of him, I know, as it does of all who take no care of themselves. Ah, Sir Miles, if you could but see Susan,—such a nurse, too, in illness! I have the honour to be, Sir Miles,

Your most **humble**, poor servant, to command,
Matthew Fielden.

French

actuate: déclencher, remuer, mouvoir, mettre en action.
ardour: ardeur.
calendar: calendrier, analyse, liste chronologique de documents, régestes.
conclude: conclure, terminer.
dutiful: dévoué, consciencieux.
enforce: mettre en vigueur, réalisez, imposez.
expressly: expressément.
fanciful: fantaisiste, capricieux,
imaginaire.
feminine: féminin.
frozen: gelé, congelé.
humble: humble, modeste.
implying: impliquant.
incontinently: de façon incontinente, de manière incontinente.
insalubrious: insalubre.
lacked: manqua.
mercy: pitié, miséricorde, compassion.
offending: offensant, insultant.
parochial: paroissial.
pond: étang, bassin, mare.
prays: prie.
propinquity: proximité.
reluctantly: à regret, de façon peu disposée, de manière peu disposée, à contrecœur.
tassel: gland, houppe.
thanking: remerciant.
vulgarly: de façon vulgaire, de manière vulgaire, vulgairement.

Sir Miles put this letter in his niece's hand, and said kindly, "Why not have gone to see your sister before? I should not have been angry. Go, my child, as soon as you like. To-morrow is Sunday,—no **travelling** that day; but the next, the carriage shall be at your order."

Lucretia hesitated a moment. To leave Dalibard in **sole possession** of the field, even for a few days, was a thought of alarm; but what evil could he do in that time? And her **pulse** beat quickly: Mainwaring could come to Southampton; she should see him again, after more than six weeks' absence! She had so much to **relate** and to hear; she fancied his last letter had been colder and **shorter**; she **yearned** to hear him say, with his own lips, that he loved her still. This idea **banished** or prevailed over all others. She thanked her uncle cheerfully and gayly, and the journey was settled.

"Be at watch early on Monday," said Olivier to his son.

Monday came; the baronet had ordered the carriage to be at the door at ten. A little before eight, Lucretia stole out, and took her way to Guy's Oak. Gabriel had placed himself in **readiness**; he had climbed a tree at the bottom of the park (near the place where hitherto he had lost sight of her); she passed under it,—on through a dark grove of **pollard** oaks. When she was at a sufficient distance, the boy dropped from his **perch**; with the stealth of an Indian he crept on her **trace**, following from tree to tree, always sheltered, always **watchful**. He saw her pause at the dell and look round; she **descended** into the hollow; he slunk through the **fern**; he gained the **marge** of the dell, and looked down,—she was lost to his sight. At length, to his surprise, he saw the **gleam** of her **robe emerge** from the hollow of a tree,— her head stooped as she came through the **aperture**; he had time to shrink back amongst the fern; she passed on hurriedly, the same way she had taken, back to the house; then into the dell crept the boy. Guy's Oak, vast and venerable, with **gnarled** green boughs below, and **sere** branches above, that told that its day of fall was **decreed** at last, rose high from the **abyss** of the hollow, high and far-seen amidst the trees that stood on the vantage-ground above,—even as a great name **soars** the loftier when it springs from the grave. A dark and irregular **fissure** gave entrance to the heart of the oak. The

French

abyss: abîme, abysse, gouffre.
aperture: ouverture, orifice, trou.
banished: exila, bannîtes.
decreed: décrété.
descended: descendu, issu.
emerge: émerger, surgir, apparaître, paraître.
fern: fougère.
fissure: fissure, fente, scissure, crevasse.
gleam: lueur, luire.
gnarled: noueux.

marge: marger.
perch: perche, jucher, se percher, porteuse, fixation oculaire, machine à raccoutrer.
pollard: arbre étêté, têtard.
possession: possession, jouissance.
pulse: pouls, impulsion, pulsation.
readiness: disponibilité, empressement.
relate: raconter, conter, être en relation avec, concerner, relater.
robe: robe, peignoir.

sere: série.
shorter: plus court.
soar: monter en flèche, faire du vol à voile.
sole: sole, semelle, seul, plante, pur.
trace: trace, décalquer, calquer, empreinte, impression, retracer, piste, trait.
travelling: itinérant, voyageant.
watchful: vigilant, attentif.
yearned: soupiré, languîtes.

boy glided in and looked round; he saw nothing, yet something there must be. The rays of the early sun did not **penetrate** into the hollow, it was as **dim** as a cave. He felt slowly in every crevice, and a startled **moth** or two flew out. It was not for moths that the girl had come to Guy's Oak! He drew back, at last, in despair; as he did so, he heard a low sound close at hand,—a low, **murmuring,** angry sound, like a hiss; he looked round, and through the dark, two burning eyes fixed his own: he had startled a **snake** from its bed. He drew out in time, as the **reptile** sprang; but now his task, search, and object were forgotten. With the **versatility** of a child, his thoughts were all on the enemy he had **provoked**. That zest of prey which is inherent in man's breast, which makes him love the sport and the chase, and **maddens** boyhood and age with the passion for **slaughter, leaped** up within him; anything of danger and contest and excitement gave Gabriel Varney a strange fever of pleasure. He sprang up the sides of the dell, climbed the park pales on which it bordered, was in the wood where the young shoots rose green and strong from the underwood. To cut a staff for the strife, to **descend** again into the dell, **creep** again through the fissure, look round for those **vengeful** eyes, was quick done as the joyous play of the impulse. The poor snake had slid down in content and fancied security; its young, perhaps, were not far off; its wrath had been the instinct Nature gives to the mother. It hath done thee no harm yet, boy; leave it in peace! The young hunter had no ear to such whisper of prudence or mercy. Dim and blind in the fissure, he struck the ground and the tree with his stick, shouted out, bade the eyes gleam, and defied them. Whether or not the reptile had spent its **ire** in the first **fruitless** spring, and this unlooked-for return of the intruder rather **daunted** than **exasperated**, we leave those better **versed** in natural history to **conjecture**; but instead of **obeying** the challenge and **courting** the contest, it glided by the sides of the oak, close to the very feet of its foe, and emerging into the light, dragged its gray **coils** through the grass; but its hiss still betrayed it. Gabriel sprang through the fissure and struck at the **craven, insulting** it with a laugh of scorn as he struck. Suddenly it halted, suddenly reared its **crest**; the throat swelled with venom, the tongue darted

---

French

coil: bobine, serpentin, rouleau, enroulement.
conjecture: conjecturer, prévoir, se douter de.
courting: briguant.
craven: lâche, poltron.
creep: ramper, fluage, glissement, traîner.
crest: crête, sommet.
daunted: découragea, intimidai.
descend: descendre, baisser, s'abaisser.

dim: faible, sombre, obscur, brouiller, rendre confus.
exasperated: exaspérâtes.
fruitless: stérile, infructueux.
insulting: insultant, offensant, agonissant, injurieux.
ire: courroux.
leaped: sauté.
maddens: exaspère.
moth: mite, phalène.
murmuring: murmurer.
obeying: obéissant, obtempérant.

penetrate: pénétrer, pénètres, entrer.
provoked: provoqua, chiffonnées.
reptile: reptile.
slaughter: abattre, massacre, carnage, tuerie.
snake: serpent, traînée, casse en long, multicâble, sardine.
vengeful: vindicatif.
versatility: versatilité, polyvalence.
versed: versé.

out, and again, green as **emeralds**, glared the spite of its eyes. No fear felt Gabriel Varney; his arm was **averted**; he gazed, **spelled** and **admiringly**, with the eye of an artist. Had he had pencil and tablet at that moment, he would have dropped his **weapon** for the **sketch**, though the snake had been as deadly as the **viper** of Sumatra. The sight sank into his memory, to be **reproduced** often by the wild, morbid fancies of his hand. Scarce a moment, however, had he for the gaze; the reptile sprang, and fell, baffled and **bruised** by the **involuntary blow** of its **enemy**. As it writhed on the grass, how its colours came out; how graceful were the movements of its pain! And still the boy gazed, till the eye was **sated** and the cruelty returned. A blow, a second, a third,—all the beauty is gone; **shapeless**, and clotted with **gore**, that **elegant** head; mangled and dissevered the airy **spires** of that **delicate** shape, which had glanced in its **circling** involutions, free and **winding** as a poet's thought through his verse. The boy **trampled** the **quivering relics** into the **sod**, with a fierce animal joy of conquest, and turned once more towards the hollow, for a last almost hopeless survey. Lo, his object was found! In his search for the snake, either his staff or his foot had disturbed a **layer** of moss in the corner; the **faint** ray, ere he entered the hollow, gleamed upon something white. He **emerged** from the **cavity** with a letter in his hand; he read the address, thrust it into his **bosom**, and as **stealthily**, but more rapidly, than he had come, took his way to his father.

French

admiringly: de façon admirative, de manière admirative.
averted: détourné.
blow: coup, souffler, bataille.
bosom: sein, poitrine.
bruised: contusionné, coupure, meurtri.
cavity: cavité, creux, caverne.
circling: coupage circulaire.
delicate: délicat, tendre, fragile.
elegant: élégant, excellent, chic, distingué.
emerald: émeraude.
emerged: émergeâtes, surgi.
enemy: ennemi, adversaire.
faint: s'évanouir, faible, défaillir.
gore: encorner, fuseau, godet.
involuntary: involontaire.
layer: couche, gisement, feuille de placage, assise, marcotte, strate.
quivering: frisson, tremblant.
relic: relique, vestige.
reproduced: reproduisîmes.
sated: assouvîmes, repu, saturé.
shapeless: informe, difforme.
sketch: esquisse, croquis, ébauche.
sod: gazon, motte.
spelled: épela.
spire: flèche, spire, aiguille.
stealthily: de manière furtive, furtivement, de façon furtive.
trampled: piétiné.
viper: vipère, couleuvre.
weapon: arme.
winding: bobinage, enroulement, sinueux.

CHAPTER V

HOUSEHOLD TREASON

The Provencal took the letter from his son's hand, and looked at him with an **approbation** half-complacent, half-ironical. "Mon fils!" said he, patting the boy's head gently, "why should we not be friends? We want each other; we have the strong world to **fight** against."

"Not if you are **master** of this place."

"Well answered,—no; then we shall have the strong world on our side, and shall have only **rogues** and the poor to make war upon." Then, with a **quiet** gesture, he dismissed his son, and gazed slowly on the letter. His pulse, which was usually low, **quickened**, and his lips were **tightly** compressed; he shrank from the **contents** with a **jealous pang**; as a light **quivers** strugglingly in a **noxious** vault, love descended into that hideous breast, gleamed upon **dreary** horrors, and warred with the noxious atmosphere: but it shone still. To this **dangerous** man, every art that gives power to the household **traitor** was **familiar**: he had no fear that the **violated seals** should betray the fraud which gave the contents to the eye that, at length, **steadily** fell upon the following lines:—

Dearest, and ever dearest,—Where art thou at this moment? What are thy thoughts,—are they upon me? I write this at the dead of night. I picture you

French

approbation: approbation, autorisation.
content: contenu, satisfait.
dangerous: dangereux, périlleux, redoutable.
dreary: morne, triste, maussade, sombre, affreux, épouvantable, repoussant, mélancolique, horrible, foncé, désolé.
familiar: familier.
fight: combattre, lutter, batailler, luter.

household: ménage, famille.
jealous: jaloux.
master: maître, patron, maestro, apprendre à fond, capitaine, principal.
noxious: nocif, nuisible.
pang: douleur.
quickened: hâtâtes, hâté, hâtas, accéléré, hâtèrent.
quiet: calme, tranquille, paisible, quiet, silencieux, abattre, rassurer, repos.

quiver: trembler, frisson, frémir.
rogue: gredin, canaille, fripon, polisson, escroc.
seal: sceau, phoque, sceller, cachet, plomber, joint, obturer.
steadily: de façon régulier, de manière régulire.
tightly: de façon stricte, de manière stricte.
traitor: traître, criminel d'État.
violated: violé, enfreignîtes, attentèrent.

to myself as my hand glides over the paper. I think I see you, as you look on these words, and envy them the gaze of those dark eyes. Press your lips to the paper. Do you feel the kiss that I leave there? Well, well! it will not be for long now that we shall be **divided**. Oh, what joy, when I think that I am about to see you! Two days more, at most three, and we shall meet, shall we not? I am going to see my sister. I **subjoin** my address. Come, come, come; I thirst to see you once more. And I did well to say, "Wait, and be patient;" we shall not wait long: before the year is out I shall be free. My uncle has had another and more deadly attack. I see its trace in his face, in his step, in his whole form and **bearing**. The only obstacle between us is **fading** away. Can I **grieve** when I think it,—grieve when life with you spreads **smiling** beyond the old man's grave? And why should age, that has **survived** all passion, stand with its chilling frown, and the miserable prejudices the world has not conquered, but **strengthened** into a creed,—why should age stand between youth and youth? I feel your **mild** eyes **rebuke** me as I write. But chide me not that on earth I see only you. And it will be mine to give you wealth and **rank**! Mine to see the homage of my own heart reflected from the crowd who **bow**, not to the **statue**, but the **pedestal**. Oh, how I shall enjoy your revenge upon the proud! For I have drawn no pastoral scenes in my picture of the future. No; I see you leading **senates**, and **duping fools**. I shall be by your side, your partner, step after step, as you **mount** the height, for I am ambitious, you know, William; and not less because I love,—rather ten thousand times more so. I would not have you born great and noble, for what then could we look to,—what use all my schemes, and my plans, and aspirings? Fortune, accident, would have taken from us the great zest of life, which is desire.

When I see you, I shall tell you that I have some fears of Olivier Dalibard; he has evidently some wily project in view. He, who never interfered before with the **blundering** physician, now thrusts him aside, affects to have saved the old man, **attends** him always. Dares he think to win an influence, to turn against me,—against us? **Happily**, when I shall come back, my uncle will probably be restored to the false strength which deceives him; he will have

French

attends: assiste, soigne.
bearing: coussinet, relèvement, palier, roulement, support.
blundering: embrouillant, gaffe, maladroit.
bow: arc, proue, archet, s'incliner, saluer, avant.
divided: divisa, partageâtes, séparas, trié, débitai, tria, trièrent, triâtes.
duping: contretypage.
fading: évanouissement, fondu, pâlissant, fading, décoloration, déteignant, fluctuation.
fool: sot, imbécile, mystifier, idiot, duper, fou.
grieve: affliger, chagriner, attrister, désoler.
happily: heureusement, de façon heureuse, de manière heureuse.
mild: doux, suave, léger, faible, bénin.
mount: monter, support, adapter, bague de raccordement.
pedestal: socle, piédestal, décollement du niveau du noir.
rank: rang, grade, file, tour.
rebuke: réprimander, gronder, reprocher, sermonner, repousser.
senate: sénat.
smiling: souriant.
statue: statue.
strengthened: fortifièrent, renforcé.
subjoin: adjoindre.
survived: survécûmes.

less need of Dalibard; and then—then let the Frenchman beware! I have already a plot to turn his schemes to his own banishment. Come to Southampton, then, as soon as you can,—perhaps the day you receive this; on Wednesday, at **farthest**. Your last letter implies blame of my policy with respect to Vernon. Again I say, it is necessary to **amuse** my uncle to the last. Before Vernon can **advance** a claim, there will be **weeping** at Laughton. I shall weep, too, perhaps; but there will be joy in those tears, as well as sorrow,—for then, when I clasp thy hand, I can murmur, "It is mine at last, and forever!"

Adieu! No, not adieu,—to our meeting, my lover, my beloved! Thy
Lucretia.

An hour after Miss Clavering had departed on her visit, Dalibard returned the letter to his son, the seal seemingly **unbroken**, and bade him **replace** it in the hollow of the tree, but sufficiently in sight to betray itself to the first that **entered**. He then communicated the plan he had formed for its detection,—a plan which would prevent Lucretia ever suspecting the agency of his son or himself; and this done, he joined Sir Miles in the **gallery**. Hitherto, in **addition** to his other apprehensions in **revealing** to the baronet Lucretia's **clandestine** intimacy with Mainwaring, Dalibard had shrunk from the thought that the **disclosure** would lose her the **heritage** which had first **tempted** his avarice or ambition; but now his jealous and his vindictive passions were aroused, and his whole plan of strategy was changed. He must **crush** Lucretia, or she would crush him, as her threats **declared**. To ruin her in Sir Miles's eyes, to **expel** her from his house, might not, after all, **weaken** his own position, even with regard to power over herself. If he remained **firmly** established at Laughton, he could affect intercession,—he could delay, at least, any **precipitate** union with Mainwaring, by practising on the ambition which he still saw at work beneath her love; he might become a necessary ally; and then—why, then, his **ironical** smile glanced across his lips. But beyond this, his quick eye saw fair **prospects** to self-interest: Lucretia banished; the heritage not hers; the will to be altered;

French

addition: addition, ajout, adjonction, rajout, appendice, extension.
advance: avance, s'approcher, promouvoir, progrès, acompte, suggérer, proposer, accélérer, inspirer, hâter.
amuse: amuser, divertir, faire rire.
clandestine: clandestin.
crush: piler, écraser, briser, broyer, foule, réduire en miettes, fracasser, presse, aplatir.
declared: déclarâtes.
disclosure: divulgation, révélation.
entered: entré, introduisit.
expel: expulser, renvoyer, repousser.
farthest: le plus loin.
firmly: fermement, de façon ferme, de manière ferme.
gallery: galerie, tribune.
heritage: héritage, patrimoine.
ironical: ironique.
precipitate: précipité, hâter, hâtif, irréfléchi.
prospect: perspective, prospecter.
replace: remplacer, substituer, mettre en place de, replacer.
revealing: révélant, décelant.
tempted: tentai.
unbroken: intact, non cassé.
weaken: affaiblir, atténuer, abattre, s'affaiblir.
weeping: pleurant, sourdant, larmoyant.

Dalibard esteemed **indispensable** to the life of the baronet. Come, there was hope here,—not for the heritage, indeed, but at least for a munificent **bequest**.

At noon, some **visitors, bringing strangers** from London whom Sir Miles had invited to see the house (which was one of the **lions** of the neighbourhood, though not **professedly** a show-place), were expected. Aware of this, Dalibard **prayed** the baronet to rest quiet till his company arrived, and then he said carelessly,—

"It will be a **healthful diversion** to your spirits to **accompany** them a little in the park; you can go in your garden-chair; you will have new companions to talk with by the way; and it is always warm and sunny at the **slope** of the hill, towards the bottom of the park."

Sir Miles assented cheerfully; the guests came, strolled over the house, admired the pictures and the **armour** and the hall and the staircase, paid due respect to the substantial old-fashioned **luncheon**, and then, **refreshed**, and in great good-humour, **acquiesced** in Sir Miles's **proposition** to saunter through the park.

The poor baronet was more lively than usual. The younger people clustered gayly round his chair (which was **wheeled** by his valet), smiling at his **jests** and charmed with his courteous high-breeding. A little in the rear walked Gabriel, **paying** special attention to the prettiest and **merriest** girl of the company, who was a great favourite with Sir Miles,—perhaps for those reasons.

"What a **delightful** old gentleman!" said the young lady. "How I envy Miss Clavering such an uncle!"

"Ah, but you are a little out of favour to-day, I can tell you," said Gabriel, **laughingly**; "you were close by Sir Miles when we went through the picture-gallery, and you never asked him the history of the old knight in the **buff** doublet and blue sash."

"Dear me, what of that?"

French

accompany: accompagner.
acquiesced: acquiesçâtes.
armour: armure, blinder.
bequest: legs, promesse de don.
bringing: apportant, amenant.
buff: polir, peau de buffle, feutre à polir, buffle.
delightful: délicieux, ravissant, superbe, charmant.
diversion: distraction, déviation, amusement, détente, récréation, déroutement, détournement, diversion.
healthful: salubre.
indispensable: indispensable.
jest: badiner, plaisanter.
laughingly: de façon riante, de manière riante.
lion: lion.
luncheon: déjeuner.
merriest: le plus joyeux.
paying: payant, payer, rétribuant, salariant, soldant.
prayed: prièrent, prié, priâtes, prias.
professedly: de façon professée, de manière professé.
proposition: proposition.
refreshed: rafraîchîmes, actualisas.
slope: pente, côte, talus, inclinaison, versant, déclivité.
stranger: étranger, inconnu.
visitor: visiteur.
wheeled: mobile, roues, sur roues, à roues.

"Why, that was **brave** Colonel Guy St. John, the Cavalier, the pride and boast of Sir Miles; you know his weakness. He looked so **displeased** when you said, 'What a droll-looking figure!' I was on **thorns** for you!"

"What a pity! I would not offend dear Sir Miles for the world."

"Well, it's easy to make it up with him. Go and tell him that he must take you to see Guy's Oak, in the dell; that you have heard so much about it; and when you get him on his **hobby**, it is hard if you can't make your peace."

"Oh, I'll certainly do it, Master Varney;" and the young lady lost no time in obeying the hint. Gabriel had set other tongues on the same cry, so that there was a general exclamation when the girl **named** the subject,—"Oh, Guy's Oak, by all means!"

Much pleased with the **enthusiasm** this **memorial** of his **pet** ancestor produced, Sir Miles led the way to the dell, and pausing as he reached the verge, said,—

"I fear I cannot do you the honours; it is too **steep** for my chair to descend safely."

Gabriel whispered the fair companion whose side he still kept to.

"Now, my dear Sir Miles," cried the girl, "I **positively** won't **stir** without you; I am sure we could get down the chair without a **jolt**. Look there, how **nicely** the ground slopes! Jane, Lucy, my dears, let us take charge of Sir Miles. Now, then."

The gallant old gentleman would have **marched** to the **breach** in such **guidance**; he **kissed** the fair hands that lay so **temptingly** on his chair, and then, rising with some difficulty, said,—

"No, my dears, you have made me so young again that I think I can walk down the steep with the best of you."

So, **leaning** partly on his valet, and by the help of the hands **extended** to him, step after step, Sir Miles, with well-disguised effort, reached the huge **roots** of the oak.

French

brave: courageux, vaillant, brave.
breach: brèche, infraction, trouée, violation.
displeased: mécontent, déplut.
enthusiasm: enthousiasme.
extended: étendîtes, prorogeai, allongé, débordant.
guidance: guidage, tutorat, conseil, direction.
hobby: hobby, violon d'Ingres, faucon hobereau.
jolt: secousse, cahoter.
kissed: baisée, embrassé.
leaning: penchant, tendance, appui, adossé.
marched: marché.
memorial: mémorial, commémoratif, écrit mémorial, monument.
named: nommé.
nicely: bien, de façon agréable, de manière agréable.
pet: animal de compagnie, dorloter, choyer, chouchou.
positively: de façon positive, de manière positive.
root: racine, enraciner, s'enraciner, radical, origine.
steep: raide, escarpé, à pic, abrupt, tremper.
stir: remuer, battre, émouvoir, affecter, faire tournoyer, vigueur, agiter, bouger.
temptingly: de façon tentante, de manière tentante.
thorn: épine.

"The hollow then was much smaller," said he, "so he was not so easily detected as a man would be now, the **damned** crop-ears—I beg pardon, my dears; the rascally rebels—poked their **swords** through the fissure, and two went, one through his **jerkin**, one through his arm; but he took care not to swear at the liberty, and they went away, not suspecting him."

While thus speaking, the young people were already **playfully** struggling which should first enter the oak. Two got **precedence**, and went in and out, one after the other. Gabriel **breathed** hard. "The **blind** owlets!" thought he; "and I put the letter where a **mole** would have seen it!"

"You know the **spell** when you enter an oak-tree where the **fairies** have been," he whispered to the fair object of his notice. "You must turn round three times, look carefully on the ground, and you will see the face you love best. If I was but a little older, how I should pray—"

"Nonsense!" said the girl, **blushing**, as she now slid through the crowd, and went **timidly** in; **presently** she uttered a little exclamation.

The gallant Sir Miles stooped down to see what was the matter, and offering his hand as she came out, was startled to see her holding a letter.

"Only think what I have found!" said the girl. "What a strange place for a post-office! Bless me! It is **directed** to Mr. Mainwaring!"

"Mr. Mainwaring!" cried three or four voices; but the baronet's was mute. His eye **recognized** Lucretia's hand; his tongue **clove** to the roof of his mouth; the blood **surged**, like a sea, in his **temples**; his face became **purple**. Suddenly Gabriel, peeping over the girl's shoulder, **snatched** away the letter.

"It is my letter,—it is mine! What a shame in Mainwaring not to have come for it as he **promised**!"

Sir Miles looked round and breathed more **freely**.

"Yours, Master Varney!" said the young lady, **astonished**. "What can make your letters to Mr. Mainwaring such a secret?"

"Oh! you'll **laugh** at me; but—but—I wrote a **poem** on Guy's Oak, and Mr. Mainwaring promised to get it into the county paper for me; and as he

---

French

astonished: étonné, stupéfait, époustoufla.
blind: aveugle, store, éblouir.
blushing: rougissant, voile d'un film, ternissement dû à l'eau, opalescence, louchissement, formation d'un voile.
breathed: respiré.
clove: clou de girofle, fendîtes, clivâmes, girofle.
damned: damné, maudit.
directed: dirigé.
fairy: fée, lutin.
freely: librement, de façon gratuite, de manière gratuite.
jerkin: justaucorps, pourpoint.
laugh: rire, rigoler.
mole: taupe, mole, môle, grain de beauté, tunnelier.
playfully: de manière espiègle, de façon espiègle.
poem: poème, poésie.
precedence: priorité, préséance.
presently: actuellement, à présent.
promised: promîmes.
purple: pourpre, violet.
recognized: reconnu, retrouvâmes, admis.
snatched: saisi.
spell: épeler, sortilège, charme.
surged: enflées.
sword: épée, sabre, glaive.
temple: temple, branche.
timidly: timidement, de façon timide, de manière timide.

was to pass close by the park **pales**, through the **wood** yonder, on his way to D—last Saturday, we agreed that I should leave it here; but he has **forgotten** his promise, I see."

Sir Miles grasped the boy's arm with a **convulsive** pressure of gratitude. There was a general cry for Gabriel to read his poem on the spot; but the boy looked **sheepish**, and **hung** down his head, and seemed rather more disposed to cry than to **recite**. Sir Miles, with an **effort** at **simulation** that all his long practice of the world never could have nerved him to, unexcited by a motive less strong than the honour of his blood and house, came to the **relief** of the young wit that had just come to his own.

"Nay," he said, almost calmly, "I know our young **poet** is too **shy** to **oblige** you. I will take charge of your verses, Master Gabriel;" and with a grave air of command, he took the letter from the boy and placed it in his pocket.

The return to the house was less gay than the visit to the oak. The baronet himself made a feverish effort to appear **blithe** and debonair as before; but it was not successful. **Fortunately**, the carriages were all at the door as they reached the house, and luncheon being over, nothing **delayed** the **parting** compliments of the guests. As the last carriage drove away, Sir Miles beckoned to Gabriel, and bade him follow him into his room.

When there, he dismissed his valet and said,—

"You know, then, who wrote this letter. Have you been in the secret of the correspondence? Speak the **truth**, my dear boy; it shall cost you nothing."

"Oh, Sir Miles!" cried Gabriel, earnestly, "I know nothing whatever beyond this,—that I saw the hand of my dear, kind Miss Lucretia; that I felt, I **hardly** knew why, that both you and she would not have those people **discover** it, which they would if the letter had been **circulated** from one to the other, for some one would have known the hand as well as myself, and therefore I **spoke**, without thinking, the first thing that came into my head."

"You—you have obliged me and my niece, sir," said the baronet, tremulously; and then, with a **forced** and **sickly smile**, he added: "Some

French

blithe: joyeux.
circulated: circulé, dégorgeai.
convulsive: convulsif, spasmodique.
delayed: retardé, différé.
discover: découvrir, dépouiller.
effort: effort, peine, requête, démarche.
forced: forcé, forçâmes.
forgotten: oublié, désappris.
fortunately: heureusement, de manière heureuse, de façon heureuse.
hardly: à peine, péniblement, lourdement, difficilement, durement, de manière dure, de façon dure.
hung: pendu.
oblige: obliger.
pale: pâle, blême.
parting: raie, séparation.
poet: poète.
recite: réciter.
relief: soulagement, allégement, relief, relève, secours, détalonnage.
sheepish: penaud.
shy: timide, ombrageux.
sickly: maladif, malsain, écoeurant, de manière malade, de façon malade.
simulation: simulation.
smile: sourire.
spoke: parlâmes, rayon.
truth: vérité, définition.
wood: bois, au bois.

foolish **vagary** of Lucretia, I suppose; I must **scold** her for it. Say nothing about it, however, to any one."

"Oh, no, sir!"

"Good-by, my dear Gabriel!"

"And that boy saved the honour of my niece's name,—my mother's grandchild! O God! this is bitter,—in my old age too!"

He bowed his head over his hands, and tears forced themselves through his fingers. He was long before he had courage to read the letter, though he little **foreboded** all the shock that it would give him. It was the first letter, not destined to himself, of which he had ever broken the seal. Even that recollection made the honourable old man pause; but his duty was **plain** and evident, as head of the house and guardian to his niece. Thrice he **wiped** his spectacles; still they were dim, still the tears would come. He rose **tremblingly**, walked to the window, and saw the stately **deer** grouped in the distance, saw the church spire that rose above the **burial** vault of his ancestors, and his heart sank **deeper** and deeper as he muttered: "Vain pride! pride!" Then he crept to the door and locked it, and at last, **seating** himself firmly, as a **wounded** man to some terrible operation, he read the letter.

Heaven support thee, old man! thou hast to pass through the bitterest trial which honour and affection can undergo,—household **treason**. When the wife lifts high the blushless front and **brazens** out her guilt; when the child, with **loud** voice, throws off all control and makes boast of disobedience,—man revolts at the **audacity**; his spirit arms against his wrong: its face, at least, is bare; the blow, if **sacrilegious**, is direct. But when mild words and soft **kisses** conceal the worst foe Fate can arm; when amidst the confidence of the heart starts up the form of Perfidy; when out from the reptile **swells** the **fiend** in its terror; when the breast on which man leaned for comfort has taken counsel to deceive him; when he **learns** that, day after day, the life **entwined** with his own has been a lie and a stage-mime,—he feels not the softness of grief, nor the **absorption** of rage; it is mightier than grief, and more **withering** than rage,—it is a horror that **appalls**. The heart

---

French

absorption: absorption, amortissement.
appalls: consterne, épouvante.
audacity: audace.
brazen: effronté.
burial: enterrement, obsèques, ensevelissement, enfouissement.
deeper: plusieurs traductions selon le contexte.
deer: cerf, chevreuil.
entwined: entrelacèrent.
fiend: démon, monstre, enragé.

foreboded: présagèrent.
heaven: ciel, paradis.
kisses: baise, bisous.
learns: apprend.
loud: fort, sonore, bruyant, haut, criard.
plain: plaine, clair, uni, net, ordinaire, limpide, évident.
sacrilegious: sacrilège.
scold: réprimander, gronder, sommer, admonester, reprocher, exhorter, sermonner.

seating: places assises, portée, appui, assise.
swell: gonfler, houle, enfler, s'enfler, se gonfler, grossir.
treason: trahison, haute trahison.
tremblingly: de façon tremblante, de manière tremblante.
vagary: caprice.
wiped: essuyé, torchas.
withering: flétrissure, fanaison, desséchant.
wounded: blessé.

does not bleed, the tears do not flow, as in **woes** to which humanity is commonly subjected; it is as if something that **violates** the course of nature had taken place,—something **monstrous** and out of all thought and **forewarning**; for the domestic traitor is a being apart from the orbit of criminals: the **felon** has no fear of his innocent children; with a price on his head, he lays it in safety on the bosom of his wife. In his home, the ablest man, the most subtle and suspecting, can be as much a **dupe** as the simplest. Were it not so as the rule, and the exceptions most rare, this world were the riot of a hell!

And therefore it is that to the household **perfidy**, in all lands, in all ages, God's **curse** seems to **cleave**, and to God's curse man abandons it; he does not honour it by hate, still less will he **lighten** and share the guilt by descending to revenge. He turns aside with a sickness and **loathing**, and leaves Nature to **purify** from the earth the **ghastly** phenomenon she **abhors**.

Old man, that she **wilfully** deceived thee, that she abused thy belief and denied to thy question and profaned maidenhood to stealth,—all this might have galled thee; but to these wrongs old men are subjected,—they give mirth to our **farces**; maid and lover are privileged **impostors**. But to have counted the sands in thine hour-glass, to have sat by thy side, marvelling when the **worms** should have thee, and looked smiling on thy face for the signs of the death-writ—Die quick, old man; the **executioner** hungers for the fee!

There were no tears in those eyes when they came to the close; the letter fell noiselessly to the floor, and the head sank on the breast, and the hands drooped upon the poor **crippled** limbs, whose **crawl** in the sunshine hard youth had grudged. He felt humbled, **stunned**, crushed; the pride was clean gone from him; the cruel words struck home. Worse than a **cipher**, did he then but cumber the earth? At that moment old Ponto, the setter, shook himself, looked up, and laid his head in his master's lap; and Dash, jealous, rose also, and sprang, not actively, for Dash was old, too, upon his knees, and **licked** the **numbed**, **drooping** hands. Now, people praise the **fidelity** of

French

abhors: abhorre, exécre.
cipher: chiffre, zéro.
cleave: fendre, cliver, se fendre.
crawl: ramper, crawl.
crippled: infirme, estropié.
curse: maudire, malédiction, blasphémer.
drooping: tombant, fanaison.
dupe: internégatif, contretype.
executioner: bourreau, exécuteur.
farce: farce.
felon: criminel, panaris.

fidelity: fidélité, exactitude, loyauté.
forewarning: préavis, prévenant, avertissant.
ghastly: horrible, désagréable, repoussant, abominable, maussade, odieux.
impostor: imposteur, charlatan.
licked: léché.
lighten: alléger, éclaircir, allègent.
loathing: abhorrant, abominant, haïssant, répugnance.

monstrous: monstrueux, colossal.
numbed: engourdis.
perfidy: perfidie.
purify: purifier, épurer, assainir.
stunned: étourdîmes, abasourdîmes, assommé, abruti.
violates: viole, attente, enfreint.
wilfully: de façon obstinée, de manière obstinée.
woe: hélas, aïe, malheur.
worm: ver, vis sans fin.

dogs till the **theme** is **worn** out; but **nobody** knows what a **dog** is, unless he has been deceived by men,—then, that honest face; then, that sincere caress; then, that coaxing **whine** that never **lied**! Well, then,—what then? A dog is long-lived if he live to ten years,—small **career** this to truth and friendship! Now, when Sir Miles felt that he was not **deserted**, and his look **met** those four fond **eyes**, **fixed** with that strange wistfulness which in our hours of **trouble** the eyes of a dog sympathizingly **assume**, an **odd** thought for a sensible man **passed** into him, **showing**, more than **pages** of sombre **elegy**, how **deep** was the **sudden misanthropy** that **blackened** the world around. "When I am dead," **ran** that thought, "is there one human being whom I can trust to take **charge** of the old man's dogs?"

So, let the **scene** close!

French

assume: assumer, prendre, supposer, présumer.
blackened: noirci, mâchurâtes.
career: carrière, parcours.
charge: charger, accusation, plainte, taxe, imputation, chef d'accusation.
deep: profond, foncé, fosse, grave, mouille.
deserted: déserté, abandonné.
dog: chien, clébard, toc.
elegy: élégie.
eye: oeil, trou, chas, anneau.
fixed: fixe, fixèrent, fixa, fixâmes, fixé, réparèrent, remédia.
lied: menti, gésie.
met: rencontré.
misanthropy: misanthropie.
nobody: personne, nul.
odd: bizarre, impair, singulier, étrange, drôle.
page: page, paginer.
passed: passé.
ran: courûmes, coulèrent.
scene: scène, lieu.
showing: montrant, manifestant, marquant, affichant, exposition.
sudden: subit, soudain.
theme: thème, sujet, composition.
trouble: gêner, problème, dérangement, panne, difficulté, trouble, ennui.
whine: plainte, geindre, sifflement, se lamenter, gémissons, crie, geignez, crions.
worn: usé, porté, usagé.

CHAPTER VI

THE WILL

The next day, or rather the next evening, Sir Miles St. John was seated before his unshared chicken,—seated **alone**, and **vaguely surprised** at himself, in a large, **comfortable** room in his old hotel, Hanover Square. Yes, he had escaped. Hast thou, O Reader, **tasted** the luxury of **escape** from a home where the charm is broken,—where Distrust looks askant from the Lares? In vain had Dalibard remonstrated, **conjured** up **dangers**, and asked at **least** to accompany him. **Excepting** his dogs and his old valet, who was too like a dog in his fond fidelity to rank **amongst bipeds**, Sir Miles did not wish to have about him a single face familiar at Laughton, Dalibard especially. Lucretia's letter had hinted at plans and designs in Dalibard. It might be unjust, it might be ungrateful; but he **grew sick** at the thought that he was the centre-stone of stratagems and plots. The **smooth** face of the Provencal took a wily **expression** in his eyes; nay, he thought his very footmen watched his **steps** as if to **count** how long before they followed his bier. So, breaking from all **roughly**, with a shake of his head and a **laconic assertion** of business in London, he got into his carriage,—his own old bachelor's lumbering travelling-carriage,—and bade the post-boys drive **fast**, fast! Then, when he felt alone,—quite alone,—and the **gates** of the lodge

---

French

alone: seul.
amongst: parmi, entre.
assertion: assertion, affirmation.
biped: bipède.
comfortable: confortable, douillet, commode, à l'aise.
conjured: conjura, escamotèrent.
count: compter, comte, calculer, coup, chef d'accusation.
danger: danger, péril.
escape: échapper, s'échapper, évasion, fuite, enfuir, fuir.
excepting: sauf, excepté.
expression: expression, terme, locution, mine, air.
fast: rapide, vite, jeûner, ferme, prompt, carême.
gate: porte, vanne, grille, barrière, gâchette, berceau, doigt, entrée.
grew: grandirent, crût, crûmes, crûs, crûrent.
laconic: laconique.
least: moindre, le moins.
roughly: de façon brute, de manière brute, rudement.
sick: malade, malsain.
smooth: lisse, uni, plat, polir, égaliser, douce.
step: pas, marche, étape, gradin, faire les cent pas, échelon, palier.
surprised: surpris, étonné.
tasted: goûté.
vaguely: vaguement, de manière vague, de façon vague.

swung behind him, he **rubbed** his hands with a schoolboy's **glee**, and chuckled aloud, as if he enjoyed, not only the sense, but the fun of his safety; as if he had done something **prodigiously cunning** and clever.

So when he saw himself **snug** in his old, well-remembered hotel, in the same room as of **yore**, when returned, **brisk** and gay, from the breezes of Weymouth or the brouillards of Paris, he thought he shook hands again with his youth. Age and lameness, apoplexy and treason, all were forgotten for the moment. And when, as the excitement died, those grim **spectres** came back again to his thoughts, they found their victim **braced** and prepared, standing erect on that **hearth** for whose **hospitality** he paid his guinea a day,—his front proud and **defying**. He felt yet that he had fortune and power, that a movement of his hand could raise and strike down, that at the verge of the tomb he was armed, to **punish** or reward, with the balance and the sword. Tripped in the **smug waiter**, and announced "Mr. Parchmount."

"Set a chair, and show him in." The lawyer entered.

"My dear Sir Miles, this is indeed a surprise! What has brought you to town?"

"The common **whim** of the old, sir. I would alter my will."

Three days did lawyer and client **devote** to the task; for Sir Miles was minute, and Mr. Parchmount was precise, and little difficulties arose, and changes in the first outline were made, and Sir Miles, from the very depth of his disgust, desired not to act only from passion. In that last **deed** of his life, the old man was **sublime**. He sought to rise out of the **mortal**, fix his eyes on the Great Judge, weigh circumstances and excuses, and keep justice even and serene.

Meanwhile, unconscious of the train laid **afar**, Lucretia reposed on the mine,—reposed, indeed, is not the word; for she was **agitated** and **restless** that Mainwaring had not obeyed her **summons**. She wrote to him again from Southampton the third day of her arrival; but before his answer came she received this short **epistle** from London:—

French

afar: loin.
agitated: agitèrent, débattîtes, troubla, nerveux, remuas, émurent, émûmes, émus, émut, émûtes, inquiet.
braced: contreventé.
brisk: vif, actif, alerte, vigilant.
cunning: rusé, malin, astucieux, ruse, artificieux, rouerie, sournois.
deed: acte, action.
defying: défiant, provoquant.
devote: consacrer, dédier, adonner.
epistle: épître.
glee: joie.
hearth: foyer, cheminée, sole.
hospitality: hospitalité, dépense de représentation, salon de réception.
mortal: mortel.
prodigiously: de façon prodigieuse, de manière prodigieuse, prodigieusement.
punish: punir.
restless: remuant, agité.
rubbed: frotté.
smug: suffisant.
snug: confortable, douillet, ergot, oreille de châssis.
spectre: spectre.
sublime: sublimer.
summons: sommation, citation, appel, assignation, intimation, convocation, commandement.
waiter: garçon, serveur.
whim: caprice, lubie, manège à chevaux.
yore: jadis.

"Mr. Parchmount presents his compliments to Miss Clavering, and, by desire of Sir Miles St. John, requests her not to return to Laughton. Miss Clavering will hear further in a few days, when Sir Miles has **concluded** the business that has brought him to London."

This letter, if it excited much curiosity, did not produce alarm. It was natural that Sir Miles should be busy in winding up his affairs; his journey to London for that purpose was no ill **omen** to her prospects, and her thoughts **flew** back to the one subject that **tyrannized** over them. Mainwaring's reply, which came two days afterwards, **disquieted** her much more. He had not found the letter she had left for him in the tree. He was full of apprehensions; he **condemned** the imprudence of calling on her at Mr. Fielden's; he **begged** her to **renounce** the idea of such a risk. He would return again to Guy's Oak and search more **narrowly**: had she changed the spot where the former letters were placed? Yet now, not even the non-receipt of her letter, which she **ascribed** to the care with which she had concealed it amidst the dry leaves and moss, disturbed her so much as the **evident** constraint with which Mainwaring wrote,—the **cautious** and **lukewarm** remonstrance which answered her **passionate** appeal. It may be that her very doubts, at times, of Mainwaring's affection had increased the ardour of her own attachment; for in some natures the **excitement** of fear **deepens** love more than the **calmness** of trust. Now with the doubt for the first time flashed the resentment, and her answer to Mainwaring was vehement and imperious. But the next day came a **messenger** express from London, with a letter from Mr. Parchmount that **arrested** for the moment even the fierce current of love.

When the task had been completed,—the will signed, **sealed**, and delivered,—the old man had felt a load lifted from his heart. Three or four of his old friends, bons vivants like himself, had seen his arrival duly **proclaimed** in the newspapers, and had **hastened** to welcome him. **Warmed** by the **genial** sight of faces associated with the frank joys of his youth, Sir Miles, if he did not forget the prudent counsels of Dalibard, conceived a proud **bitterness** of joy in **despising** them. Why take such care of the worn-out **carcass**? His will was made. What was left to life so peculiarly attractive?

French

arrested: arrêté.
ascribed: attribuèrent.
begged: mendiai, quémandèrent, supplièrent.
bitterness: amertume, âcreté.
calmness: calme, repos.
carcass: carcasse, gros œuvre.
cautious: prudent, circonspect.
concluded: conclûmes, clôturé.
condemned: condamnèrent, réprouvèrent, dangereuse.
deepen: approfondir, foncer, rembrunissons, épaissir, devenir plus profond, creuser.
despising: méprisant, dédaignant.
disquieted: perturbâtes, dérangeâtes.
evident: évident, manifeste.
excitement: excitation, agitation.
flew: vola, volâmes, volèrent.
genial: génien.
hastened: hâtâmes, hâté, hâtai, hâtèrent.
lukewarm: tiède.
messenger: messager, coursier.
narrowly: de façon étroite, étroitement, de manière étroite.
omen: augure, présage.
passionate: passionné, brûlant.
proclaimed: proclamai.
renounce: renoncer, abandonner, abjurer, résigner, renier.
sealed: scellé, étanche, hermétique, fermé.
tyrannized: tyrannisai.
warmed: bassinâmes, chauffâmes.

He invited his friends to a **feast** worthy of old. **Seasoned revellers** were they, with a free gout for a vent to all **indulgence**. So they came; and they **drank**, and they laughed, and they talked back their young days. They saw not the nervous **irritation**, the **strain** on the spirits, the **heated membrane** of the brain, which made Sir Miles the most jovial of all. It was a night of nights; the old fellows were lifted back into their **chariots** or **sedans**. Sir Miles alone seemed as steady and **sober** as if he had supped with Diogenes. His servant, whose **respectful** admonitions had been awed into silence, lent him his arm to bed, but Sir Miles **scarcely** touched it. The next morning, when the servant (who slept in the same room) awoke, to his surprise the **glare** of a **candle** streamed on his eyes. He rubbed them: could he see right? Sir Miles was seated at the table; he must have got up and lighted a candle to write,— noiselessly, indeed. The servant looked and looked, and the **stillness** of Sir Miles awed him: he was seated on an **armchair**, leaning back. As awe **succeeded** to suspicion, he sprang up, approached his master, took his hand: it was cold, and fell heavily from his clasp. Sir Miles must have been dead for hours.

The **pen** lay on the ground, where it had dropped from the hand; the letter on the table was scarcely commenced: the words ran thus,—

"*Lucretia*,—You will return no more to my house. You are free as if I were dead; but I shall be just. Would that I had been so to your mother, to your sister! But I am old now, as you say, and—"

To one who could have seen into that poor proud heart at the moment the hand paused **forever**, what remained **unwritten** would have been clear. There was, first, the sharp struggle to conquer loathing repugnance, and address at all the false and degraded one; then came the sharp **sting** of **ingratitude**; then the idea of the life grudged and the grave desired; then the stout victory over scorn, the resolution to be just; then the reproach of the conscience that for so far less an offence the sister had been thrown aside, the comfort, perhaps, found in her gentle and **neglected** child obstinately repelled; then the **conviction** of all **earthly** vanity and nothingness,—the look on into life, with the chilling sentiment that affection was gone, that he could

French

armchair: fauteuil, de salon, chaire à bras.
candle: bougie, chandelle, cierge.
chariot: char.
conviction: conviction, condamnation.
drank: burent.
earthly: terrestre.
feast: fête, banqueter, festin.
forever: pour toujours, toujours.
glare: éblouissement, éclat, reflet.
heated: chauffé, échauffé.
indulgence: indulgence, tolérance.
ingratitude: ingratitude.
irritation: irritation, agacement.
membrane: membrane, paroi étanche, feuillet de parchemin, masque amont.
neglected: négligé.
pen: stylo, plume, enclos.
respectful: respectueux.
reveller: fêtard, noceur.
scarcely: à peine, de façon rare, de manière rare.
seasoned: assaisonné, épicé.
sedan: berline, sedan.
sober: sobre, dessoûler, modéré, sérieux.
stillness: calme, tranquillité.
sting: piquer, aiguillon, piqûre, dard.
strain: tension, souche, fatigue, effort, tendre.
succeeded: réussis, succédâmes, about a.
unwritten: non écrit, verbal.

never trust again, that he was too old to open his arms to new ties; and then, before felt singly, all these thoughts united, and snapped the **cord**.

In **announcing** his mournful intelligence, with more feeling than might have been expected from a lawyer (but even his lawyer loved Sir Miles), Mr. Parchmount observed that "as the **deceased** lay at a hotel, and as Miss Clavering's presence would not be needed in the performance of the last **rites**, she would probably forbear the journey to town. Nevertheless, as it was Sir Miles's wish that the will should be opened as soon as possible after his death, and it would **doubtless** contain instructions as to his funeral, it would be well that Miss Clavering and her sister should immediately **depute** some one to attend the reading of the **testament** on their **behalf**. Perhaps Mr. Fielden would kindly **undertake** that melancholy office."

To do justice to Lucretia, it must be said that her first emotions, on the **receipt** of this letter, were those of a **poignant** and **remorseful** grief, for which she was unprepared. But how different it is to count on what shall follow death, and to know that death has come! Susan's **sobbing** sympathy availed not, nor Mr. Fielden's **pious** and **tearful exhortations**; her own **sinful** thoughts and hopes came back to her, **haunting** and stern as **furies**. She insisted at first upon going to London, gazing once more on the clay,—nay, the carriage was at the door, for all yielded to her vehemence; but then her heart misgave her: she did not dare to face the dead. Conscience **waved** her back from the solemn offices of nature; she hid her face with her hands, shrank again into her room; and Mr. Fielden, assuming **unbidden** the responsibility, went alone.

Only Vernon (summoned from Brighton), the good clergyman, and the lawyer, to whom, as sole **executor**, the will was addressed, and in whose **custody** it had been left, were present when the seal of the testament was broken. The will was long, as is common when the dust that it **disposes** of covers some fourteen or fifteen thousand acres. But out of the mass of **technicalities** and **repetitions** these points of interest rose salient: To Charles Vernon, of Vernon Grange, Esq., and his heirs by him **lawfully begotten**, were left all the lands and woods and **manors** that covered that space in the

French

announcing: annonçant, affichant.
begotten: engendré.
behalf: part.
cord: corde, câble, fil.
custody: garde, détention.
deceased: décédé, défunt.
depute: députes.
dispose: disposer.
doubtless: sans aucun doute.
executor: exécuteur.
exhortation: sommation, observation, recommandation.
fury: fureur, furie.
haunting: hanter.
lawfully: de façon légale, de manière légale, légalement.
manor: manoir.
pious: pieux.
poignant: intense.
receipt: reçu, quittance, récépissé, réception, acquit, accusé de réception, ticket de caisse, recette.
remorseful: plein de remords.
repetition: répétition, reprise.
rite: rite.
sinful: coupable, honteux.
sobbing: sanglotant.
tearful: éploré, larmoyant.
technicality: subtilité, détail de procédure, point de détail, terme technique.
testament: testament.
unbidden: spontanément.
undertake: entreprendre, se démener.
waved: ondulé.

Hampshire map known by the name of the "Laughton property," on condition that he and his heirs assumed the name and arms of St. John; and on the failure of Mr. Vernon's issue, the estate passed, first (with the same conditions) to the issue of Susan Mivers; next to that of Lucretia Clavering. There the entail ceased; and the **contingency** fell to the **rival** ingenuity of lawyers in **hunting** out, amongst the remote and forgotten **descendants** of some ancient St. John, the heir-at-law. To Lucretia Clavering, without a word of endearment, was **bequeathed** 10,000 pounds,—the usual portion which the house of St. John had **allotted** to its daughters; to Susan Mivers the same sum, but with the addition of these words, withheld from her sister: "and my blessing!" To Olivier Dalibard an **annuity** of 200 pounds a year; to Honore Gabriel Varney, 3,000 pounds; to the Rev. Matthew Fielden, 4,000 pounds; and the same sum to John Walter Ardworth. To his favourite servant, Henry Jones, an ample provision, and the charge of his dogs Dash and Ponto, with an allowance therefor, to be paid **weekly**, and cease at their deaths. Poor old man! he made it the interest of their guardian not to **grudge** their **lease** of life. To his other **attendants**, suitable and munificent bequests, proportioned to the length of their services. For his body, he desired it to be **buried** in the vault of his ancestors without pomp, but without a pretence to a **humility** which he had not **manifested** in life; and he requested that a small **miniature** in his **writing-desk** should be placed in his **coffin**. That last **injunction** was more than a sentiment,—it bespoke the moral conviction of the happiness the original might have **conferred** on his life. Of that happiness his pride had **deprived** him; nor did he **repent**, for he had deemed pride a duty. But the mute likeness, buried in his grave,—that told the might of the sacrifice he had made! Death removes all distinctions, and in the coffin the Lord of Laughton might choose his partner.

When the will had been read, Mr. Parchmount produced two letters, one **addressed**, in the hand of the deceased, to Mr. Vernon, the other in the lawyer's own hand to Miss Clavering. The last **enclosed** the **fragment** found on Sir Miles's table, and her own letter to Mainwaring, **redirected** to her in

---

French

addressed: adressé, accessibles.
allotted: attribua.
annuity: annuité, rente.
attendant: surveillant, serviteur, gardien, préposé.
bequeathed: léguai.
buried: enterra, inhumas, ensevelîmes.
coffin: cercueil, château, lacune.
conferred: conférâtes.
contingency: contingence, éventualité, imprévu.
deprived: privai, dépouilla.
descendant: descendant.
enclosed: enserras, inclus, clos, enclos.
fragment: fragment.
grudge: rancune.
humility: humilité, modestie.
hunting: chasse, lacet, pompage.
injunction: injonction, avant dire droit, arrêt de la suspension.
lease: bail, affermer, prendre à bail, location, louer, concession, encroix, contrat de location.
manifested: manifesté.
miniature: miniature, maquette.
redirected: redirigeâmes, réorientèrent.
repent: se repentir, regretter, repentir.
rival: rival, concourir.
weekly: hebdomadaire, chaque semaine.
writing-desk: secrétaire, commode à tablette pour écrire.

Sir Miles's boldest and stateliest **autograph**. He had, no doubt, meant to return it in the letter left **uncompleted**.

The letter to Vernon contained a copy of Lucretia's fatal epistle, and the following lines to Vernon himself: —

My dear Charles, — With much **deliberation**, and with natural reluctance to reveal to you my niece's shame, I feel it my duty to **transmit** to you the accompanying **enclosure**, **copied** from the original with my own hand, which the task sullied.

I do so first, because otherwise you might, as I should have done in your place, feel bound in honour to **persist** in the offer of your hand, — feel bound the more, because Miss Clavering is not my heiress; secondly, because had her attachment been stronger than her interest, and she had refused your offer, you might still have deemed her hardly and **capriciously** dealt with by me, and not only sought to **augment** her portion, but have profaned the house of my ancestors by receiving her there as an honoured and welcome relative and guest. Now, Charles Vernon, I believe, to the utmost of my poor judgment, I have done what is right and just. I have taken into consideration that this young person has been brought up as a daughter of my house, and what the daughters of my house have received, I **bequeath** her. I put aside, as far as I can, all resentment of mere family pride; I show that I do so, when I repair my **harshness** to my poor sister, and leave both her children the same provision. And if you exceed what I have done for Lucretia, unless, on more **dispassionate** consideration than I can give, you **conscientiously** think me wrong, you **insult** my memory — and **impugn** my justice. Be it in this as your conscience dictates; but I **entreat**, I **adjure**, I command, at least that you never **knowingly** admit by a hearth, hitherto sacred to unblemished truth and honour, a person who has **desecrated** it with treason. As gentleman to gentleman, I impose on you this solemn injunction. I could have wished to leave that young woman's children **barred** from the entail; but our old tree has so few branches! You are unwedded; Susan too. I must take my chance that Miss Clavering's children, if ever they **inherit**, do not **imitate** the mother. I conclude she will **wed** that Mainwaring; her children will have a

French

adjure: adjurer.
augment: augmenter, accroître, agrandir, amplifier, étendre, redoubler.
autograph: autographe, signer.
barred: barrâtes, exclu, forclos.
bequeath: léguer, lègues.
capriciously: de façon capricieuse, de manière capricieuse.
conscientiously: de façon consciencieuse, de manière consciencieuse.
copied: copié.
deliberation: délibération.
desecrated: profané.
dispassionate: impartial.
enclosure: enceinte, pièce jointe, clôture, enclos, enveloppe, encoffrement, annexe, boîtier.
entreat: implore, supplient.
harshness: rudesse, dureté, sévérité.
imitate: imiter, copier, contrefaire.
impugn: contester, attaquer.
inherit: hériter.
insult: insulte, offenser, injure, affront.
knowingly: sciemment, de manière connaissante.
persist: persister, s'obstiner.
transmit: transmettre, envoyer, adresser.
uncompleted: inachevé.
wed: marier, me marie, vous mariez, te maries, se marient, nous marions.

low-born father. Well, her **race** at least is pure,—Clavering and St. John are names to guarantee **faith** and honour; yet you see what she is! Charles Vernon, if her issue inherit the **soul** of gentlemen, it must come, after all, not from the well-born mother! I have **lived** to say this,—I who— But perhaps if we had looked more **closely** into the pedigree of those Claverings—.

Marry yourself,—marry soon, Charles Vernon, my dear kinsman; keep the old house in the old line, and true to its old fame. Be kind and good to my poor; don't strain on the **tenants**. By the way, Farmer Strongbow **owes** three years' rent,—I forgive him. **Pension** him off; he can do no good to the land, but he was born on it, and must not fall on the **parish**. But to be kind and good to the poor, not to strain the tenants, you must **learn** not to **waste**, my dear Charles. A **needy** man can never be **generous** without being unjust. How give, if you are in **debt**? You will think of this now,—now,—while your good heart is **soft**, while your feelings are moved. Charley Vernon, I think you will shed a tear when you see my armchair still and **empty**. And I would have left you the care of my dogs, but you are thoughtless, and will go much to London, and they are used to the country now. Old Jones will have a **cottage** in the village,—he has promised to live there; **drop** in now and then, and see poor Ponto and Dash. It is late, and old friends come to **dine** here. So, if anything happens to me, and we don't meet again, good-by, and God bless you.

Your affectionate kinsman,
Miles St. John.

French

closely: étroitement, attentivement.
cottage: cabanon, chaumière, petite maison.
debt: dette, créance, endettement.
dine: dîner, dînons, souper.
drop: goutte, tomber, chute, faire tomber, abattre, s'amoindrir, s'abattre, laisser tomber, baisse, abandonner.
empty: vide, vidanger.
faith: foi, confiance, croyance.
generous: généreux, abondant, copieux.
learn: apprendre, instruire.
lived: vécut, vécûmes, habitâmes, logeâmes, logé, logèrent.
marry: marier, me marie, vous mariez, te maries, se marient, nous marions, épouser.
needy: indigent, vide, nécessiteux.
owes: doit.
parish: paroisse, commune.
pension: pension, retraite.
race: course, race, s'élancer, se précipiter, raz, chemin de roulement.
soft: doux, mou, tendre, moelleux, sucré, gentil, suave.
soul: âme, soul.
tenant: locataire, preneur, fermier, habiter comme locataire.
waste: gaspiller, déchets, dissiper, perte, rebut, gâcher, prodiguer, déperdition.

CHAPTER VII

THE ENGAGEMENT

It is somewhat less than three months after the death of Sir Miles St. John; November **reigns** in London. And "reigns" seems scarcely a metaphorical expression as applied to the sullen, absolute sway which that dreary **month** (first in the dynasty of Winter) **spreads** over the passive, dejected city.

Elsewhere in England, November is no such gloomy, grim fellow as he is **described**. Over the **brown** glebes and **changed** woods in the country, his still face looks contemplative and mild; and he has soft smiles, too, at times,—lighting up his taxed vassals the groves; gleaming where the **leaves** still cling to the boughs, and **reflected** in dimples from the **waves** which still glide free from his **chains**. But as a conqueror who makes his home in the **capital**, weighs down with **hard** policy the mutinous citizens long ere his **iron influence** is felt in the province, so the first tyrant of Winter has only rigour and frowns for London. The very **aspect** of the wayfarers has the look of men **newly** enslaved: cloaked and muffled, they steal to and fro through the dismal fogs. Even the children creep timidly through the **streets**; the carriages go cautious and hearse-like **along**; daylight is dim and obscure; the **town** is not filled, **nor** the brisk mirth of Christmas commenced; the unsocial **shadows** flit amidst the mist, like men on the eve of a fatal conspiracy. Each

French

along: le long de, avec, d'après.
aspect: aspect, allure, spectacle, apparence, air, exposition, faciès.
brown: brun, marron, faire dorer, rissoler, dorer.
capital: capital, fonds, chapiteau, majuscule.
chain: chaîne, enchaîner.
changed: changé.
described: décrivirent.
hard: dur, pénible, difficile.
influence: influence, empire.

iron: fer, fer à repasser, repasser.
leave: partir, pars, abandonner, laisser, quitter, permission, congé, s'en aller, délaisser, livrer, sortir.
month: mois.
newly: de façon nouvelle, de manière nouveau, récemment.
nor: ni.
reflected: refléta, réfléchîmes, renvoyèrent.
reign: règne, tenue, commandement, gouvernement.

shadow: ombre, prendre en filature.
spread: enduire, étaler, étendre, écart, dispersion, propagation, se propager, se répandre, tartiner, diffusion.
street: rue, pavé.
town: ville, cité, localité.
wave: onde, vague, brandir, agiter, onduler, lame.

other month in London has its charms for the **experienced**. Even from August to October, when The Season lies dormant, and Fashion forbids her sons to be seen within **hearing** of Bow, the true lover of London finds pleasure still at hand, if he search for her duly. There are the early walks through the parks and green Kensington Gardens, which now change their character of **resort**, and seem rural and countrylike, but yet with more life than the country; for on the benches beneath the trees, and along the sward, and up the malls, are living beings enough to interest the eye and divert the thoughts, if you are a guesser into character, and amateur of the human face,—fresh nursery-maid and playful children; and the old shabby-genteel, buttoned-up officer, musing on half-pay, as he sits alone in some alcove of Kenna, or leans pensive over the **rail** of the vacant Ring; and early tradesman, or **clerk** from the suburban lodging, trudging brisk to his business,—for business never ceases in London. Then at noon, what delight to escape to the banks at Putney or Richmond,—the row up the river; the **fishing** punt; the ease at your inn till dark! or if this tempt not, still Autumn shines clear and **calm** over the **roofs**, where the **smoke** has a holiday; and how clean gleam the vistas through the tranquillized thoroughfares; and as you saunter along, you have all London to yourself, Andrew Selkirk, but with the mart of the world for your **desert**. And when October comes on, it has one **characteristic** of spring,—life busily returns to the city; you see the shops bustling up, trade flowing back. As **birds** scent the April, so the children of **commerce** plume their **wings** and prepare for the first slack returns of the season. But November! Strange the taste, stout the lungs, grief-defying the heart, of the visitor who finds charms and joy in a London November.

In a small lodging-house in Bulstrode Street, Manchester Square, grouped a family in mourning who had had the temerity to come to town in November, for the purpose, no doubt, of raising their spirits. In the dull, small drawing-room of the dull, small house we **introduce** to you, first, a middle-aged gentleman whose **dress** showed what dress now **fails** to show,—his profession. Nobody could **mistake** the cut of the **cloth** and the

French

bird: oiseau, volaille, poisson, objet volant, l'oiseau, type.
calm: calme, tranquille, quiet, repos, rassurer, abattre, paisible, accalmie.
characteristic: caractéristique, typique, qualité, démographique.
clerk: commis, greffier.
cloth: tissu, étoffe, linge, toile, chiffon.
commerce: commerce, négoce, affaires.
desert: désert, abandonner, quitter, délaisser, livrer.
dress: robe, habiller, vêtir, panser, s'habiller, revêtir, garnir, apprêter, dresser.
experienced: expérimenté, éprouvé.
fail: échouer, avorter, rater, manquer, faillir.
fishing: pêche, repêchage, sauvetage.
hearing: entendant, audition, ouïe, oyant.
introduce: présenter, introduire, offrir.
mistake: erreur, faute, méprise, se tromper.
rail: rail, barre, rampe, rambarde, longeron.
resort: lieu de vacances, recours.
roof: toit, voûte.
smoke: fumée, fumer, fumons.
wing: aile, voilure.

shape of the hat, for he had just come in from a walk, and not from **discourtesy**, but **abstraction**, the broad brim still shadowed his pleasant, **placid** face. **Parson** spoke out in him, from **beaver** to **buckle**. By the coal fire, where, through volumes of smoke, fussed and flickered a pretension to flame, sat a middle-aged lady, whom, without being a **conjurer**, you would pronounce at once to be wife to the parson; and **sundry** children sat on stools all about her, with one book between them, and a low whispered murmur from their two or three pursed-up lips, announcing that that book was **superfluous**. By the last of three dim-looking windows, made **dimmer** by brown moreen draperies, **edged genteelly** with black cotton velvet, stood a girl of very soft and pensive expression of features, — pretty **unquestionably**, **excessively** pretty; but there was something so delicate and elegant about her, — the bend of her head, the shape of her slight figure, the little fair hands crossed one on each other, as the face mournfully and **listlessly** turned to the window, that "pretty" would have seemed a word of praise too often proffered to **milliner** and serving-maid. Nevertheless, it was perhaps the right one: "handsome" would have implied something statelier and more commanding; "beautiful," greater **regularity** of feature, or **richness** of colouring. The parson, who since his entrance had been walking up and down the small room with his hands behind him, glanced now and then at the young lady, but not speaking, at length paused from that monotonous exercise by the chair of his wife, and touched her shoulder. She stopped from her work, which, more engrossing than elegant, was nothing less than what is technically called "the taking in" of a certain blue jacket, which was about to pass from Matthew, the eldest born, to David, the second, and looked up at her husband **affectionately**. Her husband, however, spoke not; he only made a sign, partly with his eyebrow, partly with a **jerk** of his thumb over his right shoulder, in the direction of the young lady we have described, and then completed the **pantomime** with a melancholy shake of the head. The wife turned round and looked hard, the scissors **horizontally** raised in one hand, while the other reposed on the **cuff** of the jacket. At this moment a low knock was heard at the street-door. The worthy pair saw the girl shrink back,

French

abstraction: abstraction, distraction, inattention.
affectionately: affectueusement, de façon affectueuse, de manière affectueuse.
beaver: castor, flanelle.
buckle: boucle, gondolement.
conjurer: conjurateur, illusionniste, prestidigitateur.
cuff: manchette, poignet, ballonnet, revers.
dimmer: gradateur, variateur.
discourtesy: impolitesse.
edged: déligné.
excessively: de façon excessive, de manière excessive, excessivement.
genteelly: de façon distinguée, de manière distinguée.
horizontally: de façon horizontale, de manière horizontale.
jerk: secousse, saccade, suraccélération.
listlessly: de manière indifférente, de façon indifférente.
milliner: modiste, chapelier.
pantomime: pantomime, mime.
parson: pasteur, curé, prêtre.
placid: placide, serein, calme.
regularity: régularité.
richness: richesse, pouvoir couvrant.
sundry: divers.
superfluous: superflu.
unquestionably: de façon incontestable, de manière incontestable.

with a kind of tremulous movement; presently there came the sound of a **footstep** below, the creak of a **hinge** on the ground-floor, and again all was silent.

"That is Mr. Mainwaring's knock," said one of the children.

The girl left the room abruptly, and, light as was her step, they heard her steal up the stairs.

"My dears," said the parson, "it wants an hour yet to dark; you may go and walk in the **square**."

"'T is so dull in that **ugly** square, and they won't let us into the green. I am sure we'd rather stay here," said one of the children, as spokesman for the rest; and they all nestled **closer** round the hearth.

"But, my dears," said the parson, simply, "I want to talk alone with your mother. However, if you like best to go and keep quiet in your own room, you may do so."

"Or we can go into Susan's?"

"No," said the parson; "you must not **disturb** Susan."

"She never used to care about being disturbed. I wonder what's come to her?"

The parson made no **rejoinder** to this half-petulant question. The children consulted together a moment, and resolved that the square, though so dull, was less dull than their own little **attic**. That being decided, it was the mother's turn to **address** them. And though Mr. Fielden was as anxious and fond as most fathers, he grew a little **impatient** before **comforters**, **kerchiefs**, and muffettees were **arranged**, and minute **exordiums** as to the danger of **crossing** the street, and the risk of patting strange dogs, etc., were half-way concluded; with a **shrug** and a smile, he at length **fairly pushed** out the children, **shut** the door, and drew his chair close to his wife's.

"My dear," he began at once, "I am **extremely** uneasy about that poor girl."

French

address: adresse, destination, interpeller, aborder, allocution, discours.
arranged: arrangé, disposâtes, rangea, ordonnas, accommoda, agencèrent.
attic: grenier, mansarde.
closer: clausoir, clé de voûte, dispositif de fermeture, piqueur.
comforter: aspirateur, soucette, consolateur.
crossing: croisement, traversée, intersection.
disturb: déranger, gêner, gênons, troubler, perturber.
exordium: exorde.
extremely: extrêmement, de façon extrême, de manière extrême.
fairly: assez, relativement, de façon foire, de manière foire, équitablement.
footstep: pas, marche.
hinge: charnière, gond, articulation, paumelle.
impatient: impatient.
kerchief: mouchoir, marmotte, carré.
pushed: poussé.
rejoinder: réplique.
shrug: hausser les épaules.
shut: fermer, arrêter.
square: carré, place, équerre, droit, rectangle, esplanade, case, square.
ugly: laid, vilain, moche, mauvais.

"What, Miss Clavering? Indeed, she **eats** almost nothing at all, and **sits** so moping alone; but she sees Mr. Mainwaring every day. What can we do? She is so proud, I'm **afraid** of her."

"My dear, I was not **thinking** of Miss Clavering, though I did not interrupt you, for it is very true that she is much to be pitied."

"And I am sure it was for her **sake** alone that you **agreed** to Susan's **request**, and got Blackman to do **duty** for you at the **vicarage**, while we all came up here, in **hopes** London town would divert her. We left all at sixes and sevens; and I should not at all wonder if John made away with the apples."

"But, I say," resumed the parson, without heeding that mournful foreboding,—"I say, I was then only thinking of Susan. You see how pale and sad she is grown."

"Why, she is so very soft-hearted, and she must feel for her **sister**."

"But her sister, though she thinks much, and keeps aloof from us, is not sad herself, only reserved. On the contrary. I believe she has now got over even **poor** Sir Miles's death." "And the loss of the great property!"

"Fie, Mary!" said Mr. Fielden, almost **austerely**.

Mary looked down, rebuked, for she was not one of the high-spirited wives who despise their **husbands** for goodness.

"I beg pardon, my dear," she said **meekly**; "it was very **wrong** in me; but I cannot—do what I will—I cannot like that Miss Clavering."

"The more need to **judge** her with **charity**. And if what I **fear** is the case, I'm sure we can't feel too much compassion for the poor blinded young lady."

"Bless my **heart**, Mr. Fielden, what is it you mean?"

The parson looked round, to be sure the door was quite **closed**, and replied, in a whisper: "I mean, that I fear William Mainwaring loves, not Lucretia, but Susan."

French

afraid: timide, peureux, effrayé.
agreed: consenti, ça va, convenu, soit.
austerely: de façon austère, de manière austère.
charity: charité, bienfaisance, aumône, compassion.
closed: fermas, clos.
duty: devoir, droit, service, taxe, obligation.
eats: mange, bouffe.
fear: peur, crainte, angoisse, redouter, appréhension, avoir peur.
heart: coeur, le coeur.
hope: espoir, espérer, espères, souhaiter.
husband: mari, époux.
judge: juge, magistrat assis, assesseur, arbitre, estimateur.
meekly: de façon humble, de manière humble.
poor: pauvre, mauvais, misérable, maigre, malheureux, méchant, mal, médiocre, faible.
request: demande, prier, requête.
sake: saké.
sister: soeur, la soeur.
sit: être assis, couver, asseoir, m'assieds, nous asseyons, s'asseyent, siéger, t'assieds, vous asseyez, siéger.
thinking: pensant, rationnel.
vicarage: presbytère.
wrong: faux, tort, abusif, incorrect, erroné, injustice, mal.

The scissors **fell** from the hand of Mrs. Fielden; and though one point **stuck** in the ground, and the other point **threatened** war upon **flounces** and **toes**, strange to say, she did not even stoop to **remove** the chevaux-de-frise.

"Why, then, he's a most false-hearted young man!"

"To blame, certainly," said Fielden; "I don't say to the contrary,—though I like the young man, and am sure that he's more timid than false. I may now tell you—for I want your **advice**, Mary—what I **kept** secret before. When Mainwaring **visited** us, many months ago, at Southampton, he **confessed** to me that he felt warmly for Susan, and asked if I thought Sir Miles would **consent**. I knew too well how proud the poor old **gentleman** was, to give him any such hopes. So he left, very honourably. You remember, after he went, that Susan's **spirits** were low,—you **remarked** it."

"Yes, indeed, I remember. But when the first **shock** of Sir Miles's death was over, she got back her **sweet colour**, and looked cheerful enough."

"Because, perhaps, then she felt that she had a fortune to **bestow** on Mr. Mainwaring, and thought all obstacle was over."

"Why, how clever you are! How did you get at her thoughts?"

"My own folly,—my own **rash** folly," almost groaned Mr. Fielden. "For not **guessing** that Mr. Mainwaring could have got **engaged meanwhile** to Lucretia, and suspecting how it was with Susan's poor little heart, I let out, in a jest—Heaven forgive me!—what William had said; and the dear child blushed, and kissed me, and—why, a day or two after, when it was fixed that we should come up to London, Lucretia informed me, with her **freezing** politeness, that she was to marry Mainwaring herself as soon as her first mourning was over."

"Poor, dear, dear Susan!"

"Susan **behaved** like an angel; and when I broached it to her, I thought she was calm; and I am sure she prayed with her whole heart that both might be happy."

French

advice: conseil, avis, renseignement.
behaved: comporté.
bestow: accorder, octroyer.
colour: couleur, teinte, colorier.
confessed: confessas, avoué.
consent: consentement, admettre, donner son accord, être d'accord, agrément.
engaged: engageai, occupé.
fell: tombai, abattre, chut, chûtes, chus, churent, chûmes.

flounce: volant.
freezing: congélation, gel, glacial, gelant, blocage.
gentleman: monsieur, gentilhomme.
guessing: devinant.
kept: garda, élevèrent, remplit.
meanwhile: dans l'intervalle, en attendant, pendant ce temps.
rash: éruption, irréfléchi, rougeur, inconsidéré.
remarked: remarqué.

remove: supprimer, ôter, enlever, ôtez, ôtent, ôtes, ôte, ôtons, enlève, retirer, déplacer.
shock: choc, choquer, secouer, heurter, moyette.
spirit: esprit, vigueur.
stuck: collé, être embourbé.
sweet: sucré, doux, suave, bonbon, friandise, gentil, dessert.
threatened: menaçâtes.
toe: orteil, doigt du pied, bout.
visited: visita.

"I'm sure she did. What is to be done? I understand it all now. Dear me, dear me! a sad piece of work indeed." And Mrs. Fielden **abstractedly picked** up the scissors.

"It was not till our coming to town, and Mr. Mainwaring's visits to Lucretia, that her **strength** gave way."

"A hard **sight** to bear,—I never could have borne it, my love. If I had seen you paying court to another, I should have—I don't know what I should have done! But what an **artful wretch** this young Mainwaring must be."

"Not very artful; for you see that he looks even sadder than Susan. He got entangled **somehow**, to be sure. Perhaps he had given up Susan in despair; and Miss Clavering, if haughty, is no doubt a very **superior** young lady; and, I dare say, it is only now in **seeing** them both together, and **comparing** the two, that he feels what a **treasure** he has lost. Well, what do you **advise**, Mary? Mainwaring, no doubt, is bound in honour to Miss Clavering; but she will be sure to discover, sooner or later, the state of his feelings, and then I **tremble** for both. I'm sure she will never be happy, while he will be **wretched**; and Susan—I dare not think upon Susan; she has a **cough** that goes to my heart."

"So she has; that cough—you don't know the money I **spend** on black-currant **jelly**! What's my advice? Why, I'd speak to Miss Clavering at once, if I **dared**. I'm sure love will never **break** her heart; and she's so proud, she'd throw him off without a sigh, if she knew how things stood."

"I believe you are right," said Mr. Fielden; "for truth is the best policy, after all. Still, it's scarce my business to **meddle**; and if it were not for Susan— Well, well, I must think of it, and pray Heaven to direct me."

This conference suffices to **explain** to the reader the stage to which the history of Lucretia had **arrived**. Willingly we pass over what it were scarcely possible to describe,—her first shock at the fall from the expectations of her life; fortune, rank, and what she **valued** more than either, power, **crushed** at a blow. From the dark and sullen despair into which she was first **plunged**, she was roused into hope, into something like joy, by Mainwaring's letters.

French

abstractedly: de façon distraite, de manière distraite.
advise: conseiller, recommander.
arrived: arrivâtes.
artful: astucieux, rusé, malin.
break: rompre, pause, briser, casser, rupture, interruption, violer, repos, fracture, trêve, coupure.
comparing: comparant.
cough: toux, tousser.
crushed: écrasé, broyé, accablé.
dared: osa, osèrent, osé, osâtes, osas, osâmes, osai, aventurèrent.
explain: expliquer, développer.
jelly: gelée, gélation.
meddle: mêlez, se mêler, mêlons.
picked: cueillirent, piquâmes.
plunged: plongé.
seeing: voyant, sciant.
sight: vue, spectacle, visée, apparence, mire, air, aspect, apercevoir, allure.
somehow: d'une façon ou d'une autre, de façon ou d'autre.
spend: dépenser, passer, donner.
strength: force, puissance, résistance mécanique.
superior: supérieur, suprême, surplombant, dominant.
treasure: trésor, cassette.
tremble: trembler, frémir.
valued: estimé, précieux.
wretch: malheureux, scélérat.
wretched: misérable, pauvre, pitoyable, infortuné, malheureux.

Never had they been so warm and so **tender**; for the young man felt not only poignant remorse that he had been the cause of her downfall (though she broke it to him with more delicacy than might have been expected from the state of her feelings and the **hardness** of her character), but he felt also **imperiously** the obligations which her loss rendered more **binding** than ever. He persuaded, he urged, he forced himself into affection; and probably without a murmur of his heart, he would have gone with her to the altar, and, once **wedded**, **custom** and duty would have strengthened the chain imposed on himself, had it not been for Lucretia's fatal **eagerness** to see him, to come up to London, where she **induced** him to meet her,—for with her came Susan; and in Susan's averted face and **trembling** hand and mute **avoidance** of his eye, he read all which the poor dissembler fancied she concealed. But the die was cast, the union announced, the time fixed, and day by day he came to the house, to leave it in anguish and despair. A feeling they shared in common caused these two unhappy persons to **shun** each other. Mainwaring rarely came into the usual sitting-room of the family; and when be did so, **chiefly** in the evening, Susan usually took **refuge** in her own room. If they met, it was by accident, on the stairs, or at the sudden opening of a door; then not only no word, but scarcely even a look was exchanged: neither had the courage to face the other. Perhaps, of the two, this **reserve weighed** most on Susan; perhaps she most yearned to break the silence,—for she thought she divined the cause of Mainwaring's gloomy and mute constraint in the upbraidings of his conscience, which might doubtless recall, if no positive pledge to Susan, at least those words and tones which betray the one heart, and seek to **allure** the other; and the profound melancholy **stamped** on his whole person, apparent even to her hurried glance, touched her with a compassion free from all the bitterness of selfish reproach. She fancied she could die happy if she could remove that cloud from his brow, that shadow from his conscience. Die; for she thought not of life. She loved gently, quietly,—not with the vehement passion that belongs to stronger natures; but it was the love of which the young and the pure have died. The face of the Genius was calm and soft; and only by the **lowering** of

French

allure: attrait, séduisez, attirez.
avoidance: évitement, action d'éviter, dérobade, évasion.
binding: bandeau, obligatoire, reliure, liaison, contraignant, fixation.
chiefly: principalement, surtout, particulièrement, de façon chef, de manière chef.
custom: coutume, habitude, usage.
eagerness: avidité, empressement, ardeur, impatience.
hardness: crudité, degré du vide, difficulté, Dureté, compacité.
imperiously: de façon impérieuse, de manière impérieuse.
induced: induit, bouton de vapeur, bilame.
lowering: abaissement, baissant.
refuge: refuge, abri, réserve, retraite.
reserve: réserver, retenir, commander, demander.
shun: fuir, évite, fuyons, fuis, fuient, fuyez.
stamped: affranchi, timbré.
tender: offre, tendre, adjudication, doux, annexe, suave, proposition, présenter, soumission, sucré, gentil.
trembling: tremblant, frémissant.
wedded: se maria, vous mariâtes, te marias, nous mariâmes, me mariai, marié.
weighed: pesèrent, pesa, pesâmes, pesé.

the hand do you see that the **torch burns** out, and that the image too serene for earthly love is the **genius** of loving Death.

Absorbed in the **egotism** of her passion (increased, as is ever the case with women, even the worst, by the sacrifices it had cost her), and if that passion paused, by the energy of her ambition, which already began to scheme and **reconstruct** new **scaffolds** to **repair** the **ruined** walls of the past,—Lucretia as yet had not detected what was so apparent to the simple sense of Mr. Fielden. That Mainwaring was grave and thoughtful and abstracted, she ascribed only to his grief at the thought of her loss, and his anxieties for her altered future; and in her efforts to console him, her attempts to convince him that **greatness** in England did not **consist** only in lands and manors,—that in the higher walks of life which conduct to the Temple of Renown, the leaders of the **procession** are the aristocracy of knowledge and of intellect,—she so betrayed, not generous **emulation** and high-souled aspiring, but the dark, unscrupulous, **tortuous** ambition of cunning, stratagem, and intrigue, that instead of feeling grateful and encouraged, he shuddered and revolted. How, accompanied and led by a spirit which he felt to be stronger and more **commanding** than his own,— how **preserve** the **whiteness** of his soul, the **uprightness** of his honour? Already he felt himself **debased**. But in the still trial of domestic intercourse, with the daily, hourly **dripping** on the stone, in the many struggles between truth and falsehood, guile and candour, which men—and, above all, ambitious men—must wage, what darker angel would whisper him in his **monitor**? Still, he was bound,—bound with an iron band; he writhed, but dreamed not of escape.

The day after that of Fielden's conference with his wife, an unexpected visitor came to the house. Olivier Dalibard called. He had not seen Lucretia since she had left Laughton, nor had any correspondence passed between them. He came at **dusk**, just after Mainwaring's daily visit was over, and Lucretia was still in the parlour, which she had appropriated to herself. Her brow contracted as his name was announced, and the maid-servant lighted the candle on the table, **stirred** the fire, and gave a **tug** at the curtains. Her

---

French

burn: brûler, s'allumer.
commanding: commandant, dominant, ordonner.
consist: consister, composition de traction, bulletin de composition, avis de composition, rame.
debased: abâtardis, avilîtes.
dripping: égouttement, bavure, dégoulinade, ruissellement, suintement.
dusk: crépuscule.
egotism: égotisme, égoïsme.
emulation: émulation.
genius: génie.
greatness: grandeur.
monitor: moniteur, appareil de surveillance, contrôler, surveiller.
preserve: conserver, confire, préserver, maintenir, retenir, mettre en conserve, réserve.
procession: procession, cortège.
reconstruct: reconstruire, rebâtissez.
repair: réparation, refaire, dépanner, restaurer, remédier, réformer, réfection, radouber, remettre en état.
ruined: ruiné, foutu.
scaffold: échafaud.
stirred: remué.
torch: torche, lampe de poche, flambeau.
tortuous: tortueux.
tug: remorqueur, tirer.
uprightness: intégrité.
whiteness: blancheur, pâleur.

eye, glancing from his, round the mean room, with its **dingy horsehair furniture**, involuntarily implied the contrast between the past state and the present, which his sight could scarcely help to impress on her. But she **welcomed** him with her usual stately composure, and without reference to what had been. Dalibard was **secretly** anxious to discover if she **suspected** himself of any agency in the detection of the eventful letter; and assured by her manner that no such thought was yet harboured, he thought it best to imitate her own reserve. He **assumed**, however, a manner that, far more respectful than he ever before observed to his pupil, was nevertheless sufficiently kind and familiar to **restore** them gradually to their old footing; and that he succeeded was apparent, when, after a pause, Lucretia said abruptly: "How did Sir Miles St. John discover my correspondence with Mr. Mainwaring?"

"Is it possible that you are **ignorant**? Ah, how—how should you know it?" And Dalibard so simply explained the **occurrence**, in which, indeed, it was impossible to trace the hand that had moved springs which seemed so entirely set at work by an accident, that despite the **extreme suspiciousness** of her nature, Lucretia did not see a pretence for **accusing** him. Indeed, when he related the little **subterfuge** of Gabriel, his attempt to save her by taking the letter on himself, she felt **thankful** to the boy, and deemed Gabriel's conduct quite in keeping with his attachment to herself. And this accounted **satisfactorily** for the only circumstance that had ever **troubled** her with a doubt,—namely, the **legacy** left to Gabriel. She knew enough of Sir Miles to be aware that he would be grateful to any one who had saved the name of his niece, even while most **embittered** against her, from the shame **attached** to clandestine correspondence.

"It is strange, nevertheless," said she, **thoughtfully**, after a pause, "that the girl should have detected the letter, concealed as it was by the leaves that covered it."

"But," answered Dalibard, readily, "you see two or three persons had entered before, and their feet must have **displaced** the leaves."

French

accusing: accusant.
assumed: assumâtes, supposé.
attached: attachâtes, apposa.
dingy: terne.
displaced: déplaçâmes, dérégla, décalèrent.
embittered: aigri, acharnées.
extreme: extrême, cuir léger, hors tout.
furniture: meubles, mobilier, les meubles, garniture, ameublement.
horsehair: crin.
ignorant: ignorant.
legacy: legs, héritage.
occurrence: événement, cas, indice, occurrence, venue.
restore: restaurer, rétablir, rénover, réparer.
satisfactorily: de façon satisfaisante, de manière satisfaisante.
secretly: secrètement, de façon secrte, de manière secrète, en secret.
subterfuge: artifice, subterfuge.
suspected: soupçonné.
suspiciousness: caractère suspect.
thankful: reconnaissant.
thoughtfully: de façon réfléchie, de manière réfléchie.
troubled: inquiet, gêné, préoccupé, gênai, agité, gênâmes.
welcomed: accueillis.

"Possibly; the evil is now past recall."

"And Mr. Mainwaring? Do you still **adhere** to one who has cost you so much, poor child?"

"In three months more I shall be his wife."

Dalibard sighed **deeply**, but offered no remonstrance.

"Well," he said, taking her hand with mingled reverence and affection, — "well, I oppose your inclinations no more, for now there is nothing to risk; you are **mistress** of your own fortune; and since Mainwaring has **talents**, that fortune will suffice for a career. Are you at length convinced that I have conquered my folly; that I was disinterested when I **incurred** your displeasure? If so, can you restore to me your friendship? You will have some struggle with the world, and, with my long experience of men and life, even I, the poor exile, may **assist** you."

And so thought Lucretia; for with some **dread** of Dalibard's **craft**, she yet **credited** his attachment to herself, and she felt profound admiration for an **intelligence** more **consummate** and **accomplished** than any ever yet **submitted** to her **comprehension**. From that time, Dalibard became an habitual visitor at the house; he never interfered with Lucretia's interviews with Mainwaring; he took the union for **granted**, and **conversed** with her cheerfully on the prospects before her; he ingratiated himself with the Fieldens, played with the children, made himself at home, and in the evenings when Mainwaring, as often as he could find the **excuse**, absented himself from the family **circle**, he contrived to draw Lucretia into more social intercourse with her **homely** companions than she had before condescended to **admit**. Good Mr. Fielden **rejoiced**; here was the very person, — the old friend of Sir Miles, the **preceptor** of Lucretia herself, evidently most attached to her, having influence over her, — the very person to whom to confide his **embarrassment**. One day, therefore, when Dalibard had touched his heart by noticing the paleness of Susan, he took him aside and told him all. "And now," concluded the pastor, **hoping** he had found one to **relieve** him of his

---

French

accomplished: accomplîmes, réalisas, confectionnâmes, remplîtes, expérimenté, qualifié, compétent.
adhere: adhérer, adhères, correspondre, coller, concorder.
admit: admettre, reconnaître, avouer, confesser, laisser entrer, permettre.
assist: assister, aider, aidons, secourir.
circle: cercle, rond, encercler.
comprehension: compréhension.
consummate: consommé.
conversed: conversé.
craft: métier, embarcation, engin, artisanat.
credited: crédité.
deeply: profondément, de façon profonde, de manière profonde.
dread: crainte, redouter.
embarrassment: embarras, gêne.
excuse: excuser, dispenser, pardonner.
granted: alloua, accordé.
homely: simple, sans charme.
hoping: espérant, souhaitant.
incurred: encouru, contractai.
intelligence: intelligence, renseignement.
mistress: maîtresse, madame.
preceptor: précepteur.
rejoiced: réjouis.
relieve: soulager, relayer.
submitted: soumîmes.
talent: talent, don, aptitude.

dreaded and **ungracious** task, "don't you think that I—or rather you—as so old a friend, should speak frankly to Miss Clavering herself?"

"No, indeed," said the Provencal, quickly; "if we spoke to her, she would disbelieve us. She would no doubt appeal to Mainwaring, and Mainwaring would have no choice but to **contradict** us. Once put on his guard, he would control his very sadness. Lucretia, offended, might leave your house, and certainly she would regard her sister as having **influenced** your confession,—a position unworthy Miss Mivers. But do not fear: if the evil be so, it carries with it its **inevitable** remedy. Let Lucretia discover it herself; but, pardon me, she must have seen, at your first **reception** of Mainwaring, that he had before been acquainted with you?"

"She was not in the room when we first received Mainwaring; and I have always been **distant** to him, as you may suppose, for I felt **disappointed** and displeased. Of course, however, she is aware that we knew him before she did. What of that?"

"Why, do you think, then, he told her at Laughton of this acquaintance,— that he spoke of Susan? I suspect not."

"I cannot say, I am sure," said Mr. Fielden.

"Ask her that question **accidentally**; and for the rest, be **discreet**, my dear sir. I thank you for your **confidence**. I will watch well over my poor young pupil. She must not, indeed, be sacrificed to a man whose affections are engaged elsewhere."

Dalibard trod on air as he left the house; his very countenance had changed; he seemed ten years **younger**. It was evening; and suddenly, as he came into Oxford Street, he **encountered** a **knot** of young men—noisy and **laughing** loud—obstructing the **pavement**, breaking jests on the more sober **passengers**, and **attracting** the **especial** and admiring attention of sundry ladies in **plumed hats** and **scarlet pelisses**; for the streets then **enjoyed** a gay liberty which has vanished from London with the **lanterns** of the watchmen. **Noisiest** and most **conspicuous** of these descendants of the Mohawks, the sleek and **orderly** scholar beheld the childish figure of his son. Nor did

French

accidentally: accidentellement, de manière accidentelle, par hasard, de façon accidentelle.
attracting: attirant, alléchant, appâtant.
confidence: confiance, foi.
conspicuous: visible, apparent.
contradict: contredire, démentir.
disappointed: déçu, trompa, déçûtes.
discreet: discret, prudent.
distant: lointain, distant, éloigné.

encountered: rencontrèrent.
enjoyed: jouirent, jouîtes.
especial: exceptionnel, particulier, spécial.
hat: chapeau, le chapeau, bonnet, casque.
inevitable: inévitable, inéluctable.
influenced: influencé.
knot: noeud, nouer, bécasseau maubèche, larme, nodule, nœud lâche.
lantern: lanterne, fanal.

laughing: riant, rieur, rire.
noisiest: le plus bruyant.
orderly: ordonné, méthodique.
passenger: passager, voyageur.
pavement: pavé, trottoir, chaussée.
pelisse: pelisse.
plumed: empanaché.
reception: réception, accueil.
scarlet: écarlate, rouge écarlate.
ungracious: incivil.
younger: plus jeune, puîné.

Gabriel shrink from his father's eye, stern and **scornful** as it was, but rather braved the glance with an **impudent leer**.

Right, however, in the midst of the group, strode the Provencal, and **laying** his hand very gently on the boy's shoulder, he said: "My son, come with me."

Gabriel looked irresolute, and glanced at his companions. Delighted at the prospect of a scene, they now **gathered** round, with countenances and gestures that seemed little disposed to acknowledge the **parental** authority.

"Gentlemen," said Dalibard, turning a shade more pale, for though **morally** most resolute, **physically** he was not brave,—"gentlemen, I must beg you to excuse me; this child is my son!"

"But Art is his mother," replied a tall, raw-boned young man, with long **tawny** hair **streaming** down from a hat very much **battered**. "At the **juvenile** age, the child is **consigned** to the mother! Have I said it?" and he turned round **theatrically** to his **comrades**.

"Bravo!" cried the rest, **clapping** their hands.

"Down with all tyrants and fathers! **hip**, hip, Hurrah!" and the hideous **diapason** nearly split the drum of the ears into which it **resounded**.

"Gabriel," whispered the father, "you had better follow me, had you not? Reflect!" So saying, he bowed low to the unpropitious assembly, and as if **yielding** the victory, stepped aside and crossed over towards Bond Street.

Before the **din** of **derision** and **triumph** died away, Dalibard looked back, and saw Gabriel behind him.

"Approach, sir," he said; and as the boy stood still, he added, "I promise peace if you will accept it."

"Peace, then," answered Gabriel, and he joined his father's side.

"So," said Dalibard, "when I consented to your **studying** Art, as you call it, under your mother's most respectable brother, I ought to have contemplated what would be the natural and becoming companions of the rising Raphael I have given to the world."

French

battered: en pâte à frire, battu, cabossé.
clapping: claquage, physiothérapie respiratoire, applaudir.
comrade: camarade.
consigned: consigné.
derision: dérision.
diapason: diapason.
din: vacarme, tapage.
gathered: ramassée, rassemblé, cueilli.
hip: hanche, arête, fruit de l'églantier, cuisse.
impudent: effronté, impudent.
juvenile: juvénile, jeune, mineur.
laying: pose, posant, ponte, pondant, couchant, levée.
leer: regard mauvais, lorgner.
morally: moralement, de manière morale, de façon morale.
parental: parental.
physically: physiquement, de façon physique, de manière physique.
resounded: résonnèrent, retentîtes.
scornful: dédaigneux, méprisant.
streaming: effet de canalisation, lecture en transit, courant, continu, fuite, coulant.
studying: étude.
tawny: fauve.
theatrically: de façon théâtrale, de manière théâtrale.
triumph: triomphe.
yielding: cédant, rendant, rapportant, produire, élastique, complaisant, coulissant.

"I own, sir," replied Gabriel, **demurely**, "that they are riotous fellows; but some of them are clever, and—"

"And excessively **drunk**," interrupted Dalibard, **examining** the **gait** of his son. "Do you learn that accomplishment also, by way of **steadying** your hand for the easel?"

"No, sir; I like wine well enough, but I would not be drunk for the world. I see people when they are drunk are mere fools,—let out their secrets, and show themselves up."

"Well said," replied the father, almost admiringly. "But a **truce** with this bantering, Gabriel. Can you imagine that I will permit you any longer to remain with that **vagabond** Varney and yon **crew** of vauriens? You will come home with me; and if you must be a **painter**, I will look out for a more **trustworthy** master."

"I shall stay where I am," answered Gabriel, firmly, and **compressing** his lips with a force that left them **bloodless**.

"What, boy? Do I hear right? Dare you **disobey** me? Dare you defy?"

"Not in your house, so I will not enter it again." Dalibard **laughed mockingly**.

"Peste! but this is **modest**! You are not of age yet, Mr. Varney; you are not free from a father's tyrannical control."

"The law does not own you as my father, I am told, sir. You have said my name rightly,—it is Varney, not Dalibard. We have no rights over each other; so at least says Tom Passmore, and his father's a lawyer!"

Dalibard's hand griped his son's arm **fiercely**. Despite his pain, which was **acute**, the child uttered no cry; but he **growled** beneath his teeth, "Beware! beware! or my mother's son may **avenge** her death!"

Dalibard removed his hand, and **staggered** as if struck. **Gliding** from his side, Gabriel seized the occasion to escape; he paused, however, midway in the dull, lamp-lit **kennel** when he saw himself out of reach, and then approaching **cautiously**, said: "I know. I am a boy, but you have made me

French

acute: aigu, perçant, intense, sagace, piquant, coupant, aigre, rude, âcre, acéré, tranchant.
avenge: venger.
bloodless: exsangue, pâle.
cautiously: avec précaution, de façon prudente, de manière prudente.
compressing: comprimant.
crew: équipage, personnel navigant.
demurely: de manière modeste, de façon modeste.
disobey: désobéir.
drunk: ivre, bu, soûl.
examining: examinant, fouillant.
fiercely: de façon féroce, de manière féroce.
gait: démarche, allure, marche.
gliding: vol à voile, glissement.
growled: grogné.
kennel: chenil, niche, ruisseau.
laughed: ries, rit, rirent, rie, ris.
mockingly: de façon dérisionnelle, de manière dérisionnelle.
modest: modeste, modique, pudique.
painter: peintre, tricoteuse double, artiste peintre, bosse, gouacheur.
staggered: disposé en quinconce.
steadying: assujettissant.
truce: trêve.
trustworthy: sûr, digne de confiance, fiable.
vagabond: vagabond, clochard, chemineau.

man enough to take care of myself. Mr. Varney, my uncle, will **maintain** me; when of age, old Sir Miles has provided for me. Leave me in peace, **treat** me as free, and I will visit you, help you when you want me, obey you still,— yes, follow your **instructions**; for I know you are," he paused, "you are wise. But if you seek again to make me your slave, you will only find your foe. Good-night; and remember that a **bastard** has no father!"

With these words he moved on, and **hurrying** down the street, turned the **corner** and vanished.

Dalibard **remained motionless** for some minutes; at **length** he muttered: "Ay, let him go, he is dangerous! What son ever revolted even from the **worst** father, and throve in life? Food for the **gibbet**! What matters?"

When next Dalibard visited Lucretia, his **manner** was changed; the **cheerfulness** he had before assumed gave place to a kind of melancholy compassion; he no longer entered into her plans for the future, but would look at her mournfully, start up, and **walk** away. She would have attributed the change to some return of his ancient passion, but she heard him once murmur with unspeakable pity, "Poor child, poor child!" A **vague** apprehension seized her,—first, indeed, **caught** from some remarks dropped by Mr. Fielden, which were less discreet than Dalibard had **recommended**. A day or two afterwards, she asked Mainwaring, carelessly, why he had never **spoken** to her at Laughton of his acquaintance with Fielden.

"You asked me that before," he said, somewhat **sullenly**.

"Did I? I **forget**! But how was it? Tell me again."

"I scarcely know," he replied **confusedly**; "we were always talking of each other or poor Sir Miles,—our own hopes and fears."

This was true, and a lover's natural excuse. In the present of love all the past is forgotten.

"Still," said Lucretia, with her sidelong glance,—"still, as you must have seen much of my own sister—"

French

bastard: bâtard, métis, roche massive, salaud, enfant naturel.
caught: attrapâtes, prit, prîmes, prirent, prîtes, pris, capturas, frappai.
cheerfulness: gaieté, bonne humeur.
confusedly: de manière confuse, de façon confuse.
corner: coin, accaparer, monopoliser, corner, angle.
forget: oublier, désapprenons.
gibbet: gibet.
hurrying: dépêchant.
instruction: instruction, enseignement.
length: longueur, traînée, portant, étendue, délai d'amortissement, durée de validité.
maintain: maintenir, conserver, retenir, entretenir.
manner: manière, façon.
motionless: immobile, fixe, au repos.
recommended: recommandai, préconisa.
remained: restâtes.
spoken: parlé.
sullenly: de façon maussade, de manière maussade.
treat: traiter, soigner, régaler, guérir.
vague: vague, imprécis, flou.
walk: marcher, promenade, se promener, démarche.
worst: pire, le plus mauvais.

Mainwaring, while she spoke, was at work on a **button** on his **gaiter** (gaiters were then worn **tight** at the ankle); the effort brought the blood to his forehead.

"But," he said, still **stooping** at his **occupation**, "you were so little intimate with your sister; I feared to offend. Family differences are so difficult to approach."

Lucretia was satisfied at the moment; for so vast was her **stake** in Mainwaring's heart, so did her whole heart and soul **grapple** to the rock left serene amidst the **deluge**, that she habitually and **resolutely** thrust from her mind all the doubts that at times **invaded** it.

"I know," she would often say to herself,—"I know he does not love as I do; but man never can, never ought to love as woman! Were I a man, I should scorn myself if I could be so absorbed in one emotion as I am proud to be now,—I, poor woman! I know," again she would think,—"I know how **suspicious** and **distrustful** I am; I must not distrust him,—I shall only **irritate**, I may lose him: I dare not distrust,—it would be too dreadful."

Thus, as a system **vigorously** embraced by a determined mind, she had schooled and forced herself into **reliance** on her lover. His words now, we say, satisfied her at the moment; but afterwards, in absence, they were **recalled**, in spite of herself,—in the midst of fears, shapeless and **undefined**. Involuntarily she began to examine the countenance, the movements, of her sister,—to court Susan's society more than she had done; for her previous indifference had now **deepened** into bitterness. Susan, the neglected and despised, had become her equal,—nay, more than her equal: Susan's children would have precedence to her own in the heritage of Laughton! Hitherto she had never deigned to talk to her in the sweet familiarity of sisters so placed; never deigned to confide to her those feelings for her future husband which **burned lone** and ardent in the close vault of her guarded heart. Now, however, she began to name him, wind her arm into Susan's, talk of love and home, and the days to come; and as she spoke, she read the workings of her sister's face. That part of the secret grew clear almost at the

---

French

burned: brûlé.
button: bouton, bourrelet, collier, insigne syndical, manette, mouche, touche, bosse.
deepened: approfondirent, rembrunîtes.
deluge: déluge, inondation.
distrustful: méfiant, défiant.
gaiter: guêtre, emplâtre.
grapple: grappin, attraper, saisir, capturer.
invaded: envahîtes, invadées.
irritate: irriter, énerver, agacer.
lone: solitaire, seul.
occupation: occupation, métier, profession, emploi.
recalled: rappelé.
reliance: confiance.
resolutely: de façon résolue, de manière résolue, résolument.
stake: pieu, poteau, échalas, jalon, piquet, perche.
stooping: penché, perchage, mirage raccourcissant verticalement l'image, baisse, dépilage.
suspicious: méfiant, soupçonneux, sinistre, suspect.
tight: strict, serré, tendu, étanche, étroit.
undefined: indéfini, non défini, vague.
vigorously: vigoureusement, de façon vigoureuse, de manière vigoureuse.

first glance. Susan loved,—loved William Mainwaring; but was it not a love hopeless and unreturned? Might not this be the cause that had made Mainwaring so reserved? He might have seen, or conjectured, a conquest he had not sought; and hence, with manly delicacy, he had **avoided naming** Susan to Lucretia; and now, perhaps, sought the excuses which at times had chafed and wounded her for not **joining** the household circle. If one of those who glance over these pages chances to be a person more than usually able and acute,—a person who has loved and been deceived,—he or she, no matter which, will perhaps recall those first moments when the doubt, long put off, insisted to be heard. A weak and foolish heart gives way to the doubt at once; not so the subtler and more powerful,—it rather, on the contrary, recalls all the little circumstances that justify trust and make head against suspicion; it will not render the citadel at the mere sound of the **trumpet**; it arms all its forces, and bars its gates on the foe. Hence it is that the persons most easy to dupe in matters of affection are usually those most **astute** in the larger affairs of life. Moliere, reading every **riddle** in the vast **complexities** of human character, and **clinging**, in self-imposed **credulity**, to his **profligate** wife, is a type of a **striking** truth. Still, a **foreboding**, a warning instinct withheld Lucretia from **plumbing** farther into the deeps of her own fears. So horrible was the thought that she had been deceived, that rather than face it, she would have **preferred** to deceive herself. This poor, bad heart shrank from inquiry, it trembled at the idea of **condemnation**. She **hailed**, with a sentiment of release that partook of rapture, Susan's abrupt **announcement** one morning that she had accepted an invitation from some relations of her father to spend some time with them at their **villa** near Hampstead; she was to go the end of the week. Lucretia hailed it, though she saw the cause,— Susan shrank from the name of Mainwaring on Lucretia's lips; shrank from the familiar intercourse so **ruthlessly** forced on her! With a bright eye, that day, Lucretia met her lover; yet she would not tell him of Susan's intended **departure**, she had not the courage.

Dalibard was foiled. This contradiction in Lucretia's temper, so suspicious, so determined, puzzled even his penetration. He saw that bolder

French

announcement: annonce, avis, renseignement.
astute: astucieux, avisé, sagace.
avoided: évité, esquivas.
clinging: se cramponnant, adhérant, collant.
complexity: complexité, degré de complexité.
condemnation: condamnation.
credulity: crédulité.
departure: départ, disparition.
foreboding: pressentiment, présage.
hailed: grêlé.
joining: joignant, reliant, accouplant, associant, nouant, raccordement, rattachement.
naming: nomination, tests d'appellation, nommage, dénomination.
plumbing: plomberie, tuyauterie.
preferred: préféra, privilégiâmes.
profligate: débauché, libertin.
riddle: énigme, puzzle, devinette, cribler.
ruthlessly: de façon impitoyable, de manière impitoyable, impitoyablement.
striking: frappant, saisissant, reprise, radiation, impressionnant, éclatant, coup de talon, battage, assénant, amorçage d'un arc, développement de la couleur.
trumpet: trompette, barrir.
villa: villa, pavillon.

tactics were required. He waylaid Mainwaring on the young man's way to his lodgings, and after talking to him on indifferent matters, asked him carelessly whether he did not think Susan far gone in a **decline**. Affecting not to notice the convulsive start with which the question was received, he went on,—

"There is evidently something on her mind; I **observe** that her eyes are often red, as with weeping, poor girl. Perhaps some **silly** love-affair. However, we shall not see her again before your marriage; she is going away in a day or two. The change of air may **possibly** yet restore her,—I own, though, I fear the worst. At this time of the year, and in your **climate**, such **complaints** as I take hers to be are **rapid**. Good-day. We may meet this evening."

Terror-stricken at these barbarous words, Mainwaring no sooner reached his lodging than he wrote and despatched a note to Fielden, **entreating** him to call.

The **vicar** obeyed the summons, and found Mainwaring in a state of mind bordering on **distraction**. Nor when Susan was named did Fielden's words take the **shape** of comfort; for he himself was **seriously** alarmed for her health. The sound of her low cough rang in his **ears**, and he rather **heightened** than removed the picture which haunted Mainwaring,—Susan stricken, **dying**, broken-hearted!

Tortured both in heart and conscience, Mainwaring felt as if he had but one wish left in the world,—to see Susan once more. What to say, he scarce knew; but for her to depart,—depart perhaps to her grave, **believing** him coldly indifferent,—for her not to know at least his **struggles**, and pronounce his pardon, was a thought beyond **endurance**. After such an **interview** both would have new fortitude,—each would unite in **encouraging** the other in the only step left to honour. And this desire he **urged** upon Fielden with all the eloquence of passionate grief as he **entreated** him to permit and procure one last conference with Susan. But this, the plain sense and **straightforward** conscience of the good man long **refused**. If Mainwaring had been left in the

---

French

believing: croyant.
climate: Climat.
complaint: réclamation, accusation.
decline: déclin, diminuer, baisse, refuser, dépérir, régression.
distraction: distraction, récréation, amusement, détente.
dying: mourant, décédant.
ear: oreille, épi.
encouraging: encourageant, incitant, réconfortant.
endurance: endurance, résistance, autonomie.
entreated: supplia, implorèrent.
entreating: implorant, suppliant.
heightened: aggravai, rehaussâtes.
interview: entrevue, interview.
observe: observer, respecter, accomplir, réaliser, suivre, remplir, agir selon, assurer.
possibly: de façon possible, de manière possible.
rapid: rapide, prompt.
refused: refusé.
seriously: sérieusement, de manière sérieuse, gravement, de façon sérieuse.
shape: forme, façonner, modeler, profil.
silly: idiot, stupide, bête.
straightforward: simple, pur, franc.
struggle: lutter, combat, se débattre, bataille, luter.
tactic: tactique.
urged: exhorté.
vicar: curé, pasteur.

position to explain his heart to Lucretia, it would not have been for Fielden to object; but to have a clandestine interview with one sister while **betrothed** to the other, **bore** in itself a character too **equivocal** to meet with the simple vicar's approval.

"What can you apprehend?" exclaimed the young man, almost fiercely; for, **harassed** and tortured, his mild nature was driven to bay. "Can you suppose that I shall encourage my own misery by the guilty **pleadings** of **unavailing** love? All that I ask is the luxury—yes, the luxury, long unknown to me, of candour—to place fairly and **manfully** before Susan the position in which fate has involved me. Can you suppose that we shall not both take comfort and strength from each other? Our duty is plain and obvious; but it **grows** less painful, encouraged by the lips of a companion in suffering. I tell you fairly that see Susan I will and must. I will watch round her home, wherever it be, hour after hour; come what may, I will find my occasion. Is it not better that the interview should be under your roof, within the same walls which shelter her sister? There, the place itself **imposes restraint** on despair. Oh, sir, this is no time for formal scruples; be **merciful**, I beseech you, not to me, but to Susan. I judge of her by myself. I know that I shall go to the altar more **resigned** to the future if for once I can give vent to what weighs upon my heart. She will then see, as I do, that the path before me is inevitable; she will **compose** herself to face the fate that **compels** us. We shall swear **tacitly** to each other, not to love, but to conquer love. Believe me, sir, I am not selfish in this prayer; an instinct, the **intuition** which human grief has into the secrets of human grief, assures me that that which I ask is the best **consolation** you can afford to Susan. You own she is ill,—suffering. Are not your fears for her very life—O Heaven? for her very life—gravely awakened? And yet you see we have been silent to each other! Can speech be more fatal in its results than silence? Oh, for her sake, hear me!"

The good man's tears fell fast. His scruples were shaken; there was truth in what Mainwaring urged. He did not yield, but he promised to reflect, and **inform** Mainwaring, by a line, in the evening. Finding this was all he could effect, the young man at last suffered him to leave the house, and Fielden

---

French

betrothed: se fiancé, vous fiançâtes, nous fiançâmes, me fiançai, fiancé, te fianças.
bore: ennuyer, forer, percer, alésage, rencontrer, lasser, fatiguer, vrille, toucher, calibre.
compel: obliger, imposer, contraindre, astreindre.
compose: composer, écrire.
consolation: consolation.
equivocal: équivoque, douteux, incertain, ambigu.
grows: grandit, croît.
harassed: harcelâtes, tracassâtes.
imposes: impose, contraint.
inform: informer, renseigner, faire part de.
intuition: intuition.
manfully: de façon vaillante, de manière vaillante.
merciful: indulgent, Clément, sensible, miséricordieux.
pleading: plaidant, excipant, implorant.
resigned: démissionnèrent, résignâmes.
restraint: contrainte, mesure d'austérité, sollicitation, retenue, modération, maîtrise de soi, bridage, punition corporelle.
tacitly: de façon tacite, de manière tacite, tacitement.
unavailing: inutile, inefficace.

hastened to take counsel of Dalibard; that wily persuader soon **reasoned** away Mr. Fielden's last faint objection. It now only remained to procure Susan's **assent** to the interview, and to **arrange** that it should be **undisturbed**. Mr. Fielden should take out the children the next morning. Dalibard volunteered to **contrive** the absence of Lucretia at the hour **appointed**. Mrs. Fielden alone should remain within, and might, if it were **judged** proper, be present at the interview, which was fixed for the **forenoon** in the usual drawing-room. Nothing but Susan's consent was now necessary, and Mr. Fielden **ascended** to her room. He **knocked** twice,—no sweet voice bade him enter; he opened the door gently,—Susan was in **prayer**. At the **opposite** corner of the room, by the side of her bed, she knelt, her face buried in her hands, and he heard, low and **indistinct**, the murmur broken by the **sob**. But **gradually**, as he stood unperceived, sob and murmur ceased,— prayer had its customary and blessed effect with the pure and earnest. And when Susan rose, though the tears yet **rolled** down her cheeks, the face was serene as an angel's.

The pastor approached and took her hand; a **blush** then **broke** over her countenance,—she trembled, and her eyes fell on the ground. "My child," he said **solemnly**, "God will hear you!" And after those words there was a long silence. He then drew her passively towards a seat, and sat down by her, embarrassed how to begin. At length he said, looking somewhat aside, "Mr. Mainwaring has made me a request,—a prayer which relates to you, and which I **refer** to you. He asks you to grant him an interview before you leave us,—to-morrow, if you will. I refused at first,—I am in doubt still; for, my dear, I have always found that when the feelings move us, our duty becomes less clear to the human heart,—corrupt, we know, but still it is often a safer **guide** than our reason. I never knew reason **unerring**, except in **mathematics**; we have no Euclid," and the good man smiled mournfully, "in the problems of real life. I will not urge you one way or the other; I put the case before you: Would it, as the young man says, give you comfort and strength to see him once again while, while—in short, before your sister is—I

French

appointed: nommèrent, fixé, appointâmes, attitré.
arrange: arranger, disposer, ranger, régler, ordonner, accommoder, agencer, organiser.
ascended: montai.
assent: assentiment, affirmation, consentement, avis conforme.
blush: rougir, blush, opalescence.
broke: fauché, cassés de fabrication.
contrive: inventer.

forenoon: matinée.
gradually: petit à petit, peu à peu, graduellement, de proche en proche, de façon graduelle, de manière graduelle.
guide: guide, diriger, conduire, mener, régler, aboutir.
indistinct: confus, touffu, trouble, indistinct.
judged: jugé.
knocked: frappâmes.
mathematics: mathématiques.

opposite: opposé, en face de, contraire.
prayer: prière, oraison.
reasoned: raisonné.
refer: référer, réfère, déférer.
rolled: roulé, enroula, laminé.
sob: sanglot, pleurer.
solemnly: solennellement, de façon solennelle, de manière solennelle.
undisturbed: paisible, non détériorée, calme.
unerring: infaillible, sûr.

mean before—that is, would it **soothe** you now, to have an **unreserved communication** with him? He **implores** it. What shall I answer?"

"This trial, too!" muttered Susan, almost inaudibly,—"this trial which I once **yearned** for; "and the hand clasped in Fielden's was as **cold** as **ice**. Then, **turning** her eyes to her guardian somewhat **wildly**, she cried: "But to what end, what **object**? Why should he **wish** to see me?"

"To take greater courage to do his duty; to feel less **unhappy** at—at—"

"I will see him," interrupted Susan, firmly,—"he is right; it will **strengthen** both. I will see him!"

"But **human nature** is **weak**, my child; if my heart be so now, what will be yours?"

"Fear me not," answered Susan, with a sad, **wandering** smile; and she repeated **vacantly**: "I will see him!"

The good man looked at her, **threw** his arms round her wasted form, and **lifting** up his eyes, his lips **stirred** with such half-syllabled **words** as fathers breathe on high.

French

cold: froid, rhume.
communication: communication, renseignement.
human: humain.
ice: glace, crème glacée.
implore: implorer, conjurer.
lifting: levage, relevage, remontage, scarification, soulevé, prise, transfert, passerelle de chargement relevable, arrachage, levée du revêtement comme suite du revernissage, élevant.
nature: nature, caractère.
object: objet, chose.
soothe: abattre, rassurer, calmer, apaiser.
stirred: remué.
strengthen: fortifier, renforcer, raffermir.
threw: jetèrent, jeta, jetâmes.
turning: tournant, changeant, retournant, déviant, virage, rotation.
unhappy: malheureux, mécontent.
unreserved: non réservé.
vacantly: de façon vide, de manière vide.
wandering: errant, vaguant, vagabond, nomade.
weak: faible, mou, lâche, débile.
wildly: de façon sauvage, de manière sauvage.
wish: souhait, désir, vouloir, volonté, gré.
word: mot, parole, promesse.
yearned: soupiré, languîtes.

CHAPTER VIII

THE DISCOVERY

Dalibard had **undertaken** to get Lucretia from the house,—in fact, her approaching **marriage** rendered necessary a communication with Mr. Parchmount, as executor to her uncle's will, **relative** to the **transfer** of her portion; and she had asked Dalibard to accompany her **thither**; for her pride shrank from **receiving** the lawyer in the **shabby** parlour of the shabby lodging-house; she therefore, that evening, fixed the next day, before noon, for the **visit**. A carriage was **hired** for the **occasion**, and when it drove off, Mr. Fielden took his children a walk to Primrose Hill, and called, as was agreed, on Mainwaring by the way.

The carriage had scarcely rattled **fifty yards** through the street when Dalibard fixed his eyes with deep and solemn **commiseration** on Lucretia. Hitherto, with **masterly** art, he had kept aloof from **direct explanations** with his pupil; he knew that she would distrust no one like himself. The plot was now **ripened**, and it was time for the main **agent** to **conduct** the catastrophe. The look was so **expressive** that Lucretia felt a chill at her heart, and could not, help **exclaiming**, "What has **happened**? You have some **terrible** tidings to communicate!"

French

agent: agent, représentant, mandataire, intermédiaire, ustensile, outil, instrument, commissionnaire, produit.
commiseration: commisération.
conduct: conduire, guider, mener, diriger, aboutir, procédé, régler.
direct: direct, diriger, guider, régler, droit.
exclaiming: exclamant.
explanation: explication, interprétation, libellé.
expressive: expressif.
fifty: cinquante.
happened: arrivâmes, advinrent, advenu.
hired: louai, louèrent, loué, louâtes, embauché.
marriage: mariage, noces, alliance.
masterly: magistral.
occasion: occasion, lieu, fois.
receiving: recevant, accueillant, réception.
relative: parent, relatif.
ripened: mûrîmes, mûrit.
shabby: mesquin, miteux, usé.
terrible: terrible, affreux.
thither: là.
transfer: transfert, mutation, cession, virement, dépasser, remuer, report, muter, passer, mutons, décalquer.
undertaken: entrepris.
visit: visite, aller voir.
yard: cour, yard, chantier, dépôt, parc, vergue.

"I have indeed to say that which may, perhaps, cause you to **hate** me forever; as we hate those who report our **afflictions**. I must **endure** this; I have **struggled** long between my indignation and my compassion. **Rouse** up your strong mind, and hear me. Mainwaring loves your sister!"

Lucretia uttered a cry that seemed scarcely to come from a human voice,—

"No, no!" she gasped out; "do not tell me. I will hear no more; I will not believe you!"

With an inexpressible pity and softness in his tone, this man, whose career had given him such profound experience in the **frailties** of the human heart, **continued**: "I do not ask you to believe me, Lucretia; I would not now speak, if you had not the opportunity to convince yourself. Even those with whom you live are false to you; at this moment they have arranged all, for Mainwaring to steal, in your **absence**, to your sister. In a few moments more he will be with her; if you yourself would learn what **passes** between them, you have the power."

"I have—I have not—not—the courage; drive on—faster—faster."

Dalibard again was foiled. In this strange **cowardice** there was something so terrible, yet so touching, that it became sublime,—it was the **grasp** of a **drowning** soul at the last **plank**.

"You are right perhaps," he said, after a pause; and **wisely forbearing** all taunt and **resistance**, he left the heart to its own workings.

Suddenly, Lucretia caught at the check-string. "Stop," she exclaimed,— "stop! I will not, I cannot, endure this suspense to last through a life! I will learn the worst. **Bid** him drive back."

"We must descend and walk; you forget we must **enter** unsuspected;" and Dalibard, as the carriage **stopped**, **opened** the door and let down the steps.

French

absence: absence, manque, privation, défaut, vice, insuffisance.
affliction: affliction, chagrin, désolation.
bid: offre, soumission, demander, enchère, prier, tentative de prise, mise dans les enchères, annonce.
continued: continuai, duras, durèrent, durâtes, duré.
cowardice: lâcheté, faiblesse.
drowning: noyant, noyer, submersion, la noyade, couvrant, asphyxie des racines.
endure: supporter, endurer, souffrir, durer, durons, subir, tolérer, soutenir, continuer.
enter: entrer, introduire, inscrire, pénétrer.
forbearing: patient.
frailty: fragilité, faiblesse.
grasp: saisir, agripper, empoigner, compréhension, prise, étreindre.
hate: haïr, haine, détester.
opened: ouvert, ouvrîmes.
passe: dépassé, fané.
plank: planche, panneau.
resistance: résistance, défense.
rouse: exciter, stimuler, irriter, inciter, agacer, hérisser, réveiller.
stopped: arrêtèrent, cessa, stoppâmes, interrompîmes, bouché.
struggled: lutté.
wisely: sagement, de manière sensée, de façon sensée.

Lucretia recoiled, then **pressing** one hand to her heart, she descended, without touching the arm held out to her. Dalibard bade the **coachman** wait, and they walked back to the house.

"Yes, he may see her," exclaimed Lucretia, her face **brightening**. "Ah, there you have not deceived me; I see your stratagem,—I despise it; I know she loves him; she has sought this interview. He is so mild and gentle, so fearful to give pain; he has consented, from pity,—that is all. Is he not pledged to me? He, so **candid**, so ingenuous! There must be truth somewhere in the world. If he is false, where find truth? Dark man, must I look for it in you,—you?"

"It is not my truth I require you to test; I **pretend** not to truth **universal**; I can be true to one, as you may yet discover. But I own your belief is not impossible; my interest in you may have made me rash and unjust,—what you may **overhear**, far from **destroying**, may **confirm** forever your happiness. Would that it may be so!"

"It must be so," returned Lucretia, with a fearful gloom on her brow and in her **accent**; "I will **interpret** every word to my own salvation."

Dalibard's countenance changed, despite his usual control over it. He had set all his chances upon this cast, and it was more **hazardous** than he had deemed. He had **counted** too much upon the jealousy of common natures. After all, how little to the ear of one resolved to deceive herself might pass between these two young persons, meeting not to **avow** attachment, but to take courage from each other! What restraint might they **impose** on their feelings! Still, the game must be played out.

As they now neared the house, Dalibard looked carefully round, lest they should **encounter** Mainwaring on his way to it. He had counted on **arriving** before the young man could get there.

"But," said Lucretia, breaking silence, with an ironical smile,—"but—for your tender **anxiety** for me has, no doubt, provided all means and **contrivance**, all necessary aids to **baseness** and eavesdropping, that can assure my happiness—how am I to be present at this interview?"

French

accent: accent, souligner, emphase.
anxiety: anxiété, inquiétude, angoisse.
arriving: arrivant.
avow: avouer, confesser.
baseness: bassesse.
brightening: surbrillance, avivage, azurage, brillantage, éclaircissant, polissage.
candid: franc, impartial, sincère, candide.
coachman: cocher.
confirm: confirmer, ratifier.
contrivance: invention, ingéniosité, dispositif.
counted: compté.
destroying: détruisant, ravageant.
encounter: rencontre, abord.
hazardous: hasardeux, périlleux, dangereux.
impose: imposer, obliger, contraindre.
interpret: interpréter, traduire.
overhear: entendre par hasard, surprendre.
pressing: pressage, urgent, pièce forgée par pression, moulage, mise en balle, impression, formage à la presse, emboutissage, compression, chargement par introduction d'un bloc préformé, cas particulier d'emboutissage.
pretend: feindre, prétendre, feignent, simuler, se retrancher, faire semblant.
universal: universel, large plat.

"I have provided, as you say," answered Dalibard, in the tone of a man deeply **hurt**, "those means which I, who have found the world one foe and one traitor, deemed the best to distinguish falsehood from truth. I have arranged that we shall enter the house **unsuspected**. Mainwaring and your sister will be in the drawing-room; the room next to it will be vacant, as Mr. Fielden is from home: there is but a glass-door between the two chambers."

"Enough, enough!" and Lucretia turned round and placed her hand **lightly** on the Provencal's arm. "The next hour will **decide** whether the means you **suggest** to learn truth and **defend safety** will be familiar or **loathsome** to me for life,—will decide whether trust is a madness; whether you, my youth's **teacher**, are the wisest of men, or only the most dangerous."

"Believe me, or not, when I say I would rather the decision should **condemn** me; for I, too, have need of confidence in men."

Nothing further was said; the dull street was quiet and **desolate** as usual. Dalibard had taken with him the **key** of the house-door. The door opened noiselessly; they were in the house. Mainwaring's cloak was in the hall; he had arrived a few moments before them. Dalibard **pointed** silently to that evidence in favour of his tale. Lucretia bowed her head. but with a look that implied **defiance**; and (still without a word) she ascended the stairs, and entered the room appointed for concealment. But as she entered, at the farther corner of the chamber she saw Mrs. Fielden seated,—seated, remote and out of hearing. The good-natured woman had yielded to Mainwaring's prayer, and Susan's silent look that **enforced** it, to let their interview be unwitnessed. She did not **perceive** Lucretia till the last **walked** glidingly, but firmly, up to her, placed a **burning** hand on her lips, and whispered: "Hush, betray me not; my happiness for life—Susan's—his—are at stake; I must hear what passes: it is my fate that is **deciding**. Hush! I command; for I have the right."

Mrs. Fielden was awed and startled; and before she could **recover** even **breath**, Lucretia had quitted her side and taken her post at the fatal door. She lifted the corner of the curtain from the glass **panel**, and looked in.

French

breath: souffle, haleine, respiration, le souffle.
burning: brûlant, combustion, cuisson.
condemn: condamner, repousser.
decide: décider, juge.
deciding: décidant, jugeant.
defend: défendre, contester, protéger, soutenir.
defiance: défi.
desolate: sombre, désolé, morne.
enforced: imposèrent, réalisé, forcé.
hurt: blesser, offenser, vexer, nuire, faire mal, endommager, mal.
key: clé, touche, clef, clavette, code, manipulateur.
lightly: légèrement, de façon légre, de manière légre.
loathsome: détestable, répugnant.
panel: panneau, lambris, panel, tableau, jury.
perceive: apercevoir, percevoir, saisir, discerner, perçoivent, s'apercevoir, se rendre compte.
pointed: pointu, aigu.
recover: récupérer, recouvrer, guérir, regagner, retrouver, se remettre.
safety: sécurité, sûreté.
suggest: suggérer, proposer, indiquer, désigner, inspirer.
teacher: enseignant, instituteur, maître, professeur.
unsuspected: insoupçonné.
walked: marcha, promena, déambula.

Mainwaring was seated at a little **distance** from Susan, whose face was turned from her. Mainwaring's countenance was in full view. But it was Susan's voice that met her ear; and though sweet and **low**, it was **distinct**, and even **firm**. It was evident from the words that the **conference** had but just **begun**.

"Indeed, Mr. Mainwaring, you have nothing to explain, nothing of which to **accuse yourself**. It was not for this, believe me,"—and here Susan turned her face, and its aspect of **heavenly innocence** met the **dry**, **lurid** eye of the **unseen** witness,—"not for this, believe me, that I consented to see you. If I did so, it was only because I thought, because I feared from your manner, when we met at times, still more from your evident avoidance to **meet** me at all, that you were unhappy (for I know you kind and honest),—unhappy at the thought that you had wounded me, and my heart could not **bear** that, nor, perhaps, my pride either. That you should have forgotten me—"

"Forgotten you!"

"That you should have been captivated," continued Susan, in a more hurried tone, "by one so superior to me in all things as Lucretia, is very **natural**. I thought, then—thought only—that nothing could cloud your happiness but some reproach of a conscience too **sensitive**. For this I have met you,—met you without a thought which Lucretia would have a right to blame, could she read my heart; met you," and the voice for the first time **faltered**, "that I might say, 'Be at peace; it is your sister that **addresses** you. **Requite** Lucretia's love,—it is deep and strong; give her, as she gives to you, a whole heart; and in your happiness I, your sister—sister to both—I shall be blest.'" With a smile **inexpressibly** touching and ingenuous, she held out her hand as she ceased. Mainwaring sprang **forward**, and despite her struggle, pressed it to his lips, his heart.

"Oh," he exclaimed, in **broken** accents, which gradually became more clear and loud, "what—what have I lost!—lost forever! No, no, I will be worthy of you! I do not, I dare not, say that I love you still! I feel what I owe

---

French

accuse: accuser, dénoncer, incriminer, livrer.
addresses: adresses.
bear: ours, endurer, souffrir, produire, subir, mettre au monde, baisser, faire naître, porter, supporter.
begun: commencé, débuté.
broken: cassé, brisé, rompu.
conference: conférence, séance, association, colloque, congrès.
distance: distance, éloignement.
distinct: net, clair, limpide, distinct.
dry: sec, sécher, sèche.
faltered: hésitai, chancelâmes.
firm: ferme, solide, firme, robuste, entreprise, stable.
forward: en avant, avancer.
heavenly: céleste, divin, du ciel, merveilleux, paradisiaque.
inexpressibly: de façon inexprimable, de manière inexprimable.
innocence: innocence, naïveté.
low: bas, basse, lâche, dépression, abject.
lurid: aigu, acéré, âcre, rude, tranchant, piquant, coupant, aigre, perçant.
meet: rencontrer, réunir, se réunir.
natural: naturel, marche, bécarre, au naturel, simple, inné.
requite: récompenser.
sensitive: sensible, délicat.
unseen: inaperçu, invisible.
yourself: vous.

to Lucretia. How I became first ensnared, **infatuated**; how, with your **image** graven so deeply here—"

"Mainwaring—Mr. Mainwaring—I must not hear you. Is this your promise?"

"Yes, you must hear me yet. How I became engaged to your sister,—so different indeed from you,—I start in amaze and **bewilderment** when I seek to conjecture. But so it was. For me she has forfeited fortune, rank, all which that proud, stern heart so prized and **coveted**. Heaven is my **witness** how I have struggled to **repay** her affection with my own! If I cannot succeed, at least all that faith and gratitude can give are hers. Yes, when I leave you, **comforted** by your **forgiveness**, your prayers, I shall have strength to tear you from my heart; it is my duty, my fate. With a firm step I will go to these abhorred nuptials. Oh, shudder not, turn not away. Forgive the word; but I must speak,—my heart will out; yes, abhorred nuptials! Between my grave and the altar, would—would that I had a choice!"

From this burst, which in vain from time to time Susan had sought to **check**, Mainwaring was startled by an **apparition** which **froze** his veins, as a **ghost** from the grave. The door was **thrown** open, and Lucretia stood in the aperture,—stood, gazing on him, face to face; and her own was so **colourless**, so **rigid**, so locked in its livid and **awful solemnity** of aspect that it was, indeed, as one risen from the dead.

Dismayed by the abrupt cry and the changed face of her lover, Susan turned and beheld her sister. With the impulse of the **pierced** and loving heart, which divined all the agony inflicted, she sprang to Lucretia's side, she fell to the ground and clasped her **knees**.

"Do not heed, do not believe him; it is but the **frenzy** of a moment. He spoke but to deceive me,—me, who loved him once! Mine alone, mine is the **crime**. He knows all your worth. Pity—pity—pity on yourself, on him, on me!"

Lucretia's eyes fell with the glare of a fiend upon the imploring face lifted to her own. Her lips **moved**, but no sound was audible. At length she drew

---

French

apparition: apparition.
awful: horrible, abominable, hideux, terrible, abject, odieux.
bewilderment: égarement, ahurissement, confusion.
check: chèque, vérifier, contrôle, réprimer, surveiller, retenir, enrayer, bride, examiner, enregistrer, cocher.
colourless: incolore, sans couleur.
comforted: soulagé.
coveted: convoitèrent.

crime: crime, délit, infraction.
forgiveness: pardon, rémission.
frenzy: frénésie.
froze: gela, gelâmes, gelèrent.
ghost: fantôme, apparition, image fantôme, revenant, spectre, hématie dépigmentée.
image: image, figure.
infatuated: infatué, entiché.
knee: genou, le genou, coude.
moved: ému, émurent, remuèrent, mus, mouvé, émus, déplacé.

pierced: perça, percèrent.
repay: rembourser, reprendre.
rigid: rigide, raide.
solemnity: solennité.
thrown: jeté, faillé, rappel publicitaire.
witness: témoin, assister, être présent.

herself from her sister's clasp, and walked steadily up to Mainwaring. She **surveyed** him with a calm and cruel gaze, as if she enjoyed his shame and terror. Before, however, she spoke, Mrs. Fielden, who had watched, as one spellbound, Lucretia's movements, and, without hearing what had passed, had the full foreboding of what would **ensue**, but had not stirred till Lucretia herself terminated the suspense and broke the charm of her awe,—before she spoke, Mrs. Fielden rushed in, and **giving** vent to her agitation in loud sobs, as she threw her arms round Susan, who was still kneeling on the **floor**, brought something of **grotesque** to the more tragic and fearful character of the scene.

"My uncle was right; there is **neither** courage nor honour in the low-born! He, the schemer, too, is right. All hollow,—all false!" Thus said Lucretia, with a strange sort of musing accent, at first scornful, at last only **quietly** abstracted. "**Rise**, sir," she then **added**, with her most imperious tone; "do you not hear your Susan weep? Do you fear in my **presence** to console her? **Coward** to her, as **forsworn** to me! Go, sir, you are free!"

"Hear me," faltered Mainwaring, **attempting** to **seize** her hand; "I do not ask you to forgive; but—"

"Forgive, sir!" interrupted Lucretia, rearing her head, and with a look of freezing and unspeakable majesty. "There is only one person here who needs a pardon; but her fault is inexpiable: it is the woman who stooped **beneath** her—"

With these words, hurled from her with a scorn which crushed while it galled, she **mechanically** drew round her form her black mantle; her eye glanced on the deep mourning of the **garment**, and her memory recalled all that love had cost her; but she added no other reproach. **Slowly** she turned away. **Passing** Susan, who **lay** senseless in Mrs. Fielden's arms, she paused, and kissed her forehead.

"When she recovers, madam," she said to Mrs. Fielden, who was moved and astonished by this softness, "say that Lucretia Clavering uttered a **vow** when she kissed the brow of William Mainwaring's future wife!"

French

added: ajouta, additionnas, adjoignit.
attempting: essayant, attentant.
beneath: sous, dessous.
coward: lâche, peureux, couard, poltron.
ensue: s'ensuivre, résultez.
floor: plancher, étage, sol, taux plancher, mur.
forsworn: abjuré.
garment: vêtement, habit.
giving: donnant, offrant, aboulant.
grotesque: ubuesque, grotesque.
lay: poser, posons, laïque, coucher, pondre, commettage.
mechanically: de façon mécanique, de manière mécanique, mécaniquement.
neither: ni, non plus, personne, nul.
passing: passant, dépassement, écoulement.
presence: présence, prestance, degré de présence.
quietly: paisiblement, tranquillement, de façon calme, de manière calme, calmement.
rise: monter, surgir, lever, sursauter, se soulever, se lever, hausse, augmenter, hauteur, s'élever, élévation.
seize: saisir, agripper, s'emparer de, gripper, attraper.
slowly: lentement, de façon lente, de manière lente, doucement.
surveyed: levé, examiné.
vow: voeu, vouer, serment.

Olivier Dalibard was still **seated** in the **parlour below** when Lucretia entered. Her face yet **retained** its almost **unearthly rigidity** and calm; but a sort of **darkness** had come over its **ashen** pallor,—that **shade** so **indescribable**, which is seen in the human face, after long **illness**, a day or two before death. Dalibard was **appalled**; for he had too often seen that **hue** in the dying not to recognize it now. His **emotion** was sufficiently genuine to give more than usual **earnestness** to his voice and gesture, as he **poured** out every word that spoke **sympathy** and **soothing**. For a long time Lucretia did not **seem** to **hear** him; at last her face softened,—the ice broke.

"**Motherless, friendless, lone,** alone **forever, undone,** undone!" she **murmured**. Her head sank upon the shoulder of her **fearful counsellor, unconscious** of its resting-place, and she burst into tears,—tears which perhaps saved her **reason** or her life.

French

appalled: consternai, épouvantâtes.
ashen: cendreux.
below: sous, dessous, en bas.
counsellor: conseiller, guide.
darkness: obscurité, ténèbres.
earnestness: sérieux, gravité.
emotion: émotion, attendrissement, sentiment.
fearful: effrayant, affreux, craintif.
forever: pour toujours, toujours.
friendless: sans amis.
hear: entendre, ouïr, oyons, oient, écouter, ois, oyez.
hue: teinte, nuance, tonalité chromatique.
illness: maladie, infirmité.
indescribable: indescriptible.
lone: solitaire, seul.
motherless: sans mère.
murmured: murmuré.
parlour: salon.
poured: versé, en vrac.
reason: raison, cause, motif.
retained: retînmes, retint, retenu.
rigidity: rigidité, raideur.
seated: assis.
seem: sembler, paraître.
shade: ombre, nuance, teinte.
soothing: calmant, lénitif, rassurant, abattant, apaisant.
sympathy: sympathie, compassion.
unconscious: inconscient, évanoui, sans connaissance.
undone: défait, annulé.
unearthly: surnaturel, sinistre.

CHAPTER IX

A SOUL WITHOUT HOPE

When Mr. Fielden **returned** home, Lucretia had **quitted** the house. She left a line for him in her usual bold, clear handwriting, **referring** him to his **wife** for explanation of the reasons that forbade a further **residence** beneath his roof. She had removed to an **hotel** until she had **leisure** to arrange her **plans** for the **future**. In a **few** months she should be of age; and in the meanwhile, who now **living claimed authority** over her? For the rest, she added, "I **repeat** what I told Mr. Mainwaring: all engagement between us is at an end; he will not insult me either by **letter** or by visit. It is natural that I should at **present** shrink from seeing Susan Mivers. Hereafter, if permitted, I will visit Mrs. Mainwaring."

Though all had chanced as Mr. Fielden had desired (if, as he once half **meditated**, he had spoken to Lucretia herself); though a marriage that could have brought happiness to **none**, and would have made the misery of two, was at an end,—he yet felt a **bitter** pang, almost of remorse, when be **learned** what had **occurred**. And Lucretia, before secretly **disliked** (if any one he could dislike), became dear to him at once, by sorrow and compassion. Forgetting every other person, he hurried to the hotel Lucretia had **chosen**; but her **coldness** deceived and her pride **repelled** him. She listened **dryly** to

---

French

authority: autorité, pouvoir, instance.
bitter: amer, âcre, acerbe.
chosen: choisi, élu, opté.
claimed: réclamé, arrogeâmes.
coldness: froideur.
disliked: détestâtes.
dryly: sèchement.
few: peu, peu de.
future: avenir, futur.
hotel: hôtel.
learned: apprit, cultivé, savant,
érudit.
leisure: loisir.
letter: lettre, missive, la lettre, caractère.
living: vivant, habitant, en vie, logeant, bénéfice.
meditated: méditâtes, songea.
none: aucun, personne, nul.
occurred: arriva, survins.
plan: plan, projet, dessein, organiser, intention, esquisser, propos.
present: présent, cadeau, actuel, offrir, don.
quitted: quittèrent.
referring: référant, déférant.
repeat: répéter, répète, reprise, redire.
repelled: repoussas, refusé.
residence: résidence, domicile, habitation, demeure, logement, gîte, logis.
returned: retourné, renvoyé.
wife: femme, épouse.

all he said, and merely replied: "I feel only gratitude at my escape. Let this subject now close forever."

Mr. Fielden left her presence with less anxious and commiserating feelings,—perhaps all had chanced for the best. And on returning home, his whole mind became absorbed in alarm for Susan. She was **delirious**, and in great danger; it was many weeks before she **recovered**. Meanwhile, Lucretia had removed into private apartments, of which she withheld the address. During this time, therefore, they lost sight of her.

If amidst the **punishments** with which the sombre imagination of poets has **diversified** the Realm of the tortured Shadows, it had **depicted** some soul condemned to look **evermore** down into an abyss, all change to its gaze forbidden, **chasm** upon chasm **yawning** deeper and deeper, darker and darker, endless and **infinite**, so that, **eternally** gazing, the soul became, as it were, a part of the abyss,—such an image would **symbol** forth the state of Lucretia's mind.

It was not the mere **desolation** of one whom love has **abandoned** and betrayed. In the abyss were mingled **inextricably** together the gloom of the past and of the future,—there, the broken fortunes, the crushed ambition, the ruin of the worldly expectations long inseparable from her schemes; and amidst them, the angry shade of the more than father, whose heart she had **wrung**, and whose old age she had speeded to the grave. These sacrifices to love, while love was left to her, might have haunted her at moments; but a smile, a word, a glance, banished the **regret** and the remorse. Now, love being **razed** out of life, the ruins of all else loomed dismal amidst the darkness; and a voice rose up, **whispering**: "Lo, fool, what thou hast lost because thou didst believe and love!" And this thought grasped together the two worlds of being,—the what has been, and the what shall be. All hope seemed stricken from the future, as a man strikes from the **calculations** of his income the returns from a property **irrevocably** lost. At her age but few of her sex have parted with religion; but even such **mechanical** faith as the lessons of her childhood, and the constrained **conformities** with Christian **ceremonies**, had instilled, had long since **melted** away in the hard scholastic

French

abandoned: abandonné, délaissa, immoral, malsain, abject.
calculation: calcul, note, addition.
ceremony: cérémonie.
chasm: abîme, gouffre.
conformity: conformité.
delirious: délirant.
depicted: peignîmes, dépeignirent, peint.
desolation: désolation, dévastation, solitude.
diversified: diversifié.
eternally: éternellement, de façon éternelle, de manière éternelle.
evermore: toujours.
inextricably: inextricablement, de façon inextricable, de manière inextricable.
infinite: infini, illimité.
irrevocably: de façon irrévocable, de manière irrévocable.
mechanical: mécanique, maquette, machinal.
melted: fondu, cuit.
punishment: punition, peine, châtiment, sanction.
razed: rasa, rasâmes, rasé, rasèrent.
recovered: récupéra, recouvra.
regret: regret, ménager.
symbol: symbole, attribut, emblème, signe.
whispering: chuchotement, murmure.
wrung: tordu, essoré.
yawning: bâillement, béant.

scepticism of her fatal tutor,—a scepticism which had won, with little effort, a reason delighting in the **maze** of doubt, and easily narrowed into the cramped and iron logic of **disbelief** by an intellect that **scorned** to **submit** where it failed to comprehend. Nor had faith given place to those large moral truths from which philosophy has sought to restore the proud statue of Pagan Virtue as a substitute for the meek symbol of the Christian cross. By temperament unsocial, nor readily moved to the genial and **benevolent**, that absolute egotism in which Olivier Dalibard **centred** his dreary **ethics** seemed **sanctioned** to Lucretia by her studies into the motives of man and the history of the world. She had read the **chronicles** of States and the **memoirs** of statesmen, and seen how craft carries on the movements of an age. Those Viscontis, Castruccios, and Medici; those Richelieus and Mazarins and De Retzs; those Loyolas and Mohammeds and Cromwells; those Monks and Godolphins; those Markboroughs and Walpoles; those founders of history and dynasties and **sects**; those leaders and dupers of men, greater or lesser, **corrupters** or corrupt, all standing out prominent and **renowned** from the **guiltless** and laurelless obscure,—seemed to win, by the homage of **posterity**, the rewards that attend the **deceivers** of their time. By a superb **arrogance** of **generalization**, she transferred into private life, and the rule of commonplace actions, the policy that, to the **abasement** of honour, has so often triumphed in the guidance of States. Therefore, betimes, the whole frame of society was changed to her eye, from the calm aspect it wears to those who live united with their kind; she viewed all seemings with suspicion; and before she had entered the world, prepared to live in it as a **conspirator** in a city **convulsed**, **spying** and espied, schemed against and scheming,—here the crown for the **crafty**, there the **axe** for the **outwitted**.

But her love—for love is trust—had led her half way forth from this maze of the intellect. That fair youth of inexperience and candour which seemed to bloom out in the face of her betrothed; his very **shrinking** from the schemes so natural to her that to her they seemed even innocent; his apparent reliance on mere masculine ability, with the plain aids of **perseverance** and honesty,—all had an attraction that **plucked** her back from herself. If she

French

abasement: abaissement, humiliation.
arrogance: arrogance.
axe: hache, cognée.
benevolent: bienveillant.
centred: centré.
chronicle: chronique.
conspirator: conspirateur, comploteur.
convulsed: convulsionna, bouleversé.
corrupter: corrupteur.
crafty: astucieux, malin, rusé.
deceiver: trompeur.
disbelief: incrédulité.
ethic: éthique.
generalization: généralisation.
guiltless: innocent.
maze: labyrinthe, dédale.
memoir: mémoire, livre mémorial.
outwitted: dépista.
perseverance: persévérance, ténacité.
plucked: plumé.
posterity: postérité.
renowned: renommé, célèbre.
sanctioned: sanctionné.
scepticism: scepticisme.
scorned: dédaigné.
sect: secte.
shrinking: rétrécissant, perte de volume, décatissage, contraction, retrait.
spying: espionnage, épiant.
submit: soumettre, abdiquer, se soumettre.

clung to him firmly, **blindly**, **credulously**, it was not as the lover alone. In the lover she beheld the good angel. Had he only died to her, still the angel smile would have survived and **warned**. But the man had not died; the angel itself had deceived; the wings could **uphold** her no more,—they had touched the **mire**, and were sullied with the **soil**; with the **stain**, was forfeited the strength. All was deceit and **hollowness** and treachery. Lone again in the **universe** rose the **eternal** I. So down into the abyss she looked, depth upon depth, and the darkness had no relief, and the deep had no end.

Olivier Dalibard alone, of all she knew, was **admitted** to her **seclusion**. He played his part as might be expected from the singular patience and penetration which belonged to the genius of his character. He forbore the most distant allusion to his attachment or his hopes. He evinced sympathy rather by **imitating** her silence, than attempts to console. When he spoke, he sought to interest her mind more than to **heal** directly the deep **wounds** of her heart. There is always, to the **afflicted**, a certain charm in the depth and bitterness of eloquent misanthropy. And Dalibard, who **professed** not to be a man-hater, but a world-scorner, had powers of language and of **reasoning commensurate** with his astute intellect and his profound research. His society became not only a relief, it grew almost a want, to that stern sorrower. But whether alarmed or not by the influence she felt him gradually **acquiring**, or whether, through some haughty desire to rise once more **aloft** from the state of her rival and her lover, she made one sudden effort to grasp at the rank from which she had been hurled. The only living person whose **connection** could re-open to her the great world, with its splendours and its **scope** to ambition, was Charles Vernon. She scarcely admitted to her own mind the idea that she would now accept, if offered, the suit she had before despised; she did not even contemplate the **renewal** of that suit,—though there was something in the gallant and disinterested character of Vernon which should have made her believe he would regard their altered fortunes rather as a claim on his honour than a release to his engagements. But hitherto no communication had passed between them; and this was strange if he retained the same intentions which he had announced at Laughton.

French

acquiring: acquérant.
admitted: admîmes, admirent.
afflicted: affligeas, désolèrent.
aloft: en haut, en l'air, vol.
blindly: de façon aveugle, aveuglément, de manière aveugle.
commensurate: proportionné.
connection: connexion, raccord, liaison, ligue, chaîne de connexion, rapport, branchement, relation, réunion, jonction, communication.
credulously: de façon crédule, de manière crédule.
eternal: éternel, perpétuel.
heal: guérir, assainir, cicatriser.
hollowness: creux, son caverneux, cavité.
imitating: imitant, copiant.
mire: mire, bourbier, boue.
professed: confessé, professai.
reasoning: raisonnement.
renewal: renouvellement, reconduction.
scope: portée, champ d'application, étendue, cadre, compétence.
seclusion: solitude.
soil: sol, terre, souiller, salir, barbouiller.
stain: tache, salir, souiller, colorant, teinture.
universe: univers.
uphold: soutenir, maintenir.
warned: avertîmes, alertâmes.
wound: blessure, plaie.

Putting aside, we say, however, all such **considerations**, Vernon had sought her friendship, called her "cousin," enforced the distant relationship between them. Not as lover, but as kinsman,—the only kinsman of her own rank she possessed,—his position in the world, his connections, his brilliant range of acquaintance, made his counsel for her future plans, his aid in the re-establishment of her **consequence** (if not—as wealthy, still as well-born), and her **admission** amongst her equals, of price and value. It was worth sounding the depth of the friendship he had offered, even if his love had passed away with the fortune on which doubtless it had been based.

She took a bold step,—she wrote to Vernon: not even to allude to what had passed between them; her pride forbade such unwomanly vulgarity. The baseness that was in her took at least a more delicate exterior. She wrote to him simply and **distantly**, to state that there were some books and trifles of hers left at Laughton, which she prized beyond their **trivial** value, and to request, as she believed him to be **absent** from the Hall, **permission** to call at her old home, in her way to a visit in a neighbouring county, and point out to whomsoever he might **appoint** to meet her, the effects she deemed herself privileged to claim. The letter was one merely of business, but it was a sufficient test of the **friendly** feelings of her former suitor.

She sent this letter to Vernon's house in London, and the next day came the answer.

Vernon, we must own, entirely **sympathized** with Sir Miles in the solemn injunctions the old man had bequeathed. Immediately after the death of one to whom we owe gratitude and love, all his desires take a **sanctity** irresistible and **ineffable**; we **adopt** his affection, his **dislikes**, his **obligations**, and his wrongs. And after he had read the copy of Lucretia's letter, inclosed to him by Sir Miles, the conquest the poor baronet had made over resentment and vindictive emotion, the evident effort at **passionless** justice with which he had provided **becomingly** for his niece, while he **cancelled** her claims as his heiress, had filled Vernon with a reverence for his wishes and decisions that silenced all those inclinations to over-generosity which an **unexpected** inheritance is apt to create towards the less **fortunate** expectants.

French

absent: absent.
admission: admission, entrée, aveu, confession, accueil, réception, abord, accès.
adopt: adopter, approuver, choisir.
appoint: nommer, désigner, appointer.
becomingly: de façon convenable, de manière convenable.
cancelled: annulé.
consequence: conséquence, répercussion, suite, aboutissement.
consideration: considération, rémunération, provision, étude, délibération, cause, contrepartie.
dislike: antipathie, détester, dédaigner.
distantly: de façon lointaine, de manière lointaine.
fortunate: heureux, chanceux.
friendly: amical, aimable, gentil, affable, amène.
ineffable: ineffable.
obligation: obligation, engagement.
passionless: sans passion.
permission: autorisation, permission, licence.
sanctity: sainteté.
sympathized: compatis, sympathisa.
trivial: insignifiant, banal.
unexpected: inattendu, imprévu, inespéré.

Nevertheless, Lucretia's direct application, her formal appeal to his common courtesy as host and kinsman, perplexed greatly a man ever accustomed to a certain **chivalry** towards the sex; the usual **frankness** of his disposition suggested, however, plain dealing as the best escape from his dilemma, and therefore he answered thus: —

Madam, — Under other circumstances it would have given me no common pleasure to place the house that you so long **inhabited** again at your disposal; and I feel so **painfully** the position which my refusal of your request **inflicts** upon me, that rather than resort to excuses and **pretexts**, which, while **conveying** an impression of my sincerity, would seem almost like an insult to yourself, I venture frankly to inform you that it was the dying wish of my **lamented** kinsman, in consequence of a letter which came under his eye, that the welcome you had hitherto received at Laughton should be withdrawn. Pardon me, Madam, if I express myself thus bluntly; it is somewhat necessary to the **vindication** of my character in your eyes, both as regards the honour of your request and my **tacit** resignation of hopes **fervently** but too **presumptuously entertained**. In this most painful candour, Heaven forbid that I should add **wantonly** to your self-reproaches for the fault of youth and inexperience, which I should be the last person to judge rigidly, and which, had Sir Miles's life been spared, you would doubtless have **amply repaired**. The feelings which **actuated** Sir Miles in his latter days might have changed; but the injunction those feelings prompted I am bound to respect.

For the mere matter of business on which you have done me the honour to address me, I have only to say that any orders you may give to the **steward**, or transmit through any person you may send to the Hall, with regard to the effects you so naturally desire to claim, shall be **implicitly** obeyed.

And believe me, Madam (though I do not **presume** to add those expressions which might rather **heighten** the offence I fear this letter will give you), that the assurance of your happiness in the choice you have made,

---

French

actuated: déclenchai, actionné.
amply: amplement, de façon ample, de manière ample.
chivalry: chevalerie.
conveying: acheminant, transmettant, véhiculant.
entertained: distrait, divertites, vous régalâtes, te régalas, se régalèrent, nous régalâmes, me régalai.
fervently: ardemment, de façon fervente, de manière fervente.
frankness: franchise.
heighten: aggraver, amplifier, rehausser, augmenter.
implicitly: implicitement, de façon implicite, de manière implicite.
inflict: infliger, imposer.
inhabited: habitèrent.
lamented: lamenté.
painfully: de manière pénible, péniblement, de façon pénible.
presume: présumer, supposer.
presumptuously: présomptueusement, de façon présomptueuse, de manière présomptueuse.
pretext: prétexte.
repaired: réparé.
steward: intendant, commissaire, économe, steward.
tacit: tacite.
vindication: justification, revendication, défense.
wantonly: de façon dévergondée, de manière dévergondée.

and which now no obstacle can oppose, will considerably—lighten the **pain** with which I shall long **recall** my ungracious reply to your communication.

I have the honour to be, etc.,
C. *Vernon St. John.*
Brook Street, Dec. 28, 18—.

The receipt of such a letter could hardly add to the profounder grief which preyed in the innermost **core** of Lucretia's heart; but in repelling the effort she had made to distract that grief by ambition, it blackened the sullen despondency with which she **regarded** the future. As the **insect** in the hollow **snare** of the ant-lion, she felt that there was no footing up the sides of the **cave** into which she had **fallen**; the **sand** gave way to the step. But despondency in her brought no meekness; the cloud did not descend in **rain**; resting over the **horizon**, its darkness was tinged with the fires which it **fed**. The heart, already so embittered, was **stung** and **mortified** into **intolerable** shame and wrath. From the home that should have been hers, in which, as acknowledged heiress, she had **smiled** down on the ruined Vernon, she was banished by him who had **supplanted** her, as one worthless and **polluted**. Though, from motives of obvious delicacy, Vernon had not said expressly that he had seen the letter to Mainwaring, the **unfamiliar** and **formal** tone which he assumed indirectly declared it, and betrayed the **impression** it had made, in spite of his reserve. A living man then was in possession of a secret which justified his **disdain**, and that man was master of Laughton! The suppressed rage which embraced the lost lover extended **darkly** over this witness to that baffled and miserable love. But what availed rage against either? Abandoned and despoiled, she was **powerless** to avenge. It was at this time, when her prospects seemed most dark, her pride was most crushed, and her despair of the future at its **height**, that she turned to Dalibard as the only friend left to her under the sun. Even the vices she **perceived** in him became merits, for they forbade him to despise her. And now, this man rose suddenly into another and higher aspect of character. Of late, though **equally deferential** to her, there had been something more lofty

French

cave: grotte, caverne, creux.
core: noyau, coeur, âme, centre, trognon, carotte, mandrin, tore.
darkly: de façon foncée, de manière foncée.
deferential: respectueux, déférent.
disdain: dédain.
equally: également, pareillement, de même, de façon égale.
fallen: tombé, déchu, abattu, chu.
fed: alimentas, nourrîtes.
formal: formel, officiel.

height: hauteur, altitude, taille.
horizon: horizon.
impression: impression, effet, empreinte, tirage.
insect: insecte.
intolerable: intolérable, insupportable.
mortified: mortifiai, humiliâmes.
pain: douleur, mal, peine.
perceived: aperçûmes, perçûtes, discernèrent.
polluted: polluas, vicié.

powerless: impuissant.
rain: pluie, pleuvoir, la pluie.
recall: rappel, se rappeler, se souvenir, retenir, remémorer.
regarded: considérâtes.
sand: sable, arène.
smiled: souri.
snare: piège, collet.
stung: piqué.
supplanted: supplantâtes.
unfamiliar: inconnu, peu familier.

in his mien, more assured on his brow; gleams of a secret **satisfaction**, even of a joy, that he appeared anxious to **suppress**, as ill in **harmony** with her causes for **dejection**, broke out in his looks and words. At length, one day, after some **preparatory hesitation**, he informed her that he was free to return to France; that even without the peace between England and France, which (known under the name of the Peace of Amiens) had been just concluded, he should have **crossed** the Channel. The **advocacy** and interest of friends whom he had left at Paris had already brought him under the special notice of the wonderful man who then **governed** France, and who sought to unite in its service every description and variety of intellect. He should return to France, and then—why, then, the **ladder** was on the walls of Fortune and the foot **planted** on the step! As he spoke, **confidently** and sanguinely, with the **verve** and assurance of an able man who sees clear the path to his goal, as he sketched with rapid **precision** the nature of his prospects and his hopes, all that **subtle** wisdom which had before often seemed but vague and general, took practical shape and interest, thus applied to the actual circumstances of men; the spirit of intrigue, which seemed mean when employed on mean things, swelled into **statesmanship** and masterly genius to the listener when she saw it linked with the large objects of masculine ambition. Insensibly, therefore, her attention became earnest, her mind aroused. The vision of a field, afar from the scenes of her **humiliation** and despair,—a field for energy, stratagem, and contest,—invited her restless intelligence. As Dalibard had **profoundly calculated**, there was no new channel for her affections,—the source was **dried** up, and the **parched** sands **heaped** over it; but while the heart lay dormant, the mind rose **sleepless**, chafed, and **perturbed**. Through the mind, he indirectly addressed and **subtly** wooed her.

"Such," he said, as he rose to take leave, "such is the career to which I could **depart** with joy if I did not depart alone!"

"Alone!" that word, more than once that day, Lucretia repeated to herself—"alone!" And what career was left to her?—she, too, alone!

French

advocacy: plaidoyer, art de plaider.
calculated: calculâtes, compta.
confidently: de manière confiante, de façon confiante.
crossed: croisé, traversés, décussé, barré.
dejection: abattement, découragement, mélancolie.
depart: partir, pars, s'en aller.
dried: séché, sec.
governed: gouvernâmes, régnèrent.
harmony: harmonie, concorde.
heaped: entassé.
hesitation: hésitation.
humiliation: humiliation.
ladder: échelle, maille filée.
parched: desséché.
perturbed: perturba, brouillèrent.
planted: planté.
precision: précision, exactitude.
preparatory: préparatoire.
profoundly: profondément, de manière profonde, de façon profonde.
satisfaction: satisfaction, contentement.
sleepless: sans sommeil.
statesmanship: habileté politique, sens politique.
subtle: subtil, fin.
subtly: de manière subtile, subtilement, de façon subtile.
suppress: étouffer, réprimer, suffoquer, supprimer.
verve: brio, verve.

In certain **stages** of great grief our natures **yearn** for excitement. This has made some men gamblers; it has made even women drunkards,—it had effect over the serene calm and would-be **divinity** of the poet-sage. When his **son** dies, Goethe does not mourn, he plunges into the absorption of a study **uncultivated** before. But in the great **contest** of life, in the **whirlpool** of **actual** affairs, the stricken heart finds all,—the gambling, the **inebriation**, and the study.

We pause here. We have **pursued** long enough that patient **analysis**, with all the **food** for **reflection** that it possibly affords, to which we were **insensibly** led on by an interest, dark and **fascinating**, that grew more and more upon us as we **proceeded** in our research into the early **history** of a person **fated** to **pervert** no **ordinary** powers into no commonplace guilt.

The charm is concluded, the circle closed round; the self-guided **seeker** after **knowledge** has gained the **fiend** for the familiar.

French

actual: réel, effectif, actuel.
analysis: analyse, ventilation, composition, dépouillement, étude.
contest: concours, contester, disputer.
divinity: divinité, théologie.
fascinating: fascinant, passionnant.
fated: destiné, fatal.
fiend: démon, monstre, enragé.
food: nourriture, aliment, pâture.
history: histoire, anamnèse, antécédents.
inebriation: enivrement, état d'ivresse.
insensibly: de façon insensible, de manière insensible.
knowledge: connaissance, savoir.
ordinary: ordinaire.
pervert: pervertir, fausser, dénaturer, dépraver.
proceeded: procédai, avançai.
pursued: poursuivîtes.
reflection: réflexion, reflet.
seeker: chercheur, tête chercheuse.
son: fils, fiston, le fils.
stage: étape, stade, phase, scène, tenue, station, niveau, étage, gare, mettre en scène, théâtre.
uncultivated: inculte.
whirlpool: tourbillon, marmite, récepteur de moût tangentiel.
yearn: soupirer, aspirer, languir.

CHAPTER X

THE RECONCILIATION BETWEEN FATHER AND SON

We pass over an **interval** of some months.

A painter stood at work at the **easel**, his human model before him. He was employed on a **nymph**,—the Nymph Galatea. The subject had been taken before by Salvator, whose genius found all its elements in the wild rocks, gnarled, **fantastic** trees, and **gushing waterfalls** of the **landscape**; in the huge **ugliness** of Polyphemus the lover; in the grace and suavity and unconscious abandonment of the nymph, **sleeking** her tresses dripping from the bath. The painter, on a larger canvas (for Salvator's picture, at least the one we have seen, is among the small sketches of the great **artistic creator** of the **romantic** and grotesque), had **transferred** the subject of the master; but he had left subordinate the landscape and the **giant**, to **concentrate** all his art on the person of the nymph. Middle-aged was the painter, in truth; but he looked old. His hair, though long, was gray and **thin**; his face was **bloated** by **intemperance**; and his hand trembled much, though, from habit, no trace of the **tremor** was **visible** in his work.

A boy, near at hand, was also employed on the same subject, with a **rough chalk** and a bold freedom of touch. He was sketching his design of a Galatea and Polyphemus on the wall; for the wall was only **whitewashed**,

---

French

artistic: artistique.
bloated: gonflé, bouffi.
chalk: craie, poudrer, pierre calcaire, partir en poudre blanche, marquer à la craie, fariner, chaux, calcaire, favori.
concentrate: concentrer, aliment concentrée, se concentrer.
creator: créateur.
easel: chevalet, établi.
fantastic: fantastique, formidable.
giant: géant, colosse.
gushing: jaillissement, giclage.
intemperance: intempérance.
interval: intervalle, temps mort.
landscape: paysage, texte en largeur, format à l'italienne.
nymph: nymphe.
romantic: romantique.
rough: brut, grossier, rude, rugueux, cru, rustique, maussade, rêche, râpeux.
sleeking: lissage.
thin: mince, maigre, fin.
transferred: transféré, muta, mutâmes, muté, mutèrent.
tremor: tremblement.
ugliness: laideur.
visible: visible, apparent, manifeste.
waterfall: cascade, chute d'eau.
whitewashed: blanchi, badigeonnèrent.

and covered already with the multiform vagaries whether of master or pupils,—caricatures and demigods, hands and feet, **torsos** and monsters, and Venuses. The rude creations, all mutilated, **jarring**, and mingled, gave a cynical, mocking, devil-may-care kind of aspect to the sanctum of art. It was like the dissection-room of the **anatomist**. The boy's sketch was more in harmony with the walls of the studio than the canvas of the master. His nymph, accurately drawn, from the **undressed** proportions of the model, down to the waist, terminated in the scales of a fish. The **forked** branches of the trees stretched weird and imp-like as the hands of **skeletons**. Polyphemus, **peering** over the rocks, had the leer of a demon; and in his gross features there was a certain **distorted**, hideous likeness of the grave and **symmetrical lineaments** of Olivier Dalibard.

All around was **slovenly**, squalid, and poverty-stricken,—rickety, worn-out, rush-bottom chairs; **unsold**, **unfinished** pictures, pell-mell in the corner, covered with dust; broken casts of plaster; a lay-figure battered in its basket-work arms, with its doll-like face all **smudged** and **besmeared**. A pot of porter and a noggin of **gin** on a **stained** deal table, accompanied by two or three broken, smoke-blackened pipes, some **tattered** song-books, and old numbers of the "Covent Garden Magazine," betrayed the tastes of the artist, and accounted for the shaking hand and the bloated form. A jovial, **disorderly**, **vagrant** dog of a painter was Tom Varney. A **bachelor**, of course; **humorous** and **droll**; a **boon** companion, and a terrible **borrower**. Clever enough in his calling; with pains and some method, he had easily gained subsistence and established a name; but he had one trick that soon ruined him in the business part of his profession. He took a fourth of his price in advance; and having once clutched the money, the poor customer might go hang for his picture. The only things Tom Varney ever fairly completed were those for which no order had been given; for in them, somehow or other, his fancy became interested, and on them he lavished the **gusto** which he really possessed. But the subjects were rarely **salable**. Nymphs and deities undraperied have few **worshippers** in England amongst the buyers of "furniture pictures." And, to say truth, nymph and deity had usually a very

French

anatomist: anatomiste.
bachelor: célibataire, garçon, bachelier.
besmeared: barbouillâtes.
boon: faveur, bienfait, chènevotte.
borrower: emprunteur.
disorderly: désordonné, en désordre.
distorted: déformâtes, distordîmes, oblique, tordu.
droll: drôle, comique.
forked: fourchu, bifurqué, en forme de fourche.
gin: gin, mât de levage, rouet, égreneuse, chèvre, genièvre.
gusto: vigueur, délectation, plaisir.
humorous: amusant, humoristique.
jarring: battage, broutage d'un outil, discordant.
lineament: linéament.
peering: échange de trafic.
salable: vendable.
skeleton: squelette, ossature, charpente.
slovenly: négligé.
smudged: maculé.
stained: taché, souillé.
symmetrical: symétrique.
tattered: déguenillé, en lambeaux.
torso: torse.
undressed: déshabillé, dévêtîmes.
unfinished: inachevé, incomplet.
unsold: invendu.
vagrant: vagabond, clochard, chemineau.
worshipper: adorateur.

equivocal look; and if they came from the gods, you would swear it was the gods of the galleries of Drury. When Tom Varney sold a picture, he lived upon clover till the money was gone. But the poorer and less steady **alumni** of the rising school, especially those at war with the Academy, from which Varney was excluded, pitied, despised, yet liked and courted him withal. In addition to his good qualities of blithe song-singer, droll story-teller, and stanch Bacchanalian, Tom Varney was **liberally** good-natured in communicating instruction really valuable to those who knew how to **avail** themselves of a knowledge he had made almost worthless to himself. He was a **shrewd**, though good-natured **critic**, had many little secrets of colouring and composition, which an invitation to supper, or the loan of ten shillings, was sufficient to bribe from him. **Ragged**, out of elbows, **unshaven**, and **slipshod**, he still had his set amongst the gay and the young,—a precious master, a profitable set for his nephew, Master Honore Gabriel! But the poor **rapscallion** had a heart larger than many honest, **painstaking** men. As soon as Gabriel had found him out, and entreated refuge from his fear of his father, the painter clasped him tight in his great slovenly arms, sold a Venus half-price to buy him a bed and a washstand, and **swore** a tremendous **oath** that the son of his poor guillotined sister should share the last shilling in his pocket, the last drop in his can.

Gabriel, fresh from the cheer of Laughton, and **spoiled** by the prodigal gifts of Lucretia, had little gratitude for shillings and **porter**. Nevertheless, he condescended to take what he could get, while he sighed, from the depths of a heart in which cupidity and vanity had become the **predominant rulers**, for a destiny more worthy his genius, and more in keeping with the sphere from which he had descended.

The boy finished his sketch, with an impudent **wink** at the model, flung himself back on his chair, folded his arms, cast a **discontented** glance at the whitened **seams** of the **sleeves**, and soon seemed lost in his own reflections. The painter worked on in silence. The model, whom Gabriel's wink had aroused, half-flattered, half-indignant for a moment, **lapsed** into a **doze**. Outside the window, you heard the song of a canary,—a dingy, smoke-

French

alumni: anciens élèves.
avail: profiter, avantage.
critic: critique, censeur.
discontented: mécontent.
doze: sommeiller, somnoler, remuer la terre avec un bulldozer, faire un petit somme.
lapsed: dévolu par péremption, vieux, périmé, infirme, caduc, délabré.
liberally: de manière libérale, libéralement, de façon libérale.

oath: serment, juron.
painstaking: assidu, soigneux.
porter: porteur, bagagiste, concierge.
predominant: prédominant, principal.
ragged: déchiqueté, déguenillé, dépenaillé, ébavuré, en haillons, en lambeaux, loqueteux.
rapscallion: vaurien.
ruler: règle, dominateur, souverain.
seam: couture, joint, veine, filon,

couche, paille.
shrewd: sagace, avisé, perspicace.
sleeve: manche, douille, bague, chemise, gaine.
slipshod: négligé.
spoiled: gâté, abîmé, défectueux, invalidé.
swore: jura, jurâtes, jurèrent.
unshaven: non rasé.
wink: clin d'oeil, clignement, faire un clin d'oeil.

coloured **canary** that seemed **shedding** its plumes, for they were as ragged as the garments of its master; still, it contrived to sing, trill-trill-trill-trill-trill, as **blithely** as if free in its native woods, or **pampered** by fair hands in a gilded cage. The bird was the only true artist there, it sang as the poet sings,—to obey its nature and vent its heart. Trill-trill-trillela-la-la-trill-trill, went the song,—louder, gayer than usual; for there was a gleam of April sunshine struggling over the **rooftops**. The song at length roused up Gabriel; he turned his chair round, laid his head on one side, listened, and looked **curiously** at the bird.

At length an idea seemed to cross him; he rose, opened the window, drew in the cage, placed it on the chair, then took up one of his uncle's pipes, walked to the fireplace, and thrust the **shank** of the pipe into the bars. When it was red-hot he took it out by the bowl, having first protected his hand from the heat by **wrapping** round it his handkerchief; this done, he returned to the cage. His movements had **wakened** up the dozing model. She **eyed** them at first with dull curiosity, then with lively suspicion; and presently starting up with an exclamation such as no novelist but Fielding dare put into the mouth of a female,—much less a nymph of such **renown** as Galatea,—she sprang across the room, wellnigh upsetting easel and painter, and **fastened** firm hold on Gabriel's shoulders.

"The varment!" she cried **vehemently**; "the good-for-nothing varment! If it had been a **jay**, or a nasty **raven**, well and good; but a poor little canary!"

"Hoity-toity! what are you about, nephew? What's the matter?" said Tom Varney, coming up to the strife. And, indeed, it was time; for Gabriel's teeth were set in his **catlike** jaws, and the **glowing** point of the pipe-shank was within an inch of the cheek of the model.

"What's the matter?" replied Gabriel, suddenly; "why, I was only going to try a little experiment."

"An experiment? Not on my canary, poor dear little thing! The hours and hours that creature has **strained** its throat to say 'Sing and be merry,' when I had not a **rap** in my pocket! It would have made a stone feel to hear it."

French

blithely: de façon joyeuse, de manière joyeuse.
canary: Canari, indicateur, mouchard, serin.
catlike: félin.
curiously: de manière curieuse, avec curiosité, de façon curieuse.
eyed: embryonné.
fastened: attachâtes, verrouillai, liai, lié, lia, liâtes, lias, liâmes, lièrent.
glowing: incandescence, rougeoyant, feu avec incandescence, luire.
jay: geai.
pampered: choyé, dorlotas.
rap: rap, ébranler, rapper.
raven: corbeau, grand corbeau.
renown: renommée, distinction, gloire, réputation.
rooftop: toit.
shank: tige, jambe, jarret, hampe, queue.
shedding: perte, relargage, formation de la foule, chute, déchaussement, foulée.
strained: tendu, contraint, forcé.
vehemently: de façon véhémente, de manière véhémente.
wakened: réveillèrent.
wrapping: emballage, encartage de deux cahiers, banderolage, mise en forme, enveloppement, enrobage, ruban de placage pour mise en forme, capage, cellophanage.

"But I think I can make it **sing** much better than ever,—only just let me try! They say that if you put out the eyes of a canary, it—"

Gabriel was not allowed to conclude his sentence; for here rose that **clamour** of horror and indignation from both painter and model which usually **greets** the announcement of every philosophical discovery,—at least, when about to be **practically** applied; and in the midst of the **hubbub**, the poor little canary, who had been **fluttering** about the **cage** to escape the hand of the benevolent **operator**, set up no longer the cheerful trill-trillela-la-trill, but a **scared** and heart-breaking chirp,—a **shrill**, **terrified** twit-twit-twitter-twit.

"Damn the bird! Hold your tongues!" cried Gabriel Varney, reluctantly giving way, but still eying the bird with the scientific regret with which the illustrious Majendie might contemplate a dog which some brute of a master refused to **disembowel** for the good of the **colics** of **mankind**.

The model seized on the cage, shut the door of the **wires**, and carried it off. Tom Varney **drained** the rest of his porter, and wiped his forehead with the sleeve of his **coat**.

"And to use my **pipe** for such cruelty! Boy, boy, I could not have **believed** it! But you were not in earnest; oh, no, impossible! Sukey, my love—Galatea the divine—calm thy breast; Cupid did but jest.

'Cupid is the God of Laughter,
Quip and jest and **joke**, sir.'"

"If you don't **whip** the little wretch within an inch of his life, he'll have a gallows end on't," replied Galatea.

"Go, Cupid, go and kiss Galatea, and make your peace.

'Oh, leave a kiss within the cup,
And I'll not ask for wine.'

French

believed: crurent, crut, crus, crûtes, cru, crûmes.
cage: cage, soupape à cage, tambour perforé, foulon grillagé, encager, couvercle protecteur, corbeille à matrices, case, camp.
clamour: clameur.
coat: manteau, enduire, pardessus, capote, paletot, couche, napper, pelage, enrober.
colic: colique.
disembowel: éventre.
drained: drainé, assécha.
fluttering: battement des gouvernes, flottant.
greets: salue, accueille.
hubbub: vacarme, brouhaha.
joke: plaisanterie, badiner, blague, farce.
mankind: humanité, genre humain, l'humanité.
operator: opérateur, téléphoniste, entité exploitante.
pipe: tuyau, tube, pipe, conduite, retassure.
practically: de façon pratique, de manière pratique, pratiquement.
scared: effrayé.
shrill: aigu, perçant, strident, criard.
sing: chanter.
terrified: terrifié.
whip: fouet, flageller, battre, faire tournoyer, cravache.
wire: fil, câbler, toile, fil de fer, brin.

And 't is no use asking for wine, or for gin either,—not a drop in the noggin!"

All this while Gabriel, disdaining the **recommendations** held forth to him, was employed in **brushing** his jacket with a very mangy-looking **brush**; and when he had completed that operation he approached his uncle, and **coolly** thrust his hands into that gentleman's waistcoat-pockets.

"Uncle, what have you done with those seven shillings? I am going out to spend the day."

"If you give them to him, Tom, I'll **scratch** your eyes out," cried the model; "and then we'll see how you'll sing. Whip him, I say, whip him!"

But, strange to say, this liberty of the boy quite **reopened** the heart of his uncle,—it was a pleasure to him, who put his hands so habitually into other people's pockets, to be **invested** with the novel **grandeur** of the man **sponged** upon. "That's right, Cupid, son of Cytherea; all's common property amongst friends. Seven shillings, I have 'em not. 'They now are five who once were seven;' but such as they are, we'll share.

> 'Let old Timotheus yield the prize,
> Or both **divide** the crown.'"

"Crowns bear no division, my uncle," said Gabriel, dryly; and he **pocketed** the five shillings. Then, having first **secured** his escape by gaining the **threshold**, he suddenly seized one of the **rickety** chairs by its leg, and **regardless** of the gallantries due to the sex, sent it right against the model, who was shaking her **fist** at him. A **scream** and a fall and a sharp **twit** from the cage, which was hurled nearly into the fireplace, told that the **missive** had taken effect. Gabriel did not wait for the probable reaction; he was in the streets in an **instant**. "This won't do," he muttered to himself; "there is no getting on here. Foolish **drunken** vagabond! no good to be got from him. My father is terrible, but he will make his way in the world. Umph! if I were but

---

French

brush: brosse, pinceau, balai.
brushing: brossage, peignage, fibrillation, thermobrossage, balayage, application au pinceau, affleurer, levée.
coolly: de façon refroidissante, froidement.
divide: diviser, partager, disperser, séparer, répartir, trier, débiter, dissiper, trions.
drunken: ivre.
fist: poing, main.
grandeur: noblesse, grandeur.
instant: instant, moment.
invested: investîmes.
missive: missive.
pocketed: empochés.
recommendation: recommandation, liste de présentation, préconisation, proposition.
regardless: inattentif, indifférent.
reopened: réexaminai, rouvert.
rickety: délabré, vieux, infirme, caduc, rachitique.
scratch: gratter, égratignure, griffer, éraflure, rayure, écorchure, raie, effacer en grattant, accroc, strie.
scream: crier, cri, clameur, hurler.
secured: fixa, fixèrent, fixé, fixâtes.
sponged: épongé.
threshold: seuil, valeur de seuil, limite de circulation.
twit: taquiner, idiot.

his match,—and why not? I am brave, and he is not. There's **fun**, too, in danger."

Thus musing, he took his way to Dalibard's lodgings. His father was at home. Now, though they were but lodgings, and the street not in **fashion**, Olivier Dalibard's apartments had an air of **refinement**, and even elegance, that contrasted both the wretched squalor of the **abode** Gabriel had just left and the meanness of Dalibard's former **quarters** in London, The change seemed to imply that the Provencal had already made some way in the world. And, truth to say, at all times, even in the **lowest ebb** of his fortunes, there was that indescribable **neatness** and **formality** of precision about all the exterior seemings of the ci-devant friend of the **prim** Robespierre which belong to those in whom order and **method** are **strongly** developed,— qualities which give even to **neediness** a certain dignity. As the room and its **owner** met the eye of Gabriel, on whose senses all **externals** had considerable influence, the ungrateful young **ruffian** recalled the kind, tattered, slovenly uncle, whose purse he had just emptied, without one feeling milder than disgust. Olivier Dalibard, always **careful**, if simple, in his dress, with his brow of grave **intellectual** power, and his mien imposing, not only from its calm, but from that nameless refinement which **rarely** fails to give to the **student** the air of a gentleman,—Olivier Dalibard he might dread, he might even **detest**; but he was not ashamed of him.

"I said I would visit you, sir, if you would permit me," said Gabriel, in a tone of **respect**, not unmingled with some defiance, as if in doubt of his reception.

The father's **slow** full eye, so different from the sidelong, furtive glance of Lucretia, turned on the son, as if to penetrate his very heart.

"You look pale and haggard, child; you are fast **losing** your health and **beauty**. Good gifts these, not to be wasted before they can be duly employed. But you have taken your choice. Be an artist,—copy Tom Varney, and prosper." Gabriel remained silent, with his eyes on the floor.

French

abode: demeure, domicile, logis, gîte, habitation, localité, logement.
beauty: beauté.
careful: prudent, soigneux, attentif.
detest: détester, exécrez, abominez, haïr.
ebb: reflux, marée descendante, jusant.
external: externe, extérieur.
fashion: mode, façon.
formality: formalité.
fun: amusement, plaisir, détente, distraction, récréation.
intellectual: intellectuel.
losing: perdant, paumant.
lowest: le plus bas, déclive.
method: méthode, modalité.
neatness: netteté.
neediness: indigence.
owner: propriétaire, détenteur, possesseur, maître de la chose, titulaire, armateur.
prim: collet monté, guindé.
quarter: quartier, trimestre, le quart.
rarely: rarement, de manière rare, de façon rare.
refinement: raffinement, délicatesse, affinage.
respect: respect, égard.
ruffian: apache, brute, voyou.
slow: lent, ralentir, lourd.
strongly: fortement, de façon forte, de manière forte.
student: étudiant, élève.

"You come in time for my farewell," resumed Dalibard. "It is a comfort, at least, that I leave your youth so honourably **protected**. I am about to return to my country; my career is once more before me!"

"Your country,—to Paris?"

"There are fine pictures in the Louvre,—a good place to inspire an artist!"

"You go alone, Father!"

"You forget, young gentleman, you **disown** me as father! Go alone! I thought I told you in the times of our confidence, that I should marry Lucretia Clavering. I rarely fail in my plans. She has lost Laughton, it is true; but 10,000 pounds will make a **fair** commencement to fortune, even at Paris. Well, what do you want with me, worthy **godson** of Honore Gabriel Mirabeau?"

"Sir, if you will let me, I will go with you."

Dalibard **shaded** his brow with his hand, and reflected on the **filial proposal**. On the one hand, it might be convenient, and would certainly be **economical**, to **rid** himself evermore of the mutinous son who had already thrown off his authority; on the other hand, there was much in Gabriel, mutinous and even menacing as he had **lately** become, that promised an unscrupulous **tool** or a sharp-witted accomplice, with interests that every year the ready youth would more and more discover were bound up in his **plotting** father's. This last consideration, **joined**, if not to affection, still to habit,—to the **link** between blood and blood, which even the hardest find it difficult to sever,—prevailed. He extended his pale hand to Gabriel, and said gently,—

"I will take you, if we **rightly** understand each other. Once again in my power, I might **constrain** you to my will, it is true. But I rather confer with you as man to man than as man to boy."

"It is the best way," said Gabriel, firmly.

"I will use no harshness, inflict no punishment,—unless, indeed, amply **merited** by **stubborn disobedience** or **wilful** deceit. But if I meet with these,

French

constrain: contraindre, forcez, forçons.
disobedience: désobéissance.
disown: renier, désavouer.
economical: économique.
fair: foire, juste, kermesse, blond, marché, équitable, moral, bazar, exposition, loyal, beau.
filial: filial.
godson: filleul.
joined: joint, joignirent, relia, associas, accouplâmes, nouai, nouâmes, nouèrent, noué.
lately: dernièrement, de manière tarde, de façon tardive, récemment.
link: lien, liaison, maillon, chaînon, monter, lier, articulation, rapport, relation, biellette.
merited: mérité.
plotting: levé, traçant.
proposal: proposition, offre.
protected: protégé, préservas, sauvegardèrent, garantit, abritâtes.
rid: débarrasser, délivrer.
rightly: correctement, de façon droite, de manière droite.
shaded: ombragé, nuancé, dégradé.
stubborn: têtu, obstiné, entêté, tenace.
tool: outil, instrument, produit, ustensile.
wilful: obstiné, têtu, entêté, délibéré, opiniâtre.

better rot on a **dunghill** than come with me! I ask **implicit** confidence in all my **suggestions**, prompt **submission** to all my requests. **Grant** me but these, and I promise to consult your fortune as my own, to gratify your tastes as far as my means will allow, to grudge not your pleasures, and when the age for ambition comes, to **aid** your rise if I rise myself,—nay, if well contented with you, to remove the **blot** from your birth, by **acknowledging** and **adopting** you formally as my son."

"Agreed! and I thank you," said Gabriel. "And Lucretia is going? Oh, I so long to see her!"

"See her—not yet; but next week."

"Do not fear that I should let out about the letter. I should betray myself if I did," said the boy, bluntly betraying his guess at his father's delay.

The evil scholar smiled.

"You will do well to keep it secret for your own sake; for mine, I should not fear. Gabriel, go back now to your master,—you do right, like the **rats**, to run from the **falling** house. Next week I will send for you, Gabriel!"

Not, however, back to the **studio** went the boy. He sauntered leisurely through the gayest streets, eyed the **shops** and the equipages, the fair women and the well-dressed men,—eyed with envy and **longings** and **visions** of pomps and vanities to come; then, when the day began to close, he sought out a young painter, the wildest and maddest of the crew to whom his uncle had **presented** their future comrade and rival, and went with this youth, at half-price, to the **theatre**, not to gaze on the **actors** or study the play, but to **stroll** in the **saloon**. A supper in the Finish **completed** the **void** in his pockets, and concluded his day's rank experience of life. By the gray **dawn** he stole back to his bed, and as he **laid** himself down, he thought with **avid pleasure** of Paris, its gay gardens and brilliant shops and crowded streets; he thought, too, of his father's calm confidence of success, of the triumph that already had **attended** his wiles,—a confidence and a triumph which, exciting his reverence and rousing his emulation, had decided his resolution. He thought, too, of Lucretia with something of affection, recalled her **praises**

French

acknowledging: reconnaissant.
actor: acteur, comédien.
adopting: adoptant.
aid: aide, secourir, assister, adjoint.
attended: assisté, soignèrent.
avid: avide.
blot: tache, pâté.
completed: complété, achevé, terminé.
dawn: aube, aurore, point du jour.
dunghill: tas de fumier.
falling: tombant, abattant, choyant,
chute.
grant: subvention, allocation, concéder.
implicit: implicite, absolu.
laid: posèrent, posa, posâmes, posé, vergé, couchèrent, pondîmes.
longing: désir, envie, aspiration.
pleasure: plaisir, jouissance.
praise: glorifier, louange, louer, éloge.
presented: présenté.
rat: rat.
saloon: bar, berline.
shop: boutique, magasin, atelier.
stroll: promenade, se promener, flâner, faire un tour.
studio: studio, atelier.
submission: soumission, dépôt.
suggestion: suggestion, proposition.
theatre: théâtre.
vision: vision, vue.
void: vide, manque, pore, interstice.

and bribes, her **frequent mediation** with his father, and felt that they should have need of each other. Oh, no, he never would tell her of the **snare** laid at Guy's Oak,—never, not even if **incensed** with his father. An instinct told him that that **offence** could never be **forgiven**, and that, **henceforth**, Lucretia's was a destiny bound up in his own. He thought, too, of Dalibard's **warning** and **threat**. But with fear itself came a strange excitement of pleasure,—to grapple, if **necessary**, he a mere child, with such a man! His heart swelled at the thought. So at last he fell asleep, and dreamed that he saw his mother's trunkless face dripping gore and **frowning** on him,—dreamed that he **heard** her say: "Goest thou to the scene of my execution only to **fawn** upon my murderer?" Then a **nightmare** of horrors, of scaffolds and executioners and **grinning** mobs and **agonized** faces, came on him,—dark, **confused**, and indistinct. And he woke, with his **hair standing** on end, and **beard** below, in the rising **sun**, the merry song of the poor canary,—trill-lill-lill, trill-trill-lill-lill-la! Did he feel glad that his cruel hand had been **stayed**?

French

agonized: agonisâtes, tourmentâtes.
beard: barbe, blanc, talus de pied, soie, ombrage hachuré, la barbe, brosse, bec, hachures.
confused: confondîtes, embrouillèrent.
fawn: faon, fauve.
forgiven: pardonné, excusé.
frequent: fréquent, habituel.
frowning: renfrogné.
grinning: manque de pouvoir couvrant par opacité, pouvoir opacifiant insuffisant, clair, fendillement.
hair: cheveux, poil.
heard: entendirent, ouïs, ouï.
henceforth: désormais, dorénavant, à l'avenir.
incensed: courroucé.
mediation: médiation, intermédiaire, entremise.
necessary: nécessaire, indispensable, essentiel.
nightmare: cauchemar.
offence: délit, infraction, offense, agacement.
snare: piège, collet.
standing: debout, permanent.
stayed: restâtes, séjourna, haubané.
sun: soleil, ensoleillé.
threat: menace.
warning: avertissement, sommation, recommandation, alerte, avis.

EPILOGUE TO PART THE FIRST.

It is a year since the November day on which Lucretia Clavering **quitted** the roof of Mr. Fielden. And first we must recall the eye of the reader to the old-fashioned **terrace** at Laughton,—the jutting porch, the **quaint balustrades**, the **broad**, dark, changeless **cedars** on the **lawn beyond**. The day is calm, clear, and mild, for November in the country is often a gentle month. On that terrace walked Charles Vernon, now known by his new name of St. John. Is it the change of name that has so changed the person? Can the **wand** of the Herald's Office have filled up the hollows of the cheek, and **replaced** by **elastic** vigour the **listless languor** of the tread? No; there is another and a better **cause** for that **healthful** change. Mr. Vernon St. John is not alone,—a fair companion leans on his arm. See, she pauses to press closer to his side, gaze on his face, and whisper, "We did well to have hope and faith!"

The husband's faith had not been so **unshaken** as his Mary's, and a slight **blush** passed over his cheek as he thought of his **concession** to Sir Miles's wishes, and his **overtures** to Lucretia Clavering. Still, that fault had been fairly acknowledged to his wife, and she felt, the moment she had spoken, that she had committed an **indiscretion**; **nevertheless**, with an arch touch of womanly **malice** she added softly,—

"And Miss Clavering, you persist in **saying**, was not really handsome?"

French

balustrade: balustrade, rampe, accoudoir.
beyond: plus loin, ensuite, après, outre.
blush: rougir, blush, opalescence.
broad: large, ample.
cause: cause, faire, rendre, procurer, situer, déterminer, entraîner des conséquences, occasionner, motif.
cedar: cèdre.
concession: concession, acte de
concession.
elastic: élastique, souple.
healthful: salubre.
indiscretion: indiscrétion.
languor: langueur.
lawn: pelouse, gazon, linon, batiste.
listless: apathique, indifférent.
malice: méchanceté, malice, malveillance.
nevertheless: néanmoins, pourtant, cependant, tout de même, quand même.
overture: ouverture.
quaint: curieux, intéressant, singulier, étrange.
quitted: quittèrent.
replaced: remplaçâmes, substitua, replaçâmes.
saying: disant, adage, proverbe.
terrace: terrasse, maisons en bande, rangée de maisons, gradin.
unshaken: inébranlable.
wand: baguette, badine.

"My love," replied the husband, gravely, "you would oblige me by not recalling the very **painful** recollections **connected** with that name. Let it never be **mentioned** in this house."

Lady Mary bowed her graceful head in submission; she **understood** Charles's **feelings**. For though he had not shown her Sir Miles's letter and its enclosure, he had communicated enough to account for the unexpected heritage, and to **lessen** his wife's compassion for the disappointed heiress. Nevertheless, she **comprehended** that her husband felt an uneasy **twinge** at the idea that he was compelled to act hardly to the one whose hopes he had supplanted. Lucretia's banishment from Laughton was a just humiliation, but it humbled a generous heart to inflict the **sentence**. Thus, on all accounts, the remembrance of Lucretia was painful and unwelcome to the **successor** of Sir Miles. There was a **silence**; Lady Mary pressed her husband's hand.

"It is strange," said he, giving vent to his thoughts at that tender **sign** of sympathy in his feeling,—"strange that, after all, she did not marry Mainwaring, but fixed her **choice** on that subtle Frenchman. But she has settled abroad now, perhaps for life; a great relief to my mind. Yes, let us never **recur** to her."

"Fortunately," said Lady Mary, with some hesitation, "she does not seem to have **created** much interest here. The poor seldom name her to me, and our neighbours only with **surprise** at her marriage. In another year she will be forgotten!"

Mr. St. John sighed. Perhaps he felt how much more **easily** he had been forgotten, were he the banished one, Lucretia the possessor! His light nature, however, soon escaped from all thoughts and **sources** of annoyance, and he listened with complacent **attention** to Lady Mary's gentle plans for the poor, and the children's school, and the cottages that ought to be repaired, and the **labourers** that ought to be employed. For though it may seem singular, Vernon St. John, insensibly influenced by his wife's meek superiority, and **corrected** by her pure companionship, had begun to feel the charm of innocent occupations,—more, perhaps, than if he had been accustomed to

---

French

attention: attention, prévenances.
choice: choix, réponse, sélection, option, assortiment, de choix, élection.
comprehended: comprîmes.
connected: connecta, cohérent, raccordé, brancha, abouchâtes, allié, nouâmes, nouas, noué, nouèrent.
corrected: corrigé.
created: créas, créâtes, créèrent, créé.

easily: facilement, aisément, de façon facile, de manière facile.
feeling: sentiment, palpant, ressentant, tâtant.
labourer: ouvrier, manoeuvre.
lessen: diminuer, amoindrir, abréger, abaisser.
mentioned: mentionné.
painful: douloureux, pénible.
recur: se reproduire, revenir, reviens, reparaissons.
sentence: phrase, condamner, peine, sentence, verdict.
sign: signe, augure, témoignage, panneau, preuve, enseigne, écriteau, indication.
silence: silence, repos.
source: source, origine, fontaine.
successor: successeur, descendant.
surprise: surprendre.
twinge: élancement.
understood: compris, entendu.

the larger and loftier excitements of life, and **missed** that stir of intellect which is the element of those who have warred in the **democracy** of letters, or **contended** for the **leadership** of States. He had begun already to think that the country was no such exile after all. **Naturally** benevolent, he had **taught** himself to share the occupations his Mary had already found in the busy "luxury of doing good," and to conceive that **brotherhood** of charity which usually **unites** the lord of the village with its poor.

"I think, what with hunting once a week,—I will not **venture** more till my pain in the side is quite gone,—and with the help of some old friends at Christmas, we can get through the winter very well, Mary."

"Ah, those old friends, I dread them more than the hunting!"

"But we'll have your grave father and your dear, **precise**, excellent mother to keep us in order. And if I sit more than half an hour after dinner, the old **butler** shall **pull** me out by the ears. Mary, what do you say to **thinning** the grove yonder? We shall get a better view of the landscape beyond. No, hang it! dear old Sir Miles loved his trees better than the prospect; I won't **lop** a bough. But that **avenue** we are **planting** will be certainly a noble improvement—"

"Fifty years hence, Charles!"

"It is our duty to think of posterity," answered the ci-devant spendthrift, with a gravity that was actually **pompous**. "But hark! is that two o'clock? Three, by Jove! How time **flies**! and my new **bullocks** that I was to see at two! Come down to the farm, that's my own Mary. Ah, your fine ladies are not such bad **housewives** after all!"

"And your fine gentlemen—"

"Capital **farmers**! I had no idea till last week that a **prize** ox was so interesting an animal. One lives to learn. Put me in mind, by the by, to write to Coke about his sheep."

"This way, dear Charles; we can go round by the village,—and see poor Ponto and Dash."

French

avenue: avenue, allée, boulevard.
brotherhood: fraternité, confrérie.
bullock: boeuf, bouvillon.
butler: maître d'hôtel, majordome.
contended: contestés, disputa, combattîmes.
democracy: démocratie.
farmer: agriculteur, fermier, paysan, cultivateur, laboureur, exploitant agricole, agrarien.
fly: mouche, voler, volons, volant.
housewife: femme au foyer, ménagère.
leadership: direction, leadership, primauté.
lop: taille, ébrancher, clapotis.
missed: manqué.
naturally: naturellement, bien sûr, de façon naturelle, de manière naturelle.
planting: plantation, repeuplement, repiquage, encépagement, empoissonnement, peuplement.
pompous: pompeux.
precise: précis, méticuleux.
prize: prix, récompense.
pull: tirer, tirons, traction, tirage, traîner, épreuve.
taught: enseigna, instruisîtes.
thinning: éclaircissage, amincissement.
unites: unit, apparie, englobe.
venture: risquer, aventurer, oser, entreprise, hasarder.

The tears rushed to Mr. St. John's eyes. "If poor Sir Miles could have known you!" he said, with a sigh; and though the gardeners were at work on the lawn, he bowed his head and kissed the blushing cheek of his wife as **heartily** as if he had been really a farmer.

From the terrace at Laughton, **turn** to the humbler **abode** of our old **friend** the vicar,—the same day, the same **hour**. Here also the scene is without doors,—we are in the **garden** of the vicarage; the children are **playing** at hide-and-seek amongst the **espaliers** which **screen** the winding gravel-walks from the esculents more dear to Ceres than to Flora. The vicar is seated in his little parlour, from which a **glazed** door admits into the garden. The door is now open, and the good man has paused from his work (he had just **discovered** a new **emendation** in the first **chorus** of the "Medea") to look out at the rosy faces that gleam to and fro across the scene. His wife, with a **basket** in her hand, is standing without the door, but a little aside, not to **obstruct** the view.

"It does one's heart good to see them," said the vicar, "little dears!"

"Yes, they ought to be dear at this time of the year," **observed** Mrs. Fielden, who was absorbed in the contents of the basket.

"And so fresh!"

"Fresh, indeed,—how different from London! In London they were not **fit** to be seen,—as old as—-I am **sure** I can't guess how old they were. But you see here they are new laid every morning!"

"My dear," said Mr. Fielden, opening his eyes,—"new laid every morning!"

"Two **dozen** and four."

"Two dozen and four! What on earth are you **talking** about, Mrs. Fielden?"

"Why, the **eggs**, to be sure, my love!"

"Oh," said the vicar, "two dozen and four! You alarmed me a little; 't is of no consequence,—only my foolish mistake. Always prudent and **saving**, my

---

French

abode: demeure, domicile, logis, gîte, habitation, localité, logement.
basket: panier, corbeille, nacelle.
chorus: chœur, chorale.
discovered: découvris, dépouilla.
dozen: douzaine.
egg: oeuf, graine, œuf de poisson, ovule.
emendation: correction.
espalier: espalier, arbre en espalier.
fit: adapter, apoplexie, convenir, ajustement, crise, en bonne santé.

friend: ami, amie, copain, camarade, copine.
garden: jardin, faire du jardinage.
glazed: glacé, givré, lissé, vitré.
heartily: de façon cordiale, de manière cordiale, chaleureusement.
hour: heure, l'heure.
observed: observâtes, respectèrent, remplîtes.
obstruct: obstruer, barrer, entraver, bloquer, encombrer, faire

obstruction, engorger.
playing: jouant, jeu, jouer.
saving: épargnant, sauvant, économisant, enregistrant.
screen: écran, trame, paravent, filtre, grillage, blindage, crible.
sure: sûr, certain, assuré.
talking: parlant, bavardage.
turn: tourner, changer, retourner, renverser, dévier, virage, spire, serrer, rangée, file, faire tourner.

dear Sarah, — just as if poor Sir Miles had not left us that munificent fortune, I may call it."

"It will not go very far when we have our young ones to **settle**. And David is very **extravagant** already; he has **torn** such a **hole** in his jacket!"

At this moment up the gravel-walk two young persons came in sight. The children darted across them, whooping and laughing, and vanished in the further recess of the garden.

"All is for the best, blind mortals that we are; all is for the best," said the vicar, musingly, as his eyes rested upon the approaching **pair**.

"Certainly, my love; you are always right, and it is **wicked** to **grumble**. Still, if you saw what a hole it was, — past **patching**, I fear!"

"Look round," said Mr. Fielden, **benevolently**. "How we **grieved** for them both; how wroth we were with William, — how sad for Susan! And now see them; they will be the better man and wife for their trial."

"Has Susan then consented? I was almost afraid she never would consent. How often have I been almost angry with her, poor **lamb**, when I have heard her accuse herself of **causing** her sister's **unhappiness**, and declare with sobs that she felt it a crime to think of William Mainwaring as a husband."

"I trust I have reasoned her out of a morbid **sensibility** which, while it could not have rendered Lucretia the happier, must have **insured** the **wretchedness** of herself and William. But if Lucretia had not **married**, and so forever closed the door on William's **repentance** (that is, supposing he did repent), I believe poor Susan would rather have died of a broken heart than have given her hand to Mainwaring."

"It was an odd marriage of that proud young lady's, after all," said Mrs. Fielden, — "so much **older** than she; a foreigner, too!"

"But he is a very **pleasant** man, and they have known each other so long. I did not, however, quite like a sort of cunning he **showed**, when I came to

---

French

benevolently: de façon bienveillante, de manière bienveillante.
causing: causant.
extravagant: extravagant.
grieved: affligeâmes, chagrina, attristé.
grumble: grogner, râler, grommeler, ronchonner.
hole: trou, fossé, orifice, creux.
insured: assuras, maître de l'ouvrage.

lamb: agneau, mettre bas.
married: marié, te marias, se marièrent, vous mariâtes, nous mariâmes, me mariai, épousas.
older: âgé.
pair: paire, couple, apparier.
patching: retouche, correction de programme, emploi partiel, placage, raccommodage, rapiéçage, redistribution en agrégats.
pleasant: agréable, plaisant,

charmant, sympathique.
repentance: repentir.
sensibility: sensibilité.
settle: régler, règlent, s'abaisser, coloniser.
showed: montrèrent, manifesta, marquèrent.
torn: déchiré, lacéré.
unhappiness: tristesse, chagrin, malheur.
wicked: mauvais, méchant.
wretchedness: misère.

reflect on it, in bringing Lucretia back to the house; it looks as if he had laid a **trap** for her from the first."

"Ten **thousand** pounds,—a great **catch** for a foreigner!" observed Mrs. Fielden, with the shrewd instinct of her **sex**; and then she added, in the spirit of a prudent sympathy equally characteristic: "But I think you say Mr. Parchmount persuaded her to **allow** half to be settled on **herself**. That will be a **hold** on him."

"A **bad** hold, if that be all, Sarah. There is a better,—he is a learned man and a scholar. Scholars are naturally **domestic**, and make good husbands."

"But you know he must be a papist!" said Mrs. Fielden.

"Umph!" muttered the vicar, irresolutely.

While the worthy **couple** were thus conversing, Susan and her lover, not having **finished** their conference, had **turned** back through the winding walk.

"Indeed," said William, **drawing** her arm closer to his side, "these scruples, these fears, are cruel to me as well as to yourself. If you were no longer **existing**, I could be nothing to your sister. Nay, even were she not married, you must know enough of her pride to be assured that I can **retain** no place in her affections. What has chanced was not our crime. Perhaps Heaven **designed** to **save** not only us, but herself, from the certain misery of nuptials so inauspicious!"

"If she would but **answer** one of my letters!" sighed Susan; "or if I could but know that she were **happy** and contented!"

"Your letters must have miscarried,—you are not sure even of her address. **Rely** upon it, she is happy. Do you think that she would a second time have 'stooped beneath her'"—Mainwaring's lip writhed as he repeated that phrase—"if her feelings had not been **involved**? I would not wrong your sister,—I shall ever feel gratitude for the past, and remorse for my own **shameful** weakness; still, I must think that the nature of her attachment to me was more ardent than lasting."

French

allow: permettre, laisser, autoriser, admettre, accorder.
answer: réponse, réplique.
bad: mauvais, méchant, mal.
catch: attraper, prise, prenons, saisir, capturer, s'allumer, cliquet, atteindre, parvenir, frapper.
couple: couple, accoupler, mari et femme, époux, apparier, atteler, embrayer.
designed: conçu.
domestic: domestique, intérieur, aborigène, relatif à la maison, national.
drawing: dessin, puisant, étirage, tirage, appâtant, traçant.
existing: existant, présent.
finished: termina, finîtes, finit, acheva, prêt.
happy: heureux, joyeux, content.
herself: même, se.
hold: tenir, maintien, prise, cale, retenir, contenir, pause, tenue, blocage.
involved: impliqué, compliqué.
rely: comptez, fient, fiez, fions.
retain: retenir, retiennent, réprimer.
save: épargner, sauver, économiser, enregistrer, préserver.
sex: sexe, bagatelle.
shameful: honteux, scandaleux.
thousand: mille.
trap: piège, trappe, piéger, siphon.
turned: tournèrent, retournâmes, changeas, déviâmes.

"Ah, William, how can you know her heart?"

"By comparing it with yours. Oh, there indeed I may **anchor** my faith! Susan, we were formed for each other! Our natures are alike, save that yours, despite its surpassing sweetness, has greater strength in its **simple** candour. You will be my guide to good. Without you I should have no **aim** in life, no courage to **front** the contests of this world. Ah, this hand trembles still!"

"William, William, I cannot **repress** a foreboding, a **superstition**! At night I am haunted with that pale face as I saw it last,—pale with suppressed despair. Oh, if ever Lucretia could have need of us,—need of our services, our affections,—if we could but repair the grief we have **caused** her!"

Susan's head sank on her lover's shoulder. She had said "need of us," "need of our services." In those simple monosyllables the union was pledged, the **identity** of their lots in the dark **urn** was implied.

From this scene turn again; the **slide shifts** in the lantern,—we are at Paris. In the **antechamber** at the Tuileries a **crowd** of expectant **courtiers** and **adventurers** gaze upon a figure who passes with modest and downcast eyes through the throng; he has just left the **closet** of the First Consul.

"Par Dieu!" said B—, "power, like misery, makes us acquainted with strange **bedfellows**. I should like to hear what the First Consul can have to say to Olivier Dalibard."

Fouche, who at that period was scheming for the **return** to his old dignities of minister of police, smiled **slightly**, and answered: "In a time when the air is filled with **daggers**, one who was familiar with Robespierre has his uses. Olivier Dalibard is a **remarkable** man. He is one of those children of the Revolution **whom** that great mother is bound to save."

"By betraying his brethren?" said B—, dryly.

"I do not allow the **inference**. The simple fact is that Dalibard has **spent** many years in England; he has married an Englishwoman of birth and connections; he knows well the English language and the English people; and just now when the First Consul is so anxious to approfondir the **popular**

French

adventurer: aventurier.
aim: but, viser, visons, peiner, dessein, avoir pour but, se démener, objectif.
anchor: ancre, mouiller, fixer, relâcher.
antechamber: antichambre.
bedfellow: camarade de lit.
caused: causé.
closet: armoire, placard.
courtier: courtisan.
crowd: foule, masse, amas, multitude, tas, cohue.
dagger: poignard, dague.
front: front, devant, avant, face.
identity: identité.
inference: inférence, corollaire.
popular: populaire, célèbre.
remarkable: remarquable, saillant, insigne.
repress: refouler, réprimer.
return: retour, revenir, rentrée, renvoyer, rendre, restituer, rappel, déclaration.
shift: décalage, équipe, poste, déplacer, changement.
simple: simple, pur.
slide: diapositive, glissière, coulisse, lame.
slightly: légèrement, de manière légère, de façon légère.
spent: dépensa, passas, épuisé.
superstition: superstition.
urn: urne.
whom: qui, lequel, auquel, que.

feelings of that strange nation, with whose government he is compelled to go to war, he may naturally have much to say to so acute an observer as Olivier Dalibard."

"Um!" said B—; "with such **patronage**, Robespierre's friend should hold his head somewhat higher!"

Meanwhile, Olivier Dalibard, crossing the gardens of the palace, took his way to the Faubourg St. Germain. There was no change in the aspect of this man: the same meditative tranquillity **characterized** his **downward** eyes and **bonded** brow; the same precise **simplicity** of dress which had pleased the prim taste of Robespierre gave decorum to his **slender**, stooping form. No expression more cheerful, no footstep more elastic, bespoke the exile's return to his **native** land, or the **sanguine** expectations of Intellect restored to a career. Yet, to all appearance, the prospects of Dalibard were bright and **promising**. The First Consul was at that stage of his greatness when he sought to employ in his service all such talent as the Revolution had made manifest, provided only that it was not stained with **notorious bloodshed**, or too strongly associated with the Jacobin clubs. His quick eye seemed to have discovered already the abilities of Dalibard, and to have **appreciated** the sagacity and knowledge of men which had **enabled** this subtle person to obtain the friendship of Robespierre, without **sharing** in his crimes. He had been frequently closeted with Bonaparte; he was in the declared favour of Fouche, who, though not at that period at the head of the police, was too necessary amidst the dangers of the time, deepened as they were by the **rumours** of some terrible and profound conspiracy, to be laid aside, as the First Consul had at one moment designed. One man alone, of those high in the State, appeared to distrust Olivier Dalibard,—the **celebrated** Cambaceres. But with his aid the Provencal could **dispense**. What was the secret of Dalibard's power? Was it, in truth, owing **solely** to his native talent, and his **acquired** experience, especially of England? Was it by honourable means that he had won the ear of the First Consul? We may be sure of the contrary; for it is a striking attribute of men once thoroughly **tainted** by the indulgence of **vicious** schemes and stratagems that they become **wholly**

French

acquired: acquîmes, appris.
appreciated: appréciâtes, aimé, aimâtes, aimas, aimèrent.
bloodshed: carnage, effusion de sang, massacre.
bonded: garanti par une obligation, lié à la masse, sous douane, encollé, cautionné, couvert par une garantie.
celebrated: célébra, fêtâtes, fêté, fêtas, fêtèrent.
characterized: caractérisai.
dispense: dispenser, délivrer un médicament, distribuer, exempter.
downward: descendant, vers le bas.
enabled: permis, habilité, opérationnel.
native: autochtone, naturel, natif, inné, aborigène, indigène, natal.
notorious: notoire, mal famé.
patronage: patronage, clientèle.
promising: promettant.
rumour: renommée, réputation, rumeur.
sanguine: sanguin, optimiste.
sharing: partageant.
simplicity: simplicité, naïveté.
slender: mince, svelte, maigre.
solely: seulement, de façon sole, de manière sole, uniquement.
tainted: corrompu, vicié, pollué, infecté, entachées, avarié, altéré.
vicious: méchant, vicieux, perfide, malin.
wholly: complètement, entièrement, totalement, tout.

blinded to those plain paths of ambition which common-sense makes manifest to ordinary ability. If we regard narrowly the lives of great criminals, we are often very much startled by the extraordinary acuteness, the profound calculation, the patient, meditative energy which they have employed upon the conception and execution of a crime. We feel **inclined** to think that such intellectual power would have commanded great distinction, **worthily** used and **guided**; but we never find that these great criminals seem to have been sensible of the opportunities to real **eminence** which they have thrown away. Often we observe that there have been before them vistas into worldly greatness which, by no uncommon prudence and exertion, would have **conducted** honest men half as clever to fame and power; but, with a strange **obliquity** of vision, they appear to have looked from these broad clear avenues into some dark, **tangled defile**, in which, by the subtlest ingenuity, and through the most **besetting** perils, they might attain at last to the success of a fraud or the enjoyment of a vice. In crime once indulged there is a wonderful fascination, and the fascination is, not rarely, great in proportion to the intellect of the criminal. There is always hope of reform for a dull, **uneducated**, **stolid** man, led by accident or temptation into guilt; but where a man of great ability, and highly **educated**, besots himself in the **intoxication** of dark and terrible excitements, takes **impure** delight in tortuous and **slimy** ways, the good angel **abandons** him forever.

Olivier Dalibard walked musingly on, gained a house in one of the most desolate quarters of the abandoned faubourg, **mounted** the **spacious** stairs, and rang at the door of an attic next the roof. After some moments the door was slowly and cautiously opened, and two small, fierce eyes, peering through a mass of black, tangled curls, gleamed through the aperture. The gaze seemed **satisfactory**.

"Enter, friend," said the **inmate**, with a sort of complacent **grunt**; and as Dalibard obeyed, the man reclosed and barred the door.

The room was **bare** to **beggary**; the **ceiling**, low and **sloping**, was blackened with smoke. A wretched bed, two chairs, a table, a strong chest, a small **cracked** looking-glass, completed the inventory. The dress of the

French

abandon: abandonner, délaisser, quitter, renoncer, abdiquer, livrer, résigner.
bare: nu, dénudé, mettre à nu.
beggary: mendicité.
besetting: assaillant.
ceiling: plafond, tillac, vaigrage, parquet.
conducted: conduite, amenée, mené.
cracked: fêlé, craqué, criqué, fendu, timbré, toqué, cassé.
defile: col, violer, défilé.
educated: éduqua, cultivé.
eminence: éminence.
grunt: grognement.
guided: guidé, dirigé.
impure: impur.
inclined: enclin, incliné.
inmate: détenu, interne, occupant, résident d'institution.
intoxication: ivresse, intoxication, ébriété, empoisonnement, griserie.
mounted: monté, porté.
obliquity: obliquité.
satisfactory: satisfaisant.
slimy: visqueux, limoneux, vaseux.
sloping: talutage, déclive, en pente, incliné.
spacious: spacieux, ample, étendu, large.
stolid: flegmatique, impassible.
tangled: embrouillé.
uneducated: inculte.
worthily: de façon digne, de manière digne, dignement.

occupier was not in keeping with the chamber; true that it was not such as was worn by the wealthier classes, but it betokened no sign of poverty. A blue coat with high **collar**, and half of military fashion, was **buttoned** tight over a chest of vast **girth**; the nether garments were of leather, **scrupulously** clean, and solid, heavy riding-boots came half-way up the **thigh**. A more **sturdy**, **stalwart**, strong-built **knave** never excited the admiration which physical power always has a right to command; and Dalibard gazed on him with envy. The pale scholar absolutely sighed as he thought what an **auxiliary** to his own scheming mind would have been so tough a frame!

But even less in form than face did the man of thews and sinews contrast the man of wile and craft. Opposite that high forehead, with its massive development of organs, scowled the low front of one to whom thought was unfamiliar,—protuberant, indeed, over the **shaggy** brows, where phrenologists place the seats of practical **perception**, strongly marked in some of the brutes, as in the dog, but almost **literally** void of those higher organs by which we reason and imagine and **construct**. But in rich **atonement** for such deficiency, all the animal **reigned triumphant** in the **immense** mass and **width** of the **skull** behind. And as the hair, long before, curled in close rings to the **nape** of the bull-like neck, you saw before you one of those useful **instruments** to ambition and fraud which **recoil** at no danger, comprehend no crime, are not without certain good qualities, under virtuous guidance,—for they have the fidelity, the obedience, the stubborn courage of the animal,—but which, under evil control, turn those very qualities to unsparing evil: bull-dogs to **rend** the foe, as bull-dogs to defend the master.

For some moments the two men gazed, silently at each other. At length Dalibard said, with an air of calm superiority,—

"My friend, it is time that I should be presented to the chiefs of your party!"

"Chiefs, **par** tous les diables!" growled the other; "we Chouans are all chiefs, when it comes to blows. You have seen my **credentials**; you know that I am a man to be trusted: what more do you need?"

French

atonement: expiation.
auxiliary: auxiliaire, sortie auxiliaire, subsidiaire.
buttoned: boutonné.
collar: col, collier, bague.
construct: bâtir, construire, poser.
credential: lettre de créance, recommandations, pouvoir.
girth: circonférence, sangle, tour, ceinture.
immense: énorme, immense, formidable.
instrument: instrument, orchestrer, titre, acte instrumentaire, effet de commerce, appareil de mesure.
knave: fripon, coquin.
literally: littéralement, de façon littérale, de manière littérale.
nape: nuque.
occupier: occupant.
par: pair, égalité.
perception: perception.
recoil: recul, ancre à recul, billot.
reigned: régné.
rend: déchirer.
scrupulously: de manière scrupuleuse, de façon scrupuleuse.
shaggy: poilu, velu, hirsute.
skull: crâne, tête de mort.
stalwart: vigoureux, fidèle.
sturdy: robuste, fort.
thigh: cuisse.
triumphant: triomphant.
width: largeur, ampleur, mesure de largeur.

"For myself nothing; but my friends are more **scrupulous**. I have sounded, as I promised, the heads of the old Jacobin party, and they are favourable. This **upstart** soldier, who has suddenly seized in his iron grasp all the **fruits** of the Revolution, is as **hateful** to them as to you. But que voulez vous, mon cher? men are men! It is one thing to **destroy** Bonaparte; it is another thing to restore the Bourbons. How can the Jacobin **chiefs** depend on your assurance, or my own, that the Bourbons will forget the old offences and **reward** the new service? You **apprise** me—so do your credentials—that a prince of the **blood** is engaged in this **enterprise**, that he will **appear** at the **proper season**. Put me in direct communication with this representative of the Bourbons, and I promise in return, if his assurances are satisfactory, that you shall have an emeute, to be felt from Paris to Marseilles. If you cannot do this, I am useless; and I withdraw—"

"Withdraw! Garde a vous, Monsieur le Savant! No man withdraws **alive** from a conspiracy like ours."

We have said before that Olivier Dalibard was not physically brave; and the look of the Chouan, as those words were said, would have frozen the blood of many a bolder man. But the habitual hypocrisy of Dalibard enabled him to disguise his fear, and he replied dryly,—

"Monsieur le Chouan, it is not by threats that you will **gain adherents** to a **desperate** cause, which, on the contrary, **requires** mild words and flattering **inducements**. If you **commit** a violence,—a murder,—mon cher, Paris is not Bretagne; we have a police: you will be discovered."

"Ha, ha! What then? Do you think I fear the guillotine?"

"For yourself, no; but for your **leaders**, yes! If you are discovered, and arrested for crime, do you fancy that the police will not recognize the right arm of the terrible George Cadoudal; that they will not guess that Cadoudal is at Paris; that Cadoudal will not accompany you to the guillotine?"

The Chouan's face fell. Olivier watched him, and pursued his advantage.

"I asked you to introduce to me this shadow of a prince, under which you would march to a counter-revolution. But I will be more easily

---

French

adherent: adhérent, adepte.
alive: vivant, en vie.
appear: apparaître, sembler, paraître, avoir l'air de, surgir, comparaître.
apprise: informer, instruire.
blood: sang, le sang.
chief: chef, principal, dominant.
commit: commettre, engager, validation.
desperate: désespéré, éperdu.
destroy: détruire, ravager, démolir.
abaisser, abîmer.
enterprise: entreprise, initiative.
fruit: fruit, réponse parasite.
gain: gain, gagner, profit, bénéfice, remporter, avantage, acquisition.
hateful: odieux, haïssable.
inducement: incitation, lieu, occasion.
leader: guide, animateur, leader, conseiller, chef, amorce, dirigeant, commandant, meneur.
proper: convenable, propre, exact,
juste, approprié, adéquat.
requires: exige, requiert, réclame.
reward: récompenser, prime, rémunérer, salaire, sanction prémiale.
scrupulous: scrupuleux, méticuleux.
season: saison, assaisonner.
upstart: parvenu, bascule, arriviste.

contented. Present me to George Cadoudal, the **hero** of Morbihan; he is a man in whom I can trust, and with whom I can deal. What, you **hesitate**? How do you suppose enterprises of this nature can be carried on? If, from fear and distrust of each other, the man you would employ cannot meet the chief who **directs** him, there will be delay, **confusion**, **panic**, and you will all perish by the executioner. And for me, Pierre Guillot, consider my position. I am in some favour with the First Consul; I have a station of respectability,—a career **lies** before me. Can you think that I will **hazard** these, with my head to boot, like a rash child? Do you suppose that, in **entering** into this terrible contest, I would consent to treat only with subordinates? Do not deceive yourself. Again, I say, tell your **employers** that they must confer with me directly, or je m'en lave les mains."

"I will repeat what you say," answered Guillot, sullenly, "Is this all?"

"All for the present," said Dalibard, slowly drawing on his **gloves**, and **retreating** towards the door. The Chouan watched him with a suspicious and sinister eye; and as the Provencal's hand was on the **latch**, he laid his own rough grasp on Dalibard's shoulder,—

"I know not how it is, Monsieur Dalibard, but I **mistrust** you."

"Distrust is natural and prudent to all who conspire," replied the scholar, quietly. "I do not ask you to confide in me. Your employers bade you seek me: I have mentioned my **conditions**; let them decide."

"You carry it off well, Monsieur Dalibard, and I am under a solemn oath, which poor George made me take, **knowing** me to be a hot-headed, honest fellow,—mauvaise tete, if you will,—that I will keep my hand off **pistol** and **knife** upon mere suspicion; that nothing less than his word, or than clear and **positive proof** of treachery, shall put me out of good humour and into **warm** blood. But bear this with you, Monsieur Dalibard: if I once discover that you use our secrets to betray them; should George see you, and one hair of his head come to **injury** through your hands,—I will **wring** your **neck** as a housewife wrings a pullet's."

French

condition: condition, état, situation, manière d'être.
confusion: confusion, désordre, affolement.
directs: dirige.
employer: employeur, patron.
entering: entrant, introduisant.
glove: gant, mitaine.
hazard: risque, danger, hasard, péril, aléa, aventurer, oser.
hero: héros.
hesitate: hésiter, barguigner.
injury: blessure, lésion, préjudice, dégât.
knife: couteau, poignarder, le couteau.
knowing: connaissant, entendu, sachant.
latch: loquet, verrou, clenche, bascule.
lie: mensonge, mentir, être couché, gésir.
mistrust: méfiance, te méfies, se méfient, nous méfions, vous méfiez, me méfie, défiance.
neck: cou, col, goulot, collet, encolure.
panic: panique, affolement.
pistol: pistolet.
positive: positif, affirmatif, image positive, mère.
proof: preuve, épreuve, témoignage, démonstration.
retreating: dépilage en rabattant.
warm: chaud, cordial, chaleureux.
wring: tordre, essorez.

"I don't doubt your strength or your ferocity, Pierre Guillot; but my neck will be **safe**: you have enough to do to take care of your own. Au revoir."

With a tone and look of calm and fearless irony, the scholar thus spoke, and left the room; but when he was on the stairs, he paused, and caught at the balustrade,—the sickness as of terror at some danger past, or to be, came over him; and this **contrast** between the self-command, or simulation, which belongs to moral courage, and the feebleness of natural and **constitutional** cowardice, would have been sublime if shown in a noble cause. In one so corrupt, it but betrayed a nature **doubly** formidable; for treachery and murder **hatch** their **brood** amidst the **folds** of a hypocrite's cowardice.

While thus the interview is going on between Dalibard and the conspirator, we must bestow a glance upon the Provencal's home.

In an apartment in one of the **principal** streets between the Boulevards and the Rue St. Honore, a boy and a woman **sat** side by side, conversing in whispers. The boy was Gabriel Varney, the woman Lucretia Dalibard. The apartment was furnished in the then **modern** taste, which **affected** classical forms; and though not without a certain elegance, had something **meagre** and comfortless in its **splendid tripods** and thin-legged **chairs**. There was in the apartment that air which **bespeaks** the struggle for appearances,—that struggle familiar to those of **limited income** and vain aspirings, who want the taste which smooths all **inequalities** and gives a smile to home; that taste which affection seems to prompt, if not to **create**, which shows itself in a thousand nameless, costless trifles, each a grace. No sign was there of the household cares or industry of women. No flowers, no music, no embroidery-frame, no work-table. Lucretia had none of the sweet feminine habits which betray so lovelily the whereabout of women. All was formal and precise, like rooms which we enter and leave,—not those in which we settle and **dwell**.

Lucretia herself is changed; her air is more assured, her complexion more pale, the evil character of her **mouth** more firm and pronounced.

French

affected: affecté, maniéré, artificiel, émus, influé, émut, émûmes, ému, émurent, émûtes, touché.
bespeaks: annonce, retient.
brood: couvée, nichée, progéniture.
chair: chaise, siège, fauteuil.
constitutional: constitutionnel.
contrast: contraste, mettre en contraste, opposition, antithèse, réglage du contraste.
create: créer, créons, écrire, composer.
doubly: de façon double, de manière double, doublement.
dwell: demeurer, habiter, loger.
fold: pli, plier, repli, plisser, pliure.
hatch: écoutille, trappe, hachurer, couvée, panneau, éclosion.
income: revenu, recette, produit, rente.
inequality: inégalité, inéquation.
limited: limité, borné.
meagre: maigre.
modern: moderne.
mouth: bouche, embouchure, bec, gueule, ouverture, entrée, goulot.
principal: principal, commettant, mandant, directeur, donneur d'ordre, dominant, capital.
safe: sûr, en sûreté, sans danger, sauf, à l'abri.
sat: couva, s'assirent, t'assis, vous assîtes, nous assîmes, m'assis, assis.
splendid: splendide, magnifique.
tripod: trépied, tripode.

Gabriel, still a mere **boy** in years, has a premature look of man. The down shades his lip. His dress, though **showy** and **theatrical**, is no longer that of boyhood. His **rounded** cheek has **grown** thin, as with the care and thought which beset the anxious step of youth on entering into life.

Both, as before remarked, spoke in whispers; both from time to time glanced fearfully at the door; both felt that they belonged to a hearth round which smile not the jocund graces of trust and love and the heart's open ease.

"But," said Gabriel, — "but if you would be safe, my father must have no secrets hid from you."

"I do not know that he has. He **speaks** to me frankly of his hopes, of the **share** he has in the **discovery** of the plot against the First Consul, of his interviews with Pierre Guillot, the Breton."

"Ah, because there your courage supports him, and your **acuteness** assists his own. Such secrets belong to his public life, his political **schemes**; with those he will trust you. It is his **private** life, his private **projects**, you must know."

"But what does he conceal from me? **Apart** from **politics**, his whole mind seems bent on the very natural object of **securing** intimacy with his **rich** cousin, M. Bellanger, from whom he has a right to **expect** so large an inheritance."

"Bellanger is rich, but he is not much older than my father."

"He has bad health."

"No," said Gabriel, with a **downcast** eye and a strange smile, "he has not bad health; but he may not be long-lived."

"How do you mean?" asked Lucretia, **sinking** her voice into a still **lower** whisper, while a shudder, she scarce knew why, passed over her **frame**.

"What does my father do," resumed Gabriel, "in that room at the **top** of the house? Does he tell you that secret?"

French

acuteness: intensité, acuité.
apart: particulier, à part, séparément.
boy: garçon, gosse, serviteur, gamin, domestique.
discovery: découverte, trouvaille, communication préalable, invention.
downcast: abattu, abaissé, baissé.
expect: attendre, espérer.
frame: cadre, trame, châssis, encadrer, image, charpente, membrure, carcasse, couple, bâti, photogramme.
grown: crû, grandi.
lower: baisser, abaisser, inférieur.
politic: politique.
private: privé, personnel, simple pompier, soldat, confidentiel.
project: projet, plan.
rich: riche.
rounded: arrondi.
scheme: schéma, projet, plan.
securing: fixant, arrimage.
share: action, part, prendre part, portion, ration, diviser, débiter, contingent.
showy: voyant, frimeur, prétentieux, tapageur.
sinking: affaissement, naufrage.
speaks: parle.
theatrical: théâtral, commercial.
top: sommet, haut, faîte, mutiler, summon, comble, supérieur, cime, tête, toupie, couvercle.

"He makes **experiments** in **chemistry**. You know that that was always his favourite study. You smile again! Gabriel, do not smile so; it **appalls** me. Do you think there is some **mystery** in that chamber?"

"It **matters** not what we think, belle-mere; it matters much what we know. If I were you, I would know what is in that chamber. I repeat, to be safe, you must have all his secrets, or none. Hush, that is his step!"

The door-handle turned noiselessly, and Olivier entered. His look fell on his son's face, which betrayed only **apparent** surprise at his unexpected return. He then glanced at Lucretia's, which was, as usual, cold and **impenetrable**.

"Gabriel," said Dalibard, gently, "I have come in for you. I have promised to take you to spend the day at M. Bellanger's; you are a great favourite with Madame. Come, my boy. I shall be back **soon**, Lucretia. I shall but drop in to leave Gabriel at my cousin's."

Gabriel **rose** cheerfully, as if only alive to the expectation of the bon-bons and compliments he **received** habitually from Madame Bellanger.

"And you can take your drawing **implements** with you," continued Dalibard. "This good M. Bellanger has given you permission to **copy** his Poussin."

"His Poussin! Ah, that is placed in his **bedroom** [It is scarcely necessary to observe that bedchambers in Paris, when **forming** part of the **suite** of reception-rooms, are often **decorated** no less **elaborately** than the other apartments], is it not?"

"Yes," answered Dalibard, **briefly**.

Gabriel lifted his **sharp**, **bright** eyes to his father's face. Dalibard turned away.

"Come!" he said with some **impatience**; and the boy took up his hat.

In another minute Lucretia was alone.

"Alone," in an English home, is a word implying no dreary solitude to an accomplished woman; but alone in that **foreign** land, alone in those half-

---

French

appalls: consterne, épouvante.
apparent: évident, apparent.
bedroom: chambre à coucher.
briefly: brièvement, de manière courte, de façon courte.
bright: clair, lumineux, luisant, brillant, magnifique, vif, éclatant.
chemistry: chimie, composition chimique, produit de traitement.
copy: copier, exemplaire, reproduire, imiter.
decorated: décora, agrémenté.
elaborately: de manière élaborée, de façon élaborée.
experiment: expérience, essai.
foreign: étranger, extérieur.
forming: formation, profilage.
impatience: impatience.
impenetrable: impénétrable, imperméable.
implement: instrument, outil, exécuter, implémenter.
matter: matière, substance, affaire, cas, chose, question.
mystery: mystère.
received: reçûtes, reçurent, accueillis.
rose: rose, rosace.
sharp: aigu, acéré, coupant, tranchant, précisément, piquant, perçant, dièse, rude, justement, à l'heure.
soon: bientôt, tout à l'heure.
suite: suite, clique, cortège, escorte.

furnished, desolate apartments,—few books, no **musical** instruments, no companions during the day to drop in,—that loneliness was wearying. And that mind so **morbidly** active! In the old Scottish **legend**, the spirit that serves the **wizard** must be kept constantly employed; **suspend** its work for a moment, and it rends the **enchanter**. It is so with minds that **crave** for excitement, and live, without relief of heart and affection, on the hard tasks of the intellect.

Lucretia mused over Gabriel's words and warning: "To be safe, you must know all his secrets, or none." What was the secret which Dalibard had not communicated to her?

She rose, stole up the cold, **cheerless** stairs, and ascended to the attic which Dalibard had lately hired. It was locked; and she observed that the lock was small,—so small that the key might be worn in a ring. She descended, and entered her husband's usual cabinet, which **adjoined** the sitting-room. All the books which the house **contained** were there,—a few works on metaphysics, Spinoza in especial, the great Italian histories, some volumes of **statistics**, many on physical and mechanical philosophy, and one or two works of **biography** and memoirs. No light literature,—that grace and flower of human culture, that best philosophy of all, **humanizing** us with gentle art, making us wise through the humours, elevated through the passions, tender in the affections of our kind. She took out one of the volumes that seemed less **arid** than the rest, for she was weary of her own thoughts, and began to read. To her surprise, the first passage she opened was **singularly** interesting, though the title was nothing more **seductive** than the "Life of a Physician of Padua in the Sixteenth Century." It related to that singular **epoch** of terror in Italy when some **mysterious** disease, **varying** in a thousand symptoms, baffled all remedy, and long defied all conjecture,—a disease **attacking** chiefly the heads of families, father and husband; rarely women. In one city, seven hundred husbands **perished**, but not one wife! The disease was **poison**. The hero of the memoir was one of the earlier **discoverers** of the true cause of this household **epidemic**. He had been a chief authority in a commission of inquiry. **Startling** were the details given in

French

adjoined: about it.
arid: aride, ingrat.
attacking: attaquant.
biography: biographie.
cheerless: morne.
contained: continrent, renfermas.
crave: sollicitons.
discoverer: découvreur, premier témoin.
enchanter: enchanteur, sorcier.
epidemic: épidémie.
epoch: époque, ère, période.

humanizing: humanisant.
legend: légende, marquage.
morbidly: de façon morbide, de manière morbide.
musical: musical, comédie musicale.
mysterious: mystérieux.
perished: péri, pérîtes.
poison: poison, venin, empoisonner, intoxiquer, substance toxique.
seductive: séduisant, aguichant.

singularly: de façon singulière, de manière singulière, singulièrement.
startling: surprenant, alarmant, ébouriffant, effarouchant, effrayant.
statistic: statistique, fonction des observations.
suspend: suspendre.
varying: variant, changeant.
wizard: sorcier, assistant, magicien, enchanteur.

the work,—the anecdotes, the histories, the **astonishing** craft brought daily to bear on the victim, the wondrous perfidy of the subtle means, the **variation** of the certain murder,—here **swift** as **epilepsy**, there slow and **wasting** as long decline. The lecture was absorbing; and absorbed in the book Lucretia still was, when she heard Dalibard's voice behind: he was looking over her shoulder.

"A strange selection for so fair a student! En fant, play not with such weapons."

"But is this all true?"

"True, though scarce a fragment of the truth. The physician was a sorry **chemist** and a worse **philosopher**. He **blundered** in his analysis of the means; and if I remember rightly, he whines like a **priest** at the motives,—for see you not what was really the cause of this **spreading pestilence**? It was the Saturnalia of the Weak,—a burst of mocking **license** against the Strong; it was more,—it was the **innate** force of the individual waging war against the many."

"I do not understand you."

"No? In that age, husbands were indeed lords of the household; they married mere children for their lands; they neglected and betrayed them; they were **inexorable** if the wife committed the faults set before her for example. Suddenly the wife found herself armed against her tyrant. His life was in her hands. So the weak had no mercy on the strong. But man, too, was then, even more than now, a **lonely wrestler** in a crowded **arena**. Brute force alone gave him distinction in courts; wealth alone brought him justice in the halls, or gave him safety in his home. Suddenly the **frail puny** lean saw that he could reach the mortal part of his giant foe. The noiseless **sling** was in his hand,—it smote Goliath from afar. Suddenly the poor man, ground to the **dust**, spat upon by contempt, saw through the crowd of richer **kinsmen**, who shunned and bade him rot; saw those whose death made him heir to **lordship** and gold and palaces and power and esteem. As a worm through a **wardrobe**, that man **ate** through velvet and **ermine**, and **gnawed**

French

arena: arène, piste.
astonishing: étonnant, époustouflant, surprenant.
ate: mangea, bouffèrent.
blundered: embrouillai.
chemist: chimiste, pharmacien, apothicaire.
dust: poussière, poudre, saupoudrer, épousseter.
epilepsy: épilepsie.
ermine: hermine.
frail: fragile, frêle.
gnawed: rongea.
inexorable: inexorable.
innate: inné, naturel, congénital.
kinsmen: parents.
license: licence, permis, autoriser.
lonely: solitaire, seul, de façon solitaire, de manière solitaire, isolé.
lordship: seigneurie.
pestilence: peste.
philosopher: philosophe.
priest: prêtre, curé, abbé.
puny: chétif.
sling: écharpe, fronde, élingue, bretelle.
spreading: diffusion, enduisage, épandage.
swift: rapide, prompt, martinet.
variation: variation, déclinaison, fluctuation.
wardrobe: penderie, armoire.
wasting: gaspillant, prodiguant, gâchant.
wrestler: lutteur, catcheur.

out the hearts that beat in his way. No. A great intellect can comprehend these criminals, and account for the crime. It is a mighty thing to feel in one's **self** that one is an army,—more than an army! What thousands and millions of men, with trumpet and **banner**, and under the sanction of **glory**, **strive** to do,—destroy a foe,—that, with little more than an effort of the will,—with a drop, a **grain**, for all his arsenal,—one man can do!"

There was a horrible enthusiasm about this reasoning **devil** as he spoke thus; his crest rose, his breast expanded. That **animation** which a noble thought gives to generous hearts **kindled** in the face of the **apologist** for the darkest and basest of human crimes. Lucretia shuddered; but her gloomy **imagination** was spelled; there was an interest mingled with her terror.

"Hush! you appall me," she said at last, timidly. "But, happily, this fearful art **exists** no more to tempt and destroy?"

"As a more philosophical discovery, it might be amusing to a chemist to learn exactly what were the **compounds** of those ancient poisons," said Dalibard, not directly **answering** the implied question. "Portions of the art are indeed lost, unless, as I suspect, there is much **credulous** exaggeration in the accounts **transmitted** to us. To kill by a flower, a pair of gloves, a soap-ball,—kill by means which elude all possible suspicion,—is it **credible**? What say you? An amusing research, indeed, if one had leisure! But enough of this now; it grows late. We dine with M. de—; he wishes to let his hotel. Why, Lucretia, if we knew a little of this old art, par Dieu! we could soon **hire** the hotel! Well, well; perhaps we may **survive** my cousin Jean Bellanger!"

Three days afterwards, Lucretia stood by her husband's side in the secret chamber. From the hour when she left it, a change was perceptible in her countenance, which gradually removed from it the character of youth. Paler the cheek could scarce become, nor more cold the discontented, restless eye. But it was as if some great care had settled on her brow, and contracted yet more the stern **outline** of the lips. Gabriel **noted** the **alteration**, but he did not attempt to win her confidence. He was **occupied** rather in **considering**, first, if it were well for him to sound deeper into the mystery he suspected;

French

alteration: modification, transformation, altération, changement, retouche.
animation: animation.
answering: répondant.
apologist: apologiste.
banner: bannière, drapeau, pavillon, banderole, étendard.
compound: composé, combiné, mot composé.
considering: considérant, envisageant, étant donné.
credible: croyable.
credulous: crédule.
devil: diable, tourbillon, poêle à flamber, démon.
exists: existe.
glory: gloire, renommée, réputation.
grain: grain, bloc de poudre, fil, pépin, blé.
hire: louer, louons, embaucher, location.
imagination: imagination, fantaisie.
kindled: allumâtes, enflammé.
noted: noté, annoté, célèbre.
occupied: occupâtes.
outline: contour, silhouette, esquisse, profil, résumer, schéma, tracé, ébauche.
self: même, soi.
strive: s'efforcer, combats, se battre.
survive: survivre, subsister.
transmitted: transmit, adressa.

and, **secondly,** to what extent, and on what terms, it became his interest to aid the designs in which, by Dalibard's hints and kindly treatment, he **foresaw** that he was meant to **participate.**

A word now on the rich kinsman of the Dalibards. Jean Bellanger had been one of those prudent Republicans who had put the Revolution to profit. By birth a Marseillais, he had settled in Paris, as an epicier, about the year 1785, and had **distinguished** himself by the **adaptability** and **finesse** which become those who fish in such troubled waters. He had sided with Mirabeau, next with Vergniaud and the Girondins. These he **forsook** in time for Danton, whose **facile corruptibility** made him a seductive patron. He was a large **purchaser** in the sale of the emigrant property; he **obtained** a contract for the supply of the army in the Netherlands; he abandoned Danton as he had abandoned the Girondins, but without taking any active part in the after-proceedings of the Jacobins. His next connection was with Tallien and Barras, and he enriched himself yet more under the Directory than he had done in the earlier stages of the Revolution. Under cover of an **appearance** of bonhomie and good humour, a **frank** laugh and an open countenance, Jean Bellanger had always retained general **popularity** and good-will, and was one of those whom the policy of the First Consul led him to **conciliate.** He had long since **retired** from the more vulgar departments of trade, but continued to **flourish** as an army **contractor.** He had a large hotel and a splendid **establishment**; he was one of the great **capitalists** of Paris. The relationship between Dalibard and Bellanger was not very close,—it was that of cousins twice removed; and during Dalibard's previous residence at Paris, each **embracing** different parties, and each **eager** in his career, the blood-tie between them had not been much thought of, though they were good friends, and each respected the other for the **discretion** with which he had kept aloof from the more sanguinary **excesses** of the time. As Bellanger was not many years older than Dalibard; as the former had but just married in the year 1791, and had naturally before him the prospect of a family; as his fortunes at that time, though rising, were **unconfirmed**; and as some nearer relations stood between them, in the shape of two promising, sturdy

---

French

adaptability: adaptabilité, faculté d'adaptation.
appearance: aspect, apparence, comparution, allure, spectacle, air.
capitalist: capitaliste.
conciliate: concilier, réconcilier.
contractor: entrepreneur, façonnier, maître des travaux, contrôleur délégué, prestataire.
corruptibility: corruptibilité.
discretion: discrétion, prudence, précaution.
distinguished: distinguas, dégageâtes.
eager: avide, désireux.
embracing: embrassant.
establishment: établissement, implantation.
excesses: excès.
facile: facile.
finesse: finesse, impasse.
flourish: prospérer, rinceau, parafe, trait de plume, fleurir.
foresaw: prévis.
forsook: abandonnâtes, délaissai.
frank: franc, affranchir.
obtained: obtint, obtîntes, obtenu.
participate: participer, prendre part.
popularity: popularité, banalité.
purchaser: acheteur, acquéreur.
retired: retiré, retraité.
secondly: deuxièmement, de manière seconde, de façon seconde.
unconfirmed: non confirmé.

nephews,—Dalibard had not then calculated on any inheritance from his cousin. On his return, circumstances were widely altered: Bellanger had been married some years, and no issue had blessed his nuptials. His nephews, draughted into the conscription, had perished in Egypt. Dalibard apparently became his **nearest** relative.

To avarice or to worldly ambition there was **undoubtedly** something very dazzling in the prospect thus opened to the eyes of Olivier Dalibard. The contractor's splendid **mode** of living, **vying** with that of the fermier-general of old, the colossal masses of capital by which he **backed** and **supported speculations** that **varied** with an ingenuity rendered practical and profound by experience, **inflamed** into **fever** the morbid restlessness of fancy and intellect which characterized the evil scholar; for that restlessness seemed to supply to his nature vices not constitutional to it. Dalibard had not the avarice that belongs either to a miser or a spendthrift. In his youth, his books and the simple desires of an **abstract** student sufficed to his wants, and a habit of method and order, a mechanical calculation which **accompanied** all his acts, from the least to the greatest, **preserved** him, even when most poor, from neediness and want. Nor was he by nature vain and ostentatious,—those infirmities accompany a larger and more luxurious nature. His philosophy rather despised, than inclined to, show. Yet since to plot and to scheme made his sole amusement, his absorbing excitement, so a man **wrapped** in himself, and with no generous ends in view, has little to plot or to scheme for but objects of worldly **aggrandizement**. In this Dalibard **resembled** one whom the intoxication of gambling has **mastered**, who neither wants nor greatly prizes the stake, but who has grown wedded to the venture for it. It was a madness like that of a certain rich nobleman in our own country who, with more money than he could spend, and with a **skill** in all games where skill **enters** that would have secured him success of itself, having learned the art of **cheating**, could not **resist** its indulgence. No hazard, no warning, could **restrain** him,—cheat he must; the **propensity** became iron-strong as a Greek destiny.

French

abstract: abstrait, résumé, abrégé, déduire, retrancher, réduction de texte, ôter, conclure, extrait.
accompanied: accompagnâtes.
aggrandizement: accroissement, agrandissement.
backed: chemisé, soutenu, doublage.
cheating: tricherie, escroquerie, fraude, tromperie.
enters: entre, introduit.
fever: fièvre, la fièvre.
inflamed: enflammé.
mastered: gravé, maîtrisé.
mode: mode, manière.
nearest: plus proche.
preserved: conservé.
propensity: propension, prédisposition.
resembled: ressembla, rejoignîmes.
resist: résister, épargne, enduit protecteur.
restrain: retenir, réprimer, retiennent, gouverner, surveiller, régner, restreindre.
skill: habileté, compétence, adresse.
speculation: spéculation.
supported: soutenu, appuyé.
undoubtedly: sans doute, indubitablement, de façon indubitable, de manière indubitable.
varied: variâmes, divers.
vying: rivalisant.
wrapped: enrobé.

That the possible chance of an inheritance so magnificent should **dazzle** Lucretia and Gabriel, was yet more natural; for in them it appealed to more direct and eloquent, though not more powerful, propensities. Gabriel had every vice which the **greed** of gain most **irritates** and **excites**. **Intense covetousness** lay at the core of his heart; he had the sensual temperament, which yearns for every enjoyment, and takes pleasure in every pomp and show of life. Lucretia, with a hardness of mind that disdained luxury, and a certain grandeur (if such a word may be applied to one so perverted) that was **incompatible** with the **sordid** infirmities of the miser, had a **determined** and **insatiable** ambition, to which **gold** was a necessary instrument. Wedded to one she loved, like Mainwaring, the ambition, as we have said in a former chapter, could have lived in another, and become **devoted** to intellectual efforts, in the nobler desire for power based on fame and genius. But now she had the gloomy **cravings** of one fallen, and the uneasy desire to restore herself to a lost position; she fed as an **aliment** upon scorn to bitterness of all beings and all things around her. She was gnawed by that false fever which **riots** in those who seek by outward seemings and **distinctions** to console themselves for the want of their own self-esteem, or who, despising the world with which they are brought in contact, sigh for those worldly advantages which alone justify to the world itself their contempt.

To these diseased infirmities of vanity or pride, whether exhibited in Gabriel or Lucretia, Dalibard administered without apparent effort, not only by his conversation, but his habits of life. He **mixed** with those much wealthier than himself, but not better born; those who, in the hot and fierce **ferment** of that new society, were rising fast into new aristocracy,—the fortunate soldiers, daring **speculators**, **plunderers** of many an argosy that had been **wrecked** in the Great Storm. Every one about them was actuated by the **keen** desire "to make a fortune;" the desire was **contagious**. They were not **absolutely** poor in the proper sense of the word "poverty," with Dalibard's annuity and the interest of Lucretia's fortune; but they were poor **compared** to those with whom they associated,—poor enough for **discontent**. Thus, the image of the mighty **wealth** from which, perhaps, but a

French

absolutely: absolument, vraiment, en réalité, sûrement, sans faute, en vérité, en fait, de manière absolue, de façon absolue.
aliment: aliment.
compared: comparâmes.
contagious: contagieux.
covetousness: avidité.
craving: désir ardent, envie, sollicitant.
dazzle: aveugler, éblouissement.
determined: déterminâtes, décidé.

devoted: dévoué, consacrâmes, affectueux, attaché.
discontent: mécontentement.
distinction: distinction.
excites: excite, hérisse.
ferment: fermenter, humidifier.
gold: or, l'or.
greed: avidité, avarice, cupidité.
incompatible: incompatible, inalliable, marchandises incompatibles.
insatiable: insatiable.

intense: intense, fort, aigu, vif, violent.
irritates: irrite, énerve.
keen: vif, aiguisé, vigilant, alerte, actif, affilé.
mixed: mélangé, mixte, mêlé.
plunderer: pillard.
riot: émeute, baroufle, bagarre.
sordid: sordide, vil.
speculator: spéculateur.
wealth: richesse, fortune.
wrecked: démoli, naufragé.

single life divided them, became horribly haunting. To Gabriel's sensual vision the image presented itself in the shape of **unlimited** pleasure and prodigal riot; to Lucretia it wore the solemn majesty of power; to Dalibard himself it was but the Eureka of a calculation,—the **palpable** reward of wile and scheme and **dexterous combinations**. The devil had temptations suited to each.

Meanwhile, the Dalibards were more and more with the Bellangers. Olivier glided in to talk of the chances and changes of the State and the market. Lucretia sat for hours **listening mutely** to the contractor's boasts of past frauds, or submitting to the martyrdom of his **victorious** games at tric-trac. Gabriel, a spoiled **darling**, copied the pictures on the walls, **complimented** Madame, flattered Monsieur, and fawned on both for **trinkets** and crowns. Like three birds of night and omen, these three evil natures settled on the rich man's roof.

Was the rich man himself blind to the motives which **budded** forth into such attentive affection? His penetration was too acute, his ill opinion of mankind too strong, perhaps, for such amiable self-delusions. But he took all in good part; availed himself of Dalibard's hints and suggestions as to the employment of his capital; was polite to Lucretia, and readily condemned her to be **beaten** at tric-trac; while he accepted with bonhomie Gabriel's spirited copies of his pictures. But at times there was a gleam of satire and malice in his round gray eyes, and an **inward** chuckle at the caresses and **flatteries** he received, which perplexed Dalibard and humbled Lucretia. Had his wealth been wholly at his own **disposal**, these signs would have been **inauspicious**; but the new law was strict, and the **bulk** of Bellanger's property could not be **alienated** from his nearest **kin**. Was not Dalibard the nearest?

These hopes and speculations did not, as we have seen, **absorb** the restless and rank energies of Dalibard's **crooked**, but **capacious** and grasping intellect. **Patiently** and ingeniously he pursued his main political object,—the detection of that **audacious** and **complicated** conspiracy against the First Consul, which **ended** in the tragic deaths of Pichegru, the Duc d'Enghien,

French

absorb: absorber, amortir, disposer, assimiler.
alienated: aliénèrent.
audacious: audacieux, hardi.
beaten: battu, abattue.
budded: bourgeonné.
bulk: vrac, grandeur, masse, ampleur, importance, volume, taille.
capacious: vaste.
combination: combinaison, couplage, complexe, coalition, agrégat, assemblage.
complicated: compliquèrent, embrouillé, tarabiscoté.
complimented: complimenté.
crooked: tordu, de travers.
darling: chéri, favori, charmant.
dexterous: adroit, habile.
disposal: disposition, vente.
ended: terminé, sortie, finirent.
flattery: flatterie, adulation.
inauspicious: peu propice.
inward: intérieur, vers l'intérieur.
kin: parenté, famille.
listening: écoutant, interrogation.
mutely: de façon muete, de manière muette.
palpable: palpable.
patiently: de façon patiente, de manière patiente, patiemment.
trinket: colifichet, bibelot.
unlimited: illimité, indéfini, sans bornes.
victorious: victorieux, vainqueur.

and the erring but illustrious hero of La Vendee, George Cadoudal. In the midst of these dark plots for personal aggrandizement and political fortune, we leave, for the moment, the sombre, sullen soul of Olivier Dalibard.

Time has passed on, and spring is over the world. The seeds buried in the earth burst to flower; but man's breast knoweth not the sweet division of the seasons. In winter or summer, autumn or spring alike, his thoughts **sow** the **germs** of his actions, and day after day his destiny **gathers** in her **harvests**.

The joy-bells ring clear through the groves of Laughton,—an heir is born to the old name and fair lands of St. John. And, as usual, the present race welcomes **merrily** in that which shall succeed and replace it,—that which shall thrust the enjoyers down into the black graves, and **wrest** from them the pleasant goods of the world. The joy-bell of birth is a note of warning to the **knell** for the dead; it wakes the worms beneath the mould: the new-born, every year that it grows and flourishes, speeds the parent to their feast. Yet who can **predict** that the infant shall become the heir? Who can tell that Death sits not side by side with the nurse at the **cradle**? Can the mother's hand measure out the **woof** of the Parcae, or the father's eye detect through the darkness of the **morrow** the gleam of the fatal **shears**?

It is market-day at a town in the midland districts of England. There Trade takes its **healthiest** and most animated form. You see not the **stunted** form and hollow eye of the mechanic,—poor slave of the capitalist, poor agent and victim of the arch disequalizer, Civilization. There strides the **burly** form of the farmer; there waits the ruddy **hind** with his **flock**; there, patient, sits the miller with his samples of corn; there, in the **booths**, gleam the humble **wares** which form the luxuries of cottage and farm. The thronging of men, and the clacking of whips, and the dull sound of wagon or dray, that parts the crowd as it passes, and the lowing of herds and the bleating of sheep,—all are sounds of movement and **bustle**, yet **blend** with the pastoral associations of the **primitive** commerce, when the link between market and farm was visible and direct.

French

blend: mélanger, mêler, retourner, coupage.
booth: cabine, baraque.
burly: robuste.
bustle: tournure, se démener, s'affairer.
cradle: berceau, arceau, nacelle, cerceau.
flock: troupeau, bourre, tontisse, flocon.
gather: rassembler, ramasser, réunir, recueillir, déduire, conclure, collectionner, assembler, froncer, grappiller, récolter.
germ: germe, microbe.
harvest: récolte, moisson, recueillir, vendange.
healthiest: le plus sain.
hind: biche, suivant, de derrière.
knell: glas.
merrily: joyeusement, de façon joyeuse, de manière joyeuse.
morrow: lendemain.
predict: prédire, présager.
primitive: primitif.
shear: tondre, découper, cisaillement, couper avec des ciseaux.
sow: semer, truie, coche, ensemencer.
stunted: rabougri.
ware: articles, marchandise.
woof: trame, aboiement, aboyer, retraité bien nanti.
wrest: arrache.

Towards one large house in the centre of the brisk life **ebbing** on, you might see stream after stream **pour** its way. The large doors **swinging** light on their hinges, the gilt letters that shine above the threshold, the windows, with their **shutters** outside **cased** in iron and **studded** with **nails**, **announce** that that house is the bank of the town. Come in with that **yeoman** whose broad face tells its tale, sheepish and down-eyed,—he has come, not to **invest**, but to **borrow**. What matters? War is breaking out **anew**, to bring the time of high prices and paper money and credit. Honest yeoman, you will not be refused. He scratches his rough head, pulls a leg, as he calls it, when the clerk leans over the **counter**, and asks to see "Muster Mawnering hisself." The clerk points to the little office-room of the new **junior** partner, who has brought 10,000 pounds and a clear head to the firm. And the yeoman's great boots creak heavily in. I told you so, honest yeoman; you come out with a smile on your brown face, and your hand, that might fell an ox, buttons up your huge breeches pocket. You will **ride** home with a light heart; go and dine, and be merry.

The yeoman tramps to the ordinary; plates **clatter**, tongues **wag**, and the borrower's full heart finds vent in a good word for that kind "Muster Mawnering." For a wonder, all join in the praise. "He's an honour to the town; he's a pride to the country. Thof he's such a friend at a **pinch**, he's a **rale** mon of business. He'll make the baunk worth a million! And how well he spoke at the great county meeting about the war, and the laund, and them bloodthirsty Mounseers! If their members were loike him, Muster Fox would look small!"

The day declines; the town empties; **whiskeys**, horses, and **carts** are giving life to the roads and the lanes; and the market is deserted, and the bank is shut up, and William Mainwaring walks back to his home at the skirts of the town. Not villa nor cottage, that plain English house, with its cheerful face of red **brick**, and its **solid squareness** of shape,—a symbol of **substance** in the fortunes of the owner! Yet as he passes, he sees through the distant trees the hall of the member for the town. He pauses a moment, and sighs unquietly. That pause and that sigh betray the germ of ambition and

---

French

anew: de nouveau, encore.
announce: annoncer, publier, introduire.
borrow: emprunter, prêter, retenue.
brick: brique, brik, la brique, maçonner.
cart: charrette, camionner.
cased: retourné.
clatter: cliquetis, bavarder, bruit.
counter: compteur, guichet, voûte, contrefort.
ebbing: baissant, jusant.

invest: investir, placer d'argent.
junior: junior, cadet, débutant, jeune.
nail: clou, ongle, river, pointe, cheville.
pinch: pincer, serrer.
pour: verser, servir, déverser, couler, affluer, fondre.
rale: râle.
ride: chevaucher, monter à cheval, tour, aller, se déplacer.
shutter: obturateur, volet.

solid: solide, massif.
squareness: perpendicularité, équerrage, forme carrée.
studded: clouté, pointes de diamant.
substance: substance, fond.
swinging: balancement, pivotant, oscillation.
wag: remuer, farceur.
whiskey: whisky.
yeoman: secrétaire militaire.

discontent. Why should not he, who can speak so well, be member for the town, instead of that **stammering** squire? But his reason has soon silenced the **querulous** murmur. He **hastens** his step,—he is at home! And there, in the neat-furnished drawing-room, which looks on the garden behind, hisses the welcoming tea-urn; and the piano is open, and there is a **packet** of new books on the table; and, best of all, there is the glad face of the sweet English wife. The happy scene was characteristic of the time, just when the simpler and more innocent luxuries of the higher class spread, not to **spoil**, but **refine** the middle. The dress, air, mien, movements of the young couple; the unassuming, suppressed, sober elegance of the house; the flower-garden, the books, and the music, evidences of cultivated taste, not **signals** of display,— all bespoke the gentle **fusion** of ranks before **rude** and uneducated wealth, made in **looms** and **lucky** hits, rushed in to separate forever the gentleman from the **parvenu**.

Spring smiles over Paris, over the spires of Notre Dame and the crowded alleys of the Tuileries, over thousands and thousands eager, joyous, aspiring, reckless,—the New Race of France, bound to one man's destiny, children of glory and of carnage, whose blood the **wolf** and the **vulture** scent, **hungry**, from afar!

The conspiracy against the life of the First Consul has been detected and **defeated**. Pichegru is in prison, George Cadoudal **awaits** his trial, the Duc d'Enghien sleeps in his bloody grave; the **imperial** crown is prepared for the great soldier, and the great soldier's creatures bask in the **noonday** sun. Olivier Dalibard is in high and **lucrative** employment; his rise is ascribed to his talents, his opinions. No service connected with the detection of the conspiracy is traced or **traceable** by the public eye. If such exist, it is known but to those who have no desire to **reveal** it. The old apartments are retained, but they are no longer dreary and comfortless and deserted. They are gay with draperies and **ormolu** and **mirrors**; and Madame Dalibard has her nights of reception, and Monsieur Dalibard has already his **troops** of clients. In that **gigantic concentration** of egotism which under Napoleon is called the

---

French

await: attendre.
concentration: concentration.
defeated: vaincu, battu.
fusion: fusion.
gigantic: gigantesque, énorme, formidable, colossal.
hasten: hâter, hâtons.
hungry: affamé, anémique.
imperial: impérial.
loom: métier à tisser, manche, gaine isolante, lueur.
lucky: chanceux, heureux.

lucrative: lucratif.
mirror: miroir, glace, rétroviseur.
noonday: midi.
ormolu: or moulu.
packet: paquet, colis, entassement.
parvenu: parvenu, nouveau riche.
querulous: quérulant, ronchon.
refine: raffiner, épurer, affiner.
reveal: révéler, révèle, publier, développer, déceler, jouée.
rude: grossier, impoli, mal élevé.
signal: signal, transmettre des signalisations, témoignage, lampe de signalisation, attaquer, indiquer, feu, cavalier.
spoil: abîmer, gâcher, gâter, détériorer, déblais.
stammering: bégaiement, balbutiement.
traceable: traçable.
troop: troupe, bande.
vulture: vautour.
wolf: loup, le loup, quinte du loup.

State, Dalibard has found his place. He has **served** to swell the power of the **unit**, and the cipher gains **importance** by its position in the **sum**.

Jean Bellanger is no more. He died, not **suddenly**, and yet of some quick disease,—nervous exhaustion; his schemes, they said, had worn him out. But the state of Dalibard, though prosperous, is not that of the heir to the dead millionnaire. What mistake is this? The bulk of that wealth must go to the nearest kin,—so runs the law. But the will is read; and, for the first time, Olivier Dalibard learns that the dead man had a son,—a son by a former marriage,—the marriage **undeclared**, **unknown**, amidst the riot of the Revolution; for the wife was the **daughter** of a proscrit. The son had been reared at a distance, put to school at Lyons, and unavowed to the second wife, who had brought an ample dower, and whom that discovery might have **deterred** from the altar. Unacknowledged through life, in death at least the son's rights are proclaimed; and Olivier Dalibard feels that Jean Bellanger has died in vain! For days has the pale Provencal been closeted with lawyers; but there is no hope in **litigation**. The proofs of the marriage, the birth, the identity, come out clear and **clearer**; and the **beardless schoolboy** at Lyons **reaps** all the **profit** of those nameless schemes and that mysterious death. Olivier Dalibard desires the friendship, the intimacy of the heir; but the heir is consigned to the **guardianship** of a **merchant** at Lyons, near of kin to his mother, and the guardian **responds** but coldly to Olivier's letters. Suddenly the defeated aspirant seems **reconciled** to his loss. The widow Bellanger has her own **separate** fortune, and it is large beyond expectation. In addition to the wealth she brought the deceased, his affection had led him to invest **vast** sums in her name. The widow then is rich,—rich as the heir himself. She is still fair. Poor woman, she needs consolation! But, meanwhile, the nights of Olivier Dalibard are disturbed and broken. His eye in the **daytime** is haggard and anxious; he is seldom seen on **foot** in the streets. Fear is his companion by day, and sits at night on his **pillow**. The Chouan, Pierre Guillot, who looked to George Cadoudal as a god, knows that George Cadoudal has been betrayed, and suspects Olivier Dalibard; and the Chouan has an arm of iron, and a heart steeled against all mercy. Oh, how the pale scholar thirsted for

French

beardless: imberbe.
clearer: purgeur, nettoyeur.
daughter: fille, la fille.
daytime: journée.
deterred: dissuadâtes.
foot: pied, patte, bordure, le pied.
guardianship: curatelle, tutelle, garde.
importance: importance.
litigation: litige, contentieux.
merchant: négociant, marchand, commerçant.
pillow: oreiller, coussin.
profit: bénéfice, profit, gain, avantage.
reaps: moissonne.
reconciled: réconciliâtes, rapprochèrent, raccommodèrent.
responds: répond, réplique.
schoolboy: écolier, collégien, élève.
separate: séparer, particulier, disperser, diviser, dissiper, trier, débiter, indépendant.
served: servîmes, desservîmes.
suddenly: soudainement, tout à coup, subitement, de manière subite, brusquement, de façon subite.
sum: somme, montant, addition.
undeclared: non déclaré.
unit: unité, élément, bloc, groupe.
unknown: inconnu, ignoré.
vast: étendu, large, vaste, ample.

that Chouan's blood! With what relentless **pertinacity**, with what ingenious research, he had set all the **hounds** of the police upon the track of that single man! How **notably** he had **failed**! An **avenger** lived; and Olivier Dalibard started at his own shadow on the wall. But he did not the less continue to plot and to intrigue—nay, such occupation became more necessary, as an escape from himself.

And in the mean while, Olivier Dalibard sought to take courage from the recollection that the Chouan had taken an oath (and he knew that oaths are held **sacred** with the Bretons) that he would keep his hand from his knife unless he had clear evidence of treachery; such evidence existed, but only in Dalibard's **desk** or the **archives** of Fouche. Tush, he was safe! And so, when from **dreams** of fear he started at the depth of night, so his bolder wife would whisper to him with firm, uncaressing lips: "Olivier Dalibard, thou fearest the living: dost thou never fear the dead? Thy dreams are haunted with a spectre. Why takes it not the accusing shape of thy mouldering kinsman?" and Dalibard would answer, for he was a philosopher in his cowardice: "Il n'y a que les morts qui ne reviennent pas."

It is the **notable convenience** of us narrators to **represent**, by what is called "soliloquy," the thoughts, the **interior** of the personages we **describe**. And this is almost the master-work of the tale-teller,—that is, if the soliloquy be really in words, what self-commune is in the dim and tangled recesses of the human heart! But to this privilege we are rarely admitted in the case of Olivier Dalibard, for he rarely communed with himself. A sort of **mental** calculation, it is true, eternally went on within him, like the **wheels** of a destiny; but it had become a mechanical operation, seldom disturbed by that **consciousness** of thought, with its struggles of fear and doubt, conscience and crime, which gives its **appalling** interest to the soliloquy of tragedy. Amidst the **tremendous secrecy** of that profound intellect, as at the **bottom** of a sea, only monstrous images of terror, things of **prey**, stirred in cold-blooded and devouring life; but into these deeps Olivier himself did not **dive**. He did not face his own soul; his **outer** life and his **inner** life seemed separate **individualities**, just as, in some complicated State, the social

---

French

appalling: épouvantable, consternant, effroyable.
archive: archives.
avenger: vengeur.
bottom: fond, derrière, cul, bas, croupe, inférieur, dessous.
consciousness: conscience, connaissance.
convenience: convenance, commodité.
describe: décrire, représenter, dépeindre.
desk: pupitre, bureau.
dive: plonger, piqué.
dream: rêve, songe.
failed: faillies, échoué, manqué.
hound: chien de chasse, talonner, traquer, jottereau, capelage.
individuality: individualité.
inner: interne, intérieur.
interior: intérieur.
mental: mental, intellectuel.
notable: notable.
notably: notamment, de façon notable, de manière notable.
outer: extérieur, externe.
pertinacity: entêtement.
prey: proie.
represent: représenter, figurer.
sacred: sacré, saint.
secrecy: secret, discrétion.
tremendous: énorme, terrible, prodigieux, immense, formidable, épouvantable, fantastique.
wheel: roue, volant, galet.

machine goes on through all its **numberless cycles** of vice and dread, **whatever** the acts of the government, which is the representative of the State, and **stands** for the State in the **shallow** judgment of history.

Before this time Olivier Dalibard's manner to his son had greatly changed from the indifference it betrayed in England,—it was kind and affectionate, almost caressing; while, on the other hand, Gabriel, as if in possession of some secret which gave him power over his father, took a more careless and **independent** tone, often absented himself from the house for days together, joined the **revels** of young **profligates** older than himself, with whom he had formed acquaintance, indulged in **spendthrift expenses**, and plunged prematurely into the stream of vicious pleasure that **oozed** through the **mud** of Paris.

One morning Dalibard, **returning** from a visit to Madame Bellanger, found Gabriel alone in the **salon**, contemplating his fair face and gay dress in one of the mirrors, and **smoothing** down the hair, which he wore long and sleek, as in the portraits of Raphael. Dalibard's lip curled at the boy's coxcombry,—though such tastes he himself had fostered, according to his **ruling principles**, that to govern, you must find a **foible**, or instil it; but the sneer changed into a smile.

"Are you satisfied with yourself, joli garcon?" he said, with **saturnine playfulness**.

"At least, **sir**, I hope that you will not be ashamed of me when you formally legitimatize me as your son. The time has come, you know, to keep your promise."

"And it shall be kept, do not fear. But first I have an **employment** for you,—a **mission**; your first **embassy**, Gabriel."

"I **listen**, sir."

"I have to send to England a communication of the utmost importance—public importance—to the secret agent of the French government. We are on the eve of a descent on England. We are in correspondence with some in London on whom we count for support. A man might be suspected and

French

cycle: cycle, bicyclette, vélo, bécane, manœuvrer.
embassy: ambassade.
employment: emploi, occupation, travail, embauche.
expense: dépense, frais.
foible: faible.
independent: indépendant, impartial.
listen: écouter, entendre, être en mode Réception.
machine: machine, usiner.
mission: mission.
mud: boue, vase, bourbe, limon.
numberless: innombrable.
oozed: suinta, exsudé.
playfulness: enjouement.
principle: principe, loi.
profligate: débauché, libertin.
returning: renvoyant, retournant.
revel: se divertir, s'amuser.
ruling: réglage, dominant, décision.
salon: salon.
saturnine: saturnin.
shallow: peu profond, superficiel.
sir: monsieur.
smoothing: amortissement, ajustement, modulation.
spendthrift: dépensier, gaspilleur, prodigue.
stand: stand, être debout, kiosque, support, échoppe, se dresser, peuplement, socle, pied, sursauter, position.
whatever: quoi que, n'importe quel, quel que, tout ce que.

searched,—mind, searched. You, a boy, with English name and **speech**, will be my safest **envoy**. Bonaparte approves my **selection**. On your return, he permits me to present you to him. He loves the rising **generation**. In a few days you will be **prepared** to start."

Despite the calm tone of the father, so had the son, from the instinct of fear and self-preservation, studied every accent, every glance of Olivier,—so had he **constituted** himself a spy upon the heart whose perfidy was ever **armed**, that he detected at once in the proposal some scheme hostile to his interests. He made, however, no opposition to the plan **suggested**; and seemingly satisfied with his obedience, the father dismissed him.

As soon as he was in the streets, Gabriel went **straight** to the house of Madame Bellanger. The hotel had been **purchased** in her name, and she therefore retained it. Since her husband's death he had avoided that house, before so familiar to him; and now he grew pale and breathed hard as he passed by the porter's lodge up the lofty stairs.

He knew of his father's recent and **constant** visits at the house; and without conjecturing **precisely** what were Olivier's designs, he connected them, in the natural and acquired **shrewdness** he possessed, with the wealthy widow. He resolved to **watch**, observe, and **draw** his own **conclusions**. As he entered Madame Bellanger's room rather abruptly, he observed her **push** aside amongst her papers something she had been gazing on,—something which **sparkled** to his eyes. He sat himself down close to her with the caressing manner he usually **adopted** towards women; and in the midst of the **babbling** talk with which ladies generally honour boys, he suddenly, as if by **accident**, displaced the papers, and saw his father's miniature set in brilliants. The start of the widow, her blush, and her exclamation strengthened the light that flashed upon his mind. "Oh, ho! I see now," he said laughing, "why my father is always praising black hair; and—nay, nay—gentlemen may admire ladies in Paris, surely?"

"Pooh, my dear child, your father is an old friend of my poor husband, and a near relation too! But, Gabriel, mon petit ange, you had better not say

French

accident: accident, sinistre.
adopted: adoptas.
armed: armé, armâmes, armai.
babbling: babiller, bavardant.
conclusion: conclusion, résultat.
constant: constant, continuel, permanent, invariable, perpétuel.
constituted: constitué.
draw: dessiner, puiser, tirer, appâter, solliciter, abaisser, allécher, tracer, match nul, tirage, traçons.
envoy: envoyé, ambassadeur, émissaire, représentant.
generation: génération, production.
precisely: précisément, de façon précise, de manière précise.
prepared: prépara, apprêtai, prêt.
purchased: acheté.
push: pousser, imposer, coup extérieur, charge incorrecte, biaiser, appuyer.
searched: cherché.
selection: sélection, choix.
shrewdness: perspicacité, sagacité.
sparkled: brillâmes.
speech: discours, parole, langage, allocution, élocution.
straight: droit, direct, franc, tout droit, rectiligne, honnête, ligne droite.
suggested: suggéras.
watch: montre, regarder, horloge, veiller, être spectateur de, surveiller, pendule, garde, voir, observer, guetter.

at home that you have seen this **picture**; Madame Dalibard might be foolish enough to be angry."

"To be sure not. I have kept a secret before now!" and again the boy's cheek grew pale, and he looked **hurriedly** round.

"And you are very fond of Madame Dalibard too; so you must not **vex** her."

"Who says I'm fond of Madame Dalibard? A stepmother!"

"Why, your father, of course,—il est si bon, ce pauvre Dalibard; and all men like cheerful faces. But then, poor lady,—an Englishwoman, so strange here; very natural she should **fret**, and with bad health, too."

"Bad health! Ah, I **remember**! She, also, **does** not seem likely to **live** long!"

"So your poor father **apprehends**. Well, well; how **uncertain** life is! Who would have thought dear Bellanger would have—"

Gabriel rose hastily, and interrupted the widow's **pathetic** reflections. "I only ran in to say Bon jour. I must leave you now."

"Adieu, my dear boy,—not a word on the miniature! By the by, here's a shirt-pin for you,—tu es joli comme un amour."

All was clear now to Gabriel; it was necessary to get rid of him, and forever. Dalibard might dread his attachment to Lucretia,—he would dread still more his closer intimacy with the widow of Bellanger, should that widow wed again, and Dalibard, **freed** like her (by what means?), be her choice! Into that **abyss** of **wickedness**, **fathomless** to the innocent, the young villanous eye plunged, and surveyed the **ground**; a terror seized on him,—a terror of life and death. Would Dalibard **spare** even his own son, if that son had the power to **injure**? This mission, was it exile only,—only a **fall** back to the old squalor of his uncle's studio; only the laying aside of a useless tool? Or was it a **snare** to the grave? **Demon** as Dalibard was, doubtless the boy wronged him. But guilt **construes** guilt for the worst.

French

abyss: abîme, abysse, gouffre.
apprehends: appréhende, craint.
construes: analyse.
demon: démon.
doe: biche, hase, lapine, daine.
fall: chute, tomber, baisse, choir, s'abattre, s'amoindrir, décrue, choyez, abats, pente.
fathomless: impénétrable, insondable.
freed: libéré.
fret: frette, mousser fortement, cloison, tracasser.
ground: terre, sol, fond, masse, échouer, motif.
hurriedly: à la hâte, de façon hâtive, de manière hâtive, précipitamment.
injure: abîmer, détériorer, blesser.
live: vivre, vis, vivent, vivons, habiter, demeurer, loger, vivant, actif, sous tension.
pathetic: pathétique, pitoyable.
picture: image, figure, tableau, photo.
remember: se rappeler, se souvenir, retenir, rappeler, retiens.
snare: piège, collet.
spare: épargner, économiser, être indulgent, rechange, pièce de rechange.
uncertain: incertain, aléatoire, vague.
vex: chagriner, vexer, vexons.
wickedness: méchanceté, atrocité, cruauté.

Gabriel had **formerly** enjoyed the thought to **match** himself, should danger come, with Dalibard; the hour had come, and he felt his impotence. Brave his father, and **refuse** to leave France! From that, even his reckless hardihood shrank, as from inevitable **destruction**. But to depart,—be the poor **victim** and dupe; after having been let **loose** amongst the riot of pleasure, to return to labour and privation,—from that **option** his vanity and his senses **vindictively** revolted. And Lucretia, the only being who seemed to have a human kindness to him! Through all the vicious egotism of his nature, he had some grateful sentiments for her; and even the egotism **assisted** that **unwonted** amiability, for he felt that, Lucretia gone, he had no hold on his father's house, that the home of her successor never would be his. While thus **brooding**, he lifted his eyes, and saw Dalibard pass in his carriage towards the Tuileries. The house, then, was clear; he could see Lucretia alone. He formed his resolution at once, and turned homewards. As he did so, he observed a man at the angle of the street, whose eyes followed Dalibard's carriage with an expression of **unmistakable** hate and revenge; but scarcely had he **marked** the countenance, before the man, looking hurriedly round, darted away, and was lost amongst the crowd.

Now, that countenance was not quite unfamiliar to Gabriel. He had seen it before, as he saw it now,—hastily, and, as it were, by fearful **snatches**. Once he had marked, on returning home at twilight, a figure **lurking** by the house; and something, in the quickness with which it turned from his gaze, joined to his knowledge of Dalibard's apprehensions, made him **mention** the circumstance to his father when he entered. Dalibard bade him hasten with a **note**, written hurriedly, to an agent of the police, whom he kept **lodged** near at hand. The man was still on the threshold when the boy went out on this **errand**, and he caught a **glimpse** of his face; but before the police-agent **reached** the spot, the ill-omened apparition had vanished. Gabriel now, as his eye rested full upon that **threatening** brow and those burning eyes, was convinced that be saw before him the terrible Pierre Guillot, whose very name blenched his father's cheek. When the figure retreated, he resolved at once to **pursue**. He hurried through the crowd amidst which the man had

French

assisted: assista, aida, aidé, aidâtes, aidèrent.
brooding: élevage des poussins.
destruction: destruction, ravage, annihilation.
errand: commission, message, course.
formerly: autrefois, auparavant, devant, anciennement, jadis.
glimpse: entrevoir.
lodged: logé.
loose: détaché, lâche.
lurking: badaudage.
marked: marqué.
match: allumette, apparier, match, s'entremettre, assortir, partie, égal, rencontre.
mention: mentionner, citer.
note: note, billet, nota, remarque, mention, ticket.
option: option, alternative, choix, faculté.
pursue: poursuivre, continuer, rechercher.
reached: parvenu.
refuse: refuser, rejeter, déchets, détritus, repousser, ordures.
snatch: arraché en flexion, saisir, fragment, chercher à attraper.
threatening: menaçant, sinistre.
unmistakable: indubitable.
unwonted: insolite.
victim: victime.
vindictively: de façon vindicative, de manière vindicative.

disappeared, and looked eagerly into the faces of those he jostled; sometimes at the distance he caught sight of a figure which appeared to resemble the one which he pursued, but the likeness faded on approach. The chase, however, vague and desultory as it was, led him on till his way was lost amongst **labyrinths** of narrow and unfamiliar streets. Heated and **thirsty**, he paused, at last, before a small **cafe**, entered to ask for a draught of **lemonade**, and behold, chance had **favoured** him! The man he sought was seated there before a **bottle** of wine, and **intently** reading the newspaper. Gabriel sat himself down at the adjoining table. In a few moments the man was joined by a **newcomer**; the two conversed, but in whispers so low that Gabriel was unable to hear their conversation, though he caught more than once the name of "George." Both the men were **violently** excited, and the expression of their countenances was menacing and sinister. The first comer pointed often to the newspaper, and read **passages** from it to his companion. This suggested to Gabriel the demand for another **journal**. When the waiter brought it to him, his eye rested upon a long **paragraph**, in which the name of George Cadoudal frequently occurred. In fact, all the journals of the day were filled with speculations on the conspiracy and trial of that **fiery** martyr to an erring **adaptation** of a noble principle. Gabriel knew that his father had had a principal share in the detection of the defeated enterprise; and his previous persuasions were **confirmed**.

His sense of hearing grew **sharper** by continued effort, and at length he heard the first comer say distinctly, "If I were but sure that I had brought this fate upon George by **introducing** to him that **accursed** Dalibard; if my oath did but justify me, I would—" The **concluding** sentence was lost. A few moments after, the two men rose, and from the familiar words that passed between them and the master of the cafe, who approached, himself, to receive the **reckoning**, the shrewd boy perceived that the place was no **unaccustomed** haunt. He crept nearer and nearer; and as the **landlord** shook hands with his customer, he heard distinctly the former address him by the name of "Guillot." When the men **withdrew**, Gabriel followed them at a distance (taking care first to impress on his memory the name of the cafe,

---

French

accursed: maudit.
adaptation: adaptation, transformation.
bottle: bouteille, embouteiller, flacon.
cafe: café.
concluding: concluant, final, clôturant.
confirmed: confirmâtes.
favoured: favorisé.
fiery: ardent, fougueux.
intently: attentivement, de façon intentionnelle, de manière intentionnelle.
introducing: introduisant, présentant.
journal: journal, tourillon, quotidien, revue, livre journal, magazine, portée d'arbre.
labyrinth: labyrinthe, dédale.
landlord: propriétaire, aubergiste, logeur.
lemonade: limonade, citronnade.
newcomer: novice, nouveau.
paragraph: alinéa, paragraphe.
passage: passage, couloir, corridor, traversée, canal.
reckoning: calculant, compte, estime.
sharper: tricheur, escroc.
thirsty: assoiffé, altéré.
unaccustomed: inaccoutumé, inhabituel.
violently: violemment, de façon violente, de manière violente.
withdrew: retiras.

and the street in which it was placed) and, as he thought, **unobserved**; he was mistaken. Suddenly, in one street more solitary than the rest, the man whom he was **mainly** bent on **tracking** turned round, **advanced** to Gabriel, who was on the other side of the street, and laid his hand upon him so abruptly that the boy was fairly taken by surprise.

"Who bade you **follow** us?" said he, with so dark and fell an expression of countenance that even Gabriel's courage failed him. "No **evasion**, no lies; **speak** out, and at once;" and the grasp **tightened** on the boy's **throat**.

Gabriel's readiness of resource and presence of mind did not long **forsake** him.

"Loose your hold, and I will tell you—you stifle me." The man slightly **relaxed** his grasp, and Gabriel said quickly "My mother perished on the guillotine in the Reign of Terror; I am for the Bourbons. I thought I **overheard** words which showed sympathy for poor George, the brave Chouan. I followed you; for I thought I was following friends."

The man smiled as he fixed his steady eye upon the **unflinching** child. "My poor lad," he said gently, "I believe you,—pardon me; but follow us no more,—we are dangerous!" He waved his hand, and strode away and **rejoined** his companion, and Gabriel reluctantly abandoned the pursuit and went homeward. It was long before he reached his father's house, for he had **strayed** into a strange quarter of Paris, and had **frequently** to **inquire** the way. At length he reached home, and ascended the stairs to a small room in which Lucretia usually sat, and which was divided by a **narrow** corridor from the sleeping-chamber of herself and Dalibard. His stepmother, leaning her cheek upon her hand, was seated by the **window**, so absorbed in some gloomy thoughts, which **cast** over her rigid face a shade, intense and solemn as despair, that she did not perceive the approach of the boy till he threw his arms round her neck, and then she started as in alarm.

"You! only you," she said, with a constrained smile; "see, my nerves are not so strong as they were."

"You are disturbed, belle-mere,—has he been **vexing** you?"

French

advanced: avancé, poussé.
cast: fondre, moule, couler, plâtre, distribution, acteurs.
evasion: évasion, fraude.
follow: suivre, suis, respecter, agir selon.
forsake: abandonner, délaisser, quitter, livrer.
frequently: fréquemment, souvent, beaucoup, de façon fréquente, de manière fréquente.
inquire: enquérir, m'enquiers, vous enquérez, t'enquiers, s'enquièrent, se renseigner, nous enquérons, demander.
mainly: principalement, surtout, de manière principale, en grande partie, de façon principale.
narrow: étroit, rétrécir, serré, restreint, resserré, diminuer, défilé, borné, limité.
overheard: surprirent.
rejoined: rejoignit, répliquai, rallié.
relaxed: détendu, relaxâtes, relâchâtes.
speak: parler, dire, obtenir la parole.
strayed: écartai.
throat: gorge, la gorge, gosier.
tightened: serra, resserrâmes.
tracking: poursuite, cheminement.
unflinching: décidé.
unobserved: inobservé.
vexing: chagrinant, vexant.
window: fenêtre, guichet, hublot, créneau, la fenêtre.

"He—Dalibard? No, indeed; we were only this morning **discussing** matters of business."

"Business,—that means money."

"Truly," said Lucretia, "money does make the staple of life's business. In spite of his new **appointment**, your father needs some sums in hand,— favours are to be **bought**, **opportunities** for speculation **occur**, and—"

"And my father," interrupted Gabriel, "wishes your consent to **raise** the rest of your portion?"

Lucretia looked surprised, but answered quietly: "He had my consent long since; but the **trustees** to the marriage-settlement—mere men of business, my uncle's **bankers**; for I had lost all **claim** on my kindred—refuse, or at least **interpose** such **difficulties** as amount to refusal."

"But that reply came some days since," said Gabriel, musingly.

"How did you know,—did your father tell you?"

"Poor belle-mere!" said Gabriel, almost with pity; "can you live in this house and not watch all that passes,—every stranger, every **message**, every letter? But what, then, does he wish with you?"

"He has suggested my returning to England and seeing the trustees **myself**. His interest can **obtain** my passport."

"And you have refused?"

"I have not consented."

"Consent!—hush!—your maid; Marie is not **waiting** without;" and Gabriel rose and looked forth. "No, **confound** these doors! none close as they ought in this house. Is it not a **clause** in your **settlement** that the half of your fortune now invested goes to the survivor?"

"It is," replied Lucretia, struck and thrilled at the question. "How, again, did you know this?"

"I saw my father **reading** the copy. If you die first, then, he has all. If he **merely** wanted the money, he would not send you away."

French

appointment: nomination, rencontre.
banker: banquier, plateau pour gâcher, établi de maçon.
bought: acheté.
claim: créance, revendication, réclamer, demande, requérir, exiger.
clause: clause, disposition, proposition, stipulation.
confound: confondre, déconcerter.
difficulty: difficulté, ennui, peine.
discussing: discutant, débattant.
interpose: interposer.
merely: simplement, de façon pure, de manière pure.
message: message, renseignement.
myself: me.
obtain: obtenir, obtiennent, acquérir, procurer.
occur: arriver, avoir lieu, survenir, intervenir, se présenter.
opportunity: occasion, opportunité.
raise: lever, élever, soulever, entonner, augmentation, relever, hausse, éduquer, majorer, dresser, ériger.
reading: lecture, lisant.
settlement: règlement, colonie, liquidation, tassement, possession, accord, établissement, arrangement.
trustee: fiduciaire, curateur, fidéicommissaire, dépositaire, consignataire, administrateur.
waiting: attendant, arrêt.

There was a terrible pause. Gabriel resumed: "I trust you, it may be, with my life; but I will speak out. My father goes much to Bellanger's widow; she is rich and weak. Come to England! Yes, come; for he is about to dismiss me. He fears that I shall be in the way, to warn you, perhaps, or to—to— In **short**, both of us are in his way. He gives you an escape. Once in England, the war which is breaking out will **prevent** your return. He will **twist** the laws of **divorce** to his favour; he will marry again! What then? He spares you what **remains** of your fortune; he spares your life. **Remain** here,—cross his schemes, and—No, no; come to England,—safer **anywhere** than here!"

As he spoke, great changes had passed over Lucretia's countenance. At first it was the **flash** of conviction, then the stunned shock of horror; now she rose, rose to her full height, and there was a **livid** and deadly light in her eyes,—the light of conscious courage and power and revenge. "Fool," she muttered, "with all his craft! Fool, fool! As if, in the war of household **perfidy**, the woman did not always conquer! Man's only **chance** is to be mailed in honour."

"But," said Gabriel, **overhearing** her, "but you do not remember what it is. There is nothing you can see and guard against. It is not like an enemy face to face; it is death in the food, in the **air**, in the touch. You **stretch** out your arms in the dark, you feel nothing, and you die! Oh, do not fancy that I have not thought well (for I am almost a man now) if there were no means to resist,—there are none! As well make head against the plague,—it is in the atmosphere. Come to England, and return. Live **poorly**, if you must, but live—but live!"

"Return to England poor and despised, and bound still to him, or a **disgraced** and **divorced** wife,—disgraced by the low-born **dependant** on my kinsman's house,—and **fawn** perhaps upon my sister and her husband for **bread**! Never! I am at my **post**, and I will not fly."

"Brave, brave!" said the boy, **clapping** his hands, and **sincerely** moved by a daring superior to his own; "I wish I could help you!"

French

air: air, mélodie, aérer, air de musique, aria, ventiler.
anywhere: quelque part, n'importe où.
bread: pain, paner.
chance: hasard, chance, accidentel, occasion.
clapping: claquage, physiothérapie respiratoire, applaudir.
dependant: personne à charge.
disgraced: disgraciâmes.
divorce: divorce.
divorced: divorcé.
fawn: faon, fauve.
flash: flash, éclat, clignoter, bavure.
livid: livide.
overhearing: écoute indiscrète, surprenant.
perfidy: perfidie.
poorly: pauvrement, de façon pauvre, de manière pauvre.
post: poste, poteau, pieu, fonction, emploi, afficher, courrier, coller, office, agglutiner, service.
prevent: empêcher, prévenir.
remain: rester, demeurer.
remains: reste, vestige, débris.
short: court, manquant, tube court, petite longueur, insuffisant, cycliste, brusquement, bref, culotte.
sincerely: sincèrement, de façon sincère, de manière sincère.
stretch: tendre, étendre, étirer, s'étendre, allongement.
twist: tordre, torsion.

Lucretia's eye rested on him with the full gaze, so rare in its looks. She drew him to her and kissed his brow. "Boy, through life, whatever our guilt and its **doom**, we are bound to each other. I may yet live to have wealth; if so, it is yours as a son's. I may be iron to others,—never to you. Enough of this; I must reflect!" She passed her hands over her eyes a moment, and resumed: "You would help me in my self-defence; I think you can. You have been more **alert** in your watch than I have. You must have means I have not secured. Your father guards well all his papers."

"I have keys to every desk. My foot passed the threshold of that room under the roof before yours. But no; his powers can never be yours! He has never **confided** to you half his secrets. He has **antidotes** for every—every—"

"Hist! what **noise** is that? Only the **shower** on the **casements**. No, no, child, that is not my object. Cadoudal's conspiracy! Your father has letters from Fouche which show how he has betrayed others who are stronger to **avenge** than a woman and a boy."

"Well?"

"I would have those letters. Give me the keys. But hold! Gabriel, Gabriel, you may yet **misjudge** him. This woman—wife to the **dead** man—his wife! Horror! Have you no proofs of what you imply?"

"Proofs!" echoed Gabriel, in a tone of wonder; "I can but see and conjecture. You are warned, watch and decide for yourself. But again I say, come to England; I shall go!"

Without reply, Lucretia took the keys from Gabriel's half-reluctant hand, and passed into her husband's **writing-room**. When she had entered, she locked the door. She passed at once to a **huge secretary**, of which the key was small as a fairy's work. She opened it with ease by one of the **counterfeits**. No love-correspondence—the first object of her **search**, for she was woman—met her eye. What need of letters, when interviews were so **facile**? But she soon found a **document** that told all which love-letters could tell,—it was an **account** of the moneys and possessions of Madame Bellanger; and there were pencil notes on the **margin**: "Vautran will give four **hundred**

French

account: compte, rapport, client, relation, considérer, facture, penser que, être d'avis, motif, description, croire.
alert: alerte, vif, vigilant, actif.
antidote: antidote, contrepoison.
avenge: venger.
casement: croisée, châssis, vantail.
confided: confié.
counterfeit: contrefaçon, faux.
dead: mort, perdue, tension, stérile, sourd, sans tension, hors tension, inactif, fibres mortes par suite d'un raffinage excessif, claqué, peau de qualité inférieure.
document: document, acte, pièce, titre.
doom: ruine, condamner, destin.
facile: facile.
huge: énorme, immense, gigantesque, formidable, vaste, colossal.
hundred: cent.
margin: marge, bord, couverture.
misjudge: mal juger, méjugez.
noise: bruit, tapage, souffle.
search: recherche, perquisition, chercher, fouille.
secretary: secrétaire.
shower: douche, averse, se doucher, gerbe, prendre une douche, ondée.
writing-room: salon de correspondance.

thousand **francs** for the lands in Auvergne,—to be **accepted**. Consult on the power of **sale** granted to a second husband. **Query**, if there is no chance of the heir-at-law **disputing** the moneys invested in Madame B.'s name," — and such memoranda as a man notes down in the **schedule** of **properties** about to be his own. In these **inscriptions** there was a hideous mockery of all love; like the **blue** lights of corruption, they showed the black vault of the heart. The pale reader saw what her own **attractions** had been, and, fallen as she was, she smiled superior in her bitterness of scorn. Arranged methodically with the precision of business, she found the letters she next looked for; one **recognizing** Dalibard's services in the detection of the conspiracy, and **authorizing** him to employ the police in the search of Pierre Guillot, **sufficed** for her **purpose**. She withdrew, and **secreted** it. She was about to lock up the secretary, when her eye fell on the **title** of a small **manuscript volume** in a corner; and as **shet** read, she pressed one hand **convulsively** to her heart, while **twice** with the other she grasped the volume, and twice withdrew the grasp. The title ran **harmlessly** thus: "Philosophical and Chemical Inquiries into the Nature and Materials of the Poisons in Use between the Fourteenth and Sixteenth Centuries." Hurriedly, and at last as if doubtful of herself, she left the manuscript, closed the secretary, and returned to Gabriel.

"You have got the **paper** you seek?" he said.

"Yes."

"Then whatever you do, you must be quick; he will soon discover the loss."

"I will be quick."

"It is I whom he will suspect," said Gabriel, in alarm, as that thought struck him. "No, for my sake do not take the letter till I am **gone**. Do not fear in the mean time; he will do nothing against you while I am here."

"I will replace the letter till then," said Lucretia, meekly. "You have a right to my first thoughts." So she went back, and Gabriel (suspicious perhaps) crept after her.

French

accepted: acceptâmes, agréé.
attraction: attraction, appât.
authorizing: autorisant.
blue: bleu, azur.
convulsively: de façon convulsive, de manière convulsive.
disputing: disputant.
franc: franc.
gone: allé, parti.
harmlessly: de façon inoffensive, de manière inoffensive.
inscription: inscription, exergue,
légende.
manuscript: manuscrit, restitution photogrammétrique, stéréominute, minute.
paper: papier, document, tapisser, article, journal.
property: propriété, biens, domaine, qualité, possession, fonds, accessoire, patrimoine.
purpose: but, dessein, objet, intention.
query: requête, question.
recognizing: reconnaissant, retrouvant.
sale: vente, solde, abattement.
schedule: calendrier, tableau, horaire, programme, annexe, barème, liste, plan, ordonnancer.
secreted: sécrétas.
shet: toit éboulé.
sufficed: suffîmes.
title: titre, intitulé.
twice: deux fois, bis.
volume: volume, tome.

As she replaced the document, he pointed to the manuscript which had tempted her. "I have seen that before; how I longed for it! If anything ever happens to him, I claim that as my legacy."

Their hands met as he said this, and grasped each other convulsively; Lucretia relocked the secretary, and when she gained the next room, she **tottered** to a chair. Her strong nerves gave way for the moment; she uttered no cry, but by the whiteness of her face, Gabriel saw that she was senseless,—senseless for a minute or so; scarcely more. But the return to consciousness with a **clenched** hand, and a brow of defiance, and a **stare** of mingled **desperation** and **dismay**, seemed rather the awaking from some **frightful** dream of **violence** and struggle than the slow, languid **recovery** from the **faintness** of a **swoon**. Yes, henceforth, to **sleep** was to couch by a serpent,—to breathe was to listen for the **avalanche**! Thou who didst trifle so wantonly with Treason, now gravely front the grim comrade thou hast **won**; thou scheming desecrator of the Household Gods, now learn, to the last page of dark knowledge, what the hearth is without them!

Gabriel was **strangely** moved as he beheld that proud and solitary despair. An instinct of nature had hitherto **checked** him from **actively aiding** Lucretia in that struggle with his father which could but end in the destruction of one or the other. He had contented himself with forewarnings, with hints, with **indirect** suggestions; but now all his sympathy was so strongly roused on her behalf that the last faint scruple of filial conscience vanished into the abyss of blood over which stood that lonely Titaness. He drew near, and clasping her hand, said, in a quick and broken voice,—

"Listen! You know where to find proof of my fa—that is, of Dalibard's treason to the conspirators, you know the name of the man he dreads as an avenger, and you know that he **waits** but the proof to **strike**; but you do not know where to find that man, if his revenge is **wanting** for yourself. The police have not **hunted** him out: how can you? Accident has made me acquainted with one of his haunts. Give me a single promise, and I will put you at least upon that clew,—weak, perhaps, but as yet the sole one to be followed. Promise me that, only in defence of your own life, not for mere

French

actively: activement, de façon active, de manière active.
aiding: aider.
avalanche: avalanche.
checked: quadrillé, à carreaux.
clenched: rivé.
desperation: désespoir.
dismay: consterner, stupéfier, abasourdir, atterrer.
faintness: malaise, faiblesse.
frightful: affreux, effroyable, épouvantable.
hunted: chassâtes.
indirect: indirect, détourné.
recovery: récupération, rétablissement, reprise, guérison, recouvrement, salut.
sleep: sommeil, dormir, dors, pioncer.
stare: dévisager, regarder fixement, fixer.
strangely: étrangement, de façon étrange, de manière étrange.
strike: grève, frapper, heurter, forer, toucher, s'allumer, battre, saisir, rencontrer, atteindre, parvenir.
swoon: s'évanouir, se pâmer, pâmoison, évanouissement.
tottered: vacillé, titubé, chancelèrent.
violence: violence.
wait: attendre, servir.
wanting: voulant, désirant.
won: gagnèrent, remportèrent.

jealousy, you will avail yourself of the knowledge, and you shall know all I do!"

"Do you think," said Lucretia, in a calm, cold voice, "that it is for jealousy, which is love, that I would murder all hope, all peace? For we have here"—and she smote her breast—"here, if not elsewhere, a heaven and a hell! Son, I will not harm your father, except in self-defence. But tell me nothing that may make the son a party in the father's doom."

"The father **slew** the mother," muttered Gabriel, between his clenched teeth; "and to me, you have wellnigh supplied her place. Strike, if need be, in her name! If you are driven to want the arm of Pierre Guillot, seek news of him at the Cafe Dufour, Rue S—, Boulevard du Temple. Be calm now; I hear your husband's step."

A few days more, and Gabriel is gone! Wife and husband are alone with each other. Lucretia has refused to depart. Then that mute **coma** of horror, that suspense of two foes in the conflict of death; for the subtle, **prying** eye of Olivier Dalibard sees that he himself is suspected,—further he shuns from **sifting**! Glance **fastens** on glance, and then **hurries smilingly** away. From the cup **grins** a skeleton, at the board warns a spectre. But how kind still the words, and how gentle the tone; and they lie down side by side in the marriage-bed,—brain plotting against brain, heart loathing heart. It is a **duel** of life and death between those **sworn** through life and beyond death at the altar. But it is carried on with all the forms and courtesies of duel in the age of chivalry. No **conjugal** wrangling, no slip of the tongue; the oil is on the surface of the wave,—the **monsters** in the hell of the abyss war **invisibly** below. At length, a dull **torpor** creeps over the woman; she feels the **taint** in her veins,—the slow victory is begun. What mattered all her **vigilance** and **caution**? Vainly glide from the **fangs** of the serpent,—his very breath suffices to destroy! Pure seems the draught and **wholesome** the viand,—that master of the science of murder needs not the means of the **bungler**! Then, keen and strong from the **creeping lethargy** started the fierce instinct of self and the ruthless impulse of revenge. Not too late yet to escape; for those subtle **banes**, that are to defy all detection, work but slowly to their end.

French

bane: fléau, peste.
bungler: bousilleur, maladroit, saboteur, gâcheur.
caution: prudence, avertir, alerter, précaution, attention.
coma: coma, comète.
conjugal: conjugal.
creeping: rampant, traînant, usure du presseur, reptation de talus, fluent, fluage, débordement de l'application, contraction, boursouflement du sol,
cheminant, glissant.
duel: duel.
fang: croc.
fastens: attache, verrouille, lie.
grin: sourire, rictus.
hurry: se dépêcher, hâte, presser, être urgent, dépêcher, se presser, se hâter.
invisibly: de façon invisible, de manière invisible, invisiblement.
lethargy: léthargie.
monster: monstre, clébard.
prying: fureteur, indiscret.
sifting: tamisant, criblage.
slew: tuâmes, tuèrent, tuâtes, tuas, tua, tuai.
smilingly: de façon souriante, de manière souriante.
sworn: juré, assermenté.
taint: entacher, infection.
torpor: torpeur.
vigilance: vigilance, état de veille.
wholesome: sain, salubre.

One **evening** a woman, closely mantled, stood at watch by the angle of a **wall**. The light came dim and muffled from the window of a cafe hard at hand; the reflection slept amidst the shadows on the dark pavement, and save a solitary lamp **swung** at distance in the vista over the centre of the narrow street, no ray broke the gloom. The night was clouded and **starless**, the **wind moaned** in **gusts**, and the rain fell **heavily**; but the gloom and the loneliness did not appall the eye, and the wind did not chill the heart, and the rain fell **unheeded** on the head of the woman at her post. At times she paused in her slow, sentry-like **pace** to and fro, to look through the window of the cafe, and her gaze fell always on one **figure** seated apart from the rest. At length her pulse **beat** more **quickly**, and the patient lips smiled sternly. The figure had risen to depart. A man came out and walked quickly up the street; the woman approached, and when the man was under the single lamp swung aloft, he felt his arm touched: the woman was at his side, and looking steadily into his face—

"You are Pierre Guillot, the Breton, the friend of George Cadoudal. Will you be his avenger?"

The Chouan's first impulse had been to place his hand in his vest, and something shone bright in the lamp-light, clasped in those iron **fingers**. The voice and the manner **reassured** him, and he answered readily,—

"I am he whom you seek, and I only live to avenge."

"Read, then, and act," answered the woman, as she placed a paper in his hands.

At Laughton the **babe** is on the breast of the fair mother, and the father sits beside the **bed**; and mother and father **dispute** almost **angrily** whether mother or father those soft, rounded **features** of slumbering infancy resemble most. At the **red** house, near the market-town, there is a hospitable bustle. William is home **earlier** than usual. Within the last hour, Susan has been thrice into every room. Husband and wife are now **watching** at the window. The good Fieldens, with a coach full of children, are **expected**, every moment, on a week's visit at least.

French

angrily: de manière fâchée, de façon fâchée.
babe: bébé.
beat: battement, frapper, heurter, temps, rythme.
bed: lit, planche, couche, banc.
dispute: dispute, se disputer, contester, différend, conflit, débattre.
earlier: plus tôt, avant.
evening: soir, égalisage.
expected: attendit, prévu.
feature: trait, caractéristique, fonction, grand film.
figure: figure, chiffre, compter, calculer, forme, silhouette.
finger: doigt, tâter.
gust: rafale, coup de vent.
heavily: fortement, de manière lourde, lourdement, de façon lourde.
moaned: gémi, bêla, bêlèrent, bêlés.
pace: pas, allure, faire les cent pas, rythme.
quickly: rapidement, vite, de façon rapide, de manière rapide.
reassured: rassuré.
red: rouge.
starless: sans étoiles.
swung: pivotai, balancé.
unheeded: ignoré, inaperçu, négligé.
wall: mur, paroi, cloison, muraille.
watching: regarder.
wind: vent, enrouler, emmailloter, bobiner.

In the **cafe** in the Boulevard du Temple sit Pierre Guillot, the Chouan, and another of the old **band** of **brigands** whom George Cadoudal had mustered in Paris. There is an expression of content on Guillot's countenance,—it seems more open than usual, and there is a **complacent** smile on his lips. He is **whispering** low to his friend in the intervals of eating,—an employment pursued with the **hearty gusto** of a hungry man. But his friend **does** not seem to **sympathize** with the cheerful feelings of his **comrade**; he is pale, and there is terror on his face; and you may see that the journal in his hand **trembles** like a **leaf**.

In the gardens of the Tuileries some **score** or so of gossips group together.

"And no news of the murderer?" asked one.

"No; but the man who had been friend to Robespierre must have made secret enemies enough."

"Ce pauvre Dalibard! He was not mixed up with the Terrorists, nevertheless."

"Ah, but the more deadly for that, perhaps; a **sly** man was Olivier Dalibard!"

"What's the matter?" said an **employee**, lounging up to the group. "Are you talking of Olivier Dalibard? It is but the other day he had Marsan's appointment. He is now to have Pleyel's. I heard it two days ago; a capital thing! Peste! il ira **loin**. We shall have him a **senator** soon."

"Speak for yourself," quoth a ci-devant abbe, with a laugh; "I should be **sorry** to see him again soon, **wherever** he be."

"Plait-il? I don't **understand** you!"

"Don't you know that Olivier Dalibard is **murdered**, found stabbed,—in his own house, too!"

"Ciel! Pray tell me all you know. His place, then, is vacant!"

"Why, it seems that Dalibard, who had been brought up to medicine, was still fond of **chemical** experiments. He hired a room at the top of the house for such **scientific** amusements. He was **accustomed** to spend part of his

French

accustomed: accoutumé, se 'habitua, nous 'habituâmes, me 'habituai, te 'habituas, vous 'habituâtes, habituel.
band: bande, orchestre, tranche, fanfare, troupeau, ruban, zone.
brigand: brigand.
cafe: café.
chemical: chimique, produit chimique.
complacent: complaisant.
comrade: camarade.
doe: biche, hase, lapine, daine.
employee: employé, salarié, travailleur, ouvrier.
gusto: vigueur, délectation, plaisir.
hearty: cordial, chaleureux.
leaf: feuille, rallonge, vantail, pousse, lamelle, volant, aile.
loin: lombes, reins, longe.
murdered: assassiné.
scientific: scientifique.
score: orchestrer, note, rayure, partition, marque, score, adapter,
cote.
senator: sénateur, père conscrit.
sly: rusé, malin, astucieux, artificieux.
sorry: désolé, navré, pardon.
sympathize: compatir, sympathisez.
tremble: trembler, frémir.
understand: comprendre, entendre.
wherever: partout où, là où.
whispering: chuchotement, murmure.

nights there. They found him at morning **bathed** in his blood, with three ghastly wounds in his side, and his fingers cut to the **bone**. He had struggled hard with the knife that butchered him."

"In his own house!" said a lawyer. "Some servant or spendthrift heir."

"He has no heir but young Bellanger, who will be riche a millions, and is now but a schoolboy at Lyons. No; it seems that the window was left open, and that it **communicates** with the rooftops. There the **murderer** had entered, and by that way escaped; for they found the leads of the **gutter dabbled** with blood. The next house was uninhabited, — easy enough to get in there, and lie perdu till night."

"Hum!" said the lawyer. "But the **assassin** could only have learned Dalibard's habits from some one in the house. Was the deceased married?"

"Oh, yes, — to an Englishwoman."

"She had lovers, perhaps?"

"Pooh, lovers! The happiest couple ever known; you should have seen them together! I **dined** there last week."

"It is strange," said the lawyer.

"And he was getting on so well," muttered a hungry-looking man.

"And his place is vacant!" repeated the employee, as he quitted the crowd abstractedly.

In the house of Olivier Dalibard sits Lucretia alone, and in her own usual morning-room. The **officer** appointed to such **tasks** by the French law has **performed** his visit, and made his notes, and **expressed condolence** with the widow, and promised justice and **retribution**, and placed his seal on the locks till the representatives of the heir-at-law shall **arrive**; and the heir-at-law is the very boy who had succeeded so **unexpectedly** to the wealth of Jean Bellanger the contractor! But Lucretia has obtained beforehand all she wishes to save from the rest. An open **box** is on the floor, into which her hand drops noiselessly a volume in manuscript. On the **forefinger** of that hand is a **ring**, **larger** and more **massive** than those usually worn by

French

arrive: arriver, atteindre, parvenir, réussir.
assassin: assassin.
bathed: baignèrent.
bone: os, désosser, arête.
box: boîte, caisse, boxer, coffret, case, boite, loge, encadré, carton, buis, bac.
communicates: communique.
condolence: condoléances.
dabbled: mouillâtes, barboté.
dined: dîné, dînèrent, dinâmes,
dîna.
expressed: exprimas, extériorisa, émise.
forefinger: index.
gutter: gouttière, caniveau, rigole, petits fonds, lézarde, rue, blanc de fond, logement de bavure, crochet de jante, dalot, goulotte.
larger: plus grand.
massive: massif, énorme.
murderer: meurtrier, assassin.
officer: officier, fonctionnaire.
performed: réalisé, accomplîmes, effectua, rempli, exécuté.
retribution: châtiment, récompense.
ring: anneau, bague, sonner, tinter, cercle, couronne, rondelle, cerne, ring, cycle, son.
task: tâche, devoir.
unexpectedly: de façon inattendue, de manière inattendue, inopinément.

women, — by Lucretia never worn before. Why should that ring have been **selected** with such care from the dead man's **hoards**? Why so **precious** the dull **opal** in that cumbrous setting? From the hand the volume drops without sound into the box, as those whom the secrets of the volume **instruct** you to destroy may drop without noise into the grave. The trace of some illness, recent and deep, nor conquered yet, has **ploughed** lines in that young countenance, and **dimmed** the light of those searching eyes. Yet courage! the poison is arrested, the **poisoner** is no more. Minds like thine, stern woman, are cased in **coffers** of **steel**, and the **rust** as yet has gnawed no deeper than the surface. So over that face, stamped with **bodily suffering**, plays a calm smile of triumph. The schemer has baffled the schemer! Turn now to the right, pass by that narrow corridor: you are in the marriage-chamber; the windows are closed; **tall** tapers burn at the foot of the bed. Now go back to that narrow corridor. Disregarded, thrown aside, are a cloth and a besom: the cloth is **wet** still; but here and there the red stains are dry, and clotted as with bloody **glue**; and the hairs of the besom start up, torn and ragged, as if the **bristles** had a sense of some horror, as if things **inanimate** still partook of men's dread at men's deeds. If you passed through the corridor and saw in the shadow of the wall that homeliest of instruments cast away and forgotten, you would smile at the slatternly **housework**. But if you knew that a **corpse** had been borne down those stairs to the left, — borne along those floors to that marriage-bed, — with the blood **oozing** and gushing and plashing below as the **bearers** passed with their **burden**, then straight that dead thing would take the awe of the dead being; it told its own tale of violence and murder; it had dabbled in the gore of the violated **clay**; it had become an evidence of the crime. No wonder that its hairs bristled up, sharp and ragged, in the shadow of the wall.

The first part of the tragedy ends; let fall the curtain. When next it rises, years will have passed away, graves uncounted will have wrought fresh hollows in our merry sepulchre, — sweet earth! Take a sand from the **shore**, take a drop from the ocean, — less than sand-grain and drop in man's **planet** one Death and one Crime! On the **map**, trace all **oceans**, and search out every

French

bearer: porteur, support, traverse.
bodily: corporel, physique.
bristle: soie, poil, crin.
burden: fardeau, charge, alourdir, grever, lit de fusion.
clay: argile, colloïde minéral, glaise, terre glaise.
coffer: plafonnier encastré, coffre.
corpse: cadavre, corps.
dimmed: estompé.
glue: colle, adhésif.
hoard: amas, thésaurisation, stocker, trésor.
housework: travaux domestiques, ménage.
inanimate: inanimé.
instruct: instruire, donner des instructions, enseigner.
map: carte, plan, mappe, application.
ocean: océan, mer.
oozing: suintement, exsudant.
opal: opale.
planet: planète.
ploughed: labouré.
poisoner: empoisonneur.
precious: précieux, rare.
rust: rouille, se rouiller.
selected: sélectionna, choisi.
shore: rive, bord, côte, rivage, accore, étai, étançon, étayer.
steel: acier, aciérer.
suffering: souffrant, subissant.
tall: haut, grand.
wet: mouillé, humide.

shore,—more than **seas**, more than **lands**, in God's **balance** shall **weigh** one Death and one Crime!

French

balance: solde, balance, équilibre, bilan, reliquat, reste.
land: terre, atterrir, pays, aborder, contrée, s'abattre.
sea: mer, marin.
weigh: peser, pèses, pesons.

PART THE SECOND.

PROLOGUE TO PART THE SECOND.

The century has advanced. The **rush** of the deluge has ebbed back; the old **landmarks** have **reappeared**; the dynasties Napoleon willed into life have **crumbled** to the dust; the **plough** has passed over Waterloo; **autumn** after autumn the harvests have glittered on that grave of an empire. Through the immense ocean of universal change we look back on the **single track** which our frail **boat** has **cut** through the waste. As a **star** shines impartially over the measureless **expanse**, though it seems to **gild** but one broken line into each eye, so, as our memory gazes on the past, the light spreads not over all the **breadth** of the waste where **nations** have **battled** and argosies gone down,—it falls narrow and **confined** along the single course we have taken; we lean over the small **raft** on which we **float**, and see the **sparkles** but reflected from the waves that it divides.

On the terrace at Laughton but one step paces slowly. The **bride** clings not now to the bridegroom's arm. Though pale and worn, it is still the same gentle face; but the blush of woman's love has gone from it evermore.

Charles Vernon (to **call** him still by the name in which he is best known to us) sleeps in the vault of the St. Johns. He had lived longer than he himself had expected, than his physician had hoped,—lived, cheerful and happy, amidst quiet pursuits and innocent excitements. Three sons had blessed his hearth, to mourn over his grave. But the two elder were delicate and sickly.

French

autumn: automnal, arrière, saison.
battled: lutté.
boat: bateau, barque, canot, embarcation, navire.
breadth: largeur, travers.
bride: fiancée, mariée, accordée.
call: appel, communication, nommer, visite, escale.
confined: confiné, enfermé, accouchâmes.
crumbled: froissa, émietta.
cut: couper, tailler, trancher, hacher, balafre, découper, tondre, faucher, réduction, entaille, incision.
expanse: étendue.
float: flotter, planer, nager, taloche.
gild: dorer, dorons.
landmark: point de repère, repère.
nation: nation, peuple.
plough: charrue, labourer.
raft: radeau, radier, rame, tapée.
reappeared: reparûmes, réapparu.
rush: ruée, jonc, se dépêcher, épreuve, congestion, afflux de sang, urgent, précipiter, hâte.
single: célibataire, unique, seul, simple, individuel.
sparkle: étincelle, éclat, scintiller, pétiller, briller.
star: étoile, vedette, star, astral.
track: piste, voie, route, trace, empreinte, impression, chenille, chemin de roulement, rail.

They did not long survive him, and **died** within a few months of each other. The third seemed formed of a different mould and **constitution** from his **brethren**. To him descended the ancient heritage of Laughton, and he promised to **enjoy** it long.

It is Vernon's widow who walks alone in the stately terrace; sad still, for she loved well the choice of her youth, and she **misses** yet the children in the grave. From the **date** of Vernon's death, she wore mourning without and within; and the sorrows that came later broke more the bruised reed,—sad still, but resigned. One son **survives**, and earth yet has the troubled hopes and the holy fears of affection. Though that son be afar, in **sport** or in earnest, in pleasure or in toil, working out his destiny as man, still that step is less solitary than it seems. When does the son's image not walk beside the mother? Though she lives in seclusion, though the gay world **tempts** no more, the gay world is yet **linked** to her thoughts. From the distance she hears its murmurs in **music**. Her fancy still **mingles** with the crowd, and **follows** on, to her eye, **outshining** all the rest. Never vain in herself, she is vain now of another; and the small triumphs of the young and well-born seem **trophies** of renown to the eyes so tenderly deceived.

In the old-fashioned market-town still the business goes on, still the doors of the **bank** open and **close** every moment on the great day of the week; but the names over the threshold are partially changed. The junior partner is **busy** no more at the desk; not wholly forgotten, if his name still is spoken, it is not with **thankfulness** and praise. A something rests on the name,—that something which dims and attaints; not **proven**, not certain, but suspected and **dubious**. The head shakes, the voice whispers; and the **attorney** now lives in the solid red house at the verge of the town.

In the vicarage, Time, the old scythe-bearer, has not paused from his work. Still employed on Greek **texts**, little changed, save that his hair is gray and that some lines in his kindly face tell of sorrows as of years, the vicar sits in his parlour; but the children no longer, blithe-voiced and rose-cheeked, **dart** through the **rustling** espaliers. Those children, grave men or staid matrons (save one whom Death **chose**, and therefore now of all best

French

attorney: mandataire, avocat, procureur.
bank: banque, rive, bord, banc, berge, talus.
brethren: frères.
busy: occupé, actif, affairé.
chose: choisirent, optèrent, opta, optâmes.
close: fermer, proche, près, auprès, intime.
constitution: constitution, classement, loi fondamentale, statuts, structure d'une forêt.
dart: dard, fléchette.
date: date, datte, rencontre.
died: mourûmes, mort, décéda.
dubious: douteux, suspect, véreux, discutable.
enjoy: jouir, être joyeux, savourer.
follows: suit, talonne, ensuit, s'ensuit.
linked: lié.
mingle: mélanger, mêler, mêlons, retourner.
misses: manque.
music: musique, partition.
outshining: éclipsant, surpassant.
proven: prouvé.
rustling: bruissement, froissement.
sport: sport.
survives: survit.
tempts: tente.
text: texte.
thankfulness: gratitude, reconnaissance.
trophy: trophée.

beloved!) are at their posts in the world. The young ones are **flown** from the nest, and, with anxious wings, here and there, search food in their turn for their young. But the blithe voice and rose-cheek of the child make not that loss which the hearth misses the most. From childhood to manhood, and from manhood to departure, the natural changes are gradual and prepared. The absence most missed is that household life which **presided**, which kept things in order, and must be coaxed if a chair were displaced. That **providence** in trifles, that clasp of small links, that dear, bustling agency,— now pleased, now complaining,—dear alike in each change of its humour; that **active** life which has no self of its own; like the mind of a poet, though its prose be the humblest, **transferring** self into others, with its right to be cross, and its **charter** to scold; for the motive is clear,—it takes what it loves too **anxiously** to heart. The door of the parlour is open, the garden-path still passes before the threshold; but no step now has full right to **halt** at the door and interrupt the grave thought on Greek texts; no small talk on **details** and wise sayings **chimes** in with the wrath of "Medea." The Prudent Genius is gone from the household; and perhaps as the good scholar now **wearily** pauses, and looks out on the silent garden, he would have given with joy all that Athens **produced**, from Aeschylus to Plato, to hear again from the old familiar lips the **lament** on torn **jackets**, or the **statistical economy** of eggs.

But see, though the wife is no more, though the children have departed, the vicar's home is not **utterly** desolate. See, along the same walk on which William soothed Susan's fears and won her consent,—see, what fairy advances? Is it Susan returned to youth? How like! Yet look again, and how **unlike**! The same, the pure, candid regard; the same, the clear, **limpid** blue of the eye; the same, that fair hue of the hair,—light, but not auburn; more subdued, more **harmonious** than that equivocal colour which too nearly approaches to red. But how much more blooming and joyous than Susan's is that exquisite face in which all Hebe smiles forth; how much airier the tread, light with health; how much **rounder**, if slighter still, the wave of that **undulating** form! She smiles, her lips move, she is conversing with herself; she cannot be all silent, even when alone, for the sunny **gladness** of her

French

active: actif, agissant, laborieux.
anxiously: de manière inquiète, de façon inquiète.
charter: charte, affrètement.
chime: carillon, peigne.
detail: détail, particularité.
economy: économie, système économique.
flown: volé.
gladness: joie, allégresse.
halt: arrêt, s'arrêter, halte.
harmonious: harmonieux, mélodieux.
jacket: veste, jaquette, chemise, enveloppe, blouson, pochette, gaine.
lament: lamentation, se lamenter, complainte.
limpid: limpide.
presided: présidai.
produced: produisîmes, apparaissant p prés.
providence: providence, prévoyance.
rounder: bouleuse.
statistical: statistique.
transferring: transférant, mutant.
undulating: ondulant, ondoyant.
unlike: à la différence de, différent, dissemblable.
utterly: complètement, de façon répandre, de manière répandre, totalement.
wearily: de manière lasse, de façon lasse.

nature must have vent like a bird's. But do not fancy that that gladness speaks the **levity** which comes from the absence of thought; it is rather from the depth of thought that it **springs**, as from the depth of a sea comes its music. See, while she pauses and listens, with her finger half-raised to her lip, as amidst that careless **jubilee** of birds she hears a note more grave and sustained,—the **nightingale singing** by day (as sometimes, though rarely, he is heard,—perhaps because he misses his **mate**; perhaps because he sees from his **bower** the creeping form of some foe to his race),—see, as she listens now to that **plaintive**, low-chanted **warble**, how quickly the smile is sobered, how the shade, soft and **pensive**, steals over the brow. It is but the **mystic** sympathy with Nature that **bestows** the smile or the shade. In that heart lightly moved beats the **fine** sense of the poet. It is the exquisite sensibility of the nerves that sends its **blithe play** to those spirits, and from the **clearness** of the atmosphere comes, warm and **ethereal**, the ray of that light.

And does the roof of the pastor give shelter to Helen Mainwaring's youth? Has Death taken from her the natural protectors? Those forms which we saw so full of youth and youth's heart in that very spot, has the grave closed on them yet? Yet! How few attain to the age of the Psalmist! Twenty-seven years have passed since that date: how often, in those years, have the dark doors opened for the young as for the old! William Mainwaring died first, **careworn** and shamebowed; the blot on his name had cankered into his heart. Susan's life, always **precarious**, had struggled on, while he lived, by the **strong** power of affection and will; she would not die, for who then could console him? But at his death the power gave way. She lingered, but lingered dyingly, for three years; and then, for the first time since William's death, she smiled: that smile remained on the lips of the corpse. They had had many trials, that young couple whom we left so prosperous and happy. Not till many years after their marriage had one sweet consoler been born to them. In the season of poverty and shame and grief it came; and there was no pride on Mainwaring's brow when they placed his first-born in his arms. By her will, the widow **consigned** Helen to the **joint guardianship** of Mr. Fielden and her sister; but the **latter** was abroad, her address unknown, so the vicar

French

bestow: accorder, octroyer.
blithe: joyeux.
bower: tonnelle, ancre de bossoir.
careworn: rongé par les soucis.
clearness: clarté, limpidité, netteté.
consigned: consigné.
ethereal: éthéré.
fine: amende, fin, excellent, beau, délicat, tendre, éminent, accompli, à merveille, contravention.
guardianship: curatelle, tutelle, garde.
joint: articulation, commun, joint, raccord, pétard, interarmées, diaclase, charnière, mors.
jubilee: jubilé.
latter: dernier.
levity: légèreté.
mate: s'accoupler, compagnon, accoupler, camarade.
mystic: mystique.
nightingale: rossignol.
pensive: pensif, songeur.
plaintive: plaintif.
play: jouer, pièce de théâtre, jouons, jeu, représenter, passer.
precarious: précaire.
singing: chantant, amorçage.
spring: ressort, source, fontaine, sauter, émaner, mouillère, sortir de.
strong: fort, puissant, vigoureux, solide, robuste.
warble: gazouiller, bosse de varron, chanter, hululement, modulation de fréquence, varron.

for two years had had sole charge of the orphan. She was not unprovided for. The sum that Susan brought to her husband had been long since gone, it is **true**,—lost in the **calamity** which had wrecked William Mainwaring's name and **blighted** his prospects; but Helen's **grandfather**, the landagent, had died some time **subsequent** to that **event**, and, indeed, just before William's death. He had never forgiven his son the stain on his name,— never assisted, never even seen him since that fatal day; but he left to Helen a sum of about 8,000 **pounds**; for she, at least, was innocent. In Mr. Fielden's eyes, Helen was therefore an heiress. And who amongst his small range of acquaintance was good enough for her?—not only so **richly** portioned, but so lovely,—accomplished, too; for her **parents** had of **late** years lived chiefly in France, and languages there are easily learned, and masters **cheap**. Mr. Fielden knew but one, whom Providence had also consigned to his charge,— the **supposed** son of his old pupil Ardworth; but though a tender affection existed between the two young persons, it seemed too like that of **brother** and sister to **afford** much ground for Mr. Fielden's anxiety or hope.

From his window the vicar observed the still **attitude** of the young orphan for a few moments; then he pushed aside his books, rose, and approached her. At the **sound** of his tread she woke from her revery and bounded lightly towards him.

"Ah, you would not see me before!" she said, in a voice in which there was the slightest possible foreign accent, which betrayed the country in which her childhood had been passed; "I peeped in twice at the window. I wanted you so much to walk to the **village**. But you will come now, will you not?" added the **girl**, coaxingly, as she looked up at him under the shade of her **straw** hat.

"And what do you want in the village, my **pretty** Helen?"

"Why, you know it is fair day, and you promised Bessie that you would **buy** her a fairing,—to say nothing of me."

"Very true, and I ought to look in; it will help to keep the poor people from **drinking**. A clergyman should **mix** with his **parishioners** in their

---

French

afford: produire, permettre.
attitude: attitude, assiette, orientation.
blighted: rouillé.
brother: frère, frangin, le frère, confrère.
buy: acheter, achat, acquérir.
calamity: calamité, plaie, fléau.
cheap: bon marché, abordable.
drinking: buvant, fait de boire.
event: événement, occasion, fait, manifestation.
girl: fille, jeune fille, gosse, la fille.
grandfather: aïeul.
late: tard, en retard.
mix: mélanger, mêler, mixer, malaxer, retourner, gâcher, allier.
parent: parent, antériologue.
parishioner: paroissien.
pound: livre, piler, broyer, fourrière, marteler, battre.
pretty: joli, mignon, aimable, bath, assez.
richly: de façon riche, de manière riche, richement.
sound: son, sonner, résonner, bruit, sain, sonder, solide, vibration acoustique, détroit, oscillation acoustique.
straw: paille, chalumeau, chaume.
subsequent: subséquent, postérieur, suivant.
supposed: supposâmes, prétendu.
true: vrai, véritable, réel, exact, qui a raison, juste.
village: village, localité.

holidays. We must not associate our office only with grief and sickness and **preaching**. We will go. And what **fairing** are you to have?"

"Oh, something very brilliant, I promise you! I have formed **grand notions** of a fair. I am sure it must be like the bazaars we read of last night in that **charming** 'Tour in the East.'"

The vicar smiled, half **benignly**, half anxiously. "My dear child, it is so like you to **suppose** a village fair must be an Eastern **bazaar**. If you always thus judge of things by your fancy, how this sober world will deceive you, poor Helen!"

"It is not my fault; ne me grondez pas, mechant," answered Helen, **hanging** her head. "But come, sir, allow, at least, that if I let my romance, as you call it, run away with me now and then, I can still content myself with the **reality**. What, you shake your head still? Don't you remember the **sparrow**?"

"Ha! ha! yes, — the sparrow that the **pedlar sold** you for a **goldfinch**; and you were so proud of your **purchase**, and **wondered** so much why you could not **coax** the goldfinch to sing, till at last the **paint** wore away, and it was only a poor little sparrow!"

"Go on! Confess: did I **fret** then? Was I not as pleased with my dear sparrow as I should have been with the **prettiest** goldfinch that ever **sang**? Does not the sparrow follow me about and **nestle** on my shoulder, dear little thing? And I was right after all; for if I had not fancied it a goldfinch, I should not have bought it, perhaps. But now I would not change it for a goldfinch, — no, not even for that **nightingale** I heard just now. So let me still fancy the poor fair a bazaar; it is a **double** pleasure, first to fancy the bazaar, and then to be surprised at the fair."

"You **argue** well," said the vicar, as they now entered the village; "I really think, in **spite** of all your turn for **poetry** and Goldsmith and Cowper, that you would take as kindly to mathematics as your cousin John Ardworth, poor lad!

French

argue: se disputer, argumenter, arraisonner.
bazaar: bazar, foire, marché.
benignly: de manière Bénine, de façon Bénine.
charming: charmant, ravissant, gentil, mignon.
coax: cajoler, amadouer.
double: double, redoubler, sosie.
fairing: carénage, coiffe.
fret: frette, mousser fortement, cloison, tracasser.
goldfinch: chardonneret.
grand: grandiose, magnifique.
hanging: pendaison, suspension, mise à la pente.
holiday: jour férié, vacance, fête, blanc, congé, défaut d'enrobage, villégiature.
nestle: se nicher, se pelotonner.
nightingale: rossignol.
notion: notion, idée.
paint: peinture, couleur, dépeindre.
pedlar: colporteur, camelot.
poetry: poésie.
preaching: prêchant, sermon.
prettiest: le plus joli.
purchase: achat, acheter, emplette, acquérir, palan.
reality: réalité.
sang: chanta.
sold: vendirent, bradées.
sparrow: moineau, passereau.
spite: rancune, dépit.
suppose: supposer, croire.
wondered: demandé.

"Not if mathematics have made him so grave, and so **churlish**, I was going to say; but that word does him wrong, dear cousin, so kind and so rough!"

"It is not mathematics that are to blame if he is grave and absorbed," said the **vicar**, with a **sigh**; "it is the two cares that **gnaw** most,—poverty and ambition."

"Nay, do not sigh; it must be such a pleasure to feel, as he does, that one must triumph at last!"

"Umph! John must have **nearly** reached London by this time," said Mr. Fielden, "for he is a **stout walker**, and this is the third day since he left us. Well, now that he is about fairly to be called to the Bar, I hope that his **fever** will **cool**, and he will settle **calmly** to work. I have felt great pain for him during this last visit."

"Pain! But why?"

"My dear, do you remember what I read to you both from Sir William Temple the night before John left us?"

Helen put her hand to her **brow**, and with a **readiness** which showed a memory equally quick and **retentive**, replied, "Yes; was it not to this effect? I am not sure of the **exact** words: 'To have something we have not, and be something we are not, is the root of all evil.'"

"Well **remembered**, my darling!"

"Ah, but," said Helen, archly, "I remember too what my cousin replied: 'If Sir William Temple had practised his **theory**, he would not have been **ambassador** at the Hague, or—"

"Pshaw! the boy's always **ready** enough with his answers," **interrupted** Mr. Fielden, rather **petulantly**. "There's the fair, my dear,—more in your way, I see, than Sir William Temple's philosophy."

And Helen was right; the fair was no Eastern bazaar, but how delighted that young, **impressionable** mind was, notwithstanding,—delighted with the **swings** and the **roundabouts**, the shows, the **booths**, even down to the

---

French

ambassador: ambassadeur.
booth: cabine, baraque.
brow: sourcil, front.
calmly: de façon calme, de manière calme.
churlish: grossier.
cool: refroidir, frais, froid.
exact: exact, juste.
fever: fièvre, la fièvre.
gnaw: ronger.
impressionable: impressionnable.
interrupted: interrompit.

nearly: presque, quasiment, de manière près, à peu près, de façon près.
petulantly: de façon maussade, de manière maussade.
readiness: disponibilité, empressement.
ready: prêt, disponible.
remembered: retint, rappelâmes, retîntes, retenu.
retentive: fidèle.
roundabout: alentour, carrefour

giratoire, détourné, manège, autour.
sigh: soupir.
stout: corpulent, fort, gros, stout.
swing: balançoire, brandir, agiter, osciller, marge de découvert réciproque.
theory: théorie.
vicar: curé, pasteur.
walker: marcheur, promeneur, déambulateur.

gilt **gingerbread** kings and queens! All minds **genuinely poetical** are peculiarly susceptible to movement,—that is, to the excitement of numbers. If the movement is sincerely joyous, as in the mirth of a village holiday, such a nature shares insensibly in the joy; but if the movement is a false and **spurious** gayety, as in a state ball, where the **impassive** face and languid step are out of harmony with the evident object of the scene, then the nature we speak of feels chilled and dejected. **Hence** it really is that the more delicate and **ideal** order of minds soon **grow** inexpressibly weary of the **hack routine** of what are called **fashionable** pleasures. Hence the same person most alive to a dance on the green, would be without enjoyment at Almack's. It was not because one scene is a village green, and the other a room in King Street, nor is it because the actors in the one are of the humble, in the others of the noble class; but simply because the enjoyment in the first is visible and hearty, because in the other it is a listless and melancholy pretence. Helen fancied it was the swings and the booths that gave her that innocent exhilaration,—it was not so; it was the unconscious sympathy with the crowd around her. When the poetical nature quits its own dreams for the actual world, it enters and **transfuses** itself into the hearts and humours of others. The two wings of that spirit which we call Genius are revery and sympathy. But poor little Helen had no idea that she had genius. Whether **chasing** the **butterfly** or talking fond fancies to her birds, or whether with earnest, musing eyes watching the stars come forth, and the dark pine-trees gleam into **silver**; whether with airy **daydreams** and credulous wonder poring over the **magic** tales of Mirglip or Aladdin, or whether spellbound to awe by the solemn woes of Lear, or following the blind great **bard** into "the heaven of heavens, an earthly guest, to draw empyreal air,"—she obeyed but the honest and varying impulse in each change of her **pliant mood**, and would have ascribed with genuine humility to the vagaries of childhood that prompt **gathering** of pleasure, that quick-shifting sport of the fancy by which Nature **binds** to itself, in chains undulating as **melody**, the lively senses of genius.

While Helen, leaning on the vicar's arm, thus **surrendered** herself to the innocent excitement of the moment, the vicar himself smiled and nodded to

---

French

bard: barde.
bind: attacher, lier, relier, nouer.
butterfly: papillon, le papillon, butterfly, oreilles.
chasing: ciselure, chassant, filetage au peigne.
daydream: rêve, songer, rêvasser.
fashionable: à la mode, dernier cri, moderne, actuel, dans le vent.
gathering: réunion, ramassage, rassemblement, cueillage, roulage.
genuinely: réellement, en réalité, de façon authentique, authentiquement, de manière authentique.
gingerbread: pain d'épice.
grow: grandir, croître, cultiver, croissez, augmenter, devenir, s'accroître, redoubler.
hack: hacher, tailler, rainette.
hence: par conséquent, donc, c'est pourquoi, d'où.
ideal: idéal.
impassive: impassible.
magic: magie, enchantement, sorcellerie.
melody: mélodie, chant.
mood: humeur, ambiance.
pliant: flexible, souple, docile.
poetical: poétique.
routine: routine, habituel.
silver: argent, hareng argenté.
spurious: faux, fallacieux, parasite, simulé.
surrendered: rendu.
transfuses: transfuse.

his parishioners, or paused to **exchange** a friendly word or two with the youngest or the eldest loiterers (those two extremes of **mortality** which the Church so tenderly unites) whom the scene drew to its **tempting vortex**, when a rough-haired lad, with a leather bag **strapped** across his **waist**, turned from one of the gingerbread booths, and touching his hat, said, "Please you, sir, I was a **coming** to your house with a letter."

The vicar's correspondence was confined and rare, **despite** his distant children, for letters but a few years ago were **costly** luxuries to persons of narrow income, and therefore the juvenile letter-carrier who **plied** between the post-town and the village failed to excite in his breast that indignation for being an hour or more behind his time which would have animated one to whom the post **brings** the usual event of the day. He took the letter from the boy's hand, and **paid** for it with a **thrifty** sigh as he glanced at a handwriting unfamiliar to him,—perhaps from some clergyman poorer than himself. However, that was not the place to read letters, so he put the epistle into his pocket, until Helen, who watched his countenance to see when he grew tired of the scene, kindly **proposed** to return home. As they gained a **stile** half-way, Mr. Fielden remembered his letter, took it forth, and put on his spectacles. Helen stooped over the bank to gather **violets**; the vicar seated himself on the stile. As he again looked at the address, the handwriting, before unfamiliar, seemed to grow indistinctly on his recollection. That bold, firm hand—thin and fine as woman's, but large and **regular** as man's—was too peculiar to be forgotten. He uttered a **brief** exclamation of surprise and **recognition**, and hastily broke the seal. The contents ran thus:—

Dear Sir,—So many years have passed since any communication has taken place between us that the name of Lucretia Dalibard will seem more strange to you than that of Lucretia Clavering. I have **recently** returned to England after long residence abroad. I perceive by my deceased sister's will that she has confided her only daughter to my guardianship, conjointly with yourself. I am anxious to participate in that tender charge. I am alone in the world,—an habitual **sufferer**; afflicted with a **partial paralysis** that **deprives**

French

brief: court, dossier, bref, sommaire, mémoire, passager.
brings: apporte, amène.
coming: venant, approche, venir, prochain, futur.
costly: coûteux, cher.
deprives: prive, dépouille.
despite: en dépit de, malgré.
exchange: échange, central, change, commutateur, troquer, bourse.
mortality: mortalité.
paid: payai, payé, payèrent, payâtes.
paralysis: paralysie, immobilisation.
partial: partiel.
plied: manié.
proposed: proposèrent.
recently: récemment, dernièrement, de façon récente, de manière récente.
recognition: reconnaissance, identification, récognition.
regular: régulier, cyclique, réglé, normal, standard, conforme, client habitué, habitué.
stile: échalier, montant.
strapped: fauché, sanglé, câblé.
sufferer: victime, malade.
tempting: tentant, attrayant, séduisant.
thrifty: économe, épargnant.
violet: violet.
vortex: tourbillon, vortex.
waist: taille, corset.

me of the use of my limbs. In such circumstances, it is the more natural that I should turn to the only relative left me. My **journey** to England has so exhausted my strength, and all **movement** is so painful, that I must request you to excuse me for not coming in person for my niece. Your **benevolence**, however, will, I am sure, prompt you to afford me the comfort of her society, and as soon as you can, **contrive** some **suitable arrangement** for her journey. **Begging** you to express to Helen, in my name, the assurance of such a **welcome** as is **due** from me to my sister's child, and waiting with great anxiety your reply, I am, dear Sir,

Your very faithful servant,
Lucretia Dalibard.

P. S. I can scarcely venture to **ask** you to **bring** Helen yourself to town, but I should be glad if other inducements to take the journey **afforded** me the pleasure of seeing you once again. I am anxious, in addition to such details of my late sister as you may be enabled to give me, to learn something of the history of her connection with Mr. Ardworth, in whom I felt much **interested** years ago, and who, I am recently informed, left an **infant**, his supposed son, under your care. So long absent from England, how much have I to learn, and how little the mere **gravestones** tell us of the dead!

While the vicar is absorbed in this letter, equally unwelcome and unexpected; while, unconscious as the daughter of Ceres, gathering flowers when the Hell King drew **near**, of the change that awaited her and the grim presence that approached on her fate, Helen **bends** still over the bank **odorous** with shrinking violets, — we turn where the new generation equally invites our gaze, and make our first acquaintance with two persons connected with the progress of our tale.

The britzska stopped. The servant, who had been gradually **accumulating** present dust and future rheumatisms on the "bad **eminence**" of a rumble-tumble, **exposed** to the **nipping** airs of an English **sky**, leaped to the ground and opened the carriage-door.

French

accumulating: accumulant, entassant, s'amoncelant.
afforded: produisîmes.
arrangement: disposition, arrangement, agencement, classement, aménagement, construction.
ask: demander, poser une question, prier.
begging: mendiant, suppliant, quémandant.
bend: courber, fléchir, coude, incliner, ployer, plier, cintrer, virage, pencher, nœud, tournant.
benevolence: bienveillance.
bring: apporter, amener, amènent.
contrive: inventer.
due: dû, exigible, droit, arrivé à échéance, normal.
eminence: éminence.
exposed: exposé, irradié.
gravestone: pierre tombale.
infant: enfant, nourrisson, poupon.
interested: intéressé.
journey: voyage, trajet, parcours, périple.
movement: mouvement, déplacement.
near: près, proche, auprès, à.
nipping: éclat, pilon, pinçage.
odorous: odorant.
sky: ciel, le ciel.
suitable: convenable, approprié, propice, raisonnable.
welcome: bienvenue, accueillir, recevoir solennellement.

"This is the best place for the view, sir,—a little to the right."

Percival St. John threw aside his book (a volume of Voyages), **whistled** to a **spaniel dozing** by his side, and descended lightly. Light was the step of the young man, and merry was the **bark** of the dog, as it **chased** from the road the startled sparrow, rising high into the clear air,—favourites of Nature both, man and dog. You had but to glance at Percival St. John to know at once that he was of the race that toils not; the assured step spoke confidence in the world's fair smile. No care for the morrow **dimmed** the bold eye and the **radiant** bloom.

About the **middle** height,—his slight figure, yet undeveloped, seemed not to have attained to its full growth,—the **darkening** down only just shaded a cheek somewhat sunburned, though naturally fair, round which locks black as **jet played** sportively in the **fresh** air; about him **altogether** there was the **inexpressible** charm of happy youth. He scarcely looked **sixteen**, though above four years older; but for his firm though careless step, and the open **fearlessness** of his frank eye, you might have almost taken him for a girl in men's clothes,—not from effeminacy of feature, but from the **sparkling** bloom of his youth, and from his unmistakable newness to the cares and sins of man. A more delightful vision of **ingenuous boyhood** opening into life under happy auspices never inspired with pleased yet melancholy interest the eye of half-envious, half-pitying age.

"And that," mused Percival St. John,—"that is London! Oh for the Diable Boiteux to unroof me those distant houses, and show me the pleasures that **lurk** within! Ah, what long letters I shall have to **write** home! How the dear old **captain** will laugh over them, and how my dear good mother will put down her work and sigh! Home!—um, I miss it already. How strange and grim, after all, the huge city seems!"

His glove fell to the ground, and his spaniel **mumbled** it into **shreds**. The young man laughed, and **throwing** himself on the grass, played gayly with the dog.

French

altogether: tout, entièrement.
bark: écorce, aboyer, barque, coque, glapir.
boyhood: enfance, adolescence.
captain: capitaine, commandant.
chased: chassé, ciselé.
darkening: fonçant, noircissement, assombrissant.
dimmed: estompé.
dozing: sommeillant.
fearlessness: intrépidité.
fresh: frais, nouveau.

inexpressible: inexprimable, indicible.
ingenuous: ingénu, candide, naïf.
jet: jais, jet, avion à réaction, gicleur.
lurk: se cacher, badauder.
middle: milieu, moyen, intermédiaire, centre.
mumbled: marmonna, bredouillèrent, mâchonnèrent.
played: jouèrent, jouai, jouâmes, joué.

radiant: rayonnant, radieux.
shred: lambeau, déchiqueter.
sixteen: seize.
spaniel: épagneul.
sparkling: brillant, étincelant, mousseux, pétillant.
throwing: lancement, tournassage, abattage directionnel, balle accompagnée, jet, jetant, moulinage.
whistled: sifflé.
write: écrire, composer, rédiger.

"Fie, Beau, sir, fie! gloves are **indigestible**. Restrain your **appetite**, and we'll lunch together at the Clarendon."

At this moment there arrived at the same **patch** of greensward a pedestrian some years older than Percival St. John,—a tall, **muscular**, raw-boned, dust-covered, travel-stained pedestrian; one of your pedestrians in good earnest,—no amateur in **neat** gambroon **manufactured** by Inkson, who leaves his carriage behind him and walks on with his fishing-rod by choice, but a sturdy **wanderer**, with thick **shoes** and strapless trousers, a **threadbare** coat and a **knapsack** at his back. Yet, withal, the young man had the air of a gentleman,—not gentleman as the word is understood in St. James's, the gentleman of the noble and idle class, but the gentleman as the title is accorded, by courtesy, to all to whom both education and the habit of **mixing** with educated persons gives a claim to the distinction and **imparts** an air of refinement. The new-comer was strongly built, at once lean and large,—far more strongly built than Percival St. John, but without his look of cheerful and comely health. His complexion had not the **florid** hues that should have accompanied that strength of body; it was pale, though not sickly; the expression grave, the lines deep, the face strongly marked. By his side trotted painfully a **wiry**, **yellowish**, **footsore** Scotch **terrier**. Beau sprang from his master's caress, cocked his handsome head on one side, and **suspended** in silent halt his right fore-paw. Percival cast over his left shoulder a careless glance at the intruder. The last heeded neither Beau nor Percival. He **slipped** his knapsack to the ground, and the Scotch terrier sank upon it, and curled himself up into a ball. The wayfarer folded his arms tightly upon his breast, heaved a short, **unquiet** sigh, and cast over the giant city, from under deep-pent, lowering brows, a look so earnest, so searching, so full of inexpressible, dogged, determined power, that Percival, roused out of his gay indifference, rose and regarded him with **curious** interest.

In the mean while Beau had very leisurely approached the bilious-looking terrier; and after walking three times round him, with a stare and a small **sniff** of **superb** impertinence, halted with great composure, and lifting his hind leg— O Beau, Beau, Beau! your **historian** blushes for your **breeding**,

French

appetite: appétit, faim.
breeding: reproduction, élevage, surgénération.
curious: curieux, intéressant, singulier.
florid: fleuri, florissant.
footsore: aux pieds endoloris.
historian: historien.
impart: donner, communiquer.
indigestible: indigeste.
knapsack: havresac, sac tyrolien.
manufactured: fabriquâtes, manufacturâmes, ouvré.
mixing: mélange, malaxage, brassage, mixage.
muscular: musculaire.
neat: net, propre.
patch: rapiécer, pièce, rustine, parcelle, réparer, correction, plaque, tache.
shoe: chaussure, soulier, sabot, ferrer.
slipped: glissé.
sniff: renifler, flairer, respirer.
superb: superbe, magnifique, grandiose.
suspended: suspendu, en suspens, flottant.
terrier: registre foncier, terrier.
threadbare: usé, tissu trop découvert.
unquiet: inquiet.
wanderer: vagabond.
wiry: raide, nerveux, tordu, vigoureux.
yellowish: jaunâtre.

and, like Sterne's **recording** angel, drops a tear upon the stain which washes it from the register—but not, alas, from the back of the **bilious** terrier! The space around was wide, Beau; you had all the world to choose: why select so **specially** for insult the single spot on which reposed the wornout and unoffending? O **dainty** Beau! O dainty world! Own the truth, both of ye. There is something **irresistibly provocative** of insult in the back of a shabby-looking dog! The poor terrier, used to **affronts**, raised its heavy **eyelids**, and shot the gleam of just indignation from its dark eyes. But it neither stirred nor growled, and Beau, extremely pleased with his achievement, wagged his **tail** in triumph and returned to his master,—perhaps, in parliamentary **phrase**, to "report **proceedings** and ask leave to sit again."

"I wonder," soliloquized Percival St. John, "what that poor fellow is thinking of? Perhaps he is poor; indeed, no doubt of it, now I look again. And I so rich! I should like to—Hem! let's see what he's made of."

Herewith Percival approached, and with all a boy's half-bashful, half-saucy frankness, said: "A fine prospect, sir." The pedestrian started, and threw a rapid glance over the brilliant figure that accosted him. Percival St. John was not to be **abashed** by stern looks; but that glance might have abashed many a more experienced man. The glance of a squire upon a corn-law **missionary**, of a Crockford **dandy** upon a Regent Street **tiger**, could not have been more **disdainful**.

"Tush!" said the pedestrian, **rudely**, and turned upon his heel.

Percival **coloured**, and—shall we own it?—was boy enough to double his fist. Little would he have been deterred by the **brawn** of those great arms and the girth of that Herculean chest, if he had been quite sure that it was a proper thing to **resent** pugilistically so **discourteous** a monosyllable. The "tush!" stuck greatly in his throat. But the man, now removed to the farther verge of the hill, looked so tranquil and so lost in thought that the short-lived **anger** died.

French

abashed: confus, décontenançai.
affront: insulter, affront, offenser.
anger: colère, courroucer, emportement, irriter, mettre en colère, rage.
bilious: bilieux.
brawn: fromage de tête, hure.
coloured: coloré.
dainty: délicat, tendre, aimable.
dandy: chouette, dandy.
discourteous: impoli, discourtois.
disdainful: dédaigneux.

eyelid: paupière, déflecteur.
irresistibly: irrésistiblement, de manière irrésistible, de façon irrésistible.
missionary: missionnaire.
phrase: locution, phrase, groupe de mots.
proceeding: procédant, avançant.
provocative: provocant.
recording: enregistrement, archivage.
resent: s'indigner de, ressentez.

rudely: de façon grossière, de manière grossière.
specially: spécialement, particulièrement, surtout, de manière spéciale, de façon spéciale.
tail: queue, talon, pointe, pivot, piste, pile, pan, orgette, naissance du pivot, la queue, fouet.
tiger: tigre.

"And after all, if I were as poor as he looks, I dare say I should be just as proud," muttered Percival. "However, it's his own fault if he goes to London on foot, when I might at least have given him a lift. Come, Beau, sir."

With his face still a little flushed, and his hat **unconsciously** cocked fiercely on one side, Percival **sauntered** back to his britzska.

As in a **whirl** of dust the light carriage was borne by the four **posters** down the **hill**, the **pedestrian** turned for an instant from the view before to the cloud behind, and muttered: "Ay, a fine prospect for the rich,—a noble **field** for the poor!" The tone in which those words were said told volumes; there spoke the pride, the hope, the **energy**, the ambition which make youth **laborious**, **manhood** prosperous, age renowned.

The stranger then threw himself on the sward, and continued his silent and intent **contemplation** till the clouds grew red in the **west**. When, then, he rose, his eye was bright, his **mien** erect, and a smile, playing round his firm, full lips, stole the moody **sternness** from his hard face. Throwing his **knapsack** once more on his back, John Ardworth went **resolutely** on to the great **vortex**.

French

contemplation: contemplation, méditation, recueillement.
energy: énergie.
field: champ, domaine, zone, trame, terrain, corps, gisement.
hill: colline, terrer, butter, coteau.
knapsack: havresac, sac tyrolien.
laborious: laborieux, pénible.
manhood: virilité, âge d'homme.
mien: mine.
pedestrian: piéton, pédestre.
poster: placard, mural, poster.
resolutely: de façon résolue, de manière résolue, résolument.
sauntered: flânas.
sternness: sévérité.
unconsciously: de façon inconsciente, de manière inconsciente, inconsciemment.
vortex: tourbillon, vortex.
west: ouest, occident, à l'ouest, vers l'ouest.
whirl: faire tournoyer, tourbillon, battre.

CHAPTER I

THE CORONATION

The 8th of September, 1831, was a holiday in London. William the Fourth received the **crown** of his ancestors in that mighty church in which the most **impressive** monitors to human **pomp** are the **monuments** of the dead. The dust of **conquerors** and statesmen, of the wise heads and the bold hands that had guarded the **thrones** of departed kings, slept around; and the great men of the Modern time were **assembled** in homage to the **monarch** to whom the **prowess** and the liberty of generations had **bequeathed** an empire in which the sun never sets. In the Abbey—thinking little of the past, **caring** little for the future—the immense **audience** gazed eagerly on the **pageant** that **occurs** but once in that **division** of history,—the **lifetime** of a **king**. The **assemblage** was brilliant and imposing. The galleries **sparkled** with the **gems** of women who still **upheld** the **celebrity** for form and feature which, from the remotest times, has been **awarded** to the great English race. Below, in their robes and **coronets**, were men who neither in the senate nor the field have shamed their fathers. Conspicuous amongst all for grandeur of mien and **stature** towered the brothers of the king; while, commanding yet more the universal gaze, were seen, here the **eagle** features of the old hero of Waterloo, and there the majestic brow of the **haughty statesman** who was **leading** the

---

French

assemblage: montage, réunion.
assembled: monta, assembla.
audience: audience, assistance.
awarded: faveur.
bequeathed: léguai.
caring: soin, prise en charge globale.
celebrity: célébrité, star, vedette.
conqueror: conquérant, vainqueur.
coronet: couronne.
crown: couronne, sommet, cime, sacrer, voûte.
division: division, partage, section.
eagle: aigle.
gem: gemme, pierre précieuse.
haughty: hautain, arrogant.
impressive: impressionnant, grandiose, imposant.
king: roi, dame.
leading: conduisant, menant, guidant, aboutissant, plombage, principal, laissant.
lifetime: vie, durée de vie.
monarch: monarque.
monument: monument, borne cadastrale.
occurs: arrive, survient.
pageant: reconstitution historique, réflecteur.
pomp: pompe, splendeur.
prowess: prouesse, exploit.
sparkled: brillâmes.
statesman: homme d'Etat.
stature: stature, taille.
throne: trône.
upheld: soutînmes.

people (while the last of the Bourbons, whom Waterloo had restored to the Tuileries, had left the **orb** and purple to the kindred house so fatal to his name) through a stormy and **perilous transition** to a bloodless **revolution** and a new charter.

Tier upon tier, in the division set apart for them, the members of the Lower House moved and murmured above the pageant; and the **coronation** of the new **sovereign** was connected in their minds with the great **measure** which, still **undecided**, made at that time a link between the People and the King, and **arrayed** against both, if not, indeed, the real Aristocracy, at least the Chamber recognized by the Constitution as its representative. Without the space was one dense mass. Houses, from **balcony** to balcony, window to window, were filled as some immense theatre. Up, through the long thoroughfare to Whitehall, the eye saw that audience,—A *people*; and the gaze was bounded at the spot where Charles the First had passed from the banquet-house to the scaffold.

The ceremony was over, the procession had **swept** slowly by, the last huzza had died away; and after staring a while upon Orator Hunt, who had **clambered** up the iron **palisade** near Westminster Hall, to exhibit his **goodly** person in his court **attire**, the serried crowds, hurrying from the shower which then unseasonably descended, broke into large masses or **lengthening columns**.

In that part of London which may be said to form a **boundary** between its old and its new world, by which, on the one hand, you pass to Westminster, or through that **gorge** of the Strand which leads along endless **rows** of shops that have grown up on the **sites** of the ancient **halls** of the Salisburys and the Exeters, the Buckinghams and Southamptons; to the heart of the City **built** around the **primeval palace** of the "Tower;" while, on the other hand, you pass into the new city of aristocracy and letters, of art and fashion, embracing the whilom chase of Marylebone, and the once sedge-grown waters of Pimlico,—by this **ignoble** boundary (the crossing from the Opera House, at the bottom of the Haymarket, to the commencement of Charing Cross) stood a person whose discontented countenance was in singular contrast with the

French

arrayed: rangé.
attire: vêtir, vêtement, habit, mise.
balcony: balcon, le balcon.
boundary: limite, frontière, borne.
built: construit, édifiés.
clambered: grimpâtes.
column: colonne, pilier, rubrique, file, montant, chronique.
coronation: couronnement.
goodly: de façon bonne, de manière bonne.
gorge: gorge, anglaise.
hall: salle, hall, couloir, vestibule.
ignoble: ignoble.
lengthening: allongeant, rallongement, prolongation.
measure: mesure, taille, jauger.
orb: orbe.
palace: palais, le palais.
palisade: palissade.
perilous: périlleux.
primeval: primitif.
revolution: révolution, tour, rotation.
row: rangée, ramer, file, tour, ligne.
site: site, emplacement, endroit, chantier.
sovereign: souverain.
swept: balayé.
tier: plan, étage, gradin, rangée.
transition: transition, pente concave, passage, mutation, conduite de transition.
undecided: indécis, hésitant, incertain.

general gayety and animation of the day. This person, O gentle reader, this sour, querulous, discontented person, was a king, too, in his own walk! None might dispute it. He feared no **rebel**; he was harassed by no **reform**; he **ruled** without ministers. Tools he had; but when worn out, he replaced them without a pension or a sigh. He lived by taxes, but they were **voluntary**; and his Civil List was supplied without **demand** for the **redress** of **grievances**. This person, nevertheless, not **deposed**, was suspended from his empire for the day. He was pushed aside; he was forgotten. He was not distinct from the crowd. Like Titus, he had **lost** a day,—his vocation was gone. This person was the Sweeper of the Crossing!

He was a character. He was young, in the fairest **prime** of youth; but it was the face of an old man on young shoulders. His hair was long, thin, and prematurely **streaked** with gray; his face was pale and deeply **furrowed**; his eyes were hollow, and their stare gleamed, cold and stolid, under his bent and shaggy brows. The figure was at once **fragile** and **ungainly**, and the narrow shoulders **curved** in a **perpetual** stoop. It was a person, once **noticed**, that you would easily remember, and associate with some undefined, painful impression. The manner was humble, but not meek; the voice was **whining**, but without pathos. There was a meagre, passionless dulness about the aspect, though at times it quickened into a kind of avid acuteness. No one knew by what human **parentage** this personage came into the world. He had been reared by the charity of a stranger, crept through childhood and misery and **rags** mysteriously; and suddenly succeeded an old **defunct negro** in the **profitable** crossing whereat he is now standing. All education was unknown to him, so was all love. In those **festive** haunts at St. Giles's where he who would see "life in London" may often discover the boy who has held his **horse** in the morning dancing merrily with his chosen damsel at night, our sweeper's character was austere as Charles the Twelfth's. And the poor creature had his good qualities. He was **sensitively** alive to kindness,—little enough had been shown him to make the luxury the more prized from its **rarity**! Though fond of money, he would part with it (we do not say cheerfully, but part with it still),—not to mere want, indeed (for he had been

French

curved: courbe, arqué, cintré, incurvé.
defunct: défunt, décédé.
demand: demande, exiger, revendication, abattement, puissance.
deposed: destituai, déposâtes.
festive: de fête.
fragile: fragile, délicat.
furrowed: ridé, sillonné.
grievance: grief, réclamation.
horse: cheval, le cheval.

lost: perdit, non vu.
negro: nègre, noir.
noticed: remarqué.
parentage: naissance, filiation.
perpetual: perpétuel, éternel.
prime: amorcer, prime, apprêter.
profitable: rentable, profitable, lucratif.
rag: chiffon, lambeau, torchon, guenille, haillon.
rarity: rareté.
rebel: rebelle, se révolter.

redress: réparation, redresser.
reform: réformer, reformer, transformation, redresser.
ruled: hachuré.
sensitively: de façon sensible, de manière sensible.
streaked: bigarrés, taché d'auréole.
ungainly: dégingandé, disgracieux, gauche.
voluntary: volontaire, bénévole.
whining: criant, geignant, gémissant.

too **pinched** and **starved** himself, and had grown too **obtuse** to pinching and to **starving** for the **sensitiveness** that prompts to charity), but to any of his companions who had done him a good service, or who had even warmed his dull heart by a friendly smile. He was honest, too,—honest to the **backbone**. You might have trusted him with gold **untold**. Through the heavy **clod** which man's care had not **moulded**, nor books enlightened, nor the priest's solemn lore informed, still natural rays from the great parent source of Deity struggled, **fitful** and dim. He had no **lawful** name; none knew if **sponsors** had ever stood security for his sins at the sacred **fount**. But he had **christened** himself by the strange, **unchristian** like name of "Beck." There he was, then, seemingly without origin, parentage, or kindred tie,—a **lonesome**, squalid, bloodless thing, which the great monster, London, seemed to have **spawned** forth of its own self; one of its sickly, miserable, rickety **offspring**, whom it puts out at nurse to Penury, at school to Starvation, and, finally, and literally, gives them stones for bread, with the option of the gallows or the dunghill when the desperate offspring calls on the giant mother for return and home.

And this creature did love something,—loved, perhaps, some fellow-being; of that hereafter, when we dive into the secrets of his **privacy**. Meanwhile, openly and frankly, he loved his crossing; he was proud of his crossing; he was grateful to his crossing. God help thee, son of the street, why not? He had in it a double affection,—that of serving and being served. He kept the crossing, if the crossing kept him. He smiled at times to himself when he saw it lie fair and brilliant amidst the mire around; it bestowed on him a sense of property! What a man may feel for a fine estate in a ring fence, Beck felt for that **isthmus** of the kennel which was subject to his **broom**. The coronation had made one **rebellious** spirit when it swept the **sweeper** from his crossing.

He stood, then, half under the **colonnade** of the Opera House as the crowd now rapidly grew **thinner** and more scattered: and when the last carriage of a long string of vehicles had passed by, he muttered audibly,—

"It'll take a deal of pains to make she right agin!"

French

backbone: épine dorsale, réseau fédérateur, dorsale, colonne vertébrale.
broom: balai, genêt, le balai.
christened: baptisâmes.
clod: boule, motte.
colonnade: colonnade.
fitful: irrégulier.
fount: source, fonte, réservoir de lampe.
isthmus: isthme.
lawful: légal, légitime, licite.
lonesome: seul, solitaire.
moulded: membres, moulé.
obtuse: obtus, borné.
offspring: descendant, progéniture, successeur.
pinched: pincé.
privacy: intimité, vie privée, secret, respect de la vie privée.
rebellious: rebelle, révolté.
sensitiveness: sensibilité, susceptibilité.
spawned: pondîmes.
sponsor: parrain, commanditaire, promoteur, sponsor, mécène.
starved: affamèrent.
starving: affamant.
sweeper: balayeuse, arrière latéral, bétonneur, libero, verrouilleur, analyseur panoramique.
thinner: diluant, dissolvant, éclaircisseuse, démarieuse.
unchristian: peu chrétien.
untold: jamais dévoilé.

"So you be's 'ere to-day, Beck!" said a **ragamuffin** boy, who, **pushing** and **scrambling** through his betters, now halted, and wiped his forehead as he looked at the sweeper. "Vy, ve are all out pleasuring. Vy von't you come with ve? Lots of fun!"

The sweeper scowled at the **urchin**, and made no answer, but began **sedulously** to apply himself to the crossing.

"Vy, there isn't another **sweep** in the streets, Beck. His Majesty King Bill's currynation makes all on us so 'appy!"

"It has made she unkimmon dirty!" returned Beck, **pointing** to the dingy crossing, scarce distinguished from the rest of the road.

The ragamuffin laughed.

"But ve be's goin' to 'ave Reform now, Beck. The peopul's to have their rights and libties, hand the luds is to be put down, hand **beefsteaks** is to be a **penny** a pound, and—"

"What good will that do to she?"

"Vy, man, ve shall take turn about, and sum vun helse will sveep the crossings, and ve shall ride in sum vun helse's coach and four, p'r'aps,—cos vy? ve shall hall be hequals!"

"Hequals! I tells you vot, if you keeps jawing there, atween me and she, I shall vop you, Joe,—cos vy? I be's the biggest!" was the answer of Beck the sweeper to Joe the ragamuffin.

The jovial Joe laughed **aloud**, **snapped** his fingers, threw up his ragged **cap** with a **shout** for King Bill, and set off scampering and whooping to join those **festivities** which Beck had so **churlishly** disdained.

Time crept on; evening began to close in, and Beck was still at his crossing, when a young gentleman on **horseback**, who, after seeing the procession, had **stolen** away for a quiet ride in the **suburbs**, reined in close by the crossing, and looking round, as for some one to hold his horse, could discover no loiterer worthy that honour **except** the solitary Beck. So young was the **rider** that he seemed still a boy. On his smooth countenance all that

French

aloud: à haute voix, fort, haut.
beefsteak: bifteck, tranche de bœuf.
cap: casquette, bonnet, toque, chapeau, calotte, capsule, capuchon, coiffe, bouchon, culot, plafond.
churlishly: de façon grossière, de manière grossière.
except: sauf, excepter, hormis, exempter, dispenser, en outre, exclure, à moins que.
festivity: festivité, fête, réjouissance.
horseback: à cheval.
penny: sou, grain inférieur, penny.
pointing: pointage, repérage dans l'espace, jointement, collage de poils, braquant, appointage, précalibrage, piquage des nervures.
pushing: poussant, dynamique.
ragamuffin: gueux.
rider: cavalier, avenant, annexe, clause additionnelle, écuyer, acte additionnel.
scrambling: embrouillage, brouillant.
sedulously: de façon assidue, de manière assidue.
shout: cri, crier, pousser des cris.
snapped: pressionné.
stolen: volé.
suburb: banlieue, faubourg.
sweep: balayer, courbure, draguer.
urchin: galopin, gamin, hérisson, oursin, polisson.

most prepossesses in early youth left its witching **stamp**. A smile, at once gay and sweet, played on his lips. There was a charm, even in a certain impatient **petulance**, in his quick eye and the slight contraction of his delicate brows. Almaviva might well have been jealous of such a page. He was the beau-ideal of Cherubino. He **held** up his whip, with an arch sign, to the sweeper. "Follow, my man," he said, in a tone the very command of which sounded gentle, so blithe was the movement of the lips, and so **silvery** the **easy** accent; and without waiting, he cantered carelessly down Pall Mall.

The sweeper cast a **rueful** glance at his melancholy domain. But he had gained but little that day, and the **offer** was too tempting to be **rejected**. He heaved a sigh, shouldered his broom, and murmuring to himself that he would give her a last brush before he retired for the night, he put his long limbs into that swinging, shambling **trot** which characterizes the **motion** of those **professional jackals** who, having once caught sight of a groomless rider, fairly **hunt** him down, and appear when he least **expects** it, the instant he **dismounts**. The young rider lightly swung himself from his sleek, high-bred gray at the door of one of the clubs in St. James's Street, patted his horse's neck, chucked the **rein** to the sweeper, and sauntered into the house, whistling musically,—if not from want of thought, **certainly** from want of care.

As he entered the **club**, two or three men, young indeed, but much older, to appearance at least, than himself, who were dining together at the same table, nodded to him their friendly greeting.

"Ah, Perce," said one, "we have only just sat down; here is a **seat** for you."

The boy blushed **shyly** as he accepted the proposal, and the young men made room for him at the table, with a smiling alacrity which showed that his shyness was no **hindrance** to his popularity.

"Who," said an **elderly** dandy, dining apart with one of his contemporaries,—"who is that lad? One ought not to admit such mere boys into the club."

French

certainly: certainement, sûrement, assurément, si, d'abord, de façon certaine, de manière certaine.
club: club, trèfle.
dismount: descends, mettre pied à terre, sors, sortent, démontent.
easy: facile.
elderly: de façon sureau, de manière sureau, âgé.
expects: attend, espère.
held: tenu, tinrent.
hindrance: obstacle, entrave.
hunt: chasser, poursuivre.
jackal: chacal.
motion: mouvement, motion, résolution, marche, requête.
offer: offre, proposition, présenter, sacrifier, faire offrande, consacrer.
petulance: irritabilité.
professional: professionnel, spécialiste, membre d'une profession libérale, pro.
rein: rêne, bride.
rejected: rejeté, rebutée, refusé.
rueful: triste.
seat: siège, assiette, banquette, selle, place.
shyly: timidement.
silvery: argenté.
stamp: timbre, estampiller, tampon, poinçon, cachet, empreinte, emboutir, marque.
trot: trotter, aller au trot.

"He is the only **surviving** son of an old friend of ours," answered the other, dropping his eyeglass, — "young Percival St. John."

"St. John! What! Vernon St. John's son?"

"Yes."

"He has not his father's good air. These young fellows have a tone, a something, — a want of self-possession, eh?"

"Very true. The fact is, that Percival was **meant** for the **navy**, and even served as a **mid** for a year or so. He was a younger son, then, — third, I think. The two elder ones died, and Master Percival walked into the inheritance. I don't think he is quite of age yet."

"Of age! he does not look seventeen."

"Oh, he is more than that; I remember him in his jacket at Laughton. A fine property!"

"Ay, I don't wonder those fellows are so **civil** to him. This **claret** is **corked**! **Everything** is so bad at this d—d club, — no wonder, when a troop of boys are let in! Enough to spoil any club; don't know Larose from Lafitte! Waiter!"

Meanwhile, the **talk** round the table at which sat Percival St. John was **animated**, lively, and various, — the talk **common** with young **idlers**; of horses, and **steeplechases**, and opera-dancers, and **reigning** beauties, and good-humoured **jests** at each other. In all this **babble** there was a **freshness** about Percival St. John's conversation which showed that, as yet, for him life had the **zest** of **novelty**. He was more at home about horses and steeplechases than about opera-dancers and beauties and the small **scandals** of town. Talk on these latter topics did not seem to interest him, on the contrary, almost to pain. Shy and modest as a girl, he coloured or looked aside when his more **hardened** friends **boasted** of **assignations** and love-affairs. **Spirited**, gay, and **manly** enough in all really manly points, the **virgin** bloom of innocence was yet visible in his frank, charming manner; and often, out of respect for his **delicacy**, some **hearty** son of pleasure

---

French

animated: animé.
assignation: attribution, affectation.
babble: murmure confus, babiller, bavarder.
boasted: vanté.
civil: civil.
claret: vin de Bordeaux, bordeaux.
common: commun, ordinaire, vulgaire.
corked: bouché.
delicacy: friandise, délicatesse, finesse.
everything: tout, tous.
freshness: fraîcheur.
hardened: durci, trempé, endurci.
hearty: cordial, chaleureux.
idler: roue folle, oisif, paresseux, poulie de tension, fainéant, galet d'entraînement, rouleau, laveur.
jest: badiner, plaisanter.
manly: viril, mâle.
meant: signifié.
mid: mi.
navy: marine.
novelty: nouveauté, gadget, innovation.
reigning: régnant.
scandal: scandale, agacement.
spirited: vif, animé, fougueux.
steeplechase: steeple.
surviving: survivant, dernier mourant, rescapé.
talk: parler, causerie, discuter, entretien.
virgin: vierge, virginal.
zest: zeste, vigueur, enthousiasme.

stopped short in his narrative, or lost the point of his anecdote. And yet so **lovable** was Percival in his good humour, his **naivete**, his joyous **entrance** into innocent joy, that his companions were scarcely conscious of the **gene** and restraint he imposed on them. Those merry, dark eyes and that **flashing** smile were **conviviality** of themselves. They brought with them a contagious **cheerfulness** which **compensated** for the want of corruption.

Night had set in. St. John's companions had departed to their several haunts, and Percival himself stood on the steps of the club, **resolving** that he would **join** the crowds that swept through the streets to gaze on the **illuminations**, when he perceived Beck (still at the rein of his **dozing** horse), whom he had quite forgotten till that moment. Laughing at his own want of memory, Percival put some silver into Beck's hand,—more silver than Beck had ever before received for **similar** service,—and said,—

"Well, my man, I suppose I can trust you to take my horse to his stables,—No.—, the Mews, behind Curzon Street. Poor fellow, he wants his supper,—and you, too, I suppose!"

Beck smiled a pale, hungry smile, and **pulled** his **forelock politely**.

"I can take the 'oss werry **safely**, your 'onor."

"Take him, then, and good evening; but don't get on, for your life."

"Oh, no, sir; I never **gets** on,—'t aint in my ways."

And Beck slowly led the horse through the crowd, till he vanished from Percival's eyes.

Just then a man passing through the street paused as he saw the young gentleman on the steps of the club, and said gayly, "Ah! how do you do? Pretty faces in **plenty** out to-night. Which way are you going?"

"That is more than I can tell you, Mr. Varney. I was just thinking which turn to take,—the right or the left."

"Then let me be your guide;" and Varney **offered** his arm.

Percival accepted the courtesy, and the two walked on towards Piccadilly. Many a kind glance from the milliners—and maid-servants whom

---

French

cheerfulness: gaieté, bonne humeur.
compensated: compensa, récompensas.
conviviality: convivialité.
dozing: sommeillant.
entrance: admission, porte, ravir, point d'entrée, façons de l'avant.
flashing: clignotement, étincelable, solin, séchage à la vapeur, latensification, postlumination, tache, ébarbage, rappel sur
supervision, doublage, brillant inégal.
forelock: toupet, goujon d'arrêt, mèche.
gene: gène.
gets: obtient.
illumination: éclairage, illumination, enluminure.
join: joindre, joignent, unir, relier, réunir, associer, accoupler, attacher, adhérer, nouer, raccorder.
lovable: aimable.
naivete: naïveté.
offered: offert, offrie.
plenty: abondance, beaucoup.
politely: poliment, de manière polie, de façon polie.
pulled: tirèrent, tiré, tirâtes, tiras.
resolving: résolvant.
safely: de façon sûre, de manière sûre.
similar: semblable, pareil, similaire, analogue.

the illuminations drew abroad, roved, somewhat impartially, towards St. John and his companion; but they dwelt longer on the last, for there at least they were sure of a return. Varney, if not in his first youth, was still in the prime of life, and Time had **dealt** with him so leniently that he retained all the **personal** advantages of youth itself. His complexion still was clear; and as only his **upper** lip, decorated with a slight silken and well-trimmed **mustache**, was unshaven, the contour of the face added to the **juvenility** of his appearance by the rounded **symmetry** it betrayed. His hair escaped from his hat in fair **unchanged luxuriance**. And the **nervous** figure, **agile** as a panther's, though broad-shouldered and deep-chested, **denoted** all the slightness and **elasticity** of twenty-five, **combined** with the muscular power of **forty**. His dress was rather fantastic,—too showy for the good taste which is habitual to the English gentleman,—and there was a **peculiarity** in his gait, almost approaching to a **strut**, which bespoke a desire of effect, a consciousness of personal advantages, equally **opposed** to the mien and manner of Percival's usual companions; yet withal, even the most fastidious would have hesitated to **apply** to Gabriel Varney the **epithet** of "vulgar."

Many turned to look again, but it was not to remark the dress or the slight swagger; an expression of reckless, sinister power in the countenance, something of vigour and **determination** even in that very walk, foppish as it would have been in most, made you **sink** all **observation** of the mere externals, in a sentiment of curiosity towards the man himself. He seemed a **somebody**,—not a somebody of **conventional** rank, but a somebody of personal individuality; an **artist**, perhaps a poet, or a soldier in some foreign service, but certainly a man whose name you would expect to have heard of. Amongst the common mob of passengers he stood out in marked and distinct relief.

"I feel at home in a crowd," said Varney. "Do you understand me?"

"I think so," answered Percival. "If ever I could become distinguished, I, too, should feel at home in a crowd."

"You have ambition, then; you mean to become distinguished?" asked Varney, with a sharp, searching look.

French

agile: agile, alerte, vif, vigilant, actif.
apply: appliquer, pratiquer.
artist: artiste.
combined: combiné.
conventional: classique, conventionnel, traditionnel.
dealt: opéré.
denoted: indiquâtes.
determination: détermination, dosage, résolution.
elasticity: élasticité.
epithet: épithète.
forty: quarante.
juvenility: juvénilité.
luxuriance: luxuriance, exubérance.
mustache: moustache, la moustache.
nervous: nerveux, intimidé, agité, excitable, inquiet.
observation: observation, remarque, réflexion.
opposed: opposé, rouspétâmes.
peculiarity: particularité, bizarrerie, singularité.
personal: personnel, propre.
sink: évier, forer, couler, lavabo, sombrer, rencontrer, puits, enfoncer, toucher, collecteur.
somebody: quelqu'un, un.
strut: entretoise, étrésillon, jambe de force, étai, support.
symmetry: symétrie.
unchanged: inchangé, intact, stationnaire.
upper: supérieur, empeigne.

There was a deeper and steadier flash than usual from Percival's dark eyes, and a manlier glow over his cheek, at Varney's question. But he was slow in answering; and when he did so, his manner had all its **wonted mixture** of **graceful** bashfulness and gay **candour**.

"Our rise does not always depend on ourselves. We are not all born great, nor do we all have 'greatness thrust on us.'"

"One can be what one likes, with your fortune," said Varney; and there was a **growl** of envy in his voice.

"What, be a painter like you! Ha, ha!"

"Faith," said Varney, "at least, if you could paint at all, you would have what I have not,—praise and fame."

Percival pressed kindly on Varney's arm. "Courage! you will get justice some day."

Varney **shook** his head. "Bah! there is no such thing as justice; all are underrated or **overrated**. Can you name one man who you think is **estimated** by the public at his precise **value**? As for present popularity, it depends on two **qualities**, each **singly**, or both united,—cowardice and charlatanism; that is, **servile compliance** with the taste and **opinion** of the moment, or a quack's **spasmodic** efforts at **originality**. But why bore you on such matters? There are things more **attractive** round us. A good **ankle** that, eh? Why, pardon me, it is strange, but you don't seem to care much for women?"

"Oh, yes, I do," said Percival, with a **sly demureness**. "I am very fond of—my mother!"

"Very proper and filial," said Varney, laughing; "and does your love for the sex **stop** there?"

"Well, and in truth I fancy so,—pretty nearly. You know my grandmother is not alive! But that is something really **worth** looking at!" And Percival pointed, almost with a child's delight, at an **illumination** more brilliant than the rest.

French

ankle: cheville, la cheville.
attractive: attrayant, attirant, alléchant, affriolant, attachant, séduisant.
candour: candeur, franchise, sincérité.
compliance: conformité, souplesse, acquiescement, élasticité.
demureness: modestie.
estimated: estimé, évaluai, taxa, taxâmes, taxèrent, taxé.
graceful: gracieux, élégant,

mignon.
growl: grogner, râler, grondement.
illumination: éclairage, illumination, enluminure.
mixture: mélange, mixture.
opinion: avis, opinion, vœu.
originality: originalité.
overrated: surtaxèrent, surfis, surévaluas.
quality: qualité, propriété.
servile: aplaventriste, servile.
shook: secouas, ébranlâtes.

singly: de façon célibataire, de manière célibataire.
sly: rusé, malin, astucieux, artificieux.
spasmodic: spasmodique.
stop: arrêter, cesser, stopper, halte, interrompre, s'arrêter, station, butée, gare, faire cesser, taquet.
value: valeur, apprécier, mérite, évaluer.
wonted: habituel, accoutumé.
worth: valeur, mérite.

"I suppose, when you come of age, you will have all the **cedars** at Laughton hung with coloured lamps. Ah, you must ask me there some day; I should so like to see the old place again."

"You never saw it, I think you say, in my poor father's time?"

"Never."

"Yet you knew him."

"But slightly."

"And you never saw my mother?"

"No; but she seems to have such influence over you that I am sure she must be a very superior person,—rather proud, I suppose."

"Proud, no,—that is, not **exactly** proud, for she is very **meek** and very **affable**. But yet—"

"'But yet—' You **hesitate**: she would not like you to be seen, perhaps, **walking** in Piccadilly with Gabriel Varney, the natural son of old Sir Miles's librarian,—Gabriel Varney the painter; Gabriel Varney the adventurer!"

"As long as Gabriel Varney is a man without **stain** on his character and honour, my mother would only be pleased that I should know an able and **accomplished** person, whatever his **origin** or **parentage**. But my mother would be sad if she knew me intimate with a Bourbon or a Raphael, the first in rank or the first in genius, if either prince or artist had lost, or even sullied, his scutcheon of gentleman. In a word, she is most sensitive as to honour and conscience; all else she disregards."

"Hem!" Varney stooped down, as if examining the polish of his boot, while he continued **carelessly**: "Impossible to walk the streets and keep one's boots out of the **mire**. Well—and you **agree** with your mother?"

"It would be strange if I did not. When I was scarcely four years old, my poor father used to **lead** me through the long **picture-gallery** at Laughton and say: 'Walk through life as if those brave gentlemen looked down on you.' And," added St. John, with his **ingenuous** smile, "my mother would put in her word,—'And those **unstained** women too, my Percival.'"

French

accomplished: accomplîmes, réalisas, confectionnâmes, remplîtes, expérimenté, qualifié, compétent.
affable: affable, aimable, gentil, amène.
agree: consentir, être d'accord, s'accorder, donner son accord, s'harmoniser, admettre, approuver, accorder, accepter.
carelessly: de façon négligente, négligemment, de manière négligente.
cedar: cèdre.
exactly: exactement, justement, précisément, à l'heure, proprement, de façon exacte, de manière exacte.
hesitate: hésiter, barguigner.
ingenuous: ingénu, candide, naïf.
lead: plomb, mener, conduire, guider, mènes, menons, aboutir, avance, diriger, régler, mine.
meek: humble, doux.
mire: mire, bourbier, boue.
origin: origine, provenance, source.
parentage: naissance, filiation.
picture-gallery: pinacothèque.
stain: tache, salir, souiller, colorant, teinture.
unstained: sans tache.
walking: marchant, promenade.

There was something noble and touching in the boy's low accents as he said this; it gave the key to his **unusual** modesty and his frank, **healthful** innocence of character.

The devil in Varney's lip **sneered** mockingly.

"My young friend, you have never loved yet. Do you think you ever shall?"

"I have dreamed that I could love one day. But I can wait."

Varney was about to reply, when he was accosted abruptly by three men of that **exaggerated style** of dress and manner which is implied by the vulgar appellation of "Tigrish." Each of the three men had a **cigar** in his mouth, each seemed flushed with **wine**. One wore long brass **spurs** and immense **mustaches**; another was distinguished by an **enormous surface** of black **satin** cravat, across which meandered a Pactolus of gold chain; a third had his coat **laced** and **braided** a la Polonaise, and pinched and **padded** a la Russe, with trousers **shaped** to the **calf** of a **sinewy leg**, and a glass **screwed** into his right eye.

"Ah, Gabriel! ah, Varney! ah, prince of good fellows, well met! You **sup** with us to-night at little Celeste's; we were just going in search of you."

"Who's your friend,—one of us?" whispered a second. And the third screwed his arm tight and **lovingly** into Varney's.

Gabriel, despite his habitual assurance, looked abashed foz a moment, and would have **extricated** himself from **cordialities** not at that moment welcome; but he saw that his friends were too far gone in their **cups** to be easily shaken off, and he felt **relieved** when Percival, after a **dissatisfied** glance at the three, said quietly: "I must detain you no longer; I shall soon look in at your studio;" and without waiting for an answer, slid off, and was lost among the crowd.

Varney walked on with his new-found friends, **unheeding** for some moments their loose remarks and familiar **banter**. At length he shook off his abstraction, and surrendering himself to the coarse humours of his

French

banter: badinage, plaisanterie.
braided: tresse de paille.
calf: veau, mollet.
cigar: cigare.
cordiality: cordialité.
cup: tasse, coupe, godet.
dissatisfied: mécontent.
enormous: énorme, immense, formidable.
exaggerated: exagéré, outras.
extricated: dégagèrent.
healthful: salubre.

laced: triangulé, lacé.
leg: jambe, patte, gigot, branche, cuisse, pied, montant, étançon.
lovingly: de façon amoureuse, de manière amoureuse.
mustache: moustache, la moustache.
padded: rembourré.
relieved: soulagé, relayâmes, exonéré.
satin: satin, de satin.
screwed: vissé, soûl.

shaped: façonné, profilé.
sinewy: tendineux.
sneered: ricané.
spur: éperon, inciter, embase de poteau, ergot.
style: style, mode.
sup: souper, super.
surface: surface, superficie, comble, faîte, summon, haut, sommet.
unheeding: insouciant.
unusual: inhabituel, insolite.
wine: vin, rouge vin.

companions, soon eclipsed them all by the gusto of his **slang** and the mocking **profligacy** of his sentiments; for here he no longer played a part, or suppressed his grosser instincts. That uncurbed **dominion** of the senses, to which his very boyhood had abandoned itself, found a willing slave in the man. Even the talents themselves that he **displayed** came from the cultivation of the sensual. His eye, studying externals, made him a painter,— his ear, quick and practised, a **musician**. His wild, prodigal fancy rioted on every excitement, and brought him in a vast harvest of experience in knowledge of the frailties and the vices on which it indulged its vagrant experiments. Men who over-cultivate the art that **connects** itself with the senses, with little **counterpoise** from the reason and pure intellect, are apt to be dissipated and irregular in their lives. This is frequently **noticeable** in the biographies of musicians, **singers**, and painters; less so in poets, because he who deals with words, not signs and tones, must **perpetually compare** his senses with the pure images of which the senses only see the appearances,— in a word, he must employ his intellect, and his self-education must be large and comprehensive. But with most real genius, however fed merely by the senses,—most really great painters, singers, and musicians, however easily led **astray** into temptation,—the richness of the soil throws up **abundant** good qualities to countervail or **redeem** the evil; they are usually **compassionate**, generous, **sympathizing**. That Varney had not such beauties of soul and temperament it is **unnecessary** to add,—principally, it is true, because of his **nurture**, education, parental example, the **utter** corruption in which his childhood and youth had passed; partly because he had no real genius,—-it was a false apparition of the **divine** spirit, reflected from the exquisite **perfection** of his frame (which rendered all his senses so vigorous and acute) and his riotous fancy and his fitful energy, which was capable at times of great application, but not of **definite** purpose or earnest study. All about him was **flashy** and hollow. He had not the natural subtlety and depth of mind that had characterized his terrible father. The **graft** of the opera-dancer was visible on the stock of the scholar; wholly without the habits of method and order, without the patience, without the **mathematical**

French

abundant: abondant, copieux.
astray: égaré.
compare: comparer, conférer.
compassionate: compatissant.
connect: connecter, joindre, relier, réunir, brancher, allier, aboucher, attacher, raccorder, nouer, associer.
counterpoise: contrepoids, balancier.
definite: définitif, ferme.
displayed: affichâmes, en affichage, montré.
divine: divin.
dominion: domination, fédéral, territoire, autorité.
flashy: tapageur, voyant.
graft: greffe, garnir, corruption.
mathematical: mathématique.
musician: musicien.
noticeable: perceptible, évident.
nurture: nourriture, élever, entretenir, milieu.
perfection: perfection, mise en état.
perpetually: perpétuellement, de façon perpétuelle, de manière perpétuelle.
profligacy: débauche.
redeem: racheter, rembourser.
singer: chanteur.
slang: argot.
sympathizing: compatissant, sympathisant.
unnecessary: inutile.
utter: répandre, émettre, proférer, prononcer.

calculating **brain** of Dalibard, he played **wantonly** with the horrible and **loathsome** wickedness of which Olivier had made dark and solemn study. Extravagant and **lavish**, he spent money as fast as he gained it; he threw away all chances of **eminence** and career. In the midst of the direst plots of his villany or the most **energetic** pursuit of his **art**, the poorest excitement, the **veriest bauble** would draw him aside. His heart was with Falri in the **sty**, his fancy with Aladdin in the palace. To make a show was his darling object; he loved to create effect by his person, his talk, his dress, as well as by his talents. Living from hand to mouth, crimes through which it is not our intention to follow him had at times made him rich to-day, for vices to make him poor again to-morrow. What he called "luck," or "his star," had favoured him,—he was not hanged!—he lived; and as the greater part of his unscrupulous career had been conducted in foreign lands and under other names, in his own name and in his own country, though something scarcely to be **defined**, but **equivocal** and provocative of suspicion, made him **displeasing** to the prudent, and vaguely alarmed the experience of the sober, still, no positive **accusation** was attached to the general **integrity** of his character, and the mere **dissipation** of his habits was naturally little known out of his familiar circle. Hence he had the most **presumptuous** confidence in himself,—a confidence native to his courage, and confirmed by his experience. His conscience was so utterly **obtuse** that he might almost be said to present the **phenomenon** of a man without conscience at all. Unlike Conrad, he did not "know himself a villain;" all that he knew of himself was that he was a **remarkably** clever fellow, without prejudice or superstition. That, with all his gifts, he had not succeeded better in life, he ascribed carelessly to the **surpassing** wisdom of his philosophy. He could have done better if he had enjoyed himself less; but was not enjoyment the be-all and end-all of this little life? More often, **indeed**, in the moods of his bitter envy, he would lay the fault upon the world. How great he could have been, if he had been rich and high-born! Oh, he was made to spend, not to save,—to command, not to **fawn**! He was not formed to **plod** through the dull **mediocrities** of fortune; he must toss up for the All or the Nothing! It was no

---

French

accusation: accusation, plainte, dénonciation.
art: art.
bauble: babiole, marotte.
brain: cerveau, encéphale.
defined: défini, précisèrent.
displeasing: déplaisant, mécontentant.
dissipation: dissipation, noce.
eminence: éminence.
energetic: énergique.
equivocal: équivoque, douteux, incertain, ambigu.
fawn: faon, fauve.
indeed: vraiment, certes, en vérité, si, réellement, en effet, en réalité, en fait, d'abord, voire, effectivement.
integrity: intégrité, honnêteté, probité.
lavish: généreux, prodigue.
loathsome: détestable, répugnant.
mediocrity: médiocrité.
obtuse: obtus, borné.
phenomenon: phénomène.
plod: chemines.
presumptuous: présomptueux.
remarkably: de façon remarquable, de manière remarquable, remarquablement.
sty: étable, écurie, orgelet.
surpassing: surpassant, dépassant, maîtrisant.
veriest: le plus très.
wantonly: de façon dévergondée, de manière dévergondée.

control over himself that made Varney now turn his thoughts from certain grave **designs** on Percival St. John to the **brutal debauchery** of his three companions,—rather, he then yielded most to his natural self. And when the morning star rose over the night he passed with low profligates and **venal** nymphs; when over the fragments on the **board** and emptied bottles and drunken riot dawn gleamed and saw him in all the pride of his magnificent **organization** and the **cynicism** of his **measured** vice, fair, fresh, and blooming amidst those **maudlin** eyes and flushed cheeks and **reeling** figures, laughing **hideously** over the spectacle he had provoked, and **kicking** aside, with a devil's scorn, the **prostrate** form of the favoured partner whose head had rested on his bosom, as alone with a steady step, he passed the threshold and walked into the fresh, healthful air,—Gabriel Varney enjoyed the fell triumph of his hell-born vanity, and revelled in his sentiment of superiority and power.

Meanwhile, on **quitting** Varney young Percival strolled on as the whim directed him. Turning down the Haymarket, he gained the colonnade of the Opera House. The crowd there was so dense that his footsteps were arrested, and he leaned against one of the columns in admiration of the various **galaxies** in view. In front blazed the rival stars of the United Service Club and the Athenaeum; to the left, the quaint and peculiar **device** which lighted up Northumberland House; to the right, the anchors, **cannons**, and **bombs** which typified ingeniously the **martial** attributes of the Ordnance Office.

At that moment there were three persons connected with this narrative within a few feet of each other, distinguished from the **multitude** by the feelings with which each regarded the scene, and felt the **jostle** of the crowd. Percival St. John, in whom the **harmless** sense of pleasure was yet vivid and unsatiated, caught from the assemblage only that **physical hilarity** which heightened his own spirits. If in a character as yet so undeveloped, to which the large passions and stern ends of life were as yet unknown, stirred some deeper and more musing thoughts and speculations, giving gravity to the habitual smile on his rosy lip, and steadying the play of his sparkling eyes,

French

board: planche, carte, panneau, conseil, comité, pension, monter à bord, commission, aborder.
bomb: bombe.
brutal: maussade, brutal.
cannon: canon, rond.
cynicism: cynisme.
debauchery: noce, débauche.
design: dessin, conception, projet, plan, esquisse, modèle, élaborer, design, esthétique industrielle, stylique.
device: dispositif, appareil, périphérique, organe, engin.
galaxy: galaxie, poivré.
harmless: inoffensif, anodin, innocent.
hideously: de façon hideuse, de manière hideuse.
hilarity: hilarité.
jostle: bousculer, jouer des coudes.
kicking: puits actif, coups de pied au ballon, bottant.
martial: martial.
maudlin: larmoyant.
measured: mesuré.
multitude: multitude, amas, foule, masse, tas.
organization: organisation, implantation.
physical: physique.
prostrate: prosterné.
quitting: quittant, sortie des employés.
reeling: bobinage, dévidage.
venal: vénal.

he would have been at a loss himself to explain the dim sentiment and the vague desire.

Screened by another column from the **pressure** of the mob, with his arms folded on his breast, a man some few years older in point of time,—many years older in point of character,—gazed (with thoughts how turbulent,— with ambition how profound!) upon the dense and dark masses that **covered** space and street far as the eye could **reach**. He, indeed, could not have said, with Varney, that he was "at home in a crowd." For a crowd did not **fill** him with the sense of his own individual being and importance, but grappled him to its mighty breast with the thousand **tissues** of a common destiny. Who shall explain and **disentangle** those high and restless and interwoven emotions with which intellectual ambition, honourable and ardent, gazes upon that solemn thing with which, in which, for which it lives and labours,—the Human Multitude? To that abstracted, solitary man, the illumination, the festivity, the curiosity, the holiday, were nothing, or but as **fleeting phantoms** and vain seemings. In his heart's eye he saw before him but the *people*, the shadow of an **everlasting** audience,—audience at once and judge.

And literally touching him as he stood, the ragged sweeper, who had returned in vain to devote a last care to his beloved charge, stood arrested with the rest, gazing **joylessly** on the **blazing** lamps, dead as the **stones** he heeded, to the young vivacity of the one man, the solemn visions of the other. So, O London, amidst the universal holiday to monarch and to mob, in those three souls lived the three **elements** which, duly mingled and administered, make thy vice and thy virtue, thy glory and thy shame, thy labour and thy luxury; **pervading** the palace and the street, the hospital and the prison,—enjoyment, which is pleasure; energy, which is action; torpor, which is want!

French

blazing: en flammes, flamboyer, griffade, éclatant, étincelant, enflammé.
covered: couvert, revêtu, bâché, guipé.
disentangle: démêler, dénouer, débrouillez.
element: élément, bloc de plaques, ouvrage, organe, matière de base, foyer de cuisson, cartouche, crayon.
everlasting: éternel, permanent, perpétuel, interminable, immortelle, infini, inusable.
fill: remplir, obturer, plomber, compléter, charger, bourrer, remblai, emplir.
fleeting: fugace, fugitif.
joylessly: de manière triste, de façon triste.
pervading: imprégnant.
phantom: fantôme, apparition.
pressure: pression, instance, impulsion, oppression, vive sollicitation.
reach: atteindre, parvenir, portée, remporter, aboutir, toucher, bief, étendue.
screened: trié, triâmes, trièrent, blindé, tria, tramé, simili.
stone: pierre, lapider, calcul, noyau, dénoyauter, de pierre, caillou.
tissue: tissu, écran, mouchoir en papier, papier mousseline, serpente.

CHAPTER II

LOVE AT FIRST SIGHT

Suddenly across the gaze of Percival St. John there flashed a face that woke him from his **abstraction**, as a light awakes the **sleeper**. It was as a recognition of something seen **dimly** before,—a truth coming out from a dream. It was not the mere beauty of that face (and **beautiful** it was) that arrested his eye and made his heart beat more quickly, it was rather that **nameless** and **inexplicable** sympathy which **constitutes** love at first sight,— a sort of impulse and instinct common to the dullest as the quickest, the hardest reason as the **liveliest** fancy. Plain Cobbett, seeing before the cottage-door, at her homeliest of house-work, the girl of whom he said, "That girl should be my wife," and Dante, first thrilled by the vision of Beatrice,—are alike true **types** of a common experience. Whatever of love sinks the **deepest** is felt at first sight; it streams on us **abrupt** from the cloud, a **lightning** flash,—a destiny **revealed** to us face to face.

Now, there was nothing **poetical** in the place or the **circumstance**, still less in the **companionship** in which this fair creature startled the virgin heart of that **careless** boy; she was leaning on the arm of a **stout**, rosy-faced **matron** in a puce-coloured **gown**, who was **flanked** on the other side by a very small, very spare man, with a very **wee** face, the lower part of which was

French

abrupt: abrupt, brusque, raide, subit, soudain, escarpé, inattendu, à pic.
abstraction: abstraction, distraction, inattention.
beautiful: beau, belle, joli, très beau.
careless: négligent, distrait, étourdi, insouciant.
circumstance: circonstance, état de fait.
companionship: compagnie, équipe, camaraderie.
constitutes: constitue.
deepest: le plus profond.
dimly: de façon faible, de manière faible.
flanked: flanqué.
gown: robe, toge.
inexplicable: inexplicable.
lightning: éclair, foudre.
liveliest: le plus vif.
matron: matrone, directrice, mère de famille, surveillante.
nameless: anonyme, inconnu.
poetical: poétique.
revealed: révéla, décelas.
sleeper: dormeur, traverse.
stout: corpulent, fort, gros, stout.
type: type, taper, dactylographier, modèle, espèce, genre, caractère.
wee: faire pipi, tout petit.

enveloped in an immense belcher. Besides these two incumbrances, the stout **lady** contrived to **carry** in her hands an **umbrella**, a basket, and a pair of pattens.

In the midst of the strange, unfamiliar emotion which his eye conveyed to his heart, Percival's ear was displeasingly jarred by the loud, **bluff**, hearty voice of the girl's **female** companion—

"Gracious me! if that is not John Ardworth. Who'd have thought it? Why, John,—I say, John!" and lifting her umbrella horizontally, she **poked** aside two city clerks in front of her, wheeled round the little man on her left, upon whom the clerks simultaneously **bestowed** the **appellation** of "feller," and **driving** him, as being the sharpest and thinnest **wedge** at hand, through a dense knot of some half-a-dozen **gapers**, while, following his involuntary progress, she looked defiance on the **malcontents**, she succeeded in **clearing** her way to the spot where stood the young man she had discovered. The ambitious **dreamer**, for it was he, thus detected and disturbed, looked embarrassed for a moment as the stout lady, touching him with the umbrella, said,—

"Well, I declare if this is not too bad! You **sent** word that you should not be able to come out with us to see the 'luminations, and here you are as large as life!"

"I did not think, at the moment you **wrote** to me, that-"

"Oh, stuff!" interrupted the stout woman, with a **significant**, good-humoured shake of her head; "I know what's what. Tell the truth, and shame the gentleman who objects to showing his **feet**. You are a wild fellow, John Ardworth, you are! You like looking after the pretty faces, you do, you do—ha, ha, ha! very natural! So did you once,—did not you, Mr. Mivers, did not you, eh? Men must be men,—they always are men, and it's my **belief** that men they always will be!"

With this **sage conjecture** into the future, the lady turned to Mr. Mivers, who, thus appealed to, **extricated** with some difficulty his **chin** from the

---

French

appellation: nom, surnom.
belief: croyance, conviction, foi.
bestowed: accordas, me octroyai, nous octroyâmes, se octroya, te octroyas, vous octroyâtes.
bluff: bluffer, écore.
carry: porter, report, transporter, retenir.
chin: menton, le menton, houppe du menton.
clearing: clairière, défrichement, dégagement, éclaircie.
conjecture: conjecturer, prévoir, se douter de.
dreamer: rêveur, songeur.
driving: poussant, conduisant, pourchassant, actionnant, pilotant.
enveloped: enveloppa.
extricated: dégagèrent.
feet: pieds, les pieds, faute de pied.
female: femelle, féminin, femme.
gaper: badaud, mactre du Pacifique.
lady: dame, madame, demoiselle noble.
malcontent: mécontent.
poked: poussé.
sage: sauge, sensé, raisonnable.
sent: envoyai, adressâmes.
significant: significatif, appréciable, important, considérable.
umbrella: parapluie, pébroc.
wedge: cale, coin, clavette.
wrote: écrivîmes, notâmes, notèrent, notas.

folds of his belcher, and **putting** up his small face, said, in a small voice, "Yes, I was a wild fellow once; but you have **tamed** me, you have, Mrs. M.!"

And **therewith** the chin sank again into the belcher, and the small voice died into a small sigh.

The stout lady glanced **benignly** at her **spouse**, and then **resuming** her address, to which Ardworth listened with a half-frown and a half-smile, observed encouragingly,—

"Yes, there's nothing like a **lawful** wife to break a man in, as you will find some day. Howsomever, your time's not come for the altar, so suppose you give Helen your arm, and come with us."

"Do," said Helen, in a sweet, **coaxing** voice.

Ardworth bent down his rough, **earnest** face to Helen's, and an evident pleasure relaxed its **thoughtful** lines. "I cannot resist you," he began, and then he paused and frowned. "Pish!" he added, "I was talking folly; but what head would not you turn? Resist you I must, for I am on my way now to my **drudgery**. Ask me anything some years hence, when I have time to be happy, and then see if I am the bear you now call me."

"Well," said Mrs. Mivers, **emphatically**, "are you coming, or are you not? Don't stand there shilly-shally."

"Mrs. Mivers," returned Ardworth, with a kind of **sly** humour, "I am sure you would be very angry with your husband's **excellent** shopmen if that was the way they spoke to your customers. If some unhappy dropper-in,—some lady who came to buy a yard or so of Irish,—was suddenly dazzled, as I am, by a luxury wholly **unforeseen** and **eagerly** coveted,—a splendid **lace veil**, or a **ravishing cashmere**, or whatever else you ladies desiderate,—and while she was **balancing** between **prudence** and temptation, your **foreman** exclaimed: 'Don't stand shilly-shally'—come, I put it to you."

"Stuff!" said Mrs. Mivers.

French

balancing: équilibrage, balancement.
benignly: de manière Bénine, de façon Bénine.
cashmere: cachemire.
coaxing: cajolerie, câlin.
drudgery: corvée.
eagerly: de façon avide, de manière avide.
earnest: sérieux, sincère, grave.
emphatically: énergiquement, de façon emphatique, de manière emphatique.
excellent: excellent, parfait, exquis.
fold: pli, plier, repli, plisser, pliure.
foreman: contremaître, chef d'équipe.
lace: dentelle, lacet.
lawful: légal, légitime, licite.
prudence: prudence, précaution.
putting: mettant, lancement, rouler.
ravishing: enchanteur, ravissant.
resuming: reprenant, recommençant.
sly: rusé, malin, astucieux, artificieux.
spouse: époux, conjoint.
tamed: apprivoisé.
therewith: avec cela.
thoughtful: réfléchi, pensif.
unforeseen: imprévu.
veil: voile, dissimuler.

"Alas! unlike your **imaginary customer** (I hope so, at least, for the sake of your till), prudence gets the better of me; unless," added Ardworth, **irresolutely**, and glancing at Helen,—"unless, indeed, you are not sufficiently protected, and—"

"Purtected!" exclaimed Mrs. Mivers, in an **indignant** tone of **astonishment**, and **agitating** the formidable umbrella; "as if I was not enough, with the help of this here domestic **commodity**, to purtect a dozen such. Purtected, indeed!"

"John is right, Mrs. M.,—business is business," said Mr. Mivers. "Let us **move** on; we stop the way, and those idle lads are listening to us, and sniggering."

"Sniggering!" exclaimed the gentle **helpmate**. "I should like to see those who presume for to snigger;" and as she spoke, she threw a look of defiance around her. Then, having thus satisfied her resentment, she prepared to obey, as no doubt she always did, her **lord** and master. Suddenly, with a practised movement, she wheeled round Mr. Mivers, and taking care to **protrude** before him the sharp point of the umbrella, cut her way through the crowd like the scythed car of the Ancient Britons, and was soon lost amidst the **throng**, although her way might be guessed by a slight **ripple** of peculiar agitation along the general stream, accompanied by a **prolonged murmur** of **reproach** or expostulation which gradually died in the distance.

Ardworth gazed after the fair form of Helen with a look of regret; and when it vanished, with a slight start and a suppressed sigh he turned away, and with the long, steady stride of a strong man, cleared his **path** through the Strand towards the printing-office of a journal on which he was **responsibly** engaged.

But Percival, who had caught much of the conversation that took place so near him,—Percival, happy child of **idleness** and whim,—had no motive of labour and occupation to **stay** the free impulse of his heart, and his heart drew him on, with **magnetic** attraction, in the track of the first being that had ever touched the sweet instincts of youth.

French

agitating: agitant, débattant, troublant, émouvant, remuant.
astonishment: étonnement, surprise.
commodity: denrée, marchandise, produit, article.
customer: client, abonné, acheteur, chaland.
helpmate: compagnon.
idleness: oisiveté, désœuvrement.
imaginary: imaginaire, fantastique, fictif.
indignant: indigné.
irresolutely: de façon indécise, de manière indécise.
lord: seigneur, monsieur.
magnetic: magnétique, aimanté.
move: émouvoir, remuer, déplacer, mouvoir, se déplacer, coup, déménagement, affecter, bouger, proposer.
murmur: murmure, bruit.
path: chemin, sentier, trajectoire, piste.
prolonged: prolongeâtes.
protrude: dépasser.
reproach: reproche, gronder, réprimander, sermonner.
responsibly: de façon responsable, de manière responsable.
ripple: ondulation, ride.
stay: séjour, rester, étai, hauban, demeurer.
throng: affluer, cohue, foule, multitude, se presser.

Meanwhile, Mrs. Mivers was destined to learn—though perhaps the lesson little availed her—that to get **smoothly** through this world it is necessary to be **supple** as well as strong; and though, up to a certain point, man or woman may force the way by poking umbrellas into people's **ribs** and **treading mercilessly** upon people's toes, yet the endurance of ribs and toes has its appointed **limits**.

Helen, half terrified, also half amused by her companion's **robust** resolution of purpose, had in Mrs. Mivers's general courage and success that confidence which the weak repose in the strong; and though **whenever** she turned her eyes from the illuminations, she besought Mrs. Mivers to be more gentle, yet, seeing that they had gone safely from St. Paul's to St. James's, she had no distinct apprehension of any practically ill results from the energies she was **unable** to **mitigate**. But now, having just gained the end of St. James's Street, Mrs. Mivers at last found her match. The crowd here halted, **thick** and serried, to gaze in peace upon the brilliant vista which the shops and clubs of that street presented. Coaches and carriages had paused in their line, and **immediately** before Mrs. Mivers stood three very thin, small women, whose dress bespoke them to be of the humblest class.

"Make way, there; make way, my good women, make way!" cried Mrs. Mivers, equally disdainful of the size and the rank of the **obstructing** parties.

"Arrah, and what shall we make way for the like of you, you old busybody?" said one of the **dames**, turning round, and **presenting** a very formidable **squint** to the broad **optics** of Mrs. Mivers.

Without **deigning** a reply, Mrs. Mivers had **recourse** to her usual tactics. Umbrella and husband went right between two of the feminine obstructives; and to the **inconceivable** astonishment and horror of the **assailant**, husband and umbrella **instantly** vanished. The three small furies had **pounced** upon both. They were torn from their natural owner; they were hurried away; the stream behind, long fretted at the path so abruptly made amidst it, closed in, joyous, with a thousand waves. Mrs. Mivers and Helen were borne forward

French

assailant: attaquant, assaillant.
dame: demoiselle noble, dame.
deigning: condescendant, daignant.
immediately: immédiatement, tout de suite, aussitôt, directement, sitôt, d'abord, de manière immédiate, de façon immédiate.
inconceivable: inconcevable, abracadabrant, inimaginable.
instantly: aussitôt, directement, tout d'abord, d'abord, de façon instante, de manière instante, à l'instant.
limit: limite, frontière.
mercilessly: de façon impitoyable, de manière impitoyable.
mitigate: mitiger, adoucir, atténuer.
obstructing: obstruant, entravant.
optic: optique, moulure optique.
pounced: bondis.
presenting: présentant.
recourse: recours, garantie.
rib: côte, nervure, membre.
robust: robuste, vigoureux.
smoothly: de façon lisse, de manière lisse, facilement.
squint: loucher, strabisme, angle de strabisme.
supple: souple.
thick: épais, dense, gros.
treading: côchage, marcher, piétinage.
unable: incapable.
whenever: chaque fois que, toutes les fois que.

in one way, the umbrella and the husband in the other; in the distance a small voice was heard: "Don't you! don't! Be quiet! Mrs.—Mrs. M.! Oh, oh, Mrs. M.!" At that last repetition of the beloved and familiar **initial**, uttered in a tone of almost **superhuman** anguish, the **conjugal** heart of Mrs. Mivers was afflicted beyond control.

"Wait here a moment, my dear; I'll just give it them, that's all!" And in another moment Mrs. Mivers was heard bustling, **scolding**, till all trace of her whereabout was gone from the eyes of Helen. Thus left alone, in **exceeding** shame and dismay, the poor girl cast a glance around. The glance was caught by two young men, **whose** station, in these days when dress is an equivocal **designator** of rank, could not be guessed by their exterior. They might be **dandies** from the west,—they might be clerks from the **east**.

"By Jove," exclaimed one, "that's a sweet pretty girl!" and, by a sudden movement of the crowd, they both found themselves close to Helen.

"Are you alone, my dear?" said a voice rudely familiar. Helen made no reply; the tone of the voice **frightened** her. A **gap** in the mob showed the **space** towards Cleveland Row, which, leading to no illuminations, was vacant and solitary. She instantly made towards this spot; the two men **followed** her, the bolder and elder one occasionally **trying** to catch hold of her arm. At last, as she passed the last house to the left, a house then owned by one who, at once far-sighted and **impetuous**, affable and haughty, characterized alike by solid virtues and brilliant faults, would, but for hollow friends, have triumphed over **countless** foes, and enjoyed at last that brief day of stormy power for which statesmen **resign** the health of manhood and the hope of age,—as she passed that **memorable** mansion, she suddenly perceived that the space before her had no **thoroughfare**; and, while she paused in dismay, her **pursuers** blockaded her escape.

One of them now fairly seized her hand. "Nay, pretty one, why so cruel? But one kiss,—only one!" He endeavoured to pass his arm round her waist while he spoke. Helen **eluded** him, and darted forward, to find her way stopped by her persecutor's companion, when, to her astonishment, a third

French

conjugal: conjugal.
countless: incalculable, innombrable.
dandy: chouette, dandy.
designator: indicateur, code.
east: est, orient.
eluded: éludas, déjouèrent.
exceeding: dépassant, excédant, maîtrisant, outrepassant.
followed: suivis, talonnâtes, ensuivues, vous ensuivîtes, t'ensuivis, s'ensuivit, m'ensuivis, nous ensuivîmes.
frightened: effrayé, redouta.
gap: brèche, écart, lacune, interstice, espace inter électrode, créneau, trou, couloir, fente, jeu, goulet.
impetuous: impétueux, fougueux.
initial: initiale, parapher.
memorable: mémorable.
pursuer: poursuivant.
resign: démissionner, résigner, abandonner, abdiquer, re retirer, renoncer.
scolding: réprimande, grondeur.
space: espace, écartement, case, blanc, interligne, place, repos, spatial.
superhuman: surhumain.
thoroughfare: voie de communication.
trying: essayant, fastidieux, pénible.
whose: dont, de qui, duquel.

person gently pushed aside the form that **impeded** her path, approached, and looking **mute** defiance at the unchivalric molesters, offered her his arm. Helen gave but one **timid**, hurrying glance to her unexpected protector; something in his face, his air, his youth, appealed at once to her confidence. **Mechanically**, and scarce knowing what she did, she laid her trembling hand on the arm held out to her.

The two Lotharios looked foolish. One pulled up his shirt-collar, and the other turned, with a forced laugh, on his heel. Boy as Percival seemed, and little more than boy as he was, there was a dangerous **fire** in his eye, and an expression of spirit and ready courage in his whole **countenance**, which, if it did not awe his tall rivals, made them at least **unwilling** to have a scene and provoke the interference of a **policeman**; one of whom was now seen walking slowly up to the spot. They therefore preserved a discomfited silence; and Percival St. John, with his heart going ten knots a beat, **sailed triumphantly** off with his prize.

Scarcely knowing **whither** he went, certainly **forgetful** of Mr. Mivers, in his anxiety to escape at least from the crowd, Percival walked on till he found himself with his fair charge under the **trees** of St. James's Park.

Then Helen, recovering herself, paused, and said, alarmed: "But this is not my way; I must go back to the street!"

"How foolish I am! That is true," said Percival, looking confused. "I—I felt so happy to be with you, feel your hand on my arm, and think that we were all by ourselves, that—that—-But you have dropped your flowers!"

And as a **bouquet** Helen wore, **dislodged** somehow or other, fell to the ground, both stooped to **pick** it up, and their hands met. At that touch, Percival felt a strange **tremble**, which perhaps communicated itself (for such things are **contagious**) to his fair companion. Percival had got the **nosegay**, and seemed **willing** to **detain** it; for he bent his face **lingeringly** over the flowers. At length he turned his bright, ingenuous eyes to Helen, and **singling** one rose from the rest, said **beseechingly**: "May I keep this? See, it is not so fresh as the others."

French

beseechingly: de façon adjurante, de manière adjurante.
bouquet: bouquet.
contagious: contagieux.
countenance: encourager, figure, mine, visage.
detain: détenir, retenir, détiens, retiens, réprimer.
dislodged: délogé.
fire: feu, incendie, tirer, renvoyer, licencier, suspendre, partir, le feu.
forgetful: distrait, oublieux.
impeded: empêchâmes.
lingeringly: de façon prolongée, de manière prolongé.
mechanically: de façon mécanique, de manière mécanique, mécaniquement.
mute: muet, sourdine, commutateur de sourdine.
nosegay: petit bouquet odorant.
pick: cueillir, piquer, pioche, ramasser, pic, choisir.
policeman: policier, agent de police.
sailed: navigué.
singling: démariage, pli cassé.
timid: timide, peureux, craintif.
tree: arbre, arborescence.
tremble: trembler, frémir.
triumphantly: de manière triomphante, triomphalement, de façon triomphante.
unwilling: peu disposé, rétif.
whither: où.
willing: volontaire, disposé, prêt.

"I am sure, sir," said Helen, **colouring**, and looking down, "I owe you so much that I should be glad if a poor flower could repay it."

"A poor flower! You don't know what a prize this is to me!" Percival placed the rose **reverently** in his **bosom**, and the two moved back slowly, as if **reluctant** both, through the old palace-court into the street.

"Is that lady **related** to you?" asked Percival, looking another way, and **dreading** the reply, — "not your mother, surely!"

"Oh, no! I have no mother!"

"Forgive me!" said Percival; for the tone of Helen's voice told him that he had touched the spring of a household sorrow. "And," he added, with a jealousy that he could scarcely restrain from making itself evident in his accent, "that gentleman who spoke to you under the Colonnade, — I have seen him before, but where I cannot remember. In fact, you have put everything but yourself out of my head. Is he related to you?"

"He is my cousin."

"Cousin!" repeated Percival, **pouting** a little; and again there was silence.

"I don't know how it is," said Percival at last, and very **gravely**, as if much **perplexed** by some **abstruse** thought, "but I feel as if I had known you all my life. I never felt this for any one before."

There was something so **irresistibly** innocent in the boy's **serious**, wondering tone as he said these words that a smile, in **spite** of herself, broke out amongst the thousand **dimples** round Helen's charming lips. Perhaps the little **witch** felt a touch of **coquetry** for the first time.

Percival, who was looking **sidelong** into her face, saw the smile, and said, drawing up his head, and shaking back his **jetty curls**: "I dare say you are laughing at me as a mere boy; but I am older than I look. I am sure I am much older than you are. Let me see, you are seventeen, I suppose?"

Helen, getting more and more at her ease, nodded **playful** assent.

French

abstruse: mystérieux, abstrus.
bosom: sein, poitrine.
colouring: coloration, prétannage, teinture, encrage.
coquetry: coquetterie.
curl: boucle, friser, rotationnel, coiffer, faire tournoyer, battre, roulage, gode, fourche.
dimple: fossette, trace de coup, ride, alvéole, contraction latérale, cribler, dépression de l'émail, dermatomycose descaprins.
dreading: option marchandises diverses.
gravely: gravement, de façon tombe, de manière tombe.
irresistibly: irrésistiblement, de manière irrésistible, de façon irrésistible.
jetty: jetée, débarcadère, embarcadère.
perplexed: embarrassâtes, perplexe.
playful: espiègle, ludique, badin.
pouting: bouder, gode, tacaud.
related: racontai, contèrent, apparenté, concerna.
reluctant: peu disposé, réticent.
reverently: de manière respectueuse, de façon respectueuse.
serious: sérieux, grave, important, considérable, majeur.
sidelong: de côté, oblique.
spite: rancune, dépit.
witch: sorcière.

"And I am not far from twenty-one. Ah, you may well look surprised, but so it is. An hour ago I felt a mere boy; now I shall never feel a boy again!"

Once more there was a long pause, and before it was broken, they had gained the very spot in which Helen had lost her friend.

"Why, bless us and save us!" exclaimed a voice "loud as a trumpet," but not "with a silver sound," "there you are, after all;" and Mrs. Mivers (husband and umbrella both **regained**) planted herself full before them.

"Oh, a pretty **fright** I have been in! And now to see you coming along as cool as if nothing had happened; as if the humbrella had not lost its hivory 'andle,—it's quite purvoking. Dear, dear, what we have gone through! And who is this young gentleman, pray?"

Helen whispered some **hesitating** explanation, which Mrs. Mivers did not seem to **receive** as **graciously** as Percival, poor fellow, had a right to expect. She stared him full in the face, and shook her head **suspiciously** when she saw him a little confused by the **survey**. Then, **tucking** Helen tightly under her arm, she walked back towards the Haymarket, merely saying to Percival,—

"Much **obligated**, and good-night. I have a long journey to take to set down this here young lady; and the best thing we can all do is to get home as fast as we can, and have a **refreshing** cup of tea—that's my mind, sir. Excuse me!"

Thus abruptly dismissed, poor Percival gazed **wistfully** on his Helen as she was borne along, and was somewhat **comforted** at seeing her look back with (as he thought) a touch of regret in her **parting** smile. Then suddenly it flashed across him how **sadly** he had wasted his time. **Novice** that he was, he had not even learned the name and address of his new acquaintance. At that thought he hurried on through the crowd, but only reached the object of his pursuit just in time to see her placed in a coach, and to catch a full view of the **luxuriant proportions** of Mrs. Mivers as she followed her into the **vehicle**.

French

comforted: soulagé.
fright: peur, effroi, anxiété, frayeur, terreur.
graciously: de façon gracieuse, de manière gracieuse.
hesitating: hésitant, barguignant.
luxuriant: luxuriant, exubérant.
novice: débutant, novice.
obligated: obligé.
parting: raie, séparation.
proportion: proportion, pourcentage, fréquence.
receive: recevoir, reçois, accueillir, admettre, agréer, recueillir, accepter, réception.
refreshing: rafraîchissant, actualisant.
regained: regagna, rattrapai.
sadly: tristement, de façon triste, de manière triste.
survey: enquête, étude, levé, inspection, sondage, arpenter, campagne d'évaluation.
suspiciously: de manière méfiante, de façon méfiante.
tucking: charge, serrage aux doigts, accrochage, tassement, bourrage.
vehicle: véhicule, voiture, bagnole.
wistfully: de façon mélancolique, de manière mélancolique.

As the lumbering **conveyance** (the only coach on the stand) heaved itself into motion, Percival's eye fell on the sweeper, who was still leaning on his broom, and who, in grateful recognition of the **unwonted** generosity that had repaid his service, touched his ragged hat, and smiled **drowsily** on his young customer. Love **sharpens** the wit and **animates** the timid; a thought worthy of the most experienced inspired Percival St. John; he hurried to the sweeper, laid his hand on his **patchwork** coat, and said breathlessly,—

"You see that coach turning into the square? Follow it,—find out where it sets down. There's a sovereign for you; another if you succeed. Call and tell me your success. Number—Curzon Street! Off, like a shot!"

The sweeper nodded and grinned; it was possibly not his first **commission** of a similar kind. He darted down the street; and Percival, following him with **equal speed**, had the satisfaction to see him, as the coach traversed St. James's Square, **comfortably** seated on the **footboard**.

Beck, dull **clod**, knew nothing, cared nothing, felt nothing as to the motives or purpose of his employer. Honest love or selfish vice, it was the same to him. He saw only the one sovereign which, with **astounded** eyes, he still gazed at on his **palm**, and the vision of the sovereign that was yet to come.

"Scandit aeratas vitiosa **naves**
Cura; nee turmas equitum relinquit."

It was the Selfishness of London, calm and **stolid**, whether on the track of innocence or at the command of guile.

At half-past ten o'clock Percival St. John was seated in his room, and the sweeper stood at the threshold. Wealth and **penury** seemed brought into visible **contact** in the persons of the visitor and the host. The **dwelling** is held by some to give an **index** to the character of the owner; if so, Percival's apartments differed much from those **generally** favoured by young men of rank and fortune. On the one hand, it had none of that affectation of superior

French

animates: anime.
astounded: confondit, stupéfièrent, étonné.
clod: boule, motte.
comfortably: agréablement, confortablement, de façon confortable, de manière confortable.
commission: commission, groupe de travail, mandat.
contact: contact, s'aboucher avec.
conveyance: moyen de transport, transport, acte de cession.
drowsily: de façon somnolente, de manière somnolente.
dwelling: demeurant, habitation, domicile, logis, logeant, gîte.
equal: égal, pareil, conforme.
footboard: marchepied, pied de lit, planchette, petit dossier.
generally: généralement, en général, ordinairement, de manière générale, de façon générale.
index: indice, index, tableau, liste, répertoire.
nave: moyeu, nef.
palm: palmier, paume.
patchwork: patchwork, mosaïque.
penury: indigence, pénurie.
sharpen: affiler, affûter, acérer, appointer, acères.
speed: vitesse, rapidité, allure, hâte.
stolid: flegmatique, impassible.
unwonted: insolite.

taste **evinced** in marqueterie and **gilding,** or the more picturesque discomfort of high-backed chairs and **mediaeval** curiosities which **prevails** in the daintier abodes of fastidious bachelors; nor, on the other hand, had it the **sporting** character which **individualizes** the ruder juveniles qui gaudent equis, betrayed by **engravings** of **racers** and celebrated fox-hunts, relieved, perhaps, if the Nimrod **condescend** to a cross of the Lovelace, with portraits of figurantes, and ideals of French sentiment **entitled**, "Le Soir," or "La Reveillee," "L'Espoir," or "L'Abandon." But the rooms had a **physiognomy** of their own, from their exquisite neatness and cheerful simplicity. The chintz draperies were lively with gay flowers; books filled up the niches; here and there were small pictures, chiefly sea-pieces,—well chosen, well placed.

There might, indeed, have been something almost **effeminate** in a certain **inexpressible purity** of taste, and a **cleanliness** of detail that seemed actually brilliant, had not the folding-doors **allowed** a glimpse of a plainer apartment, with fencing-foils and boxing-gloves ranged on the wall, and a cricket-bat resting carelessly in the corner. These gave a **redeeming** air of **manliness** to the rooms; but it was the manliness of a boy,—half-girl, if you **please**, in the purity of thought that **pervaded** one room, all boy in the playful pursuits that were made manifest in the other. Simple, however, as this abode really was, poor Beck had never been admitted to the sight of anything half so fine. He stood at the door for a moment, and stared about him, bewildered and dazzled. But his natural torpor to things that **concerned** him not soon brought to him the same **stoicism** that philosophy gives the strong; and after the first surprise, his eye quietly settled on his employer. St. John rose eagerly from the **sofa**, on which he had been contemplating the **starlit treetops** of Chesterfield Gardens,—

"Well, well?" said Percival.

"Hold Brompton," said Beck, with a **brevity** of word and **clearness** of perception worthy a Spartan.

French

allowed: permîmes, autorisé, admis.
brevity: brièveté, concision.
cleanliness: propreté, netteté.
clearness: clarté, limpidité, netteté.
concerned: concerné, intéressé.
condescend: condescendre, daignent.
effeminate: efféminé.
engraving: gravure, tracé sur couche, ciselure, engravant.
entitled: habilité, titrèrent, intitulé,
autorisèrent.
evinced: montré.
gilding: dorant, dorure.
individualizes: individualise.
inexpressible: inexprimable, indicible.
manliness: virilité.
mediaeval: du moyen âge, médiéval.
pervaded: imprégnas.
physiognomy: physionomie.
please: s'il vous plaît, plaire,
contenter, faire plaisir, satisfaire.
prevail: prévaloir, régner, prédominer.
purity: pureté, propreté.
racer: coureur, aspe, couleuvre agile, racer.
redeeming: rachetant.
sofa: canapé, sofa.
sporting: sportif.
starlit: étoilé.
stoicism: stoïcisme.
treetop: cime d'un arbre.

"Old Brompton?" **repeated** Percival, thinking the **reply** the most natural in the world.

"In a big 'ous by hisself," continued Beck, "with a 'igh vall in front."

"You would know it again?"

"In **course**; he's so wery peculiar."

"He,—who?"

"Vy, the 'ous. The young lady got out, and the hold **folks** driv back. I did not go arter them!" and Beck looked sly.

"So! I must find out the name."

"I axed at the public," said Beck, **proud** of his **diplomacy**. "They keeps a sarvant vot takes half a **pint** at her **meals**. The young lady's mabe a foriner."

"A **foreigner**! Then she lives there with her mother?"

"So they s'pose at the public."

"And the name?"

Beck shook his head. "'T is a French 'un, your **honour**; but the sarvant's is Martha."

"You must meet me at Brompton, near the **turnpike**, **tomorrow**, and show me the house."

"Vy, I's in bizness all day, please your honour."

"In business?"'

"I's the place of the crossing," said Beck, with much **dignity**; "but arter **eight** I goes vere I likes."

"To-morrow evening, then, at half-past eight, by the turnpike."

Beck pulled his **forelock** assentingly.

"There's the **sovereign** I **promised** you, my poor **fellow**; much good may it do you. Perhaps you have some father or mother whose heart it will glad."

"I never had no such thing," replied Beck, turning the **coin** in his hand.

"Well, don't spend it in drink."

French

coin: pièce de monnaie, dresser, monnaie.
course: cours, route, plat, parcours, direction, leçon, piste, trivial, met, trajet, rangée.
dignity: dignité.
diplomacy: diplomatie.
eight: huit.
fellow: homme, individu, camarade, ensemble, mâle.
folk: peuple, folklorique, gens.
foreigner: étranger, inconnu.
forelock: toupet, goujon d'arrêt, mèche.
honour: honneur, honorer.
meal: repas, farine.
pint: pinte, chope, petite bouteille.
promised: promîmes.
proud: fier, altier, orgueilleux.
repeated: répéta, redirent, redîtes.
reply: réponse, répliquer.
sovereign: souverain.
tomorrow: demain.
turnpike: autoroute à péage, route à péage, barrière de péage.

"I never **drinks** nothing but svipes."

"Then," said Percival, **laughingly**, "what, my good friend, will you ever do with your money?"

Beck put his finger to his **nose**, **sunk** his voice into a whisper, and replied **solemnly**: "I 'as a mattris."

"A mistress," said Percival. "Oh, a **sweetheart**. Well, but if she's a good girl, and loves you, she'll not let you spend your money on her."

"I haint such a **ninny** as that," said Beck, with **majestic** contempt. "I 'spises the **flat** that is done brown by the blowens. I 'as a mattris."

"A **mattress**! a mattress! Well, what has that to do with the money?"

"Vy, I lines it."

Percival looked puzzled. "Oh," said he, after a thoughtful pause, and in a tone of **considerable compassion**, "I understand: you **sew** your money in your mattress. My poor, poor lad, you can do better than that! There are the savings banks."

Beck looked frightened. "I 'opes your honour von't tell no vun. I 'opes no vun von't go for to put my **tin** vere I shall know nothing vatsomever about it. Now, I knows vere it is, and I lays on it."

"Do you sleep more **soundly** when you lie on your treasure?"

"No. It's hodd," said Beck, **musingly**, "but the more I lines it, the vorse I sleeps."

Percival laughed, but there was **melancholy** in his **laughter**; something in the **forlorn, benighted, fatherless, squalid miser** went to the core of his open, generous heart.

"Do you ever read your Bible," said he, after a pause, "or even the newspaper?"

"I does not read nothing; cos vy? I haint been made a scholard, like **swell** Tim, as was lagged for a forgery."

"You go to church on a Sunday?"

French

benighted: surpris par la nuit.
compassion: compassion, pitié, apitoiement.
considerable: considérable, imposant, majeur.
drink: boisson, boire, consommation, s'enivrer.
fatherless: sans père.
flat: plat, appartement, aplati, bémol, uni, mat.
forlorn: désespéré, délaissé, triste, abandonné.

laughingly: de façon riante, de manière riante.
laughter: rire.
majestic: majestueux, imposant.
mattress: matelas, clayonnage, entrelacs de protection.
melancholy: mélancolie, sombre, abattement.
miser: avare, ladre.
musingly: de façon rêveuse, de manière rêveuse.
ninny: nigaud.

nose: nez, bec.
sew: coudre, cousons.
solemnly: solennellement, de façon solennelle, de manière solennelle.
soundly: de façon sensée ad, judicieusement, solidement.
squalid: misérable, sordide.
sunk: enfoncés, sombré.
sweetheart: amoureux, trésor.
swell: gonfler, houle, enfler, s'enfler, se gonfler, grossir.
tin: étain, tôle, étamer.

"Yes; I 'as a **weekly** hingagement at the New Road."

"What do you mean?"

"To see arter the **gig** of a gemman vot comes from 'Igate."

Percival **lifted** his **brilliant eyes**, and they were **moistened** with a **heavenly dew**, on the **dull** face of his fellow-creature. Beck made a **scrape**, looked round, shambled back to the door, and **ran** home, through the lamp-lit streets of the great **mart** of the Christian **universe**, to sew the **gold** in his mattress.

French

brilliant: brillant, magnifique, luisant, génial, éclatant.
dew: rosée.
dull: terne, mat, obtus, abêtir, sot, bébête, ennuyeux, monotone.
eye: oeil, trou, chas, anneau.
gig: engagement d'un soir, machine d'extraction, guigue, gig.
gold: or, l'or.
heavenly: céleste, divin, du ciel, merveilleux, paradisiaque.
lifted: élevai, soulevé.
mart: centre commercial, marché.
moistened: humidifia, humectâtes.
ran: courûmes, coulèrent.
scrape: gratter, racler, effacer en grattant.
universe: univers.
weekly: hebdomadaire, chaque semaine.

CHAPTER III

EARLY TRAINING FOR AN UPRIGHT GENTLEMAN

Percival St. John had been brought up at home under the eye of his mother and the care of an excellent man who had been tutor to himself and his brothers. The tutor was not much of a classical scholar, for in great measure he had educated himself; and he who does so, **usually lacks** the polish and **brilliancy** of one whose **footsteps** have been led early to the Temple of the Muses. In fact, Captain Greville was a **gallant** soldier, with whom Vernon St. John had been **acquainted** in his own brief **military** career, and whom circumstances had so **reduced** in life as to **compel** him to **sell** his commission and live as he could. He had always been known in his regiment as a reading man, and his authority looked up to in all the disputes as to history and dates, and **literary anecdotes**, which might occur at the mess-table. Vernon **considered** him the most learned man of his acquaintance; and when, accidentally **meeting** him in London, he learned his fallen fortunes, he **congratulated** himself on a very brilliant idea when he suggested that Captain Greville should assist him in the education of his boys and the management of his **estate**. At first, all that Greville **modestly** undertook, with respect to the **former**, and, indeed, was expected to do, was to prepare the young gentlemen for Eton, to which Vernon, with the natural **predilection** of an Eton man, destined his sons. But the sickly constitutions of the two elder

---

French

acquainted: renseignai, informé.
anecdote: anecdote.
brilliancy: éclat, brillance, intensité d'image.
compel: obliger, imposer, contraindre, astreindre.
congratulated: félicitèrent, congratulé, complimentèrent.
considered: considérâtes, envisagé.
estate: domaine, propriété, bien, fonds, succession.
footstep: pas, marche.
former: ancien, précédent.
gallant: vaillant, brave, galant, courageux.
lack: manque, défaut, privation, insuffisance, vice.
literary: littéraire.
meeting: réunion, rencontrant, séance, croisement, assemblée.
military: militaire.
modestly: modestement, de manière modeste, de façon modeste.
predilection: prédilection.
reduced: réduisîtes, modéra, comprimâtes, minora, amaigris, abaissai, amenuisa.
sell: vendre, brader, écouler.
usually: ordinairement, habituellement, d'habitude, généralement, de façon habituelle, normalement, de manière habituelle.

justified Lady Mary in her **opposition** to a public school; and Percival conceived early so strong an affection for a sailor's life that the father's intentions were frustrated. The two elder continued their education at home, and Percival, at an earlier age than usual, went to sea. The last was fortunate enough to have for his captain one of that new race of **naval** officers who, well educated and accomplished, form a notable contrast to the old heroes of Smollett. Percival, however, had not been long in the service before the deaths of his two elder brothers, **preceded** by that of his father, made him the head of his ancient house, and the sole prop of his mother's **earthly** hopes. He conquered with a generous effort the passion for his noble profession, which service had but confirmed, and returned home with his fresh, **childlike** nature uncorrupted, his constitution strengthened, his lively and **impressionable** mind **braced** by the experience of danger and the habits of duty, and quietly resumed his reading under Captain Greville, who moved from the Hall to a small house in the village.

Now, the education he had received, from first to last, was less **adapted prematurely** to **quicken** his intellect and **excite** his imagination than to warm his heart and **elevate**, while it **chastened**, his moral qualities; for in Lady Mary there was, amidst singular sweetness of temper, a high cast of character and thought. She was not what is **commonly** called clever, and her experience of the world was limited, compared to that of most women of similar rank who pass their lives in the vast theatre of London. But she became superior by a certain single-heartedness which made truth so **habitual** to her that the light in which she lived rendered all objects around her clear. One who is always true in the great duties of life is nearly always wise. And Vernon, when he had fairly buried his faults, had felt a noble shame for the excesses into which they had led him. Gradually more and more **wedded** to his home, he dropped his old companions. He set grave guard on his talk (his habits now **required** no guard), lest any of the ancient **levity** should **taint** the ears of his children. Nothing is more common in parents than their desire that their children should escape their faults. We scarcely know ourselves till we have children; and then, if we love them

---

French

adapted: adapté.
braced: contreventé.
chastened: châtièrent.
childlike: enfantin.
commonly: de façon commune, de manière commune.
earthly: terrestre.
elevate: élever, hausser, élève.
excite: exciter, irriter, agacer, hérisser.
habitual: habituel.
impressionable: impressionnable.
levity: légèreté.
naval: naval, douanier.
opposition: opposition, résistance.
preceded: précédèrent, avançâmes.
prematurely: de façon prématurée, de manière prématurée.
quicken: hâte, accélérez, hâtons.
required: exigeas, requîtes, réclamé.
taint: entacher, infection.
wedded: se maria, vous mariâtes, te marias, nous mariâmes, me mariai, marié.

duly, we look narrowly into **failings** that become vices, when they serve as examples to the young.

The **inborn** gentleman, with the native courage and spirit and horror of **trick** and falsehood which belong to that **chivalrous** abstraction, survived almost alone in Vernon St. John; and his boys sprang up in the atmosphere of generous sentiments and **transparent** truth. The tutor was in harmony with the parents,—a soldier every inch of him; not a mere **disciplinarian**, yet with a profound sense of duty, and a knowledge that duty is to be found in attention to details. In **inculcating** the habit of **subordination**, so graceful to the young, he knew how to make himself beloved, and what is harder still, to be understood. The soul of this poor soldier was white and unstained, as the arms of a maiden knight; it was full of suppressed but lofty enthusiasm. He had been ill used, whether by Fate or the Horse Guards; his career had been a failure; but he was as **loyal** as if his hand held the field-marshal's **truncheon**, and the **garter** bound his knee. He was above all querulous discontent. From him, no less than from his parents, Percival caught, not only a spirit of honour worthy the antiqua fides of the poets, but that peculiar cleanliness of thought, if the expression may be used, which belongs to the ideal of youthful chivalry. In mere booklearning, Percival, as may be supposed, was not very **extensively** read; but his mind, if not largely **stored**, had a certain unity of culture, which gave it **stability** and individualized its operations. Travels, **voyages**, narratives of heroic **adventure**, biographies of great men, had made the favourite **pasture** of his enthusiasm. To this was added the more **stirring**, and, perhaps, the more genuine order of poets who make you feel and glow, rather than doubt and ponder. He knew at least enough of Greek to enjoy old Homer; and if he could have come but ill through a college examination into Aeschylus and Sophocles, he had dwelt with fresh delight on the rushing **storm** of **spears** in the "Seven before Thebes," and **wept** over the heroic calamities of Antigone. In science, he was no **adept**; but his clear good sense and quick **appreciation** of positive truths had led him easily through the elementary mathematics, and his somewhat martial spirit had made him delight in the old captain's lectures on military

French

adept: adepte, expérimenté, maestro, maître.
adventure: aventure, spéculation hasardée, péripétie, entreprise maritime.
appreciation: appréciation, estimation.
chivalrous: chevaleresque, galant.
disciplinarian: disciplinaire.
extensively: de manière étendue, largement, de façon étendue.
failing: défaillant, échouer, faillant.
garter: jarretière.
inborn: inné, naturel, congénital.
inculcating: inculquant.
loyal: loyal, dévoué, droit, fidèle, honnête.
pasture: pâturage, pacage.
spear: lance, javelot.
stability: stabilité, constance, permanence d'une couleur, résistibilité.
stirring: agitation, mise en suspension par agitation, brassage, guinandage, malaxage.
stored: entreposé, stockées.
storm: tempête, orage, donner l'assaut.
subordination: subordination.
transparent: transparent, limpide.
trick: artifice, truc, mystifier, ruse, tour, astuce.
truncheon: matraque, souchet.
voyage: voyage.
wept: pleurâtes, sourdis, larmoyèrent.

tactics. Had he remained in the navy, Percival St. John would doubtless have been distinguished. His talents **fitted** him for straightforward, **manly** action; and he had a generous desire of distinction, vague, perhaps, the moment he was taken from his profession, and **curbed** by his diffidence in himself and his sense of deficiencies in the ordinary routine of **purely** classical education. Still, he had in him all the elements of a true man,—a man to go through life with a firm step and a clear conscience and a **gallant** hope. Such a man may not **win** fame,—that is an accident; but he must **occupy** no **despicable** place in the movement of the world.

It was at first **intended** to send Percival to Oxford; but for some reason or other that design was abandoned. Perhaps Lady Mary, over cautious, as mothers left alone sometimes are, feared the **contagion** to which a young man of brilliant expectations and no **studious** turn is **necessarily** exposed in all places of **miscellaneous** resort. So Percival was sent abroad for two years, under the **guardianship** of Captain Greville. On his return, at the age of nineteen, the great world lay before him, and he longed **ardently** to enter. For a year Lady Mary's fears and fond anxieties **detained** him at Laughton; but though his great **tenderness** for his mother **withheld** Percival from **opposing** her wishes by his own, this interval of **inaction** affected visibly his health and spirits. Captain Greville, a man of the world, saw the cause sooner than Lady Mary, and one morning, earlier than usual, he walked up to the Hall.

The captain, with all his **deference** to the sex, was a plain man enough when business was to be done. Like his great **commander**, he came to the point in a few words.

"My dear Lady Mary, our boy must go to London,—we are **killing** him here."

"Mr. Greville!" cried Lady Mary, turning pale and putting aside her embroidery,—"killing him?"

"Killing the man in him. I don't mean to alarm you; I dare say his lungs are sound enough, and that his heart would bear the **stethoscope** to the

French

ardently: ardemment, de façon ardante, de manière ardante.
commander: commandant, capitaine de frégate.
contagion: contagion.
curbed: bridai.
deference: déférence, ajournement.
despicable: méprisable, ignoble.
detained: détinrent, retîntes, retint, retenu, détîntes, détenu.
fitted: ajusté.
gallant: vaillant, brave, galant, courageux.
guardianship: curatelle, tutelle, garde.
inaction: inaction.
intended: visé, visa, visâmes, visèrent, projetas, destiné.
killing: meurtre, abattage.
manly: viril, mâle.
miscellaneous: divers.
necessarily: nécessairement, forcément, de manière nécessaire, de façon nécessaire.
occupy: occuper, habiter, remplir.
opposing: opposant, rouspétant.
purely: purement, de façon pure, de manière pure.
stethoscope: stéthoscope, lunette de visée.
studious: studieux.
tenderness: tendresse, sensibilité à la palpation, câlinerie, endolorissement.
win: gagner, remporter.
withheld: retint, retîntes, retenu.

satisfaction of the College of Surgeons. But, my dear ma'am, Percival is to be a man; it is the man you are killing by **keeping** him tied to your apron-string."

"Oh, Mr. Greville, I am sure you don't wish to wound me, but—"

"I beg ten thousand pardons. I am rough, but truth is rough sometimes."

"It is not for my sake," said the mother, **warmly**, and with tears in her eyes, "that I have wished him to be here. If he is dull, can we not fill the house for him?"

"Fill a **thimble**, my dear Lady Mary. Percival should have a **plunge** in the ocean."

"But he is so young yet,—that **horrid** London; such temptations,—fatherless, too!"

"I have no fear of the result if Percival goes now, while his principles are strong and his imagination is not **inflamed**; but if we keep him here much longer against his bent, he will learn to **brood** and to **muse**, write bad poetry perhaps, and think the world withheld from him a thousand times more delightful than it is. This very **dread** of temptation will **provoke** his curiosity, **irritate** his fancy, make him **imagine** the temptation must be a very delightful thing. For the first time in my life, ma'am, I have caught him sighing over fashionable novels, and **subscribing** to the Southampton Circulating Library. Take my word for it, it is time that Percival should **begin** life, and **swim** without corks."

Lady Mary had a profound confidence in Greville's judgment and affection for Percival, and, like a sensible woman, she was **aware** of her own weakness. She remained silent for a few moments, and then said, with an effort,—

"You know how **hateful** London is to me now,—how **unfit** I am to return to the **hollow** forms of its society; still, if you think it right, I will take a house for the season, and Percival can still be under our eye."

French

aware: conscient, averti.
begin: commencer, débuter, aborder.
brood: couvée, nichée, progéniture.
dread: crainte, redouter.
hateful: odieux, haïssable.
hollow: creux, cavité, caver.
horrid: horrible, affreux, méchant.
imagine: imaginer, se figurer, se représenter, s'imaginer.
inflamed: enflammé.
irritate: irriter, énerver, agacer.
keeping: gardant, élevant, remplissant.
muse: muse, songer, méditer, rêver.
plunge: plonger, se jeter, se précipiter, risquer de grosses sommes, piquer du nez, inclinaison, chute, enfoncer.
provoke: provoquer, irriter, agacer.
subscribing: souscrivant, signant, abonnant, s'abonnant.
swim: nager, baignade.
thimble: dé à coudre, dé, cosse, tulipe, chaussette, doigt de gant.
unfit: inapte, impropre, incapable de combattre, indigne.
warmly: chaudement, de façon chaude, de manière chaude.

"No, ma'am,—pardon me,—that will be the surest way to make him either **discontented** or **hypocritical**. A young man of his prospects and temper can hardly be expected to **chime** in with all our **sober**, old-fashioned habits. You will impose on him—if he is to **conform** to our hours and notions and quiet set—a thousand **irksome** restraints; and what will be the consequence? In a year he will be of age, and can throw us off altogether, if he **pleases**. I know the boy; don't seem to **distrust** him,—he may be trusted. You place the true restraint on temptation when you say to him: 'We **confide** to you our dearest treasure,—your honour, your morals, your conscience, yourself!'"

"But at least you will go with him, if it must be so," said Lady Mary, after a few **timid arguments**, from which, one by one, she was driven.

"I! What for? To be a **jest** of the young **puppies** he must know; to make him ashamed of himself and me,—himself as a milksop, and me as a dry nurse?"

"But this was not so abroad."

"Abroad, ma'am, I gave him full swing I promise you; and when we went abroad he was two years younger."

"But he is a mere child still."

"Child, Lady Mary! At his age I had gone through two **sieges**. There are younger faces than his at a mess-room. Come, come! I know what you fear,—he may commit some follies; very likely. He may be taken in, and **lose** some money,—he can afford it, and he will get experience in return. Vices he has none. I have seen him,—ay, with the **vicious**. Send him out against the world like a saint of old, with his Bible in his hand, and no spot on his **robe**. Let him see fairly what is, not stay here to dream of what is not. And when he's of age, ma'am, we must get him an object, a pursuit; start him for the **county**, and make him serve the State. He will understand that business pretty well. Tush! tush! what is there to cry at?"

The captain **prevailed**. We don't say that his advice would have been equally **judicious** for all youths of Percival's age; but he knew well the

---

French

argument: argument, dispute, débat, discussion.
chime: carillon, peigne.
confide: confier.
conform: conformer, correspondre, concorder.
county: comté, circonscription électorale.
discontented: mécontent.
distrust: méfiance, se méfier, défiance.
hypocritical: hypocrite.
irksome: ennuyeux.
jest: badiner, plaisanter.
judicious: judicieux.
lose: perdre, s'égarer, succomber, se perdre, paumez, être vaincu.
pleases: plaît, plait.
prevailed: prévalus.
puppy: chiot, caniche, jeune chien.
robe: robe, peignoir.
siege: siège.
sober: sobre, dessoûler, modéré, sérieux.
timid: timide, peureux, craintif.
vicious: méchant, vicieux, perfide, malin.

nature to which he confided; he knew well how strong was that young heart in its healthful simplicity and instinctive **rectitude**; and he appreciated his manliness not too highly when he felt that all evident props and aids would be but irritating **tokens** of distrust.

And thus, armed only with letters of **introduction**, his mother's tearful admonitions, and Greville's experienced warnings, Percival St. John was **launched** into London life. After the first month or so, Greville came up to visit him, do him sundry kind, **invisible** offices amongst his old friends, help him to **equip** his apartments, and mount his **stud**; and wholly satisfied with the result of his experiment, returned in high spirits, with flattering reports, to the anxious mother.

But, indeed, the tone of Percival's letters would have been **sufficient** to allay even maternal anxiety. He did not write, as sons are apt to do, short excuses for not writing more at length, **unsatisfactory compressions** of details (exciting worlds of conjecture) into a hurried sentence. Frank and **overflowing**, those delightful epistles gave accounts fresh from the first impressions of all he saw and did. There was a **racy**, wholesome gusto in his enjoyment of novelty and **independence**. His balls and his **dinners** and his **cricket** at Lord's, his partners and his companions, his general gayety, his **occasional** ennui, furnisbed ample materials to one who felt he was **corresponding** with another heart, and had nothing to fear or to conceal.

But about two months before this portion of our narrative opens with the coronation, Lady Mary's favourite sister, who had never married, and who, by the death of her parents, was left alone in the worse than **widowhood** of an old maid, had been **ordered** to Pisa for a complaint that betrayed **pulmonary** symptoms; and Lady Mary, with her usual **unselfishness**, conquered both her aversion to movement and her wish to be in reach of her son, to accompany abroad this beloved and solitary relative. Captain Greville was pressed into service as their joint cavalier. And thus Percival's habitual intercourse with his two principal **correspondents** received a **temporary** check.

French

compression: compression, écrasement.
correspondent: correspondant, chroniqueur.
corresponding: correspondant.
cricket: grillon, cricket.
dinner: dîner, déjeuner, souper.
equip: équiper, outillez, armez, armons.
independence: indépendance, autonomie.
introduction: introduction, présentation.
invisible: invisible.
launched: lancé, lançai.
occasional: occasionnel, de circonstance, intermittent.
ordered: commandé, ordonné.
overflowing: débordant, dégorgement.
pulmonary: pulmonaire.
racy: risqué, piquant, osé, plein de verve.
rectitude: rectitude.
stud: goujon, clou, poteau, crampon, tige, montant.
sufficient: suffisant.
temporary: temporaire, provisoire, intérimaire.
token: jeton, témoignage, signe, marque, preuve, gage.
unsatisfactory: insatisfaisant, peu satisfaisant.
unselfishness: générosité, désintéressement.
widowhood: veuvage, viduité.

CHAPTER IV

JOHN ARDWORTH

At noon the next day Beck, restored to his grandeur, was at the **helm** of his state; Percival was **vainly** trying to be amused by the talk of two or three **loungers** who did him the honour to smoke a cigar in his rooms; and John Ardworth sat in his dingy **cell** in Gray's Inn, with a **pile** of law books on the table, and the **daily newspapers carpeting** a **footstool** of Hansard's Debates upon the floor,—no unusual combination of studies amongst the poorer and more ardent students of the law, who often owe their **earliest**, nor perhaps their least noble, **earnings** to employment in the empire of the Press. By the power of a mind **habituated** to labour, and backed by a frame of remarkable strength and endurance, Ardworth grappled with his arid studies not the less **manfully** for a night mainly spent in a printer's office, and stinted to less than four hours' actual sleep. But that sleep was profound and refreshing as a peasant's. The nights thus devoted to the Press (he was employed in the sub-editing of a daily journal), the mornings to the law, he kept distinct the two separate **callings** with a stern **subdivision** of labour which in itself **proved** the vigour of his energy and the resolution of his will. Early compelled to shift for himself and **carve** out his own way, he had obtained a small **fellowship** at the small **college** in which he had passed his **academic**

French

academic: académique, universitaire, étudiant, scolaire.
calling: appelant, vocation, criant, prénommant.
carpeting: moquette.
carve: ciseler, tailler, cisèle, buriner, découper.
cell: cellule, cachot, prison, compartiment, alvéole.
college: collège, université.
daily: quotidien, journellement, tous les jours, chaque jour.
earliest: le plus tôt.
earning: gagnant, salaire.
fellowship: camaraderie, confrérie, titre universitaire, corporation, communion fraternelle, bourse universitaire, association, amitié.
footstool: tabouret.
habituated: te 'habituas, vous 'habituâtes, se 'habituèrent, nous 'habituâmes, me 'habituai.
helm: gouvernail, barre, timon.
lounger: fainéant.
manfully: de façon vaillante, de manière vaillante.
newspaper: journal, gazette, quotidien.
pile: tas, amas, foule, pieu, pilotis, pile, multitude, hémorrhoïde, masse, empiler.
proved: prouvas, éprouvâmes.
subdivision: subdivision, lotissement, compartimentage.
vainly: de manière vaniteuse, vainement, de façon vaniteuse.

career. Previous to his arrival in London, by contributions to political **periodicals** and a high reputation at that noble **debating** society in Cambridge which has **trained** some of the most **eminent** of living public men [Amongst those whom the "Union" almost **contemporaneously** prepared for public life, and whose distinction has kept the promise of their youth, we may mention the eminent barristers, Messrs. Austin and Cockburn; and amongst statesmen, Lord Grey, Mr. C. Buller, Mr. Charles Villiers, and Mr. Macaulay. Nor ought we to forget those brilliant **competitors** for the prizes of the University, Dr. Kennedy (now head-master of Shrewsbury School) and the late Winthrop M. Praed.], he had established a name which was immediately useful to him in obtaining employment on the Press. Like most young men of practical ability, he was an eager **politician**. The popular passion of the day kindled his enthusiasm and stirred the depths of his soul with magnificent, though exaggerated, hopes in the destiny of his race. He identified himself with the people; his stout heart beat loud in their stormy cause. His **compositions**, if they wanted that knowledge of men, that subtle comprehension of the true state of parties, that happy **temperance** in which the **crowning** wisdom of statesmen must consist,—qualities which experience alone can give,—excited considerable attention by their bold eloquence and hardy **logic**. They were suited to the time. But John Ardworth had that **solidity** of understanding which **betokens** more than talent, and which is the usual **substratum** of genius. He would not depend alone on the precarious and often unhonoured toils of **polemical** literature for that distinction on which he had fixed his steadfast heart. Patiently he **plodded** on through the formal drudgeries of his new profession, **lighting** up dulness by his own acute comprehension, **weaving** complexities into simple system by the grasp of an intellect inured to **generalize**, and learning to love even what was most **distasteful**, by the sense of difficulty **overcome**, and the clearer vision which every step through the mists and up the hill gave of the land beyond. Of what the **superficial** are apt to consider genius, John Ardworth had but little. He had some imagination (for a true **thinker** is never without that), but he had a very

---

French

betoken: présager.
competitor: concurrent, compétiteur.
composition: composition, arrangement.
contemporaneously: de manière contemporaine, de façon contemporaine.
crowning: bombé longitudinal, capsulage, couronnement.
debating: débattant.
distasteful: déplaisant,
désagréable, répugnant.
eminent: éminent, excellent, accompli.
generalize: généraliser.
lighting: éclairage, allumage.
logic: logique.
overcome: triompher de, vaincre.
periodical: périodique, revue, gazette, journal.
plodded: cheminèrent.
polemical: polémique.
politician: politicien, homme politique.
solidity: solidité, coefficient de plénitude.
substratum: substrat.
superficial: superficiel.
temperance: modération, tempérance.
thinker: penseur, théoricien.
trained: diplômé, dressé.
weaving: tissage, entrecroisement.

slight share of fancy. He did not **flirt** with the Muses; on the **granite** of his mind few flowers could spring. His style, rushing and earnest, admitted at times of a humour not without delicacy,—though less delicate than **forcible** and deep,—but it was little adorned with wit, and still less with poetry. Yet Ardworth had genius, and genius ample and magnificent. There was genius in that **industrious** energy so patient in the conquest of detail, so triumphant in the perception of results. There was genius in that kindly sympathy with mankind; genius in that stubborn determination to succeed; genius in that vivid comprehension of affairs, and the large interests of the world; genius fed in the labours of the closet, and **evinced** the instant he was brought into contact with men,—evinced in readiness of thought, grasp of memory, even in a rough, **imperious** nature, which showed him born to speak strong truths, and in their name to struggle and command.

Rough was this man often in his exterior, though really gentle and kind-hearted. John Ardworth had sacrificed to no Graces; he would have thrown Lord Chesterfield into a fever. Not that he was ever vulgar, for **vulgarity** implies **affectation** of refinement; but he **talked** loud and laughed loud if the whim seized him, and rubbed his great hands with a **boyish heartiness** of glee if he discomfited an **adversary** in argument. Or, sometimes, he would sit **abstracted** and moody, and answer briefly and **boorishly** those who interrupted him. Young men were **mostly** afraid of him, though he wanted but fame to have a set of admiring **disciples**. Old men **censured** his presumption and **recoiled** from the novelty of his ideas. Women alone liked and appreciated him, as, with their **finer insight** into character, they generally do what is honest and **sterling**. Some strange failings, too, had John Ardworth,—some of the usual **vagaries** and contradictions of clever men. As a system, he was rigidly **abstemious**. For days together he would drink nothing but water, **eat** nothing but bread, or hard **biscuit**, or a couple of eggs; then, having wound up some allotted portion of work, Ardworth would **indulge** what he called a self-saturnalia,—would stride off with old college friends to an inn in one of the suburbs, and spend, as he said triumphantly, "a day of blessed **debauch**!" Innocent enough, for the most

---

French

abstemious: sobre, frugal.
abstracted: distrait, abstraits, abrégé.
adversary: antagoniste, ennemi.
affectation: affectation, minauderie, afféterie.
biscuit: biscuit, galette, gâteau sec.
boorishly: rustrement.
boyish: puéril, de garçon, enfantin.
censured: censuré.
debauch: faire la noce, bamboucher.

disciple: disciple.
eat: manger, déjeuner, nourrir.
evinced: montré.
finer: affineur.
flirt: flirter, voltiger, conter fleurette.
forcible: de force, par force.
granite: granit, de granit.
heartiness: cordialité.
imperious: impérieux.
indulge: être indulgent, gâter.
industrious: laborieux, appliqué,

assidu, industrieux, travailleur.
insight: perspicacité, connaissance intuitive, intéroception, compréhension de soi, intuition.
mostly: plupart, surtout.
recoiled: reculé.
sterling: de bon aloi, sterling, de confiance.
talked: parlèrent, bavardas.
vagary: caprice.
vulgarity: vulgarité.

part, the debauch was, **consisting** in **cracking** jests, **stringing puns**, a **fish** dinner, perhaps, and an **extra** bottle or two of fiery **port**. Sometimes this jollity, which was always loud and **uproarious**, found its scene in one of the cider-cellars or **midnight taverns**; but Ardworth's labours on the Press made that latter dissipation extremely rare. These **relaxations** were always succeeded by a mien more than usually grave, a manner more than usually **curt** and ungracious, an **application** more than ever **rigorous** and intense. John Ardworth was not a good-tempered man, but he was the best-natured man that ever breathed. He was, like all ambitious persons, very much occupied with self; and yet it would have been a **ludicrous** misapplication of words to call him selfish. Even the desire of fame which absorbed him was but a part of benevolence,—a desire to promote justice and to serve his kind.

John Ardworth's shaggy brows were bent over his open volumes when his clerk entered noiselessly and placed on his table a letter which the twopenny-postman had just delivered. With an impatient shrug of the shoulders, Ardworth glanced towards the **superscription**; but his eye became earnest and his interest aroused as he recognized the hand. "Again!" he muttered. "What mystery is this? Who can feel such interest in my fate?" He broke the seal and read as follows:—

Do you neglect my advice, or have you begun to act upon it? Are you contented only with the slow process of mechanical application, or will you make a triumphant effort to **abridge** your **apprenticeship** and emerge at once into fame and power? I repeat that you **fritter** away your talents and your opportunities upon this miserable task-work on a journal. I am impatient for you. Come forward yourself, put your force and your knowledge into some work of which the world may know the **author**. Day after day I am examining into your destiny, and day after day I believe more and more that you are not fated for the **tedious** drudgery to which you doom your youth. I would have you great, but in the senate, not a wretched casuist at the Bar. Appear in public as an **individual** authority, not one of that

French

abridge: abréger, abrèges, raccourcir, abaisser, diminuer, amoindrir, limiter.
application: application, demande, requête.
apprenticeship: apprentissage, années d'apprentissage.
author: auteur, écrivain.
consisting: consistant.
cracking: fissuration, craquage, concassage, fendillement.
curt: brusque, sec.
extra: extra, figurant, supplémentaire.
fish: poisson, pêcher.
fritter: beignet, gaspiller.
individual: individu, particulier.
ludicrous: grotesque, ridicule, risible.
midnight: minuit.
port: port, bâbord, accès, lumière, orifice.
pun: calembour.
relaxation: relaxation, relâchement, décontraction, détente, assouplissement.
rigorous: rigoureux, sévère.
stringing: déroulage, enfilage, enguirlandage, rangée de cordes, tamis.
superscription: inscription, suscription.
tavern: taverne.
tedious: ennuyeux, fastidieux.
uproarious: hilarant.

nameless troop of shadows contemned while dreaded as the Press. Write for renown. Go into the world, and make friends. **Soften** your **rugged** bearing. Lift yourself above that herd whom you call "the people." What if you are born of the noble class! What if your career is as gentleman, not **plebeian** Want not for money. Use what I send you as the young and the well-born should use it; or let it at least gain you a **respite** from toils for bread, and support you in your struggle to **emancipate** yourself from **obscurity** into fame.

Your unknown friend

A bank-note for 100 pounds dropped from the **envelope** as Ardworth silently replaced the letter on the table.

Thrice before had he received communications in the same handwriting, and much to the same effect. Certainly, to a mind of less strength there would have been something very **unsettling** in those vague hints of a station **higher** than he owned, of a future at **variance** with the **toilsome lot** he had **drawn** from the urn; but after a single glance over his lone position in all its bearings and probable expectations, Ardworth's steady sense shook off the slight **disturbance** such **misty** vaticinations had effected. His mother's family was indeed unknown to him, he was even ignorant of her maiden name. But that very obscurity seemed unfavourable to much hope from such a quarter. The connections with the rich and well-born are seldom left obscure. From his father's family he had not one expectation. More had he been moved by exhortation now generally repeated, but in a **previous** letter more precisely **detailed**; **namely**, to **appeal** to the reading public in his acknowledged person, and by some striking and **original** work. This idea he had often contemplated and **revolved**; but **partly** the necessity of keeping pace with the many **exigencies** of the hour had deterred him, and partly also the conviction of his sober judgment that a man does himself no good at the Bar even by the most brilliant distinction gained in **discursive** fields. He had the natural **yearning** of the Restless Genius; and the Patient Genius (higher power of the two) had suppressed the longing. Still, so far, the whispers of

French

appeal: appel, recours, faire appel, pourvoi, attrait, charme.
detailed: détaillé.
discursive: discursif, décousu.
disturbance: perturbation, dérangement, trouble, désordre, émeute.
drawn: dessiné, puisé, tracé, tiré, appâté.
emancipate: émanciper.
envelope: enveloppe, ampoule.
exigency: exigence.
higher: plus haut.
lot: lot, sort.
misty: brumeux, embué, vague, vaporeux.
namely: à savoir.
obscurity: obscurité, ténèbres.
original: original, inédit.
partly: en partie, partiellement.
plebeian: plébéien.
previous: précédent, antérieur, préalable.
respite: répit, sursis.
revolved: tournai, ruminèrent.
rugged: robuste, raboteux, accidenté.
soften: adoucir, amollir, attendrir, ramollir, te ramollis, se ramollissent, vous ramollissez, me ramollis, nous ramollissons.
toilsome: pénible.
unsettling: perturbant.
variance: variance, désaccord.
yearning: soupirant, désir ardent, languissant.

his correspondent tempted and aroused. But hitherto he had sought to **persuade** himself that the communications thus strangely forced on him **arose** perhaps from idle motives,—a jest, it might be, of one of his old college friends, or at best the vain enthusiasm of some more **credulous admirer**. But the enclosure now sent to him **forbade** either of these **suppositions**. Who that he knew could afford so costly a jest or so **extravagant** a **tribute**? He was **perplexed**, and with his **perplexity** was mixed a kind of fear. Plain, earnest, **unromantic** in the common **acceptation** of the word, the mystery of this **intermeddling** with his fate, this arrogation of the license to spy, the right to counsel, and the privilege to **bestow**, gave him the **uneasiness** the bravest men may feel at noises in the dark. That day he could apply no more, he could not settle back to his Law Reports. He took two or three **unquiet** turns up and down his smoke-dried cell, then locked up the letter and enclosure, seized his hat, and strode, with his usual **lusty**, swinging strides, into the open air.

But still the letter haunted him. "And if," he said almost audibly,—"if I were the heir to some higher station, why then I might have a heart like idle men; and Helen, beloved Helen—" He paused, sighed, shook his rough head, **shaggy** with neglected curls, and added: "As if even then I could steal myself into a girl's good graces! Man's esteem I may command, though poor; woman's love could I win, though rich? Pooh! pooh! every wood does not make a Mercury; and faith, the wood I am made of will scarcely cut up into a lover."

Nevertheless, though thus soliloquizing, Ardworth **mechanically** bent his way towards Brompton, and halted, half-ashamed of himself, at the house where Helen lodged with her **aunt**. It was a **building** that stood apart from all the cottages and villas of that charming suburb, half-way down a narrow **lane**, and enclosed by high, **melancholy** walls, deep set in which a small door, with the paint **blistered** and weather-stained, gave **unfrequented** entrance to the demesne. A woman servant of middle age and **starched**, **puritanical** appearance answered the loud ring of the **bell**, and Ardworth seemed a privileged visitor, for she asked him no question as, with

French

acceptation: acception.
admirer: admirateur.
arose: naquit.
aunt: tante.
bell: cloche, sonnette.
bestow: accorder, octroyer.
blistered: cloqué.
building: bâtiment, construction, édifice.
credulous: crédule.
extravagant: extravagant.
forbade: interdit.
intermeddling: immixtion.
lane: voie, ruelle, couloir.
lusty: vigoureux, robuste.
mechanically: de façon mécanique, de manière mécanique, mécaniquement.
melancholy: mélancolie, sombre, abattement.
perplexed: embarrassâtes, perplexe.
perplexity: perplexité, embarras.
persuade: persuader, convaincre, inspirer.
puritanical: puritain.
shaggy: poilu, velu, hirsute.
starched: amidonné.
supposition: hypothèse, supposition.
tribute: tribut, hommage.
uneasiness: inquiétude, malaise.
unfrequented: peu fréquenté.
unquiet: inquiet.
unromantic: peu romantique.

a slight **nod** and a smileless, stupid expression in a face otherwise comely, she led the way across a **paved** path, much weed-grown, to the house. That house itself had somewhat of a stern and sad exterior. It was not ancient, yet it looked old from shabbiness and neglect. The **vine**, **loosened** from the **rusty** nails, **trailed** rankly against the wall, and fell in **crawling** branches over the ground. The house had once been whitewashed; but the colour, worn off in great patches, distained with **damp**, struggled here and there with the dingy, **chipped** bricks beneath. There was no peculiar want of what is called "tenantable repair;" the windows were whole, and doubtless the roof sheltered from the rain. But the **woodwork** that encased the **panes** was **decayed**, and **houseleek** covered the **tiles**. Altogether, there was that forlorn and cheerless aspect about the place which chills the visitor, he **defines** not why. And Ardworth **steadied** his usual careless step, and crept, as if timidly, up the **creaking** stairs.

On entering the drawing-room, it seemed at first deserted; but the eye, searching round, perceived something stir in the recess of a huge chair set by the fireless hearth. And from amidst a mass of **coverings** a pale face emerged, and a thin hand waved its welcome to the visitor.

Ardworth approached, pressed the hand, and drew a seat near to the sufferer's.

"You are better, I hope?" he said cordially, and yet in a tone of more respect than was often perceptible in his deep, blunt voice.

"I am always the same," was the quiet answer; "come nearer still. Your visits cheer me."

And as these last words were said, Madame Dalibard raised herself from her **recumbent posture** and gazed long upon Ardworth's face of power and front of thought. "You overfatigue yourself, my poor kinsman," she said, with a certain tenderness; "you look already too old for your young years."

"That's no **disadvantage** at the Bar."

"Is the Bar your means, or your end?"

French

chipped: ébréché, écaillé, égrisé, émoussé.
covering: revêtement, couverture, habillage, saillie, recouvrement, housse.
crawling: rampage, rétraction, refus à l'application, retrait, retirement d'émail, reptation.
creaking: grinçant, craquant.
damp: humide, amortir, mouiller.
decayed: délabré, caduc, infirme, vieux, carié, pourri.
defines: définit, précise.
disadvantage: inconvénient, désavantage.
houseleek: joubarbe.
loosened: desserrâtes, se détendirent, nous détendîmes, te détendis, ameublîmes, me détendis, déliés, vous détendîtes.
nod: signe de tête, somnoler, se balancer, incliner la tête, hochement, faire signe que oui.
pane: volet, vitre, carreau.
paved: pavé, pavai, pavâmes, pavèrent.
posture: posture, attitude, maintien.
recumbent: étendu, alité, allongé, couché.
rusty: rouillé, rubigineux.
steadied: assujetti.
tile: carreau, tuile, mosaïque, dalle.
trailed: traîné.
vine: vigne, plante grimpante.
woodwork: menuiserie, boiseries.

"My dear Madame Dalibard, it is my profession."

"No, your profession is to rise. John Ardworth," and the low voice swelled in its volume, "you are bold, able, and aspiring; for this, I love you,—love you almost—almost as a mother. Your fate," she continued hurriedly, "interests me; your energies inspire me with admiration. Often I sit here for hours, musing over your destiny to be, so that at times I may almost say that in your life I live."

Ardworth looked embarrassed, and with an **awkward attempt** at compliment he began, hesitatingly: "I should think too **highly** of myself if I could really believe that you—"

"Tell me," interrupted Madame Dalibard,—"we have had many conversations upon grave and subtle matters; we have **disputed** on the secret mysteries of the human mind; we have compared our several experiences of outward life and the **mechanism** of the social world,—tell me, then, and frankly, what do you think of me? Do you regard me merely as your sex is apt to regard the woman who **aspires** to equal men,—a thing of **borrowed** phrases and **unsound** ideas, feeble to guide, and **unskilled** to **teach**; or do you recognize in this miserable body a mind of **force** not unworthy yours, ruled by an experience larger than your own?"

"I think of you," answered Ardworth, frankly, "as the most remarkable woman I have ever met. Yet—do not be angry—I do not like to **yield** to the influence which you gain over me when we meet. It disturbs my convictions, it **disquiets** my reason; I do not settle back to my life so easily after your breath has passed over it."

"And yet," said Lucretia, with a solemn sadness in her voice, "that influence is but the natural power which cold **maturity exercises** on ardent youth. It is my mournful ad **vantage** over you that disquiets your happy calm. It is my experience that **unsettles** the **fallacies** which you name 'convictions.' Let this pass. I asked your opinion of me, because I wished to place at your service all that knowledge of life which I possess. In proportion as you esteem me you will **accept** or reject my counsels."

French

accept: accepter, agréer, admettre, accueillir, recevoir, recueillir.
aspire: aspirer.
attempt: tentative, essai, effort, requête, démarche, se démener, peiner, attentat.
awkward: maladroit, gênant, embarrassant.
borrowed: emprunté.
disputed: disputé, contesté.
disquiet: déranger, perturber, rendre trouble, brouiller, inquiétude.
exercise: exercice, instruire, pratique, levée.
fallacy: erreur, fausseté.
force: force, contraindre, imposer, obliger, violer, puissance, faire accepter.
highly: hautement, fortement, extrêmement, de façon haute, de manière haute.
maturity: maturité, échéance.
mechanism: mécanisme.
teach: enseigner, instruire, apprendre.
unsettle: perturbe.
unskilled: inexpérimenté, non qualifié.
unsound: véreux, hasardeux, précaire, tiqueur.
vantage: avantage.
yield: rendement, céder, cédons, cèdes, abandonner, produire, reculer, abdiquer, récolte, rapporter, mise au mille.

"I have benefited by them already. It is the tone that you **advised** me to assume that gave me an importance I had not before with that old **formalist** whose paper I serve, and whose prejudices I shock; it is to your **criticisms** that I owe the more **practical** turn of my **writings**, and the greater hold they have taken on the public."

"Trifles indeed, these," said Madame Dalibard, with a half smile. "Let them at least **induce** you to listen to me if I **propose** to make your path more pleasant, yet your **ascent** more rapid."

Ardworth **knit** his **brows**, and his countenance assumed an expression of doubt and curiosity. However, he only replied, with a **blunt** laugh,—

"You must be wise indeed if you have discovered a **royal** road to distinction.

'Ah, who can tell how hard it is to **climb**
The steep where
Fame's proud temple **shines** afar!'

A more sensible **exclamation** than poets usually **preface** with their **whining** 'Ahs' and 'Ohs!'"

"What we are is nothing," pursued Madame Dalibard; "what we seem is much."

Ardworth thrust his hands into his pockets and shook his head. The wise woman continued, **unheeding** his **dissent** from her premises,—

"Everything you are taught to value has a **likeness**, and it is that likeness which the world values. Take a man out of the streets, poor and **ragged**, what will the world do with him? Send him to the **workhouse**, if not to the **jail**. Ask a great painter to take that man's portrait,—rags, squalor, and all,—and kings will bid for the picture. You would thrust the man from your doors, you would place the portrait in your palaces. It is the same with qualities; the portrait is worth more than the truth. What is virtue without character? But a man without virtue may **thrive** on a character! What is

French

advised: conseillé, recommandai, avisée, informé.
ascent: ascension, montée, phase propulsée, remontée.
blunt: émoussé, épointer.
brow: sourcil, front.
climb: grimper, gravir, monter.
criticism: critique.
dissent: dissentiment, faire valoir sa dissidence, différer.
exclamation: exclamation.
formalist: formaliste.
induce: induire, conclure, provoquer, persuader.
jail: prison, geôle, emprisonner.
knit: tricoter, mailler, prendre.
likeness: ressemblance, similitude, portrait.
practical: pratique, réel.
preface: introduction, préface.
propose: proposer, soumettre, suggérer.
ragged: déchiqueté, déguenillé, dépenaillé, ébavuré, en haillons, en lambeaux, loqueteux.
royal: royal, cacatois, bleu roi.
shine: briller, luire, être lumineux, éclat, lustre, reluire.
thrive: prospérer, pousser, se développer.
unheeding: insouciant.
whining: criant, geignant, gémissant.
workhouse: asile de pauvres.
writing: écrivant, inscription.

genius without success? But how often you bow to success without genius! John Ardworth, possess yourself of the portraits,—win the character; seize the success."

"Madame," exclaimed Ardworth, **rudely**, "this is horrible!"

"Horrible it may be," said Madame Dalibard, gently, and feeling, perhaps, that she had gone too far; "but it is the world's judgment. Seem, then, as well as be. You have virtue, as I believe. Well, **wrap** yourself in it—in your **closet**. Go into the world, and **earn** character. If you have genius, let it comfort you. Rush into the crowd, and get success."

"Stop!" cried Ardworth; "I recognize you. How could I be so blind? It is you who have **written** to me, and in the same strain; you have **robbed** yourself,—you, poor sufferer,—to throw **extravagance** into these strong hands. And why? What am I to you?" An expression of actual **fondness softened** Lucretia's face as she looked up at him and replied: "I will tell you **hereafter** what you are to me. First, I confess that it is I whose letters have perplexed, perhaps **offended** you. The sum that I sent I do not miss. I have more,—will ever have more at your command; never fear. Yes, I wish you to go into the world, not as a **dependant**, but as an equal to the world's favourites. I wish you to know more of men than mere law-books teach you.

I wish you to be in men's mouths, create a circle that shall talk of young Ardworth; that talk would **travel** to those who can advance your career. The very possession of money in certain stages of life gives assurance to the manner, gives attraction to the address."

"But," said Ardworth, "all this is very well for some favourite of birth and fortune; but for me—Yet speak, and plainly. You throw out hints that I am what I know not, but something less **dependent** on his nerves and his brain than is plain John Ardworth. What is it you mean?"

Madame Dalibard bent her face over her breast, and **rocking** herself in her chair, seemed to **muse** for some moments before she answered.

"When I first came to England, some months ago, I desired naturally to learn all the particulars of my family and **kindred**, from which my long

---

French

closet: armoire, placard.
dependant: personne à charge.
dependent: dépendant, personne à charge, subordonné, charge de famille.
earn: gagner, remporter.
extravagance: extravagance.
fondness: affection, penchant, prédilection, tendresse.
hereafter: après, désormais, dorénavant.
kindred: parenté, famille.

muse: muse, songer, méditer, rêver.
offended: offensas, insultèrent.
robbed: pilla, ravi, ravîmes, dévalisa.
rocking: balancement, basculant.
rudely: de façon grossière, de manière grossière.
softened: amollîmes, adoucit, attendrit, se ramollit, me ramollis, nous ramollîmes, vous ramollîtes, te ramollis.
travel: voyage, course, aller, se déplacer, déplacement.
wrap: envelopper, emballer.
written: écrit, noté.

residence abroad had **estranged** me. John Walter Ardworth was related to my half-sister; to me he was but a mere connection. However, I knew something of his history, yet I did not know that he had a son. **Shortly** before I came to England, I learned that one who passed for his son had been brought up by Mr. Fielden, and from Mr. Fielden I have since learned all the grounds for that belief from which you take the name of Ardworth."

Lucretia paused a moment; and after a glance at the impatient, wondering, and eager countenance that bent intent upon her, she resumed:

"Your **reputed** father was, you are doubtless aware, of reckless and **extravagant** habits. He had been put into the **army** by my uncle, and he entered the profession with the careless **buoyancy** of his **sanguine** nature. I remember those days,—that day! Well, to return—where was I?—Walter Ardworth had the folly to **entertain** strong notions of **politics**. He dreamed of being a soldier, and yet persuaded himself to be a republican. His notions, so **hateful** in his profession, got wind; he **disguised** nothing, he neglected the portraits of things,—appearances. He excited the **rancour** of his **commanding** officer; for politics then, more even than now, were **implacable** ministrants to hate. Occasion presented itself. During the short Peace of Amiens he had been recalled. He had to head a **detachment** of soldiers against some mob,—in Ireland, I believe; he did not fire on the mob, **according** to orders,—so, at least, it was said. John Walter Ardworth was **tried** by a court-martial, and broke! But you know all this, perhaps?"

"My poor father! Only in part; I knew that he had been dismissed the army,—I believed **unjustly**. He was a soldier, and yet he dared to think for himself and be humane!"

"But my uncle had left him a legacy; it brought no blessing,—none of that old man's gold did. Where are they all now,—Dalibard, Susan, and her fair-faced husband,—where? Vernon is in his grave,—but one son of many left! Gabriel Varney lives, it is true, and I! But that gold,—yea, in our hands there was a **curse** on it! Walter Ardworth had his legacy. His nature was gay; if **disgraced** in his profession, he found men to pity and praise him,—Fools of

---

French

according: selon, s'accorder.
army: armée.
buoyancy: flottabilité, fermeté, élasticité, poussée d'Archimède.
commanding: commandant, dominant, ordonner.
curse: maudire, malédiction, blasphémer.
detachment: détachement, équipe, groupe, commando, séparation, décollement.
disgraced: disgraciâmes.
disguised: déguisé.
entertain: distraire, régaler, divertir, se régalent, te régales, vous régalez, recevoir des visiteurs, abriter, nous régalons, me régale, amuser.
estranged: aliéné.
extravagant: extravagant.
hateful: odieux, haïssable.
implacable: implacable.
politic: politique.
rancour: rancune.
reputed: réputé.
sanguine: sanguin, optimiste.
shortly: prochainement, bientôt, de façon courte, de manière courte.
tried: essayé, éprouvé.
unjustly: de façon injuste, de manière injuste.

Party like himself. He lived **joyously**, drank or gamed, or lent or borrowed,—what matters the **wherefore**? He was in debt; he lived at last a wretched, **shifting, fugitive** life, **snatching** bread where he could, with the **bailiffs** at his heels. Then, for a short time, we met again."

Lucretia's brow grew black as night as her voice dropped at that last sentence, and it was with a start that she continued,—

"In the midst of this hunted **existence**, Walter Ardworth appeared, late one night, at Mr. Fielden's with an infant. He seemed—so says Mr. Fielden—ill, worn, and haggard. He entered into no explanations with respect to the child that accompanied him, and retired at once to rest. What follows, Mr. Fielden, at my request, has noted down. Read, and see what claim you have to the honourable **parentage** so vaguely ascribed to you."

As she spoke, Madame Dalibard opened a box on her table, drew forth a paper in Fielden's writing, and placed it in Ardworth's hand. After some **preliminary statement** of the writer's intimacy with the elder Ardworth, and the appearance of the latter at his house, as related by Madame Dalibard, etc., the document went on thus:—

The next day, when my poor guest was still in bed, my servant Hannah came to advise me that two persons were without, waiting to see me. As is my **wont**, I bade them be **shown** in. On their entrance (two rough, farmer-looking men they were, who I thought might be coming to hire my little pasture field), I prayed them to speak low, as a sick gentleman was just **overhead. Whereupon**, and without saying a word further, the two strangers made a rush from the room, **leaving** me dumb with **amazement**; in a few moments I heard voices and a **scuffle** above. I recovered myself, and thinking **robbers** had entered my **peaceful** house, I called out **lustily**, when Hannah came in, and we both, taking courage, went upstairs, and found that poor Walter was in the hands of these supposed robbers, who in truth were but bailiffs. They would not trust him out of their sight for a moment. However, he took it more **pleasantly** than I could have supposed possible; prayed me in a whisper to take care of the child, and I should soon hear from

---

French

amazement: étonnement, stupéfaction, abasourdissement.
bailiff: huissier, bailli.
existence: existence.
fugitive: fugitif, réfugié, couleur qui déteint, non solide à la lumière.
joyously: de façon joyeuse, de manière joyeuse.
leaving: partant, départ.
lustily: de façon vigoureuse, de manière vigoureuse.

overhead: aérien, en haut, dessus, sur, temps système, frais généraux.
parentage: naissance, filiation.
peaceful: paisible, pacifique.
pleasantly: agréablement, de manière agréable, de façon agréable.
preliminary: préliminaire, partie liminaire, préalable.
robber: voleur, ravisseur.
scuffle: bagarre, combat, bataille,

baroud, rixe, se bagarrer.
shifting: déplacement, ripage, désarrimage.
shown: montré, manifesté, marqué.
snatching: arrachement.
statement: déclaration, constatation, instruction, énoncé.
wherefore: pourquoi.
whereupon: après quoi, sur quoi.
wont: coutume, accoutumé, habitude.

him again. In less than an hour he was gone. Two days **afterwards** I received from him a hurried letter, without address, of which this is a copy:—

Dear friend,—I slipped from the bailiffs, and here I am in a safe little **tavern** in sight of the sea! Mother Country is a very bad parent to me! Mother Brownrigg herself could scarcely be **worse**. I shall work out my passage to some foreign land, and if I can recover my health (sea-air is bracing), I don't despair of getting my bread honestly, somehow. If ever I can pay my debts, I may return. But, meanwhile, my good old tutor, what will you think of me? You to whom my sole return for so much pains, taken in **vain**, is another mouth to feed! And no money to pay for the board! Yet you'll not **grudge** the child a place at your table, will you? No, nor kind, saving Mrs. Fielden either,—God **bless** her tender, **economical** soul! You know quite enough of me to be sure that I shall very soon either free you of the boy, or send you something to prevent its being an **encumbrance**. I would say, love and pity the child for my sake. But I own I feel—-By Jove, I must be off; I hear the first signal from the **vessel** that—

Yours in **haste**,
J. W. A.

Young Ardworth stopped from the lecture, and sighed heavily. There seemed to him in this letter worse than a **mock** gayety,—a certain levity and **recklessness** which jarred on his own high principles. And the want of affection for the child thus abandoned was evident,—not one fond word. He resumed the statement with a **gloomy** and **disheartened** attention.

This was all I heard from my poor, **erring** Walter for more than three years; but I knew, in spite of his follies, that his heart was sound at bottom (the son's eyes **brightened** here, and he kissed the paper), and the child was no burden to us; we loved it, not only for Ardworth's sake, but for its own, and for charity's and Christ's. Ardworth's second letter was as follows:—

French

afterward: après, plus tard.
bless: bénir.
brightened: avivas, éclaircîtes, blanchi.
disheartened: décourageâtes.
economical: économique.
encumbrance: encombrement, servitude.
erring: errant, aberrant.
gloomy: sombre, morne.
grudge: rancune.
haste: hâte, précipitation.
mock: bafouer, railler, se moquer de, faux.
recklessness: imprudence, témérité, insouciance.
tavern: taverne.
vain: vain, vaniteux, abortif, frivole.
vessel: navire, vaisseau, bateau, vase, pot, récipient, bac, baquet.
worse: pire, plus mauvais.

En iterum Crispinus! I am still alive, and getting on in the world,—ay, and honestly too; I am no longer **spending heedlessly**; I am saving for my debts, and I shall live, I trust, to pay off every farthing. First, for my debt to you I send an order, not **signed** in my name, but equally **valid**, on Messrs. Drummond, for 250 pounds. **Repay** yourself what the boy has **cost**. Let him be educated to get his own living,—if clever, as a scholar or a lawyer; if dull, as a **tradesman**. Whatever I may gain, he will have his own way to make. I ought to tell you the **story** connected with his birth; but it is one of pain and shame, and, on reflection, I feel that I have no right to **injure** him by **affixing** to his early birth an **opprobrium** of which he himself is **guiltless**. If ever I return to England, you shall know all, and by your counsels I will **abide**. Love to all your happy family.

Your grateful
Friend and pupil.

From this letter I began to suspect that the poor boy was probably not born in **wedlock**, and that Ardworth's silence arose from his **compunction**. I conceived it best never to mention this suspicion to John himself as he grew up. Why should I **afflict** him by a doubt from which his own father **shrank**, and which might only exist in my own **inexperienced** and **uncharitable interpretation** of some vague words? When John was fourteen, I received from Messrs. Drummond a further sum of 500 pounds, but without any line from Ardworth, and only to the effect that Messrs. Drummond were directed by a correspondent in Calcutta to pay me the said sum on behalf of expenses **incurred** for the **maintenance** of the child left to my charge by John Walter Ardworth. My young pupil had been two years at the University when I received the letter of which this is a copy:—

"How are you? Still well, still happy? Let me hope so! I have not written to you, dear old friend, but I have not been **forgetful** of you; I have **inquired** of you through my correspondents, and have learned, from time to time, such accounts as satisfied my grateful affection for you. I find that you have given the boy my name. Well, let him bear it,—it is nothing to **boast** of such

---

French

abide: endurer, demeurer, persévérer, supporter, soutenir, attendre, subir, souffrir.
affixing: apposition.
afflict: affliger, désoler, attrister.
boast: fanfaronner, vanter, se vanter, faire le malin.
compunction: componction, remords.
cost: coût, dépense, prix de revient.
forgetful: distrait, oublieux.
guiltless: innocent.

heedlessly: de façon insouciante, de manière insouciante.
incurred: encouru, contractai.
inexperienced: inexpérimenté.
injure: abîmer, détériorer, blesser.
inquired: vous enquîtes, t'enquis, s'enquit, nous enquîmes, m'enquis.
interpretation: interprétation, décodage, définition.
maintenance: entretien, maintenance, garde.

opprobrium: opprobre.
repay: rembourser, reprendre.
shrank: rétrécies.
signed: signé.
spending: dépensant, passant.
story: histoire, étage, récit, conte, relation, intrigue.
tradesman: marchand, commerçant.
uncharitable: peu charitable.
valid: valable, valide.
wedlock: mariage.

as it became in my person; but, mind, I do not, therefore, acknowledge him as my son. I wish him to think himself without parents, without other aid in the career of life than his own **industry** and talent—if talent he has. Let him go through the healthful **probation** of toil; let him search for and find independence. Till he is of age, 150 pounds **per** annum will be paid **quarterly** to your account for him at Messrs. Drummond's. If then, to set him up in any business or profession, a sum of money be necessary, name the **amount** by a line, signed A. B., Calcutta, to the care of Messrs. Drummond, and it will reach and find me disposed to follow your instructions. But after that time all further **supply** from me will cease. Do not suppose, because I send this from India, that I am **laden** with **rupees**; all I can hope to attain is a **competence**. That boy is not the only one who has claims to share it. Even, therefore, if I had the wish to rear him to the extravagant habits that ruined myself, I have not the power. Yes, let him lean on his own strength. In the letter you send me, write **fully** of your family, your sons, and write as to a man who can perhaps help them in the world, and will be too happy thus in some slight **degree** to repay all he owes you. You would smile **approvingly** if you saw me now,—a steady, money-getting man, but still yours as ever."

"P.S.—Do not let the boy write to me, nor give him this **clew** to my address."

On the receipt of this letter, I wrote fully to Ardworth about the excellent promise and conduct of his poor neglected son. I told him **truly** he was a son any father might be proud of, and rebuked, even to harshness, Walter's **unseemly** tone **respecting** him. One's child is one's child, however the father may have wronged the mother. To this letter I never received any answer. When John was of age, and had made himself independent of want by obtaining a college fellowship, I spoke to him about his prospects. I told him that his father, though **residing** abroad and for some reason keeping himself concealed, had munificently paid hitherto for his maintenance, and would

---

French

amount: montant, somme, quantité, nombre, total.
approvingly: de façon approuvante, de manière approuvante.
clew: point d'écoute.
competence: compétence, capacité, attributions.
degree: degré, grade, titre, intitulé, diplôme, rang.
fully: entièrement, complètement, de façon pleine, de manière pleine, pleinement.
industry: industrie, application.
laden: chargé.
per: par, dans, à, parmi, pour, en, au milieu de, à raison de, afin de.
probation: probation, liberté surveillée, période d'essai, stage.
quarterly: trimestriel, revue trimestrielle, publication trimestrielle.
residing: résidant, demeurant.
respecting: respectant, en ce qui concerne.
rupee: roupie.
supply: fourniture, provision, approvisionnement, ravitaillement, alimentation, livrer, munir, réserve, pourvoir, de manière souple, de façon souple.
truly: vraiment, en vérité, réellement, en fait, en réalité, véritablement.
unseemly: inconvenant, malséant.

lay down what might be necessary to start him in business, or perhaps place him in the army, but that his father might be better pleased if he could show a love of independence, and **henceforth** maintain himself. I knew the boy I spoke to! John thought as I did, and I never applied for another **donation** to the elder Ardworth. The allowance ceased; John since then has **maintained** himself. I have heard no more from his father, though I have written often to the address he gave me. I begin to fear that he is dead. I once went up to town and saw one of the heads of Messrs. Drummond's firm, a very polite gentleman, but he could give me no information, except that he **obeyed** instructions from a correspondent at Calcutta, — one Mr. Macfarren. Whereon I wrote to Mr. Macfarren, and asked him, as I thought very **pressingly**, to tell me all he knew of poor Ardworth the elder. He answered shortly that he knew of no such person at all, and that A. B. was a French merchant, settled in Calcutta, who had been dead for above two years. I now gave up all hopes of any further intelligence, and was more convinced than ever that I had **acted** rightly in **withholding** from poor John my correspondence with his father. The lad had been curious and **inquisitive** naturally; but when I told him that I thought it my duty to his father to be so reserved, he forebore to press me. I have only to **add**, first, that by all the **inquiries** I could make of the surviving **members** of Walter Ardworth's family, it seemed their full belief that he had never been married, and therefore I fear we must conclude that he had no **legitimate** children, — which may account for, though it cannot excuse, his neglect; and secondly, with respect to the sums received on dear John's account, I put them all by, capital and interest, **deducting** only the expense of his first year at Cambridge (the which I could not **defray** without **injuring** my own children), and it all stands in his name at Messrs. Drummond's, **vested** in the Three per Cents. That I have not told him of this was by my poor dear wife's advice; for she said, very sensibly, — and she was a **shrewd** woman on money matters, — "If he knows he has such a large sum all in the **lump**, who knows but he may grow **idle** and extravagant, and spend it at once, like his father before him? **Whereas**, some

French

acted: agi, agirent, agies.
add: ajouter, additionner, joindre, adjoindre, rajouter.
deducting: prélevant, défalquant, décomptant.
defray: paies, payer, remboursons, payons, défraie.
donation: don, donation.
henceforth: désormais, dorénavant, à l'avenir.
idle: inactif, tourner au ralenti, ralenti, fainéant, inoccupé, paresseux, au repos.
injuring: détériorant, abîmant, blessant.
inquiry: enquête, demande de renseignements, interrogation, investigation.
inquisitive: curieux, inquisiteur.
legitimate: légitime, logique.
lump: masse, bloc, morceau, boule, motte, pièce, fragment, gros morceau, grumeau, bosse, pan.
maintained: maintîntes, conservai, entretenu.
member: membre, adhérent, affilié, partisan.
obeyed: obéis, obéites.
pressingly: de manière pressage.
shrewd: sagace, avisé, perspicace.
vested: investi.
whereas: tandis que, attendu que, durant, lors, pendant, alors que.
withholding: retenant, rétention, refus.

time or other he will want to marry, or need money for some particular purpose, — then what a **blessing** it will be!"

However, my dear madam, as you know the world better than I do, you can now do as you please, both as to **communicating** to John all the information **herein** contained as to his parentage, and as to **apprising** him of the large sum of which he is **lawfully** possessed.

Matthew Fielden.

P.S. — In justice to poor John Ardworth, and to show that whatever **whim** he may have **conceived** about his own child, he had still a heart kind enough to remember mine, though Heaven knows I said nothing about them in my letters, my **eldest** boy received an offer of an excellent place in a West India merchant's house, and has got on to be chief clerk; and my second son was presented to a living of 117 pounds a year by a gentleman he never heard of. Though I never traced these good acts to Ardworth, from whom else could they come?

Ardworth put down the paper without a word; and Lucretia, who had watched him while he read, was struck with the self-control he evinced when he came to the end of the **disclosure**. She laid her hand on his and said, —

"Courage! you have lost nothing!"

"Nothing!" said Ardworth, with a bitter smile. "A father's love and a father's name, — nothing!"

"But," **exclaimed** Lucretia, "is this man your father? Does a father's heart beat in one line of those hard sentences? No, no; it seems to me probable, — it seems to me almost certain, that you are—" She stopped, and continued, with a calmer accent, "near to my own blood. I am now in England, in London, to **prosecute** the inquiry built upon that hope. If so, if so, you shall—" Madame Dalibard again stopped **abruptly**, and there was something terrible in the very **exultation** of her countenance. She drew a

French

abruptly: brusquement, abruptement, sèchement, de façon abrupte, de manière abrupte.
apprising: informant.
blessing: bénissant, bénédiction.
communicating: communiquant.
conceived: conçurent.
disclosure: divulgation, révélation.
eldest: aîné.
exclaimed: exclamâtes.
exultation: exultation.
herein: en ceci.
lawfully: de façon légale, de manière légale, légalement.
prosecute: poursuivre.
whim: caprice, lubie, manège à chevaux.

long breath, and resumed, with an evident effort at self-command, "If so, I have a right to the interest I feel for you. **Suffer** me yet to be silent as to the grounds of my belief, and—and—love me a little in the mean while!"

Her voice **trembled**, as if with rushing tears, at these last words, and there was almost an agony in the tone in which they were said, and in the gesture of the clasped hands she held out to him.

Much moved (amidst all his **mingled** emotions at the tale thus made known to him) by the manner and voice of the narrator, Ardworth bent down and kissed the extended hands. Then he rose abruptly, walked to and fro the room, **muttering** to himself, paused opposite the window, threw it open, as for air, and, indeed, fairly gasped for breath. When he turned round, however, his face was **composed**, and **folding** his arms on his large breast with a sudden action, he said aloud, and yet rather to himself than to his listener,—

"What matter, after all, by what name men call our fathers? We ourselves make our own fate! Bastard or noble, not a **jot** care I. Give me ancestors, I will not disgrace them; **raze** from my lot even the very name of father, and my sons shall have an **ancestor** in me!"

As he thus spoke, there was a rough **grandeur** in his hard face and the strong ease of his **powerful** form. And while thus standing and thus looking, the door opened, and Varney walked in abruptly.

These two men had met occasionally at Madame Dalibard's, but no intimacy had been **established** between them. Varney was formal and distant to Ardworth, and Ardworth felt a **repugnance** to Varney. With the instinct of sound, sterling, **weighty** natures, he detected at once, and disliked **heartily**, that something of **gaudy**, false, exaggerated, and hollow which **pervaded** Gabriel Varney's talk and manner,—even the trick of his walk and the cut of his dress. And Ardworth wanted that **boyish** and beautiful **luxuriance** of character which belonged to Percival St. John, easy to please and to be pleased, and **expanding** into the **warmth** of admiration for all talent and all distinction. For art, if not the **highest**, Ardworth cared not a

French

ancestor: ancêtre, ascendant.
boyish: puéril, de garçon, enfantin.
composed: composa, tranquille, calme.
established: établi, constatâtes.
expanding: développant, croissance, expansion, mandrinage, moussant, renflement.
folding: pliant, plissement.
gaudy: voyant, criard.
grandeur: noblesse, grandeur.

heartily: de façon cordiale, de manière cordiale, chaleureusement.
highest: le plus haut.
jot: brin, noter.
luxuriance: luxuriance, exubérance.
mingled: mélangeâtes, mêlé, mêlâtes, mêlas, mêlèrent.
muttering: barbotant.
pervaded: imprégnas.
powerful: puissant.
raze: rases, rasons.

repugnance: répugnance, aversion.
suffer: souffrir, subir, endurer.
trembled: tremblé.
warmth: chaleur, cordialité.
weighty: important, lourd.

straw; it was nothing to him that Varney **painted** and composed, and ran showily through the jargon of literary **babble**, or toyed with the puzzles of **unsatisfying** metaphysics. He saw but a **charlatan**, and he had not yet learned from experience what strength and what danger lie hid in the **boa** parading its colours in the sun, and shifting, in the **sensual** sportiveness of its being, from **bough** to bough.

Varney halted in the middle of the room as his eye rested first on Ardworth, and then glanced towards Madame Dalibard. But Ardworth, jarred from his revery or **resolves** by the sound of a voice **discordant** to his ear at all times, **especially** in the mood which then possessed him, scarcely returned Varney's **salutation**, **buttoned** his coat over his **chest**, seized his hat, and **upsetting** two chairs, and very **considerably disturbing** the gravity of a round table, forced his way to Madame Dalibard, pressed her hand, and said in a whisper, "I shall see you again soon," and vanished.

Varney, **smoothing** his hair with fingers that shone with rings, slid into the seat next Madame Dalibard, which Ardworth had lately occupied, and said: "If I were a Clytemnestra, I should dread an Orestes in such a son!"

Madame Dalibard **shot** towards the **speaker** one of the **sidelong**, suspicious glances which of old had characterized Lucretia, and said, —

"Clytemnestra was happy! The Furies slept to her crime, and haunted but the avenger."

"Hist!" said Varney.

The door opened, and Ardworth **reappeared**.

"I quite **forgot** what I half came to know. How is Helen? Did she return home safe?"

"Safe — yes!"

"Dear girl, I am glad to hear it! Where is she? Not gone to those Miverses again? I am no **aristocrat**, but why should one couple together refinement and vulgarity?"

French

aristocrat: aristocrate.
babble: murmure confus, babiller, bavarder.
boa: boa.
bough: branche, rameau.
buttoned: boutonné.
charlatan: charlatan.
chest: poitrine, coffre, caisse, sein, commode, bac, bahut.
considerably: considérablement, de façon considérable, de manière considérable.
discordant: discordant.
disturbing: dérangeant, gênant.
especially: surtout, principalement, tout d'abord, notamment, de façon spéciale, spécialement, particulièrement, de manière spéciale.
forgot: oubliâtes, désapprîtes.
painted: peint, peignirent, fardé.
reappeared: reparûmes, réapparu.
resolve: résoudre, décider.
salutation: salut.
sensual: sensuel, voluptueux.
shot: tirèrent, tiré, tirâtes, tiras, tir, coup, grenaille, piqûre, injection.
sidelong: de côté, oblique.
smoothing: amortissement, ajustement, modulation.
speaker: orateur, conférencier, locuteur, enceinte, intervenant.
unsatisfying: insuffisant.
upsetting: bouleversant, déranger, forgeage par refoulement, matage, refoulage, vexant, aplatissement.

"Mr. Ardworth," said Madame Dalibard, with **haughty coldness**, "my niece is under my care, and you will permit me to judge for myself how to **discharge** the trust. Mr. Mivers is her own relation,—a nearer one than you are."

Not at all **abashed** by the **rebuke**, Ardworth said **carelessly**: "Well, I shall talk to you again on that **subject**. Meanwhile, pray give my love to her,—Helen, I mean."

Madame Dalibard half rose in her chair, then sank back again, motioning with her hand to Ardworth to **approach**. Varney rose and walked to the window, as if sensible that something was about to be said not meant for his ear.

When Ardworth was close to her chair, Madame Dalibard grasped his hand with a vigour that surprised him, and drawing him nearer still, whispered as he bent down,—

"I will give Helen your love, if it is a cousin's, or, if you will, a brother's love. Do you intend—do you feel—an other, a **warmer** love? Speak, sir!" and drawing suddenly back, she gazed on his face with a stern and **menacing** expression, her teeth set, and the lips firmly pressed together.

Ardworth, though a little startled, and half angry, answered with the low, **ironical** laugh not uncommon to him, "Pish! you ladies are apt to think us men much greater fools than we are. A briefless lawyer is not very **inflammable tinder**. Yes, a cousin's love,—quite enough. Poor little Helen! time enough to put other notions into her head; and then—she will have a **sweetheart**, gay and handsome like herself!"

"Ay," said Madame Dalibard, with a slight smile, "ay, I am satisfied. Come soon."

Ardworth nodded, and hurried down the **stairs**. As he gained the door, he caught sight of Helen at a distance, **bending** over a flower-bed in the neglected garden. He paused, **irresolute**, a moment. "No," he muttered to himself, "no; I am fit company only for myself! A long walk into the fields,

French

abashed: confus, décontenançai.
approach: approche, aborder, s'avancer, méthode, s'approcher, voie d'abord, démarche.
bending: pliage, flexion, courbure, cintrage.
carelessly: de façon négligente, négligemment, de manière négligente.
coldness: froideur.
discharge: décharge, congé, renvoyer, débit, écoulement, licencier, partir, quitus, suspendre, acquittement, rejet.
haughty: hautain, arrogant.
inflammable: inflammable.
ironical: ironique.
irresolute: indécis, hésitant, irrésolu.
menacing: menaçant, sinistre.
rebuke: réprimander, gronder, reprocher, sermonner, repousser.
stair: marche, escalier.
subject: sujet, thème, composition, objet.
sweetheart: amoureux, trésor.
tinder: amadou.
warmer: plus chaud.

and then away with these **mists** round the Past and Future; the Present at **least** is mine!"

French

least: moindre, le moins.
mist: brume, brouillard, buée, voile.

CHAPTER V

THE WEAVERS AND THE WOOF

"And what," said Varney,—"what, while we are **pursuing** a **fancied clew**, and **seeking** to provide first a name, and then a fortune for this young lawyer,—what steps have you really taken to meet the danger that **menaces** me,—to **secure**, if our inquiries fail, an independence for yourself? Months have **elapsed**, and you have still **shrunk** from **advancing** the great scheme upon which we built, when the daughter of Susan Mainwaring was admitted to your hearth."

"Why recall me, in these rare moments when I feel myself human still,—why recall me back to the nethermost **abyss** of revenge and crime? Oh, let me be sure that I have still a son! Even if John Ardworth, with his gifts and energies, be **denied** to me, a son, though in **rags**, I will give him wealth!—a son, though ignorant as the merest **boor**, I will pour into his brain my dark wisdom! A son! a son! my heart swells at the word. Ah, you **sneer**! Yes, my heart swells, but not with the **mawkish fondness** of a feeble mother. In a son, I shall live again,—transmigrate from this **tortured** and horrible life of mine; drink back my youth. In him I shall rise from my fall,—strong in his power, great in his **grandeur**. It is because I was born a woman,—had woman's poor passions and **infirm** weakness,—that I am what I am. I would transfer

French

abyss: abîme, abysse, gouffre.
advancing: avançant.
boor: goujat, malotru, rustre, abruti.
clew: point d'écoute.
denied: nié, nia, niai, niâmes, nias, niâtes, nièrent.
elapsed: passé, écoulé.
fancied: imaginaire.
fondness: affection, penchant, prédilection, tendresse.
grandeur: noblesse, grandeur.

infirm: infirme, irrésolu.
mawkish: fade.
menace: menacer, gronder.
pursuing: poursuivant.
rag: chiffon, lambeau, torchon, guenille, haillon.
secure: fixer, sûr, fixons, en sûreté, attacher, à l'abri, obtenir, assurer.
seeking: cherchant, raillant.
shrunk: rétréci, retrait.
sneer: ricaner, tourner en ridicule, remarque moqueuse.

tortured: torturé.

myself into the soul of man,—man, who has the strength to act, and the privilege to rise. Into the **bronze** of man's nature I would pour the experience which has broken, with its fierce elements, the **puny** vessel of clay. Yes, Gabriel, in return for all I have done and sacrificed for you, I ask but co-operation in that one hope of my **shattered** and storm-beat being. Bear, **forbear**, await; **risk** not that hope by some wretched, **peddling** crime which will bring on us both detection,—some **wanton** revelry in guilt, which is not worth the terror that treads upon its heels."

"You forget," answered Varney, with a kind of **submissive** sullenness,—for whatever had passed between these two persons in their secret and fearful intimacy, there was still a power in Lucretia, surviving her fall amidst the **fiends**, that **impressed** Varney with the only respect he felt for man or woman,—"you forget strangely the nature of our **elaborate** and master project when you speak of 'peddling crime,' or 'wanton revelry' in guilt! You forget, too, how every hour that we waste **deepens** the peril that surrounds me, and may sweep from your side the sole companion that can aid you in your objects,—nay, without whom they must wholly fail. Let me speak first of that most urgent danger, for your memory seems short and troubled, since you have learned only to hope the recovery of your son. If this man Stubmore, in whom the trust created by my uncle's will is now vested, once comes to town, once begins to bustle about his **accursed** projects of transferring the money from the Bank of England, I tell you again and again that my **forgery** on the bank will be detected, and that **transportation** will be the **smallest penalty** inflicted. Part of the forgery, as you know, was committed on your behalf, to find the moneys necessary for the research for your son,—committed on the clear understanding that our project on Helen should repay me, should **enable** me, perhaps undetected, to restore the sums **illegally abstracted**, or, at the worst, to confess to Stubmore—whose character I well know—that, **oppressed** by difficulties, I had yielded to temptation, that I had **forged** his name (as I had forged his father's) as an authority to sell the capital from the bank, and that now, in **replacing** the money, I repaid my **error** and threw myself on his indulgence, on his silence.

French

abstracted: distrait, abstraits, abrégé.
accursed: maudit.
bronze: bronze, airain.
deepen: approfondir, foncer, rembrunissons, épaissir, devenir plus profond, creuser.
elaborate: élaborer, soigné, compliqué, développer, raffiné.
enable: permettre, habiliter.
error: erreur, faute, méprise.
fiend: démon, monstre, enragé.
forbear: s'abstenir.
forged: forgé, contrefait.
forgery: falsification, faux, contrefaçon.
illegally: illégalement, de façon illégale, de manière illégale.
impressed: impressionné.
oppressed: opprimé, serrâtes.
peddling: colportage, commerce ambulant, vente à la chine.
penalty: pénalité, penalty, punition, amende.
puny: chétif.
replacing: remplaçant, substituant, replaçant.
risk: risque, aléa, aventurer, oser, péril.
shattered: brisa, fracassa.
smallest: le plus petit.
submissive: soumis, docile.
transportation: transport, moyen de transport.
wanton: dévergondé, impudique, licencieux.

I say that I know enough of the man to know that I should be thus **cheaply** saved, or at the worst, I should have but to strengthen his compassion by a **bribe** to his **avarice**; but if I cannot replace the money, I am lost."

"Well, well," said Lucretia; "the money you shall have, let me but find my son, and—"

"Grant me patience!" cried Varney, **impetuously**. "But what can your son do, if found, **unless** you **endow** him with the heritage of Laughton? To do that, Helen, who comes next to Percival St. John in the course of the **entail**, must cease to live! Have I not **aided**, am I not **aiding** you **hourly**, in your grand objects? This evening I shall see a man whom I have long lost sight of, but who has acquired in a lawyer's life the true scent after evidence: if that evidence exist, it shall be found. I have just learned his address. By tomorrow he shall be on the track. I have stinted myself to save from the results of the last forgery the gold to **whet** his **zeal**. For the rest, as I have said, your design **involves** the **removal** of two lives. Already over the one more difficult to **slay** the shadow creeps and the **pall** hangs. I have won, as you wished, and as was necessary, young St. John's familiar acquaintance; when the hour comes,   he is in my hands."

Lucretia smiled **sternly**. "So!" she said, between her ground teeth, "the father **forbade** me the house that was my heritage! I have but to lift a finger and breathe a word, and, **desolate** as I am, I thrust from that home the son! The **spoiler** left me the world,—I leave his son the grave!"

"But," said Varney, **doggedly** pursuing his **dreadful** object, "why force me to repeat that his is not the only life between you and your son's inheritance? St. John gone, Helen still remains. And what, if your researches fail, are we to lose the rich harvest which Helen will yield us,—a harvest you **reap** with the same **sickle** which gathers in your revenge? Do you no longer see in Helen's face the features of her mother? Is the **perfidy** of William Mainwaring forgotten or forgiven?"

"Gabriel Varney," said Lucretia, in a hollow and **tremulous** voice, "when in that hour in which my whole being was revulsed, and I heard the cord

---

French

aided: assisté.
aiding: aider.
avarice: avarice, cupidité.
bribe: corrompre, soudoyer.
cheaply: de manière bon marchée, à bon marché, de façon bon marchée.
desolate: sombre, désolé, morne.
doggedly: de façon obstinée, de manière obstinée.
dreadful: terrible, affreux, épouvantable.
endow: doter, dotons.
entail: comporter, entraîner.
forbade: interdit.
hourly: horaire, constant.
impetuously: de façon impétueuse, de manière impétueuse.
involve: impliquer, comprendre.
pall: drap mortuaire, manteau.
perfidy: perfidie.
reap: moissonner, faucher.
removal: enlèvement, déménagement, renvoi, révocation, piégeage, dépose.
sickle: faucille, serpe.
slay: tuer, tuons, tuez, tues, tue, tuent, abattre, rectifier.
spoiler: déporteur, spoiler, déflecteur.
sternly: de manière poupe, sévèrement.
tremulous: timide, tremblotant.
unless: à moins que, sauf.
whet: aiguiser, affûter, stimuler.
zeal: zèle, ferveur.

snap from the anchor, and saw the **demons** of the storm gather round my bark; when in that hour I stooped calmly down and kissed my rival's brow,—I murmured an oath which seemed not inspired by my own soul, but by an influence henceforth given to my fate: I vowed that the perfidy dealt to me should be repaid; I vowed that the ruin of my own existence should fall on the brow which I kissed. I vowed that if shame and disgrace were to supply the inheritance I had **forfeited**, I would not stand alone amidst the scorn of the **pitiless** world. In the vision of my agony, I saw, **afar**, the altar dressed and the bride-chamber prepared; and I breathed my curse, strong as **prophecy**, on the marriage-hearth and the marriage-bed. Why dream, then, that I would **rescue** the **loathed** child of that loathed **union** from your grasp? But is the time come? Yours may be come: is mine?"

Something so awful there was in the look of his **accomplice**, so intense in the hate of her low voice, that Varney, **wretch** as he was, and contemplating at that very hour the foulest and most hideous guilt, drew back, appalled.

Madame Dalibard resumed, and in a somewhat softer tone, but softened only by the anguish of despair.

"Oh, had it been **otherwise**, what might I have been! Given over from that hour to the very **incarnation** of plotting crime, none to resist the evil impulse of my own **maddening** heart, the partner, forced on me by fate, leading me deeper and deeper into the **inextricable** hell,—from that hour fraud upon fraud, guilt upon guilt, **infamy heaped** on infamy, till I stand a **marvel** to myself that the **thunderbolt** falls not, that Nature thrusts not from her breast a living **outrage** on all her laws! Was I not justified in the desire of retribution? Every step that I fell, every glance that I gave to the **gulf** below, **increased** but in me the desire for revenge. All my acts had **flowed** from one **fount**: should the stream **roll pollution**, and the fount spring pure?"

"You have had your revenge on your rival and her husband."

"I had it, and I passed on!" said Lucretia, with **nostrils dilated** as with haughty triumph; "they were crushed, and I **suffered** them to live! Nay, when, by chance, I heard of William Mainwaring's death, I bowed down my

---

French

accomplice: complice.
afar: loin.
demon: démon.
dilated: dilatâtes.
flowed: coulé.
forfeited: forfaits, perdu.
fount: source, fonte, réservoir de lampe.
gulf: golfe, abîme, gouffre.
heaped: entassé.
incarnation: incarnation.
increased: augmenté.

inextricable: inextricable.
infamy: infamie.
loathed: abominâtes, haï, haïtes, haïrent, abhorrai, haïs, haïmes.
maddening: à rendre fou, enrageant, exaspérant.
marvel: merveille, s'étonner.
nostril: narine, naseau.
otherwise: sinon, autrement.
outrage: outrage, scandale, attentat, infraction correctionnelle.
pitiless: impitoyable.

pollution: pollution, contamination.
prophecy: prophétie.
rescue: sauver, secours, délivrance.
roll: rouleau, petit pain, enrouler, tableau, cylindre.
snap: mousqueton, claquement.
suffered: souffrit, subîtes, subi.
thunderbolt: chute de la foudre.
union: union, syndicat, raccord.
wretch: malheureux, scélérat.

head, and I almost think I **wept**. The old days came back upon me. Yes, I wept! But I had not **destroyed** their love. No, no; there I had **miserably** failed. A pledge of that love lived. I had left their hearth **barren**; Fate sent them a comfort which I had not **foreseen**. And suddenly my hate returned, my wrongs rose again, my **vengeance** was not **sated**. The love that had destroyed more than my life,—my soul,—rose again and **cursed** me in the face of Helen. The oath which I took when I kissed my rival's brow, **demanded** another prey when I kissed the child of those nuptials."

"You are prepared at last, then, to act?" cried Varney, in a tone of **savage** joy.

At that moment, close under the window, rose, sudden and sweet, the voice of one singing,—the young voice of Helen. The words were so distinct that they came to the ears of the dark-plotting and **guilty** pair. In the song itself there was little to remark or **peculiarly apposite** to the consciences of those who heard; yet in the extreme and touching purity of the voice, and in the innocence of the general spirit of the words, **trite** as might be the image they conveyed, there was something that **contrasted** so **fearfully** their own thoughts and minds that they sat silent, looking **vacantly** into each other's faces, and **shrinking** perhaps to turn their eyes within themselves.

HELEN'S HYMN.

Ye fade, yet still how sweet, ye Flowers!
Your scent outlives the bloom!
So, Father, may my mortal hours
Grow sweeter towards the tomb!

In **withered** leaves a **healing cure**
The simple **gleaners** find; So may our withered hopes endure
In virtues left behind!

French

apposite: juste, à propos, approprié, pertinent.
barren: stérile, aride, infertile.
contrasted: contrasté.
cure: guérir, traitement, remédier, assainir, soigner, cure, cuisson, vulcanisation, durcissement d'un adhésif, prise.
cursed: maudit.
demanded: exigé.
destroyed: détruisîmes, ravageai.
fearfully: de manière effrayante, de façon effrayante.
foreseen: prévu.
gleaner: glaneur.
guilty: coupable.
healing: guérissant, curatif, assainissant, cicatrisation.
miserably: de façon misérable, de manière misérable.
peculiarly: de façon étrange, de manière étrange.
sated: assouvîmes, repu, saturé.
savage: sauvage, attaquer férocement, barbare, brutal, féroce.
shrinking: rétrécissant, perte de volume, décatissage, contraction, retrait.
trite: banal.
vacantly: de façon vide, de manière vide.
vengeance: revanche, vengeance.
wept: pleurâtes, sourdis, larmoyèrent.
withered: flétri, fané.

> Oh, not to me be **vainly** given
> The lesson ye bestow,
> Of thoughts that rise in sweets to Heaven,
> And turn to use below.

The song died, but still the listeners remained silent, till at length, shaking off the effect, with his laugh of **discordant** irony, Varney said,—

"Sweet innocence, fresh from the **nursery**! Would it not be sin to suffer the world to **mar** it? You hear the prayer: why not grant it, and let the flower 'turn to use below'?"

"Ah, but could it **wither** first!" muttered Lucretia, with an accent of suppressed rage. "Do you think that her—that his—daughter is to me but a **vulgar** life to be **sacrificed** merely for gold? Imagine away your sex, man! Women only know what I—such as I, woman still—feel in the presence of the pure! Do you fancy that I should not have held death a blessing if death could have found me in youth such as Helen is? Ah, could she but live to suffer! Die! Well, since it must be, since my son requires the sacrifice, do as you will with the victim that death **mercifully snatches** from my grasp. I could have wished to **prolong** her life, to **load** it with some fragment of the curse her parents **heaped** upon me,—baffled love, and ruin, and despair! I could have **hoped**, in this division of the spoil, that mine had been the vengeance, if yours the gold. You want the life, I the heart,—the heart to **torture** first; and then—why then more **willingly** than I do now, could I have thrown the **carcass** to the jackal!"

"Listen!" began Varney; when the door opened and Helen herself stood **unconsciously** smiling at the threshold.

French

carcass: carcasse, gros œuvre.
discordant: discordant.
heaped: entassé.
hoped: espéra, souhaitâtes.
load: charger, fardeau.
mar: gâter, gâtons.
mercifully: de façon indulgente, de manière indulgente.
nursery: pépinière, pouponnière, nourricerie, nursery, crèche, garderie.
prolong: prolonger, étaler.
sacrificed: sacrifié.
snatch: arraché en flexion, saisir, fragment, chercher à attraper.
torture: torture, supplice.
unconsciously: de façon inconsciente, de manière inconsciente, inconsciemment.
vainly: de manière vaniteuse, vainement, de façon vaniteuse.
vulgar: vulgaire, trivial.
willingly: volontiers, de manière volontaire, de façon volontaire.
wither: se faner, dessécher.

CHAPTER VI

THE LAWYER AND THE BODY-SNATCHER

That same evening Beck, **according** to appointment, met Percival and showed him the dreary-looking house which held the fair stranger who had so **attracted** his **youthful** fancy. And Percival looked at the high walls with the sailor's bold desire for adventure, while confused visions reflected from plays, **operas**, and novels, in which **scaling** walls with rope-ladders and dark-lanterns was **represented** as the natural **vocation** of a lover, **flitted** across his brain; and certainly he gave a deep sigh as his common-sense **plucked** him back from such romance. However, having now **ascertained** the house, it would be easy to learn the name of its **inmates**, and to watch or make his opportunity. As slowly and reluctantly he walked back to the spot where he had left his **cabriolet**, he entered into some **desultory** conversation with his strange guide; and the pity he had before conceived for Beck increased upon him as he talked and listened. This **benighted** mind, only illumined by a kind of miserable **astuteness** and that "cunning of the **belly**" which is born of want to **engender avarice**; this joyless temperament; this age in youth; this living **reproach**, rising up from the stones of London against our social indifference to the souls which wither and **rot** under the hard eyes

---

French

according: selon, s'accorder.
ascertained: constatai.
astuteness: finesse, sagacité.
attracted: attirai, allécha, appâtèrent.
avarice: avarice, cupidité.
belly: ventre, panse, abdomen.
benighted: surpris par la nuit.
cabriolet: cabriolet.
desultory: décousu.
engender: engendrer, produire.
flitted: voltigé, flirtâmes.
inmate: détenu, interne, occupant, résident d'institution.
opera: opéra.
plucked: plumé.
represented: représenta, figuré.
reproach: reproche, gronder, réprimander, sermonner.
rot: pourrir, se gâter, rouir à l'excès, se pourrir, carie, clavelée, gâter.
scaling: mise à l'échelle, écaillage, escalade.
vocation: vocation.
youthful: jeune, juvénile.

of **science** and the **deaf** ears of wealth,—had a **pathos** for his lively sympathies and his fresh heart.

"If ever you want a friend, come to me," said St. John, abruptly.

The **sweeper** stared, and a gleam of **diviner** nature, a ray of gratitude and **unselfish** devotion, darted through the fog and darkness of his mind. He stood, with his hat off, watching the wheels of the cabriolet as it bore away the happy child of fortune, and then, shaking his head, as at some puzzle that perplexed and defied his comprehension, strode back to the town and bent his way homeward.

Between two and three hours after Percival thus parted from the sweeper, a man whose dress was little in **accordance** with the scene in which we present him, **threaded** his way through a foul labyrinth of alleys in the worst part of St. Giles's,—a neighbourhood, indeed, **carefully shunned** at dusk by wealthy passengers; for here dwelt not only **Penury** in its grimmest shape, but the desperate and dangerous guilt which is not to be lightly encountered in its haunts and **domiciles**. Here children **imbibe** vice with their mother's **milk**. Here Prostitution, **commencing** with childhood, grows fierce and **sanguinary** in the **teens**, and **leagues** with **theft** and murder. Here slinks the **pickpocket**, here emerges the **burglar**, here skulks the **felon**. Yet all about and all around, here, too, may be found virtue in its rarest and noblest form,—virtue **outshining** circumstance and defying temptation; the virtue of utter poverty, which **groans**, and yet sins not. So **interwoven** are these webs of penury and fraud that in one court your life is not safe; but turn to the right hand, and in the other, you might sleep safely in that worse than Irish shealing, though your pockets were full of gold. Through these haunts the ragged and penniless may walk unfearing, for they have nothing to dread from the lawless,—more, perhaps, from the law; but the wealthy, the respectable, the **spruce**, the **dainty**, let them beware the spot, unless the policeman is in sight or day is in the skies!

As this passenger, whose appearance, as we have implied, was certainly not that of a **denizen**, turned into one of the alleys, a rough hand seized him

---

French

accordance: accord, conformité, convention, entente, concordance.
burglar: cambrioleur, voleur.
carefully: soigneusement, de façon prudente, de manière prudente.
commencing: commençant.
dainty: délicat, tendre, aimable.
deaf: sourd.
denizen: habitant.
diviner: devin.
domicile: domicile.
felon: criminel, panaris.
groan: gémir, geindre.
imbibe: absorber, buvons, boire, bois, boivent, buvez.
interwoven: entremêlé.
league: ligue, lieue.
milk: lait, traire.
outshining: éclipsant, surpassant.
pathos: pathétique.
penury: indigence, pénurie.
pickpocket: pickpocket, voleur à la tire.
sanguinary: sanguinaire.
science: science.
shunned: éviteraient, fui, fuîtes, fuit, fuis, fuirent, fuîmes.
spruce: épicéa, impeccable, sapin.
sweeper: balayeuse, arrière latéral, bétonneur, libero, verrouilleur, analyseur panoramique.
teen: adolescent.
theft: vol, chapardage.
threaded: enfilé, visser, fileté.
unselfish: désintéressé, généreux.

by the arm, and suddenly a group of girls and tatterdemalions **issued** from a house, in which the lower shutters unclosed showed a light burning, and **surrounded** him with a **hoarse whoop**.

The passenger whispered a word in the ear of the grim **blackguard** who had seized him, and his arm was instantly **released**.

"Hist! a pal,—he has the catch," said the blackguard, **surlily**. The group gave way, and by the light of the clear starlit skies, and a single lamp hung at the entrance of the alley, gazed upon the stranger. But they made no effort to detain him; and as he disappeared in the distant shadows, hastened back into the wretched hostlery where they had been merry-making. Meanwhile, the stranger gained a narrow court, and stopped before a house in one of its angles,—a house taller than the rest, so much taller than the rest that it had the effect of a tower; you would have supposed it (perhaps rightly) to be the last remains of some ancient building of importance, around which, as **population thickened** and fashion changed, the **huts** below it had **insolently** sprung up. Quaint and massive pilasters, black with the mire and **soot** of **centuries**, flanked the deep-set door; the windows were **heavy** with mullions and **transoms**, and strongly barred in the lower floor; but few of the panes were whole, and only here and there had any attempt been made to keep out the wind and rain by rags, paper, old shoes, old hats, and other ingenious contrivances. Beside the door was **conveniently** placed a row of some ten or **twelve** bell-pulls, **appertaining** no doubt to the **various** lodgments into which the building was **subdivided**. The stranger did not seem very familiar with the **appurtenances** of the place. He stood in some suspense as to the proper bell to **select**; but at last, guided by a brass **plate annexed** to one of the pulls, which, though it was too dark to **decipher** the inscription, denoted a claim to superior gentility to the rest of that nameless class, he hazarded a tug, which brought forth a 'larum loud enough to **startle** the whole court from its stillness.

In a minute or less, the casement in one of the upper stories opened, a head peered forth, and one of those voices peculiar to low debauch—raw, cracked, and hoarse—called out: "Who waits?"

French

annexed: annexé.
appertaining: appartenant.
appurtenance: appartenance, dépendance locative, droit accessoire, accessoires.
blackguard: canaille, vaurien.
century: siècle.
conveniently: de façon commode, de manière commode.
decipher: déchiffrer, décrypte.
heavy: lourd, fort.
hoarse: rauque, enroué.

hut: hutte, cabane, chaumière, baraque.
insolently: de façon insolente, de manière insolente.
issued: émis.
plate: plaque, assiette, plat, lame, cliché, met, planche.
population: population, peuplement.
released: libéré, relâché.
select: sélectionner, choisir.
soot: suie.

startle: effarouches, surprenons, alarment.
subdivided: subdivisèrent.
surlily: de façon maussade, de manière maussade.
surrounded: entoura, environnâtes.
thickened: grossi, épaissis.
transom: traverse, tableau, imposte.
twelve: douze.
various: divers, varié, différents.
whoop: chant du coq, cri, reprise.

"Is it you, Grabman?" asked the stranger, **dubiously**.

"Yes,—Nicholas Grabman, attorney-at-law, sir, at your service; and your name?"

"Jason," answered the stranger.

"Ho, there! ho, Beck!" cried the cracked voice to some one within; "go down and open the door."

In a few moments the heavy **portal** swung and **creaked** and yawned **sullenly**, and a **gaunt** form, half-undressed, with an inch of a farthing rushlight **glimmering** through a battered **lantern** in its hand, presented itself to Jason. The last eyed the ragged porter **sharply**.

"Do you live here?"

"Yes," answered Beck, with the **cringe habitual** to him. "H-up the ladder, vith the rats, drat 'em."

"Well, lead on; hold up the lantern. A devil of a dark place this!" grumbled Jason, as he nearly **stumbled** over **sundry** broken **chattels**, and gained a **flight** of rude, black, broken **stairs**, that creaked under his **tread**.

"'St! 'st!" said Beck between his teeth, as the stranger, **halting** at the second floor, demanded, in no gentle tones, whether Mr. Grabman lived in the chimney-pots.

"'St! 'st! Don't make such a **rumpus**, or No. 7 will be at you."

"What do I care for No. 7? And who the devil is No. 7?"

"A body-snatcher!" whispered Beck, with a **shudder**. "He's a dillicut sleeper,—can't **abide** having his night's rest sp'ilt. And he's the houtrageoustest great cretur when he's h-up in his **tantrums**; it makes your 'air stand on ind to 'ear him!"

"I should like very much to hear him, then," said the stranger, curiously. And while he spoke, the door of No. 7 opened abruptly. A huge head, covered with **matted** hair, was thrust for a moment through the **aperture**,

---

French

abide: endurer, demeurer, persévérer, supporter, soutenir, attendre, subir, souffrir.
aperture: ouverture, orifice, trou.
chattel: biens meubles.
creaked: grincé, craquai.
cringe: reculer.
dubiously: de manière douteuse, de façon douteuse.
flight: vol, fuite, volée, essor.
gaunt: morne, maigre, désert, désolé, sombre, maussade, mince,
angulaire, décharné, mélancolique.
glimmering: éclat, miroitant.
habitual: habituel.
halting: arrêter, hésitant, immobilisation.
lantern: lanterne, fanal.
matted: maté, feutré.
portal: portail, tête de tunnel, entrée de tunnel.
rumpus: chahut, bagarre, boucan.
sharply: de façon aigue, de manière
aigue, nettement, brusquement.
shudder: frisson, frémissement.
stair: marche, escalier.
stumbled: trébuché, bronchai.
sullenly: de façon maussade, de manière maussade.
sundry: divers.
tantrum: crise de colère, colère.
tread: piétiner, fouler aux pieds, semelle, marcher sur, giron, bande de roulement, faire les cent pas, chape.

and two dull eyes, that seemed covered with a film like that of the birds which feed on the dead, met the stranger's bold, sparkling orbs.

"**Hell** and fury!" **bawled** out the voice of this **ogre**, like a **clap** of near **thunder**, "if you two keep tramp, tramp, there close at my door, I'll make you **meat** for the **surgeons**, b—you!"

"Stop a moment, my civil friend," said the stranger, advancing; "just stand where you are: I should like to make a sketch of your head."

That head **protruded** farther from the door, and with it an enormous bulk of chest and shoulder. But the adventurous visitor was not to be daunted. He took out, very coolly, a pencil and the back of a letter, and began his sketch.

The body-snatcher stared at him an instant in mute astonishment; but that **operation** and the composure of the artist were so new to him that they actually inspired him with terror. He slunk back, **banged** to the door; and the stranger, putting up his implements, said, with a disdainful laugh, to Beck, who had slunk away into a corner,—

"No. 7 knows well how to take care of No. 1. Lead on, and be quick, then!"

As they continued to mount, they heard the body-snatcher **growling** and **blaspheming** in his **den**, and the sound made Beck **clamber** the **quicker**, till at the next landing-place he took breath, threw open a door, and Jason, pushing him aside, entered first.

The interior of the room bespoke better circumstances than might have been supposed from the approach; the floor was covered with sundry **scraps** of **carpet**, formerly of different hues and **patterns**, but mellowed by time into one threadbare mass of **grease** and canvas. There was a good fire on the hearth, though the night was warm; there were sundry volumes **piled** round the walls, in the binding peculiar to law books; in a corner stood a tall desk, of the fashion used by clerks, perched on tall, **slim** legs, and companioned by a tall, slim stool. On a table before the fire were **scattered** the remains of the nightly meal,—broiled bones, the skeleton of a **herring**; and the **steam** rose from a tumbler containing a **liquid** colourless as water, but **poisonous** as gin.

French

banged: frappé.
bawled: braillé.
blaspheming: blasphémant.
carpet: tapis, moquette.
clamber: grimper.
clap: claquer, applaudir.
den: nid, repaire.
grease: graisse, lubrifiant.
growling: grondement, grognement.
hell: enfer, géhenne.
herring: hareng.

liquid: liquide, flot, fluide.
meat: viande, chair.
ogre: ogre.
operation: opération, exploitation, fonctionnement, manoeuvre.
pattern: patron, modèle, schéma, motif, pattern, forme, configuration, dessin.
piled: entassé.
poisonous: toxique, venimeux, vénéneux.
protruded: dépassèrent.

quicker: plus vite.
scattered: dispersa, répandis, disséminé, éparpillèrent.
scrap: ferraille, chiffon, lambeau, déchets, fragment, mettre au rebut, rebut, débris.
slim: mince, amincir, amaigrir, maigrir.
steam: vapeur, buée, étuver.
surgeon: chirurgien.
thunder: tonnerre, retenir.

The room was squalid and dirty, and bespoke mean and slovenly habits; but it did not **bespeak** penury and want, it had even an air of **filthy** comfort of its own,—the comfort of the **swine** in its warm sty. The **occupant** of the chamber was in keeping with the **localities**. Figure to yourself a man of middle height, not thin, but void of all muscular flesh,—bloated, **puffed**, **unwholesome**. He was dressed in a gray-flannel gown and short breeches, the **stockings wrinkled** and distained, the feet in **slippers**. The stomach was that of a **portly** man, the legs were those of a skeleton; the cheeks full and **swollen**, like a ploughboy's, but livid, bespeckled, of a dull lead-colour, like a patient in the **dropsy**. The head, covered in patches with thin, yellowish hair, gave some promise of intellect, for the forehead was high, and appeared still more so from partial **baldness**; the eyes, **embedded** in fat and wrinkled skin, were small and **lustreless**, but they still had that acute look which education and ability **communicate** to the human orb; the mouth most showed the animal,—full-lipped, coarse, and sensual; while behind one of two great ears stuck a pen.

You see before you, then, this slatternly figure,—slipshod, half-clothed, with a sort of shabby demi-gentility about it, half ragamuffin, half clerk; while in strong contrast appeared the new-comer, scrupulously neat, new, with bright black-satin stock, coat cut **jauntily** to the waist, **varnished** boots, **kid** gloves, and **trim** mustache.

Behind this sleek and comely personage, on knock-knees, in torn shirt open at the throat, with **apathetic**, listless, unlighted face, stood the lean and **gawky** Beck.

"Set a chair for the gentleman," said the inmate of the chamber to Beck, with a dignified wave of the hand.

"How do you do, Mr.—Mr.—humph—Jason? How do you do? Always smart and blooming; the world **thrives** with you."

"The world is a farm that thrives with all who till it properly, Grabman," answered Jason, dryly; and with his handkerchief he carefully dusted the chair, on which he then **daintily deposited** his person.

French

apathetic: apathique, indifférent.
baldness: calvitie, platitude.
bespeak: retenez, retiens, annonçons.
communicate: communiquer, transmettre.
daintily: de façon délicate, de manière délicate.
deposited: déposé.
dropsy: hydropisie.
embedded: enfonçai, incorporai, enrobas, inclus, imbriqué, intégré.

encastras.
filthy: sale, dégoûtant, crasseux.
gawky: dégingandé, gauche, maladroit.
jauntily: de façon désinvolte, de manière désinvolte.
kid: gosse, chevreau, gamin.
locality: localité, lieu.
lustreless: éclat, mat, terne.
occupant: occupant, habitant, locataire.
portly: corpulent.

puffed: soufflé, bouffant.
slipper: pantoufle, mule, chausson.
stocking: bas, stockage, chaussette.
swine: porc, cochon.
swollen: gonflé, enflé.
thrives: prospère.
trim: garnir, tailler, rogner, égaliser, décorer, ébarber, assiette.
unwholesome: malsain, nocif, pernicieux.
varnished: verni.
wrinkled: ridé, moiré.

"But who is your Ganymede, your **valet**, your gentleman-usher?"

"Oh, a lad about town who lodges above and does odd jobs for me,—brushes my coat, **cleans** my shoes, and after his day's work goes an **errand** now and then. Make yourself **scarce**, Beck! **Anatomy**, vanish!"

Beck grinned, nodded, pulled hard at a **flake** of his hair, and closed the door.

"One of your **brotherhood**, that?" asked Jason, carelessly.

"He, **oaf**? No," said Grabman, with profound contempt in his **sickly visage**. "He works for his bread,—instinct! Turnspits and truffle-dogs and some silly men have it! What an age since we met! Shall I mix you a tumbler?"

"You know I never drink your **vile** spirits; though in Champagne and Bordeaux I am any man's match."

"And how the devil do you keep old black thoughts out of your mind by those **washy** potations?"

"Old black thoughts—of what?"

"Of black actions, Jason. We have not met since you paid me for **recommending** the **nurse** who attended your uncle in his last illness."

"Well, poor **coward**?"

Grabman knit his thin eyebrows and **gnawed** his **blubber** lips.

"I am no coward, as you know."

"Not when a thing is to be done, but after it is done. You brave the substance, and tremble at the shadow. I dare say you see ugly **goblins** in the dark, Grabman?"

"Ay, ay; but it is no use talking to you. You call yourself Jason because of your **yellow** hair, or your love for the **golden fleece**; but your old **comrades** call you 'Rattlesnake,' and you have its blood, as its venom."

"And its charm, man," added Jason, with a strange smile, that, though **hypocritical** and constrained, had yet a certain **softness**, and added greatly

---

French

anatomy: anatomie.
blubber: graisse de baleine, lard.
brotherhood: fraternité, confrérie.
clean: propre, pur, purifier, nettoyer, affiner, laver, ramoner, net.
comrade: camarade.
coward: lâche, peureux, couard, poltron.
errand: commission, message, course.
flake: flocon, écaille, paillette, s'écailler, miette, doublure débouchante.
fleece: toison, tondre, polaire.
gnawed: rongea.
goblin: lutin, gnome.
golden: doré, en or, d'or.
hypocritical: hypocrite.
nurse: infirmière, soigner, nourrice, veiller sur, allaiter.
oaf: balourd, mufle, dadais, lourdaud.
recommending: recommandant, préconisant.
scarce: insuffisant, rare.
sickly: maladif, malsain, écoeurant, de manière malade, de façon malade.
softness: douceur, mollesse.
valet: valet.
vile: vil, abject, lâche, infâme.
visage: visage.
washy: délavé.
yellow: jaune, froussard.

to the comeliness of features which many might call beautiful, and all would allow to be regular and **symmetrical**. "I shall find at least ten love-letters on my table when I go home. But enough of these fopperies, I am here on business."

"Law, of course; I am your man. Who's the victim?" and a hideous grin on Grabman's face contrasted the **sleek** smile that yet **lingered** upon his visitor's.

"No; something less hazardous, but not less lucrative than our old **practices**. This is a business that may bring you hundreds, thousands; that may take you from this **hovel** to **speculate** at the West End; that may change your gin into Lafitte, and your **herring** into **venison**; that may lift the broken attorney again upon the wheel,—again to roll down, it may be; but that is your affair."

"'Fore Gad, open the case," cried Grabman, eagerly, and **shoving** aside the **ignoble relics** of his supper, he leaned his elbows on the table and his chin on his damp palms, while eyes that positively **brightened** into an expression of **greedy** and relentless intelligence were fixed upon his visitor.

"The case runs thus," said Jason. "Once upon a time there lived, at an old house in Hampshire called Laughton, a wealthy **baronet** named St. John. He was a bachelor, his estates at his own disposal. He had two nieces and a more distant **kinsman**. His eldest niece lived with him,—she was supposed to be destined for his heiress; circumstances **needless** to relate brought upon this girl her uncle's displeasure,—she was dismissed his house. Shortly **afterwards** he died, leaving to his kinsman—a Mr. Vernon—his estates, with **remainder** to Vernon's **issue**, and in **default thereof**, first to the issue of the younger niece, next to that of the elder and **disinherited** one. The elder married, and was left a widow without children. She married again, and had a son. Her second husband, for some reason or other, conceived ill opinions of his wife. In his last illness (he did not live long) he resolved to punish the wife by **robbing** the mother. He sent away the son, nor have we been able to discover him since. It is that son whom you are to find."

French

afterward: après, plus tard.
baronet: baronnet.
brightened: avivas, éclaircîtes, blanchi.
default: par défaut, défaut.
disinherited: exhéréda, déshérité.
greedy: avide, glouton, gourmand, cupide, goulu.
herring: hareng.
hovel: taudis, masure.
ignoble: ignoble.
issue: émission, éditer, livraison, question, parution, problème, numéro, émettre, proclamer.
kinsman: parent.
lingered: traîné.
needles: aiguilles.
practice: pratique, exercice, appliquer, usage, cabinet, clientèle.
relic: relique, vestige.
remainder: reste, débris, reliquat, culot.
robbing: pillant, ravissant, dévalisant.
shoving: bourrelet.
sleek: lisse, onctueux, filandre, film d'huile, ligne de ferrasse.
speculate: spéculer, boursicoter.
symmetrical: symétrique.
thereof: de cela.
venison: venaison, viande de cerf, cerf.

"I see, I see; go on," said Grabman. "This son is now the **remainderman**. How lost? When? What year? What trace?"

"Patience. You will find in this paper the date of the loss and the age of the child, then a mere infant. Now for the trace. This husband—did I tell you his name? No? Alfred Braddell—had one friend more intimate than the rest,—John Walter Ardworth, a cashiered officer, a **ruined** man, pursued by bill-brokers, Jews, and **bailiffs**. To this man we have **lately** had reason to believe that the child was given. Ardworth, however, was shortly afterwards obliged to fly his **creditors**. We know that he went to India; but if **residing** there, it must have been under some new name, and we fear he is now dead. All our inquiries, at least after this man, have been **fruitless**. Before he went abroad, he left with his old **tutor** a child corresponding in age to that of Mrs. Braddell's. In this child she thinks she **recognizes** her son. All that you have to do is to trace his identity by good **legal** evidence. Don't smile in that **foolish** way,—I mean sound, bona fide evidence that will stand the fire of cross-examination; you know what that is! You will therefore find out,—first, whether Braddell did **consign** his child to Ardworth, and, if so, you must then follow Ardworth, with that child in his keeping, to Matthew Fielden's house, whose address you find noted in the paper I gave you, together with many other memoranda as to Ardworth's creditors and those whom he is likely to have come across."

"John Ardworth, I see!"

"John Walter Ardworth,—commonly called Walter; he, like me, perferred to be known only by his second baptismal name. He, because of a favourite Radical **godfather**; I, because Honore is an **inconvenient** Gallicism. And perhaps when Honore Mirabeau (my godfather) went out of fashion with the sans-culottes, my father thought Gabriel a safer **designation**. Now I have told you all."

"What is the mother's **maiden** name?"

"Her maiden name was Clavering; she was married under that of Dalibard, her first husband."

French

bailiff: huissier, bailli.
consign: consigner, expédier.
creditor: créancier, créditeur.
designation: désignation, indication, libellé.
foolish: sot, idiot, stupide, abracadabrant, insensé.
fruitless: stérile, infructueux.
godfather: parrain.
inconvenient: difficile, pénible, dur, inopportun, incommode, gênant.
lately: dernièrement, de manière tarde, de façon tardive, récemment.
legal: légal, légitime, juridique.
maiden: brin, vierge.
recognizes: reconnaît, retrouve.
remainderman: héritier substitué, résiduaire, dernier bénéficiaire après distribution de tous les autres legs, appelé, titulaire d'un droit révisible.
residing: résidant, demeurant.
ruined: ruiné, foutu.
tutor: tuteur, précepteur.

"And," said Grabman, looking over the notes in the paper given to him, "it is at Liverpool that the husband died, and **whence** the child was sent away?"

"It is so; to Liverpool you will go first. I tell you fairly, the task is difficult, for hitherto it has foiled me. I knew but one man who, without **flattery**, could succeed, and therefore I spared no pains to find out Nicholas Grabman. You have the true ferret's faculty; you, too, are a lawyer, and **snuff** evidence in every breath. Find us a son,—a legal son,—a son to be shown in a court of law, and the moment he steps into the lands and the Hall of Laughton, you have five thousand pounds."

"Can I have a **bond** to that effect?"

"My bond, I fear, is worth no more than my word. Trust to the last; if I break it, you know enough of my secrets to hang me!"

"Don't talk of hanging; I hate that subject. But stop. If found, does this son succeed? Did this Mr. Vernon leave no **heir**; this other sister **continue** single, or **prove** barren?"

"Oh, true! He, Mr. Vernon, who by will took the name of St. John, he left issue; but only one son still **survives**, a **minor** and **unmarried**. The sister, too, left a daughter; both are poor, **sickly** creatures,—their lives not worth a straw. Never mind them. You find Vincent Braddell, and he will not be long out of his property, nor you out of your 5,000 pounds! You see, under these **circumstances** a bond might become dangerous evidence!"

Grabman **emitted** a **fearful** and **tremulous** chuckle,—a laugh like the laugh of a **superstitious** man when you talk to him of ghosts and churchyards. He chuckled, and his hair bristled. But after a pause, in which he seemed to **wrestle** with his own conscience, he said: "Well, well, you are a strange man, Jason; you love your joke. I have nothing to do except to find out this **ultimate** remainderman; mind that!"

"Perfectly; nothing like **subdivision** of labour."

"The search will be expensive."

French

bond: obligation, lien, liaison, cautionnement, coller, lier, bon, titres, adhérence.
circumstance: circonstance, état de fait.
continue: continuer, durer, durons, reconduire, maintenir, prolonger.
emitted: émis, émit, émirent, émîmes, émîtes.
fearful: effrayant, affreux, craintif.
flattery: flatterie, adulation.
heir: héritier, légataire.
minor: mineur, secondaire, matière secondaire, enfant mineur.
prove: prouver, démontrer.
sickly: maladif, malsain, écoeurant, de manière malade, de façon malade.
snuff: tabac à priser, effleurer, moucher.
subdivision: subdivision, lotissement, compartimentage.
superstitious: superstitieux.
survives: survit.
tremulous: timide, tremblotant.
ultimate: ultime.
unmarried: célibataire, double bande.
whence: d'où.
wrestle: lutter, catcher, se débattre.

"There is **oil** for your wheels," answered Jason, putting a note-book into his confidant's hands. "But mind you waste it not. No tricks, no false play, with me; you know Jason, or, if you like the name better, you know the Rattlesnake!"

"I will account for every penny," said Grabman, eagerly, and clasping his hands, while his pale face grew **livid**.

"I do not doubt it, my quill-driver. Look sharp, start to-morrow. Get thyself **decent clothes**, be sober, **cleanly**, and respectable. Act as a man who sees before him 5,000 pounds. And now, light me downstairs."

With the candle in his hand, Grabman stole down the rugged steps even more **timorously** than Beck had **ascended** them, and put his finger to his mouth as they came in the dread **vicinity** of No. 7. But Jason, or rather Gabriel Varney, with that **fearless**, reckless **bravado** of temper which, while causing half his guilt, threw at times a false **glitter** over its **baseness**, piqued by the **cowardice** of his comrade, gave a **lusty kick** at the closed door, and shouted out: "Old grave-stealer, come out, and let me **finish** your picture. Out, out! I say, out!" Grabman left the candle on the steps, and made but three bounds to his own room.

At the third shout of his disturber the resurrection-man threw open his door violently and appeared at the gap, the **upward flare** of the candle showing the deep lines ploughed in his hideous face, and the immense strength of his gigantic trunk and limbs. Slight, fair, and delicate as he was, Varney eyed him **deliberately**, and **trembled** not.

"What do you want with me?" said the terrible voice, tremulous with rage.

"Only to finish your portrait as Pluto. He was the **god** of Hell, you know."

The next moment the vast hand of the **ogre** hung like a great cloud over Gabriel Varney. This last, ever on his guard, sprang aside, and the light **gleamed** on the steel of a pistol. "Hands off! Or—"

French

ascended: montai.
baseness: bassesse.
bravado: bravade.
cleanly: de façon propre, de manière propre, proprement.
clothe: vêtir, vêtent, vêts, vêtons, habiller, revêtir.
cowardice: lâcheté, faiblesse.
decent: convenable, décent, honnête.
deliberately: exprès, délibérément, de manière délibérée, de façon délibérée.
fearless: intrépide, courageux.
finish: terminer, finir, achever, achève, cesser, apprêter, fin, confectionner, arrivée.
flare: fusée éclairante, vaciller, arrondi, lumière parasite, ondoyer, scintiller, torche, évasement, dévers.
gleamed: luie, luis.
glitter: briller, scintillement.
god: dieu, créateur.
kick: coup de pied, recul, donner un coup de pied, botter.
livid: livide.
lusty: vigoureux, robuste.
ogre: ogre.
oil: huile, graisser, pétrole.
timorously: de façon timorée, de manière timorée.
trembled: tremblé.
upward: ascendant, vers le haut.
vicinity: voisinage, environs, proximité.

The **click** of the pistol-cock finished the sentence. The **ruffian** halted. A glare of disappointed fury gave a **momentary lustre** to his dull eyes. "P'r'aps I shall meet you again one o' these days, or nights, and I shall know ye in ten thousand."

"Nothing like a bird in the hand, Master Grave-stealer. Where can we ever meet again?"

"P'r'aps in the fields, p'r'aps on the road, p'r'aps at the Old Bailey, p'r'aps at the gallows, p'r'aps in the convict-ship. I knows what that is! I was **chained** night and day once to a **chap** jist like you. Didn't I break his spurit; didn't I **spile** his sleep! Ho, ho! you looks a **bit** less varmently howdacious now, my flash cove!"

Varney hitherto had not known one **pang** of fear, one quicker beat of the heart before. But the image presented to his **irritable** fancy (always **prone** to **brood** over terrors),—the image of that companion chained to him night and day,—suddenly **quelled** his courage; the image stood before him **palpably** like the Oulos Oneiros,—the Evil Dream of the Greeks.

He breathed loud. The body-stealer's **stupid** sense saw that he had produced the usual effect of terror, which **gratified** his brutal self-esteem; he retreated slowly, inch by inch, to the door, followed by Varney's **appalled** and staring eye, and closed it with such violence that the candle was **extinguished**.

Varney, not daring,—yes, literally not daring,—to call aloud to Grabman for another light, crept down the dark stairs with hurried, ghostlike steps; and after **groping** at the door-handle with one hand, while the other grasped his pistol with a strain of horror, he succeeded at last in **winning access** to the street, and stood a moment to **collect** himself in the open air,—the damps upon his forehead, and his limbs trembling like one who has escaped by a hairbreadth the **crash** of a falling house.

French

access: accès, attaque, accéder, abord, entrée, impulsion, incitation, assaut.
appalled: consternai, épouvantâtes.
bit: morceau, bit, pièce, mors, fragment, pan, mordis, taillant, bout, embout.
brood: couvée, nichée, progéniture.
chained: enchaîné.
chap: individu, gercer, type, gerçure.
click: claquement, clic, déclic.
cliquer.
collect: recueillir, rassembler, collectionner, ramasser, assembler, encaisser.
crash: krach, fracas, s'écraser, accident.
extinguished: éteignîtes.
gratified: satisfîtes, gratifièrent, contentés.
groping: palpant, tâtant, tâtonnant.
irritable: irritable, irascible.
lustre: lustre, éclat.
momentary: momentané.
palpably: de façon palpable, de manière palpable.
pang: douleur.
prone: enclin.
quelled: étouffé.
ruffian: apache, brute, voyou.
spile: épite, fausset, goulotte, tuyau d'alimentation des sillons.
stupid: stupide, sot, idiot, bébête, bête, abruti.
winning: gagnant, remportant.

CHAPTER VII

THE RAPE OF THE MATTRESS

That Mr. Grabman slept calmly that night is probable enough, for his gin-bottle was empty the next morning; and it was with eyes more than usually heavy that he **dozily** followed the movements of Beck, who, according to custom, opened the **shutters** of the little den **adjoining** his sitting-room, brushed his **clothes**, made his fire, set on the **kettle** to **boil**, and laid his **breakfast** things, **preparatory** to his own departure to the duties of the day. **Stretching** himself, however, and shaking off **slumber**, as the **remembrance** of the enterprise he had undertaken glanced pleasantly across him, Grabman sat up in his bed and said, in a voice that, if not **maudlin**, was **affectionate**, and if not affectionate, was maudlin,—

"Beck, you are a good fellow. You have faults, you are human,— humanism est errare; which means that you some times **scorch** my **muffins**. But, take you all in all, you are a kind creature. Beck, I am going into the country for some days. I shall leave my key in the hole in the wall,—you know; take care of it when you come in. You were out late last night, my poor fellow. Very wrong! Look well to yourself, or who knows? You may be **clutched** by that **blackguard** resurrection-man, No. 7. Well, well, to think of that Jason's **foolhardiness**! But he's the worse devil of the two. Eh! what was

---

French

adjoining: adjacent, attenant, contigu, aboutissant.
affectionate: affectueux, tendre, attaché, dévoué, amoureux.
blackguard: canaille, vaurien.
boil: bouillir, furoncle.
breakfast: petit déjeuner, déjeuner, le petit déjeuner.
clothe: vêtir, vêtent, vêts, vêtons, habiller, revêtir.
clutched: agriffa, saisi.
dozily: de façon sommeillée.
foolhardiness: imprudence, témérité.
kettle: bouilloire, chaudron.
maudlin: larmoyant.
muffin: muffin.
preparatory: préparatoire.
remembrance: souvenir, mémoire.
scorch: roussir, brûler.
shutter: obturateur, volet.
slumber: dormir, sommeil.
stretching: étirement, câble de tension, extension des coutures, cintrage à plat, allongement, élasticité conférée, croquage.

I saying? And always give a look into my room every night before you go to **roost**. The place **swarms** with cracksmen, and one can't be too cautious. Lucky dog, you, to have nothing to be robbed of!"

Beck winced at that last remark. Grabman did not seem to notice his confusion, and proceeded, as he put on his stockings: "And, Beck, you are a good fellow, and have served me **faithfully**; when I come back, I will bring you something handsome,—a backey-box or—who knows?—a beautiful silver watch. Meanwhile, I think—let me see—yes, I can give you this elegant pair of small-clothes. Put out my best,—the black ones. And now, Beck, I'll not keep you any longer."

The poor sweep, with many pulls at his forelock, acknowledged the munificent donation; and having finished all his **preparations**, hastened first to his room, to **examine** at leisure, and with great admiration, the **drab** small-clothes. "Room," indeed, we can scarcely style the wretched enclosure which Beck called his own. It was at the top of the house, under the roof, and hot— oh, so hot—in the summer! It had one small begrimed window, through which the light of heaven never came, for the **parapet**, beneath which ran the **choked** gutter, prevented that; but the rain and the wind came in. So sometimes, through four glassless frames, came a fugitive tom-cat. As for the rats, they held the place as their own. Accustomed to Beck, they cared nothing for him.

They were the Mayors of that Palace; he only le roi faineant. They ran over his bed at night; he often felt them on his face, and was convinced they would have **eaten** him, if there had been anything worth **eating** upon his bones; still, perhaps out of **precaution** rather than charity, he generally left them a **potato** or two, or a **crust** of bread, to take off the **edge** of their appetites. But Beck was far better off than most who occupied the various settlements in that Alsatia,—he had his room to himself. That was necessary to his sole luxury,—the **inspection** of his **treasury**, the safety of his mattress; for it he paid, without **grumbling**, what he thought was a very high **rent**. To this hole in the roof there was no lock,—for a very good reason, there was no door to it. You went up a ladder, as you would go into a **loft**. Now, it had

French

choked: étouffé, étranglé, choké.
crust: croûte, abaisse.
drab: terne, gris.
eaten: mangé, bouffé.
eating: mangeant, bouffant.
edge: bord, rive, lisière, arête, tranche, affiler, carre, rebord.
examine: examiner, explorer, fouiller, reconnaître, rechercher, vérifier, inspecter.
faithfully: de façon fidèle, de manière fidèle, fidèlement, loyalement.
grumbling: grognon, rouspétance.
inspection: inspection, contrôle.
loft: grenier, angle d'ouverture, coup bombé, empêchement libre, gonflant, lober, reconverti, séchoir à l'air.
parapet: balustrade, parapet, rampe.
potato: pomme de terre, patate.
precaution: précaution.
preparation: préparation, rédaction, prise d'élan, établissement, élaboration, agréage.
rent: loyer, louer, location.
roost: perchoir, se jucher.
swarm: grouiller, essaim, fourmiller.
treasury: trésorerie, fisc, ministère du Revenu.

often been matter of much intense cogitation to Beck whether or not he should have a door to his chamber; and the result of the cogitation was **invariably** the same,—he dared not! What should he want with a door,—a door with a lock to it? For one followed as a consequence to the other. Such a novel **piece** of grandeur would be an **ostentatious advertisement** that he had something to guard. He could have no pretence for it on the ground that he was intruded on by neighbours; no step but his own was ever caught by him ascending that ladder; it led to no other room. All the offices required for the lodgment he performed himself. His supposed poverty was a better **safeguard** than doors of iron. Besides this, a door, if dangerous, would be superfluous; the moment it was suspected that Beck had something worth guarding, that moment all the **picklocks** and skeleton keys in the neighbourhood would be in a **jingle**. And a cracksman of high **repute** lodged already on the ground-floor. So Beck's treasure, like the bird's nest, was deposited as much out of sight as his instinct could **contrive**; and the locks and **bolts** of **civilized** men were equally **dispensed** with by bird and Beck.

On a rusty nail the sweep suspended the drab small-clothes, stroked them down lovingly, and murmured, "They be 's too good for I; I should like to **pop** 'em! But vould n't that be a shame? Beck, be n't you be a hungrateful **beast** to go for to think of nothin' but the tin, ven your 'art ought to varm with hemotion? I vill vear 'em ven I vaits on him. Ven he sees his own smalls bringing in the **muffins**, he will say, 'Beck, you **becomes** 'em!'"

Fraught with this noble resolution, the sweep caught up his broom, crept down the ladder, and with a furtive glance at the door of the room in which the cracksman lived, let himself out and shambled his way to his crossing. Grabman, in the mean while, dressed himself with more care than usual, **shaved** his beard from a four days' **crop**, and while seated at his breakfast, read attentively over the notes which Varney had left to him, pausing at times to make his own pencil memoranda. He then **packed** up such few **articles** as so **moderate** a **worshipper** of the Graces might **require**, deposited them in an old blue brief-bag, and this done, he opened his door, and

French

advertisement: annonce, publicité, réclame.
article: article, objet, chose.
beast: bête, animal, grosse fusée.
becomes: devient.
bolt: boulon, verrouiller, pêne, cheville.
civilized: civilisé, poli, cultivé.
contrive: inventer.
crop: récolte, jabot, rogner, couper, lot de gemmage.
dispensed: dispensé.

invariably: invariablement, de façon invariable, de manière invariable.
jingle: tinter, sonal.
moderate: modéré, ralentir, raisonnable, abordable, retenir.
muffin: muffin.
ostentatious: prétentieux, ostentatoire.
packed: emballé, monté sous boîtier, tassé, bourré.
picklock: crocheteur, rossignol.

piece: pièce, morceau, fragment, part, pan, contingent.
pop: dépiler, sauter, pop, petit coup de mine.
repute: réputation, renommée.
require: exiger, requérir, demander, réclamer, avoir besoin de.
safeguard: sauvegarde, garantie.
shaved: rasé, rasai, rasâmes, rasèrent, écroûté.
worshipper: adorateur.

creeping to the threshold, listened carefully. Below, a few sounds might be heard,—here, the **wail** of a child; there, the shrill scold of a woman in that accent above all others adapted to scold,—the Irish. Farther down still, the deep bass oath of the **choleric** resurrection-man; but above, all was silent. Only one floor **intervened** between Grabman's apartment and the ladder that led to Beck's loft. And the inmates of that room gave no sound of life. Grabman took courage, and **shuffling** off his shoes, ascended the stairs; he passed the closed door of the room above; he seized the ladder with a shaking hand; he mounted, step after step; he stood in Beck's room.

Now, O Nicholas Grabman! some **moralists** may be **harsh** enough to condemn thee for what thou art doing,—kneeling yonder in the dim light, by that curtainless **pallet**, with greedy fingers feeling here and there, and a placid, self-hugging smile upon thy pale lips. That poor **vagabond** whom thou art about to **despoil** has served thee well and faithfully, has borne with thine ill-humours, thy sarcasms, thy swearings, thy kicks, and **buffets**; often, when in the **bestial** sleep of **drunkenness** he has found thee stretched **helpless** on thy floor, with a kindly hand he has moved away the sharp **fender**, too near that knavish head, now bent on his ruin, or closed the open window, lest the keen air, that thy breath tainted, should visit thee with rheum and fever. Small has been his guerdon for uncomplaining sacrifice of the few hours spared to this weary **drudge** from his daily toil,—small, but **gratefully** received. And if Beck had been taught to pray, he would have prayed for thee as for a good man, O miserable sinner! And thou art going now, Nicholas Grabman, upon an enterprise which promises thee large gains, and thy purse is filled; and thou wantest nothing for thy wants or thy swinish luxuries. Why should those shaking fingers **itch** for the poor beggar-man's hoards?

But hadst thou been bound on an errand that would have given thee a million, thou wouldst not have left unrifled that secret **store** which thy prying eye had discovered, and thy hungry heart had coveted. No; since one night,—fatal, alas! to the owner of loft and treasure, when, **needing** Beck for some service, and **fearing** to call aloud (for the resurrection-man in the floor

French

bestial: bestial.
buffet: buffet, bar.
choleric: cholérique, colérique.
despoil: spolie.
drudge: trimer, peiner, bête de somme.
drunkenness: ivresse, ivrognerie.
fearing: craignant.
fender: défense, aile, rehausse, rambarde de traînage.
gratefully: de manière reconnaissante, avec reconnaissance, de façon reconnaissante.
harsh: vulgaire, rude, grossier, rustique, maussade, dur, acerbe, astringent, âpre.
helpless: impuissant, abandonné, faible, délaissé.
intervened: intervînmes.
itch: démanger, prurit.
moralist: moraliste.
needing: nécessitant.
pallet: palette, soupape, tringle de clouage, petite planche dont se sert le colleur, ancre, levée, filet à dorer.
shuffling: réarrangement, entrelacement.
store: magasin, boutique, stocker, entreposer, mémoire, emmagasiner, ôter, enlever, réserve, dépôt, conserver.
vagabond: vagabond, clochard, chemineau.
wail: se lamenter, gémir.

below thee, whose oaths even now **ascend** to thine ear, sleeps ill, and has threatened to make thee **mute** forever if thou disturbest him in the few nights in which his dismal calling **suffers** him to sleep at all), thou didst creep up the ladder, and didst see the unconscious **miser** at his nightly work, and after the sight didst steal down again, smiling,—no; since that night, no schoolboy ever more **rootedly** and ruthlessly set his mind upon nest of **linnet** than thine was set upon the stores in Beck's mattress.

And yet why, O lawyer, should rigid moralists blame thee more than such of thy **tribe** as live, honoured and respectable, upon the frail and the poor? Who among them ever left loft or mattress while a rap could be **wrung** from either? Matters it to Astraea whether the **spoliation** be made thus **nakedly** and briefly, or by all the acknowledged forms in which, **item** on item, six-and-eightpence on six-and-eightpence, the **inexorable** hand closes at length on the last farthing of **duped** despair? Not—Heaven forbid!—that we make thee, foul Nicholas Grabman, a type for all the class called attorneys-at-law! Noble hearts, **liberal** minds, are there amongst that brotherhood, we know and have experienced; but a type art thou of those whom want and error and need have proved—alas! too well—the lawyers of the poor. And even while we write, and even while ye read, many a Grabman steals from helpless **toil** the savings of a life.

Ye poor hoards,—darling delights of your otherwise joyless owner,—how easily has his very fondness made ye the prey of the **spoiler**! How **gleefully**, when the pence swelled into a shilling, have they been exchanged into the new bright piece of silver, the newest and brightest that could be got; then the shillings into crowns, then the crowns into gold,—got slyly and at a distance, and contemplated with what **rapture**; so that at last the **total** lay **manageable** and light in its **radiant** compass. And what a total! what a surprise to Grabman! Had it been but a sixpence, he would have taken it; but to grasp sovereigns by the **handful**, it was too much for him; and as he rose, he positively laughed, from a sense of fun.

But amongst his **booty** there was found one thing that specially moved his **mirth**: it was a child's **coral**, with its little bells. Who could have given

French

ascend: monter, se soulever.
booty: butin.
coral: corail, de corail.
duped: dupé.
gleefully: de façon joyeuse, de manière joyeusese.
handful: poignée.
inexorable: inexorable.
item: article, item, individu, élément, entité, point, rubrique, poste.
liberal: libéral, généreux.
linnet: linotte.
manageable: maniable, conciliant.
mirth: gaieté, allégresse.
miser: avare, ladre.
mute: muet, sourdine, commutateur de sourdine.
nakedly: de façon nue, de manière nue.
radiant: rayonnant, radieux.
rapture: ravissement.
rootedly: de façon enracinée, de manière enracinée.
spoiler: déporteur, spoiler, déflecteur.
spoliation: pillage.
suffers: souffre, subit.
toil: labeur, travailler dur.
total: total, additionner.
tribe: peuplade.
wrung: tordu, essoré.

Beck such a bauble, or how Beck could have refrained from turning it into money, would have been a fit matter for speculation. But it was not that at which Grabman chuckled; he laughed, first because it was an **emblem** of the utter **childishness** and folly of the creature he was leaving penniless, and secondly, because it furnished his ready wit with a capital contrivance to shift Beck's indignation from his own shoulders to a party more **liable** to suspicion. He left the coral on the floor near the bed, stole down the ladder, reached his own room, took up his brief-bag, locked his door, slipped the key in the rat-hole, where the **trusty**, **plundered** Beck alone could find it, and went boldly **downstairs**; passing **successively** the doors within which still stormed the resurrection-man, still wailed the child, still shrieked the Irish **shrew**, he paused at the ground-floor occupied by Bill the cracksman and his long-fingered, slender, quick-eyed **imps**, trained already to pass through broken window-panes, on their precocious progress to the **hulks**.

The door was open, and gave a pleasant sight of the worthy family within. Bill himself, a stout-looking fellow with a florid, **jolly** countenance, and a pipe in his mouth, was **sitting** at his window, with his **brawny** legs **lolling** on a table covered with the remains of a very tolerable breakfast. Four small Bills were employed in certain sports which, no doubt, according to the fashionable mode of education, instilled useful lessons under the artful **guise** of playful amusement. Against the wall, at one corner of the room, was **affixed** a row of bells, from which were suspended **exceedingly** tempting **apples** by slender wires. Two of the boys were engaged in the innocent **entertainment** of **extricating** the apples without occasioning any alarm from the bells; a third was amusing himself at a table, covered with mock rings and trinkets, in a way that seemed really **surprising**; with the end of a finger, dipped probably in some **glutinous** matter, he just touched one of the gewgaws, and lo, it vanished!—vanished so **magically** that the quickest eye could scarcely trace whither; sometimes up a cuff, sometimes into a shoe,—here, there, anywhere, except back again upon the table. The **fourth**, an urchin **apparently** about five years old,—he might be much younger, **judging** from his stunted size; somewhat older, judging from the vicious

French

affixed: apposé.
apparently: apparemment, évidemment, de façon apparente, de manière apparente.
apple: pomme, la pomme.
brawny: musculeux.
childishness: enfantillage.
downstairs: dessous, en bas.
emblem: emblème.
entertainment: divertissement, amusement, distraction.
exceedingly: extrêmement, de façon excédante, de manière excédante.
extricating: dégageant.
fourth: quatrième, quart.
glutinous: glutineux.
guise: apparence.
hulk: ponton.
imp: lutin, diablotin.
jolly: gai, enjoué, joyeux.
judging: jugement, taxation.
liable: responsable, assujetti, passible.
lolling: pendant.
magically: de façon magique, de manière magique.
plundered: pillé.
shrew: mégère, musaraigne.
sitting: couvant, séance, s'asseyant, service, sédentaire.
successively: de façon successive, de manière successive, successivement.
surprising: surprenant, étonnant.
trusty: sûr, loyal.

acuteness of his face,—on the floor under his father's chair, was **diving** his little hand into the **paternal** pockets in search for a marble sportively **hidden** in those **capacious** recesses. On the rising **geniuses** around him Bill the cracksman looked, and his father's heart was proud. Pausing at the threshold, Grabman looked in and said **cheerfully**, "Good-day to you; good-day to you all, my little dears."

"Ah, Grabman," said Bill, rising, and making a bow,—for Bill valued himself much on his politeness,—"come to blow a cloud, eh? Bob," this to the eldest born, "manners, sir; **wipe** your nose, and set a chair for the **gent**."

"Many **thanks** to you, Bill, but I can't stay now; I have a long journey to take. But, **bless** my soul, how stupid I am! I have forgotten my clothes-brush. I knew there was some thing on my mind all the way I was coming downstairs. I was saying, 'Grabman, there is something forgotten!'"

"I know what that 'ere feelin' is," said Bill, **thoughtfully**; "I had it myself the night afore last; and sure enough, when I got to the—. But that's neither here nor there. Bob, run upstairs and **fetch** down Mr. Grabman's clothes-brush. 'T is the least you can do for a gent who saved your father from the fate of them 'ere innocent apples. Your fist, Grabman. I have a heart in my buzzom; cut me open, and you will find there 'Halibi, and Grabman!' Give Bob your key."

"The brush is not in my room," answered Grabman; "it is at the top of the house, up the ladder, in Beck's loft,—Beck, the **sweeper**. The stupid dog always keeps it there, and forgot to give it me. Sorry to occasion my friend Bob so much trouble."

"Bob has a soul above trouble; his father's heart beats in his buzzom. Bob, track the **dancers**. Up like a **lark**, and down like a dump."

Bob grinned, made a **mow** at Mr. Grabman, and scampered up the stairs.

"You never **attends** our free-and-easy," said Bill; "but we **toasts** you with three times three, and up standing. "'T is a hungrateful world! But some men has a heart; and to those who has a heart, Grabman is a trump!"

French

acuteness: intensité, acuité.
attends: assiste, soigne.
bless: bénir.
capacious: vaste.
cheerfully: de manière gaie, de façon gaie.
dancer: danseur.
diving: plongée.
fetch: apporter, amener, amènes, hente, aller chercher.
geniuses: génies.
gent: monsieur.
hidden: caché, dissimulé, masqué.
lark: alouette, blague.
mow: faucher, tas de balles.
paternal: paternel.
sweeper: balayeuse, arrière latéral, bétonneur, libero, verrouilleur, analyseur panoramique.
thanks: remercie, merci.
thoughtfully: de façon réfléchie, de manière réfléchie.
toast: toast, griller, rôtir, pain grillé.
wipe: essuyer, effacer.

"I am sure, whenever I can do you a service, you may **reckon** on me. Meanwhile, if you could get that **cursed bullying** fellow who lives under me to be a little more civil, you would **oblige** me."

"Under you? No. 7? No. 7, is it? Grabman, h-am I a man? Is this a h-arm, and this a **bunch** of fives? I dares do all that does become a man; but No. 7 is a body-snatcher! No. 7 has **bullied** me, and I bore it! No. 7 might whop me, and this h-arm would let him whop! He lives with **graves** and churchyards and **stiff** 'uns, that damnable No. 7! Ask some'at else, Grabman. I dares not touch No. 7 any more than the ghostesses."

Grabman **sneered** as he saw that **Bill**, stout **rogue** as he was, turned pale while he spoke; but at that moment Bob **reappeared** with the clothes-brush, which the ex-attorney thrust into his pocket, and shaking Bill by the hand, and patting Bob on the head, he set out on his journey.

Bill reseated himself, **muttering**, "Bully a body-snatcher! Drot that Grabman, does he want to get rid of poor Bill?"

Meanwhile Bob exhibited slyly, to his second brother, the sight of Beck's stolen **coral**. The children took care not to show it to their father. They were already inspired by the **laudable ambition** to set up in business on their own account.

French

ambition: ambition, souhait, aspiration.
bill: bec, addition, note, facture, billet, projet de loi, traite, ticket, effet, proposition de loi, lettre de change.
bullied: brutalisâmes.
bullying: brutalisant, intimidation.
bunch: botte, bouquet, paquet, tas.
coral: corail, de corail.
cursed: maudit.
grave: tombe, grave, sérieux.
laudable: louable.
muttering: barbotant.
oblige: obliger.
reappeared: reparûmes, réapparu.
reckon: calculer, estimer.
rogue: gredin, canaille, fripon, polisson, escroc.
sneered: ricané.
stiff: rigide, raide.

CHAPTER VIII

PERCIVAL VISITS LUCRETIA

Having once **ascertained** the house in which Helen lived, it was no difficult matter for St. John to learn the name of the guardian whom Beck had supposed to be her mother. No common delight **mingled** with Percival's **amaze** when in that name he recognized one borne by his own **kinswoman**. Very little indeed of the family history was known to him. Neither his father nor his mother ever willingly **conversed** of the fallen heiress,—it was a subject which the children had felt to be **proscribed**; but in the neighbourhood, Percival had of course heard some mention of Lucretia as the haughty and accomplished Miss Clavering, who had, to the astonishment of all, stooped to a mesalliance with her uncle's French librarian. That her loss of the St. John property, the **succession** of Percival's father, were unexpected by the **villagers** and **squires** around, and perhaps set down to the **caprice** of Sir Miles, or to an **intellect** impaired by **apoplectic attacks**, it was not likely that he should have heard. The rich have the polish of their education, and the poor that instinctive **tact**, so **wonderful** amongst the **agricultural peasantry**, to prevent such **unmannerly** disclosures or unwelcome hints; and both by rich and poor, the Vernon St. Johns were too popular and respected for **wanton allusions** to subjects calculated to pain

---

French

agricultural: agricole, agronomique, agrarien.
allusion: allusion.
amaze: étonner, stupéfier, abasourdis.
apoplectic: apoplectique.
ascertained: constatai.
attack: attaque, assaut, accès, agression.
caprice: caprice.
conversed: conversé.
intellect: intellect, esprit, raison.
kinswoman: parente.
mingled: mélangeâtes, mêlé, mêlâtes, mêlas, mêlèrent.
peasantry: paysannerie.
proscribed: proscrivirent.
squire: chaperonner, châtelain.
succession: succession.
tact: tact, mesure.
unmannerly: mal élevé.
villager: villageois.
wanton: dévergondé, impudique, licencieux.
wonderful: merveilleux, formidable.

them. All, therefore, that Percival knew of his relation was that she had **resided** from infancy with Sir Miles; that after their uncle's death she had married an inferior in rank, of the name of Dalibard, and settled abroad; that she was a person of peculiar manners, and, he had heard **somewhere**, of rare gifts. He had been unable to learn the name of the young lady **staying** with Madame Dalibard; he had learned only that she went by some other name, and was not the daughter of the lady who **rented** the house. Certainly it was possible that this last might not be his kinswoman, after all. The name, though strange to English ears, and not common in France, was no sufficient warrant for Percival's high spirits at the thought that he had now won legitimate and regular access to the house; still, it allowed him to call, it furnished a fair excuse for a visit.

How long he was at his **toilet** that day, poor boy! How **sedulously**, with **comb** and brush, he sought to smooth into straight precision that **luxuriant labyrinth** of **jetty** curls, which had never cost him a thought before! Gil Blas says that the toilet is a pleasure to the young, though a labour to the old; Percival St. John's toilet was no pleasure to him that anxious morning.

At last he tore himself, dissatisfied and desperate, from the glass, caught his hat and his whip, threw himself on his horse, and rode, at first very fast, and at last very slowly, to the old, **decayed**, shabby, neglected house that lay hid, like the poverty of fallen pride, amidst the trim villas and **smart** cottages of fair and **flourishing** Brompton.

The same servant who had opened the gate to Ardworth appeared to his summons, and after eying him for some moments with a **listless**, stupid stare, said: "You'll be after some mistake!" and turned away.

"Stop, stop!" cried Percival, trying to intrude himself through the gate; but the servant **blocked** up the entrance **sturdily**. "It is no mistake at all, my good lady. I have come to see Madame Dalibard, my—my relation!"

"Your relation!" and again the woman stared at Percival with a look through the dull **vacancy** of which some **distrust** was **dimly perceptible**. "**Bide** a bit there, and give us your name."

French

bide: attendent.
blocked: bloqué.
comb: peigne, crête, rayon.
decayed: délabré, caduc, infirme, vieux, carié, pourri.
dimly: de façon faible, de manière faible.
distrust: méfiance, se méfier, défiance.
flourishing: florissant, prospérant.
jetty: jetée, débarcadère, embarcadère.
labyrinth: labyrinthe, dédale.
listless: apathique, indifférent.
luxuriant: luxuriant, exubérant.
perceptible: perceptible, apercevable.
rented: loué, louèrent, accensa.
resided: résidâmes, demeurai.
sedulously: de façon assidue, de manière assidue.
smart: rusé, intelligent, malin, astucieux, artificieux, roublard, dégourdi, habile.
somewhere: quelque part.
staying: restant, chaînage, entretoisement, étayage, haubanant, séjournant.
sturdily: de façon robuste, de manière robuste.
toilet: toilette, cabinet.
vacancy: vacance, poste vacant.

Percival gave his **card** to the servant with his sweetest and most **persuasive** smile. She took it with one hand, and with the other turned the key in the gate, leaving Percival **outside**. It was five minutes before she returned; and she then, with the same **prim**, smileless expression of countenance, opened the gate and motioned him to follow.

The kind-hearted boy sighed as he cast a glance at the **desolate** and poverty-stricken appearance of the house, and thought within himself: "Ah, pray Heaven she may be my relation; and then I shall have the right to find her and that sweet girl a very different home!" The old woman threw open the drawing-room door, and Percival was in the presence of his **deadliest** foe! The armchair was turned towards the entrance, and from amidst the coverings that hid the form, the remarkable countenance of Madame Dalibard emerged, sharp and earnest, **directly fronting** the intruder.

"So," she said slowly, and, as it were, **devouring** him with her keen, **steadfast** eyes, — "so you are Percival St. John! Welcome! I did not know that we should ever meet. I have not sought you, you seek me! Strange—yes, strange—that the young and the rich should seek the suffering and the poor!"

Surprised and embarrassed by this singular greeting, Percival halted abruptly in the middle of the room; and there was something **inexpressibly** winning in his shy, yet graceful confusion. It seemed, with silent **eloquence**, to **apologize** and to **deprecate**. And when, in his silvery voice, scarcely yet **tuned** to the fulness of **manhood**, he said feelingly, "Forgive me, madam, but my mother is not in England," the excuse evinced such delicacy of idea, so exquisite a sense of high breeding, that the calm assurance of worldly ease could not have more **attested** the **chivalry** of the native gentleman.

"I have nothing to forgive, Mr. St. John," said Lucretia, with a softened manner. "Pardon me rather that my **infirmities** do not allow me to rise to receive you. This seat, — here, — next to me. You have a strong **likeness** to your father."

French

apologize: s'excuser, excusez.
attested: attesta.
card: carte, fiche, carde.
chivalry: chevalerie.
deadliest: le plus mortel.
deprecate: désapprouver.
desolate: sombre, désolé, morne.
devouring: dévorant, engloutissant.
directly: directement, debout, sans détour, de manière directe, de façon directe.
eloquence: éloquence.
fronting: façade, diffusion frontale.
inexpressibly: de façon inexprimable, de manière inexprimable.
infirmity: infirmité.
likeness: ressemblance, similitude, portrait.
manhood: virilité, âge d'homme.
outside: dehors, extérieur, en dehors de, à l'extérieur.
persuasive: persuasif, convaincant.
prim: collet monté, guindé.
steadfast: ferme, inébranlable, constant.
tuned: accordé.

Percival received this last remark as a compliment, and bowed. Then, as he lifted his ingenuous brow, he took for the first time a steady view of his new-found relation. The **peculiarities** of Lucretia's countenance in youth had naturally deepened with middle age. The **contour**, always too sharp and pronounced, was now strong and **bony** as a man's; the line between the eyebrows was **hollowed** into a **furrow**. The eye retained its old uneasy, sinister, sidelong glance, or at rare moments (as when Percival entered), its searching penetration and assured command; but the **eyelids** themselves, red and **injected**, as with grief or **vigil**, gave something **haggard** and wild, whether to glance or gaze. Despite the paralysis of the frame, the face, though pale and thin, showed no bodily **decay**. A vigour **surpassing** the strength of woman might still be seen in the play of the bold **muscles**, the **firmness** of the contracted lips. What physicians call "vitality," and trace at once (if experienced) on the **physiognomy** as the **prognostic** of long life, undulated **restlessly** in every aspect of the face, every movement of those thin, nervous hands, which, contrasting the rest of that motionless form, never seemed to be at rest. The teeth were still white and regular, as in youth; and when they shone out in **speaking**, gave a strange, **unnatural** freshness to a face otherwise so worn.

As Percival gazed, and, while gazing, saw those wandering eyes bent down, and yet felt they watched him, a **thrill** almost of fear shot through his heart. Nevertheless, so much more **impressionable** was he to **charitable** and **trustful** than to suspicious and timid emotions that when Madame Dalibard, suddenly looking up and shaking her head gently, said, "You see but a sad wreck, young **kinsman**," all those instincts, which Nature itself seemed to dictate for self-preservation, vanished into heavenly tenderness and pity.

"Ah!" he said, rising, and pressing one of those deadly hands in both his own, while tears rose to his eyes, — "Ah! since you call me kinsman, I have all a kinsman's privileges. You must have the best advice, the most skilful surgeons. Oh, you will recover; you must not despond."

Lucretia's lips moved **uneasily**. This kindness took her by surprise. She turned **desperately** away from the human gleam that shot across the

French

bony: osseux, plein d'os, maigre, décharné.
charitable: indulgent, sensible.
contour: contour, courbe de niveau.
decay: abaissement, pourriture, déclin, désastre, décomposition, se délabrer, carie.
desperately: de façon désespérée, de manière désespérée, désespérément.
eyelid: paupière, déflecteur.
firmness: fermeté, résistance.
furrow: sillon, ride, raie.
haggard: hâve, blème, égaré, maigre.
hollowed: cavèrent, cavées, cava.
impressionable: impressionnable.
injected: injectai, réinjectas.
kinsman: parent.
muscle: muscle, le muscle.
peculiarity: particularité, bizarrerie, singularité.
physiognomy: physionomie.
prognostic: pronostique.
restlessly: de façon remuante, de manière remuante.
speaking: parlant.
surpassing: surpassant, dépassant, maîtrisant.
thrill: frémissement, frisson, tressaillement.
trustful: confiant.
uneasily: de façon inquiète, de manière inquiète.
unnatural: anormal, contre nature.
vigil: veille, vigile.

sevenfold gloom of her soul. "Do not think of me," she said, with a forced smile; "it is my **peculiarity** not to like **allusion** to myself, though this time I provoked it. Speak to me of the old cedar-trees at Laughton,—do they stand still? You are the master of Laughton now! It is a noble heritage!"

Then St. John, thinking to please her, talked of the old manor-house, described the **improvements** made by his father, spoke gayly of those which he himself contemplated; and as he ran on, Lucretia's brow, a moment ruffled, grew smooth and **smoother**, and the gloom settled back upon her soul.

All at once she interrupted him. "How did you discover me? Was it through Mr. Varney? I bade him not mention me: yet how else could you learn?" As she spoke, there was an anxious trouble in her tone, which increased while she observed that St. John looked confused.

"Why," he began **hesitatingly**, and brushing his hat with his hand, "why—perhaps you may have heard from the—that is—I think there is a young—. Ah, it is you, it is you! I see you once again!" And **springing** up, he was at the side of Helen, who at that instant had entered the room, and now, her eyes **downcast**, her cheeks **blushing**, her breast gently **heaving**, heard, but answered not that passionate burst of joy.

Startled, Madame Dalibard (her hands firmly grasping the sides of her chair) contemplated the two. She had heard nothing, guessed nothing of their former meeting. All that had passed before between them was unknown to her. Yet there was evidence unmistakable, **conclusive**: the son of her despoiler loved the daughter of her rival; and—if the virgin heart speaks by the outward sign—those downcast eyes, those blushing cheeks, that heaving breast, told that he did not love in vain!

Before her **lurid** and **murderous** gaze, as if to **defy** her, the two **inheritors** of a revenge unglutted by the grave stood, **united mysteriously** together. Up, from the vast ocean of her hate, rose that poor **isle** of love; there, unconscious of the horror around them, the victims found their footing! How beautiful at that hour their youth; their very ignorance of their own

---

French

allusion: allusion.
blushing: rougissant, voile d'un film, ternissement dû à l'eau, opalescence, louchissement, formation d'un voile.
conclusive: concluant, décisif, convaincant.
defy: défier, provoquer.
downcast: abattu, abaissé, baissé.
heaving: pilonnement, gonflement.
hesitatingly: de façon hésitante, de manière hésitante.
improvement: amélioration, perfectionnement.
inheritor: héritier.
isle: île, îlot.
lurid: aigu, acéré, âcre, rude, tranchant, piquant, coupant, aigre, perçant.
murderous: meurtrier, homicide.
mysteriously: de manière mystérieuse, de façon mystérieuse.
peculiarity: particularité, bizarrerie, singularité.
sevenfold: septuple.
smoother: lisseuse.
springing: naissance, sautage par mines pochées, gauchissement, détente mécanique, compensation, bondir, agrandissement par explosion du fond d'un trou de mine, retombée.
united: unit, unîtes, uni, unîmes, unirent, unis, apparîâmes.

emotions; their **innocent gladness**; their **sweet** trouble! The fell gazer drew a long **breath** of fiendlike complacency and **glee**, and her hands **opened wide**, and then **slowly closed**, as if she felt them in her **grasp**.

French

breath: souffle, haleine, respiration, le souffle.
closed: fermas, clos.
emotion: émotion, attendrissement, sentiment.
gladness: joie, allégresse.
glee: joie.
grasp: saisir, agripper, empoigner, compréhension, prise, étreindre.
innocent: innocent.
opened: ouvert, ouvrîmes.
slowly: lentement, de façon lente, de manière lente, doucement.
sweet: sucré, doux, suave, bonbon, friandise, gentil, dessert.
wide: large, ample, étendu, vaste, grand.

CHAPTER IX

THE ROSE BENEATH THE UPAS

And from that day Percival had his privileged **entry** into Madame Dalibard's house. The little narrative of the circumstances connected with his first meeting with Helen, partly drawn from Percival, partly afterwards from Helen (with **blushing** and **faltered** excuses from the latter for not having mentioned before an **incident** that might, perhaps **needlessly**, **vex** or alarm her aunt in so delicate a state of health), was received by Lucretia with rare **graciousness**. The connection, not only between herself and Percival, but between Percival and Helen, was allowed and even dwelt upon by Madame Dalibard as a natural reason for **permitting** the **artless intimacy** which immediately sprang up between these young persons. She permitted Percival to call daily, to remain for hours, to share in their simple meals, to **wander** alone with Helen in the garden, assist her to **bind** up the **ragged** flowers, and sit by her in the old ivy-grown **arbour** when their work was done. She affected to look upon them both as children, and to leave to them that happy **familiarity** which childhood only **sanctions**, and compared to which the affection of maturer years seems at once **coarse** and cold.

As they grew more familiar, the **differences** and **similarities** in their characters came out, and nothing more delightful than the harmony into

---

French

arbour: tonnelle.
artless: ingénu, sans art, naïf, naturel.
bind: attacher, lier, relier, nouer.
blushing: rougissant, voile d'un film, ternissement dû à l'eau, opalescence, louchissement, formation d'un voile.
coarse: grossier, vulgaire, rude, rustique, brut.
difference: différence, divergence.
entry: entrée, inscription, présentation, article, écriture, introduction.
faltered: hésitai, chancelâmes.
familiarity: familiarité.
graciousness: élégance, grâce.
incident: incident, événement, pollution accidentelle.
intimacy: intimité.
needlessly: de façon inutile, de manière inutile, inutilement.
permitting: permettant.
ragged: déchiqueté, déguenillé, dépenaillé, ébavuré, en haillons, en lambeaux, loqueteux.
sanction: sanction.
similarity: similarité, ressemblance.
vex: chagriner, vexer, vexons.
wander: errer, errons, vaguer, rôder, voyager au loin, dérapage, vagabonder.

which even the contrasts **blended** ever invited the guardian angel to pause and smile. As flowers in some trained **parterre** relieve each other, now softening, now **heightening**, each several hue, till all unite in one **concord** of interwoven beauty, so these two blooming natures, brought together, seemed, where varying still, to **melt** and **fuse** their affluences into one wealth of innocence and sweetness. Both had a native buoyancy and cheerfulness of spirit, a noble trustfulness in others, a singular candour and freshness of mind and feeling. But beneath the gayety of Helen there was a soft and holy under-stream of thoughtful melancholy, a high and **religious** sentiment, that **vibrated** more **exquisitely** to the subtle mysteries of **creation**, the solemn **unison** between the bright world without and the grave destinies of that world within (which is an imperishable soul), than the **lighter** and more vivid **youthfulness** of Percival had yet conceived. In him lay the germs of the active mortal who might win distinction in the bold career we run upon the surface of the earth. In her there was that finer and more **spiritual essence** which lifts the poet to the golden atmosphere of dreams, and reveals in glimpses to the saint the **choral** Populace of Heaven. We do not say that Helen would ever have found the **utterance** of the poet, that her reveries, undefined and unanalyzed, could have taken the sharp, clear form of words; for to the poet practically developed and made manifest to the world, many other gifts besides the mere **poetic** sense are needed,—stern study, and **logical** generalization of scattered truths, and patient observation of the characters of men, and the wisdom that comes from sorrow and passion, and a sage's experience of things actual, embracing the dark secrets of human infirmity and crime. But despite all that has been said in **disparagement** or disbelief of "mute, **inglorious** Miltons," we maintain that there are natures in which the divinest element of poetry exists, the purer and more delicate for escaping from bodily form and **evaporating** from the coarser vessels into which the poet, so called, must pour the ethereal **fluid**. There is a certain virtue within us, **comprehending** our subtlest and noblest emotions, which is poetry while untold, and grows pale and poor in proportion as we strain it into poems. Nay, it may be said of this airy property of our **inmost** being

---

French

blended: mélangé.
choral: chorale.
comprehending: comprenant.
concord: accord, concorde.
creation: création, établissement, constitution.
disparagement: dénigrement, dépréciation.
essence: essence.
evaporating: s'évaporant, évaporant.
exquisitely: de manière exquise, de façon exquise.
fluid: fluide, liquide, flot, coulant.
fuse: fusible, mèche, cordeau, fusée.
heightening: aggravant, rehaussant.
inglorious: déshonorant.
inmost: le plus profond.
lighter: briquet, allège, allumeur, péniche.
logical: logique.
melt: fondre, dégeler, faire fondre, fonte.
parterre: parterre.
poetic: poétique.
religious: religieux, dévot.
spiritual: spirituel, ecclésiastique, religieux.
unison: unisson, harmonie.
utterance: expression, déclaration.
vibrated: vibrèrent, trépidâmes.
youthfulness: fraîcheur, jeunesse, juvénilité.

that, more or less, it departs from us according as we give it forth into the world, even, as only by the loss of its **particles**, the rose wastes its **perfume** on the air. So this more spiritual sensibility dwelt in Helen as the **latent mesmerism** in water, as the invisible fairy in an **enchanted** ring. It was an essence or **divinity**, shrined and **shrouded** in herself, which gave her more intimate and **vital** union with all the influences of the universe, a companion to her loneliness, an angel hymning low to her own listening soul. This made her enjoyment of Nature, in its merest trifles, exquisite and profound; this gave to her tenderness of heart all the **delicious** and **sportive variety** love borrows from imagination; this lifted her **piety** above the mere forms of conventional **religion**, and breathed into her prayers the **ecstasy** of the saint.

But Helen was not the less filled with the sweet humanities of her age and sex; her very gravity was **tinged** with rosy light, as a **western** cloud with the sun. She had sportiveness and **caprice**, and even whim, as the butterfly, though the **emblem** of the soul, still **flutters wantonly** over every wildflower, and **expands** its glowing wings on the sides of the beaten road. And with a sense of weakness in the common world (growing out of her very strength in nobler atmospheres), she leaned the more **trustfully** on the strong arm of her young **adorer**, not fancying that the difference between them arose from superiority in her; but rather as a bird, once **tamed**, flies at the sight of the **hawk** to the breast of its owner, so from each airy flight into the loftier heaven, let but the thought of danger **daunt** her wing, and, as in a more powerful nature, she took refuge on that **fostering** heart.

The love between these children—for so, if not literally in years, in their newness to all that steals the freshness and the dew from maturer life they may be rightly called—was such as befitted those whose souls have not **forfeited** the Eden. It was more like the love of fairies than of human beings. They showed it to each other **innocently** and frankly; yet of love as we of the grosser creation call it, with its impatient pains and burning hopes, they never spoke nor dreamed. It was an **unutterable**, ecstatic fondness, a clinging to each other in thought, desire, and heart, a joy more than mortal in

French

adorer: adorateur.
caprice: caprice.
daunt: intimide, découragez.
delicious: délicieux, savoureux.
divinity: divinité, théologie.
ecstasy: extase, ecstasie.
emblem: emblème.
enchanted: enchanté.
expands: développe, mousse.
flutter: voltiger, scintillement, flottement, flirter, voleter, flutter, battement, conter fleurette,
chevrotement, pleurage.
forfeited: forfaits, perdu.
fostering: encourager.
hawk: autour, colporter, faucon.
innocently: de manière innocente, innocemment, de façon innocente.
latent: latent, caché.
mesmerism: mesmérisme.
particle: particule, grain.
perfume: parfum, le parfum.
piety: piété.
religion: religion, confession, culte.
shrouded: enveloppé.
sportive: sportif, folâtre.
tamed: apprivoisé.
tinged: teinté.
trustfully: de façon confiante, de manière confiante.
unutterable: inexprimable.
variety: variété, diversité.
vital: vital.
wantonly: de façon dévergondée, de manière dévergondée.
western: occidental, western.

each other's presence; yet, in parting, not that idle and empty sorrow which unfits the weak for the homelier demands on time and life, and this because of the wondrous trust in themselves and in the future, which made a main part of their **credulous**, happy natures. Neither felt fear nor jealousy, or if jealousy came, it was the pretty, childlike jealousies which have no sting,—of the bird, if Helen listened to its note too long; of the flower, if Percival left Helen's side too quickly to **tie** up its drooping **petals** or **refresh** its **dusty** leaves. Close by the stir of the great city, with all its fret and **chafe** and storm of life, in the desolate garden of that sombre house, and under the withering eyes of relentless Crime, **revived** the Arcady of old,—the scene **vocal** to the **reeds** of idyllist and **shepherd**; and in the midst of the iron Tragedy, harmlessly and unconsciously arose the strain of the Pastoral Music.

It would be a vain effort to describe the state of Lucretia's mind while she watched the progress of the affection she had favoured, and gazed on the spectacle of the fearless happiness she had **promoted**. The image of a **felicity** at once so great and so holy wore to her gloomy sight the aspect of a mocking Fury. It rose in contrast to her own ghastly and crime-stained life; it did not **upbraid** her conscience with guilt so **loudly** as it scoffed at her intellect for folly. These children, playing on the verge of life, how much more of life's true secret did they already know than she, with all her vast native powers and wasted **realms** of blackened and charred experience! For what had she studied, and **schemed**, and calculated, and toiled, and sinned? As a conqueror stricken unto death would render up all the **regions vanquished** by his sword for one drop of water to his burning lips, how **gladly** would she have given all the knowledge bought with blood and fire, to feel one moment as those children felt! Then, from out her silent and grim despair, stood forth, fierce and **prominent**, the great fiend, Revenge.

By a **monomania** not uncommon to those who have made self the centre of being, Lucretia **referred** to her own sullen history of wrong and passion all that bore **analogy** to it, however distant. She had never been enabled, without an intolerable pang of hate and envy, to contemplate **courtship** and love in others. From the rudest shape to the most refined, that master-

French

analogy: analogie.
chafe: frictionner, irriter, raguer, s'irriter, user.
courtship: cour, balz.
credulous: crédule.
dusty: poussiéreux.
felicity: félicité.
gladly: volontiers, avec plaisir, de façon joyeuse, de manière joyeuse.
loudly: fort, à haute voix, bruyamment, de façon forte, de manière forte.

monomania: monomanie.
petal: pétale.
prominent: proéminent, marquant.
promoted: promu, favorisai.
realm: règne, royaume, puissance, domaine.
reed: roseau, anche, peigne.
referred: référé, déféré, adresser.
refresh: rafraîchir, actualiser.
region: région, contrée, district, zone.
revived: ranimai, revivifièrent,

ravivèrent, réanima, aviva, ragaillardîmes.
schemed: comploté.
shepherd: berger, pasteur, pâtre, soigner.
tie: cravate, attacher, lien, nouer, relier, lier, tirant, liaison, traverse.
upbraid: morigénez, réprimandons.
vanquished: vainquîtes.
vocal: vocal.

passion in the existence, at least of woman,—reminding her of her own brief **episode** of human tenderness and devotion,—opened every wound and **wrung** every **fibre** of a heart that, while crime had **indurated** it to most emotions, memory still left **morbidly** sensitive to one. But if tortured by the sight of love in those who had had no connection with her fate, who stood apart from her lurid **orbit** and were gazed upon only afar (as a lost soul, from the abyss, sees the gleam of angels' wings within some planet it never has explored), how **ineffably** more fierce and intolerable was the wrath that seized her when, in her haunted imagination, she saw all Susan's **rapture** at the vows of Mainwaring mantling in Helen's face! All that might have **disarmed** a heart as hard, but less diseased, less **preoccupied** by revenge, only **irritated** more the **consuming** hate of that inexorable spirit. Helen's **seraphic** purity, her exquisite, overflowing kindness, ever forgetting self, her airy **cheerfulness**, even her very moods of melancholy, calm and seemingly causeless as they were, perpetually galled and **blistered** that **writhing**, **preternatural** susceptibility which is formed by the consciousness of **infamy**, the dreary **egotism** of one cut off from the charities of the world, with whom all mirth is **sardonic convulsion**, all sadness rayless and unresigned despair.

Of the two, Percival inspired her with feelings the most akin to humanity. For him, despite her bitter memories of his father, she felt something of compassion, and shrank from the touch of his frank hand in remorse. She had often need to whisper to herself that his life was an obstacle to the heritage of the son of whom, as we have seen, she was in search, and whom, indeed, she believed she had already found in John Ardworth; that it was not in wrath and in vengeance that this victim was to be swept into the grave, but as an indispensable sacrifice to a cherished object, a determined policy. As, in the studies of her youth, she had adopted the Machiavelism of ancient State-craft as a **rule admissible** in private life, so she seemed scarcely to admit as a crime that which was but the removal of a **barrier** between her aim and her end. Before she had become **personally** acquainted with Percival she had rejected all occasion to know him. She had suffered Varney

French

admissible: recevable, admissible.
barrier: barrière, bar, obstacle.
blistered: cloqué.
cheerfulness: gaieté, bonne humeur.
consuming: consommant.
convulsion: convulsion, bouleversement.
disarmed: désarmai.
egotism: égotisme, égoïsme.
episode: épisode.
fibre: fibre, brin, nerf, filament, enveloppe cellulosique.
indurated: induré.
ineffably: de façon ineffable, de manière ineffable.
infamy: infamie.
irritated: irrité, énervèrent, agacé.
morbidly: de façon morbide, de manière morbide.
orbit: orbite, mettre en orbite, graviter sur une orbite, satelliser.
personally: personnellement, de façon personnelle, de manière personnelle.
preoccupied: préoccupèrent.
preternatural: surnaturel.
rapture: ravissement.
rule: règle, gouverner, régner, règne, surveiller, tenue, commandement, filet, régler.
sardonic: sardonique.
seraphic: séraphique.
writhing: contorsions.
wrung: tordu, essoré.

to call upon him as the old protege of Sir Miles, and to wind into his intimacy, **meaning** to leave to her accomplice, when the hour should arrive, the dread task of destruction. This not from cowardice, for Gabriel had once rightly described her when he said that if she lived with shadows she could **quell** them, but **simply** because, more intellectually **unsparing** than **constitutionally** cruel (save where the old vindictive memories thoroughly unsexed her), this was a victim whose pangs she desired not to witness, over whose fate it was no luxury to **gloat** and revel. She wished not to see nor to know him living, only to learn that he was no more, and that Helen alone stood between Laughton and her son. Now that he had himself, as if with **predestined** feet, crossed her threshold, that he, like Helen, had delivered himself into her toils, the hideous guilt, before removed from her hands, became haunting, fronted her face to face, and filled her with a superstitious awe.

Meanwhile, her outward manner to both her **meditated** victims, if moody and **fitful** at times, was not such as would have provoked suspicion even in less credulous hearts. From the first entry of Helen under her roof she had been formal and measured in her welcome,—kept her, as it were, aloof, and affected no prodigal superfluity of **dissimulation**; but she had never been positively harsh or **unkind** in word or in deed, and had coldly **excused** herself for the repulsiveness of her manner.

"I am irritable," she said, "from long suffering, I am **unsocial** from habitual solitude; do not expect from me the fondness and warmth that should belong to our **relationship**. Do not **harass** yourself with vain **solicitude** for one whom all seeming attention but **reminds** more painfully of infirmity, and who, even thus stricken down, would be independent of all cares not bought and paid for. Be satisfied to live here in all **reasonable** liberty, to follow your own habits and caprices **uncontrolled**. Regard me but as a piece of necessary furniture. You can never **displease** me but when you **notice** that I live and suffer."

If Helen wept **bitterly** at these hard words when first spoken, it was not with anger that her loving heart was so thrown back upon herself. On the

---

French

bitterly: amèrement, de manière amère, de façon amère.
constitutionally: de façon constitutionnelle, de manière constitutionnelle.
displease: déplaire, mécontentons, contrarier.
dissimulation: dissimulation.
excused: excusé.
fitful: irrégulier.
gloat: jubiler, exulter.
harass: harceler, tracasser, troubler, déranger l'adversaire, tourmenter.
meaning: signification, sens, intention, importance, dessein, propos.
meditated: méditâtes, songea.
notice: avis, remarquer, apercevoir, préavis, discerner, placard, saisir, renseignement, réflexion, percevoir, observation.
predestined: prédestinâtes.
quell: étouffer, suffoquer.
reasonable: raisonnable, modéré, prudent, abordable.
relationship: relation, parenté, rapport.
remind: rappeler.
simply: simplement, de façon simple, de manière simple.
solicitude: sollicitude.
uncontrolled: incontrôlé.
unkind: maussade, méchant, peu aimable.
unsocial: antisocial.
unsparing: prodigue, généreux.

contrary, she became inspired with a compassion so great that it took the character of reverence. She regarded this very coldness as a **mournful** dignity. She felt grateful that one who could thus dispense with, should yet have sought her. She had heard her mother say that she had been under great obligations to Lucretia; and now, when she was forbidden to repay them even by a kiss on those weary eyelids, a daughter's hand to that sleepless pillow; when she saw that the barrier first imposed was irremovable, that no time **diminished** the distance her aunt set between them, that the least approach to the tenderness of service beyond the most **casual** offices really seemed but to fret those **excitable** nerves, and fever the hand that she ventured **timorously** to clasp,—she retreated into herself with a sad **amaze** that increased her pity and heightened her respect. To her, love seemed so necessary a thing in the **helplessness** of human life, even when blessed with health and youth, that this **rejection** of all love in one so bowed and crippled, struck her imagination as something sublime in its dreary grandeur and **stoic** pride of independence. She regarded it as of old a tender and pious **nun** would have regarded the **asceticism** of some **sanctified** recluse,—as Theresa (had she lived in the same age) might have regarded Saint Simeon Stylites existing aloft from human sympathy on the **roofless** summit of his column of stone; and with this feeling she sought to inspire Percival. He had the heart to enter into her compassion, but not the imagination to **sympathize** with her reverence. Even the **repugnant** awe that he had first conceived for Madame Dalibard, so bold was he by temperament, he had long since cast off; he recognized only the **moroseness** and **petulance** of an habitual invalid, and shook **playfully** his **glossy** curls when Helen, with her sweet **seriousness**, **insisted** on his recognizing more.

To this house few, indeed, were the visitors admitted. The Miverses, whom the benevolent officiousness of Mr. Fielden had **originally** sent **thither** to see their young **kinswoman**, now and then came to press Helen to join some party to the theatre or Vauxhall, or a picnic in Richmond Park; but when they found their **overtures**, which had at first been politely accepted by

---

French

amaze: étonner, stupéfier, abasourdis.
asceticism: ascétisme, ascèse.
casual: désinvolte, accidentel, informel, occasionnel.
diminished: diminuèrent, décrus.
excitable: excitable, impressionnable.
glossy: lustré, vernissé, luisant, glacée, éclatant, brillant.
helplessness: impuissance, vulnérabilité, misère.

insisted: insistai, aheurté.
kinswoman: parente.
moroseness: morosité.
mournful: morne, sombre, mélancolique, triste.
nun: nonne, religieuse.
originally: de façon originale, de manière originale.
overture: ouverture.
petulance: irritabilité.
playfully: de manière espiègle, de façon espiègle.

rejection: rejet, refus.
repugnant: répugnant, inconciliable.
roofless: sans toit.
sanctified: sanctifia.
seriousness: sérieux, gravité.
stoic: stoïque.
sympathize: compatir, sympathisez.
thither: là.
timorously: de façon timorée, de manière timorée.

Madame Dalibard, were rejected, they gradually ceased their visits, wounded and indignant.

Certain it was that Lucretia had at one time eagerly caught at their well-meant **civilities** to Helen,—now she as abruptly **declined** them. Why? It would be hard to **plumb** into all the black secrets of that heart. It would have been but natural to her, who shrank from dooming Helen to no worse **calamity** than a virgin's grave, to have designed to throw her into such **uncongenial** guidance, amidst all the **manifold** temptations of the corrupt city,—to have suffered her to be seen and to be ensnared by those gallants ever on the watch for defenceless beauty; and to contrast with their elegance of **mien** and fatal **flatteries** the **grossness** of the companions selected for her, and the unloving discomfort of the home into which she had been thrown. But now that St. John had appeared, that Helen's heart and fancy were steeled alike against more dangerous temptation, the object to be obtained from the pressing courtesy of Mrs. Mivers existed no more. The vengeance flowed into other channels.

The only other visitors at the house were John Ardworth and Gabriel Varney.

Madame Dalibard watched **vigilantly** the countenance and manner of Ardworth when, after presenting him to Percival, she whispered: "I am glad you assured me as to your sentiments for Helen. She had found there the lover you wished for her,—'gay and handsome as herself.'"

And in the sudden **paleness** that overspread Ardworth's face, in his compressed lips and **convulsive** start, she read with **unspeakable** rage the **untold** secret of his heart, till the rage gave way to complacency at the thought that the last insult to her wrongs was spared her,—that her son (as son she believed he was) could not now, at least, be the **successful suitor** of her **loathed** sister's loathed child. Her discovery, perhaps, confirmed her in her countenance to Percival's **progressive wooing**, and half reconciled her to the **pangs** it inflicted on herself.

French

calamity: calamité, plaie, fléau.
civility: civilité.
convulsive: convulsif, spasmodique.
declined: déclina, dépéri.
flattery: flatterie, adulation.
grossness: grossièreté.
loathed: abominâtes, haï, haïtes, haïrent, abhorrai, haïs, haïmes.
manifold: multiple, manifold, divers, clarinette, tubulure, variété, distributeur.
mien: mine.
paleness: pâleur.
pang: douleur.
plumb: sonder, plomb.
progressive: progressif, évolutif.
successful: réussi, prospère, couronné de succès.
suitor: prétendant, soupirant.
uncongenial: antipathique.
unspeakable: indicible, indescriptible, innommable.
untold: jamais dévoilé.
vigilantly: de façon vigilante, de manière vigilante.
wooing: courtisant.

At the first introduction Ardworth had scarcely glanced at Percival. He regarded him but as the sleek flutterer in the **sunshine** of fortune. And for the idle, the gay, the fair, the well-dressed and wealthy, the sturdy **workman** of his own rough way felt something of the **uncharitable** disdain which the **laborious** have-nots too usually entertain for the prosperous haves. But the moment the unwelcome intelligence of Madame Dalibard was conveyed to him, the smooth-faced boy swelled into dignity and importance.

Yet it was not merely as a rival that that strong, manly heart, after the first natural agony, regarded Percival. No, he looked upon him less with anger than with interest,—as the one in whom Helen's happiness was henceforth to be invested. And to Madame Dalibard's astonishment,—for this nature was wholly new to her experience,—she saw him, even in that first interview, **composing** his rough face to smiles, smoothing his bluff, **imperious** accents into courtesy, listening patiently, watching **benignly**, and at last **thrusting** his large hand frankly forth, griping Percival's slender fingers in his own; and then, with an **indistinct** chuckle that seemed half laugh and half groan, as if he did not dare to trust himself further, he made his **wonted unceremonious** nod, and strode hurriedly from the room.

But he came again and again, almost daily, for about a **fortnight**. Sometimes, without entering the house, he would join the young people in the garden, assist them with awkward hands in their playful work on the garden, or sit with them in the ivied **bower**; and **warming** more and more each time he came, talk at last with the **cordial frankness** of an elder brother. There was no disguise in this; he began to love Percival,—what would seem more strange to the superficial, to admire him. Genius has a quick perception of the moral qualities; genius, which, **differing** thus from mere talent, is more **allied** to the heart than to the head, **sympathizes genially** with goodness. Ardworth respected that young, ingenuous, unpolluted mind; he himself felt better and purer in its atmosphere. Much of the affection he cherished for Helen passed thus **beautifully** and **nobly** into his sentiments for the one whom Helen not **unworthily** preferred. And they grew so fond of

---

French

allied: allié, apparenté.
beautifully: de façon belle, de manière belle.
benignly: de manière Bénine, de façon Bénine.
bower: tonnelle, ancre de bossoir.
composing: composant, montage.
cordial: cordial, chaleureux.
differing: différant.
fortnight: quinzaine.
frankness: franchise.
genially: de manière génienne, de façon génienne.
imperious: impérieux.
indistinct: confus, touffu, trouble, indistinct.
laborious: laborieux, pénible.
nobly: noblement, de manière noble, de façon noble.
sunshine: soleil, lumière du soleil.
sympathize: compatir, sympathisez.
thrusting: persuasion.
unceremonious: brusque, sans façon.
uncharitable: peu charitable.
unworthily: de manière indigne, de façon indigne.
warming: chauffant, bassinant, échauffement, réchauffant.
wonted: habituel, accoutumé.
workman: ouvrier, homme d'équipe.

him,—as the young and gentle ever will grow fond of genius, however rough, once admitted to its companionship!

Percival by this time had recalled to his mind where he had first seen that strong-featured, dark-browed countenance, and he gayly **reminded** Ardworth of his **discourtesy**, on the brow of the hill which commanded the view of London. That **reminiscence** made his new friend **writhe**; for then, amidst all his ambitious visions of the future, he had seen Helen in the distance,—the reward of every labour, the fairest star in his horizon. But he **strove stoutly** against the regret of the **illusion** lost; the vivendi causae were left him still, and for the **nymph** that had **glided** from his clasp, he clung at least to the **laurel** that was left in her place. In the folds of his robust **fortitude** Ardworth thus wrapped his secret. Neither of his young playmates suspected it. He would have disdained himself if he had so poisoned their pleasure. That he suffered when alone, much and bitterly, is not to be denied; but in that masculine and **complete** being, Love took but its legitimate rank amidst the passions and cares of man. It soured no existence, it broke no heart; the wind swept some **blossoms** from the bough, and tossed wildly the agitated **branches** from root to summit, but the trunk stood firm.

In some of these visits to Madame Dalibard's, Ardworth **renewed** with her the more private conversation which had so **unsettled** his past convictions as to his birth, and so disturbed the calm, strong currents of his mind. He was chiefly anxious to learn what conjectures Madame Dalibard had formed as to his parentage, and what ground there was for belief that he was near in blood to herself, or that he was born to a station less dependent on **continuous** exertion; but on these points the dark sibyl preserved an **obstinate** silence. She was satisfied with the hints she had already thrown out, and absolutely refused to say more till better **authorized** by the inquiries she had set on foot. **Artfully** she turned from these topics of closer and more household interest to those on which she had **previously** insisted, connected with the general knowledge of mankind, and the complicated science of practical life. To fire his genius, wing his energies, **inflame** his ambition above that slow, laborious drudgery to which he had linked the chances of

---

French

artfully: de façon astucieuse, de manière astucieuse.
authorized: autorisai.
blossom: fleur, floraison, affleurement oxydé.
branch: branche, succursale, filiale, spécialité, rameau, domaine, bureau, embranchement, apophyse, ramification.
complete: complet, entier, remplir, finir, parfaire.
continuous: continu, permanent.
discourtesy: impolitesse.
fortitude: courage, force d'âme.
glided: glissa.
illusion: illusion, imagination.
inflame: enflammer, s'enflammer.
laurel: laurier.
nymph: nymphe.
obstinate: obstiné, têtu, tenace, entêté.
previously: auparavant, précédemment, autrefois, devant, avant, de façon précédente, de manière précédente, préalablement.
reminded: rappelèrent.
reminiscence: réminiscence.
renewed: renouvelèrent, reconduisit.
stoutly: de manière corpulente, de façon corpulente.
strove: combattirent.
unsettled: perturbé, incertain, variable, instable.
writhe: se débattre, se tordre.

his career, and which her fiery and rapid intellect was wholly unable to comprehend—save as a waste of life for uncertain and distant objects—became her task. And she saw with delight that Ardworth listened to her more assentingly than he had done at first. In truth, the pain shut within his heart, the **conflict** waged **keenly** between his reason and his passion, unfitted him for the time for mere mechanical employment, in which his genius could afford him no consolation. Now, genius is given to man, not only to **enlighten** others, but to comfort as well as to **elevate** himself. Thus, in all the sorrows of actual existence, the man is doubly inclined to turn to his genius for distraction. **Harassed** in this world of action, he **knocks** at the gate of that world of idea or fancy which he is privileged to enter; he escapes from the clay to the spirit. And rarely, till some great grief comes, does the man in whom the **celestial** fire is lodged know all the gift of which he is possessed. At last Ardworth's visits ceased abruptly. He shut himself up once more in his chambers; but the law books were laid aside.

Varney, who generally **contrived** to call when Ardworth was not there, seldom interrupted the lovers in their little **paradise** of the garden; but he took occasion to **ripen** and **cement** his intimacy with Percival. Sometimes he walked or (if St. John had his **cabriolet**) drove home and **dined** with him, tete-a-tete, in Curzon Street; and as he made Helen his chief subject of conversation, Percival could not but esteem him amongst the most agreeable of men. With Helen, when Percival was not there, Varney held some secret conferences,—secret even from Percival. Two or three times, before the hour in which Percival was accustomed to come, they had been out together; and Helen's face looked more cheerful than usual on their return. It was not surprising that Gabriel Varney, so **displeasing** to a man like Ardworth, should have won little less favour with Helen than with Percival; for, to say nothing of an ease and suavity of manner which stole into the confidence of those in whom to **confide** was a natural **propensity**, his various **acquisitions** and talents, imposing from the surface over which they spread, and the **glitter** which they made, had an inevitable effect upon a mind so susceptible as Helen's to admiration for art and respect for knowledge. But what chiefly

French

acquisition: acquisition, achat, prise en charge, emplette.
cabriolet: cabriolet.
celestial: céleste.
cement: ciment, mastic, souder, liant, dissolution, conglutiner, coller, cémenter, adhésif, scellement.
confide: confier.
conflict: conflit, combat.
contrived: inventâmes.
dined: dîné, dînèrent, dinâmes, dîna.
displeasing: déplaisant, mécontentant.
elevate: élever, hausser, élève.
enlighten: éclairer, illuminer.
glitter: briller, scintillement.
harassed: harcelâtes, tracassâtes.
keenly: de façon vive, de manière vive.
knock: frapper, coup, heurter, cogner.
paradise: paradis.
propensity: propension, prédisposition.
ripen: mûrir.

conciliated her to Varney, whom she regarded, **moreover**, as her aunt's most intimate friend, was that she was persuaded he was unhappy, and wronged by the world of fortune. Varney had a habit of so **representing** himself,—of dwelling with a bitter **eloquence**, which his natural **malignity** made **forcible**, on the **injustice** of the world to superior intellect. He was a great **accuser** of Fate. It is the **illogical** weakness of some evil natures to lay all their crimes, and the consequences of crime, upon Destiny. There was a **heat**, a vigour, a rush of words, and a readiness of strong, if **trite**, **imagery** in what Varney said that deceived the young into the monstrous error that he was an enthusiast,—misanthropical, perhaps, but only so from enthusiasm. How could Helen, whose slightest thought, when a star broke forth from the cloud, or a bird **sung** suddenly from the **copse**, had more of wisdom and of poetry than all Varney's **gaudy** and painted seemings ever could even mimic,—how could she be so deceived? Yet so it was. Here stood a man whose youth she supposed had been devoted to refined and **elevating** pursuits, **gifted**, neglected, disappointed, solitary, and unhappy. She saw little beyond. You had but to touch her pity to win her interest and to **excite** her trust. Of anything further, even had Percival never existed, she could not have dreamed. It was because a secret and **undefinable repugnance**, in the midst of pity, trust, and friendship, put Varney altogether out of the light of a possible lover, that all those sentiments were so easily **kindled**. This repugnance arose not from the **disparity** between their years; it was rather that **nameless uncongeniality** which does not forbid friendship, but is **irreconcilable** with love. To do Varney justice, he never offered to **reconcile** the two. Not for love did he secretly confer with Helen; not for love did his heart beat against the hand which **reposed** so carelessly on his murderous arm.

French

accuser: accusateur.
conciliated: concilié.
copse: taillis.
disparity: disparité, inégalité.
elevating: élevant, relevant, dressant.
eloquence: éloquence.
excite: exciter, irriter, agacer, hérisser.
forcible: de force, par force.
gaudy: voyant, criard.
gifted: doué, surdoué.

heat: chaleur, chauffer, ardeur, charge de fusion, rut.
illogical: illogique.
imagery: imagerie, cliché.
injustice: injustice, iniquité.
irreconcilable: irréconciliable, inconciliable.
kindled: allumâtes, enflammé.
malignity: malveillance, malignité.
moreover: en outre, d'ailleurs, en prime, et puis, de plus.
nameless: anonyme, inconnu.

reconcile: réconcilier, raccommode, se réconcilier, concilier, rapprochez.
reposed: reposé.
representing: représentant, figurant.
repugnance: répugnance, aversion.
sung: chanté.
trite: banal.
uncongeniality: incongénialité.
undefinable: indéfinissable.

CHAPTER X

THE RATTLE OF THE SNAKE

The progress of affection between natures like those of Percival and Helen, favoured by free and constant intercourse, was naturally rapid. It was scarcely five weeks from the day he had first seen Helen, and he already regarded her as his plighted bride. During the earlier days of his **courtship**, Percival, **enamoured** and absorbed for the first time in his life, did not **hasten** to make his mother the **confidante** of his happiness. He had written but twice; and though he said briefly, in the second letter, that he had discovered two relations, both **interesting** and one charming, he had **deferred naming** them or entering into detail. This not alone from that **indescribable coyness** which all have experienced in **addressing** even those with whom they are most intimate, in the early, half-unrevealed, and **mystic** emotions of first love, but because Lady Diary's letters had been so full of her sister's **declining** health, of her own anxieties and fears, that he had **shrunk** from giving her a new subject of anxiety; and a confidence full of hope and joy seemed to him **unfeeling** and unseasonable. He knew how necessarily uneasy and **restless** an **avowal** that his heart was seriously engaged to one she had never seen, would make that tender mother, and that his **confession** would rather add to her cares than **produce** sympathy with his **transports**.

French

addressing: adressage.
avowal: aveu, confession.
confession: confession, aveu.
confidante: confident.
courtship: cour, balz.
coyness: coquetterie.
declining: déclinant, dépérissant.
deferred: différé.
enamoured: épris.
hasten: hâter, hâtons.
indescribable: indescriptible.
interesting: intéressant, curieux, singulier.
mystic: mystique.
naming: nomination, tests d'appellation, nommage, dénomination.
produce: produire, réaliser, fabriquer.
restless: remuant, agité.
shrunk: rétréci, retrait.
transport: transporter, reporter.
unfeeling: insensible.

But now, feeling impatient for his mother's assent to the formal proposals which had become due to Madame Dalibard and Helen, and taking advantage of the letter last received from her, which gave more **cheering** accounts of her sister, and expressed curiosity for further explanation as to his half disclosure, he wrote at length, and cleared his breast of all its secrets. It was the same day in which he wrote this confession and pleaded his cause that we accompany him to the house of his sweet mistress, and leave him by her side, in the accustomed garden. Within, Madame Dalibard, whose chair was set by the window, bent over certain letters, which she took, one by one, from her desk and read slowly, lifting her eyes from time to time and glancing towards the young people as they walked, hand in hand, round the small demesnes, now hid by the fading **foliage**, now **emerging** into view. Those letters were the early love-epistles of William Mainwaring. She had not **recurred** to them for years. Perhaps she now felt that food necessary to the sustainment of her **fiendish** designs. It was a strange spectacle to see this being, so full of vital energy, **mobile** and restless as a **serpent**, condemned to that helpless **decrepitude**, **chained** to the uneasy seat, not as in the resigned and passive **imbecility** of extreme age, but rather as one whom in the prime of life the **rack** has broken, leaving the limbs **inert**, the mind active, the form as one dead, the heart with **superabundant** vigour,—a, cripple's **impotence** and a Titan's will! What, in that dreary **imprisonment** and amidst the silence she habitually preserved, passed through the **caverns** of that breast, one can no more **conjecture** than one can count the **blasts** that sweep and rage through the hollows of impenetrable **rock**, or the elements that conflict in the bosom of the **volcano**, **everlastingly** at work. She had read and replaced the letters, and leaning her cheek on her hand, was gazing **vacantly** on the wall, when Varney intruded on that dismal solitude.

He closed the door after him with more than usual care; and drawing a seat close to Lucretia, said, "Belle-mere, the time has arrived for you to act; my part is wellnigh closed."

"Ay," said Lucretia, wearily, "what is the news you bring?"

French

blast: souffle, explosion, coup de mine, faire sauter.
cavern: caverne, antre.
chained: enchaîné.
cheering: ovations.
conjecture: conjecturer, prévoir, se douter de.
decrepitude: décrépitude.
emerging: émergeant, surgissant.
everlastingly: de façon éternelle, de manière éternelle.
fiendish: diabolique.
foliage: feuillage.
imbecility: imbécillité.
impotence: impuissance, impotence.
imprisonment: emprisonnement, incarcération.
inert: inerte, matière inerte, rendre incomburant.
mobile: mobile, nomade.
rack: crémaillère, grille, étagère, casier, râtelier, arack, armoire, bâti, chevalet, claie.
recurred: revenu, revînmes, revint, reparu.
rock: roche, bercer, balancer, roc, basculer.
serpent: serpent.
superabundant: surabondant.
vacantly: de façon vide, de manière vide.
volcano: volcan, artifice pour l'imitation des éruptions volcaniques.

"First," replied Varney, and as he spoke, he shut the window, as if his whisper could possibly be heard without,—"first, all this business connected with Helen is at length arranged. You know when, **agreeably** to your permission, I first suggested to her, as it were **casually**, that you were so reduced in fortune that I trembled to regard your future; that you had years ago **sacrificed** nearly half your **pecuniary** resources to maintain her parents,—she of herself reminded me that she was entitled, when of age, to a sum far **exceeding** all her wants, and—"

"That I might be a **pensioner** on the child of William Mainwaring and Susan Mivers," interrupted Lucretia. "I know that, and **thank** her not. Pass on."

"And you know, too, that in the course of my conversation with the girl I let out also **incidentally** that, even so, you were dependent on the chances of her life; that if she died (and youth itself is **mortal**) before she was of age, the sum left her by her grandfather would **revert** to her father's family; and so, by hints, I drew her on to ask if there was no mode by which, in case of her death, she might **insure subsistence** to you. So that you see the whole scheme was made at her own **prompting**. I did but, as a man of business, suggest the means,—an **insurance** on her life."

"Varney, these details are hateful. I do not doubt that you have done all to **forestall** inquiry and **elude** risk. The girl has insured her life to the amount of her fortune?"

"To that amount only? Pooh! Her death will buy more than that. As no one single office will insure for more than 5,000 pounds, and as it was easy to persuade her that such offices were liable to **failure**, and that it was usual to insure in several, and for a larger amount than the sum desired, I got her to enter herself at three of the principal offices. The amount paid to us on her death will be 15,000 pounds. It will be paid (and here I have followed the best legal advice) in trust to me for your **benefit**. Hence, therefore, even if our researches fail us, if no son of yours can be found, with sufficient evidence to prove, against the keen interests and bought **advocates** of heirs-

---

French

advocate: avocat, défenseur, préconiser.
agreeably: agréablement, de façon agréable, de manière agréable.
benefit: avantage, bénéfice, prestation, intérêt, gain, allocation, profit, indemnité.
casually: de façon désinvolte, de manière désinvolte.
elude: éluder, éviter, déjouent.
exceeding: dépassant, excédant, maîtrisant, outrepassant.
failure: défaillance, échec, panne, manque, dérangement, banqueroute, avortement, insuccès, faillite, avarie, rupture.
forestall: anticiper, devancer, empêcher, prévenir.
incidentally: incidemment, de façon incidente, de manière incidente.
insurance: assurance.
insure: assurer, s'assurer.
mortal: mortel.
pecuniary: financier, pécuniaire.
pensioner: pensionné, retraité, titulaire d'une pension.
prompting: assistance par programme souffleur, incitation, proposition, sollicitation de l'opérateur.
revert: revenir, reviens.
sacrificed: sacrifié.
subsistence: subsistance.
thank: remercier, merci.

at-law, the right to Laughton, this girl will repay us well, will replace what I have taken, at the risk of my neck, perhaps,—certainly at the risk of the hulks,—from the capital of my uncle's legacy, will **refund** what we have spent on the inquiry; and the **residue** will secure to you an independence **sufficing** for your wants almost for life, and to me what will purchase with economy," and Varney smiled, "a year or so of a gentleman's idle pleasures. Are you satisfied thus far?"

"She will die happy and innocent," muttered Lucretia, with the **growl** of **demoniac disappointment**.

"Will you wait, then, till my **forgery** is detected, and I have no power to buy the silence of the trustees,—wait till I am in **prison**, and on a trial for life and death? Reflect, every day, every hour, of delay is **fraught** with **peril**. But if my safety is nothing compared to the refinement of your revenge, will you wait till Helen marries Percival St. John? You start! But can you suppose that this innocent love-play will not pass **rapidly** to its **denouement**? It is but **yesterday** that Percival **confided** to me that he should write this very day to his mother, and communicate all his feelings and his hopes; that he **waited** but her assent to propose formally for Helen. Now one of two things must **happen**. Either this mother, haughty and vain as lady-mothers mostly are, may refuse consent to her son's marriage with the daughter of a **disgraced** banker and the niece of that Lucretia Dalibard whom her husband would not admit beneath his roof—"

"Hold, sir!" exclaimed Lucretia, **haughtily**; and amidst all the passions that darkened her countenance and **degraded** her soul, some flash of her **ancestral** spirit shot across her brow. But it passed quickly, and she added, with fierce **composure**, "You are right; go on!"

"Either—and pardon me for an insult that comes not from me—either this will be the case: Lady Mary St. John will **hasten** back in alarm to London; she exercises **extraordinary** control over her son; she may withdraw him from us altogether, from me as well as you, and the occasion now presented to us may be lost (who knows?) forever,—or she may be a weak and fond woman;

French

ancestral: ancestral.
composure: repos, calme, impassibilité.
confided: confié.
degraded: dégrada, avilit.
demoniac: démoniaque.
denouement: dénouement.
disappointment: déception, désolation, peine, désappointement.
disgraced: disgraciâmes.
extraordinary: extraordinaire,
formidable, prodigieux, singulier.
forgery: falsification, faux, contrefaçon.
fraught: chargé, plein.
growl: grogner, râler, grondement.
happen: arriver, avoir lieu, advenir, advienne, devenir, se passer, intervenir.
hasten: hâter, hâtons.
haughtily: de façon hautaine, de manière hautaine.
peril: danger, péril.
prison: prison, geôle, maison centrale, pénitencier, établissement pénitentiaire.
rapidly: rapidement, de façon rapide, de manière rapide.
refund: remboursement, ristourne.
residue: résidu, données résiduelles, reliquat, reste.
sufficing: suffisant.
waited: attendîtes.
yesterday: hier.

may be detained in Italy by her sister's illness; may be anxious that the last **lineal descendant** of the St. Johns should marry betimes, and, moved by her darling's prayers, may consent at once to the union. Or a third course, which Percival thinks the most probable, and which, though most unwelcome to us of all, I had wellnigh forgotten, may be adopted. She may come to England, and in order to judge her son's choice with her own eyes, may withdraw Helen from your roof to hers. At all events, delays are dangerous,—dangerous, putting aside my personal interest, and **regarding** only your own object,—may bring to our acts new and searching eyes; may cut us off from the habitual presence either of Percival or Helen, or both; or surround them, at the first breath of illness, with **prying** friends and formidable **precautions**. The birds now are in our hands. Why then open the cage and bid them fly, in order to spread the **net**? This morning all the **final** documents with the Insurance Companies are completed. It remains for me but to pay the first **quarterly premiums**. For that I think I am prepared, without drawing further on your **hoards** or my own **scanty** resources, which Grabman will take care to **drain** fast enough."

"And Percival St. John?" said Madame Dalibard. "We want no idle sacrifices. If my son be not found, we need not that boy's ghost amongst those who **haunt** us."

"Surely not," said Varney; "and for my part, he may be more **useful** to me alive than dead. There is no insurance on his life, and a rich friend (credulous greenhorn that he is!) is scarcely of that flock of **geese** which it were wise to **slay** from the mere hope of a golden egg. Percival St. John is your victim, not mine; not till you give the order would I lift a finger to **harm** him."

"Yes, let him live, unless my son be found to me," said Madame Dalibard, almost exultingly,—"let him live to forget **yon** fair-faced fool, leaning now, see you, so **delightedly** on his arm, and fancying **eternity** in the hollow **vows** of love; let him live to wrong and abandon her by **forgetfulness**, though even in the grave; to laugh at his boyish dreams,—to **sully** her memory in the arms of **harlots**! Oh, if the dead can suffer, let him

French

delightedly: de façon enchantée, de manière enchantée.
descendant: descendant.
drain: drainer, assécher, vidange, purge, faire écouler, égout, écoulement, évacuer, tuyau d'écoulement, vider.
eternity: éternité.
final: finale, définitif, appel, dernier.
forgetfulness: oubli, manque de mémoire.

geese: oies.
harlot: prostituée.
harm: nuire, préjudice, mal, tort, endommager.
haunt: hanter, fréquenter.
hoard: amas, thésaurisation, stocker, trésor.
lineal: linéal, direct.
net: filet, réseau, net.
precaution: précaution.
premium: prime, récompense, prix, agio.

prying: fureteur, indiscret.
quarterly: trimestriel, revue trimestrielle, publication trimestrielle.
regarding: considérant, concernant.
scanty: insuffisant, chiche.
slay: tuer, tuons, tuez, tues, tue, tuent, abattre, rectifier.
sully: souiller.
useful: utile, pratique.
vow: voeu, vouer, serment.
yon: y, là.

live, that she may feel beyond the **grave** his **inconstancy** and his fall. Methinks that that thought will **comfort** me if Vincent be no more, and I stand **childless** in the world!"

"It is so **settled**, then," said Varney, ever ready to **clinch** the business that promised gold, and **relieve** his **apprehensions** of the **detection** of his **fraud**. "And now to your **noiseless** hands, as soon as may be, I **consign** the girl; she has lived long enough!"

French

apprehension: appréhension, arrestation, inquiétude.
childless: sans enfant.
clinch: river, accrochage, coussin de jante, étalingure.
comfort: confort, consoler, réconfort.
consign: consigner, expédier.
detection: détection, dépistage, découverte.
fraud: fraude, escroquerie, tromperie, imposture, dol, filouterie.
grave: tombe, grave, sérieux.
inconstancy: inconstance, instabilité.
noiseless: silencieux, antisouffle.
relieve: soulager, relayer.
settled: réglé, sédimenté, déposé, tassé, vida, vidâmes, vidé, vidèrent, colonisa, domicilié, arrangé.

CHAPTER XI

LOVE AND INNOCENCE

During this conference between these **execrable** and **ravening** birds of night and prey, Helen and her boy-lover were thus **conversing** in the garden; while the autumn sun—for it was in the second week of October—broke **pleasantly** through the **yellowing** leaves of the **tranquil shrubs**, and the flowers, which should have died with the gone **summer**, still fresh by tender care, despite the **lateness** of the season, smiled **gratefully** as their light **footsteps** passed.

"Yes, Helen," said Percival,—"yes, you will love my mother, for she is one of those people who seem to attract love, as if it were a property **belonging** to them. Even my dog Beau (you know how fond Beau is of me!) always **nestles** at her feet when we are at home. I own she has pride, but it is a pride that never **offended** any one. You know there are some flowers that we call proud. The pride of the flower is not more **harmless** than my mother's. But perhaps pride is not the right word,—it is rather the **aversion** to anything low or mean, the admiration for everything pure and high. Ah, how that very pride—if pride it be—will make her love you, my Helen!"

"You need not tell me," said Helen, smiling seriously, "that I shall love your mother,—I love her already; **nay**, from the first moment you said you

---

French

aversion: aversion, antipathie.
belonging: appartenant, coefficient d'appartenance.
conversing: conversant.
execrable: exécrable.
footstep: pas, marche.
gratefully: de manière reconnaissante, avec reconnaissance, de façon reconnaissante.
harmless: inoffensif, anodin, innocent.
lateness: retard.
nay: non.
nestle: se nicher, se pelotonner.
offended: offensas, insultèrent.
pleasantly: agréablement, de manière agréable, de façon agréable.
ravening: vorace, rapace.
shrub: arbuste, arbrisseau.
summer: été, estival.
tranquil: tranquille, calme, paisible.
yellowing: jaunissement.

had a mother, my heart **leaped** to her. Your mother,—if ever you are really **jealous**, it must be of her! But that she should love me,—that is what I doubt and fear. For if you were my brother, Percival, I should be so ambitious for you. A **nymph** must rise from the stream, a sylphid from the rose, before I could allow another to **steal** you from my side. And if I think I should feel this only as your sister, what can be precious enough to **satisfy** a mother?"

"You, and you only," answered Percival, with his blithesome laugh,— "you, my sweet Helen, much better than nymph or sylphid, about whom, between ourselves, I never cared three straws, even in a poem. How pleased you will be with Laughton! Do you know, I was **lying** awake all last night to **consider** what room you would like best for your own? And at last I have **decided**. Come, listen,—it opens from the music-gallery that **overhangs** the hall. From the window you **overlook** the **southern** side of the **park**, and catch a view of the **lake** beyond. There are two **niches** in the wall,—one for your piano, one for your favourite books. It is just large enough to hold four persons with ease,—our mother and myself, your aunt, whom by that time we shall have petted into good humour; and if we can **coax** Ardworth there,—the best good fellow that ever lived,—I think our party will be complete. By the way, I am uneasy about Ardworth, it is so long since we have seen him; I have called three times,—nay, five,—but his odd-looking clerk always **swears** he is not at home. Tell me, Helen, now you know him so well,—tell me how I can serve him? You know, I am so **terribly** rich (at least, I shall be in a month or two), I can never get through my money, unless my friends will help me. And is it not **shocking** that that noble fellow should be so poor, and yet suffer me to call him 'friend,' as if in friendship one man should want everything, and the other nothing? Still, I don't know how to venture to propose. Come, you understand me, Helen; let us lay our wise heads together and make him well off, in spite of himself."

It was in this loose boyish talk of Percival that he had found the way, not only to Helen's heart, but to her soul. For in this she (grand, undeveloped poetess!) recognized a nobler poetry than we chain to rhythm,—the poetry of generous **deeds**. She **yearned** to kiss the warm hand she held, and drew

French

coax: cajoler, amadouer.
consider: considérer, contempler, regarder, envisager.
decided: décidai, incontestable, résolu, jugèrent, jugeâtes, jugé.
deed: acte, action.
jealous: jaloux.
lake: lac, laque.
leaped: sauté.
lying: menteur, mensonge, gisant.
niche: niche, microhabitat, lien écologique.

nymph: nymphe.
overhang: surplomber, débord, queue de vache, offre excédentaire, inclinaison de la ligne des dents, empilage en encorbellement, élancement, dépassement, saillie.
overlook: omettre, négliger, avoir vue sur.
park: parc, garer, stationner, clairière pastorale, parquer, se garer.

satisfy: satisfaire, contenter.
shocking: choquant, affreux, bouleversant, révoltant.
southern: austral, du sud, méridional.
steal: voler, dérober, dépouiller, subtiliser, d'acier.
swear: jurer, jurons, blasphémer, prêter serment.
terribly: terriblement, de façon terrible, de manière terrible.
yearned: soupiré, languîtes.

nearer to his side as she answered: "And sometimes, dear, dear Percival, you wonder why I would rather listen to you than to all Mr. Varney's bitter eloquence, or even to my dear cousin's **aspiring** ambition. They talk well, but it is of themselves; while you—"

Percival **blushed**, and checked her.

"Well," she said,—"well, to your question. Alas! you know little of my cousin if you think all our arts could **decoy** him out of his **rugged** independence; and much as I love him, I could not wish it. But do not fear for him; he is one of those who are born to succeed, and without help."

"How do you know that, pretty prophetess?" said Percival, with the superior air of manhood. "I have seen more of the world than you have, and I cannot see why Ardworth should succeed, as you call it; or, if so, why he should succeed less if he swung his **hammock** in a better **berth** than that hole in Gray's Inn, and would just let me keep him a **cab** and groom."

Had Percival talked of keeping John Ardworth an **elephant** and a palaquin, Helen could not have been more **amused**. She **clapped** her little hands in a delight that provoked Percival, and laughed out loud. Then, seeing her boy-lover's lip pouted **petulantly**, and his brow was **overcast**, she said, more seriously,—

"Do you not know what it is to feel convinced of something which you cannot explain? Well, I feel this as to my cousin's fame and fortunes. **Surely**, too, you must feel it, you **scarce** know why, when he speaks of that future which seems so **dim** and so far to me, as of something that belonged to him."

"Very true, Helen," said Percival; "he lays it out like the map of his estate. One can't laugh when he says so carelessly: 'At such an age I shall lead my **circuit**; at such an age I shall be rich; at such an age I shall enter **parliament**; and beyond that I shall look as yet—no farther.' And, poor fellow, then he will be forty-three! And in the mean while to suffer such **privations**!"

"There are no privations to one who lives in the future," said Helen, with that noble **intuition** into **lofty** natures which at times flashed from her

French

amused: amusèrent.
aspiring: aspirant, futur.
berth: couchette, poste à quai, accoster, zone d'arrêt, lit.
blushed: rougi.
cab: cabine, taxi.
circuit: circuit, maille.
clapped: claqua.
decoy: attirer, leurre, appât.
dim: faible, sombre, obscur, brouiller, rendre confus.
elephant: éléphant.

hammock: hamac, groupe d'activités.
intuition: intuition.
lofty: haut, élevé.
overcast: couvert, surjetai, surfiler, fonças, fonce.
parliament: parlement.
petulantly: de façon maussade, de manière maussade.
privation: privation.
rugged: robuste, raboteux, accidenté.

scarce: insuffisant, rare.
surely: sûrement, certes, si, d'abord, de façon sûre, de manière sûre.

childish simplicity, **foreshadowing** what, if Heaven spare her life, her maturer **intellect** may **develop**; "for Ardworth there is no such thing as poverty. He is as rich in his hopes as we are in—" She stopped short, blushed, and continued, with downcast looks: "As well might you pity me in these walks, so **dreary** without you. I do not live in them, I live in my thoughts of you."

Her voice trembled with emotion in those last words. She slid from Percival's arm, and **timidly** sat down (and he beside her) on a little **mound** under the single chestnut-tree, that threw its shade over the garden.

Both were silent for some moments,—Percival, with grateful **ecstasy**; Helen, with one of those sudden fits of mysterious melancholy to which her nature was so subjected.

He was the first to speak. "Helen," he said **gravely**, "since I have known you, I feel as if life were a more **solemn** thing than I ever regarded it before. It seems to me as if a new and more **arduous** duty were added to those for which I was prepared,—a duty, Helen, to become worthy of you! Will you smile? No, you will not smile if I say I have had my brief moments of ambition. Sometimes as a boy, with Plutarch in my hand, stretched **idly** under the old cedar-trees at Laughton; sometimes as a **sailor**, when, **becalmed** on the Atlantic, and my ears **freshly** filled with tales of Collingwood and Nelson, I stole from my comrades and leaned **musingly** over the **boundless** sea. But when this ample heritage passed to me, when I had no more my own fortunes to make, my own rank to **build** up, such dreams became less and less frequent. Is it not true that wealth makes us **contented** to be obscure? Yes; I understand, while I speak, why poverty itself befriends, not **cripples**, Ardworth's energies. But since I have known you, dearest Helen, those dreams return more **vividly** than ever. He who claims you should be—must be—something nobler than the crowd. Helen,"—and he rose by an irresistible and restless impulse,—"I shall not be contented till you are as proud of your choice as I of mine!"

French

arduous: ardu, pénible.
becalmed: encalminé.
boundless: sans bornes, illimité.
build: construire, bâtir, maçonner, charpenter, poser, version, édifier.
childish: enfantin, puéril.
contented: content, satisfait.
cripple: estropié, paralyser.
develop: développer, évoluer, révéler, entraîner des conséquences, perfectionner.
dreary: morne, triste, maussade, sombre, affreux, épouvantable, repoussant, mélancolique, horrible, foncé, désolé.
ecstasy: extase, ecstasie.
foreshadowing: présageant.
freshly: fraîchement, de façon fraiche, de manière frais.
gravely: gravement, de façon tombe, de manière tombe.
idly: de façon inactive, de manière inactive.
intellect: intellect, esprit, raison.
mound: monticule, butte.
musingly: de façon rêveuse, de manière rêveuse.
sailor: marin, matelot, navigateur.
solemn: solennel, sérieux, grave.
timidly: timidement, de façon timide, de manière timide.
vividly: de façon vive, de manière vive.

It seemed, as Percival spoke and looked, as if **boyhood** were cast from him forever. The unusual **weight** and **gravity** of his words, to which his tone gave even eloquence; the steady **flash** of his dark eyes; his **erect**, **elastic** form,—all had the dignity of man. Helen gazed on him **silently**, and with a heart so full that words would not come, and **tears overflowed instead**.

That sight sobered him at once; he **knelt** down beside her, threw his arms around her,—it was his first embrace,—and kissed the tears away.

"How have I **distressed** you? Why do you **weep**?"

"Let me weep on, Percival, dear Percival! These tears are like prayers,—they speak to Heaven—and of you!"

A step came **noiselessly** over the grass, and between the lovers and the **sunlight** stood Gabriel Varney.

French

boyhood: enfance, adolescence.
distressed: affligé.
elastic: élastique, souple.
erect: fonder, ériger, droit, bâtir, construire, édifier.
flash: flash, éclat, clignoter, bavure.
gravity: gravité, pesanteur.
instead: plutôt, à la place, au contraire, au lieu de.
knelt: agenouillé.
noiselessly: de façon silencieuse, de manière silencieuse, silencieusement.
overflowed: débordé.
silently: silencieusement, de façon silencieuse, de manière silencieuse.
sunlight: lumière du soleil.
tear: larme, déchirer, pleur.
weep: pleurer, sourdons, suinter, larmoyez.
weight: pesanteur, masse, balance, charge, coefficient de pondération, graisse.

CHAPTER XII

SUDDEN CELEBRITY AND PATIENT HOPE

Percival was **unusually gloomy** and abstracted in his way to town that day, though Varney was his companion, and in the full play of those **animal** spirits which he **owed** to his **unrivalled** physical organization and the **obtuseness** of his conscience. Seeing, at length, that his gayety did not communicate itself to Percival, he paused, and looked at him **suspiciously**. A falling leaf **startles** the **steed**, and a shadow the guilty man.

"You are sad, Percival," he said **inquiringly**. "What has **disturbed** you?"

"It is nothing,—or, at least, would seem nothing to you," answered Percival, with an effort to smile, for I have heard you laugh at the **doctrine** of presentiments. We **sailors** are more superstitious."

"What **presentiment** can you possibly entertain?" asked Varney, more **anxiously** than Percival could have anticipated.

"Presentiments are not so easily defined, Varney. But, in truth, poor Helen has **infected** me. Have you not remarked that, gay as she **habitually** is, some shadow comes over her so suddenly that one cannot trace the cause?"

French

animal: animal, bête.
anxiously: de manière inquiète, de façon inquiète.
disturbed: dérangeai, gêna, gênèrent, gêné, gênâtes.
doctrine: doctrine.
gloomy: sombre, morne.
habitually: de façon habituelle, de manière habituelle, habituellement.
infected: infectâtes, septique.
inquiringly: de façon interrogatrice, de manière interrogatrice.
obtuseness: stupidité.
owed: dûtes, dû, dûmes, durent, dus, dut.
presentiment: pressentiment.
sailor: marin, matelot, navigateur.
startle: effarouches, surprenons, alarment.
steed: coursier.
suspiciously: de manière méfiante, de façon méfiante.
unrivalled: sans égal.
unusually: de manière inhabituelle, exceptionnellement, de façon inhabituelle.

"My dear Percival," said Varney, after a short pause, "what you say does not surprise me. It would be false kindness to conceal from you that I have heard Madame Dalibard say that her mother was, when about her age, threatened with consumptive symptoms; but she lived many years afterwards. Nay, nay, **rally** yourself; Helen's appearance, despite the extreme purity of her complexion, is not that of one threatened by the terrible **malady** of our climate. The young are often haunted with the idea of early death. As we grow older, that thought is less **cherished**; in youth it is a sort of luxury. To this **mournful** idea (which you see you have remarked as well as I) we must attribute not only Helen's occasional melancholy, but a generosity of **forethought** which I cannot **deny** myself the pleasure of communicating to you, though her delicacy would be **shocked** at my **indiscretion**. You know how helpless her aunt is. Well, Helen, who is entitled, when of age, to a moderate competence, has persuaded me to insure her life and accept a trust to hold the moneys (if ever **unhappily** due) for the benefit of my mother-in-law, so that Madame Dalibard may not be left **destitute** if her niece die before she is twenty-one. How like Helen, is it not?"

Percival was too overcome to answer.

Varney resumed: "I **entreat** you not to mention this to Helen; it would offend her **modesty** to have the secret of her good deeds thus betrayed by one to whom alone she **confided** them. I could not resist her **entreaties**, though, entre **nous**, it **cripples** me not a little to advance for her the necessary sums for the premiums. **Apropos**, this brings me to a point on which I feel, as the vulgar **idiom** goes, 'very awkward,'—as I always do in these **confounded** money-matters. But you were good enough to ask me to paint you a couple of pictures for Laughton. Now, if you could let me have some portion of the sum, whatever it be (for I don't **price** my **paintings** to you), it would very much **oblige** me."

Percival turned away his face as he wrung Varney's hand, and muttered, with a choked voice: "Let me have my share in Helen's divine forethought. Good Heavens! she, so young, to look thus beyond the grave, always for others—for others!"

French

apropos: à propos, opportun.
cherished: chérîmes.
confided: confié.
confounded: confondu, déconcertâmes.
cripple: estropié, paralyser.
deny: nier, niez, nie, nient, nies, nions, renier, démentir.
destitute: dépourvu, indigent.
entreat: implore, supplient.
entreaty: imploration, supplication.
forethought: prévoyance.

idiom: idiome, formation synaptique.
indiscretion: indiscrétion.
malady: maladie.
modesty: modestie, pudeur.
mournful: morne, sombre, mélancolique, triste.
nous: nous.
oblige: obliger.
painting: peinture, tableau.
price: prix, cours.
rally: rallye, rassembler,

amélioration, railler, échange.
shocked: choqué.
unhappily: de façon malheureuse, de manière malheureuse.

Callous as the **wretch** was, Percival's emotion and his proposal struck Varney with a sentiment like **compunction**. He had designed to **appropriate** the lover's gold as it was now offered; but that Percival himself should propose it, blind to the grave to which that gold paved the way, was a horror not counted in those to which his fell **cupidity** and his goading apprehensions had **familiarized** his conscience.

"No," he said, with one of those **wayward scruples** to which the blackest **criminals** are sometimes susceptible,—"no. I have promised Helen to regard this as a **loan** to her, which she is to repay me when of age. What you may advance me is for the pictures. I have a right to do as I please with what is bought by my own labour. And the subjects of the pictures, what shall they be?"

"For one picture try and recall Helen's aspect and attitude when you came to us in the garden, and **entitle** your subject: 'The Foreboding.'"

"Hem!" said Varney, **hesitatingly**. "And the other subject?"

"Wait for that till the joy-bells at Laughton have welcomed a bride, and then—and then, Varney," added Percival, with something of his natural **joyous** smile, "you must take the expression as you find it. Once under my care, and, please Heaven, the one picture shall **laughingly upbraid** the other!"

As this was said, the **cabriolet** stopped at Percival's door. Varney dined with him that day; and if the conversation flagged, it did not revert to the subject which had so darkened the bright spirits of the host, and so tried the hypocrisy of the guest. When Varney left, which he did as soon as the dinner was concluded, Percival silently put a check into his hands, to a greater amount than Varney had anticipated even from his generosity.

"This is for four pictures, not two," he said, shaking his head; and then, with his characteristic **conceit**, he added: "Well, some years hence the world shall not call them **overpaid**. **Adieu**, my Medici; a dozen such men, and Art would **revive** in England."

French

adieu: adieu.
appropriate: convenable, approprié, raisonnable, s'approprier, juste.
cabriolet: cabriolet.
compunction: componction, remords.
conceit: vanité, prétention.
criminal: criminel, malfaiteur.
cupidity: cupidité.
entitle: intitules, titrons, autorisons.
familiarized: familiarisâtes.
hesitatingly: de façon hésitante, de manière hésitante.
joyous: joyeux, heureux.
laughingly: de façon riante, de manière riante.
loan: prêt, emprunt.
overpaid: surpayé.
revive: ranimer, raviver, réanimer.
scruple: scrupule.
upbraid: morigénez, réprimandons.
wayward: rebelle, rétif.
wretch: malheureux, scélérat.

When he was left alone, Percival sat down, and leaning his face on both hands, gave way to the gloom which his native **manliness** and the delicacy that belongs to true affection had made him struggle not to indulge in the presence of another. Never had he so loved Helen as in that hour; never had he so intimately and **intensely** felt her **matchless** worth. The image of her **unselfish**, quiet, melancholy consideration for that austere, uncaressing, unsympathizing relation, under whose shade her young heart must have **withered**, seemed to him filled with a celestial **pathos**. And he almost **hated** Varney that the **cynic** painter could have talked of it with that business-like **phlegm**. The evening deepened; the tranquil street grew still; the air seemed close; the solitude oppressed him; he rose abruptly, seized his hat, and went forth slowly, and still with a heavy heart.

As he entered Piccadilly, on the broad step of that house successively inhabited by the Duke of Queensberry and Lord Hertford,—on the step of that mansion up which so many footsteps light with **wanton** pleasure have gayly trod, Percival's eye fell upon a wretched, **squalid**, ragged object, **doubled** up, as it were, in that last **despondency** which has ceased to beg, that has no care to steal, that has no wish to live. Percival halted, and touched the **outcast**.

"What is the matter, my poor fellow? Take care; the policeman will not suffer you to rest here. Come, cheer up, I say! There is something to find you a better lodging!"

The silver fell **unheeded** on the stones. The thing of rags did not even raise its head, but a low, broken voice muttered,—

"It be too late now; let 'em take me to prison, let 'em send me 'cross the sea to Buttany, let 'em hang me, if they please. I be 's good for nothin' now,—nothin'!"

Altered as the voice was, it struck Percival as familiar. He looked down and caught a view of the **drooping** face. "Up, man, up!" he said **cheerily**. "See, Providence sends you an old friend in need, to teach you never to despair again."

French

cheerily: de façon gaie, de manière gaie.
cynic: cynique.
despondency: découragement, abattement.
doubled: doublé, en double ad.
drooping: tombant, fanaison.
hated: détesté, häirent, häimes, häi, haie.
intensely: de façon intense, de manière intense, intensément.
manliness: virilité.
matchless: incomparable, sans égal.
outcast: banni, rejeté, proscrit, exclu, exilé, paria.
pathos: pathétique.
phlegm: flegme, expectoration.
squalid: misérable, sordide.
unheeded: ignoré, inaperçu, négligé.
unselfish: désintéressé, généreux.
wanton: dévergondé, impudique, licencieux.
withered: flétri, fané.

The hearty accent, more than the words, touched and aroused the poor creature. He rose mechanically, and a sickly, grateful smile passed over his wasted features as he recognized St. John.

"Come! how is this? I have always understood that to keep a crossing was a **flourishing trade** nowadays."

"I 'as no crossin'. I 'as sold her!" groaned Beck. "I be's good for nothin' now but to **cadge** about the streets, and steal, and **filch**, and hang like the rest on us! Thank you kindly, sir," and Beck pulled his **forelock**, "but, please your honour, I vould rather make an ind on it!"

"Pooh, pooh! didn't I tell you when you wanted a friend to come to me? Why did you doubt me, foolish fellow? Pick up those **shillings**; get a bed and a supper. Come and see me to-morrow at **nine** o'clock; you know where,—the same house in Curzon Street; you shall tell me then your whole story, and it shall go hard but I'll buy you another crossing, or get you something just as good."

Poor Beck swayed a moment or two on his slender legs like a drunken man, and then, suddenly falling on his knees, he kissed the **hem** of his benefactor's garment, and fairly **wept**. Those tears relieved him; they seemed to wash the **drought** of despair from his heart.

"**Hush**, hush! or we shall have a crowd round us. You'll not forget, my poor friend, No.—Curzon Street,—nine to-morrow. Make **haste** now, and get food and rest; you look, indeed, as if you wanted them. Ah, would to Heaven all the poverty in this huge city stood here in thy person, and we could aid it as easily as I can thee!"

Percival had moved on as he said those last words, and looking back, he had the satisfaction to see that Beck was slowly **crawling** after him, and had escaped the grim question of a very **portly** policeman, who had no doubt expressed a natural indignation at the **audacity** of so ragged a skeleton not keeping itself **respectably** at home in its churchyard.

Entering one of the clubs in St. James's Street, Percival found a small knot of politicians in eager conversation **respecting** a new book which had been

French

audacity: audace.
cadge: quémander, mendie.
crawling: rampage, rétraction, refus à l'application, retrait, retirement d'émail, reptation.
drought: sécheresse, sècheresse.
filch: chipez.
flourishing: florissant, prospérant.
forelock: toupet, goujon d'arrêt, mèche.
haste: hâte, précipitation.
hem: ourlet, bord, drapelet cousu.
hush: silence, faire taire.
nine: neuf.
portly: corpulent.
respectably: de manière respectable, de façon respectable.
respecting: respectant, en ce qui concerne.
shilling: schilling.
trade: commerce, métier, faire du commerce, négoce.
wept: pleurâtes, sourdis, larmoyèrent.

published but a day or two before, but which had already seized the public attention with that strong grasp which constitutes always an **era** in an author's life, sometimes an **epoch** in a nation's **literature**. The newspapers were full of **extracts** from the work,—the gossips, of conjecture as to the **authorship**. We need scarcely say that a book which makes this kind of **sensation** must **hit** some popular feeling of the hour, supply some popular want. Ninety-nine times out of a hundred, therefore, its character is political; it was so in the present instance. It may be remembered that that year parliament sat during great part of the month of October, that it was the year in which the Reform Bill was rejected by the House of Lords, and that public feeling in our time had never been so **keenly** excited. This work appeared during the short interval between the rejection of the Bill and the **prorogation** of parliament [Parliament was prorogued October 20th; the bill rejected by the Lords, October 8th]. And what made it more remarkable was, that while stamped with the passion of the time, there was a weight of calm and **stern** reasoning **embodied** in its vigorous periods, which gave to the arguments of the advocate something of the **impartiality** of the judge. Unusually abstracted and unsocial,—for, despite his youth and that peculiar bashfulness before noticed, he was generally alive enough to all that passed around him,—Percival paid little attention to the **comments** that **circulated** round the easy-chairs in his vicinity, till a subordinate in the **administration**, with whom he was slightly **acquainted**, pushed a small volume towards him and said,—"You have seen this, of course, St. John? Ten to one you do not guess the author. It is certainly not B—m, though the Lord Chancellor has energy enough for anything. R—says it has a touch of S—r."

"Could M—y have written it?" asked a young member of parliament, **timidly**.

"M—y! Very like his **matchless** style, to be sure! You can have read very little of M—y, I should think," said the subordinate, with the true **sneer** of an **official** and a critic.

The young member could have slunk into a **nutshell**. Percival, with very **languid** interest, glanced over the volume. But despite his mood, and his

French

acquainted: renseignai, informé.
administration: administration, gouvernement.
authorship: paternité, origine d'une œuvre littéraire, profession d'auteur, qualité d'auteur.
circulated: circulé, dégorgeai.
comment: commentaire, observation.
embodied: incarnèrent.
epoch: époque, ère, période.
era: époque, ère.

extract: extrait, arracher, retirer, soutirer, morceau choisi, cession, concentré.
hit: frapper, heurter, battre, coup, succès, atteindre, toucher, parvenir, saisir.
impartiality: impartialité.
keenly: de façon vive, de manière vive.
languid: langoureux, traînant, biseau, indolent.
literature: littérature,

documentation.
matchless: incomparable, sans égal.
nutshell: coquille de noix.
official: officiel, fonctionnaire.
prorogation: prorogation, clôture.
published: publia, édité.
sensation: sensation, sentiment.
sneer: ricaner, tourner en ridicule, remarque moqueuse.
stern: poupe, arrière, sévère.
timidly: timidement, de façon timide, de manière timide.

moderate affection for political writings, the passage he opened upon struck and seized him **unawares**. Though the sneer of the official was just, and the style was not **comparable** to M—y's (whose is?), still, the steady rush of strong words, strong with strong thoughts, heaped **massively** together, showed the ease of genius and the gravity of thought. The absence of all **effeminate glitter**, the iron **grapple** with the **pith** and substance of the argument opposed, seemed familiar to Percival. He thought he heard the deep bass of John Ardworth's earnest voice when some truth **roused** his advocacy, or some **falsehood** provoked his wrath. He put down the book, bewildered. Could it be the obscure, briefless lawyer in Gray's Inn (that very morning the object of his young pity) who was thus lifted into fame? He smiled at his own **credulity**. But he listened with more attention to the **enthusiastic** praises that circled round, and the various **guesses** which accompanied them. Soon, however, his former gloom returned,—the Babel began to **chafe** and weary him. He rose, and went forth again into the air. He strolled on without purpose, but mechanically, into the street where he had first seen Helen. He paused a few moments under the **colonnade** which faced Beck's old deserted crossing. His pause attracted the notice of one of the unhappy beings whom we suffer to **pollute** our streets and rot in our **hospitals**. She approached and spoke to him,—to him whose heart was so full of Helen! He shuddered, and strode on. At length he paused before the **twin** towers of Westminster **Abbey**, on which the moon rested in solemn splendour; and in that space one man only **shared** his solitude. A figure with folded arms leaned against the iron rails near the statue of Canning, and his gaze **comprehended** in one view the walls of the Parliament, in which all passions **wage** their war, and the **glorious** abbey, which gives a Walhalla to the great. The utter stillness of the figure, so in unison with the stillness of the scene, had upon Percival more effect than would have been produced by the most **clamorous** crowd. He looked round curiously as he passed, and uttered an **exclamation** as he recognized John Ardworth.

"You, Percival!" said Ardworth. "A strange meeting-place at this hour! What can bring you hither?"

French

abbey: abbaye.
chafe: frictionner, irriter, raguer, s'irriter, user.
clamorous: bruyant.
colonnade: colonnade.
comparable: comparable.
comprehended: comprîmes.
credulity: crédulité.
effeminate: efféminé.
enthusiastic: enthousiaste.
exclamation: exclamation.
falsehood: mensonge, supercherie.
glitter: briller, scintillement.
glorious: glorieux, fameux.
grapple: grappin, attraper, saisir, capturer.
guesses: devine.
hospital: hôpital, établissement hospitalier, hospitalier, infirmerie.
massively: de façon massive, de manière massive, massivement.
pith: moelle.
pollute: polluer, contaminer.
roused: irritâtes, excitèrent, stimulâtes.
shared: partagé, commun.
twin: jumeau, macle, cristal jumeau, biface, chambre double à deux lits.
unawares: à l'improviste.
wage: salaire, appointements, gaine, paie.

"Only whim, I fear; and you?" as Percival linked his arm into Ardworth's.

"**Twenty** years hence I will tell you what brought me hither!" answered Ardworth, **moving** slowly back towards Whitehall.

"If we are alive then!"

"We live till our destinies below are fulfilled; till our uses have passed from us in this **sphere**, and rise to benefit another. For the soul is as a sun, but with this noble distinction,—the sun is confined in its career; day after day it visits the same lands, **gilds** the same planets or rather, as the **astronomers** hold, stands, the motionless centre of moving worlds. But the soul, when it sinks into seeming darkness and the deep, rises to new destinies, fresh regions unvisited before. What we call Eternity, may be but an endless **series** of those transitions which men call 'deaths,' abandonments of home after home, ever to fairer scenes and loftier heights. Age after age, the spirit, that glorious Nomad, may shift its **tent**, **fated** not to rest in the dull Elysium of the Heathen, but **carrying** with it **evermore** its elements,— Activity and Desire. Why should the soul ever **repose**? God, its Principle, reposes never. While we speak, new worlds are sparkling forth, suns are throwing off their nebulae, nebulae are **hardening** into worlds. The Almighty proves his existence by **creating**. Think you that Plato is at rest, and Shakspeare only basking on a sun-cloud? Labour is the very essence of spirit, as of **divinity**; labour is the **purgatory** of the **erring**; it may become the hell of the wicked, but labour is not less the heaven of the good!"

Ardworth spoke with unusual **earnestness** and passion, and his idea of the future was **emblematic** of his own active nature; for each of us is wisely left to shape out, amidst the **impenetrable** mists, his own ideal of the Hereafter. The warrior child of the **biting** North placed his Hela **amid snows**, and his Himmel in the banquets of victorious war; the son of the East, **parched** by relentless summer,—his hell amidst fire, and his elysium by **cooling** streams; the weary **peasant** sighs through life for rest, and rest awaits his vision beyond the grave; the **workman** of genius,—ever ardent,

---

French

amid: parmi, au milieu de.
astronomer: astronome.
biting: mordant, âpre, morsure.
carrying: portant, transportant.
cooling: refroidissement, rafraîchissement.
creating: créant.
divinity: divinité, théologie.
earnestness: sérieux, gravité.
emblematic: emblématique.
erring: errant, aberrant.
evermore: toujours.
fated: destiné, fatal.
gild: dorer, dorons.
hardening: durcissant, trempant, endurcissant.
impenetrable: impénétrable, imperméable.
moving: émouvant, attendrissant, mobile, en mouvement, déménagement.
parched: desséché.
peasant: paysan.
purgatory: purgatoire.
repose: repos, se reposer, trêve.
series: série, suite, collection.
snow: neige, blanche.
sphere: sphère, boule, réservoir sphérique, théorie de la sphère.
tent: tente, mèche.
twenty: vingt.
workman: ouvrier, homme d'équipe.

ever young,—honours **toil** as the glorious development of being, and springs **refreshed** over the abyss of the grave, to follow, from star to star, the progress that seems to him at once the **supreme felicity** and the necessary law. So be it with the **fantasy** of each! Wisdom that is **infallible**, and love that never sleeps, watch over the darkness, and bid darkness be, that we may dream!

"Alas!" said the young listener, "what **reproof** do you not **convey** to those, like me, who, **devoid** of the power which gives results to every toil, have little left to them in life, but to idle life away. All have not the gift to write, or **harangue**, or speculate, or—"

"Friend," interrupted Ardworth, bluntly, "do not **belie** yourself. There lives not a man on earth—out of a **lunatic** asylum—who has not in him the power to do good. What can **writers**, haranguers, or **speculators** do more than that? Have you ever entered a cottage, ever **travelled** in a coach, ever talked with a peasant in the field, or **loitered** with a **mechanic** at the loom, and not found that each of those men had a talent you had not, knew some things you knew not? The most useless creature that ever yawned at a club, or counted the **vermin** on his rags under the suns of Calabria, has no excuse for want of intellect. What men want is not talent, it is purpose,—in other words, not the power to **achieve**, but the will to labour. You, Percival St. John,—you **affect** to despond, lest you should not have your uses; you, with that fresh, warm heart; you, with that pure enthusiasm for what is fresh and good; you, who can even admire a thing like Varney, because, through the **tawdry** man, you recognize art and skill, even though wasted in **spoiling** canvas; you, who have only to live as you feel, in order to **diffuse** blessings all around you,—fie, foolish boy! you will own your error when I tell you why I come from my rooms at Gray's Inn to see the walls in which Hampden, a plain country squire like you, shook with plain words the **tyranny** of eight hundred years."

"Ardworth, I will not wait your time to tell me what took you **yonder**. I have penetrated a secret that you, not kindly, kept from me. This morning you rose and found yourself **famous**; this evening you have come to gaze

---

French

achieve: accomplir, atteindre, réaliser, remplir, parvenir, assurer, confectionner, poser, aboutir, faire, construire.
affect: affecter, influer, émouvoir, toucher, émeuvent, remuer, atteindre, concerner.
belie: démentir.
convey: transmettre, véhiculez, acheminent, communiquer.
devoid: dépourvu, dénué.
diffuse: diffus, produire un halo, répandent.
famous: célèbre, fameux, illustre, glorieux, renommé, réputé.
fantasy: fantaisie, imagination.
felicity: félicité.
harangue: harangue.
infallible: infaillible.
loitered: flânas.
lunatic: aliéné, fou.
mechanic: mécanicien, ouvrier mécanicien, garagiste.
refreshed: rafraîchîmes, actualisas.
reproof: reproche.
speculator: spéculateur.
spoiling: gâterie, abîmant.
supreme: suprême, souverain.
tawdry: clinquant.
toil: labeur, travailler dur.
travelled: voyagé.
tyranny: tyrannie.
vermin: vermine, animaux nuisibles, ravageurs.
writer: auteur, écrivain, rédacteur.
yonder: là, y.

upon the scene of the career to which that fame will more rapidly conduct you—"

"And upon the tomb which the proudest ambition I can form on earth must content itself to win! A poor conclusion, if all ended here!"

"I am right, however," said Percival, with boyish pleasure. "It is you whose praises have just filled my ears. You, dear, dear Ardworth! How **rejoiced** I am!"

Ardworth pressed **heartily** the hand extended to him: "I should have trusted you with my secret to-morrow, Percival; as it is, keep it for the present. A **craving** of my nature has been satisfied, a grief has found **distraction**. As for the rest, any child that throws a stone into the water with all his force can make a **splash**; but he would be a fool indeed if he supposed that the splash was a sign that he had turned a stream."

Here Ardworth ceased abruptly; and Percival, **engrossed** by a bright idea, which had suddenly occurred to him, exclaimed,—

"Ardworth, your desire, your ambition, is to enter parliament; there must be a **dissolution** shortly,—the success of your book will render you **acceptable** to many a popular **constituency**. All you can want is a sum for the necessary expenses. Borrow that sum from me; repay me when you are in the Cabinet, or attorney-general. It shall be so!"

A look so bright that even by that dull **lamplight** the glow of the cheek, the **brilliancy** of the eye were visible, flashed over Ardworth's face. He felt at that moment what ambitious man must feel when the object he has seen **dimly** and **afar** is placed within his grasp; but his reason was proof even against that strong temptation.

He passed his arm round the boy's slender waist, and drew him to his heart with grateful affection as he replied,—"And what, if now in parliament, giving up my career,—with no regular means of subsistence,— what could I be but a **venal adventurer**? Place would become so **vitally** necessary to me that I should feed but a dangerous war between my conscience and my wants. In chasing Fame, the shadow, I should lose the

French

acceptable: acceptable, satisfaisant.
adventurer: aventurier.
afar: loin.
brilliancy: éclat, brillance, intensité d'image.
constituency: circonscription, électeurs.
craving: désir ardent, envie, sollicitant.
dimly: de façon faible, de manière faible.
dissolution: dissolution.
distraction: distraction, récréation, amusement, détente.
engrossed: grossoyâmes.
heartily: de façon cordiale, de manière cordiale, chaleureusement.
lamplight: lumière artificielle.
rejoiced: réjouis.
splash: clapoter, éclabousser, barboter, gicler.
venal: vénal.
vitally: de façon vitale, de manière vitale.

substance, Independence. Why, that very thought would **paralyze** my tongue. No, no, my generous friend. As labour is the arch **elevator** of man, so patience is the essence of labour. First let me build the **foundation**; I may then calculate the height of my tower. First let me be independent of the great; I will then be the **champion** of the **lowly**. Hold! Tempt me no more; do not **lure** me to the loss of self-esteem. And now, Percival," resumed Ardworth, in the tone of one who wishes to plunge into some utterly new current of thought, "let us forget for **awhile** these solemn **aspirations**, and be **frolicsome** and human. 'Nemo mortalium **omnibus** horis sapit.' 'Neque semper arcum tendit Apollo.' What say you to a cigar?"

Percival stared. He was not yet **familiarized** to the **eccentric** whims of his friend.

"**Hot** negus and a cigar!" repeated Ardworth, while a smile, full of drollery, played round the corners of his lips and **twinkled** in his deep-set eyes.

"Are you serious?"

"Not serious; I have been serious enough," and Ardworth sighed, "for the last three weeks. Who goes 'to Corinth to be sage,' or to the Cider Cellar to be serious?"

"I **subscribe**, then, to the negus and cigar," said Percival, smiling; and he had no cause to repent his compliance as he accompanied Ardworth to one of the resorts favoured by that strange person in his rare hours of relaxation.

For, seated at his favourite table, which happened, luckily, to be vacant, with his head thrown carelessly back, and his negus **steaming** before him, John Ardworth continued to pour forth, till the clock struck three, jest upon jest, pun upon pun, broad drollery upon broad drollery, without **flagging**, without **intermission**, so varied, so **copious**, so ready, so irresistible that Percival was **transported** out of all his melancholy in **enjoying**, for the first time in his life, the **exuberant** gayety of a grave mind once set free,—all its intellect sparkling into wit, all its passion rushing into humour. And this was the man he had pitied, supposed to have no sunny side to his life! How

---

French

aspiration: aspiration, souhait, dépoussiérage.
awhile: pendant quelque temps.
champion: champion.
copious: abondant, copieux.
eccentric: excentrique, original.
elevator: ascenseur, élévateur, gouverne de profondeur.
enjoying: jouissant, plaisant, savourant.
exuberant: exubérant.
familiarized: familiarisâtes.

flagging: balisage, distorsion en drapeau.
foundation: fondation, base, assise.
frolicsome: malin, enjoué.
hot: chaud, épicé, brûlant, missile Hot.
intermission: pause, trêve, entracte, repos, intermittence.
lowly: de manière bas, modeste, de façon bas.
lure: leurre, attirer.
omnibus: omnibus, autobus.

paralyze: paralyser, méduser, pétrifier.
steaming: vaporisage, étuvage, fumant, injection de vapeur, procédé d'étuvage, stérilisation à la vapeur sous pression, traitement à la vapeur, ébouillantage.
subscribe: s'abonner, souscrire.
transported: transporté.
twinkled: scintillas, clignoté.

much greater had been his **compassion** and his **wonder** if he could have known all that had **passed**, within the last **few** weeks, through that gloomy, yet **silent breast**, which, by the very **breadth** of its **mirth, showed** what must be the **depth** of its sadness!

French

breadth: largeur, travers.
breast: poitrine, sein, mamelle, front de taille.
compassion: compassion, pitié, apitoiement.
depth: profondeur, intensité, creux.
few: peu, peu de.
mirth: gaieté, allégresse.
passed: passé.
showed: montrèrent, manifesta, marquèrent.
silent: silencieux.
wonder: s'étonner, merveille, miracle, se demander.

CHAPTER XIII

THE LOSS OF THE CROSSING

Despite the **lateness** of the hour before he got to rest, Percival had already breakfasted, when his **valet** informed him, with **raised, supercilious** eyebrows, that an uncommon ragged sort of a person insisted that he had been told to call. Though Beck had been at the house before, and the valet had admitted him, so much **thinner**, so much more ragged was he now, that the trim servant—no close observer of such folk—did not recognize him. However, at Percival's order, too well-bred to show surprise, he ushered Beck up with much **civility**; and St. John was painfully struck with the **ravages** a few weeks had made upon the sweeper's countenance. The lines were so deeply **ploughed**, the dry hair looked so thin, and was so **sown** with gray that Beck might have beat all Farren's skill in the part of an old man.

The poor sweeper's tale, **extricated** from its peculiar **phraseology**, was simple enough, and soon told. He had returned home at night to find his **hoards** stolen, and the labour of his life **overthrown**. How he passed that night he did not very well remember. We may well suppose that the little reason he possessed was wellnigh **bereft** from him. No suspicion of the exact **thief** crossed his **perturbed** mind. Bad as Grabman's character might be, he held a respectable position compared with the other **lodgers** in the house.

French

bereft: dépossédas, privé.
civility: civilité.
extricated: dégagèrent.
hoard: amas, thésaurisation, stocker, trésor.
lateness: retard.
lodger: locataire, pensionnaire.
overthrown: renversé.
perturbed: perturba, brouillèrent.
phraseology: phraséologie.
ploughed: labouré.
raised: levé, levèrent, relief,
  levâmes, levai.
ravage: ravager, dévastation.
sown: ensemencées, semé,
  emblavé.
supercilious: dédaigneux, hautain.
thief: voleur, filou, cambrioleur,
  larron, échantillonneur, cathode
  auxiliaire, chapardeur, écran
  voleur de courant.
thinner: diluant, dissolvant,
  éclaircisseuse, démarieuse.
valet: valet.

Bill the cracksman, naturally and by vocation, suggested the hand that had **despoiled** him: how hope for redress or **extort** surrender from such a quarter? Mechanically, however, when the hour arrived to return to his day's task, he stole down the stairs, and lo, at the very door of the house Bill's children were at play, and in the hand of the eldest he recognized what he called his "curril."

"Your curril!" interrupted St. John.

"Yes, curril,—vot the little 'uns **bite** afore they gets their teethin'."

St. John smiled, and supposing that Beck had some time or other been **puerile** enough to purchase such a **bauble**, nodded to him to continue. To seize upon the **urchin**, and, in spite of kicks, bites, **shrieks**, or scratches, **repossess** himself of his treasure, was the **feat** of a moment. The brat's clamour drew out the father; and to him Beck (pocketing the coral, that its golden bells might not attract the more experienced eye and influence the more formidable **greediness** of the paternal thief) loudly, and at first **fearlessly**, appealed. Him he **charged** and **accused** and threatened with all vengeance, human and divine. Then, **changing** his tone, he **implored**, he wept, he knelt. As soon as the startled cracksman recovered his astonishment at such **audacity**, and **comprehended** the nature of the charge against himself and his family, he felt the more indignant from a strange and unfamiliar consciousness of innocence. **Seizing** Beck by the nape of the neck, with a **dexterous** application of hand and foot he sent him **spinning** into the **kennel**.

"Go to Jericho, mud-scraper!" cried Bill, in a voice of thunder; "and if ever thou sayst such a vopper agin,—'sparaging the characters of them 'ere **motherless** babes,—I'll seal thee up in a 'tato-sack, and sell thee for fiv'pence to No. 7, the great body-snatcher. Take care how I ever sets eyes agin on thy h-ugly mug!"

With that Bill clapped to the door, and Beck, frightened out of his wits, **crawled** from the kennel and, bruised and **smarting**, crept to his crossing. But he was unable to discharge his duties that day; his ill-fed, miserable

French

accused: accusé, inculpé, prévenu.
audacity: audace.
bauble: babiole, marotte.
bite: mordre, morsure, bouchée, piquer.
changing: changeant, modification.
charged: chargé, saturé de fumée et de gaz, alimenté, défoncé, électrisé.
comprehended: comprîmes.
crawled: rampé.
despoiled: spolié.

dexterous: adroit, habile.
extort: extorquer, soutire, arracher.
fearlessly: de façon intrépide, de manière intrépide.
feat: exploit.
greediness: avidité.
implored: implorai.
kennel: chenil, niche, ruisseau.
motherless: sans mère.
puerile: puéril, enfantin.
repossess: reprendre possession.
seizing: saisissant, grippage, agrippant.
shriek: crier, hurler, cri perçant.
smarting: cuisant.
spinning: filage, rotation, repoussage.
urchin: galopin, gamin, hérisson, oursin, polisson.

frame was too weak for the **stroke** he had received. Long before dusk he sneaked away, and **dreading** to return to his lodging, lest, since nothing now was left worth **robbing** but his **carcass**, Bill might keep his word and sell that to the body-snatcher, he took refuge under the only roof where he felt he could sleep in safety.

And here we must pause to explain. In our first introduction of Beck we contented ourselves with implying to the ingenious and practised reader that his heart might still be large enough to hold something besides his crossing. Now, in one of the small alleys that have their vent in the great stream of Fleet Street there dwelt an old widow-woman who eked out her existence by charing,—an **industrious**, drudging creature, whose sole occupation, since her husband, the **journeyman bricklayer**, fell from a **scaffold**, and, breaking his neck, left her happily childless as well as penniless, had been **scrubbing** stone floors and **cleaning** out **dingy** houses when about to be let,—charing, in a word. And in this vocation had she kept body and soul together till a bad **rheumatism** and old age had put an end to her **utilities** and entitled her to the receipt of two shillings weekly from parochial munificence. Between this old woman and Beck there was a mysterious tie, so mysterious that he did not well comprehend it himself. Sometimes he called her "mammy," sometimes "the h-old crittur." But certain it is that to her he was **indebted** for that name which he bore, to the **puzzlement** of St. Giles's. Becky Carruthers was the name of the old woman; but Becky was one of those good creatures who are always called by their Christian names, and never rise into the importance of the **surname** and the dignity of "Mistress;" **lopping** off the last **syllable** of the familiar **appellation**, the **outcast christened** himself "Beck."

"And," said St. John, who in the course of question and answer had got thus far into the **marrow** of the sweeper's narrative, "is not this good woman really your mother?"

"Mother!" echoed Beck, with **disdain**; "no, I 'as a gritter mother nor she. Sint Poll's is my mother. But the h-old crittur tuk care on me."

"I really don't understand you. St. Paul's is your mother? How?"

French

appellation: nom, surnom.
bricklayer: maçon, briqueteur.
carcass: carcasse, gros œuvre.
christened: baptisâmes.
cleaning: nettoyage, purifiant, épuration, dégagement.
dingy: terne.
disdain: dédain.
dreading: option marchandises diverses.
indebted: endetté, redevable.
industrious: laborieux, appliqué,

assidu, industrieux, travailleur.
journeyman: compagnon, ouvrier qualifié.
lopping: élagage, taillant.
marrow: moelle, courge.
outcast: banni, rejeté, proscrit, exclu, exilé, paria.
puzzlement: perplexité.
rheumatism: rhumatisme.
robbing: pillant, ravissant, dévalisant.
scaffold: échafaud.

scrubbing: lavage, débourbage, récurage, purification, nettoyage, épuration, frottement.
stroke: caresser, coup, course, trait, rayure, apoplexie, raie.
surname: nom de famille, nom.
syllable: syllabe.
utility: utilité, service public.

Beck shook his head mysteriously, and without answering the question, resumed the tale, which we must thus paraphrastically continue to **deliver**.

When he was a little more than six years old, Beck began to earn his own **livelihood**, by **running errands**, holding horses, **scraping** together pence and halfpence. Betimes, his passion for saving began; at first with a good and **unselfish** motive,—that of surprising "mammy" at the week's end. But when "mammy," who then gained enough for herself, patted his head and called him "good boy," and bade him save for his own uses, and told him what a great thing it would be if he could lay by a pretty penny against he was a man, he turned miser on his own account; and the miserable luxury grew upon him. At last, by the permission of the police **inspector**, strengthened by that of the owner of the **contiguous** house, he made his great step in life, and succeeded a deceased **negro** in the dignity and **emoluments** of the memorable crossing. From that hour he felt himself fulfilling his proper destiny. But poor Becky, alas! had already fallen into the **sere** and yellow leaf; with her decline, her good qualities were impaired. She took to drinking,—not to positive **intoxication**, but to making herself "comfortable;"

and, to satisfy her **craving**, Beck, **waking** betimes one morning, saw her **emptying** his pockets. Then he resolved, quietly and without **upbraiding** her, to remove to a safer lodging. To save had become the **imperative** necessity of his existence. But to do him justice, Beck had a **glimmering** sense of what was due to the "h-old crittur." Every Saturday evening he called at her house and deposited with her a certain sum, not large even in proportion to his earnings, but which seemed to the poor ignorant miser, who grudged every farthing to himself, an enormous **deduction** from his total, and a sum sufficient for every possible want of **humankind**, even to **satiety**. And now, in returning, **despoiled** of all save the few pence he had **collected** that day, it is but fair to him to add that not his least bitter pang was in the **remembrance** that this was the only Saturday on which, for the first time, the weekly **stipend** would fail.

But so ill and so wretched did he look when he reached her little room that "mammy" forgot all thought of herself; and when he had told his tale, so

---

French

collected: recueillîtes, rassemblâmes, collectionnèrent, ramassâmes.
contiguous: contigu.
craving: désir ardent, envie, sollicitant.
deduction: déduction, décompte, défalcation, prélèvement.
deliver: livrer, fournir, délivrer.
despoiled: spolié.
emolument: émolument.
emptying: vidage, évacuation.
errand: commission, message, course.
glimmering: éclat, miroitant.
humankind: humanité.
imperative: impératif.
inspector: inspecteur, contrôleur.
intoxication: ivresse, intoxication, ébriété, empoisonnement, griserie.
livelihood: subsistance, vie.
negro: nègre, noir.
remembrance: souvenir, mémoire.
running: courant, marche, coulant, fonctionnement.
satiety: satiété.
scraping: raclage, grattage.
sere: série.
stipend: traitement, appointements, bourse.
unselfish: désintéressé, généreux.
upbraiding: morigénant, réprimandant.
waking: rester éveillé, réveiller.

kind was her **comforting**, so unselfish her sympathy, that his heart **smote** him for his old **parsimony**, for his hard resentment at her single act of **peculation**. Had not she the right to all he made? But remorse and grief alike soon vanished in the fever that now seized him; for several days he was **insensible**; and when he recovered sufficiently to be made aware of what was around him, he saw the widow seated beside him, within four bare walls. Everything, except the bed he slept on, had been sold to support him in his illness. As soon as he could **totter** forth, Beck hastened to his crossing. Alas! it was preoccupied. His absence had led to ambitious **usurpation**. A one-legged, sturdy sailor had mounted his throne, and **wielded** his **sceptre**. The decorum of the street forbade **altercation** to the **contending** parties; but the sailor referred **discussion** to a meeting at a flash house in the Rookery that evening. There a **jury** was appointed, and the case opened. By the conventional laws that **regulate** this useful community, Beck was still in his rights; his **reappearance sufficed** to restore his claims, and an appeal to the policeman would no doubt re-establish his authority. But Beck was still so ill and so feeble that he had a melancholy persuasion that he could not suitably **perform** the duties of his office; and when the sailor, not a bad fellow on the whole, offered to pay down on the nail what really seemed a very liberal sum for Beck's peaceful surrender of his rights, the poor wretch thought of the bare walls at his "mammy's," of the long, dreary interval that must **elapse**, even if able to work, before the furniture pawned could be **redeemed** by the daily profits of his post, and with a groan he held out his hand and concluded the **bargain**.

Creeping home to his "h-old crittur," he threw the purchase money into her **lap**; then, broken-hearted and in despair, he slunk forth again in a sort of vague, **dreamy** hope that the law, which **abhors vagabonds**, would seize and finish him.

When this tale was done, Percival did not neglect the gentle task of admonition, which the poor sweeper's softened heart and dull remorse made easier. He pointed out, in soft tones, how the avarice he had indulged had been perhaps mercifully **chastised**, and drew no ineloquent picture of the

---

French

abhors: abhorre, exécre.
altercation: altercation, dispute.
bargain: marchander, négocier, bonne affaire, affaire, occasion.
chastised: châtia.
comforting: réconfortant, consolant.
contending: contestant, combattant, disputant.
discussion: discussion, entretien.
dreamy: rêveur.
elapse: passer, s'écouler.
insensible: insensible.
jury: jury, jurés, commission d'arbitrage.
lap: clapoter, recouvrement, nappe, chevauchement, tour, giron, barboter.
parsimony: parcimonie, frugalité.
peculation: péculat.
perform: réaliser, accomplir, faire, effectuer, exécuter, construire, poser, surgir, remplir, apparaître, paraître.
reappearance: réapparition, résurgence.
redeemed: rachetèrent, remboursé.
regulate: régler, règles, régulariser.
sceptre: sceptre.
smote: frappa.
sufficed: suffîmes.
totter: titubes, vacillez, chanceler.
usurpation: usurpation.
vagabond: vagabond, clochard, chemineau.
wielded: mania.

vicious miseries of the confirmed miser. Beck listened **humbly** and **respectfully**; though so little did he understand of mercy and Providence and vice that the **diviner** part of the **homily** was quite lost on him. However, he confessed **penitently** that "the **mattress** had made him vorse nor a beast to the h-old crittur;" and that "he was **cured** of saving to the end of his days."

"And now," said Percival, "as you really seem not strong enough to bear this out-of-door work (the **winter** coming on, too), what say you to entering into my service? I want some help in my **stables**. The work is easy enough, and you are used to horses, you know, in a sort of a way."

Beck hesitated, and looked a moment **undecided**. At last he said, "Please your honour, if I bean't strong enough for the crossin', I 'se afeared I'm too h-ailing to sarve you. And voud n't I be vorse nor a **wiper** to take your vages and not vork for 'em h-as I h-ought?"

"Pooh! we'll soon make you strong, my man. Take my advice; don't let your head run on the crossing. That kind of industry **exposes** you to bad company and bad thoughts."

"That's vot it is, sir," said Beck, assentingly, laying his **dexter forefinger** on his sinister palm.

"Well! you are in my service, then. Go downstairs now and get your breakfast; by and by you shall show me your 'mammy's' house, and we'll see what can be done for her."

Beck pressed his hands to his eyes, trying hard not to cry; but it was too much for him; and as the valet, who appeared to Percival's summons, led him down the stairs, his **sobs** were heard from **attic** to **basement**.

French

attic: grenier, mansarde.
basement: cave, socle, soubassement.
cured: guéri, maturé.
dexter: dextre.
diviner: devin.
expose: exposer, montrer, mettre à nu, insoler, affleurer, démasquer, dévoiler.
forefinger: index.
homily: homélie.
humbly: humblement, de manière humble, de façon humble.
mattress: matelas, clayonnage, entrelacs de protection.
penitently: de façon pénitente, de manière pénitente.
respectfully: de manière respectueuse, de façon respectueuse.
sob: sanglot, pleurer.
stable: écurie, stable, étable, ferme.
undecided: indécis, hésitant, incertain.
winter: hiver.
wiper: balai, frotteur.

CHAPTER XIV

NEWS FROM GRABMAN

That day, opening thus **auspiciously** to Beck, was **memorable** also to other and more prominent persons in this history.

Early in the **forenoon** a **parcel** was brought to Madame Dalibard which contained Ardworth's already famous book, a **goodly assortment** of extracts from the newspapers thereon, and the following letter from the young author:—

You will see, by the **accompanying** packet, that your counsels have had weight with me. I have turned aside in my slow, legitimate career. I have, as you desired, made "men talk of me." What solid benefit I may **reap** from this I know not. I shall not openly **avow** the book. Such **notoriety** cannot help meat the Bar. But liberavi animam meam,—excuse my pedantry,—I have let my soul free for a moment; I am now catching it back to put bit and **saddle** on again. I will not tell you how you have disturbed me, how you have **stung** me into this **premature** rush **amidst** the crowd, how, after **robbing** me of name and father, you have driven me to this experiment with my own mind, to see if I was **deceived** when I groaned to myself, "The Public shall give you a name, and Fame shall be your mother." I am satisfied with the experiment.

French

accompanying: accompagnant.
amidst: parmi, au milieu de.
assortment: assortiment.
auspiciously: de manière propice, de façon propice.
avow: avouer, confesser.
deceived: trompâtes, déçu, trichâmes.
forenoon: matinée.
goodly: de façon bonne, de manière bonne.
memorable: mémorable.
notoriety: notoriété.
parcel: paquet, colis, parcelle, lot.
premature: prématuré, anticipé, avant terme, lavé, précoce.
reap: moissonner, faucher.
robbing: pillant, ravissant, dévalisant.
saddle: selle, col, ensellement.
stung: piqué.

I know better now what is in me, and I have regained my peace of mind. If in the success of this **hasty** work there be that which will **gratify** the interest you so kindly take in me, **deem** that success your own; I owe it to you,—to your **revelations**, to your **admonitions**. I wait patiently your own time for further disclosures; till then, the wheel must work on, and the **grist** be ground. Kind and generous friend, till now I would not wound you by returning the sum you sent me,—nay, more, I knew I should please you by **devoting** part of it to the risk of giving this **essay** to the world, and so making its good fortune doubly your own work. Now, when the **publisher** smiles, and the shopmen bow, and I am acknowledged to have a bank in my brains,—now, you cannot be offended to receive it back. **Adieu**. When my mind is in **train** again, and I feel my step firm on the old dull road, I will come to see you. Till then, yours—by what name? Open the Biographical Dictionary at hazard, and send me one.

Gray's Inn.

Not at the noble thoughts and the deep sympathy with mankind that glowed through that work, over which Lucretia now **tremulously** hurried, did she feel delight. All that she recognized, or desired to recognize, were those evidences of that kind of intellect which wins its way through the world, and which, strong and unmistakable, rose up in every page of that vigorous logic and commanding style. The book was soon dropped, thus read; the newspaper extracts pleased even more.

"This," she said **audibly**, in the **freedom** of her solitude, "this is the son I asked for,—a son in whom I can rise; in whom I can exchange the sense of **crushing infamy** for the old delicious ecstasy of pride! For this son can I do too much? No; in what I may do for him methinks there will be no remorse. And he calls his success mine,—mine!" Her **nostrils dilated**, and her front rose erect.

In the midst of this **exultation** Varney found her; and before he could communicate the business which had brought him, he had to listen, which

---

French

adieu: adieu.
admonition: sommation, avertissement, admonestation, observation, recommandation, remontrance.
audibly: de manière audible, de façon audible.
crushing: écrasement, broyage, concassage.
deem: croire, être d'avis, croyez, penser que, regarder.
devoting: consacrant, adonnant, vouant.
dilated: dilatâtes.
essay: essai, thèse, composition.
exultation: exultation.
freedom: liberté, la liberté, indépendance.
gratify: satisfaire, gratifient, contentons.
grist: blé à moudre, grand nombre.
hasty: précipité, hâtif.
infamy: infamie.
nostril: narine, naseau.
publisher: éditeur, propriétaire d'un journal, publication, diffuseur.
revelation: révélation.
train: train, entraîner, rame, dresser, cortège, suite, former, escorte, clique.
tremulously: de façon tremblotante, de manière tremblotante.

he did with the secret, **gnawing** envy that every other man's success occasioned him, to her haughty self-felicitations.

He could not resist saying, with a sneer, when she paused, as if to ask his sympathy, —

"All this is very fine, belle-mere; and yet I should hardly have thought that coarse-featured, **uncouth** limb of the law, who seldom moves without **upsetting** a chair, never laughs but the **panes rattle** in the window, — I should hardly have thought him the precise person to gratify your pride, or answer the family ideal of a gentleman and a St. John."

"Gabriel," said Lucretia, **sternly**, "you have a **biting** tongue, and it is folly in me to **resent** those privileges which our fearful connection gives you. But this raillery — "

"Come, come, I was wrong; forgive it!" interrupted Varney, who, **dreading** nothing else, **dreaded** much the **rebuke** of his grim stepmother.

"It is forgiven," said Lucretia, coldly, and with a slight wave of her hand; then she added, with composure, —

"Long since — even while heiress of Laughton — I parted with mere pride in the hollow **seemings** of distinction. Had I not, should I have stooped to William Mainwaring? What I then respected, amidst all the **degradations** I have known, I respect still, — talent, ambition, intellect, and will. Do you think I would exchange these in a son of mine for the mere graces which a dancing-master can sell him? Fear not. Let us give but wealth to that intellect, and the world will see no **clumsiness** in the movements that march to its high places, and hear no **discord** in the laugh that triumphs over fools. But you have some news to communicate, or some proposal to suggest."

"I have both," said Varney. "In the first place, I have a letter from Grabman!"

Lucretia's eyes **sparkled**, and she snatched eagerly at the letter her son-in-law drew forth.

Liverpool, October, 1831.

French

biting: mordant, âpre, morsure.
clumsiness: maladresse, gaucherie.
degradation: dégradation, déchéance, surcreusement.
discord: discorde, désaccord.
dreaded: redouté.
dreading: option marchandises diverses.
gnawing: rongeant.
pane: volet, vitre, carreau.
rattle: cliquetis, claquer, crécelle, hochet.
rebuke: réprimander, gronder, reprocher, sermonner, repousser.
resent: s'indigner de, ressentez.
seeming: semblant, paraissant.
sparkled: brillâmes.
sternly: de manière poupe, sévèrement.
uncouth: grossier.
upsetting: bouleversant, déranger, forgeage par refoulement, matage, refoulage, vexant, aplatissement.

Jason,—I think I am on the road to success. Having first possessed myself of the fact, **commemorated** in the parish **register**, of the birth and **baptism** of Alfred Braddell's son,—for we must proceed **regularly** in these matters,—I next set my wits to work to trace that son's **exodus** from the paternal mansion. I have hunted up an old woman-servant, Jane Prior, who lived with the Braddells. She now thrives as a **laundress**; she is a rank Puritan, and **starches** for the **godly**. She was at first very **wary** and reserved in her communications; but by **siding** with her prejudices and humours, and by the **intercession** of the Rev. Mr. Graves (of her own persuasion), I have got her to open her lips. It seems that these Braddells lived very unhappily; the husband, a pious **dissenter**, had married a lady who turned out of a very different practice and belief. Jane Prior pitied her master, and **detested** her mistress. Some circumstances in the conduct of Mrs. Braddell made the husband, who was then in his last illness, resolve, from a point of conscience, to save his child from what he deemed the **contamination** of her precepts and **example**. Mrs. Braddell was absent from Liverpool on a visit, which was thought very **unfeeling** by the husband's friends; during this time Braddell was visited constantly by a gentleman (Mr. Ardworth), who differed from him greatly in some things, and seemed one of the **carnal**, but with whom **agreement** in politics (for they were both great politicians and republicans) seems to have established a link. One evening, when Mr. Ardworth was in the house, Jane Prior, who was the only **maidservant** (for they kept but two, and one had been just discharged), had been sent out to the apothecary's. On her return, Jane Prior, going into the nursery, missed the infant: she thought it was with her master; but coming into his room, Mr. Braddell told her to shut the door, informed her that he had intrusted the boy to Mr. Ardworth, to be brought up in a **righteous** and pious manner, and **implored** and commanded her to keep this a secret from his wife, whom he was resolved, indeed, if he lived, not to receive back into his house. Braddell, however, did not survive more than two days this event. On his death, Mrs. Braddell returned; but circumstances connected with the symptoms of his **malady**, and a strong impression which haunted himself, and with which he had

---

French

agreement: accord, convention, pacte, concordance, entente, atmosphère, réglage, arrangement, contrat.
baptism: baptême.
carnal: charnel, sexuel.
commemorated: commémorèrent.
contamination: contamination, interférence d'images, pollution, impureté, infection.
detested: détestâtes, exécrâtes, abomina.

dissenter: dissident.
example: exemple, ex, modèle.
exodus: exode.
godly: pieux, dévot.
implored: implorai.
intercession: intercession.
laundress: blanchisseuse.
maidservant: domestique.
malady: maladie.
register: registre, enregistrer, recommander, inscrire, immatriculer, mettre en registre,

liste.
regularly: régulièrement, souvent, fréquemment, beaucoup, de façon régulière, de manière régulière.
righteous: moral, juste, vertueux.
siding: bardage, revêtement, voie de garage, embranchement, délignement, parement.
starch: amidon, fécule, empeser, empois.
unfeeling: insensible.
wary: prudent.

infected Jane Prior, that he had been **poisoned**, led to a **posthumous examination** of his remains. No trace of poison was, however, discovered, and suspicions that had been directed against his wife could not be **substantiated** by law; still, she was regarded in so **unfavourable** a light by all who had known them both, she met with such little kindness or sympathy in her **widowhood**, and had been so openly **denounced** by Jane Prior, that it is not to be wondered at that she left the place as soon as possible. The house, indeed, was taken from her; for Braddell's affairs were found in such confusion, and his embarrassments so great, that everything was seized and sold off,—nothing left for the widow nor for the child (if the last were ever discovered.)

As may be supposed, Mrs. Braddell was at first very **clamorous** for the lost child; but Jane Prior kept her promise and **withheld** all **clew** to it, and Mrs. Braddell was forced to quit the place, in ignorance of what had become of it. Since then no one had heard of her; but Jane Prior says that she is sure she has come to no good. Now, though much of this may be, no doubt, familiar to you, dear Jason, it is right, when I put the evidence before you, that you should know and guard against what to expect; and in any trial at law to prove the identity of Vincent Braddell, Jane Prior must be a principal witness, and will certainly not spare poor Mrs. Braddell. For the main point, however,—namely, the suspicion of **poisoning** her husband,—the **inquest** and **verdict** may set aside all alarm.

My next researches have been directed on the track of Walter Ardworth, after leaving Liverpool, which (I find by the books at the inn where he **lodged** and was known) he did in debt to the **innkeeper**, the very night he received the charge of the child. Here, as yet, I am in fault; but I have **ascertained** that a woman, one of the **sect**, of the name of Joplin, living in a village fifteen miles from the town, had the care of some infant, to replace her own, which she had lost. I am going to this village to-morrow. But I cannot expect much in that quarter, since it would seem at **variance** with your more probable belief that Walter Ardworth took the child at once to Mr.

French

ascertained: constatai.
clamorous: bruyant.
clew: point d'écoute.
denounced: dénonças.
examination: examen, vérification, inspection.
innkeeper: aubergiste, hôtelier.
inquest: enquête.
lodged: logé.
poisoned: empoisonné, arséniqué.
poisoning: empoisonnement, intoxication.
posthumous: posthume, titre posthume.
sect: secte.
substantiated: justifié, prouvâtes.
unfavourable: défavorable, désavantageux.
variance: variance, désaccord.
verdict: verdict, sentence, jugement.
widowhood: veuvage, viduité.
withheld: retint, retîntes, retenu.

Fielden's. However, you see I have already gone very far in the evidence,—the birth of the child, the **delivery** of the child to Ardworth. I see a very pretty case already before us, and I do not now doubt for a moment of ultimate success.

Yours,
N. *Grabman.*

Lucretia read steadily, and with no change of countenance, to the last line of the letter. Then, as she put it down on the table before her, she repeated, with a tone of deep **exultation**: "No doubt of ultimate success!"

"You do not fear to brave all which the spite of this woman, Jane Prior, may **prompt** her to say against you?" asked Varney.

Lucretia's brow fell. "It is another torture," she said, "even to own my marriage with a low-born **hypocrite**. But I can **endure** it for the cause," she added, more **haughtily**. "Nothing can really hurt me in these **obsolete aspersions** and this vague scandal. The inquest **acquitted** me, and the world will be charitable to the mother of him who has wealth and rank and that vigorous genius which, if proved in **obscurity**, shall command opinion in renown."

"You are now, then, **disposed** at once to proceed to action. For Helen all is prepared,—the insurances are settled, the trust for which I hold them on your behalf is signed and completed. But for Percival St. John I **await** your **directions**. Will it be best first to prove your son's identity, or when **morally** satisfied that that proof is **forthcoming**, to remove betimes both the barriers to his inheritance? If we **tarry** for the last, the removal of St. John becomes more suspicious than it does at a time when you have no visible interest in his death. Besides, now we have the occasion, or can make it, can we tell how long it will last? Again, it will seem more natural that the lover should break his heart in the first shock of—"

"Ay," interrupted Lucretia, "I would have all thought and **contemplation** of crime at an end when, clasping my boy to my heart, I can say, 'Your

---

French

acquitted: acquittai.
aspersion: aspersion.
await: attendre.
contemplation: contemplation, méditation, recueillement.
delivery: livraison, remise, transmission, accouchement, distribution, délivrance.
direction: direction, sens, orientation.
disposed: disposé.
endure: supporter, endurer, souffrir, durer, durons, subir, tolérer, soutenir, continuer.
exultation: exultation.
forthcoming: prochain.
haughtily: de façon hautaine, de manière hautaine.
hypocrite: hypocrite.
morally: moralement, de manière morale, de façon morale.
obscurity: obscurité, ténèbres.
obsolete: obsolète, désuet, périmé.
prompt: invite, ponctuel, prompt, mobile, sollicitation, souffler.
tarry: goudronneux, demeures, restons, bitumeux, s'attarder.

mother's inheritance is yours.' I would not have a murder before my eyes when they should look only on the fair prospects beyond. I would cast back all the **hideous** images of horror into the rear of memory, so that hope may for once visit me again **undisturbed**. No, Gabriel, were I to speak forever, you would **comprehend** not what I grasp at in a son. It is at a future! **Rolling** a stone over the **sepulchre** of the past, it is a **resurrection** into a fresh world; it is to know again one emotion not **impure**, one scheme not criminal, — it is, in a word, to cease to be as myself, to think in another soul, to hear my heart beat in another form. All this I **covet** in a son. And when all this should smile before me in his image, shall I be **plucked** back again into my hell by the consciousness that a new crime is to be done? No; **wade** quickly through the passage of blood, that we may dry our garments and breathe the air upon the bank where sun shines and flowers bloom!"

"So be it, then," said Varney. "Before the week is out, I must be under the same roof as St. John. Before the week is out, why not all meet in the old halls of Laughton?"

"Ay, in the halls of Laughton. On the **hearth** of our **ancestors** the **deeds** done for our **descendants** look less dark."

"And first, to prepare the way, Helen should **sicken** in these fogs of London, and want change of air."

"Place before me that desk. I will read William Mainwaring's letters again and again, till from every shadow in the past a voice comes forth, 'The child of your rival, your **betrayer**, your undoer, stands between the daylight and your son!'"

French

ancestor: ancêtre, ascendant.
betrayer: traître.
comprehend: comprendre.
covet: convoites.
deed: acte, action.
descendant: descendant.
hearth: foyer, cheminée, sole.
hideous: hideux, horrible, abominable, odieux, abject, repoussant, affreux.
impure: impur.
plucked: plumé.
resurrection: résurrection.
rolling: roulage, cylindrage, laminage.
sepulchre: sépulcre.
sicken: écoeurer, donner mal au coeur, blasons, rendre malade, tomber malade.
undisturbed: paisible, non détériorée, calme.
wade: marcher dans l'eau, patauger.

CHAPTER XV

VARIETIES

Leaving the guilty pair to **concert** their schemes and **indulge** their **atrocious** hopes, we accompany Percival to the **hovel** occupied by Becky Carruthers.

On following Beck into the room she **rented**, Percival was greatly surprised to find, seated comfortably on the only chair to be seen, no less a person than the worthy Mrs. Mivers. This good lady in her **spinster** days had **earned** her own bread by hard work. She had **captivated** Mr. Mivers when but a simple **housemaid** in the service of one of his relations. And while this humble condition in her earlier life may account for much in her **language** and manners which is nowadays inconsonant with the breeding and education that **characterize** the wives of **opulent** tradesmen, so perhaps the remembrance of it made her unusually **susceptible** to the duties of charity. For there is no class of society more prone to pity and **relieve** the poor than females in domestic service; and this virtue Mrs. Mivers had not laid aside, as many do, as soon as she was in a condition to **practise** it with effect. Mrs. Mivers **blushed** scarlet on being detected in her visit of **kindness**, and **hastened** to excuse herself by the information that she belonged to a society of ladies for "The Bettering the Condition of the Poor," and that having just

---

French

atrocious: atroce, horrible, affreux.
blushed: rougi.
captivated: captivâtes.
characterize: caractériser, décrire.
concert: concert.
earned: gagnâmes.
hastened: hâtâmes, hâté, hâtai, hâtèrent.
housemaid: femme de chambre, bonne.
hovel: taudis, masure.
indulge: être indulgent, gâter.
kindness: amabilité, gentillesse, bonté, aménité.
language: langue, libelle, parole.
opulent: opulent.
practise: exercer, instruire, pratiquer.
relieve: soulager, relayer.
rented: loué, louèrent, accensa.
spinster: célibataire, femme célibataire, vieille fille.
susceptible: sensible, susceptible.

been informed of Mrs. Becky's **destitute** state, she had looked in to **recommend** her—a **ventilator**!

"It is quite shocking to see how little the poor **attends** to the proper wentilating their houses. No wonder there's so much typus about!" said Mrs. Mivers. "And for one-and-sixpence we can introduce a stream of h-air that goes up the chimbly, and carries away all that it finds!."

"I 'umbly thank you, marm," said the poor **bundle** of **rags** that went by the name of "Becky," as with some difficulty she **contrived** to stand in the presence of the **benevolent** visitor; "but I am much afeard that the h-air will make the rheumatiz very rumpatious!"

"On the contrary, on the contrary," said Mrs. Mivers, **triumphantly**; and she proceeded **philosophically** to explain that all the fevers, **aches**, pains, and physical ills that **harass** the poor **arise** from the want of an air-trap in the **chimney** and a **perforated network** in the window-pane. Becky listened patiently; for Mrs. Mivers was only a philosopher in her talk, and she had proved herself anything but a philosopher in her actions, by the **spontaneous** present of five **shillings**, and the promise of a basket of **victuals** and some good wine to keep the cold wind she invited to the apartment out of the **stomach**.

Percival **imitated** the silence of Becky, whose spirit was so bowed down by an existence of **drudgery** that not even the sight of her foster-son could draw her attention from the respect due to a superior.

"And is this poor cranky-looking cretur your son, Mrs. Becky?" said the visitor, struck at last by the appearance of the ex-sweeper as he stood at the threshold, hat in hand.

"No, indeed, marm," answered Becky; "I often says, says I: 'Child, you be the son of Sint Poll's.'"

Beck smiled proudly.

"It was agin the **grit** church, marm— But it's a long story. My poor good man had not a long been dead,—as good a man as hever lived, marm," and

---

French

ache: douleur, mal, peine, soupirer, faire mal, aspirer.
arise: naître, nais, se soulever, surgir, se lever.
attends: assiste, soigne.
benevolent: bienveillant.
bundle: paquet, ballot, faisceau, liasse, botte, mille feuilles.
chimney: cheminée, évent.
contrived: inventâmes.
destitute: dépourvu, indigent.
drudgery: corvée.
grit: gravier, poussière, grenaille, sable.
harass: harceler, tracasse, troubler, déranger l'adversaire, tourmenter.
imitated: imitas, copia.
network: réseau, filet.
perforated: perforâtes, poinçonnai, dentela, trouèrent, piqué.
philosophically: de manière philosophique, de façon philosophique, philosophiquement.
rag: chiffon, lambeau, torchon, guenille, haillon.
recommend: recommander, conseiller.
shilling: schilling.
spontaneous: spontané.
stomach: estomac, ventre, digérer.
triumphantly: de manière triomphante, triomphalement, de façon triomphante.
ventilator: aérateur, ventilateur.
victual: approvisionne.

Becky dropped a courtesy; "he fell off a **scaffold**, and **pitched** right on his 'ead, or I should not have come on the parish, marm,—and that's the truth on it!"

"Very well, I shall call and hear all about it; a sad case, I dare say. You see, your husband should have **subscribed** to our Loan Society, and then they'd have found him a 'andsome coffin, and given three pounds to his widder. But the poor are so **benighted** in these parts. I'm sure, sir, I can't guess what brought you here; but that's no business of mine. And how are all at Old Brompton?" Here Mrs. Mivers bridled **indignantly**. "There was a time when Miss Mainwaring was very glad to come and **chat** with Mr. M. and myself; but now 'rum has riz,' as the saying is,—not but what I dare say it's not her fault, poor thing! That stiff aunt of hers,—she need not look so high; pride and poverty, forsooth!"

While **delivering** these **conciliatory** sentences, Mrs. Mivers had gathered up her gown, and was evidently in the **bustle** of departure. As she now nodded to Becky, Percival **stepped** up, and, with his irresistible smile, offered her his arm. Much surprised and much **flattered**, Mrs. Mivers accepted it. As she did so, he gently **detained** her while he said to Becky,— "My good friend, I have brought you the poor lad to whom you have been a mother, to tell you that good deeds find their reward sooner or later. As for him, make yourself easy; he will inform you of the new step he has taken, and for you, good, kind-hearted creature, thank the boy you brought up if your old age shall be made easy and cheerful. Now, Beck, silly lad, go and tell all to your nurse! Take care of this step, Mrs. Mivers."

As soon as he was in the street, Percival, who, if amused at the ventilator, had seen the five shillings **gleam** on Becky's palm, and felt that he had found under the puce-coloured gown a good woman's heart to understand him, gave Mrs. Mivers a short sketch of poor Becky's history and **misfortunes**, and so contrived to interest her in behalf of the nurse that she **willingly** promised to become Percival's **almoner**, to **execute** his commission, to **improve** the interior of Becky's **abode**, and **distribute** weekly the liberal **stipend** he proposed to settle on the old widow. They had grown, indeed,

French

abode: demeure, domicile, logis, gîte, habitation, localité, logement.
almoner: aumônier.
benighted: surpris par la nuit.
bustle: tournure, se démener, s'affairer.
chat: bavarder, causerie, babiller, conversation.
conciliatory: conciliant.
delivering: livrant, délivrant.
detained: détinrent, retîntes, retint, retenu, détîntes, détenu.
distribute: distribuer, répartir, dispenser, diffuser.
execute: exécuter, effectuer, accomplir.
flattered: flatté, adulai, amadoua.
gleam: lueur, luire.
improve: améliorer, amender, réformer, perfectionner, bonifier.
indignantly: de façon indignée, de manière indignée.
misfortune: malheur, infortune, malchance.
pitched: abattu.
scaffold: échafaud.
stepped: échelonné.
stipend: traitement, appointements, bourse.
subscribed: souscrivîtes, signâtes, s'abonné, t'abonnas, nous abonnâmes, m'abonnai, abonnèrent, vous abonnâtes.
willingly: volontiers, de manière volontaire, de façon volontaire.

quite friendly and intimate by the time he reached the smart plate-glazed **mahogany**-coloured **facade** within which the flourishing business of Mr. Mivers was **carried** on; and when, **knocking** at the private door, **promptly** opened by a lemon-coloured page, she invited him upstairs, it so chanced that the conversation had slid off to Helen, and Percival was sufficiently interested to bow assent and to enter.

Though all the way up the stairs Mrs. Mivers, turning back at every other step, did her best to impress upon her young visitor's mind the important fact that they kept their household establishment at their "willer," and that their apartments in Fleet Street were only a "conwenience," the store set by the worthy housewife upon her goods and **chattels** was sufficiently visible in the **drugget** that **threaded** its narrow way up the gay Brussels stair-carpet, and in certain layers of paper which protected from the **profanation** of **immediate** touch the mahogany hand-rail. And nothing could **exceed** the fostering care exhibited in the drawing-room, when the door thrown open admitted a view of its **damask** moreen curtains, pinned back from such **impertinent sunbeams** as could force their way through the **foggy** air of the east into the windows, and the **ells** of yellow **muslin** that guarded the frames, at least, of a **collection** of coloured **prints** and two kit-kat portraitures of Mr. Mivers and his lady from the perambulations of the flies.

But Percival's view of this interior was somewhat **impeded** by his **portly** guide, who, **uttering** a little exclamation of surprise, stood motionless on the threshold as she perceived Mr. Mivers seated by the hearth in close conference with a gentleman whom she had never seen before. At that hour it was so rare an event in the life of Mr. Mivers to be found in the drawing-room, and that he should have an acquaintance unknown to his **helpmate** was a circumstance so much rarer still, that Mrs. Mivers may well be forgiven for keeping St. John standing at the door till she had recovered her amaze.

Meanwhile Mr. Mivers rose in some confusion, and was apparently about to introduce his guest, when that gentleman **coughed**, and pinched the host's arm **significantly**. Mr. Mivers coughed also, and **stammered** out: "A

French

carried: portèrent, transportèrent.
chattel: biens meubles.
collection: collection, recueil, recouvrement, encaissement, ensemble, troupe, ramassage, quête, are, bande.
coughed: toussé.
damask: damas.
drugget: droguet.
ell: aune.
exceed: dépasser, excéder, outrepasser, maîtriser, surmonter,

dominer, excèdent.
facade: façade.
foggy: brumeux, confus.
helpmate: compagnon.
immediate: immédiat.
impeded: empêchâmes.
impertinent: hardi, impertinent.
knocking: frappant, coups.
mahogany: acajou.
muslin: mousseline, toile écrue.
portly: corpulent.
print: imprimer, estampe, épreuve,

gravure, caractères, tirer, empreinte, copie.
profanation: profanation.
promptly: ponctuellement, rapidement.
significantly: de façon significative, de manière significative, significativement.
stammered: bégayé.
sunbeam: rayon de soleil.
threaded: enfilé, visser, fileté.
uttering: prononcer.

gentleman, Mrs. M.,—a friend; stay with us a day or two. Much honoured, hum!"

Mrs. Mivers stared and courtesied, and stared again. But there was an open, good-humoured smile in the face of the visitor, as he advanced and took her hand, that attracted a heart very easily **conciliated**. Seeing that that was no moment for further explanation, she plumped herself into a seat and said,—

"But bless us and save us, I am keeping you standing, Mr. St. John!"

"St. John!" repeated the visitor, with a **vehemence** that startled Mrs. Mivers. "Your name is St. John, sir,—related to the St. Johns of Laughton?"

"Yes, indeed," answered Percival, with his shy, arch smile. "Laughton at present has no worthier owner than myself."

The gentleman made two strides to Percival and shook him heartily by the hand.

"This is pleasant indeed!" he exclaimed. "You must excuse my freedom; but I knew well poor old Sir Miles, and my heart warms at the sight of his representative."

Percival glanced at his new acquaintance, and on the whole was prepossessed in his favour. He seemed somewhere on the sunnier side of fifty, with that superb yellow bronze of complexion which **betokens** long residence under Eastern skies. Deep **wrinkles** near the eyes, and a dark circle round them, spoke of cares and fatigue, and perhaps **dissipation**. But he had evidently a vigour of constitution that had borne him **passably** through all; his frame was **wiry** and nervous; his eye bright and full of life; and there was that abrupt, **unsteady, mercurial restlessness** in his movements and manner which usually **accompanies** the man whose **sanguine** temperament prompts him to **concede** to the impulse, and who is blessed or cursed with a **superabundance** of energy, according as circumstance may favour or judgment **correct** that **equivocal** gift of constitution.

French

accompanies: accompagne.
betoken: présager.
concede: concéder.
conciliated: concilié.
correct: corriger, rectifier, juste, exact, redresser.
dissipation: dissipation, noce.
equivocal: équivoque, douteux, incertain, ambigu.
mercurial: mercuriel.
passably: de façon passable, de manière passable.

restlessness: agitation, instabilité psychomotrice.
sanguine: sanguin, optimiste.
superabundance: surabondance.
unsteady: instable, chancelant, inconstant.
vehemence: véhémence, ardeur.
wiry: raide, nerveux, tordu, vigoureux.
wrinkle: ride, sillon, pli, plisser.

Percival said something appropriate in reply to so much **cordiality** paid to the account of the Sir Miles whom he had never seen, and seated himself, **colouring** slightly under the influence of the fixed, pleased, and **earnest** look still bent upon him.

Searching for something else to say, Percival asked Mrs. Mivers if she had lately seen John Ardworth.

The guest, who had just reseated himself, turned his chair round at that question with such **vivacity** that Mrs. Mivers heard it **crack**. Her chairs were not meant for such **usage**. A shade fell over her **rosy** countenance as she replied, —

"No, indeed (please, sir, them chairs is brittle)! No, he is like Madame at Brompton, and seldom **condescends** to favour us now. It was but last Sunday we asked him to dinner. I am sure he need not turn up his nose at our **roast beef** and pudding!"

Here Mr. Mivers was taken with a violent fit of **coughing**, which drew off his wife's attention. She was afraid he had taken cold.

The stranger took out a large **snuff**-box, **inhaled** a long **pinch** of snuff, and said to St. John, —

"This Mr. John Ardworth, a **pert** enough jackanapes, I suppose, — a **limb** of the law, eh?"

"Sir," said Percival, gravely, "John Ardworth is my particular friend. It is clear that you know very little of him."

"That's true," said the stranger, — "'pon my life, that's very true. But I suppose he's like all lawyers, — cunning and **tricky**, **conceited** and **supercilious**, full of prejudice and **cant**, and a red-hot Tory into the bargain. I know them, sir; I know them!"

"Well," answered St. John, half gayly, half angrily, "your general experience serves you very little here; for Ardworth is exactly the opposite of all you have described."

"Even in politics?"

French

beef: boeuf, viande bovine.
cant: incliner, équarri, moulure biseautée, flache, canter, biseauter, tors, bille dédossée, argot, dévers.
colouring: coloration, prétannage, teinture, encrage.
conceited: vaniteux, vain, frivole, suffisant.
condescends: condescend, daigne.
cordiality: cordialité.
coughing: toussant, toux.
crack: fissure, craquer, fente, fêlure, crevasse, crack, crique, fêler, gercer, gerçure.
earnest: sérieux, sincère, grave.
inhaled: inhala, humai, humé, humâtes, humèrent.
limb: membre, limbe, flanc.
pert: méthode du chemin critique, coquin.
pinch: pincer, serrer.
roast: griller, rôtir, torréfier.
rosy: rosé, rose.
snuff: tabac à priser, effleurer, moucher.
supercilious: dédaigneux, hautain.
tricky: difficile, délicat, rusé.
usage: usage, coutume, utilisation.
vivacity: vivacité, verve.

"Why, I fear he is half a Radical,—certainly more than a Whig," answered St. John, rather **mournfully**; for his own theories were all the other way, **notwithstanding** his unpatriotic **forgetfulness** of them in his offer to assist Ardworth's entrance into parliament.

"I am very glad to hear it," cried the stranger, again taking snuff. "And this Madame at Brompton—perhaps I know her a little better than I do young Mr. Ardworth—Mrs. Brad—I mean Madame Dalibard!" and the stranger glanced at Mr. Mivers, who was slowly **recovering** from some vigorous **slaps** on the back **administered** to him by his wife as a counter-irritant to the **cough**. "Is it true that she has lost the use of her limbs?"

Percival shook his head.

"And takes care of poor Helen Mainwaring the **orphan**? Well, well, that looks **amiable** enough. I must see; I must see!"

"Who shall I say **inquired** after her, when I see Madame Dalibard?" asked Percival, with some curiosity.

"Who? Oh, Mr. Tomkins. She will not **recollect** him, though,"—and the stranger laughed, and Mr. Mivers laughed too; and Mrs. Mivers, who, indeed, always laughed when other people laughed, laughed also. So Percival thought he ought to laugh for the sake of good company, and all laughed together as he arose and took leave.

He had not, however, got far from the house, on his way to his cabriolet, which he had left by Temple Bar, when, somewhat to his surprise, he found Mr. Tomkins at his elbow.

"I beg your pardon, Mr. St. John, but I have only just returned to England, and on such occasions a man is **apt** to seem curious. This young lawyer— You see the elder Ardworth, a good-for-nothing **scamp**, was a sort of friend of mine,—not exactly friend, indeed, for, by Jove, I think he was a worse friend to me than he was to **anybody** else; still I had a foolish interest for him, and should be glad to hear something more about any one bearing his name than I can coax out of that **droll** little **linen draper**. You are really intimate with young Ardworth, eh?"

French

administered: administrâmes.
amiable: aimable.
anybody: quelqu'un, un, quiconque.
apt: doué, juste, apte, enclin, intelligent.
cough: toux, tousser.
draper: finisseur de vêtements.
droll: drôle, comique.
forgetfulness: oubli, manque de mémoire.
inquired: vous enquîtes, t'enquis, s'enquit, nous enquîmes, m'enquis.
linen: lin, linge, toile.
mournfully: de façon sombre, de manière sombre.
notwithstanding: malgré, nonobstant, néanmoins.
orphan: orphelin, bout de ligne.
recollect: se rappeler, se souvenir, retenir, retiennent.
recovering: récupérant, recouvrant.
scamp: bâcler, polisson, vaurien, galopin, garnement.
slap: gifle, claque, tape.

"Intimate! poor fellow, he will not let any one be that; he works too hard to be social. But I love him sincerely, and I admire him beyond measure."

"The dog has industry, then;—that's good. And does he make debts, like that **rascal**, Ardworth senior?"

"Really, sir, I must say this tone with respect to Mr. Ardworth's father—"

"What the devil, sir! Do you take the father's part as well as the son's?"

"I don't know anything about Mr. Ardworth senior," said Percival, **pouting**; "but I do know that my friend would not allow any one to speak ill of his father in his presence; and I beg you, sir, to consider that whatever would offend him must offend me."

"Gad's my life! He's the **luckiest** young rogue to have such a friend. Sir, I wish you a very good-day."

Mr. Tomkins took off his hat, bowed, and passing St. John with a rapid step, was soon lost to his eye amongst the crowd hurrying **westward**.

But our business being now rather with him than Percival, we leave the latter to mount his cabriolet, and we proceed with Mr. Mivers's **mercurial** guest on his eccentric way through the **throng**. There was an odd mixture of thoughtful abstraction and quick observation in the **soliloquy** in which this gentleman **indulged**, as he walked **briskly** on.

"A pretty young spark that St. John! A look of his father, but handsomer, and less affected. I like him. Fine shop that, very! London **wonderfully improved**. A **hookah** in that window,—God bless me!—a real hookah! This is all very good news about that poor boy, very. After all, he is not to blame if his mother was such a damnable—I must contrive to see and judge of him myself as soon as possible. Can't trust to others; too sharp for that. What an ugly dog that is, looking after me! It is certainly a **bailiff**. Hang it, what do I care for bailiffs? **Hem**, hem!" And the gentleman thrust his hands into his pockets, and laughed, as the **jingle** of coin reached his ear through the **din** without. "Well, I must make haste to decide; for really there is a very **troublesome** piece of business before me. **Plague** take her, what can have

---

French

bailiff: huissier, bailli.
briskly: de façon vive, de manière vive, vivement.
din: vacarme, tapage.
hem: ourlet, bord, drapelet cousu.
hookah: narguilé.
improved: améliorâtes, amendai, réformé.
indulged: gâtas, gâtâtes, gâté, gâtèrent.
jingle: tinter, sonal.
luckiest: le plus chanceux.
mercurial: mercuriel.
plague: peste, fléau.
pouting: bouder, gode, tacaud.
rascal: fripon, coquin, vaurien.
soliloquy: soliloque, monologue.
throng: affluer, cohue, foule, multitude, se presser.
troublesome: gênant, pénible.
westward: vers l'ouest.
wonderfully: merveilleusement, de façon merveilleuse, de manière merveilleuse.

become of the woman? I shall have to hunt out a sharp lawyer. But John's a lawyer himself. No, **attorneys**, I suppose, are the men. Gad! they were sharp enough when they had to hunt me. What's that great bill on the wall about? 'Down with the Lords!' Pooh, pooh! Master John Bull, you love lords a great **deal** too much for that. A prettyish girl! **English** women are very good-looking, certainly. That Lucretia, what shall I do, if— Ah, time enough to think of her when I have got over that **mighty stiff** if!"

In such cogitations and mental remarks our **traveller** whiled away the time till he found himself in Piccadilly. There, a publisher's shop (and he had that keen eye for shops which **betrays** the stranger in London), with its new **publications** exposed at the window, attracted his notice. **Conspicuous** amongst the rest was the open title-page of a book, at the foot of which was placed a **placard** with the **enticing** words, "*Fourth Edition; just out*," in red capitals. The title of the work struck his **irritable**, curious fancy; he walked into the shop, asked for the volume, and while looking over the contents with muttered **ejaculations**, "Good! capital! Why, this reminds one of Horne Tooke! What's the price? Very dear; must have it though,—must. Ha, ha! home-thrust there!"—while thus turning over the leaves, and **rending** them asunder with his **forefinger**, regardless of the paper **cutter** extended to him by the shopman, a gentleman, pushing by him, asked if the publisher was at home; and as the shopman, **bowing** very low, answered "Yes," the new-comer darted into a little **recess** behind the shop. Mr. Tomkins, who had looked up very angrily on being jostled so unceremoniously, **started** and changed colour when he saw the face of the **offender**. "Saints in heaven!" he murmured almost **audibly**, "what a look of that woman; and yet—no—it is gone!"

"Who is that gentleman?" he asked abruptly, as he paid for his book.

The shopman smiled, but answered, "I don't know, sir."

"That's a lie! You would never bow so low to a man you did not know!"

The shopman smiled again. "Why, sir, there are many who come to this house who don't wish us to know them."

French

attorney: mandataire, avocat, procureur.
audibly: de manière audible, de façon audible.
betray: trahir, révéler.
bowing: déformation en arc, bombage, cintrage.
conspicuous: visible, apparent.
cutter: coupeur, tailleur, cotre.
deal: distribuer, dispenser, traiter, affaire, transaction, bois blanc.
ejaculation: éjaculation.
english: anglais, langue anglaise.
enticing: tentant, séduisant, entraînant, attirant, aguichant, affriolant, attrayant.
forefinger: index.
irritable: irritable, irascible.
mighty: puissant, considérable.
offender: offenseur, contrevenant.
placard: afficher, placard, coller, agglutiner.
publication: publication, parution.
recess: pause, alcôve, repos, niche, trêve, vacances.
rending: déchirant.
started: démarré, commencé.
stiff: rigide, raide.
traveller: voyageur, curseur.

"Ah, I understand; you are political publishers,—afraid of **libels**, I dare say. Always the same thing in this cursed country; and then they tell us we are 'free!' So I suppose that gentleman has written something William Pitt does not like. But William Pitt—ha—he's dead! Very true, so he is! Sir, this little book seems most excellent; but in my time, a man would have been sent to Newgate for **printing** it." While thus running on, Mr. Tomkins had edged himself pretty close to the recess within which the last-comer had disappeared; and there, seated on a high stool, he contrived to read and to talk at the same time, but his eye and his ear were both turned every instant towards the recess.

The shopman, little **suspecting** that in so very eccentric, **garrulous** a person he was permitting a spy to **encroach** upon the secrets of the house, continued to make up **sundry** parcels of the new publication which had so enchanted his customer, while he **expatiated** on the **prodigious** sensation the book had created, and while the customer himself had already caught enough of the low conversation within the recess to be aware that the author of the book was the very person who had so **roused** his curiosity.

Not till that gentleman, followed to the door by the polite publisher, had quitted the shop, did Mr. Tomkins put this volume in his pocket, and, with a familiar nod at the shopman, take himself off.

He was scarcely in the street when he saw Percival St. John leaning out of his cabriolet and **conversing** with the author he had discovered. He halted a moment **irresolute**; but the young man, in whom our reader recognizes John Ardworth, declining St. John's invitation to accompany him to Brompton, resumed his way through the throng; the cabriolet drove on; and Mr. Tomkins, though with a **graver** mien and a steadier step, continued his **desultory rambles**. Meanwhile, John Ardworth strode **gloomily** back to his lonely chamber.

There, throwing himself on the well-worn chair before the crowded desk, he buried his face in his hands, and for some minutes he felt all that profound **despondency** peculiar to those who have won fame, to add to the

---

French

conversing: conversant.
despondency: découragement, abattement.
desultory: décousu.
encroach: empiéter, usurper.
expatiated: discoururent.
garrulous: loquace, bavard.
gloomily: de façon sombre, de manière sombre.
graver: burin, échoppe, gravoir, pointe à tracer.
irresolute: indécis, hésitant,
irrésolu.
libel: libelle, diffamation, calomnie écrite.
printing: impression, tirage, gravure.
prodigious: prodigieux.
ramble: excursion, randonnée.
roused: irritâtes, excitèrent, stimulâtes.
sundry: divers.
suspecting: soupçonnant.

dark volume of experience the conviction of fame's **nothingness**. For some minutes he felt an **illiberal** and **ungrateful** envy of St. John, so fair, so light-hearted, so favoured by fortune, so rich in friends,—in a mother's love, and in Helen's half-plighted **troth**. And he, from his very birth, cut off from the social ties of blood; no mother's kiss to reward the toils or **gladden** the sports of childhood; no father's cheering word up the steep hill of man! And Helen, for whose sake he had so often, when his heart grew weary, nerved himself again to labour, saying, "Let me be rich, let me be great, and then I will dare to tell Helen that I love her!"—Helen smiling upon another, unconscious of his pangs! What could fame bestow in **compensation**? What matter that strangers praised, and the babble of the world's running stream **lingered** its brief moment round the **pebble** in its way. In the bitterness of his mood, he was unjust to his rival. All that exquisite but half-concealed treasure of imagination and thought which lay beneath the surface of Helen's **childlike** smile he believed that he alone—he, soul of power and son of genius—was worthy to discover and to prize. In the pride not unfrequent with that kingliest of all aristocracies, the Chiefs of Intellect, he forgot the grandeur which invests the attributes of the heart; forgot that, in the **lists** of love, the heart is at least the equal of the mind. In the **reaction** that follows great excitement, Ardworth had **morbidly** felt, that day, his utter solitude,—felt it in the streets through which he had passed; in the home to which he had returned; the burning tears, shed for the first time since childhood, forced themselves through his clasped fingers. At length he rose, with a strong effort at self-mastery, some contempt of his weakness, and much **remorse** at his ungrateful envy. He gathered together the **soiled** manuscript and **dingy** proofs of his book, and thrust them through the **grimy bars** of his **grate**; then, opening his desk, he drew out a small packet, with tremulous fingers **unfolding** paper after paper, and gazed, with eyes still **moistened**, on the **relics** kept till then in the devotion of the only sentiment inspired by Eros that had ever, perhaps, softened his iron nature. These were two notes from Helen, some violets she had once given him, and a little purse she had **knitted** for him (with a **playful** prophecy of future fortunes) when he had

French

bar: bar, barre, abreuvoir, lingot, mesure.
childlike: enfantin.
compensation: compensation, indemnisation, dédommagement, rémunération, réparation civile.
dingy: terne.
gladden: réjouir.
grate: grille, râper, grincer, crisser.
grimy: crasseux, sale.
illiberal: intolérant.
knitted: tricoté.
lingered: traîné.
list: liste, énumérer, répertoire, inventaire.
moistened: humidifia, humectâtes.
morbidly: de façon morbide, de manière morbide.
nothingness: néant, vide.
pebble: galet, gravillon naturel.
playful: espiègle, ludique, badin.
reaction: réaction.
relic: relique, vestige.
remorse: remords.
soiled: sale, souillé, sali.
troth: foi.
unfolding: dépliant.
ungrateful: ingrat, disgracieux.

last left the **vicarage**. Nor blame him, ye who, with more habitual **romance** of temper, and richer **fertility** of imagination, can **reconcile** the tenderest memories with the sternest duties, if he, with all his strength, felt that the **associations** connected with those **tokens** would but **enervate** his resolves and **embitter** his **resignation**. You can guess not the **extent** of the **sacrifice**, the **bitterness** of the pang, when, **averting** his head, he dropped those relics on the **hearth**. The evidence of the desultory ambition, the tokens of the **visionary** love,—the same **flame leaped** up to **devour** both! It was as the **funeral** pyre of his youth!

"So," he said to himself, "let all that can **divert** me from the true ends of my life **consume**! Labour, take back your son."

An hour afterwards, and his clerk, returning home, found Ardworth employed as **calmly** as usual on his Law Reports.

French

association: association, fédération, société.
averting: détournant.
bitterness: amertume, âcreté.
calmly: de façon calme, de manière calme.
consume: consommer, dévorer.
devour: dévorer, engloutissez.
divert: distraire, détourner, amuser, dérouter.
embitter: aigrir, acharnons.
enervate: énerver, affaiblir,
débiliter.
extent: étendue, ampleur, domaine.
fertility: fertilité, fécondité.
flame: flamme, flinguer.
funeral: enterrement, obsèques, funérailles.
hearth: foyer, cheminée, sole.
leaped: sauté.
reconcile: réconcilier, raccommode, se réconcilier, concilier, rapprochez.
resignation: démission,
résignation.
romance: romance, fabuler.
sacrifice: sacrifier, offrir, faire offrande, consacrer, immoler.
token: jeton, témoignage, signe, marque, preuve, gage.
vicarage: presbytère.
visionary: visionnaire.

CHAPTER XVI

THE INVITATION TO LAUGHTON

That day, when he called at Brompton, Percival **reported** to Madame Dalibard his interview with the **eccentric** Mr. Tomkins. Lucretia seemed chafed and **disconcerted** by the inquiries with which that gentleman had honoured her, and as soon as Percival had gone, she sent for Varney. He did not come till late; she repeated to him what St. John had said of the stranger. Varney **participated** in her uneasy alarm. The name, indeed, was unknown to them, nor could they conjecture the **bearer** of so ordinary a **patronymic**; but there had been secrets enough in Lucretia's life to **render** her **apprehensive** of **encountering** those who had known her in earlier years; and Varney feared **lest** any **rumour** reported to St. John might create his **mistrust**, or **lessen** the hold obtained upon a victim **heretofore** so unsuspicious. They both agreed in the **expediency** of **withdrawing** themselves and St. John as soon as possible from London, and **frustrating** Percival's chance of closer intercourse with the stranger, who had evidently aroused his curiosity.

The next day Helen was much **indisposed**; and the **symptoms** grew so grave towards the evening that Madame Dalibard expressed alarm, and willingly suffered Percival (who had only been permitted to see Helen for a

---

French

apprehensive: appréhensif, inquiet, craintif.
bearer: porteur, support, traverse.
disconcerted: troublâtes, déroutâmes, déconcertèrent.
eccentric: excentrique, original.
encountering: rencontrant.
expediency: convenance, opportunisme.
frustrating: frustrant, déjouant.
heretofore: jusqu'ici.
indisposed: indisposé, souffrant.
lessen: diminuer, amoindrir, abréger, abaisser.
lest: de peur que.
mistrust: méfiance, te méfies, se méfient, nous méfions, vous méfiez, me méfie, défiance.
participated: participai.
patronymic: nom patronymique, patronyme.
render: rendre, plâtrez, reproduction, renformis, crépis, enduire, interpréter.
reported: rapporté.
rumour: renommée, réputation, rumeur.
symptom: symptôme, signe fonctionnel.
withdrawing: retirant.

few minutes, when her **lassitude** was so extreme that she was obliged to **retire** to her room) to go in search of a **physician**. He returned with one of the most **eminent** of the faculty. On the way to Brompton, in reply to the questions of Dr.—, Percival spoke of the **dejection** to which Helen was occasionally subject, and this circumstance confirmed Dr.—, after he had seen his patient, in his view of the case. In addition to some **feverish** and **inflammatory** symptoms which he trusted his **prescriptions** would **speedily** remove, he found great nervous **debility**, and willingly fell in with the casual suggestion of Varney, who was present, that a change of air would greatly improve Miss Mainwaring's general health, as soon as the temporary acute attack had **subsided**. He did not regard the present complaint very seriously, and **reassured** poor Percival by his cheerful mien and sanguine **predictions**. Percival remained at the house the whole day, and had the satisfaction, before he left, of hearing that the remedies had already **abated** the fever, and that Helen had fallen into a profound sleep. Walking back to town with Varney, the last said hesitatingly,—

"You were saying to me the other day that you feared you should have to go for a few days both to Vernon Grange and to Laughton, as your steward wished to point out to you some **extensive** alterations in the management of your woods to **commence** this autumn. As you were so soon coming of age, Lady Mary desired that her directions should yield to your own. Now, since Helen is recommended change of air, why not invite Madame Dalibard to visit you at one of these places? I would suggest Laughton. My poor mother-in-law I know longs to **revisit** the scenes of her youth, and you could not **compliment** or **conciliate** her more than by such an invitation."

"Oh," said Percival, **joyfully**, "it would **realize** the fondest dream of my heart to see Helen under the old roof-tree of Laughton; but as my mother is abroad, and there is therefore no lady to receive them, perhaps—"

"Why," interrupted Varney, "Madame Dalibard herself is almost the very person whom les bienseances might induce you to select to do the honours of your house in Lady Mary's absence, not only as **kinswoman** to yourself, but as the nearest surviving relative of Sir Miles,—the most immediate

French

abated: diminuèrent.
commence: commencer, débuter, aborder.
compliment: compliment, féliciter, flatterie.
conciliate: concilier, réconcilier.
debility: débilité, asthénie.
dejection: abattement, découragement, mélancolie.
eminent: éminent, excellent, accompli.
extensive: étendu, extensif, ample.

large, vaste.
feverish: fiévreux, fébrile.
inflammatory: inflammatoire, séditieux, incendiaire.
joyfully: de manière joyeuse, de façon joyeuse.
kinswoman: parente.
lassitude: lassitude.
physician: médecin, docteur.
prediction: prédiction, prévision, prophétie.
prescription: ordonnance,

prescription, recette.
realize: réaliser, comprendre.
reassured: rassuré.
retire: se retirer, retirer.
revisit: revisitent.
speedily: de façon rapide, de manière rapide, rapidement.
subsided: nous affaissâmes, t'affaissas, vous affaissâtes, s'affaissèrent, m'affaissai.

descendant of the St. Johns; her **mature** years and **decorum** of life, her joint **kindred** to Helen and yourself, surely remove every appearance of impropriety."

"If she thinks so, certainly; I am no accurate judge of such formalities. You could not oblige me more, Varney, than in pre-obtaining her consent to the proposal. Helen at Laughton! Oh, **blissful** thought!"

"And in what air would she be so likely to revive?" said Varney; but his voice was thick and **husky**.

The ideas thus presented to him almost **banished** anxiety from Percival's breast. In a thousand delightful shapes they haunted him during the **sleepless** night; and when, the next morning, he found that Helen was **surprisingly** better, he pressed his invitation upon Madame Dalibard with a warmth that made her cheek yet more pale, and the hand, which the boy grasped as he pleaded, as cold as the dead. But she briefly **consented**, and Percival, allowed a brief interview with Helen, had the rapture to see her smile in a delight as **childlike** as his own at the news he communicated, and listen with **swimming** eye when he dwelt on the walks they should take together amidst haunts to become henceforth dear to her as to himself. **Fairyland** dawned before them.

The visit of the physician justified Percival's heightened spirits. All the acuter symptoms had vanished already. He **sanctioned** his patient's departure from town as soon as Madame Dalibard's convenience would permit, and recommended only a course of **restorative** medicines to strengthen the nervous system, which was to commence with the following morning, and be **persisted** in for some weeks. He dwelt much on the effect to be **derived** from taking these medicines the first thing in the day, as soon as Helen woke. Varney and Madame Dalibard exchanged a rapid glance. **Charmed** with the success that in this instance had attended the skill of the great physician, Percival, in his usual **zealous benevolence**, now eagerly pressed upon Madame Dalibard the wisdom of **consulting** Dr.—for her own **malady**; and the **doctor**, putting on his spectacles and drawing his chair

---

French

banished: exila, bannîtes.
benevolence: bienveillance.
blissful: bienheureux, heureux.
charmed: charmé.
childlike: enfantin.
consented: consenti, acquiesçâmes.
consulting: consultant.
decorum: décorum, bienséance.
derived: dérivâtes.
doctor: docteur, médecin, toubib.
fairyland: royaume des fées.
husky: chien esquimau, husky.

kindred: parenté, famille.
malady: maladie.
mature: mûr, adulte, fait, mûrir, font, faisons, mature, échoir.
persisted: persistèrent.
restorative: fortifiant, restaurateur.
sanctioned: sanctionné.
sleepless: sans sommeil.
surprisingly: de façon surprenante, de manière surprenante, étonnamment.
swimming: nageant, natation,

baignade.
zealous: fervent, zélé.

nearer to the frowning **cripple**, began to question her of her state. But Madame Dalibard abruptly and **discourteously** put a stop to all **interrogatories**: she had already exhausted all remedies art could suggest; she had become **reconciled** to her **deplorable infirmity**, and lost all faith in physicians. Some day or other she might try the baths at Egra, but till then she must be permitted to suffer undisturbed.

The doctor, by no means **wishing** to undertake a case of **chronic paralysis**, rose **smilingly**, and with a liberal confession that the German baths were sometimes extremely **efficacious** in such complaints, pressed Percival's **outstretched** hand, then slipped his own into his pocket, and bowed his way out of the room.

Relieved from all apprehension, Percival very good-humouredly received the hint of Madame Dalibard that the excitement through which she had gone for the last twenty-four hours rendered her unfit for his society, and went home to write to Laughton and prepare all things for the reception of his guests. Varney accompanied him. Percival found Beck in the hall, already much altered, and **embellished**, by a new **suit** of **livery**. The ex-sweeper stared hard at Varney, who, without recognizing, in so smart a shape, the squalid tatterdemalion who had **lighted** him up the stairs to Mr. Grabman's apartments, passed him by into Percival's little study, on the ground-floor.

"Well, Beck," said Percival, ever **mindful** of others, and **attributing** his groom's astonished gaze at Varney to his admiration of that gentleman's **showy** exterior, "I shall send you down to the country to-morrow with two of the horses; so you may have to-day to yourself to take leave of your nurse. I **flatter** myself you will find her rooms a little more comfortable than they were yesterday."

Beck heard with a **bursting** heart; and his master, giving him a **cheering tap** on the shoulder, left him to find his way into the streets and to Becky's abode.

He found, indeed, that the last had already **undergone** the magic **transformation** which is ever at the command of **godlike** wealth. Mrs.

French

attributing: attribuant.
bursting: éclatement, ruptage.
cheering: ovations.
chronic: chronique.
cripple: estropié, paralyser.
deplorable: déplorable, lamentable.
discourteously: de façon impolie, de manière impoli.
efficacious: efficace.
embellished: embelli, enjolivas.
flatter: flatter, aduler, amadouer.
godlike: divin.

infirmity: infirmité.
interrogatory: interrogateur.
lighted: allumé, éclairé, enflammé.
livery: livrée, couleurs d'une maison.
mindful: attentif, conscient.
outstretched: étendu, déployé, tendu.
paralysis: paralysie, immobilisation.
reconciled: réconciliâtes, rapprochèrent, raccommodèrent.

showy: voyant, frimeur, prétentieux, tapageur.
smilingly: de façon souriante, de manière souriante.
suit: costume, complet, convenir, procès, couleur.
tap: robinet, taraud, forer, prise, taper, toucher, rencontrer.
transformation: transformation, métamorphose.
undergone: subi.
wishing: désirant.

Mivers, who was naturally **prompt** and active, had had pleasure in **executing** Percival's commission. Early in the morning, floors had been scrubbed, the windows **cleaned**, the **ventilator** fixed; then followed porters with chairs and tables, and a wonderful Dutch clock, and new **bedding**, and a bright piece of carpet; and then came two servants belonging to Mrs. Mivers to arrange the **chattels**; and **finally**, when all was nearly completed, the Avatar of Mrs. Mivers herself, to give the last finish with her own mittened hands and in her own housewifely **apron**.

The good lady was still employed in **ranging** a set of **teacups** on the **shelves** of the **dresser** when Beck entered; and his old nurse, in the **overflow** of her **gratitude**, **hobbled** up to her **foundling** and threw her arms round his neck.

"That's right!" said Mrs. Mivers, good-humouredly, turning round, and **wiping** the tear from her eye. "You ought to make much of him, poor lad,—he has turned out a **godsend** indeed; and, upon my word, he looks very respectable in his new clothes. But what is this,—a child's coral?" as, opening a **drawer** in the dresser, she discovered Beck's **treasure**. "Dear me, it is a very handsome one; why, these bells look like gold!" and suspicion of her protege's **honesty** for a moment **contracted** her **thoughtful** brow. "However on earth did you come by this, Mrs. Becky?"

"Sure and sartin," answered Becky, dropping her **mutilated** courtesy, "I be's glad it be found now, instead of sum days afore, or I might have been vicked enough to let it go with the rest to the pop-shop; and I'm sure the times out of mind ven that 'ere boy was a h-urchin that I've risted the timtashung and said, 'No, Becky Carruthers, that maun't go to my h-uncle's!'"

"And why not, my good woman?"

"Lor' love you, marm, if that curril could speak, who knows vot it might say,—eh, lad, who knows? You sees, marm, my good man had not a long been dead; I could not a get no vork no vays. 'Becky Carruthers,' says I, 'you must go out in the streets a begging!' I niver thought I should a come to that.

French

apron: tablier, aire de trafic, crampon.
bedding: literie, stratification, minerai homogénéisé.
chattel: biens meubles.
cleaned: purifièrent, nettoya.
contracted: contracté.
drawer: tiroir, tireur, dessinateur.
dresser: commode, habilleur.
executing: exécutant.
finally: finalement, enfin, de façon finale, de manière finale.
foundling: enfant trouvé.
godsend: aubaine.
gratitude: gratitude, reconnaissance, remerciement.
hobbled: ambleur, entravé.
honesty: honnêteté.
mutilated: mutilé, détérioré, tronqué.
overflow: déborder, déversoir, inonder, trop plein, surplus, dépassement de capacité.
prompt: invite, ponctuel, prompt, mobile, sollicitation, souffler.
ranging: télémétrie, contrôle de l'échelle, jalonnement, mesure de distance, parangonnage, recherche par rang.
shelve: enterrer, garnissez, ajourner.
teacup: tasse à thé.
thoughtful: réfléchi, pensif.
treasure: trésor, cassette.
ventilator: aérateur, ventilateur.
wiping: essuyant, torchant.

But my poor husband, you sees, marm, fell from a scaffol',—as good a man as hever—"

"Yes, yes, you told me all that before," said Mrs. Mivers, **growing** impatient, and already diverted from her interest in the **coral** by a new **cargo**, all bright from the tinman, which, indeed, no less **instantaneously**, absorbed the admiration both of Beck and his nurse. And what with the inspection of these articles, and the comments each provoked, the coral rested in peace on the dresser till Mrs. Mivers, when just about to **renew** her inquiries, was startled by the sound of the Dutch clock striking four,—a voice which reminded her of the **lapse** of time and her own dinner-hour. So, with many promises to call again and have a good chat with her humble friend, she took her departure, amidst the blessings of Becky, and the less **noisy**, but not less grateful, **salutations** of Beck.

Very happy was the evening these poor creatures passed together over their first cup of **tea** from the new bright **copper** kettle and the almost forgotten luxury of **crumpets**, in which their altered circumstances permitted them without **extravagance** to indulge. In the course of conversation Beck **communicated** how much he had been astonished by recognizing the visitor of Grabman, the provoker of the irritable grave-stealer, in the familiar companion of his master; and when Becky told him how often, in the domestic experience her **vocation** of charing had **accumulated**, she had heard of the ruin brought on rich young men by **gamblers** and **sharpers**, Beck promised to himself to keep a sharp eye on Grabman's **showy** acquaintance. "For master is but a **babe**, like," said he, **majestically**; "and I'd be cut into **mincemeat** afore I'd let an 'air on his 'ead come to 'arm, if so be's h-as 'ow I could perwent it."

We need not say that his nurse confirmed him in these good resolutions.

"And now," said Beck, when the time came for **parting**, "you'll keep from the gin-shop, old 'oman, and not shame the young master?"

"Sartin sure," answered Becky; "it is only ven vun is down in the vorld that vun goes to the Ticker-shop. Now, h-indeed,"—and she looked round

---

French

accumulated: accumulâtes, entassai, s'amoncela, vous amoncelâtes, nous amoncelâmes, t'amoncelas, m'amoncelai.
babe: bébé.
cargo: cargaison, chargement, fret, facultés.
communicated: communiquâtes.
copper: cuivre, de cuivre, le cuivre.
coral: corail, de corail.
crumpet: crumpet.
extravagance: extravagance.
gambler: joueur, parieur, spéculateur.
growing: grandissant, croissant.
instantaneously: de façon instantanée, de manière instantanée.
lapse: déchéance, défaillance, retomber.
majestically: de façon majestueuse, de manière Majestueuse, majestueusement.
mincemeat: mincemeat.
noisy: bruyant, bruité, tapageur, tumultueux.
parting: raie, séparation.
renew: renouveler, reconduire.
salutation: salut.
sharper: tricheur, escroc.
showy: voyant, frimeur, prétentieux, tapageur.
tea: thé, infusion, tisane.
vocation: vocation.

very proudly, — "I 'as a 'spectable stashion, and I vould n't go for to lower it, and let 'em say that Becky Carruthers does not know how to **conduct** herself. The curril will be **safe** enuff now; but p'r'aps you had best take it yourself, lad."

"Vot should I do vith it? I've had enuff of the 'sponsibility. Put it up in a 'ankerchiff, and p'r'aps ven **master** gets married, and 'as a babby vots teethin', he vil say, 'Thank ye, Beck, for your curril.' Vould not that make us **proud**, mammy?"

Chuckling heartily at that **vision**, Beck **kissed** his **nurse**, and trying hard to keep himself **upright**, and do **credit** to the **dignity** of his **cloth**, returned to his new room over the **stables**.

French

cloth: tissu, étoffe, linge, toile, chiffon.
conduct: conduire, guider, mener, diriger, aboutir, procédé, régler.
credit: crédit, avoir, approvisionner, accréditif, honneur, unité, virer.
dignity: dignité.
kissed: baisée, embrassé.
master: maître, patron, maestro, apprendre à fond, capitaine, principal.
nurse: infirmière, soigner, nourrice, veiller sur, allaiter.
proud: fier, altier, orgueilleux.
safe: sûr, en sûreté, sans danger, sauf, à l'abri.
stable: écurie, stable, étable, ferme.
upright: montant, droit, honnête, intègre, vertical, debout.
vision: vision, vue.

CHAPTER XVII

THE WAKING OF THE SERPENT

And how, O Poet of the sad belief, and eloquence "like **ebony**, at once dark and splendid [It was said of Tertullian that "his style was like ebony, dark and splendid"]," how couldst thou, august Lucretius, **deem** it but sweet to **behold** from the steep the **strife** of the great sea, or, safe from the **peril**, gaze on the **wrath** of the **battle**, or, **serene** in the temples of the wise, look afar on the wanderings of human error? Is it so sweet to survey the ills from which thou art delivered? Shall not the strong law of *sympathy* find thee out, and thy heart rebuke thy philosophy? Not sweet, indeed, can be man's shelter in self when he says to the storm, "I have no bark on the sea;" or to the gods of the battle, "I have no son in the slaughter;" when he smiles **unmoved** upon **Woe**, and murmurs, "Weep on, for these eyes know no tears;" when, unappalled, he beholdeth the black deeds of crime, and cries to his conscience, "Thou art calm." Yet solemn is the sight to him who lives in all life,—seeks for Nature in the storm, and Providence in the battle; **loses** self in the woe; **probes** his heart in the crime; and owns no philosophy that sets him free from the **fetters** of man. Not in vain do we **scan** all the contrasts in the large **framework** of civilized earth if we note "when the dust groweth into **hardness**, and the **clods cleave** fast together." Range, O Art, through all

---

French

battle: bataille, combat, lutte.
behold: voici, voilà, apercevoir, voir.
cleave: fendre, cliver, se fendre.
clod: boule, motte.
deem: croire, être d'avis, croyez, penser que, regarder.
ebony: ébène, ébénier.
fetter: chaîne, enchaîner.
framework: cadre, charpente, armature, structure, ossature.
hardness: crudité, degré du vide, difficulté, Dureté, compacité.
loses: perd, paume.
peril: danger, péril.
probe: sonde, enquête, scruter, palpeur, explorer.
scan: balayage, scanner, analyser, échographie.
serene: serein, tranquille.
strife: conflit.
unmoved: indifférent, insensible.
woe: hélas, aïe, malheur.
wrath: colère, courroux.

space, clasp together in extremes, shake idle wealth from its **lethargy**, and bid States look in **hovels** where the teacher is dumb, and Reason unweeded runs to rot! Bid haughty Intellect pause in its triumph, and doubt if intellect alone can deliver the soul from its **tempters**! Only that lives uncorrupt which preserves in all seasons the human affections in which the breath of God breathes and is. Go forth to the world, O Art, go forth to the innocent, the guilty, the wise, and the dull; go forth as the still voice of Fate! Speak of the **insecurity** even of goodness below; carry on the **rapt** vision of suffering Virtue through "the doors of the shadows of death;" show the dim revelation symbolled forth in the Tragedy of old,—how **incomplete** is man's destiny, how undeveloped is the justice divine, if Antigone sleep **eternally** in the ribs of the rock, and Oedipus **vanish** forever in the Grove of the Furies. Here below, "the waters are hid with a stone, and the face of the deep is frozen;" but above liveth He "who can bind the sweet influence of the Pleiades, and loose the bands of Orion." Go with Fate over the **bridge**, and she **vanishes** in the land beyond the gulf! Behold where the Eternal demands Eternity for the progress of His creatures and the **vindication** of His justice!

It was past midnight, and Lucretia sat alone in her dreary room; her head buried on her bosom, her eyes fixed on the ground, her hands resting on her knees,—it was an image of inanimate **prostration** and **decrepitude** that might have moved compassion to its depth. The door opened, and Martha entered, to assist Madame Dalibard, as usual, to retire to rest. Her mistress slowly raised her eyes at the noise of the opening door, and those eyes took their searching, penetrating acuteness as they fixed upon the florid nor **uncomely** countenance of the waiting-woman.

In her **starched** cap, her sober-coloured **stuff** gown, in her **prim**, quiet manner and a certain **sanctified demureness** of aspect, there was something in the first appearance of this woman that impressed you with the notion of **respectability**, and inspired confidence in those steady good qualities which we seek in a trusty servant. But more closely **examined**, an habitual observer might have found much to **qualify**, perhaps to disturb, his first prepossessions. The exceeding lowness of the forehead, over which that stiff,

---

French

bridge: pont, passerelle, traverse, chevalet, bridge, arête.
decrepitude: décrépitude.
demureness: modestie.
eternally: éternellement, de façon éternelle, de manière éternelle.
examined: examina, fouillas.
hovel: taudis, masure.
incomplete: incomplet, inachevé, imparfait, dépareillé.
insecurity: insécurité.
lethargy: léthargie.

prim: collet monté, guindé.
prostration: prostration.
qualify: qualifier, exprimer une réserve, être admis dans une profession, réussir à l'examen.
rapt: enthousiaste.
respectability: respectabilité, honorabilité.
sanctified: sanctifia.
starched: amidonné.
stuff: substance, fourrer, rembourrer, choses, affaires, trucs, bourrer, empailler, farcir, remplir.
tempter: tentateur.
uncomely: laid.
vanish: disparaître.
vanishes: disparaît.
vindication: justification, revendication, défense.

harsh hair was so **puritanically** parted; the **severe hardness** of those thin, small lips, so **pursed** up and **constrained**; even a certain dull cruelty in those light, cold blue eyes, — might have caused an uneasy **sentiment**, almost approaching to fear. The fat grocer's **spoilt** child **instinctively recoiled** from her when she entered the shop to make her household purchases; the old, gray-whiskered **terrier** dog at the public-house slunk into the tap when she crossed the threshold.

Madame Dalibard silently suffered herself to be **wheeled** into the **adjoining** bedroom, and the process of **disrobing** was nearly completed before she said abruptly, —

"So you attended Mr. Varney's uncle in his last illness. Did he suffer much?"

"He was a poor creature at best," answered Martha; "but he gave me a deal of trouble afore he went. He was a scranny corpse when I strecked him out."

Madame Dalibard **shrank** from the hands at that moment employed upon herself, and said, —

"It was not, then, the first corpse you have laid out for the grave?"

"Not by many."

"And did any of those you so prepared die of the same complaint?"

"I can't say, I'm sure," returned Martha. "I never **inquires** how folks die; my bizness was to nurse 'em till all was over, and then to sit up. As they say in my country, 'Riving Pike wears a **hood** when the **weather bodes** ill.'"

> If Riving Pike do **wear** a hood,
> The day, be sure, will ne'er be good.
> A Lancashire Distich.

French

adjoining: adjacent, attenant, contigu, aboutissant.
bode: présagent.
constrained: contraint, forçâtes, gêné, forcé.
disrobing: déshabillant.
hardness: crudité, degré du vide, difficulté, Dureté, compacité.
hood: capot, capuchon, cagoule, hotte, couverture, apache, garniture frontale, chapeau.
inquire: enquérir, m'enquiers, vous enquérez, t'enquiers, s'enquièrent, se renseigner, nous enquérons, demander.
instinctively: instinctivement, de façon instinctive, de manière instinctive.
puritanically: de façon puritaine, de manière puritaine.
pursed: fourreau.
recoiled: reculé.
sentiment: sentiment.
severe: sévère, austère, grave, rigoureux, difficile, dur.
shrank: rétrécies.
spoilt: gâté.
terrier: registre foncier, terrier.
wear: usure, porter, avoir, user.
weather: temps, doubler au vent, météo.
wheeled: mobile, roues, sur roues, à roues.

"And when you sat up with Mr. Varney's uncle, did you feel no fear in the dead of the night,—that corpse before you, no fear?"

"Young Mr. Varney said I should come to no harm. Oh, he's a clever man! What should I fear, ma'am?" answered Martha, with a **horrid** simplicity.

"You have belonged to a very religious **sect**, I think I have heard you say,—a sect not unfamiliar to me; a sect to which great crime is very rarely known?"

"Yes, ma'am, some of 'em be **tame** enough, but others be weel [whirlpool] deep!"

"You do not believe what they taught you?"

"I did when I was young and silly."

"And what disturbed your belief?"

"Ma'am, the man what taught me, and my mother afore me, was the first I ever kep' company with," answered Martha, without a change in her **florid hue**, which seemed fixed in her cheek, as the red in an autumn leaf. "After he had ruined me, as the girls say, he told me as how it was all sham!"

"You loved him, then?"

"The man was well enough, ma'am, and he **behaved** handsome and got me a husband. I've known better days."

"You sleep well at night?"

"Yes, ma'am, thank you; I loves my bed."

"I have done with you," said Madame Dalibard, **stifling** a **groan**, as now, placed in her bed, she turned to the wall. Martha **extinguished** the candle, leaving it on the table by the bed, with a book and a box of matches, for Madame Dalibard was a bad **sleeper**, and often read in the night. She then drew the curtains and went her way.

It might be an hour after Martha had retired to rest that a hand was stretched from the bed, that the candle was **lighted**, and Lucretia Dalibard

---

French

behaved: comporté.
extinguished: éteignîtes.
florid: fleuri, florissant.
groan: gémir, geindre.
horrid: horrible, affreux, méchant.
hue: teinte, nuance, tonalité chromatique.
lighted: allumé, éclairé, enflammé.
sect: secte.
sleeper: dormeur, traverse.
stifling: étouffant, suffoquant.
tame: apprivoisé, dresser, dompter, docile.

rose; with a sudden movement she threw aside the coverings, and stood in her long night-gear on the floor. Yes, the helpless, **paralyzed** cripple rose, was on her feet,—tall, elastic, erect! It was as a **resuscitation** from the grave. Never was change more startling than that simple action effected,—not in the form alone, but the whole character of the face. The solitary light streamed upward on a countenance on every line of which spoke sinister power and strong resolve. If you had ever seen her before in her false, crippled state, **prostrate** and helpless, and could have seen her then,—those eyes, if **haggard** still, now full of life and vigour; that frame, if spare, **towering aloft** in commanding stature, **perfect** in its proportions as a Grecian image of Nemesis,—your amaze would have **merged** into terror, so **preternatural** did the transformation appear, so did aspect and bearing contradict the very character of her sex, **uniting** the two elements most formidable in man or in fiend,—wickedness and power.

She stood a moment motionless, **breathing** loud, as if it were a joy to breathe free from restraint; and then, lifting the light, and **gliding** to the adjoining room, she unlocked a **bureau** in the corner, and bent over a small **casket**, which she opened with a secret spring.

Reader, cast back your eye to that passage in this history when Lucretia Clavering took down the volume from the niche in the tapestried chamber at Laughton, and **numbered**, in thought, the hours left to her uncle's life. Look back on the **ungrateful** thought; **behold** how it has swelled and **ripened** into the guilty deed! There, in that box, Death guards his treasure **crypt**. There, all the science of Hades numbers its murderous **inventions**. As she searched for the **ingredients** her design had pre-selected, something heavier than those small packets she **deranged** fell to the bottom of the box with a low and hollow sound. She started at the noise, and then smiled, in scorn of her momentary fear, as she took up the ring that had occasioned the sound,—a ring plain and solid, like those used as signets in the Middle Ages, with a large dull **opal** in the centre. What secret could that **bauble** have in common with its ghastly companions in Death's crypt? This had been found amongst Olivier's papers; a note in that precious manuscript, which had given to the

French

aloft: en haut, en l'air, vol.
bauble: babiole, marotte.
behold: voici, voilà, apercevoir, voir.
breathing: respirant, pompage, souffle, pulsation, exploitation par jaillissement intermittent, reniflage.
bureau: bureau, office.
casket: cercueil, coffret, mettre en bière.
crypt: crypte.
deranged: dérangé.
gliding: vol à voile, glissement.
haggard: hâve, blème, égaré, maigre.
ingredient: ingrédient, composante, élément.
invention: invention, découverte.
merged: fusionnèrent.
numbered: numéroté.
opal: opale.
paralyzed: paralysâtes, médusé.
perfect: parfait, achevé, accompli.
preternatural: surnaturel.
prostrate: prosterné.
resuscitation: réanimation, ressuscitation.
ripened: mûrîmes, mûrit.
towering: mirage allongeant verticalement l'image, très haut.
ungrateful: ingrat, disgracieux.
uniting: unissant, appariant.

hands of his successors the keys of the grave, had discovered the mystery of its uses. By the pressure of the hand, at the touch of a concealed spring, a **barbed** point flew forth **steeped** in venom more deadly than the Indian extracts from the bag of the cobar de capello,—a venom to which no antidote is known, which no **test** can detect. It corrupts the whole mass of the blood; it mounts in frenzy and fire to the brain; it rends the soul from the body in **spasm** and convulsion. But examine the dead, and how divine the effect of the cause! How go back to the records of the Borgias, and amidst all the scepticisms of times in which, happily, such arts are unknown, unsuspected, learn from the hero of Machiavel how a clasp of the hand can get rid of a foe! Easier and more natural to point to the living **puncture** in the **skin**, and the swollen **flesh** round it, and **dilate** on the danger a rusty nail—nay, a pin—can engender when the humours are **peccant** and the blood is impure! The **fabrication** of that bauble, the discovery of Borgia's device, was the masterpiece in the science of Dalibard,—a curious and philosophical triumph of research, hitherto **unused** by its **inventor** and his heirs; for that casket is rich in the choice of more gentle **materials**: but the use yet may come. As she gazed on the ring, there was a complacent and proud expression on Lucretia's face.

"Dumb token of Caesar Borgia," she murmured,—"him of the wisest head and the boldest hand that ever grasped at empire, whom Machiavel, the virtuous, rightly praised as the model of accomplished ambition! Why should I **falter** in the paths which he trod with his royal step, only because my **goal** is not a throne? Every circle is as complete in itself, whether **rounding** a **globule** or a star. Why groan in the belief that the mind defiles itself by the darkness through which it glides on its object, or the mire through which it ascends to the hill? Murderer as he was, poisoner, and **fratricide**, did blood **clog** his intellect, or crime **impoverish** the luxury of his genius? Was his verse less **melodious** [It is well known that Caesar Borgia was both a munificent patron and an exquisite **appreciator** of art; well known also are his powers of persuasion but the general reader may not, perhaps, be acquainted with the fact that this terrible criminal was also a

---

French

appreciator: appréciateur, estimateur.
barbed: barbelé, acéré.
clog: boucher, sabot, obstruer, entrave, raccommoder.
dilate: dilater.
fabrication: fabrication, invention, première transformation.
falter: hésiter, vaciller, chanceler.
flesh: chair, pulpe.
fratricide: effet fratricide, fratricide.
globule: globule.

goal: but, dessein, objectif.
impoverish: appauvrir.
inventor: inventeur.
material: matériau, tissu, étoffe, matière.
melodious: mélodieux, harmonieux.
peccant: coupable.
puncture: ponction, crevaison, perforation, piqûre.
rounding: arrondi, prédéroulage, dégradation d'angle, copeau

arrondi, crouponnage, débrutage, brochage.
skin: peau, dépouiller, pelage, fourrure, poil d'animal, revêtement, éplucher, écorcher.
spasm: spasme.
steeped: trempai.
test: essai, test, examen, épreuve, contrôle, critère, expérimenter, éprouver.
unused: inutilisé, neuf.

poet], or his love of art less intense, or his eloquence less persuasive, because he sought to remove every barrier, revenge every wrong, crush every foe?"

In the **wondrous** corruption to which her mind had descended, thus murmured Lucretia. Intellect had been so long made her sole god that the very monster of history was lifted to her **reverence** by his ruthless intellect alone,—lifted in that mood of **feverish** excitement when conscience, often less silenced, lay crushed, under the load of the deed to come, into an example and a guide.

Though at times, when looking back, oppressed by the blackest despair, no **remorse** of the past ever **weakened** those nerves when the Hour called up its demon, and the Will ruled the rest of the human being as a machine.

She replaced the ring, she reclosed the **casket**, relocked its **depository**; then passed again into the adjoining chamber.

A few minutes afterwards, and the dim light that stole from the heavens (in which the moon was partially **overcast**) through the **casement** on the staircase rested on a **shapeless** figure robed in black from head to foot,—a figure so obscure and **undefinable** in outline, so suited to the gloom in its hue, so **stealthy** and rapid in its movements, that had you started from sleep and seen it on your floor, you would **perforce** have deemed that your fancy had befooled you!

Thus darkly, through the darkness, went the Poisoner to her prey.

French

casement: croisée, châssis, vantail.
casket: cercueil, coffret, mettre en bière.
depository: dépôt, établissement de dépôt, réceptacle de dépôt.
feverish: fiévreux, fébrile.
overcast: couvert, surjetai, surfiler, fonças, fonce.
perforce: forcément, nécessairement.
remorse: remords.
reverence: révérence, vénération, respect.
shapeless: informe, difforme.
stealthy: furtif.
undefinable: indéfinissable.
weakened: affaiblîmes, faiblîmes, fragilisé, amaigrîtes.
wondrous: merveilleux, étonnant.

CHAPTER XVIII

RETROSPECT

We have now arrived at that stage in this history when it is necessary to look back on the interval in Lucretia's life,—between the death of Dalibard, and her **reintroduction** in the second portion of our tale.

One day, without previous notice or warning, Lucretia arrived at William Mainwaring's house; she was in the deep weeds of **widowhood**, and that **garb** of **mourning** sufficed to add Susan's tenderest **commiseration** to the warmth of her **affectionate** welcome. Lucretia appeared to have forgiven the past, and to have **conquered** its more painful recollections; she was gentle to Susan, though she rather suffered than returned her caresses; she was open and frank to William. Both felt **inexpressibly** grateful for her visit, the forgiveness it **betokened**, and the confidence it implied. At this time no condition could be more promising and prosperous than that of the young banker. From the first the most active partner in the bank, he had now **virtually** almost **monopolized** the business. The **senior** partner was old and **infirm**; the second had a **bucolic** turn, and was much taken up by the care of a large **farm** he had recently purchased; so that Mainwaring, more and more trusted and honoured, became the sole **managing administrator** of the firm. Business throve in his able hands; and with patient and steady **perseverance**

French

administrator: administrateur, gestionnaire.
affectionate: affectueux, tendre, attaché, dévoué, amoureux.
betokened: présagèrent.
bucolic: bucolique, pastoral.
commiseration: commisération.
conquered: conquîtes.
farm: ferme, affermer, domaine, prendre à bail, propriété, fonds, bien, bail, cultiver.
garb: costume.
inexpressibly: de façon inexprimable, de manière inexprimable.
infirm: infirme, irrésolu.
managing: administrant, dirigeant, gérant.
monopolized: monopolisa, accaparâmes.
mourning: deuil, regrettant.
perseverance: persévérance, ténacité.
reintroduction: réintroduction.
senior: aîné, premier, personne âgée, chevronné, aimé, père.
virtually: pratiquement, de façon virtuelle, de manière virtuelle.
widowhood: veuvage, viduité.

there was little doubt but that, before middle age was attained, his competence would have swelled into a fortune sufficient to justify him in realizing the secret dream of his heart,—the **parliamentary representation** of the town, in which he had already secured the affection and esteem of the **inhabitants**.

It was not long before Lucretia detected the ambition William's industry but partially concealed; it was not long before, with the ascendency natural to her will and her talents, she began to exercise considerable, though unconscious, influence over a man in whom a thousand good qualities and some great talents were unhappily accompanied by infirm purpose and weak resolutions. The ordinary conversation of Lucretia **unsettled** his mind and **inflamed** his vanity,—a conversation able, **aspiring**, full both of knowledge drawn from books and of that experience of public men which her residence in Paris (whereon, with its new and greater Charlemagne, the eyes of the world were turned) had added to her acquisitions in the **lore** of human life. Nothing more disturbs a mind like William Mainwaring's than that **species** of eloquence which rebukes its patience in the present by **inflaming** all its hopes in the future. Lucretia had none of the charming babble of women, none of that tender interest in household details, in the minutiae of domestic life, which **relaxes** the intellect while **softening** the heart. Hard and vigorous, her sentences came forth in eternal appeal to the reason, or address to the sterner passions in which love has no share. Beside this strong thinker, poor Susan's sweet talk seemed **frivolous** and **inane**. Her soft hold upon Mainwaring **loosened**. He ceased to consult her upon business; he began to repine that the partner of his lot could have little sympathy with his dreams. More often and more bitterly now did his **discontented** glance, in his way homeward, **rove** to the **rooftops** of the **rural** member for the town; more eagerly did he read the parliamentary **debates**; more heavily did he sigh at the thought of eloquence denied a vent, and ambition delayed in its career.

When arrived at this state of mind, Lucretia's conversation took a more worldly, a more practical turn. Her knowledge of the **speculators** of Paris

---

French

aspiring: aspirant, futur.
debate: débat, discussion.
discontented: mécontent.
frivolous: frivole, vain, vaniteux.
inane: bête, inepte.
inflamed: enflammé.
inflaming: enflammant.
inhabitant: habitant.
loosened: desserrâtes, se détendirent, nous détendîmes, te détendis, ameublîmes, me détendis, déliés, vous détendîtes.
lore: lorum.
parliamentary: parlementaire.
relax: relaxer, se relâcher, relâcher, se détendre.
representation: représentation, figure.
rooftop: toit.
rove: rôdes, rôdons, vagabonde, mèche, boudinons.
rural: rural, rustique.
softening: ramollissement, adoucissement, amollissant, attendrissant, assouplissement, se ramollissant.
specie: monnaie, numéraire.
speculator: spéculateur.
unsettled: perturbé, incertain, variable, instable.

instructed her pictures of bold ingenuity creating sudden wealth; she spoke of fortunes made in a day,—of **parvenus** bursting into millionnaires; of wealth as the necessary instrument of ambition, as the arch ruler of the civilized world. Never once, be it observed, in these temptations, did Lucretia address herself to the heart; the ordinary channels of vulgar **seduction** were disdained by her. She would not have stooped so low as Mainwaring's love, could she have commanded or **allured** it; she was willing to leave to Susan the husband reft from her own passionate youth, but leave him with the **brand** on his brow and the worm at his heart,—a **scoff** and a wreck.

At this time there was in that market-town one of those adventurous, **speculative** men, who are the more dangerous **impostors** because imposed upon by their own sanguine **chimeras**, who have a **plausibility** in their calculations, an earnestness in their arguments, which account for the **dupes** they daily make in our most sober and wary of civilized communities. **Unscrupulous** in their means, yet really honest in the belief that their objects can be attained, they are at once the rogues and **fanatics** of Mammon. This person was held to have been fortunate in some **adroit** speculations in the corn trade, and he was brought too frequently into business with Mainwaring not to be a frequent visitor at the house. In him Lucretia saw the very instrument of her design. She led him on to talk of business as a **game**, of money as a realizer of **cent** per cent; she drew him into details, she praised him, she admired. In his presence she seemed only to hear him; in his absence, musingly, she started from silence to **exclaim** on the acuteness of his genius and the **accuracy** of his figures. Soon the **tempter** at Mainwaring's heart gave signification to these praises, soon this **adventurer** became his most intimate friend. Scarcely knowing why, never **ascribing** the change to her sister, poor Susan wept, **amazed** at Mainwaring's transformation. No care now for the new books from London, or the roses in the garden; the music on the instrument was **unheeded**. Books, roses, music,—what are those **trifles** to a man thinking upon cent per cent? Mainwaring's very countenance altered; it lost its frank, affectionate beauty: **sullen**, abstracted,

---

French

accuracy: exactitude, précision, justesse.
adroit: adroit, habile, actif, alerte, vif, vigilant.
adventurer: aventurier.
allured: séduisîmes, attiré.
amazed: étonnèrent, abasourdi.
ascribing: attribuant.
brand: marque, positionner, tison, établir une image de marque, estampiller.
cent: cent.
chimera: chimère.
dupe: internégatif, contretype.
exclaim: exclamer, s'exclamer.
fanatic: fanatique, exalté.
game: jeu, gibier, partie, match.
impostor: imposteur, charlatan.
instructed: instruisis.
parvenu: parvenu, nouveau riche.
plausibility: plausibilité, vraisemblance.
scoff: sarcasme.
seduction: séduction.
speculative: spéculatif.
sullen: maussade, sombre, boudeur, morne, renfrogné.
tempter: tentateur.
trifle: bagatelle, babiole.
unheeded: ignoré, inaperçu, négligé.
unscrupulous: sans scrupules.

morose, it showed that some great care was at the core. Then Lucretia herself began **grievingly** to notice the change to Susan; gradually she altered her tone with regard to the speculator, and hinted vague fears, and urged Susan's remonstrance and warning. As she had anticipated, warning and remonstrance came in vain to the man who, comparing Lucretia's mental power to Susan's, had learned to despise the unlearned, timid sense of the latter.

It is unnecessary to trace this change in Mainwaring step by step, or to measure the time which sufficed to dazzle his reason and blind his honour. In the midst of schemes and hopes which the **lust** of gold now pervaded came a thunderbolt. An **anonymous** letter to the head partner of the bank provoked suspicions that led to minute examination of the accounts. It seemed that sums had been **irregularly** advanced (upon bills drawn by men of straw) to the speculator by Mainwaring; and the destination of these sums could be traced to gambling operations in trade in which Mainwaring had a private interest and **partnership**. So great, as we have said, had been the confidence placed in William's abilities and honour that the **facilities** afforded him in the disposal of the joint **stock** far **exceeded** those usually granted to the partner of a firm, and the breach of trust appeared the more **flagrant** from the extent of the confidence **misplaced**. Meanwhile, William Mainwaring, though as yet unconscious of the proceedings of his partners, was gnawed by anxiety and remorse, not **unmixed** with hope. He **depended** upon the result of a bold speculation in the purchase of shares in a Canal Company, a bill for which was then before parliament, with (as he was led to believe) a **certainty** of success. The sums he had, on his own responsibility, abstracted from the joint account were devoted to this adventure. But, to do him justice, he never dreamed of **appropriating** the profits anticipated to himself. Though knowing that the bills on which the moneys had been advanced were merely **nominal deposits**, he had confidently calculated on the certainty of success for the speculations to which the proceeds so obtained were devoted, and he looked forward to the moment when he might avow what he had done, and justify it by **doubling** the capital

French

anonymous: anonyme.
appropriating: appropriant.
certainty: certitude, assurance.
depended: dépendirent.
deposit: déposer, dépôt, arrhes, gisement, consigne, acompte, cautionnement.
doubling: doublant, renfort, cohabitation.
exceeded: dépassâtes, excédâtes, maîtrisâtes, outrepassé.
facility: facilité, moyen de transmission, installations, aménagements, organisme d'appui ou de soutien.
flagrant: flagrant.
grievingly: de façon chagrinante, de manière chagrinante.
irregularly: irrégulièrement, de façon irrégulière, de manière irrégulière.
lust: passion, volupté, convoitise, désir, luxure.
misplaced: déplacé, égarâtes, en malposition.
morose: morose, maussade, sombre.
nominal: nominal, symbolique, modique.
partnership: association, partenariat, société en nom collectif.
stock: stock, réserve, souche, action.
unmixed: pur, sans mélange.

withdrawn. But to his inconceivable horror, the bill of the Canal Company was rejected in the Lords; the shares bought at a premium went down to **zero**; and to add to his **perplexity**, the speculator abruptly disappeared from the town. In this **crisis** he was summoned to meet his indignant associates.

The evidence against him was morally **damning**, if not **legally** conclusive. The unhappy man heard all in the silence of despair. Crushed and bewildered, he **attempted** no **defence**. He asked but an hour to sum up the **losses** of the bank and his own; they amounted within a few hundreds to the 10,000 pounds he had brought to the firm, and which, in the absence of marriage-settlements, was **entirely** at his own disposal. This sum he at once resigned to his associates, on condition that they should **defray** from it his personal **liabilities**. The money thus repaid, his partners naturally **relinquished** all further inquiry. They were moved by pity for one so gifted and so fallen,—they even offered him a subordinate but lucrative **situation** in the firm in which he had been partner; but Mainwaring wanted the patience and resolution to work back the **redemption** of his name,—perhaps, **ultimately**, of his fortunes. In the fatal anguish of his shame and despair, he **fled** from the town; his flight confirmed forever the rumours against him,— rumours worse than the reality. It was long before he even admitted Susan to the knowledge of the obscure refuge he had sought; there, at length, she joined him. Meanwhile, what did Lucretia? She sold nearly half of her own fortune, constituted principally of the **moiety** of her portion which, at Dalibard's death, had passed to herself as **survivor**, and partly of the share in her deceased husband's effects which the French law awarded to her, and with the proceeds of this sum she purchased an annuity for her victims. Was this strange generosity the act of mercy, the result of repentance? No; it was one of the not least subtle and delicious refinements of her revenge. To know him who had rejected her, the rival who had supplanted, the miserable pensioners of her **bounty**, was dear to her haughty and disdainful hate. The lust of power, ever stronger in her than avarice, more than reconciled her to the sacrifice of gold. Yes, here she, the despised, the degraded, had power still; her wrath had ruined the fortunes of her victim, blasted the repute,

French

attempted: essayé, attentées.
bounty: prime, générosité, libéralité.
crisis: crise.
damning: damnant, condamner.
defence: défense, mémoire en défense.
defray: paies, payer, remboursons, payons, défraie.
entirely: entièrement, complètement, totalement, tout, de façon entière, de manière entière.
fled: fui, fuit, fuis, fuirent, fuîtes, fuîmes, échappâmes.
legally: de façon légale, de manière légale, légalement.
liability: responsabilité, passif, élément de passif.
losses: pertes, charges hors exploitation, résidus.
moiety: groupe caractéristique, fragment.
perplexity: perplexité, embarras.
redemption: rédemption, amortissement, rachat, remboursement.
relinquished: abandonné, lâchai.
situation: situation, condition, position.
survivor: survivant, rescapé.
ultimately: finalement, enfin, de façon ultime, de manière ultime.
withdrawn: retiré.
zero: zéro, division de calage, nul, mettre à zéro.

embittered and desolated **evermore** the future,—now her contemptuous charity fed the wretched lives that she spared in scorn. She had no small difficulty, it is true, in **persuading** Susan to accept this sacrifice, and she did so only by **sustaining** her sister's belief that the past could yet be **retrieved**, that Mainwaring's energies could yet **rebuild** their fortunes, and that as the annuity was at any time **redeemable**, the aid therefore was only temporary. With this understanding, Susan, **overwhelmed** with gratitude, weeping and broken-hearted, departed to join the choice of her youth. As the men **deputed** by the auctioneer to arrange and **ticket** the furniture for sale entered the desolate house, Lucretia then, with the step of a **conqueror**, passed from the threshold.

"Ah!" she murmured, as she paused, and gazed on the walls, "ah, they were happy when I first entered those doors,—happy in each other's tranquil love; happier still when they deemed I had forgiven the wrong and **abjured** the past! How honoured was then their home! How knew I then, for the first time, what the home of love can be! And who had destroyed for me, upon all the earth, a home like **theirs**? They on whom that home smiled with its serene and **taunting** peace! I—I, the guest! I—I, the abandoned, the betrayed,—what dark memories were on my soul, what a hell **boiled** within my bosom! Well might those memories take each a voice to accuse them; well, from that hell, might rise the Alecto! Their lives were in my power, my fatal **dowry** at my command,—rapid death, or slow, consuming torture; but to have seen each cheer the other to the grave, lighting every downward step with the eyes of love,—vengeance so urged would have fallen only on myself! Ha! **deceiver**, didst thou plume thyself, forsooth, on **spotless reputation**? Didst thou stand, me by thy side, amongst thy **perjured** household gods and talk of honour? Thy home, it is reft from thee; thy reputation, it is a, **scoff**; thine honour, it is a ghost that shall haunt thee! Thy love, can it **linger** yet? Shall the soft eyes of thy wife not burn into thy heart, and shame turn love into **loathing**? Wrecks of my vengeance, **minions** of my bounty, I did well to let ye live; I shake the dust from my feet on your threshold. Live on, **homeless**, hopeless, and childless! The curse is fulfilled!"

French

abjured: abjuras.
boiled: bouilli.
conqueror: conquérant, vainqueur.
deceiver: trompeur.
deputed: députas.
dowry: dot, don.
embittered: aigri, acharnées.
evermore: toujours.
homeless: sans abri.
linger: traîner, s'attarder.
loathing: abhorrant, abominant, haïssant, répugnance.
minion: favori, mignonne.
overwhelmed: comblé, abreuva, accablai.
perjured: parjuré, vous parjurâtes, te parjuras, se parjurèrent, nous parjurâmes, me parjurai.
persuading: persuadant.
rebuild: reconstruire, rechaper totalement, rebâtissez, réfection.
redeemable: rachetable, remboursable, amortissable.
reputation: réputation, prestige, renommée.
retrieved: récupérai, rapportâmes, extrait.
scoff: sarcasme.
spotless: sans tache, immaculé, impeccable.
sustaining: maintenant, appuyant, s'accotant.
taunting: raillant.
theirs: leur.
ticket: billet, ticket, le billet.

From that hour Lucretia never paused from her career to inquire further of her victims; she never entered into communication with either. They knew not her address nor her fate, nor she theirs. As she had **reckoned**, Mainwaring made no effort to recover himself from his fall. All the high objects that had lured his ambition were gone from him evermore. No place in the State, no authority in the senate, awaits in England the man with a **blighted** name. For the **lesser** objects of life he had no heart and no care. They lived in obscurity in a small village in Cornwall till the Peace allowed them to remove to France; the rest of their fate is known.

Meanwhile, Lucretia removed to one of those **smaller** Londons, resorts of pleasure and **idleness**, with which rich England **abounds**, and in which widows of limited income can make poverty seem less **plebeian**. And now, to all those passions that had hitherto raged within her, a dismal **apathy** succeeded. It was the great calm in her sea of life. The winds fell, and the **sails** drooped. Her vengeance satisfied, that which she had made so **preternaturally** the main object of existence, once fulfilled, left her in youth objectless.

She strove at first to take pleasure in the society of the place; but its **frivolities** and **pettiness** of purpose soon wearied that masculine and grasping mind, already made **insensible** to the often healthful, often innocent, excitement of trifles, by the terrible ordeal it had passed. Can the touch of the hand, **scorched** by the burning iron, feel pleasure in the softness of **silk**, or the light down of the cygnet's **plume**? She next sought such relief as study could afford; and her natural bent of thought, and her desire to **vindicate** her deeds to herself, plunged her into the **fathomless** abyss of **metaphysical** inquiry with the hope to confirm into positive assurance her earlier scepticism,—with the atheist's hope to **annihilate** the soul, and **banish** the **presiding** God. But no voice that could satisfy her reason came from those dreary deeps; contradiction on contradiction met her in the maze. Only when, wearied with book-lore, she turned her eyes to the visible Nature, and **beheld** everywhere harmony, order, system, **contrivance**, art, did she start with the amaze and awe of instinctive conviction, and the

French

abound: abonder, fourmiller, grouiller.
annihilate: anéantir, annihilent.
apathy: apathie, abattement.
banish: bannir, exilent.
beheld: vit, remarquâtes, vu, vîmes, vis, vîtes, virent, aperçûtes.
blighted: rouillé.
contrivance: invention, ingéniosité, dispositif.
fathomless: impénétrable, insondable.
frivolity: frivolité.
idleness: oisiveté, désœuvrement.
insensible: insensible.
lesser: moindre.
metaphysical: métaphysique.
pettiness: petitesse, mesquinerie.
plebeian: plébéien.
plume: panache, traînée, souffle, plumet, faisceau de fumée, gaz d'échappement.
presiding: présidant.
preternaturally: de manière surnaturelle, de façon surnaturelle.
reckoned: calcula.
sail: voile, naviguer.
scorched: échaudé.
silk: soie, soyeux.
smaller: plus petit.
vindicate: justifier, défendre.

natural religion **revolted** from her **cheerless** ethics. Then came one of those sudden reactions common with strong passions and **exploring** minds, but more common with women, however manlike, than with men. Had she lived in Italy then, she had become a nun; for in this woman, unlike Varney and Dalibard, the conscience could never be utterly silenced. In her choice of evil, she found only torture to her spirit in all the respites afforded to the occupations it indulged. When employed upon ill, remorse gave way to the zest of **scheming**; when the ill was done, remorse came with the **repose**.

It was in this peculiar period of her life that Lucretia, turning everywhere, and desperately, for escape from the past, became acquainted with some members of one of the most rigid of the sects of Dissent. At first she permitted herself to know and **commune** with these persons from a kind of contemptuous curiosity; she desired to **encourage**, in contemplating them, her experience of the follies of human nature: but in that crisis of her mind, in those struggles of her reason, whatever showed that which she most yearned to discover,—namely, earnest faith, **rooted** and genuine conviction, whether of **annihilation** or of **immortality**, a philosophy that might reconcile her to crime by destroying the providence of good, or a creed that could hold out the hope of **redeeming** the past and **exorcising** sin by the mystery of a Divine sacrifice,—had over her a power which she had not imagined or divined. Gradually the intense convictions of her new associates disturbed and infected her. Their **affirmations** that as we are born in wrath, so sin is our second nature, our mysterious heritage, seemed, to her understanding, willing to be blinded, to imply excuses for her past **misdeeds**. Their assurances that the worst **sinner** may become the most earnest saint; that through but one act of the will, resolute faith, all redemption is to be found,—these affirmations and these assurances, which have so often restored the guilty and **remodelled** the human heart, made a **salutary**, if brief, impression upon her. Nor were the lives of these Dissenters (for the most part **austerely** moral), nor the peace and self-complacency which they evidently found in the satisfaction of conscience and **fulfilment** of duty, without an influence over her that for a while both **chastened** and **soothed**.

French

affirmation: affirmation, promesse.
annihilation: annihilation.
austerely: de façon austère, de manière austère.
chastened: châtièrent.
cheerless: morne.
commune: communauté.
encourage: inciter, encourager, réconforter, stimuler.
exorcising: exorcisant.
exploring: explorant, recherchant, fouillant.
fulfilment: réalisation, accomplissement.
immortality: immortalité.
misdeed: méfait, délit.
redeeming: rachetant.
remodelled: remanié, remodelé.
repose: repos, se reposer, trêve.
revolted: révolté.
rooted: enraciné, raciné.
salutary: salutaire.
scheming: intrigant, magouille, comploter.
sinner: pécheur.
soothed: rassurèrent, calmé, abattis.

Hopeful of such a convert, the good teachers strove hard to confirm the **seeds** springing up from the granite and amidst the weeds; and amongst them came one man more eloquent, more seductive, than the rest,—Alfred Braddell. This person, a **trader** at Liverpool, was one of those strange living **paradoxes** that can rarely be found out of a **commercial** community. He himself had been a convert to the sect, and like most converts, he pushed his enthusiasm into the **bigotry** of the **zealot**; he saw no **salvation** out of the pale into which he had entered. But though his belief was sincere, it did not **genially operate** on his practical life; with the most scrupulous attention to forms, he had the worldliness and cunning of the carnal. He had **abjured** the vices of the softer senses, but not that which so seldom wars on the decorums of outer life. He was **essentially** a money-maker,—close, acute, keen, **overreaching**. Good works with him were indeed as nothing,—faith the all in all. He was one of the **elect**, and could not fall. Still, in this man there was all the **intensity** which often characterizes a mind in proportion to the **narrowness** of its compass; that intensity gave fire to his gloomy eloquence, and strength to his obstinate will. He saw Lucretia, and his zeal for her **conversion** soon expanded into love for her person; yet that love was **secondary** to his covetousness. Though **ostensibly** in a flourishing business, he was greatly distressed for money to carry on operations which swelled beyond the reach of his capital; his fingers itched for the sum which Lucretia had still at her disposal. But the seeming sincerity of the man, the persuasion of his goodness, his reputation for sanctity, deceived her; she believed herself honestly and ardently beloved, and by one who could guide her back, if not to happiness, at least to repose. She herself loved him not,—she could love no more. But it seemed to her a luxury to find some one she could trust, she could honour. If you had **probed** into the recesses of her mind at that time, you would have found that no religious belief was there settled,—only the desperate wish to believe; only the disturbance of all previous **infidelity**; only a restless, gnawing desire to escape from memory, to emerge from the gulf. In this troubled, impatient **disorder** of mind and feeling, she hurried into a second marriage as fatal as the first.

French

abjured: abjuras.
bigotry: bigoterie, sectarisme.
commercial: commercial, annonce publicitaire, film publicitaire, message publicitaire, spot publicitaire, vocation.
conversion: conversion, transformation.
disorder: désordre, trouble.
elect: choisir, désigner, opter, adopter, élire, élu, élisent.
essentially: essentiellement, de manière essentielle, de façon essentielle.
genially: de manière génienne, de façon génienne.
infidelity: infidélité.
intensity: intensité.
narrowness: étroitesse, petitesse.
operate: opérer, opère, fonctionner, actionner, exploiter, faire fonctionner, diriger, agir, manœuvrer.
ostensibly: de manière prétendue, de façon prétendue.
overreaching: zone étendue, révoquant.
paradox: paradoxe.
probed: sondé.
salvation: salut.
secondary: secondaire, accessoire, auxiliaire.
seed: semence, graine, pépin, germe, ensemencer.
trader: commerçant, marchand.
zealot: fanatique, zélote.

For a while she bore patiently all the **privations** of that **ascetic** household, assisted in all those external formalities, centred all her intellect within that iron **range** of existence. But no grace descended on her soul,—no warm ray unlocked the ice of the well. Then, gradually **becoming** aware of the **niggardly meanness**, of the harsh, **uncharitable** judgments, of the **decorous** frauds that, with unconscious hypocrisy, her husband concealed beneath the robes of **sanctity**, a weary disgust stole over her,—it stole, it deepened, it increased; it became intolerable when she discovered that Braddell had knowingly deceived her as to his worldly substance. In that mood in which she had rushed into these **ominous** nuptials, she had had no thought for vulgar advantages; had Braddell been a **beggar**, she had married him as **rashly**. But he, with the **inability** to comprehend a nature like hers,—dim not more to her terrible vices than to the sinister grandeur which made their ordinary atmosphere,—had descended **cunningly** to address the avarice he thought as **potent** in others as himself, to enlarge on the worldly **prosperity** with which Providence had blessed him; and now she saw that her **dowry** alone had saved the crippled trader from the **bankrupt** list. With this **revolting** discovery, with the scorn it produced, vanished all Lucretia's **unstable** visions of reform. She saw this man a saint amongst his tribe, and would not believe in the virtues of his **brethren**, great and **unquestionable** as they might have been proved to a more **dispassionate** and humbler **inquirer**. The imposture she detected she deemed universal in the circle in which she dwelt; and Satan once more smiled upon the subject he regained. Lucretia became a mother; but their child formed no endearing tie between the ill-assorted pair,—it rather **embittered** their **discord**. Dimly even then, as she bent over the cradle, that vision, which now, in the old house at Brompton, haunted her dreams and beckoned her over seas of blood into the fancied future, was **foreshadowed** in the face of her infant son. To be born again in that birth, to live only in that life, to aspire as man may aspire, in that future man whom she would train to knowledge and lead to power,— these were the feelings with which that sombre mother gazed upon her babe. The idea that the low-born, grovelling father had the sole right over that

---

French

ascetic: ascétique, ascète.
bankrupt: failli, banqueroutier.
becoming: devenant, convenable, raisonnable.
beggar: mendiant, gueux.
brethren: frères.
cunningly: de façon rusée, de manière rusée.
decorous: bienséant.
discord: discorde, désaccord.
dispassionate: impartial.
dowry: dot, don.
embittered: aigri, acharnées.
foreshadowed: présagèrent.
inability: incapacité, impuissance.
inquirer: demandeur.
meanness: mesquinerie, vilenie.
niggardly: pingre, mesquin.
ominous: inquiétant, menaçant, sinistre.
potent: puissant, actif, fort.
privation: privation.
prosperity: prospérité.
range: portée, gamme, plage, étendue, fourneau de cuisine, base de lancement, distance, parcours, éventail, intervalle, domaine.
rashly: de façon éruptive, de manière éruptive.
revolting: révoltant.
sanctity: sainteté.
uncharitable: peu charitable.
unquestionable: incontestable, indiscutable.
unstable: instable, incertain.

son's destiny, had the authority to **cabin** his mind in the walls of form, bind him down to the sordid apprenticeship, **debased**, not dignified, by the solemn mien, roused her indignant wrath; she **sickened** when Braddell touched her child. All her pride of intellect, that had never slept, all her pride of birth, long **dormant**, woke up to **protect** the heir of her ambition, the descendant of her race, from the **defilement** of the father's nurture. Not long after her **confinement**, she formed a plan for escape; she disappeared from the house with her child. Taking refuge in a cottage, living on the sale of the few jewels she possessed, she was for some weeks almost happy. But Braddell, less **grieved** by the loss than shocked by the scandal, was **indefatigable** in his researches,—he discovered her retreat. The scene between them was terrible. There was no resisting the power which all civilized laws give to the rights of husband and father. Before this man, whom she **scorned** so **unutterably**, Lucretia was **impotent**. Then all the **boiling** passions long suppressed beneath that command of temper. which she owed both to habitual simulation and intense disdain, rushed forth. Then she appalled the **impostor** with her indignant **denunciations** of his hypocrisy, his meanness, and his **guile**. Then, throwing off the **mask** she had worn, she hurled her **anathema** on his sect, on his faith, with the same breath that **smote** his conscience and left it **wordless**. She shocked all the notions he sincerely entertained, and he stood awed by accusations from a **blasphemer** whom he dared not rebuke. His rage broke at length from his awe. Stung, **maddened** by the scorn of himself, his blood **fired** into juster indignation by her **scoff** at his creed, he lost all self-possession and struck her to the ground. In the midst of shame and dread at disclosure of his violence, which succeeded the act so provoked, he was not less relieved than amazed when Lucretia, rising slowly, laid her hand gently on his arm and said, "Repent not, it is passed; fear not, I will be silent! Come, you are the stronger,—you prevail. I will follow my child to your home."

In this unexpected submission in one so imperious, Braddell's imperfect comprehension of character saw but fear, and his stupidity **exulted** in his triumph. Lucretia returned with him. A few days afterwards Braddell

French

anathema: anathème.
blasphemer: blasphémateur.
boiling: bouillant, ébullition, cuisson.
cabin: cabine, cabane, hutte, chaumière.
confinement: réclusion, internement, détention, emprisonnement.
debased: abâtardis, avilîtes.
defilement: souillure, profanation.
denunciation: dénonciation.

dormant: dormant, en repos, en sommeil, endormi, inactif, insensible.
exulted: exultai.
fired: traité par pointes de feu.
grieved: affligeâmes, chagrina, attristé.
guile: astuce, fourberie.
impostor: imposteur, charlatan.
impotent: impuissant, impotent.
indefatigable: infatigable, inlassable.

maddened: exaspérâtes, rendu fou.
mask: masque, cache.
protect: protéger, abriter, garantir, sauvegarder, préserver, assurer.
scoff: sarcasme.
scorned: dédaigné.
sickened: écoeura, blasèrent.
smote: frappa.
unutterably: de manière inexprimable, de façon inexprimable.
wordless: muet.

became ill; the illness increased,—slow, gradual, wearying. It broke his spirit with his health; and then the **steadfast** imperiousness of Lucretia's stern will ruled and **subjugated** him. He cowered beneath her haughty, searching gaze, he shivered at her sidelong, malignant glance; but with this fear came necessarily hate, and this hate, sometimes **sufficing** to **vanquish** the fear, **spitefully** evinced itself in **thwarting** her legitimate control over her infant. He would have it (though he had little real love for children) constantly with him, and affected to contradict all her own orders to the servants, in the sphere in which mothers **arrogate** most the right. Only on these occasions sometimes would Lucretia lose her grim self-control, and **threaten** that her child yet should be **emancipated** from his hands, should yet be taught the scorn for **hypocrites** which he had taught herself. These words sank deep, not only in the resentment, but in the conscience, of the husband. Meanwhile, Lucretia scrupled not to **evince** her **disdain** of Braddell by **markedly abstaining** from all the ceremonies she had before so rigidly observed. The sect grew **scandalized**. Braddell did not **abstain** from making known his causes of complaint. The haughty, imperious woman was condemned in the community, and hated in the household.

It was at this time that Walter Ardworth, who was then **striving** to eke out his means by political lectures (which in the earlier part of the century found ready audience) in our great towns, came to Liverpool. Braddell and Ardworth had been schoolfellows, and even at school embryo politicians of **congenial** notions; and the conversion of the former to one of the sects which had grown out of the old creeds, that, under Cromwell, had broken the **sceptre** of the son of Belial and established the Commonwealth of Saints, had only strengthened the republican **tenets** of the sour **fanatic**. Ardworth called on Braddell, and was startled to find in his schoolfellow's wife the niece of his **benefactor**, Sir Miles St. John. Now, Lucretia had never **divulged** her true parentage to her husband. In a union so much beneath her birth, she had desired to conceal from all her connections the fall of the once-honoured heiress. She had descended, in search of peace, to obscurity; but her pride **revolted** from the thought that her low-born husband might boast of her

---

French

abstain: s'abstenir, faire abstinence, se réserver, abstenir, m'abstiens, nous abstenons, t'abstiens, vous abstenez.
abstaining: s'abstenant, abstenant.
arrogate: usurper, revendiquer à tort, s'arroger, s'attribuer.
benefactor: bienfaiteur.
congenial: convenable, sympathique.
disdain: dédain.
divulged: divulgué.
emancipated: émancipa.
evince: montres.
fanatic: fanatique, exalté.
hypocrite: hypocrite.
markedly: de façon marquée, de manière marquée, nettement.
revolted: révolté.
scandalized: scandalisèrent.
sceptre: sceptre.
spitefully: de façon rancunière, de manière rancunière.
steadfast: ferme, inébranlable, constant.
striving: combattant.
subjugated: soumîtes.
sufficing: suffisant.
tenet: principe, doctrine.
threaten: menacer, gronder.
thwarting: déjouant, frustration, contrecarrant.
vanquish: vaincre.

connections and **parade** her descent to his level. Fortunately, as she thought, she received Ardworth before he was admitted to her husband, who now, growing feebler and feebler, usually kept his room. She stooped to **beseech** Ardworth not to reveal her secret; and he, **comprehending** her pride, as a man well-born himself, and **pitying** her pain, readily gave his promise. At the first interview, Braddell evinced no pleasure in the sight of his old schoolfellow. It was natural enough that one so precise should be somewhat revolted by one so careless of all form. But when Lucretia **imprudently** evinced satisfaction at his **surly** remarks on his visitor; when he perceived that it would please her that he should not **cultivate** the acquaintance offered him,—he was moved, by the spirit of contradiction, and the **spiteful** delight even in frivolous annoyance, to **conciliate** and court the intimacy he had at first disdained: and then, by degrees, sympathy in political matters and old recollections of **sportive**, careless boyhood **cemented** the intimacy into a more familiar bond than the **sectarian** had contracted really with any of his late associates.

Lucretia regarded this growing friendship with great **uneasiness**; the uneasiness increased to alarm when one day, in the presence of Ardworth, Braddell, **writhing** with a sudden spasm, said: "I cannot account for these strange seizures; I think **verily** I am poisoned!" and his dull eye rested on Lucretia's **pallid** brow. She was unusually thoughtful for some days after this remark; and one morning she informed her husband that she had received the intelligence that a relation, from whom she had **pecuniary** expectations, was **dangerously** ill, and requested his permission to visit this sick kinsman, who dwelt in a distant county. Braddell's eyes brightened at the thought of her absence; with little further **questioning** he consented; and Lucretia, sure perhaps that the **barb** was in the side of her victim, and reckoning, it may be, on greater freedom from suspicion if her husband died in her absence, left the house. It was, indeed, to the neighbourhood of her kindred that she went. In a private conversation with Ardworth, when questioning him of his news of the present **possessor** of Laughton, he had informed her that he had heard accidentally that Vernon's two sons (Percival

---

French

barb: barbe, ardillon, bavure.
beseech: implorer, solliciter, supplier, adjurer.
cemented: cimenté.
comprehending: comprenant.
conciliate: concilier, réconcilier.
cultivate: cultiver, fidéliser.
dangerously: de façon dangereuse, de manière dangereuse, dangereusement.
imprudently: de façon imprudente, de manière imprudente,
imprudemment.
pallid: pâle, blême.
parade: défilé, parade, pompe.
pecuniary: financier, pécuniaire.
pitying: compatissant.
possessor: propriétaire, possesseur, détenteur.
questioning: interrogateur, questionnant, sondage.
sectarian: sectaire.
spiteful: malveillant, méchant, rancunier.
sportive: sportif, folâtre.
surly: maussade, bourru.
uneasiness: inquiétude, malaise.
verily: en vérité, vraiment.
writhing: contorsions.

was not then born) were sickly; and she went into Hampshire secretly and unknown, to see what were really the chances that her son might yet become the lord of her lost inheritance.

During this absence, Braddell, now **gloomily** aware that his days were numbered, resolved to put into practice the idea long contemplated, and even less favoured by his spite than justified by the genuine convictions of his conscience. Whatever his faults, sincere at least in his religious belief, he might well look with dread to the prospect of the **training** and education his son would receive from the hands of a mother who had **blasphemed** his sect and openly proclaimed her **infidelity**. By will, it is true, he might create a trust, and appoint guardians to his child. But to have lived under the same roof with his wife,—nay, to have carried her back to that roof when she had left it,—afforded **tacit** evidence that whatever the **disagreement** between them, her conduct could hardly have **merited** her **exclusion** from the privileges of a mother. The guardianship might therefore **avail** little to **frustrate** Lucretia's indirect contamination, if not her positive control. Besides, where guardians are appointed, money must be left; and Braddell knew that at his death his **assets** would be found **insufficient** for his debts. Who would be guardian to a penniless infant? He resolved, therefore, to send his child from his roof to some place where, if reared **humbly**, it might at least be brought up in the right faith,—some place which might **defy** the search and be beyond the **perversion** of the **unbelieving** mother. He looked round, and discovered no instrument for his purpose that seemed so ready as Walter Ardworth; for by this time he had thoroughly excited the pity and touched the heart of that good-natured, easy man. His representations of the **misconduct** of Lucretia were the more implicitly believed by one who had always been secretly prepossessed against her; who, admitted to household intimacy, was an eye-witness to her hard indifference to her husband's sufferings; who saw in her very request not to **betray** her gentle birth, the shame she felt in her **election**; who regarded with indignation her **unfeeling desertion** of Braddell in his last moments, and who, besides all this, had some private misfortunes of his own which made him the more ready

---

French

asset: actif, bien, acquisition, atout, avoir, élément d'actif.
avail: profiter, avantage.
betray: trahir, révéler.
blasphemed: blasphéma.
defy: défier, provoquer.
desertion: désertion, abandon de poste, défection, délaissement.
disagreement: désaccord, différend, mésentente.
election: élection, choix.
exclusion: exclusion.
frustrate: frustrer, déjoue, décevoir.
gloomily: de façon sombre, de manière sombre.
humbly: humblement, de manière humble, de façon humble.
infidelity: infidélité.
insufficient: insuffisant.
merited: mérité.
misconduct: mauvaise conduite, inconduite.
perversion: perversion.
tacit: tacite.
training: formation, entraînement, instruction, dressage.
unbelieving: incrédule.
unfeeling: insensible.

listener to themes on the faults of women; and had already, by **mutual** confidences, opened the hearts of the two ancient schoolfellows to each other's complaints and wrongs. The only other **confidant** in the refuge selected for the child was a member of the same community as Braddell, who kindly undertook to search for a pious, godly woman, who, upon such pecuniary considerations as Braddell, by robbing his creditors, could afford to bestow, would **permanently** offer to the poor infant a mother's home and a mother's care. When this woman was found, Braddell confided his child to Ardworth, with such a sum as he could scrape together for its future maintenance. And to Ardworth, rather than to his fellow-sectarian, this double trust was given, because the latter feared scandal and **misrepresentation** if he should be ostensibly mixed up in so equivocal a charge. Poor and embarrassed as Walter Ardworth was, Braddell did not for once **misinterpret** character when he placed the money in his hands; and this because the characters we have known in transparent boyhood we have known forever. Ardworth was reckless, and his whole life had been wrecked, his whole nature materially degraded, by the want of common **thrift** and prudence. His own money slipped through his fingers and left him surrounded by creditors, whom, rigidly speaking, he thus **defrauded**; but direct **dishonesty** was as wholly out of the **chapter** of his vices as if he had been a man of the strictest principles and the **steadiest** honour.

The child was gone, the father died, Lucretia returned, as we have seen in Grabman's letter, to the house of death, to meet suspicion, and cold looks, and **menial** accusations, and an inquest on the dead; but through all this the reft **tigress mourned** her stolen **whelp**. As soon as all evidence against her was proved legally groundless, and she had leave to depart, she searched blindly and **frantically** for her lost child; but in vain. The utter and penniless **destitution** in which she was left by her husband's **decease** did not suffice to **terminate** her **maddening** chase. On foot she **wandered** from village to village, and begged her way wherever a false clew **misled** her steps.

At last, in reluctant despair, she resigned the pursuit, and found herself one day in the midst of the streets of London, half-famished and in rags; and

French

chapter: chapitre, section, direction.
confidant: confident.
decease: décès, décéder.
defrauded: fraudai, escroqua.
destitution: indigence, misère.
dishonesty: malhonnêteté, improbité.
frantically: de façon frénétique, de manière frénétique.
maddening: à rendre fou, enrageant, exaspérant.
menial: subalterne, de domestique, servile.
misinterpret: mal interpréter.
misled: égara, trompé.
misrepresentation: fausse déclaration, information fausse ou trompeuse, déclaration inexacte, assertion inexacte, déformation.
mourned: regretté, te lamentas, se lamenta, vous lamentâtes, me lamentai, nous lamentâmes.
mutual: réciproque, mutuel.
permanently: de manière permanente, de façon permanente.
steadiest: le plus régulier.
terminate: terminer, finir, cesser, résilier.
thrift: économie, armeria commune, épargne.
tigress: tigresse.
wandered: errâmes, errèrent, erré, erras, vagué.
whelp: petit, savon de grande longueur, chienner, couteau pour voûte de four.

before her suddenly, now grown into vigorous youth,—blooming, **sleek**, and seemingly prosperous,—stood Gabriel Varney. By her voice, as she approached and spoke, he recognized his stepmother; and after a short pause of **hesitation**, he led her to his home. It is not our purpose (for it is not necessary to those passages of their lives from which we have selected the **thread** of our tale) to follow these two, thus united, through their general career of **spoliation** and crime. Birds of prey, they searched in human follies and human errors for their food: sometimes **severed**, sometimes together, their interests remained one. Varney **profited** by the mightier and subtler genius of evil to which he had leashed himself; for, caring little for luxuries, and dead to the **softer** senses, she abandoned to him readily the larger share of their **plunder**. Under a variety of names and disguises, through a succession of frauds, some vast and some mean, but chiefly on the Continent, they had pursued their course, **eluding** all danger and **baffling** all law.

Between three and four years before this period, Varney's uncle, the painter, by one of those unexpected caprices of fortune which sometimes find heirs to a millionnaire at the weaver's **loom** or the labourer's **plough**, had suddenly, by the death of a very distant kinsman whom he had never seen, come into possession of a small estate, which he sold for 6,000 pounds. **Retiring** from all his profession, he lived as comfortably as his shattered constitution permitted upon the interest of this sum; and he wrote to his nephew, then at Paris, to communicate the good news and offer the hospitality of his hearth. Varney **hastened** to London. Shortly afterwards a nurse, recommended as an experienced, useful person in her profession, by Nicholas Grabman, who in many a **tortuous** scheme had been Gabriel's **confederate**, was **installed** in the poor painter's house. From that time his infirmities increased. He died, as his doctor said, "by **abstaining** from the **stimulants** to which his constitution had been so long accustomed;" and Gabriel Varney was summoned to the reading of the will. To his **inconceivable** disappointment, instead of **bequeathing** to his nephew the free disposal of his 6,000 pounds, that sum was **assigned** to trustees for the benefit of Gabriel and his children yet unborn,—"An inducement," said the

---

French

abstaining: s'abstenant, abstenant.
assigned: assignâtes, attribuâmes, adjugeas.
baffling: chicanage, pose de chicanes.
bequeathing: léguant.
confederate: confédéré.
eluding: éludant, déjouant.
hastened: hâtâmes, hâté, hâtai, hâtèrent.
hesitation: hésitation.
inconceivable: inconcevable,

abracadabrant, inimaginable.
installed: installâmes, emménagés.
loom: métier à tisser, manche, gaine isolante, lueur.
plough: charrue, labourer.
plunder: piller, ravir.
profited: bénéficièrent.
retiring: retirant, sortant.
severed: disjoignîmes, rompîtes, coupa.
sleek: lisse, onctueux, filandre, film d'huile, ligne de ferrasse.

softer: plus doux.
spoliation: pillage.
stimulant: stimulant, remontant.
thread: fil, filet, enfiler.
tortuous: tortueux.

poor **testator**, **tenderly**, "for the boy to marry and reform!" So that the nephew could only enjoy the interest, and had no control over the capital. The interest of 6,000 pounds invested in the Bank of England was flocci nauci to the **voluptuous spendthrift**, Gabriel Varney.

Now, these trustees were selected from the painter's earlier and more respectable associates, who had dropped him, it is true, in his days of **beggary** and **disrepute**, but whom the fortune that made him respectable had again **conciliated**. One of these trustees had lately retired to pass the remainder of his days at Boulogne; the other was a hypochondriacal **valetudinarian**,—neither of them, in short, a man of business. Gabriel was left to draw out the interest of the money as it became **periodically** due at the Bank of England. In a few months the trustee settled at Boulogne died; the trust, of course, **lapsed** to Mr. Stubmore, the valetudinarian survivor. Soon **pinched** by extravagances, and **emboldened** by the character and helpless state of the surviving trustee, Varney forged Mr. Stubmore's **signature** to an order on the bank to sell out such portion of the capital as his wants required. The **impunity** of one offence **begot** courage for others, till the whole was well-nigh **expended**. Upon these sums Varney had lived very pleasantly, and he saw with a deep sigh the approaching failure of so **facile** a resource.

In one of the melancholy moods **engendered** by this reflection, Varney happened to be in the very town in France in which the Mainwarings, in their later years, had taken refuge, and from which Helen had been removed to the roof of Mr. Fielden. By accident he heard the name, and, his curiosity leading to further inquiries, learned that Helen was made an heiress by the will of her grandfather. With this knowledge came a thought of the most treacherous, the most miscreant, and the vilest crime that even he yet had **perpetrated**; so black was it that for a while he absolutely struggled against it. But in guilt there seems ever a Necessity that urges on, step after step, to the last **consummation**. Varney received a letter to inform him that the last surviving trustee was no more, that the trust was therefore now centred in his son and heir, that that gentleman was at present very busy in **settling** his

French

beggary: mendicité.
begot: engendrâmes.
conciliated: concilié.
consummation: consommation, perfection.
disrepute: déshonneur.
emboldened: enhardi.
engendered: engendras.
expended: dépensas.
facile: facile.
impunity: impunité.
lapsed: dévolu par péremption,

vieux, périmé, infirme, caduc, délabré.
periodically: périodiquement, de façon périodique, de manière périodique.
perpetrated: perpétra.
pinched: pincé.
settling: réglant, tassement, affaissement, règlement.
signature: signature, indicatif musical, qualité, cahier, griffe, empreinte digitale, réponse.

spendthrift: dépensier, gaspilleur, prodigue.
tenderly: tendrement.
testator: testateur.
valetudinarian: valétudinaire.
voluptuous: voluptueux, sensuel.

own affairs and examining into a very mismanaged property in Devonshire which had **devolved** upon him, but that he hoped in a few months to discharge, more **efficiently** than his father had done, the duties of trustee, and that some more profitable **investment** than the Bank of England would probably occur.

This new trustee was known personally to Varney,—a **contemporary** of his own, and in earlier youth a pupil to his uncle. But, since then, he had made way in life, and retired from the profession of art. This younger Stubmore he knew to be a bustling, officious man of business, somewhat greedy and **covetous**, but withal somewhat weak of purpose, good-natured in the main, and with a little **lukewarm** kindness for Gabriel, as a quondam fellow-pupil. That Stubmore would discover the fraud was evident; that he would declare it, for his own sake, was evident also; that the bank would prosecute, that Varney would be **convicted**, was no less surely to be **apprehended**. There was only one chance left to the **forger**: if he could get into his hands, and in time, before Stubmore's bustling interference, a sum sufficient to replace what had been **fraudulently** taken, he might easily **manage**, he thought, to prevent the **forgery** ever becoming known. Nay, if Stubmore, roused into strict personal **investigation** by the new power of attorney which a new investment in the bank would render necessary, should ascertain what had occurred, his liabilities being now **indemnified**, and the money replaced, Varney thought he could confidently rely on his ci-devant fellow-pupil's assent to **wink** at the forgery and hush up the matter. But this was his only chance. How was the money to be gained? He thought of Helen's fortune, and the last **scruple** gave way to the **imminence** of his peril and the **urgency** of his fears.

With this **decision**, he repaired to Lucretia, whose **concurrence** was necessary to his designs. Long habits of crime had now deepened still more the dark and stern colour of that dread woman's sombre nature. But through all that had ground the humanity from her soul, one human sentiment, **fearfully tainted** and **adulterated** as it was, still struggled for life,—the memory of the mother. It was by this, her least criminal emotion, that Varney

---

French

adulterated: falsifié, adultérai.
apprehended: appréhendé, craignîtes.
concurrence: accord, concordance, convention, entente.
contemporary: contemporain.
convicted: condamné.
covetous: avide.
decision: décision, arrêt, résolution.
devolved: incomba.
efficiently: efficacement, de façon efficace, de manière efficace.
fearfully: de manière effrayante, de façon effrayante.
forger: faussaire, forgeur.
forgery: falsification, faux, contrefaçon.
fraudulently: de façon frauduleuse, de manière frauduleuse.
imminence: imminence.
indemnified: indemnisèrent.
investigation: enquête, examen, recherche, investigation, reconnaissance, instruction.
investment: investissement, placement.
lukewarm: tiède.
manage: administrer, diriger, gérer, gérons, gère, réussir.
scruple: scrupule.
tainted: corrompu, vicié, pollué, infecté, entachées, avarié, altéré.
urgency: urgence, instance, vive sollicitation, impulsion.
wink: clin d'oeil, clignement, faire un clin d'oeil.

led her to the worst of her crimes. He offered to sell out the remainder of the trust-money by a fresh act of forgery, to devote such proceeds to the search for her lost Vincent; he revived the hopes she had long since gloomily **relinquished**, till she began to conceive the discovery easy and certain. He then brought before her the prospect of that son's succession to Laughton: but two lives now between him and those broad lands,—those two lives **associated** with just cause of revenge. Two lives! Lucretia till then did not know that Susan had left a child, that a pledge of those nuptials, to which she **imputed** all her infamy, existed to revive a jealousy never **extinguished**, appeal to the hate that had grown out of her love. More readily than Varney had anticipated, and with fierce exultation, she fell into his horrible schemes.

Thus had she returned to England and claimed the guardianship of her niece. Varney engaged a dull house in the suburb, and looking out for a servant not likely to upset and betray, found the nurse who had watched over his uncle's last illness; but Lucretia, according to her **invariable** practice, rejected all **menial accomplices**, **reposed** no confidence in the tools of her black deeds. **Feigning** an infirmity that would mock all suspicion of the hand that mixed the draught, and the step that stole to the **slumber**, she defied the justice of earth, and stood alone under the omniscience of Heaven.

Various considerations had delayed the execution of the **atrocious** deed so coldly contemplated. Lucretia herself drew back, perhaps more **daunted** by conscience than she herself was distinctly aware, and **disguising** her scruples in those yet fouler refinements of hoped revenge which her conversations with Varney have betrayed to the reader. The failure of the earlier researches for the lost Vincent, the suspended **activity** of Stubmore, left the more impatient murderer leisure to make the acquaintance of St. John, steal into the confidence of Helen, and render the insurances on the life of the latter less open to suspicion than if effected immediately on her entrance into that shamble-house, and before she could be supposed to form that affection for her aunt which made probable so tender a **forethought**. These causes of delay now vanished, the Parcae closed the abrupt **woof**, and lifted the **impending** shears.

French

accomplice: complice.
activity: activité, occupation, vigueur, besoin d'activité.
associated: associé.
atrocious: atroce, horrible, affreux.
daunted: découragea, intimidai.
disguising: déguisant.
extinguished: éteignîtes.
feigning: feignant, simulant.
forethought: prévoyance.
impending: imminent.
imputed: imputâmes.
invariable: invariable.
menial: subalterne, de domestique, servile.
relinquished: abandonné, lâchai.
reposed: reposé.
slumber: dormir, sommeil.
woof: trame, aboiement, aboyer, retraité bien nanti.

Lucretia had long since dropped the name of Braddell. She shrank from **proclaiming** those second spousals, sullied by the **degradation** to which they had exposed her, and the suspicions implied in the **inquest** on her husband, until the hour for **acknowledging** her son should arrive. She **resumed**, therefore, the name of Dalibard, and by that we will continue to call her. Nor was Varney **uninfluential** in **dissuading** her from proclaiming her second marriage till occasion **necessitated**. If the son were discovered, and proofs of his birth in the keeping of himself and his accomplice, his avarice naturally suggested the **expediency** of **wringing** from that son some **pledge** of **adequate** reward on succession to an **inheritance** which they alone could secure to him; out of this **fancied fund** not only Grabman, but his employer, was to be paid. The **concealment** of the identity between Mrs. Braddell and Madame Dalibard might **facilitate** such an arrangement. This idea Varney locked as yet in his own breast. He did not dare to speak to Lucretia of the **bargain** he ultimately meditated with her son.

French

acknowledging: reconnaissant.
adequate: adéquat, compétent, convenable, suffisant.
bargain: marchander, négocier, bonne affaire, affaire, occasion.
concealment: dissimulation, recel, réticence.
degradation: dégradation, déchéance, surcreusement.
dissuading: dissuadant.
expediency: convenance, opportunisme.
facilitate: faciliter, soulager.
fancied: imaginaire.
fund: fonds, caisse.
inheritance: héritage, succession.
inquest: enquête.
necessitated: nécessitai.
pledge: gage, nantissement, promettre, engagement.
proclaiming: proclamant.
resumed: reprîtes, recommençâtes.
uninfluential: sans influence.
wringing: tordant, torsion, essorant.

CHAPTER XIX

MR. GRABMAN'S ADVENTURES

The **lackeys** in their dress **liveries** stood at the porch of Laughton as the postilions drove rapidly along the road, **sweeping** through **venerable** groves, **tinged** with the hues of autumn, up to that **stately** pile. From the window of the large, cumbrous vehicle which Percival, **mindful** of Madame Dalibard's infirmity, had hired for her special **accommodation**, Lucretia looked **keenly**. On the slope of the hill grouped the deer, and below, where the lake **gleamed**, the **swan** rested on the wave. Farther on to the left, **gaunt** and stag-headed, rose, living still, from the depth of the glen, Guy's memorable oak. Coming now in sight, though at a distance, the gray church-tower emerged from the **surrounding** masses of solemn foliage. Suddenly the road **curves** round, and straight before her (the **rooks** cawing above the **turrets**, the sun reflected from the **vanes**) Lucretia gazes on the halls of Laughton. And didst thou not, O Guy's oak, **murmur** warning from thine oracular hollows? And thou who sleepest below the church-tower, didst thou not turn, Miles St. John, in thy grave, when, with such tender care, the young lord of Laughton bore that silent guest across his threshold, and with credulous, **moistened** eyes, welcomed Treason and Murder to his hearth?

French

accommodation: accommodation, logement, compromis, arrangement, habitation, construction, disposition, domicile, gîte, hébergement, logis.
curve: courbe, virage, cintre, se courber.
gaunt: morne, maigre, désert, désolé, sombre, maussade, mince, angulaire, décharné, mélancolique.
gleamed: luie, luis.
keenly: de façon vive, de manière vive.
lackey: laquais, larbin.
livery: livrée, couleurs d'une maison.
mindful: attentif, conscient.
moistened: humidifia, humectâtes.
murmur: murmure, bruit.
rook: tour, corbeau freux, freux.
stately: imposant, majestueux.
surrounding: entourant, environnant.
swan: cygne.
sweeping: balayage, large.
tinged: teinté.
turret: tourelle, barillet, rotateur.
vane: ailette, girouette, pale, aube, déflecteur de volet.
venerable: vénérable.

There, at the **porch**, paused Helen, gazing with the **rapt** eye of the **poetess** on the broad landscape, **checkered** by the vast shadows cast from the **setting** sun. There, too, by her side lingered Varney, with an artist's eye for the stately scene, till a thought, not of art, changed the face of the earth, and the view without mirrored back the Golgotha of his soul.

Leave them thus; we must hurry on.

One day a traveller stopped his gig at a public-house in a village in Lancashire. He chucked the **rein** to the **hostler**, and in reply to a question what **oats** should be given to the horse, said, "Hay and water; the beast is on job." Then **sauntering** to the bar, he called for a glass of **raw brandy** for himself; and while the host drew the spirit forth from the tap, he asked carelessly if some years ago a woman of the name of Joplin had not **resided** in the village.

"It is strange," said the host, musingly. "What is strange?"

"Why, we have just had a **gent asking** the same question. I have only been here nine year come December; but my old hostler was born in the village, and never left it. So the gent had in the hostler, and he is now gone into the village to pick up what else he can learn."

This intelligence seemed to surprise and **displease** the traveller.

"What the deuce!" he muttered; "does Jason **mistrust** me? Has he set another dog on the scent? Humph!" He drained off his brandy, and sallied forth to **confer** with the hostler.

"Well, my friend," said Mr. Grabman,—for the traveller was no other than that worthy,—"well, so you remember Mrs. Joplin more than twenty years ago, eh?"

"Yees, I guess; more than twenty years since she left the pleck [Lancashire and Yorkshire **synonym** for place]."

"Ah, she seems to have been a restless body. She had a child with her?"

"Yees, I moind that."

French

asking: demandant.
brandy: cognac, brandy.
checkered: tacheté de points en damier.
confer: conférer.
displease: déplaire, mécontentons, contrarier.
gent: monsieur.
hostler: mécanicien de manœuvre.
mistrust: méfiance, te méfies, se méfient, nous méfions, vous méfiez, me méfie, défiance.
oat: avoine.
poetess: poétesse, femme poète.
porch: porche, portique, véranda.
rapt: enthousiaste.
raw: cru, brut, grossier, rustique, écru.
rein: rêne, bride.
resided: résidâmes, demeurai.
sauntering: flânant.
setting: réglage, calage, sertissage, cadre.
synonym: synonyme.

"And I dare say you heard her say the child was not her own,—that she was paid well for it, eh?"

"Noa; my missus did not loike me to chaffer much with neighbour Joplin, for she was but a bad 'un,—pretty fease, too. She lived agin the wogh [Anglice, wall] **yonder**, where you see that gent coming out."

"Oho! that is the gent who was asking after Mrs. Joplin?"

"Yes; and he giv' me half-a-croon!" said the clever hostler, holding out his hand.

Mr. Grabman, too thoughtful, too **jealous** of his rival, to take the **hint** at that moment, darted off, as fast as his thin legs could carry him, towards the **unwelcome interferer** in his own business.

Approaching the gentleman,—a tall, powerful-looking young man,—he somewhat **softened** his tone, and mechanically touched his hat as he said,—

"What, sir, are you, too, in search of Mrs. Joplin?"

"Sir, I am," answered the young man, eying Grabman deliberately; "and you, I suppose, are the person I have found before me on the same search,—first at Liverpool; next at C—, about fifteen miles from that town; **thirdly**, at I—; and now we meet here. You have had the start of me. What have you learned?"

Mr. Grabman smiled. "Softly, sir, softly. May I first ask—since open **questioning** seems the order of the day—whether I have the honour to address a brother practitioner,—one of the law, sir, one of the law?"

"I am one of the law."

Mr. Grabman **bowed** and scowled.

"And may I make **bold** to ask the name of your client?"

"Certainly you may ask. Every man has a right to ask what he **pleases**, in a civil way."

"But you'll not answer? Deep! Oh, I understand! Very good. But I am deep too, sir. You know Mr. Varney, I suppose?"

French

approaching: approchant, abordant, rapprochant, s'approcher.
bold: gras, audacieux, épais, gros, hardi, intrépide.
bowed: incliné, courbé, arqué.
hint: insinuer, faire allusion, allusion, conseil.
interferer: brouilleur.
jealous: jaloux.
pleases: plaît, plait.
questioning: interrogateur, questionnant, sondage.
softened: amollîmes, adoucit, attendrit, se ramollit, me ramollis, nous ramollîmes, vous ramollîtes, te ramollis.
thirdly: troisièmement, en troisième lieu, tertio.
unwelcome: importun, fâcheux.
yonder: là, y.

The gentleman looked surprised. His **bushy** brows met over his steady, **sagacious** eyes; but after a moment's pause the expression of his face cleared up.

"It is as I thought," he said, half to himself. "Who else could have had an interest in similar inquiries?—Sir," he added, with a quick and decided tone, "you are doubtless employed by Mr. Varney on behalf of Madame Dalibard and in search of evidence connected with the loss of an unhappy infant. I am on the same **quest**, and for the same end. The interests of your **client** are mine. Two heads are better than one; let us **unite** our **ingenuity** and endeavours."

"And share the pec, I suppose?" said Grabman, **dryly**, **buttoning** up his pockets.

"Whatever **fee** you may expect you will have, **anyhow**, whether I assist you or not. I expect no fee, for mine is a personal interest, which I serve **gratuitously**; but I can undertake to promise you, on my own part, more than the ordinary professional reward for your co-operation."

"Well, sir," said Grabman, **mollified**, "you speak very much like a gentleman. My feelings were hurt at first, I own. I am **hasty**, but I can listen to reason. Will you walk back with me to the house you have just left? And suppose we then turn in and have a **chop** together, and compare notes."

"Willingly," answered the tall stranger, and the two **inquisitors amicably** joined company. The result of their inquiries was not, however, very satisfactory. No one knew **whither** Mrs. Joplin had gone, though all agreed it was in company with a man of bad character and **vagrant** habits; all agreed, too, in the vague **recollection** of the child, and some remembered that it was dressed in clothes **finer** than would have been natural to an infant legally and filially **appertaining** to Mrs. Joplin. One old woman remembered that on her **reproaching** Mrs. Joplin for some act of great cruelty to the poor **babe**, she replied that it was not her flesh and blood, and that if she had not expected more than she had got, she would never have undertaken the charge. On comparing the information **gleaned** at the previous places of

---

French

amicably: de façon amicale, de manière amicale.
anyhow: de toute façon, n'importe comment.
appertaining: appartenant.
babe: bébé.
bushy: touffu, broussailleux.
buttoning: boutonnage, pose des boutons.
chop: hacher, côtelette, tailler, clapot, couper.
client: client, acheteur, acquéreur.
dryly: sèchement.
fee: honoraires, droit, redevance, frais, cachet.
finer: affineur.
gleaned: glanai.
gratuitously: de façon gratuite, de manière gratuite.
hasty: précipité, hâtif.
ingenuity: ingéniosité.
inquisitor: inquisiteur.
mollified: apaisâtes.
quest: recherche, quête.
recollection: souvenir, mémoire.
reproaching: reprochant.
sagacious: sensé, intelligent, raisonnable.
unite: unir, unissez, joindre, accoupler, apparier, unifier.
vagrant: vagabond, clochard, chemineau.
whither: où.

their research, they found an **entire** agreement as to the character personally borne by Mrs. Joplin. At the village to which their inquiry had been first directed, she was known as a respectable, precise young woman, one of a small **congregation** of rigid Dissenters. She had married a member of the sect, and borne him a child, which died two weeks after birth. She was then seen **nursing** another infant, though how she came by it none knew. Shortly after this, her husband, a **journeyman** carpenter of good **repute**, died; but to the surprise of the neighbours, Mrs. Joplin continued to live as comfortably as before, and seemed not to miss the wages of her husband,—nay, she rather now, as if before kept back by the **prudence** of the deceased, launched into a less **thrifty** mode of life, and a gayety of dress at variance both with the **mourning** her **recent** loss should have imposed, and the austere **tenets** of her sect. This indecorum excited angry curiosity, and drew down stern **remonstrance**. Mrs. Joplin, in apparent disgust at this **intermeddling** with her affairs, withdrew from the village to a small town, about twenty miles distant, and there set up a shop. But her moral lapse became now confirmed; her life was **notoriously** abandoned, and her house the resort of all the **reprobates** of the place. Whether her means began to be exhausted, or the scandal she provoked attracted the notice of the **magistrates** and imposed a check on her course, was not very certain, but she sold off her goods suddenly, and was next **tracked** to the village in which Mr. Grabman met his new coadjutor; and there, though her conduct was less **flagrant**, and her expenses less reckless, she made but a very unfavourable impression, which was confirmed by her flight with an **itinerant hawker** of the lowest possible character. Seated over their port wine, the two gentlemen compared their experiences, and consulted on the best mode of remending the broken thread of their research; when Mr. Grabman said coolly, "But, after all, I think it most likely that we are not on the right scent. This bantling may not be the one we search for."

"Be not **misled** by that doubt. To arrive at the evidence we desire, we must still track this wretched woman."

"You are certain of that?"

French

congregation: congrégation, rassemblement.
entire: entier, total.
flagrant: flagrant.
hawker: colporteur, camelot, marchand ambulant.
intermeddling: immixtion.
itinerant: itinérant, ambulant.
journeyman: compagnon, ouvrier qualifié.
magistrate: magistrat.
misled: égara, trompé.
mourning: deuil, regrettant.
notoriously: de façon notoire, de manière notoire.
nursing: soins infirmiers, allaitement, sciences infirmières.
prudence: prudence, précaution.
recent: récent, frais.
remonstrance: remontrance, protestation.
reprobate: réprouver.
repute: réputation, renommée.
tenet: principe, doctrine.
thrifty: économe, épargnant.
tracked: chenillé.

"Certain."

"Hem! Did you ever hear of a Mr. Walter Ardworth?"

"Yes, what of him?"

"Why, he can best tell us where to look for the child."

"I am sure he would **counsel** as I do."

"You know him, then?"

"I do."

"What, he lives still?"

"I hope so."

"Can you bring me across him?"

"If necessary."

"And that young man, who goes by his name, brought up by Mr. Fielden?"

"Well, sir?"

"Is he not the son of Mr. Braddell?"

The **stranger** was silent, and, **shading** his face with his hand, seemed **buried** in thought. He then rose, took up his **candle**, and said quietly, —

"Sir, I wish you good-evening. I have letters to write in my own room. I will consider by to-morrow, if you stay till then, whether we can really aid each other further, or whether we should **pursue** our researches separately." With these words he closed the door; and Mr. Grabman remained baffled and **bewildered**.

However, he too had a letter to write; so, calling for pen, **ink**, and paper, and a **pint** of **brandy**, he indited his **complaints** and his news to Varney.

"Jason, (he began) are you playing me false? Have you set another man on the track with a view to **bilk** me of my promised fee? Explain, or I throw up the business."

French

bewildered: effarâmes, éperdu.
bilk: rouler, mystifier.
brandy: cognac, brandy.
buried: enterra, inhumas, ensevelîmes.
candle: bougie, chandelle, cierge.
complaint: réclamation, accusation.
counsel: conseil, avis, avocat, défenseur.
ink: encre, couleur à semelles, pâte, tracé, colorer.
pint: pinte, chope, petite bouteille.
pursue: poursuivre, continuer, rechercher.
shading: ombrage, tache.
stranger: étranger, inconnu.

Herewith, Mr. Grabman gave a minute **description** of the stranger, and related pretty **accurately** what had passed between that gentleman and himself. He then added the progress of his own inquiries, and renewed, as **peremptorily** as he dared, his demand for **candour** and plain **dealing**. Now, it so happened that in **stumbling** upstairs to bed, Mr. Grabman passed the room in which his mysterious fellow-seeker was lodged, and as is the usage in hotels, a pair of boots stood outside the door, to be cleaned betimes in the morning. Though somewhat drunk, Grabman still preserved the rays of his habitual **astuteness**. A clever and a natural idea shot across his brain, **illuminating** the **fumes** of the brandy; he stooped, and while one hand on the wall **steadied** his footing, with the other he **fished** up a boot, and peering within, saw **legibly** written: "John Ardworth, Esq., Gray's Inn." At that sight he felt what a philosopher feels at the sudden **elucidation** of a troublesome problem. Downstairs again **tottered** Grabman, re-opened his letter, and wrote,—

"P.S.—I have wronged you, Jason, by my suspicions; never mind,—jubilate! This **interloper** who made me so jealous, who think you it is? Why, young Ardworth himself,—that is, the lad who goes by such name. Now, is it not clear? Of course no one else has such interest in **learning** his birth as the lost child himself,—here he is! If old Ardworth lives (as he says), old Ardworth has set him to work on his own business. But then, that Fielden,—rather a **puzzler** that! Yet—no. Now I understand,—old Ardworth gave the boy to Mrs. Joplin, and took it away from her again when he went to the parson's. Now, certainly, it may be quite necessary to prove,—first, that the boy he took from Mr. Braddell's he gave to Mrs. Joplin; secondly, that the boy he left with Mr. Fielden was the same that he took again from that woman: therefore, the necessity of **finding** out Mother Joplin, an **essential** witness. Q. E. D., Master Jason!"

It was not till the sun had been some hours risen that Mr. Grabman **imitated** that luminary's example. When he did so, he found, somewhat to his **chagrin**, that John Ardworth had long been gone. In fact, whatever the motive that had led the latter on the search, he had succeeded in **gleaning**

French

accurately: de manière précise, de façon précise.
astuteness: finesse, sagacité.
candour: candeur, franchise, sincérité.
chagrin: chagrin, contrariété.
dealing: négociation, tractation, traiter, transaction.
description: description, signalement.
elucidation: élucidation, éclaircissement.
essential: essentiel, fondamental.
finding: fondant, recherche d'une ligne appelante, trouvant.
fished: pêché.
fume: fumée, vapeur, odeur délétère, exhalaison.
gleaning: glanage, grappillage.
illuminating: illuminant, enluminant, coloriant, éclairant.
imitated: imitas, copia.
interloper: intrus.
learning: apprenant, érudition, savoir.
legibly: de façon lisible, de manière lisible, lisiblement.
peremptorily: de façon péremptoire, de manière péremptoire.
puzzler: Œdipe.
steadied: assujetti.
stumbling: trébuchant, faux pas, bronchant.
tottered: vacillé, titubé, chancelèrent.

from Grabman all that that person could **communicate**, and their interview had **inspired** him with such **disgust** of the **attorney**, and so small an opinion of the value of his co-operation (in which last belief, perhaps, he was mistaken), that he had **resolved** to continue his **inquiries** alone, and had already, in his early morning's walk through the village, ascertained that the man with whom Mrs. Joplin had quitted the place had some time after been **sentenced** to six months' **imprisonment** in the county **jail**. Possibly the prison authorities might know something to lead to his **discovery**, and through him the news of his **paramour** might be **gained**.

French

attorney: mandataire, avocat, procureur.
communicate: communiquer, transmettre.
discovery: découverte, trouvaille, communication préalable, invention.
disgust: dégoût, écoeurer.
gained: gagné.
imprisonment: emprisonnement, incarcération.
inquiry: enquête, demande de renseignements, interrogation, investigation.
inspired: inspirâtes, s'enthousiasmé, vous enthousiasmâtes, nous enthousiasmâmes, m'enthousiasmai, t'enthousiasmas.
jail: prison, geôle, emprisonner.
paramour: amant.
resolved: résolu.
sentenced: condamné.

CHAPTER XX

MORE OF MRS. JOPLIN

One day, at the hour of noon, the court **boasting** the tall residence of Mr. Grabman was startled from the quiet usually **reigning** there at broad daylight by the appearance of two men, evidently no **inhabitants** of the place. The squalid, ill-favoured **denizens** lounging before the doors stared hard, and at the **fuller** view of one of the men, most of them retreated hastily within. Then, in those houses, you might have heard a murmur of **consternation** and alarm. The **ferret** was in the burrow, — a Bow-Street officer in the court! The two men paused, looked round, and stopping before the dingy towerlike house, selected the bell which appealed to the **inmates** of the ground-floor, to the left. At that **summons** Bill the cracksman **imprudently** presented a full view of his countenance through his **barred** window; he drew it back with astonishing **celerity**, but not in time to escape the eye of the Bow-Street **runner**.

"Open the door, Bill, — there's nothing to fear; I have no summons against you, 'pon honour. You know I never **deceive**. Why should I? Open the door, I say."

No answer.

The officer **tapped** with his **cane** at the **foul** window.

French

barred: barrâtes, exclu, forclos.
boasting: vantardise, fanfaronnade, taille de pierres.
cane: canne, roseau, bâton, jonc, rotin.
celerity: célérité.
consternation: abattement, consternation, stupéfaction, abasourdissement.
deceive: tromper, tricher, décevoir.
denizen: habitant.
ferret: furet, véhicule de renseignement électronique, chasser au furet.
foul: faute, fétide, engagé, salir.
fuller: gravure de roulage.
imprudently: de façon imprudente, de manière imprudente, imprudemment.
inhabitant: habitant.
inmate: détenu, interne, occupant, résident d'institution.
reigning: régnant.
runner: coureur, patin.
summons: sommation, citation, appel, assignation, intimation, convocation, commandement.
tapped: entaillé, taraudé.

"Bill, there's a gentleman who comes to you for information, and he will pay for it handsomely."

Bill again appeared at the casement, and peeped forth very cautiously through the bars.

"Bless my vitals, Mr. R—, and it is you, is it? What were you saying about paying handsomely?"

"That your evidence is wanted,—not against a **pal**, man. It will hurt no one, and put at least five guineas in your pocket."

"Ten guineas," said the Bow-Street officer's companion. "You be's a man of honour, Mr. R—!" said Bill, **emphatically**; "and I **scorns** to doubt you, so here goes."

With that he withdrew from the window, and in another minute or so the door was opened, and Bill, with a superb bow, asked his visitors into his room.

In the interval, leisure had been given to the cracksman to remove all trace of the **wonted educational** employment of his hopeful children. The **urchins** were seated on the floor playing at push-pin; and the Bow-Street officer benignly patted a pair of **curly** heads as he passed them, drew a chair to the table, and **wiping** his forehead, sat down, quite at home. Bill then deliberately seated himself, and **unbuttoning** his **waistcoat**, permitted the butt-ends of a **brace** of **pistols** to be seen by his guests. Mr. R—'s companion seemed very **unmoved** by this significant action. He bent one **inquiring**, steady look on the cracksman, which, as Bill afterwards said, went through him "like a **gimlet** through a penny," and taking out a **purse**, through the network of which the sovereigns gleamed **pleasantly**, placed it on the table and said,—

"This purse is yours if you will tell me what has become of a woman named Joplin, with whom you left the village of —, in Lancashire, in the year 18—."

French

brace: entretoise, croisillon, parenthèse, vilebrequin, étrésillon, bras, attache, accolade, tirant.
curly: bouclé, frisé.
educational: éducatif, pédagogique.
emphatically: énergiquement, de façon emphatique, de manière emphatique.
gimlet: vrille, foret.
inquiring: interrogateur, s'enquérant.
pal: camarade, copain.
pistol: pistolet.
pleasantly: agréablement, de manière agréable, de façon agréable.
purse: sacoche, bourse, sac à main.
scorn: dédain, mépris.
unbuttoning: déboutonnant.
unmoved: indifférent, insensible.
urchin: galopin, gamin, hérisson, oursin, polisson.
waistcoat: gilet.
wiping: essuyant, torchant.
wonted: habituel, accoutumé.

"And," put in Mr. R—, "the gentleman wants to know, with no view of harming the woman. It will be to her own advantage to **inform** us where she is."

"'Pon **honour** again?" said Bill.

"'Pon honour!"

"Well, then, I has a heart in my buzzom, and if so be I can do a good turn to the 'oman wot I has loved and kep' company with, why not?"

"Why not, indeed?" said Mr. R—. "And as we want to learn, not only what has become of Mrs. Joplin, but what she did with the child she carried off from—, begin at the **beginning** and tell us all you know."

Bill mused. "How much is there in the pus?"

"Eighteen sovereigns."

"Make it twenty—you nod—twenty then? A **bargain**! Now I'll go on right **ahead**. You see as how, some months arter we—that is, Peggy Joplin and self—left—, I was put in **quod** in Lancaster **jail**; so I lost sight of the blowen. When I got out and came to Lunnun, it was a matter of **seven** year afore, all of a sudding, I came **bang** up agin her,—at the corner of Common Garden. 'Why, Bill!' says she. 'Why, Peggy!' says I; and we **bussed** each other like winky. 'Shall us come together agin?' says she. 'Why, no,' says I; 'I has a wife wots a good 'un, and gets her bread by setting up as a widder with seven small childern. By the by, Peg, what's a come of your **brat**?' for as you says, sir, Peg had a child put out to her to nurse. Lor', how she cuffed it! 'The brat!' says she, **laughing** like **mad**, 'oh, I got **rid** o' that when you were in jail, Bill.' 'As how?' says I. 'Why, there was a woman **begging** agin St. Poll's churchyard; so I purtended to see a frind at a distance: "'Old the babby a moment," says I, puffing and **panting**, "while I **ketches** my friend yonder." So she 'olds the brat, and I never sees it agin; and there's an ind of the bother!' 'But won't they ever ax for the child,—them as giv' it you?' 'Oh, no,' says Peg, 'they left it too long for that, and all the **tin** was agone; and one mouth is hard enough to **feed** in these days,—let by other **folks**' bantlings.' 'Well,' says I, 'where do you hang out? I'll pop in, in a friendly way.' So she

French

ahead: en avant, devant, auparavant, autrefois.
bang: coup, frange, boum.
bargain: marchander, négocier, bonne affaire, affaire, occasion.
begging: mendiant, suppliant, quémandant.
beginning: commençant, début, inauguration.
brat: gosse, morveux.
bussed: transporté.
feed: alimenter, nourrir, manger,
faire paître, déjeuner, avance, paître.
folk: peuple, folklorique, gens.
honour: honneur, honorer.
inform: informer, renseigner, faire part de.
jail: prison, geôle, emprisonner.
ketch: ketch.
laughing: riant, rieur, rire.
mad: fou, aberrant, agité, enragé.
panting: haletant, essoufflement, halètement, vibration.
quod: taule.
rid: débarrasser, délivrer.
seven: sept.
tin: étain, tôle, étamer.

tells me,—som'ere in Lambeth,—I **forgets** hexactly; and many's the good piece of work we ha' done togither."

"And where is she now?" asked Mr. R—'s companion.

"I doesn't know purcisely, but I can com' at her. You see, when my poor wife died, four year com' Chris'mas, and left me with as fine a famuly, though I says it, as h-old King Georgy himself walked afore, with his gold-'eaded **cane**, on the terris at Vindsor,—all heights and all h-ages to the babby in arms (for the little 'un there warn't above a year old, and had been a brought up upon spoon-meat, with a **dash** o' blueruin to make him **slim** and ginteel); as for the **bigger** 'uns wot you don't see, they be doin' well in forin parts, Mr. R—!"

Mr. R. smiled significantly.

Bill **resumed**. "Where was I? Oh, when my wife died, I wanted sum 'un to take care of the childern, so I takes Peg into the 'ous. But Lor'! how she larrupped 'em,—she has a **cruel** heart, has n't she, Bob? Bob is a 'cute child, Mr. R—. Just as I was a thinking of turning her out neck an' crop, a gemman what **lodges aloft**, wot be a laryer, and wot had just saved my **nick**, Mr. R—, by **proving** a h-alibi, said, 'That's a **tidy** body, your Peg!' (for you see he was often a wisiting here, an' h-indeed, **sin**' then, he has taken our third floor, No. 9); 'I've been a speakin' to her, and I find she has been a nuss to the sick. I has a frind wots a h-uncle that's ill: can you spare her, Bill, to attind him?' That I can,' says I; 'anything to obleedge.' So Peg **packs** off, bag and baggidge."

"And what was the sick gentleman's name?" asked Mr. R—'s companion.

"It was one Mr. Warney,—a **painter**, wot lived at Clap'am. Since thin I've lost sight of Peg; for we had 'igh words about the childern, and she was a **spiteful** 'oman. But you can larn where she be at Mr. Warney's, if so be he's still above ground."

"And did this woman still go by the name of Joplin?"

French

aloft: en haut, en l'air, vol.
bigger: plus grand.
cane: canne, roseau, bâton, jonc, rotin.
cruel: cruel, atroce, méchant.
dash: tiret, trait.
forgets: oublie, désapprend.
lodge: loge, héberger, gîte, pavillon, auberge, déposer.
nick: entaille, encoche, ébrécher.
pack: paquet, emballer, empaqueter, condenser, meute, tasser, compresse, bande, tas.
painter: peintre, tricoteuse double, artiste peintre, bosse, gouacheur.
proving: prouvant, éprouvant.
resumed: reprîtes, recommençâtes.
sin: péché, commettre une faute.
slim: mince, amincir, amaigrir, maigrir.
spiteful: malveillant, méchant, rancunier.
tidy: ranger, ordonner, régler, soigné.

Bill grinned: "She warn't such a spooney as that,—that name was in your black books too much, Mr. R—, for a 'spectable nuss for sick bodies; no, she was then called Martha Skeggs, what was her own mother's name afore marriage. Anything more, gemman?"

"I am satisfied," said the younger visitor, rising; "there is the purse, and Mr. R—will bring you ten sovereigns in addition. Good-day to you."

Bill, with **superabundant** bows and **flourishes**, showed his visitors out, and then, in high **glee**, he began to **romp** with his children; and the whole family circle was in a state of **uproarious** enjoyment when the door flew open, and in entered Grabman, his brief-bag in hand, dust-soiled and **unshaven**.

"Aha, neighbour! your servant, your servant; just come back! Always so **merry**; for the life of me, I couldn't help looking in! Dear me, Bill, why, you're in luck!" and Mr. Grabman pointed to a pile of sovereigns which Bill had **emptied** from the purse to count over and **weigh** on the **tip** of his forefinger.

"Yes," said Bill, sweeping the gold into his **corduroy** pocket; "and who do you think brought me these **shiners**? Why, who but old Peggy, the 'oman wot you put out at Clapham."

"Well, never mind Peggy, now, Bill; I want to ask you what you have done with Margaret Joplin, whom, sly **seducer** that you are, you carried off from—"

"Why, man, Peggy be Joplin, and Joplin be Peggy! And it's for that piece of noos that I got all them pretty new picters of his Majesty Bill,—my **namesake**, God bliss 'im!"

"D—n," exclaimed Grabman, **aghast**; "the young chap's **spoiling** my game again!" And **seizing** up his brief-bag, he darted out of the house, in the hope to arrive at least at Clapham before his competitors.

French

aghast: stupéfait, atterré.
corduroy: velours côtelé, ondulations transversales.
emptied: vidé, vidâmes, vidèrent.
flourish: prospérer, rinceau, parafe, trait de plume, fleurir.
glee: joie.
merry: joyeux, gai.
namesake: homonyme.
romp: batifoler, folâtrer.
seducer: séducteur.
seizing: saisissant, grippage, agrippant.
shiner: point lustré, particule de charge transparente après calandrage, fil brillant.
spoiling: gâterie, abîmant.
superabundant: surabondant.
tip: pourboire, bout, pointe, sommet, cime, tuyau, conseil.
unshaven: non rasé.
uproarious: hilarant.
weigh: peser, pèses, pesons.

CHAPTER XXI

BECK'S DISCOVERY

Under the cedar-trees at Laughton sat that **accursed** and **abhorrent** being who sat there, young, **impassioned**, hopeful, as Lucretia Clavering, — under the old cedar-trees, which, save that their vast branches cast an **imperceptibly** broader shade over the **mossy** sward, the **irrevocable** winters had left the same. Where, through the nether **boughs** the autumn **sunbeams** came **aslant**, the windows, enriched by many a haughty scutcheon, shone brightly against the western rays. From the flower-beds in the **quaint** garden near at hand, the fresh yet tranquil air wafted faint perfumes from the **lingering heliotrope** and fading rose. The **peacock** perched **dozily** on the heavy **balustrade**; the **blithe robin** hopped **busily** along the sun-track on the lawn; in the distance the **tinkling** bells of the flock, the plaining low of some wandering **heifer**, while breaking the silence, seemed still to blend with the repose. All images around lent themselves to complete that picture of stately calm which is the character of those old mansion-houses, which owner after owner has loved and heeded, leaving to them the graces of antiquity, guarding them from the **desolation** of decay.

Alone sat Lucretia under the cedar-trees, and her heart made dismal contrast to the noble tranquillity that breathed around. From whatever

---

French

abhorrent: odieux, hideux, horrible, abject, abominable.
accursed: maudit.
aslant: obliquement.
balustrade: balustrade, rampe, accoudoir.
blithe: joyeux.
bough: branche, rameau.
busily: activement, de façon occupée, de manière occupée.
desolation: désolation, dévastation, solitude.
dozily: de façon sommeillée.
heifer: génisse.
heliotrope: héliotrope, rouge hélio.
impassioned: passionné.
imperceptibly: de façon imperceptible, de manière imperceptible.
irrevocable: irrévocable.
lingering: prolongé, traînant.
mossy: moussu.
peacock: paon, le paon.
quaint: curieux, intéressant, singulier, étrange.
robin: rouge-gorge.
sunbeam: rayon de soleil.
tinkling: tintement.

softening or repentant emotions which the scene of her youth might first have awakened; from whatever of less **unholy** anguish which memory might have caused when she first, once more, sat under those remembered boughs, and, as a voice from a former world, some faint whisper of youthful love sighed across the waste and ashes of her **devastated** soul,—from all such **rekindled** humanities in the past she had now, with gloomy power, wrenched herself away. Crime such as hers admits not long the sentiment that **softens** remorse of gentler error. If there **wakes** one moment from the past the warning and melancholy ghost, soon from that abyss rises the Fury with the lifted **scourge**, and hunts on the **frantic** footsteps towards the future. In the future, the haggard intellect of crime must live, must involve itself mechanically in webs and meshes, and lose past and present in the welcome atmosphere of darkness.

Thus while Lucretia sat, and her eyes rested upon the halls of her youth, her mind overleaped the gulf that yet yawned between her and the object on which she was bent. Already, in fancy, that home was hers again, its present **possessor** swept away, the interloping race of Vernon **ending** in one of those abrupt lines familiar to **genealogists**, which branch out busily from the main tree, as if all **pith** and **sap** were **monopolized** by them, continue for a single generation, and then shrink into a printer's **bracket** with the formal **laconism**, "Died without issue." Back, then, in the pedigree would turn the eye of some curious descendant, and see the race continue in the **posterity** of Lucretia Clavering.

With all her **ineffable** vices, mere **cupidity** had not, as we have often seen, been a main characteristic of this fearful woman; and in her design to **endow**, by the most determined guilt, her son with the heritage of her ancestors, she had hitherto looked but little to mere **mercenary** advantages for herself: but now, in the sight of that venerable and broad domain, a **covetousness**, absolute in itself, broke forth. Could she have gained it for her own use rather than her son's, she would have felt a greater zest in her ruthless purpose. She looked upon the scene as a deposed monarch upon his

---

French

bracket: parenthèse, support, crochet, potence, mettre entre parenthèses, fourchette, étagère, console, tasseau.
covetousness: avidité.
cupidity: cupidité.
devastated: dévastâmes, saccageâtes.
ending: fin, bout, finissant.
endow: doter, dotons.
frantic: frénétique, effréné.
genealogist: généalogiste.

ineffable: ineffable.
laconism: laconisme.
mercenary: mercenaire.
monopolized: monopolisa, accaparâmes.
pith: moelle.
possessor: propriétaire, possesseur, détenteur.
posterity: postérité.
rekindled: raviva, rallumé.
sap: sève, suc, jus.
scourge: fléau, plaie, fouet.

softens: adoucit, amollit, attendrit, se ramollit.
unholy: profane.
wake: sillage, réveiller, se réveiller, s'éveiller, se lever.

usurped realm,—it was her right. The early sense of possession in that inheritance returned to her.

Reluctantly would she even yield her claims to her child. Here, too, in this atmosphere she tasted once more what had long been lost to her,—the luxury of that dignified respect which surrounds the well-born. Here she ceased to be the suspected **adventuress**, the **friendless** outcast, the needy **wrestler** with hostile fortune, the skulking enemy of the law. She rose at once, and without effort, to her original state,—the honoured daughter of an illustrious house. The homeliest welcome that **greeted** her from some **aged** but unforgotten **villager**, the **salutation** of homage, the **bated** breath of humble reverence,—even trifles like these were dear to her, and made her the more resolute to retain them. In her calm, relentless **onward** vision she saw herself **enshrined** in those halls, ruling in the **delegated** authority of her son, safe evermore from **prying** suspicion and **degrading** need and miserable guilt for miserable objects. Here, but one great crime, and she resumed the majesty of her youth! While thus dwelling on the future, her eye did not even turn from those **sunlit** towers to the forms below, and more immediately **inviting** its survey. On the very spot where, at the opening of this tale, sat Sir Miles St. John sharing his attention between his dogs and his guest, sat now Helen Mainwaring; against the balustrade where had lounged Charles Vernon, leaned Percival St. John; and in the same place where he had stationed himself that eventful evening, to **distort**, in his malignant sketch, the features of his father, Gabriel Varney, with almost the same smile of irony upon his lips, was engaged in transferring to his canvas a more faithful likeness of the heir's intended bride. Helen's countenance, indeed, exhibited **comparatively** but little of the **ravages** which the **pernicious aliment**, administered so **noiselessly**, made upon the frame. The girl's eye, it is true, had sunk, and there was a languid **heaviness** in its look; but the contour of the cheek was so naturally rounded, and the features so **delicately** fine, that the fall of the muscles was less evident; and the bright, warm hue of the complexion, and the **pearly** sparkle of the teeth, still gave a **fallacious** freshness to the aspect. But as yet the **poisoners** had forborne those

---

French

adventures: aventures.
aged: âgé, vieilli, vieux.
aliment: aliment.
bated: rabattîmes, diminua.
comparatively: comparativement, de façon comparative, de manière comparative.
degrading: dégradant, avilissant.
delegated: délégué.
delicately: de manière délicate, de façon délicate.
distort: déformer, fausser,

distordent, altérer.
enshrined: enchâssâtes.
fallacious: trompeur, fallacieux.
friendless: sans amis.
greeted: saluai, accueillîtes.
heaviness: lourdeur, poids.
inviting: invitant, appétissant, attrayant, conviant.
noiselessly: de façon silencieuse, de manière silencieuse, silencieusement.
onward: en avant.

pearly: nacré, perlé.
pernicious: pernicieux.
poisoner: empoisonneur.
prying: fureteur, indiscret.
ravage: ravager, dévastation.
salutation: salut.
sunlit: ensoleillé.
usurped: usurpèrent.
villager: villageois.
wrestler: lutteur, catcheur.

ingredients which **invade** the springs of life, resorting only to such as **undermine** the health and prepare the way to **unsuspected** graves. Out of the **infernal** variety of the materials at their command, they had selected a mixture which works by **sustaining** perpetual fever; which gives little pain, little suffering, beyond that of **lassitude** and **thirst**; which wastes like **consumption**, and yet puzzles the **physician**, by **betraying** few or none of its ordinary symptoms. But the disorder as yet was not incurable,—its progress would gradually cease with the **discontinuance** of the **venom**.

Although October was far advanced, the day was as mild and warm as August. But Percival, who had been watching Helen's countenance with the anxiety of love and fear, now proposed that the sitting should be **adjourned**. The sun was declining, and it was certainly no longer safe for Helen to be exposed to the air without exercise. He proposed that they should walk through the garden, and Helen, rising cheerfully, placed her hand on his arm. But she had scarcely descended the steps of the terrace when she stopped short and breathed hard and painfully. The **spasm** was soon over, and walking slowly on, they passed Lucretia with a brief word or two, and were soon out of sight amongst the cedars.

"Lean more on my arm, Helen," said Percival. "How strange it is that the change of air has done so little for you, and our country doctor still less! I should feel miserable indeed if Simmons, whom my mother always considered very clever, did not assure me that there was no ground for alarm,—that these symptoms were only nervous. Cheer up, Helen; sweet love, cheer up!"

Helen raised her face and **strove** to smile; but the tears stood in her eyes. "It would be hard to die now, Percival!" she said **falteringly**.

"To die—oh, Helen! No; we must not stay here longer,—the air is certainly too keen for you. Perhaps your aunt will go to Italy. Why not all go there, and seek my mother? And she will nurse you, Helen, and- and—" He could not trust his voice farther.

French

adjourned: ajourné.
betraying: trahissant.
consumption: consommation, phtisie.
discontinuance: désistement, interruption, arrêt, cessation.
falteringly: de manière hésitante, de façon hésitante.
infernal: infernal.
invade: envahir, invader.
lassitude: lassitude.
physician: médecin, docteur.

spasm: spasme.
strove: combattirent.
sustaining: maintenant, appuyant, s'accotant.
thirst: soif, avoir soif.
undermine: miner, minons, saper, sapons.
unsuspected: insoupçonné.
venom: venin.

Helen pressed his arm **tenderly**. "Forgive me, dear Percival, it is but at moments that I feel so **despondent**; now, again, it is past. Ah, I so long to see your mother! When shall you hear from her? Are you not too sanguine? Do you really feel sure she will consent to so **lowly** a choice?"

"Never doubt her affection, her appreciation of you," answered Percival, **gladly**, and hoping that Helen's natural anxiety might be the latent cause of her **dejected** spirits; "often, when talking of the future, under these very cedars, my mother has said: 'You have no cause to marry for ambition,—marry only for your happiness.' She never had a daughter: in return for all her love, I shall give her that blessing."

Thus talking, the lovers rambled on till the sun set, and then, returning to the house, they found that Varney and Madame Dalibard had preceded them. That evening Helen's spirits rose to their natural **buoyancy**, and Percival's heart was once more set at ease by her **silvery** laugh.

When, at their usual early hour, the rest of the family retired to sleep, Percival remained in the drawing-room to write again, and at length, to Lady Mary and Captain Greville. While thus engaged, his valet entered to say that Beck, who had been out since the early morning, in search of a horse that had **strayed** from one of the **pastures**, had just returned with the animal, who had wandered nearly as far as Southampton.

"I am glad to hear it," said Percival, **abstractedly**, and **continuing** his letter.

The valet still lingered. Percival looked up in surprise. "If you please, sir, you said you particularly wished to see Beck when he came back."

"I—oh, true! Tell him to wait; I will speak to him by and by. You need not sit up for me; let Beck **attend** to the bell."

The valet withdrew. Percival continued his letter, and filled page after page and **sheet** after sheet; and when at length the letters, not **containing** a **tithe** of what he wished to convey, were brought to a close, he fell into a revery that lasted till the candles burned low, and the clock from the **turret**

French

abstractedly: de façon distraite, de manière distraite.
attend: être présent, soigner, assister, visiter.
buoyancy: flottabilité, fermeté, élasticité, poussée d'Archimède.
containing: contenant, renfermant.
continuing: continuant, durant.
dejected: abattu, déprimé, découragé.
despondent: découragé, abattu.
gladly: volontiers, avec plaisir, de façon joyeuse, de manière joyeuse.
lowly: de manière bas, modeste, de façon bas.
pasture: pâturage, pacage.
sheet: feuille, drap, plaque, écoute, tôle.
silvery: argenté.
strayed: écartai.
tenderly: tendrement.
tithe: dîme, décime.
turret: tourelle, barillet, rotateur.

tolled one. **Starting** up in surprise at the **lapse** of time, Percival then, for the first time, remembered Beck, and rang the bell.

The ci-devant sweeper, in his smart **livery**, appeared at the door.

"Beck, my poor fellow, I am ashamed to have kept you waiting so long; but I received a letter this morning which relates to you. Let me see, — I left it in my study upstairs. Ah, you'll never find the way; follow me, — I have some questions to put to you."

"Nothin' agin my carakter, I hopes, your honour," said Beck, timidly.

"Oh, no!"

"Noos of the mattris, then?" exclaimed Beck, **joyfully**.

"Nor that either," answered Percival, laughing, as he lighted the chamber **candlestick**, and, followed by Beck, **ascended** the grand staircase to a small room which, as it **adjoined** his **sleeping** apartment, he had **habitually** used as his morning **writing-room** and study.

Percival had, indeed, received that day a letter which had occasioned him much surprise; it was from John Ardworth, and ran thus: —

My dear Percival, — It seems that you have taken into your service a young man known only by the name of Beck. Is he now with you at Laughton? If so, pray retain him, and suffer him to be in **readiness** to come to me at a day's notice if wanted, though it is probable enough that I may rather come to you. At present, strange as it may seem to you, I am **detained** in London by business connected with that important **personage**. Will you ask him carelessly, as it were, in the mean while; the following questions: —

First, how did he become possessed of a certain child's coral which he left at the house of one Becky Carruthers, in Cole's Building?

Secondly, is he aware of any **mark** on his arm, — if so, will he describe it?

Thirdly, how long has he known the said Becky Carruthers?

Fourthly, does he believe her to be honest and **truthful**?

French

adjoined: about it.
ascended: montai.
candlestick: chandelier, bougeoir.
detained: détinrent, retîntes, retint, retenu, détîntes, détenu.
fourthly: quatrièmement.
habitually: de façon habituelle, de manière habituelle, habituellement.
joyfully: de manière joyeuse, de façon joyeuse.
lapse: déchéance, défaillance,
retomber.
livery: livrée, couleurs d'une maison.
mark: marque, estampiller, signe, cachet, mark, note, repère, témoignage, repérer, tracer, marc.
personage: personnage.
readiness: disponibilité, empressement.
sleeping: dormant, pionçant, roupillant, endormi.
starting: démarrage,
commencement, début.
tolled: sonné.
truthful: véridique, honnête.
writing-room: salon de correspondance.

Take a **memorandum** of his answers, and send it to me. I am pretty well aware of what they are likely to be; but I desire you to put the questions, that I may judge if there be any **discrepancy** between his statement and that of Mrs. Carruthers. I have much to tell you, and am eager to receive your kind **congratulations** upon an event that has given me more happiness than the **fugitive** success of my little book. Tenderest regards to Helen; and hoping soon to see you,

Ever **affectionately** yours.

P.S.—Say not a word of the contents of this letter to Madame Dalibard, Helen, or to any one except Beck. Caution him to the same discretion. If you can't trust to his silence, send him to town.

When the post brought this letter, Beck was already gone on his errand, and after **puzzling** himself with vague conjectures, Percival's mind had been naturally too absorbed with his anxieties for Helen to **recur** much to the subject.

Now, **refreshing** his memory with the contents of the letter, he drew pen and ink before him, put the questions seriatim, noted down the answers as desired, and smiling at Beck's frightened curiosity to know who could possibly care about such matters, and feeling **confident** (from that very **fright**) of his discretion, dismissed the **groom** to his repose.

Beck had never been in that part of the house before; and when he got into the corridor he became **bewildered**, and knew not which turn to take, the right or the left. He had no candle with him; but the moon came clear through a high and wide **skylight**: the light, however, gave him no guide. While pausing, much perplexed, and not sure that he should even know again the door of the room he had just quitted, if venturing to apply to his young master for a clew through such a **labyrinth**, he was inexpressibly startled and appalled by a sudden **apparition**. A door at one end of the corridor opened noiselessly, and a figure, at first scarcely **distinguishable**, for it was robed from head to foot in a black, **shapeless garb**, scarcely giving

---

French

affectionately: affectueusement, de façon affectueuse, de manière affectueuse.
apparition: apparition.
bewildered: effarâmes, éperdu.
confident: confiant, assuré.
congratulation: félicitation.
discrepancy: écart, divergence, différence, désaccord, contradiction, anomalie.
distinguishable: distinguable.
fright: peur, effroi, anxiété, frayeur, terreur.
fugitive: fugitif, réfugié, couleur qui déteint, non solide à la lumière.
garb: costume.
groom: palefrenier, marié, valet d'écurie, panser.
labyrinth: labyrinthe, dédale.
memorandum: mémorandum, note, bordereau.
puzzling: curieux, mystérieux.
recur: se reproduire, revenir, reviens, reparaissons.
refreshing: rafraîchissant, actualisant.
shapeless: informe, difforme.
skylight: lucarne, tabatière, lanterneau, lumière du ciel.

even the outline of the human form, stole forth. Beck rubbed his eyes and crept mechanically close within the **recess** of one of the doors that **communicated** with the passage. The figure advanced a few steps towards him; and what words can describe his astonishment when he **beheld** thus erect, and in full possession of physical power and motion, the **palsied** cripple whose chair he had often seen **wheeled** into the garden, and whose unhappy state was the common topic of comment in the servants' hall! Yes, the moon from above shone full upon that face which never, once seen, could be forgotten. And it seemed more than **mortally** stern and pale, **contrasted** with the **sable** of the strange garb, and beheld by that mournful light. Had a ghost, indeed, risen from the dead, it could scarcely have appalled him more. Madame Dalibard did not see the **involuntary** spy; for the recess in which he had crept was on that side of the wall on which the moon's shadow was cast. With a quick step she turned into another room, opposite that which she had quitted, the door of which stood **ajar**, and vanished noiselessly as she had appeared.

Taught suspicion by his earlier acquaintance with the "night-side" of human nature, Beck had good cause for it here. This detection of an imposture most familiar to his experience,—that of a pretended cripple; the hour of the night; the evil expression on the face of the **deceitful** guest; Madame Dalibard's familiar intimacy and near connection with Varney,—Varney, the visitor to Grabman, who received no visitors but those who desire, not to go to law, but to escape from its penalties; Varney, who had dared to brave the resurrection man in his den, and who seemed so **fearlessly** at home in abodes where **nought** but poverty could protect the honest; Varney now, with that strange woman, an inmate of a house in which the master was so young, so inexperienced, so liable to be **duped** by his own generous nature,—all these ideas, vaguely combined, inspired Beck with as vague a terror. Surely something, he knew not what, was about to be **perpetrated** against his benefactor,—some scheme of villany which it was his duty to detect. He breathed hard, formed his resolves, and stealing on tiptoe, followed the **shadowy** form of the **poisoner** through the half-opened

---

French

ajar: entrouvert.
beheld: vit, remarquâtes, vu, vîmes, vis, vîtes, virent, aperçûtes.
communicated: communiquâtes.
contrasted: contrasté.
deceitful: trompeur, dolosif, fourbe, mensonger.
duped: dupé.
fearlessly: de façon intrépide, de manière intrépide.
involuntary: involontaire.
mortally: de façon mortelle, de manière mortelle.
nought: zéro.
palsied: paralysé.
perpetrated: perpétra.
poisoner: empoisonneur.
recess: pause, alcôve, repos, niche, trêve, vacances.
sable: zibeline, martre.
shadowy: ombragé, vague, indistinct.
wheeled: mobile, roues, sur roues, à roues.

doorway. The **shutters** of the room of which he thus crossed the threshold were not closed,—the moon shone in bright and still. He kept his body behind the door, peeping in with **straining**, fearful stare. He saw Madame Dalibard standing beside a bed round which the curtains were closed,—standing for a moment or so **motionless**, and as if in the act of listening, with one hand on a table beside the bed. He then saw her take from the folds of her dress something white and **glittering**, and pour from it what appeared to him but a drop or two, cautiously, slowly, into a **phial** on the table, from which she withdrew the **stopper**; that done, she left the phial where she had found it, again paused a moment, and turned towards the door. Beck retreated hastily to his former hiding-place, and gained it in time. Again the shadowy form passed him, and again the white face in the white moonlight froze his blood with its fell and horrible expression. He remained cowering and **shrinking** against the wall for some time, **striving** to collect his wits, and considering what he should do. His first thought was to go at once and inform St. John of what he had **witnessed**. But the poor have a proverbial **dread** of **deposing** aught against a superior. Madame Dalibard would deny his tale, the guest would be believed against the menial,—he would be but dismissed with **ignominy**. At that idea, he left his hiding-place, and crept along the corridor, in the hope of finding some passage at the end which might lead to the offices. But when he arrived at the other **extremity**, he was only met by great folding-doors, which evidently communicated with the state apartments; he must **retrace** his steps. He did so; and when he came to the door which Madame Dalibard had entered, and which still stood ajar, he had recovered some courage, and with courage, curiosity seized him. For what purpose could the strange woman seek that room at night thus **feloniously**? What could she have poured, and with such **stealthy** caution, into the phial? Naturally and suddenly the idea of poison flashed across him. Tales of such crime (as, indeed, of all crime) had necessarily often thrilled the ear of the **vagrant** fellow-lodger with **burglars** and **outlaws**. But poison to whom? Could it be meant for his **benefactor**? Could St. John sleep in that room? Why not? The woman had sought the chamber before her young host

---

French

benefactor: bienfaiteur.
burglar: cambrioleur, voleur.
deposing: déposant, destituant.
doorway: embrasure, baie de communication, entrée de porte, porte.
dread: crainte, redouter.
extremity: extrémité, queue.
feloniously: de manière criminelle, de façon criminelle.
glittering: scintillant, éclat.
ignominy: ignominie.

motionless: immobile, fixe, au repos.
outlaw: proscrit.
phial: fiole, flacon.
retrace: retracer, reconstituer, retour du spot.
shrinking: rétrécissant, perte de volume, décatissage, contraction, retrait.
shutter: obturateur, volet.
stealthy: furtif.
stopper: bouchon, stoppeur,

obturateur, prise de courant mâle.
straining: filtrage, sollicitation, tendre, tension, colature, cadrage, raffinage du mélange.
striving: combattant.
vagrant: vagabond, clochard, chemineau.
witnessed: témoignai.

had retired to rest, and mingled her **potion** with some **medicinal draught**. All fear vanished before the notion of danger to his employer. He stole at once through the doorway, and noiselessly approached the table on which yet lay the phial. His hand closed on it firmly. He resolved to carry it away, and consider next morning what next to do. At all events, it might **contain** some proof to back his tale and justify his suspicions. When he came once more into the corridor, he made a quick rush **onwards**, and luckily arrived at the staircase. There the blood-red stains reflected on the stone floors from the **blazoned** casements **daunted** him little less than the sight at which his hair still bristled. He scarcely drew breath till he had got into his own little **crib**, in the wing set apart for the stable-men, when, at length, he fell into broken and **agitated** sleep,—the visions of all that had **successively** disturbed him waking, united **confusedly**, as in one picture of gloom and terror. He thought that he was in his old loft in St. Giles's, that the Gravestealer was **wrestling** with Varney for his body, while he himself, lying powerless on his **pallet**, fancied he should be safe as long as he could retain, as a **talisman**, his child's coral, which he clasped to his heart. Suddenly, in that black, shapeless **garb**, in which he had beheld her, Madame Dalibard bent over him with her stern, **colourless** face, and wrenched from him his charm. Then, **ceasing** his struggle with his horrible **antagonist**, Varney laughed aloud, and the Gravestealer seized him in his deadly arms.

French

agitated: agitèrent, débattîtes, troubla, nerveux, remuas, émurent, émûmes, émus, émut, émûtes, inquiet.
antagonist: antagoniste.
blazoned: blasonna.
ceasing: cessant.
colourless: incolore, sans couleur.
confusedly: de manière confuse, de façon confuse.
contain: contenir, renfermer.
crib: berceau, lit d'enfant, copier, crèche, prise d'eau, mangeoire, encoffrement, cage, bûcher.
daunted: découragea, intimidai.
draught: tirant d'eau, prise, profondeur d'enfoncement, esquisse, épure, dépouille, courant d'air, coup, appel d'air, plan, projet.
garb: costume.
medicinal: médicinal.
onward: en avant.
pallet: palette, soupape, tringle de clouage, petite planche dont se sert le colleur, ancre, levée, filet à dorer.
potion: potion.
successively: de façon successive, de manière successive, successivement.
talisman: amulette, talisman.
wrestling: lutte, catch.

CHAPTER XXII

THE TAPESTRY CHAMBER

When Beck woke the next morning, and gradually recalled all that had so startled and **appalled** him the previous night, the grateful creature felt, less by the process of reason than by a **brute** instinct, that in the mysterious **resuscitation** and **nocturnal** wanderings of the **pretended paralytic**, some danger **menaced** his master; he became anxious to learn whether it was really St. John's room Madame Dalibard **stealthily** visited. A bright idea struck him; and in the course of the day, at an hour when the family were out of doors, he contrived to coax the good-natured valet, who had taken him under his special **protection**, to show him over the house. He had heard the other servants say there was such a power of fine things that a **peep** into the rooms was as good as a show, and the valet felt pride in being **cicerone** even to Beck. After having stared sufficiently at the banquet-hall and the drawing-room, the **armour**, the **busts**, and the pictures, and listened, open-mouthed, to his guide's **critical** observations, Beck was led up the great stairs into the old family **picture-gallery**, and into Sir Miles's ancient room at the end, which had been left **undisturbed**, with the bed still in the angle; on returning **thence**, Beck found himself in the corridor which communicated with the principal bedrooms, in which he had lost himself the night before.

French

appalled: consternai, épouvantâtes.
armour: armure, blinder.
brute: brute, ébruter, gros projecteur, sauvage.
bust: buste.
cicerone: cicérone.
critical: critique.
menaced: menacé.
nocturnal: nocturne.
paralytic: paralytique.
peep: pépier, gazouiller.
picture-gallery: pinacothèque.
pretended: feint, feignit, prétendu.
protection: protection, sauvegarde, garde.
resuscitation: réanimation, ressuscitation.
stealthily: de manière furtive, furtivement, de façon furtive.
thence: de là.
undisturbed: paisible, non détériorée, calme.

"And vot room be that vith the littul vite 'ead h-over the door?" asked Beck, pointing to the chamber from which Madame Dalibard had emerged.

"That white head, Master Beck, is Floorer the goddess; but a **heathen** like you knows nothing about goddesses. Floorer has a half-moon in her hair, you see, which shows that the **idolatrous** Turks **worship** her; for the Turkish **flag** is a half-moon, as I have seen at Constantinople. I have travelled, Beck."

"And vot room be it? Is it the master's?" **persisted** Beck.

"No, the pretty young lady, Miss Mainwaring, has it at present. There is nothing to see in it. But that one opposite," and the valet advanced to the door through which Madame Dalibard had disappeared,—"that is curious; and as Madame is out, we may just take a peep." He opened the door gently, and Beck looked in. "This, which is called the turret-chamber, was Madame's when she was a girl, I have heard old Bessy say; so Master pops her there now. For my part, I'd rather sleep in your little **crib** than have those great gruff-looking figures staring at me by the firelight, and shaking their heads with every wind on a winter's night." And the valet took a **pinch** of snuff as he drew Beck's attention to the faded **tapestry** on the walls. As they spoke, the **draught** between the door and the window caused the gloomy **arras** to wave with a life-like motion; and to those more **superstitious** than romantic, the chamber had certainly no **inviting** aspect.

"I never sees these old tapestry rooms," said the valet, "without thinking of the story of the lady who, coming from a **ball** and taking off her **jewels**, happened to look up, and saw an eye in one of the figures which she felt sure was no peeper in worsted."

"Vot vos it, then?" asked Beck, timidly lifting up the hangings, and noticing that there was a considerable space between them and the wall, which was filled up in part by **closets** and wardrobes set into the walls, with intervals more than deep enough for the hiding-place of a man.

"Why," answered the valet, "it was a thief. He had come for the jewels; but the lady had the presence of mind to say aloud, as if to herself, that she had forgotten something, slipped out of the room, locked the door, called up

French

arras: arras.
ball: bal, balle, bille, pelote, sphère, globe, boule.
closet: armoire, placard.
crib: berceau, lit d'enfant, copier, crèche, prise d'eau, mangeoire, encoffrement, cage, bûcher.
draught: tirant d'eau, prise, profondeur d'enfoncement, esquisse, épure, dépouille, courant d'air, coup, appel d'air, plan, projet.

flag: drapeau, pavillon, indicateur, fanion, étendard, dalle, cavalier, banderole, écran opaque.
heathen: païen, barbare, sauvage.
idolatrous: idolâtre.
inviting: invitant, appétissant, attrayant, conviant.
jewel: bijou, joyau.
persisted: persistèrent.
pinch: pincer, serrer.
superstitious: superstitieux.
tapestry: tapisserie.

worship: adorer, vénération.

the servants, and the thief—who was no less a person than the under-butler—was nabbed."

"And the **French** 'oman sleeps 'ere?" said Beck, musingly.

"French 'oman! Master Beck, nothing's so **vulgar** as these **nicknames** in a first-rate sitivation. It is all very well when one lives with skinflints, but with such a master as our'n, respect's the go. Besides, Madame is not a French 'oman; she is one of the family,—and as old a family it is, too, as e'er a lord's in the three **kingdoms**. But come, your curiosity is satisfied now, and you must **trot** back to your horses."

As Beck returned to the stables, his mind yet more misgave him as to the criminal designs of his master's visitor. It was from Helen's room that the false cripple had walked, and the ill health of the poor young lady was a general subject of **compassionate** comment. But Madame Dalibard was Helen's relation: from what motive could she **harbour** an evil thought against her own **niece**? But still, if those drops were poured into the healing draught for good, why so secretly? Once more he **revolved** the idea of speaking to St. John: an accident **dissuaded** him from this intention,—the only proof to back his tale was the mysterious **phial** he had carried away; but **unluckily**, forgetting that it was in his pocket, at a time when he flung off his coat to **groom** one of the horses, the bottle struck against the corn-bin and broke; all the contents were spilt. This incident made him **suspend** his intention, and wait till he could obtain some fresh evidence of evil intentions. The day passed without any other noticeable occurrence. The doctor called, found Helen somewhat better, and **ascribed** it to his medicines, especially to the effect of his **tonic** draught the first thing in the morning. Helen smiled. "**Nay**, Doctor," said she, "this morning, at least, it was forgotten. I did not find it by my bedside. Don't tell my aunt; she would be so angry." The doctor looked rather discomposed.

"Well," said he, soon recovering his good humour, "since you are certainly better to-day without the draught, **discontinue** it also to-morrow. I

French

ascribed: attribuèrent.
compassionate: compatissant.
discontinue: interrompre, discontinuer.
dissuaded: dissuadâtes.
french: langue française, Français.
groom: palefrenier, marié, valet d'écurie, panser.
harbour: port, héberger.
kingdom: royaume, règne.
nay: non.
nickname: surnom, sobriquet.
niece: nièce.
phial: fiole, flacon.
revolved: tournai, ruminèrent.
suspend: suspendre.
tonic: tonique, remontant, fortifiant.
trot: trotter, aller au trot.
unluckily: de façon malchanceuse, de manière malchanceuse.
vulgar: vulgaire, trivial.

will make an **alteration** for the day after." So that night Madame Dalibard **visited** in **vain** her niece's **chamber**: Helen had a **reprieve**.

French

alteration: modification, transformation, altération, changement, retouche.
chamber: chambre, salle, pièce, local.
reprieve: sursis, répit, grâce.
vain: vain, vaniteux, abortif, frivole.
visited: visita.

CHAPTER XXIII

THE SHADES ON THE DIAL

The following morning was indeed **eventful** to the family at Laughton; and as if conscious of what it brought forth, it rose dreary and sunless. One heavy mist covered all the landscape, and a raw, drizzling rain fell pattering through the yellow leaves.

Madame Dalibard, **pleading** her infirmities, rarely left her room before noon, and Varney **professed** himself very irregular in his hours of rising; the breakfast, therefore, **afforded** no social assembly to the family, but each took that meal in the **solitude** of his or her own chamber. Percival, in whom all habits **partook** of the healthfulness and simplicity of his character, rose habitually early, and that day, in spite of the weather, walked forth betimes to meet the person charged with the letters from the post. He had done so for the last three or four days, **impatient** to hear from his mother, and **calculating** that it was full time to receive the expected answer to his confession and his prayer. He met the **messenger** at the bottom of the park, not far from Guy's Oak. This day he was not disappointed. The letter-bag contained three letters for himself, — two with the foreign **postmark**, the third in Ardworth's hand. It contained also a letter for Madame Dalibard, and two for Varney.

French

afforded: produisîmes.
calculating: calculant, comptant.
eventful: mouvementé.
impatient: impatient.
messenger: messager, coursier.
partook: prîmes, prirent, pris, prit, prîtes.
pleading: plaidant, excipant, implorant.
postmark: cachet de la poste, empreinte de timbre à date, marque postale, oblitération, timbrer.
professed: confessé, professai.
solitude: solitude.

Leaving the messenger to take these last to the Hall, Percival, with his own prizes, **plunged** into the hollow of the glen before him, and, **seating** himself at the foot of Guy's Oak, through the vast branches of which the rain scarcely came, and only in single, mournful drops, he opened first the letter in his mother's hand, and read as follows:—

My dear, dear son,—How can I express to you the alarm your letter has given to me! So these, then, are the new relations you have discovered! I **fondly** imagined that you were **alluding** to some of my own family, and conjecturing who, amongst my many cousins, could have so captivated your attention. These the new relations,—Lucretia Dalibard, Helen Mainwaring! Percival, do you not know— No, you cannot know that Helen Mainwaring is the daughter of a disgraced man, of one who (more than suspected of fraud in the bank in which he was a partner) left his country, condemned even by his own father. If you doubt this, you have but to inquire at—, not ten miles from Laughton, where the elder Mainwaring resided. Ask there what became of William Mainwaring. And Lucretia, you do not know that the dying prayer of her uncle, Sir Miles St. John, was that she might never enter the house he bequeathed to your father. Not till after my poor Charles's death did I know the exact cause for Sir Miles's **displeasure**, though confident it was just; but then amongst his papers I found the ungrateful letter which betrayed thoughts so dark and passions so **unwomanly** that I blushed for my sex to read it. Could it be possible that that poor old man's prayers were unheeded, that that **treacherous** step could ever cross your threshold, that that cruel eye, which read with such **barbarous** joy the ravages of death on a benefactor's face, could rest on the hearth by which your frank, **truthful** countenance has so often smiled away my tears, I should feel indeed as if a thunder-cloud hung over the roof. No, if you marry the **niece**, the aunt must be banished from your house. Good heavens! and it is the daughter of William Mainwaring, the niece and ward of Lucretia Dalibard, to whom you have given your faithful affection, whom you single from the world as your wife! Oh, my son,—my beloved, my sole surviving

---

French

alluding: insinuant.
barbarous: barbare.
displeasure: déplaisir, mécontentement.
fondly: de manière tendre, de façon tendre, tendrement.
niece: nièce.
plunged: plongé.
seating: places assises, portée, appui, assise.
treacherous: traître, déloyal.
truthful: véridique, honnête.

unwomanly: peu féminin.

child,—do not think that I blame you, that my heart does not **bleed** while I write thus; but I **implore** you on my knees to pause at least, to suspend this intercourse till I myself can reach England. And what then? Why, then, Percival, I promise, on my part, that I will see your Helen with **unprejudiced** eyes, that I will put away from me, as far as possible, all visions of disappointed pride,—the remembrance of faults not her own,—and if she be as you say and think, I will take her to my heart and call her 'Daughter.' Are you satisfied? If so, come to me,—come at once, and take comfort from your mother's lip. How I long to be with you while you read this; how I tremble at the pain I so **rudely** give you! But my poor sister still chains me here, I dare not leave her, lest I should lose her last sigh. Come then, come; we will **console** each other.

Your fond (how fond!) and sorrowing mother,
Mary St. John. Sorrento, October 3, 1831.

P.S.—You see by this address that we have left Pisa for this place, recommended by our physician; hence an unhappy delay of some days in my reply. Ah, Percival, how **sleepless** will be my pillow till I hear from you!

Long, very long, was it before St. John, mute and overwhelmed with the sudden shock of his anguish, opened his other letters. The first was from Captain Greville.

What trap have you fallen into, foolish boy? That you would get into some silly **scrape** or another, was natural enough. But a scrape for life, sir,—that is serious! But—God bless you for your candour, my Percival; you have written to us in time—you are old-fashioned enough to think that a mother's consent is necessary to a young man's union; and you have left it in our power to save you yet. It is not every boyish fancy that proves to be true love. But enough of this **preaching**; I shall do better than write **scolding** letters,—I shall come and **scold** you in person. My servant is at this very

---

French

bleed: saigner, purger.
console: consoler, pupitre de commande.
implore: implorer, conjurer.
preaching: prêchant, sermon.
rudely: de façon grossière, de manière grossière.
scold: réprimander, gronder, sommer, admonester, reprocher, exhorter, sermonner.
scolding: réprimande, grondeur.
scrape: gratter, racler, effacer en grattant.
sleepless: sans sommeil.
unprejudiced: impartial, sans préjugés.

moment **packing** my **portmanteau**, the laquais-de-place is gone to Naples for my **passport**. Almost as soon as you receive this I shall be with you; and if I am a day or two later than the **mail**, be patient: do not **commit** yourself further. Break your heart if you please, but don't **implicate** your honour. I shall come at once to Curzon Street. **Adieu**!

H. Greville.

Ardworth's letter was shorter than the others,—fortunately so, for otherwise it had been unread:—

If I do not come to you myself the day after you receive this, dear Percival,—which, indeed, is most probable,—I shall send you my **proxy**, in one whom, for my sake, I know that you will **kindly** welcome. He will undertake my task, and clear up all the mysteries with which, I trust, my correspondence has thoroughly bewildered your lively imagination.

Yours ever,
John Ardworth. Gray's Inn.

Little indeed did Percival's imagination busy itself with the mysteries of Ardworth's correspondence. His mind scarcely took in the sense of the words over which his eye mechanically **wandered**.

And the letter which **narrated** the visit of Madame Dalibard to the house thus **solemnly** interdicted to her step was on its way to his mother,—nay, by this time would almost have reached her! Greville was on the road,—nay, as his tutor's letter had been **forwarded** from London, might perhaps be in Curzon Street that day. How **desirable** to see him before he could reach Laughton, to prepare him for Madame Dalibard's visit, for Helen's illness, explain the position in which he was involved, and conciliate the old soldier's rough, kind heart to his love and his **distress**.

He did not dread the meeting with Greville,—he yearned for it. He **needed** an **adviser**, a **confidant**, a friend. To **dismiss abruptly** his guests from his house,—impossible; to **abandon** Helen because of her father's crime

French

abandon: abandonner, délaisser, quitter, renoncer, abdiquer, livrer, résigner.
abruptly: brusquement, abruptement, sèchement, de façon abrupte, de manière abrupte.
adieu: adieu.
adviser: conseiller, annonceur.
commit: commettre, engager, validation.
confidant: confident.
desirable: désirable, souhaitable.
dismiss: renvoyer, licencier, débouter, suspendre, congédier.
distress: détresse, attrister.
forwarded: achemina.
implicate: entortiller, empêtrer, impliquer.
kindly: complaisamment, de façon gentille, de manière gentille.
mail: courrier, poste.
narrated: racontèrent, contâtes.
needed: nécessita.
packing: empaquetage, garniture, remplissage, bourrage, joint, colisage.
passport: passeport.
portmanteau: valise.
proxy: procuration, mandataire, fondé de pouvoir, pouvoir.
solemnly: solennellement, de façon solennelle, de manière solennelle.
wandered: errâmes, errèrent, erré, erras, vagué.

or her aunt's fault (whatever that last might be, and no clear detail of it was given),—that never entered his thoughts! Pure and **unsullied**, the **starry** face of Helen shone the holier for the cloud around it. An inexpressible and **chivalrous** compassion mingled with his love and confirmed his faith. She, poor child, to suffer for the deeds of others,—no. What availed his power as man, and dignity as gentleman, if they could not **wrap** in their own shelter the one by whom such shelter was now **doubly** needed? Thus, **amidst** all his emotions, firm and resolved at least on one point, and beginning already to recover the hope of his sanguine nature, from his reliance on his mother's love, on the promises that softened her disclosures and warnings, and on his conviction that Helen had only to be seen for every scruple to give way, Percival wandered back towards the house, and coming abruptly on the terrace, he encountered Varney, who was leaning **motionless** against the balustrades, with an open letter in his hand. Varney was deadly pale, and there was the trace of some recent and gloomy **agitation** in the relaxed muscles of his cheeks, usually so firmly rounded. But Percival did not **heed** his appearance as he took him gravely by the arm, and leading him into the garden, said, after a painful pause,—

"Varney, I am about to ask you two questions, which your close connection with Madame Dalibard may enable you to answer, but in which, from **obvious** motives, I must demand the strictest confidence. You will not hint to her or to Helen what I am about to say?"

Varney stared **uneasily** on Percival's serious countenance, and gave the promise required.

"First, then, for what offence was Madame Dalibard **expelled** her uncle's house,—this house of Laughton?

"Secondly, what is the crime with which Mr. Mainwaring, Helen's father, is charged?"

"With regard to the first," said Varney, recovering his **composure**, "I thought I had already told you that Sir Miles was a proud man, and that in consequence of discovering a **girlish flirtation** between his niece Lucretia

---

French

agitation: agitation, bagarre, brassage, barouf.
amidst: parmi, au milieu de.
chivalrous: chevaleresque, galant.
composure: repos, calme, impassibilité.
doubly: de façon double, de manière double, doublement.
expelled: expulsèrent.
flirtation: flirt.
girlish: de petite fille, efféminé.
heed: attention.
motionless: immobile, fixe, au repos.
obvious: évident, manifeste, clair, apparent.
starry: étoilé.
uneasily: de façon inquiète, de manière inquiète.
unsullied: sans tache.
wrap: envelopper, emballer.

(now Madame Dalibard) and Mainwaring, who afterwards **jilted** her for Helen's mother, he altered his will; 'expelled her his house' is too harsh a phrase. This is all I know. With regard to the second question, no crime was ever brought home to William Mainwaring; he was suspected of dealing **improperly** with the funds of the bank, and he **repaid** the **alleged deficit** by the sacrifice of all he possessed."

"This is the truth?" exclaimed Percival, **joyfully**.

"The plain truth, I believe; but why these questions at this moment? Ah, you too, I see, have had letters,—I understand. Lady Mary gives these reasons for **withholding** her consent."

"Her consent is not withheld," answered Percival; "but shall I own it? Remember, I have your promise not to wound and **offend** Madame Dalibard by the disclosure: my mother does refer to the subjects I have **alluded** to, and Captain Greville, my old friend and tutor, is on his way to England; perhaps to-morrow he may arrive at Laughton."

"Ha!" said Varney, startled, "to-morrow! And what sort of a man is this Captain Greville?"

"The best man possible for such a case as mine,—kind-hearted, yet cool, **sagacious**; the **finest** observer, the quickest judge of character,—nothing escapes him. Oh, one interview will **suffice** to show him all Helen's innocent and matchless excellence."

"To-morrow! this man comes to-morrow!"

"All that I fear is,—for he is rather rough and **blunt** in his manner,—all that I fear is his first surprise, and, dare I say displeasure, at seeing this poor Madame Dalibard, whose faults, I fear, were **graver** than you suppose, at the house from which her uncle—to whom, indeed, I owe this inheritance—"

"I see, I see!" interrupted Varney, quickly. "And Madame Dalibard is the most susceptible of women,—so well-born and so poor, so **gifted** and so helpless; it is natural. Can you not write, and put off this Captain Greville for a few days,—until, indeed, I can find some excuse for **terminating** our visit?"

French

alleged: alléguâmes, présumé, prétendu.
alluded: insinuâtes.
blunt: émoussé, épointer.
deficit: déficit, impasse, insuffisance, manque, pénurie, découvert.
finest: le plus fin.
gifted: doué, surdoué.
graver: burin, échoppe, gravoir, pointe à tracer.
improperly: de manière incorrecte, incorrectement, de façon incorrecte.
jilted: plaqua, délaissé.
joyfully: de manière joyeuse, de façon joyeuse.
offend: offenser, insulter, pécher.
repaid: remboursa.
sagacious: sensé, intelligent, raisonnable.
suffice: suffire.
terminating: terminant, d'arrivée, aboutissant, résiliant.
withholding: retenant, rétention, refus.

"But my letter may be hardly in time to reach him; he may be in town to-day."

"Go then to town at once; you can be back late at night, or at least to-morrow. Anything better than **wounding** the pride of a woman on whom, after all, you must depend for free and open **intercourse** with Helen."

"That is exactly what I thought of; but what excuse—"

"Excuse,—a thousand! Every man coming of age into such a property has business with his lawyers. Or why not say simply that you want to meet a friend of yours who has just left your mother in Italy? In short, any excuse **suffices**, and none can be offensive."

"I will order my carriage instantly."

"Right!" exclaimed Varney; and his eye followed the **receding** form of Percival with a mixture of fierce exultation and anxious fear. Then, turning towards the window of the turret-chamber in which Madame Dalibard reposed, and seeing it still closed, he muttered an impatient **oath**; but even while he did so, the shutters were slowly opened, and a **footman, stepping** from the **porch**, approached Varney with a message that Madame Dalibard would see him in five minutes, if he would then have the goodness to **ascend** to her room.

Before that time was well **expired**, Varney was in the chamber. Madame Dalibard was up and in her chair; and the **unwonted** joy which her countenance evinced was in strong contrast with the **sombre** shade upon her son-in-law's brow, and the nervous **quiver** of his lip.

"Gabriel," she said, as he drew near to her, "my son is found!"

"I know it," he answered **petulantly**. "You! From whom?"

"From Grabman."

"And I from a still better authority,—from Walter Ardworth himself. He lives; he will restore my child!" She extended a letter while she spoke. He, in return, gave her, not that still **crumpled** in his hand, but one which he drew

---

French

ascend: monter, se soulever.
crumpled: froissé, chiffonné, fripé.
expired: expira, périmé, échut.
footman: valet de pied.
intercourse: rapport sexuel, relations.
oath: serment, juron.
petulantly: de façon maussade, de manière maussade.
porch: porche, portique, véranda.
quiver: trembler, frisson, frémir.
receding: fuyant, recédant, reculant.
sombre: sombre.
stepping: gradins, modification d'instruction, exploitation en gradins renversés, étagement, bois de marche, avance d'un ou de plusieurs pas, recul d'un ou de plusieurs pas.
suffice: suffire.
unwonted: insolite.
wounding: blessant.

from his breast. These letters **severally** occupied both, begun and finished almost in the same moment.

That from Grabman ran thus:—

Dear Jason,—Toss up your hat and cry 'hip, hip!' At last, from person to person, I have **tracked** the lost Vincent Braddell. He lives still! We can maintain his identity in any court of law. Scarce in time for the post, I have not a moment for further particulars. I shall employ the next two days in **reducing** all the evidence to a regular **digest**, which I will **despatch** to you. Meanwhile, prepare, as soon as may be, to put me in possession of my fee,— 5000 pounds; and my **expedition** merits something more.

Yours,
Nicholas Grabman.

The letter from Ardworth was no less positive:—

Madam,—In **obedience** to the commands of a dying friend, I took charge of his infant and concealed its existence from his mother,—yourself. On returning to England, I need not say that I was not unmindful of my trust. Your son lives; and after mature reflection I have resolved to restore him to your arms. In this I have been decided by what I have heard, from one whom I can trust, of your altered habits, your **decorous** life, your melancholy infirmities, and the generous protection you have given to the **orphan** of my poor cousin Susan, my old friend Mainwaring. Alfred Braddell himself, if it be permitted to him to look down and read my motives, will pardon me, I venture to feel assured, this departure from his injunctions. Whatever the faults which **displeased** him, they have been **amply chastised**. And your son, grown to man, can no longer be **endangered** by example, in **tending** the **couch**, or **soothing** the **repentance** of his mother.

French

amply: amplement, de façon ample, de manière ample.
chastised: châtia.
couch: canapé, divan, presse coucheuse.
decorous: bienséant.
despatch: expédition, dépêche.
digest: digérer, condensé.
displeased: mécontent, déplut.
endangered: risquâmes, compromîtes, MIS en danger.
expedition: expédition.
obedience: obéissance, soumission.
orphan: orphelin, bout de ligne.
reducing: réduisant, abaissant.
repentance: repentir.
severally: individuellement ad.
soothing: calmant, lénitif, rassurant, abattant, apaisant.
tending: soins culturaux, surveillant, soignant.
tracked: chenillé.

These words are severe; but you will pardon them in him who gives you back your child. I shall venture to wait on you in person, with such proofs as may satisfy you as to the identity of your son. I count on arriving at Laughton to-morrow. Meanwhile, I simply sign myself by a name in which you will recognize the kinsman to one branch of your family, and the friend of your dead husband.

J. Walter Ardworth.

Craven Hotel, October, 1831.

"Well, and are you not rejoiced?" said Lucretia, gazing surprised on Varney's **sullen** and unsympathizing face.

"No! because time presses; because, even while **discovering** your son, you may fail in securing his heritage; because, in the **midst** of your triumph, I see Newgate opening to myself. Look you, I too have had my news,—less **pleasing** than yours. This Stubmore (curse him!) writes me word that he shall certainly be in town next month at **farthest**, and that he **meditates**, immediately on his **arrival**, **transferring** the legacy from the Bank of England to an excellent **mortgage** of which he has heard. Were it not for this scheme of **ours**, nothing would be left for me but flight and exile."

"A month,—that is a long time. Do you think, now that my son is found, and that son like John Ardworth (for there can be no doubt that my **surmise** was right), with genius to make station the **pedestal** to the power I **dreamed** of in my youth, but which my sex forbade me to attain,—do you think I will keep him a month from his inheritance? Before the month is out, you shall replace what you have taken, and buy your trustee's silence, if need be, either from the sums you have **insured**, or from the rents of Laughton."

"Lucretia," said Varney, whose fresh colours had grown livid, "what is to be done must be done at once. Percival St. John has heard from his mother. Attend." And Varney rapidly related the questions St. John had put to him, the **dreaded** arrival of Captain Greville, the danger of so keen an observer,

---

French

arrival: arrivée, venue, ravitaillement, fourniture.
discovering: découvrant, dépouillant.
dreaded: redouté.
dreamed: rêvé.
farthest: le plus loin.
insured: assuras, maître de l'ouvrage.
meditates: médite, songe.
midst: milieu, millieux.
mortgage: hypothèque, lettre de gage, porteur de créance hypothécaire.
ours: nôtre.
pedestal: socle, piédestal, décollement du niveau du noir.
pleasing: plaisant, flatteur, satisfaisant.
sullen: maussade, sombre, boudeur, morne, renfrogné.
surmise: conjecturer, supposer, prévoir, se douter de.
transferring: transférant, mutant.

the necessity, at all events, of **abridging** their visit, the urgency of **hastening** the catastrophe to its close.

Lucretia listened in **ominous** and steadfast silence.

"But," she said at last, "you have persuaded St. John to give this man the meeting in London,—to put off his visit for the time. St. John will return to us to-morrow. Well, and if he finds his Helen is no more! Two nights ago I, for the first time, mingled in the morning draught that which has no **antidote** and no cure. This night two drops more, and St. John will return to find that Death is in the house before him. And then for himself,—the sole **remaining** barrier between my son and this inheritance,—for himself, why, grief sometimes **kills** suddenly; and there be **drugs** whose effect **simulates** the death-stroke of grief."

"Yet, yet, this **rapidity**, if necessary, is **perilous**. Nothing in Helen's state forbodes sudden death by natural means. The **strangeness** of two deaths, both so young; Greville in England, if not here,—hastening down to examine, to inquire. With such prepossessions against you, there must be an inquest."

"Well, and what can be discovered? It was I who shrank before,—it is I who now urge **despatch**. I feel as in my proper home in these halls. I would not leave them again but to my grave. I stand on the hearth of my youth; I fight for my rights and my son's! **Perish** those who oppose me!"

A fell energy and power were in the aspect of the **murderess** as she thus spoke; and while her determination awed the inferior villany of Varney, it served somewhat to **mitigate** his fears.

As in more detail they began to arrange their **execrable** plans, Percival, while the horses were being harnessed to take him to the nearest post-town, sought Helen, and found her in the little chamber which he had described and **appropriated** as her own, when his fond fancy had sketched the fair outline of the future.

This room had been originally fitted up for the private devotions of the Roman Catholic wife of an ancestor in the reign of Charles II; and in a recess,

French

abridging: abrégeant.
antidote: antidote, contrepoison.
appropriated: approprié.
despatch: expédition, dépêche.
drug: drogue, médicament, stupéfiant, remède.
execrable: exécrable.
hastening: hâtant, s'empressant, accourant, empressant.
kill: tuer, abattre, supprimer, rectifier.
mitigate: mitiger, adoucir, atténuer.

murderess: meurtrière.
ominous: inquiétant, menaçant, sinistre.
perilous: périlleux.
perish: périr, s'abîmer.
rapidity: rapidité.
remaining: restant, qui reste, autre.
simulate: simuler.
strangeness: étrangeté, bizarrerie.

half **veiled** by a curtain, there still stood that holy symbol which, whether Protestant or Roman Catholic, no one sincerely penetrated with the solemn pathos of sacred history can behold unmoved,—the Cross of the Divine Agony. Before this holy symbol Helen stood in earnest **reverence**. She did not **kneel** (for the forms of the religion in which she had been reared were opposed to that posture of worship before the graven image), but you could see in that countenance, eloquent at once with the enthusiasm and the **meekness** of **piety**, that the soul was filled with the memories and the hopes which, age after age, have **consoled** the sufferer and inspired the **martyr**. The soul knelt to the idea, if the knee bowed not to the image, **embracing** the tender grandeur of the sacrifice and the vast inheritance opened to faith in the redemption.

The young man held his breath while he gazed. He was moved, and he was awed. Slowly Helen turned towards him, and, smiling **sweetly**, held out to him her hand. They seated themselves in silence in the depth of the **overhanging** casement; and the mournful character of the scene without, where dimly, through the **misty** rains, gloomed the dark foliage of the cedars, made them **insensibly** draw closer to each other in the instinct of love when the world frowns around it. Percival wanted the courage to say that he had come to take farewell, though but for a day, and Helen spoke first.

"I cannot guess why it is, Percival, but I am startled at the change I feel in myself—no, not in health, dear Percival; I mean in mind—during the last few months,—since, indeed, we have known each other. I remember so well the morning in which my aunt's letter arrived at the dear **vicarage**. We were returning from the village fair, and my good guardian was smiling at my notions of the world. I was then so **giddy** and light and **thoughtless**, everything presented itself to me in such gay colours, I scarcely believed in sorrow. And now I feel as if I were **awakened** to a truer sense of nature,—of the ends of our being here; I seem to know that life is a grave and solemn thing. Yet I am not less happy, Percival. No, I think rather that I knew not true happiness till I knew you. I have read somewhere that the slave is gay in

---

French

awakened: réveilla.
consoled: consolé.
embracing: embrassant.
giddy: étourdi.
insensibly: de façon insensible, de manière insensible.
kneel: s'agenouiller, agenouillement, se mettre à genoux.
martyr: martyr.
meekness: douceur de caractère, humilité.
misty: brumeux, embué, vague, vaporeux.
overhanging: surplombant, déversé, débord, inclinaison.
piety: piété.
reverence: révérence, vénération, respect.
sweetly: de façon douce, de manière douce, doucement.
thoughtless: irréfléchi, étourdi, inconsidéré.
veiled: voilé, caché.
vicarage: presbytère.

his holiday from toil; if you free him, if you **educate** him, the gayety **vanishes**, and he cares no more for the dance under the palm-tree. But is he less happy? So it is with me!"

"My sweet Helen, I would rather have one gay smile of old, the arch, careless laugh which came so naturally from those **rosy** lips, than hear you talk of happiness with that **quiver** in your voice, — those tears in your eyes."

"Yet gayety," said Helen, thoughtfully, and in the strain of her pure, truthful poetry of soul, "is only the light impression of the present moment, — the play of the mere spirits; and happiness seems a **forethought** of the future, spreading on, far and broad, over all time and space."

"And you live, then, in the future at last; you have no **misgivings** now, my Helen? Well, that comforts me. Say it, Helen, — say the future will be ours!"

"It will, it will, — forever and forever," said Helen, **earnestly**; and her eyes **involuntarily** rested on the Cross.

In his younger spirit and less **imaginative** nature Percival did not **comprehend** the depth of sadness implied in Helen's answer; taking it literally, he felt as if a load were lifted from his heart, and kissing with rapture the hand he held, he exclaimed: "Yes, this shall soon, oh, soon be mine! I fear nothing while you hope. You cannot guess how those words have cheered me; for I am leaving you, though but for a few hours, and I shall repeat those words, for they will ring in my ear, in my heart, till we meet again."

"Leaving me!" said Helen, turning pale, and her **clasp** on his hand **tightening**. Poor child, she felt **mysteriously** a sentiment of protection in his presence.

"But at most for a day. My old tutor, of whom we have so often **conversed**, is on his way to England, — perhaps even now in London. He has some wrong impressions against your aunt; his manner is blunt and rough. It is necessary that I should see him before he comes hither, — you know how

---

French

clasp: agrafe, fermoir.
comprehend: comprendre.
conversed: conversé.
earnestly: sérieusement, de façon sérieuse, de manière sérieuse.
educate: éduquer, instruire.
forethought: prévoyance.
imaginative: imaginatif.
involuntarily: de façon involontaire, de manière involontaire, involontairement.
misgiving: crainte, doute.
mysteriously: de manière mystérieuse, de façon mystérieuse.
quiver: trembler, frisson, frémir.
rosy: rosé, rose.
tightening: serrant, resserrant.
vanishes: disparaît.

susceptible is your aunt's pride,—just to prepare him for meeting her. You understand?"

"What impressions against my aunt? Does he even know her?" asked Helen. And if such a sentiment as suspicion could cross that **candid** innocence of mind, that sentiment towards this stern relation whose arms had never embraced her, whose lips had never spoken of the past, whose history was as a sealed volume, disturbed and **disquieted** her.

"It is because he has never known her that he does her wrong. Some old story of her **indiscretion** as a girl, of her uncle's displeasure,—what matters now?" said Percival, shrinking **sensitively** from one disclosure that might wound Helen in her kinswoman. "Meanwhile, dearest, you will be prudent,—you will **avoid** this damp air, and keep quietly at home, and amuse yourself, sweet **fancier** of the future, in **planning** how to improve these old halls when they and their **unworthy** master are your own. God bless you, God guard you, Helen!"

He rose, and with that loyal **chivalry** of love which felt respect the more for the careless guardianship to which his Helen was intrusted, he refrained from that parting kiss which their pure courtship **warranted**, for which his lip yearned. But as he lingered, an irresistible impulse moved Helen's heart. Mechanically she opened her arms, and her head sank upon his shoulder. In that embrace they remained some moments silent, and an angel might unreprovingly have heard their hearts beat through the stillness.

At length Percival tore himself from those arms which relaxed their **imploring** hold reluctantly; she heard his hurried step descend the stairs, and in a moment more the roll of the wheels in the court without; a dreary sense, as of some utter **desertion**, some **everlasting bereavement**, chilled and appalled her. She stood motionless, as if turned to stone, on the floor; suddenly the touch of something warm on her hand, a plaining **whine**, awoke her attention; Percival's favourite dog missed his master, and had slunk for refuge to her. The dread sentiment of loneliness vanished in that

---

French

avoid: éviter, parer, esquiver, s'abstenir de.
bereavement: deuil, perte, endeuillement.
candid: franc, impartial, sincère, candide.
chivalry: chevalerie.
desertion: désertion, abandon de poste, défection, délaissement.
disquieted: perturbâtes, dérangeâtes.
everlasting: éternel, permanent, perpétuel, interminable, immortelle, infini, inusable.
fancier: amateur.
imploring: implorant, conjurer, suppliant.
indiscretion: indiscrétion.
planning: planification, aménagement.
sensitively: de façon sensible, de manière sensible.
unworthy: indigne.
warranted: garanti, justifié.
whine: plainte, geindre, sifflement, se lamenter, gémissons, crie, geignez, crions.

humble companionship; and seating **herself** on the **ground**, she took the **dog** in her **arms**, and **bending** over it, wept in **silence**.

French

arm: bras, armer, branche, accoudoir.
bending: pliage, flexion, courbure, cintrage.
companionship: compagnie, équipe, camaraderie.
dog: chien, clébard, toc.
ground: terre, sol, fond, masse, échouer, motif.
herself: même, se.
humble: humble, modeste.
silence: silence, repos.

CHAPTER XXIV

MURDER, TOWARDS HIS DESIGN, MOVES LIKE A GHOST

The reader will doubtless have observed the **consummate** art with which the poisoner had hitherto advanced upon her prey. The design conceived from afar, and **executed** with elaborate **stealth**, **defied** every chance of detection against which the **ingenuity** of practised villany could guard. Grant even that the **deadly** drugs should betray the nature of the death they **inflicted**, that by some unconjectured secret in the science of chemistry the presence of those **vegetable** compounds which had hitherto baffled every known and positive test in the **posthumous** examination of the most experienced surgeons, should be **clearly** ascertained, not one suspicion seemed likely to fall upon the ministrant of death. The medicines were never brought to Madame Dalibard, were never given by her hand; nothing ever **tasted** by the victim could be **tracked** to her aunt. The helpless condition of the cripple, which Lucretia had assumed, forbade all notion even of her power of movement. Only in the dead of night when, as she believed, every human eye that could watch her was sealed in sleep, and then in those dark habiliments which (even as might sometimes happen, if the victim herself were awake) a chance ray of light struggling through **chink** or shutter could scarcely distinguish from the general gloom, did she steal to the chamber and **infuse** the **colourless** and **tasteless** liquid [The celebrated acqua di

---

French

chink: fente, crevasse, crique, fissure, lézarde, tapure.
clearly: clairement, de façon claire, de manière claire, nettement.
colourless: incolore, sans couleur.
consummate: consommé.
deadly: mortel, meurtrier, de façon morte, de manière morte.
defied: provoqué, défié.
executed: exécutâtes.
inflicted: infligé.
infuse: infuser, injecter.
ingenuity: ingéniosité.
posthumous: posthume, titre posthume.
stealth: furtif.
tasted: goûté.
tasteless: insipide, sans saveur, de mauvais goût, fade.
tracked: chenillé.
vegetable: légume, végétal.

Tufania (Tufania water) was wholly without taste or colour] in the morning draught, meant to bring strength and healing. Grant that the draught was **untouched**, that it was examined by the surgeon, that the fell **admixture** could be detected, suspicion would wander anywhere rather than to that crippled and helpless kinswoman who could not rise from her bed without aid.

But now this patience was to be abandoned, the folds of the **serpent** were to coil in one fell **clasp** upon its prey.

Fiend as Lucretia had become, and hardened as were all her resolves by the discovery of her son, and her impatience to **endow** him with her forfeited inheritance, she yet shrank from the face of Helen that day; on the excuse of illness, she kept her room, and admitted only Varney, who stole in from time to time, with creeping step and haggard countenance, to **sustain** her courage or his own. And every time he entered, he found Lucretia sitting with Walter Ardworth's open letter in her hand, and turning with a **preternatural** excitement that seemed almost like **aberration** of mind, from the grim and **horrid** topic which he invited, to thoughts of wealth and power and triumph and **exulting** prophecies of the fame her son should achieve. He looked but on the **blackness** of the gulf, and shuddered; her vision overleaped it, and smiled on the misty palaces her fancy built beyond.

Late in the evening, before she retired to rest, Helen knocked gently at her aunt's door. A voice, quick and startled, bade her enter; she came in, with her sweet, **caressing** look, and took Lucretia's hand, which struggled from the clasp. Bending over that haggard brow, she said simply, yet to Lucretia's ear the voice seemed that of command, "Let me kiss you this night!" and her lips pressed that brow. The **murderess** shuddered, and closed her eyes; when she opened them, the angel visitor was gone.

Night **deepened** and deepened into those hours from the first of which we number the **morn**, though night still is at her full. Moonbeam and starbeam came through the casements **shyly** and fairylike as on that night when the murderess was young and crimeless, in deed, if not in thought,—

French

aberration: aberration, erreur.
admixture: mélange, mixture, additif, adjuvant, dosage.
blackness: noirceur, obscurité.
caressing: tendre, caressant.
clasp: agrafe, fermoir.
deepened: approfondirent, rembrunîtes.
endow: doter, dotons.
exulting: exultant.
horrid: horrible, affreux, méchant.
morn: matin.
murderess: meurtrière.
preternatural: surnaturel.
serpent: serpent.
shyly: timidement.
sustain: maintenir, appuyer, soutenir, accoter, vous accotez, m'accote, nous accotons, s'accotent, t'accotes.
untouched: intact.

that night when, in the book of Leechcraft, she **meted** out the hours in which the life of her benefactor might still **interpose** between her passion and its end. Along the stairs, through the hall, marched the armies of light, **noiseless** and still and clear as the judgments of God amidst the darkness and shadow of mortal destinies. In one chamber alone, the folds, curtained close, forbade all but a single ray; that ray came direct as the stream from a **lantern**; as the **beam** reflected back from an eye,—as an eye it seemed watchful and steadfast through the dark; it shot along the floor,—it fell at the foot of the bed.

Suddenly, in the exceeding hush, there was a strange and ghastly sound,—it was the **howl** of a dog! Helen started from her sleep. Percival's dog had followed her into her room; it had **coiled** itself, grateful for the kindness, at the foot of the bed. Now it was on the pillow, she felt its heart beat against her hand,—it was trembling; its hairs bristled up, and the howl changed into a shrill bark of terror and wrath. Alarmed, she looked round; quickly between her and that ray from the **crevice** a shapeless darkness passed, and was gone, so undistinguishable, so without outline, that it had no likeness of any living form; like a cloud, like a thought, like an **omen**, it came in gloom, and it vanished.

Helen was seized with a **superstitious** terror; the dog continued to tremble and **growl** low. All once more was still; the dog sighed itself to rest. The stillness, the solitude, the **glimmer** of the moon,—all **contributed** yet more to **appall** the **enfeebled** nerves of the listening, shrinking girl. At length she buried her face under the clothes, and towards **daybreak** fell into a broken, feverish sleep, haunted with threatening dreams.

French

appall: consterner, épouvanter.
beam: poutre, faisceau, rayon, bau, barrot, balancier, ensouple, madrier, radio.
coiled: couronne.
contributed: contribuâmes, te cotisas, se cotisé, vous cotisâtes, me cotisai, nous cotisâmes.
crevice: crevasse, fente, fissure.
daybreak: aube, aurore, point du jour.
enfeebled: débilita.
glimmer: luire, briller, faible lueur.
growl: grogner, râler, grondement.
howl: hurler, mugir, gronder.
interpose: interposer.
lantern: lanterne, fanal.
meted: infligea.
noiseless: silencieux, antisouffle.
omen: augure, présage.
superstitious: superstitieux.

CHAPTER XXV

THE MESSENGER SPEEDS

Towards the **afternoon** of the following day, an elderly gentleman was **seated** in the coffee-room of an hotel at Southampton, **engaged** in writing a letter, while the **waiter** in attendance was employed on the wires that **fettered** the **petulant** spirit contained in a bottle of Schweppe's soda-water. There was something in the aspect of the old gentleman, and in the very tone of his voice, that **inspired** respect, and the waiter had cleared the other tables of their **latest** newspapers to place before him. He had only just arrived by the **packet** from Havre, and even the newspapers had not been to him that **primary attraction** they generally **constitute** to the Englishman returning to his bustling **native** land, which, somewhat to his surprise, has contrived to go on **tolerably** well during his absence.

We use our **privilege** of looking over his shoulder while he writes:—

Here I am, then, dear Lady Mary, at Southampton, and within an easy **drive** of the old Hall. A **file** of Galignani's journals, which I found on the road between Marseilles and Paris, informed me, under the head of "fashionable movements," that Percival St. John, Esquire, was gone to his seat at Laughton. According to my **customary tactics** of **marching** at once to the seat of action, I therefore made direct for Havre, instead of crossing from

---

French

afternoon: relevée.
attraction: attraction, appât.
constitute: constituer.
customary: habituel, accoutumé, coutumier.
drive: conduire, pousser, prise, pourchasser, lecteur, faire avancer, piloter, actionner.
engaged: engageai, occupé.
fettered: grevé.
file: fichier, lime, dossier, file, classeur, rang, tour, collection à consulter, déposer, porte document.
inspired: inspirâtes, s'enthousiasmé, vous enthousiasmâtes, nous enthousiasmâmes, m'enthousiasmai, t'enthousiasmas.
latest: dernier.
marching: marcher.
native: autochtone, naturel, natif, inné, aborigène, indigène, natal.
packet: paquet, colis, entassement.
petulant: malin, maussade.
primary: primaire, principal.
privilege: privilège, prérogative.
seated: assis.
tactic: tactique.
tolerably: de manière tolérable, de façon tolérable.
waiter: garçon, serveur.

Calais, and I suppose I shall find our young gentleman engaged in the **slaughter** of **hares** and **partridges**. You see it is a good sign that he can leave London. Keep up your spirits, my dear friend. If Perce has been really **duped** and taken in,—as all you mothers are so apt to fancy,—rely upon an old soldier to **defeat** the enemy and expose the **ruse**. But if, after all, the girl is such as he **describes** and believes,—innocent, **artless**, and worthy his affection,—oh, then I range myself, with your own good heart, upon his side. Never will I run the risk of **unsettling** a man's whole character for life by wantonly **interfering** with his affections. But there we are agreed.

In a few hours I shall be with our dear boy, and his whole heart will come out clear and **candid** as when it beat under his midshipman's true-blue. In a day or two I shall make him take me to town, to introduce me to the whole nest of them. Then I shall report progress. Adieu, till then! Kind regards to your poor sister. I think we shall have a mild winter. Not one warning **twinge** as yet of the old **rheumatism**. Ever your devoted old friend and preux chevalier,

H. Greville.

The captain had completed his letter, sipped his soda-water, and was **affixing** to his communication his seal, when he heard the **rattle** of a post-chaise without. Fancying it was the one he had ordered, he went to the open window which looked on the street; but the **chaise** contained travellers, only **halting** to change horses. Somewhat to his surprise, and a little to his chagrin,—for the captain did not count on finding company at the Hall,—he heard one of the travellers in the chaise ask the distance to Laughton. The countenance of the **questioner** was not familiar to him. But leaving the worthy captain to question the landlord, without any satisfactory information, and to hasten the chaise for himself, we accompany the travellers on their way to Laughton. There were but two,—the proper **complement** of a post-chaise,—and they were both of the ruder sex. The elder of the two was a man of middle age, but whom the wear and tear of

---

French

affixing: apposition.
artless: ingénu, sans art, naïf, naturel.
candid: franc, impartial, sincère, candide.
chaise: cabriolet, calèche.
complement: complément.
defeat: défaite, vaincre, abattre, surmonter.
describes: décrit.
duped: dupé.
halting: arrêter, hésitant,

immobilisation.
hare: lièvre.
interfering: interférant, importun.
partridge: perdrix.
questioner: auteur de la question, questionneur, interrogateur.
rattle: cliquetis, claquer, crécelle, hochet.
rheumatism: rhumatisme.
ruse: ruse, stratagème.
slaughter: abattre, massacre, carnage, tuerie.

twinge: élancement.
unsettling: perturbant.

active life had evidently advanced towards the state called elderly. But there was still **abundant** life in his quick, dark eye; and that **mercurial youthfulness** of character which in some happy constitutions seems to defy years and **sorrow**, evinced itself in a rapid play of countenance and as much **gesticulation** as the narrow **confines** of the vehicle and the position of a traveller will permit. The younger man, far more grave in aspect and quiet in manner, leaned back in the corner with folded arms, and listened with **respectful** attention to his companion.

"Certainly, Dr. Johnson is right,—great happiness in an English post-chaise **properly** driven; more **exhilarating** than a palanquin. 'Post equitem sedet atra cura,'—true only of such **scrubby hacks** as old Horace could have known. Black Care does not sit behind English posters, eh, my boy?" As he spoke this, the gentleman had twice let down the glass of the vehicle, and twice put it up again.

"Yet," he resumed, without noticing the brief, good-humoured reply of his companion,—"yet this is an anxious business enough that we are about. I don't feel quite easy in my conscience. Poor Braddell's injunctions were very strict, and I **disobey** them. It is on your **responsibility**, John!"

"I take it without hesitation. All the motives for so **stern** a **severance** must have ceased, and is it not a sufficient punishment to find in that hoped-for son a—"

"Poor woman!" interrupted the elder gentleman, in whom we begin to recognize the soi-disant Mr. Tomkins; "true, indeed, too true. How well I remember the impression Lucretia Clavering first produced on me; and to think of her now as a miserable cripple! By Jove, you are right, sir! Drive on, post-boy, quick, quick!"

There was a short silence.

The elder gentleman abruptly put his hand upon his companion's arm.

"What **consummate** acuteness; what patient research you have shown! What could I have done in this business without you? How often had that **garrulous** Mrs. Mivers bored me with Becky Carruthers, and the coral, and

---

French

abundant: abondant, copieux.
confine: limiter, confinent.
consummate: consommé.
disobey: désobéir.
exhilarating: exhilarant, vivifiant.
garrulous: loquace, bavard.
gesticulation: gesticulation.
hack: hacher, tailler, rainette.
mercurial: mercuriel.
properly: convenablement, proprement, de manière convenable, comme il faut, correctement, de façon convenable.
respectful: respectueux.
responsibility: responsabilité, concordance, correspondance.
scrubby: broussailleux, rabougri.
severance: disjonction, rupture.
sorrow: abattement, chagrin.
stern: poupe, arrière, sévère.
youthfulness: fraîcheur, jeunesse, juvénilité.

St. Paul's, and not a suspicion came across me,—a word was sufficient for you. And then to track this unfeeling old Joplin from place to place till you find her absolutely a servant under the very roof of Mrs. Braddell herself! Wonderful! Ah, boy, you will be an honour to the law and to your country. And what a hard-hearted **rascal** you must think me to have deserted you so long."

"My dear father," said John Ardworth, tenderly, "your love now **recompenses** me for all. And ought I not rather to **rejoice** not to have known the tale of a mother's shame until I could half forget it on a father's breast?"

"John," said the elder Ardworth, with a **choking** voice, "I ought to wear **sackcloth** all my life for having given you such a mother. When I think what I have suffered from the habit of **carelessness** in those **confounded** money-matters ('irritamenta malorum,' indeed!), I have only one consolation,—that my patient, noble son is free from my vice. You would not believe what a well-principled, honourable fellow I was at your age; and yet, how truly I said to my poor friend William Mainwaring one day at Laughton (I remember it now) 'Trust me with anything else but half-a-guinea!' Why, sir, it was that fault that threw me into low company,—that brought me in contact with my innkeeper's daughter at Limerick. I fell in love, and I married (for, with all my faults, I was never a **seducer**, John). I did not own my marriage; why should I?—my relatives had cut me already. You were born, and, **hunted** poor devil as I was, I forgot all by your **cradle**. Then, in the midst of my troubles, that ungrateful woman deserted me; then I was led to believe that it was not my own son whom I had kissed and blessed. Ah, but for that thought should I have left you as I did? And even in **infancy**, you had the features only of your mother. Then, when the death of the **adulteress** set me free, and years afterwards, in India, I married again and had new ties, my heart grew still harder to you. I **excused** myself by knowing that at least you were cared for, and trained to good by a better guide than I. But when, by so strange a hazard, the very priest who had confessed your mother on her **deathbed** (she was a Catholic) came to India, and (for he had known me at Limerick) recognized my altered person, and

---

French

adulteress: adultère, femme adultère.
carelessness: négligence, imprudence, insouciance.
choking: étranglement des gaz, obstruction, engorgement.
confounded: confondu, déconcertâmes.
cradle: berceau, arceau, nacelle, cerceau.
deathbed: lit de mort.
excused: excusé.
hunted: chassâtes.
infancy: enfance, minorité, petite enfance.
rascal: fripon, coquin, vaurien.
recompense: récompense.
rejoice: réjouir, être joyeux.
sackcloth: toile à sac, treillis.
seducer: séducteur.

obeying his penitent's last **injunctions**, **assured** me that you were my son,—oh, John, then, believe me, I hastened back to England on the wings of remorse! Love you, boy! I have left at Madras three children, young and fair, by a woman now in **heaven**, who never wronged me, and, by my soul, John Ardworth, you are dearer to me than all!"

The father's head drooped on his son's **breast** as he spoke; then, dashing away his **tears**, he resumed,—

"Ah, why would not Braddell **permit** me, as I proposed, to find for his son the same guardianship as that to which I intrusted my own? But his **bigotry besotted** him; a **clergyman** of the High Church,—that was worse than an **atheist**. I had no choice left to me but the roof of that she-hypocrite. Yet I ought to have come to England when I heard of the child's loss, braved **duns** and all; but I was money-making, money-making,—retribution for money-wasting; and—well, it's no use **repenting**! And—and there is the **lodge**, the park, the old trees! Poor Sir Miles!"

French

assured: assura, garantîtes.
atheist: athée.
besotted: fou.
bigotry: bigoterie, sectarisme.
breast: poitrine, sein, mamelle, front de taille.
clergyman: prêtre, abbé, curé, ecclésiastique, pasteur.
dun: brun foncé, isabelle, moisissure brune, relancer.
heaven: ciel, paradis.
injunction: injonction, avant dire droit, arrêt de la suspension.
lodge: loge, héberger, gîte, pavillon, auberge, déposer.
obeying: obéissant, obtempérant.
permit: permis, autoriser.
repenting: regrettant, repentant.
tear: larme, déchirer, pleur.

CHAPTER XXVI

THE SPY FLIES

Meanwhile at Laughton there was confusion and alarm. Helen had found herself more than usually **unwell** in the morning; towards **noon**, the maid who attended her informed Madame Dalibard that she was afraid the poor young lady had much fever, and **inquired** if the doctor should be sent for. Madame Dalibard seemed surprised at the intelligence, and directed her chair to be wheeled into her niece's room, in order herself to judge of Helen's state. The maid, sure that the doctor would be summoned, hastened to the stables, and seeing Beck, instructed him to **saddle** one of the horses and to **await** further orders. Beck kept her a few moments talking while he saddled his horse, and then followed her into the house, **observing** that it would save time if he were close at hand.

"That is quite true," said the maid, "and you may as well wait in the corridor. Madame may wish to speak to you herself, and give you her own message or note to the doctor."

Beck, full of gloomy suspicions, **gladly obeyed**, and while the maid entered the sick-chamber, stood **anxiously** without. Presently Varney passed him, and knocked at Helen's door; the maid half-opened it.

"How is Miss Mainwaring?" said he, **eagerly**.

French

anxiously: de manière inquiète, de façon inquiète.
await: attendre.
eagerly: de façon avide, de manière avide.
gladly: volontiers, avec plaisir, de façon joyeuse, de manière joyeuse.
inquired: vous enquîtes, t'enquis, s'enquit, nous enquîmes, m'enquis.
noon: midi.
obeyed: obéis, obéîtes.
observing: observant, respectant, remplissant.
saddle: selle, col, ensellement.
unwell: indisposé, malade, souffrant.

"I fear she is worse, sir; but Madame Dalibard does not think there is any danger."

"No danger! I am glad; but pray ask Madame Dalibard to let me see her for a few moments in her own room. If she come out, I will wheel her chair to it. Whether there is danger or not, we had better send for other advice than this country doctor, who has perhaps mistaken the case; tell her I am very uneasy, and **beg** her to join me immediately."

"I think you are quite right, sir," said the maid, **closing** the door.

Varney then, turning round for the first time, noticed Beck, and said roughly, —

"What do you do here? Wait below till you are sent for."

Beck pulled his forelock, and retreated back, not in the direction of the principal staircase, but towards that used by the servants, and which his researches into the **topography** of the **mansion** had now made known to him. To gain these back stairs he had to pass Lucretia's room; the door stood **ajar**; Varney's face was turned from him. Beck **breathed** hard, looked round, then **crept** within, and in a moment was behind the **folds** of the **tapestry**.

Soon the chair in which sat Madame Dalibard was drawn by Varney himself into the room.

Shutting the door with care, and turning the key, Gabriel said, with low, **suppressed** passion, —

"Well; your mind seems wandering, — speak!"

"It is strange," said Lucretia, in **hollow** tones, "can Nature turn accomplice, and befriend us here?"

"Nature! did you not last night **administer** the — "

"No," interrupted Lucretia. "No; she came into the room, she kissed me here, — on the brow that even then was **meditating** murder. The kiss burned; it burns still, — it **eats** into the brain like remorse. But I did not yield; I read again her false father's protestation of love; I read again the letter

---

French

administer: administrer, appliquer, gérer.
ajar: entrouvert.
beg: mendier, demander, prier, solliciter, implorer, quémander, supplier.
breathed: respiré.
closing: fermant, clôture, enclenchement.
crept: rampé, cheminâmes, traîna, glissé.
eats: mange, bouffe.
fold: pli, plier, repli, plisser, pliure.
hollow: creux, cavité, caver.
mansion: immeuble, château, mansion.
meditating: méditant, songeant.
suppressed: étouffé, réprimâmes.
tapestry: tapisserie.
topography: topographie, topique.

announcing the discovery of my son, and remorse lay still. I went forth as before, I stole into her chamber, I had the fatal **crystal** in my hand—"

"Well, well!"

"And suddenly there came the fearful **howl** of a dog, and the dog's fierce eyes glared on me. I paused, I trembled; Helen started, woke, called aloud. I turned and fled. The poison was not given."

Varney ground his teeth. "But this illness! Ha! the effect, perhaps, of the drops administered two nights ago."

"No; this illness has no symptoms like those the poison should bequeath,—it is but natural fever, a shock on the nerves; she told me she had been **wakened** by the dog's howl, and seen a dark form, like a thing from the grave, creeping along the floor. But she is really ill; send for the physician; there is nothing in her illness to betray the hand of man. Be it as it may,—that kiss still burns; I will stir in this no more. Do what you will yourself!"

"Fool, fool!" exclaimed Varney, almost rudely grasping her arm. "Remember how much we have yet to prepare for, how much to do,—and the time so short! Percival's return,—perhaps this Greville's arrival. Give me the drugs; I will mix them for her in the **potion** the physician sends. And when Percival returns,—his Helen dead or dying,—I will attend on him! Silent still? Recall your son! Soon you will clasp him in your arms as a **beggar**, or as the lord of Laughton!"

Lucretia shuddered, but did not rise; she drew forth a ring of keys from her **bosom**, and pointed towards a secretary. Varney snatched the keys, **unlocked** the secretary, seized the fatal **casket**, and sat down quietly before it.

When the **dire** selections were made, and **secreted** about his person, Varney rose, approached the fire, and **blew** the wood **embers** to a blaze.

"And now," he said, with his **icy** irony of smile, "we may dismiss these useful instruments,—perhaps forever. Though Walter Ardworth, in **restoring** your son, leaves us dependent on that son's **filial** affection, and I

French

beggar: mendiant, gueux.
blew: souffla.
bosom: sein, poitrine.
casket: cercueil, coffret, mettre en bière.
crystal: cristal, quartz.
dire: terrible.
ember: braise, tison.
filial: filial.
howl: hurler, mugir, gronder.
icy: glacé, verglacé.
potion: potion.
restoring: restaurant, rétablissant.
secreted: sécrétas.
unlocked: ouvrit, ouvert.
wakened: réveillèrent.

may have, therefore, little to hope for from the succession, to secure which I have risked and am again to risk my life, I yet trust to that influence which you never fail to obtain over others. I take it for granted that when these halls are Vincent Braddell's, we shall have no need of gold, nor of these pale **alchemies**. **Perish**, then, the mute **witnesses** of our acts, the elements we have bowed to our will! No poison shall be found in our hoards! Fire, consume your **consuming** children!"

As he spoke, he threw upon the hearth the contents of the casket, and set his heel upon the **logs**. A **bluish** flame shot up, breaking into countless sparks, and then died.

Lucretia watched him without speaking.

In coming back towards the table, Varney felt something hard beneath his tread; he stooped, and picked up the ring which has before been described as amongst the ghastly treasures of the casket, and which had rolled on the floor almost to Lucretia's feet, as he had emptied the contents on the hearth.

"This, at least, need tell no tales," said he; "a pity to destroy so rare a piece of workmanship,—one, too, which we never can replace!"

"Ay," said Lucretia, **abstractedly**; "and if detection comes, it may secure a refuge from the **gibbet**. Give me the ring."

"A refuge more terrible than the detection," said Varney,—"beware of such a thought," as Lucretia, taking it from his hand, placed the ring on her finger.

"And now I leave you for a while to **recollect** yourself,—to **compose** your countenance and your thoughts. I will send for the physician."

Lucretia, with her eyes fixed on the floor, did not **heed** him, and he withdrew.

So motionless was her attitude, so still her very breathing, that the **unseen** witness behind the tapestry, who, while struck with horror at what he had **overheard** (the general **purport** of which it was **impossible** that he

---

French

abstractedly: de façon distraite, de manière distraite.
alchemy: alchimie.
bluish: bleuâtre.
compose: composer, écrire.
consuming: consommant.
gibbet: gibet.
heed: attention.
impossible: impossible.
log: journal, rondin, loch, log.
overheard: surprirent.
perish: périr, s'abîmer.

purport: signification, portée, prétendre.
recollect: se rappeler, se souvenir, retenir, retiennent.
unseen: inaperçu, invisible.
witnesses: témoigne.

could misunderstand), was **parched** with impatience to escape to rescue his beloved master from his impending fate, and warn him of the fate hovering nearer still over Helen, ventured to creep along the wall to the threshold, to **peer** forth from the **arras**, and seeing her eyes still downcast, to emerge, and place his hand on the door. At that very moment Lucretia looked up, and saw him **gliding** from the tapestry; their eyes met: his were fascinated as the bird's by the snake's. At the sight, all her craft, her intellect, returned. With a glance, she comprehended the terrible danger that awaited her. Before he was aware of her movement, she was at his side; her hand on his own, her voice in his ear.

"Stir not a step, utter not a sound, or you are—"

Beck did not suffer her to proceed. With the violence rather of fear than of courage, he struck her to the ground; but she clung to him still, and though rendered for the moment **speechless** by the **suddenness** of the blow, her eyes took an expression of **unspeakable** cruelty and **fierceness**. He struggled with all his might to shake her off; as he did so, she placed **feebly** her other hand upon the **wrist** of the lifted arm that had **smitten** her, and he felt a sharp pain, as if the nails had fastened into the flesh. This but **exasperated** him to new efforts. He extricated himself from her grasp, which relaxed as her lips writhed into a smile of scorn and triumph, and, spurning her while she lay before the threshold, he opened the door, sprang forward, and escaped. No thought had he of **tarrying** in that House of Pelops, those human shambles, of **denouncing** Murder in its **lair**; to fly to reach his master, warn, and shield him,—that was the sole thought which crossed his confused, bewildered brain.

It might be from four to five minutes that Lucretia, half-stunned, half-senseless, lay upon those floors,—for besides the violence of her fall, the shock of the struggle upon nerves weakened by the agony of apprehension, occasioned by the **imminent** and **unforeseen** chance of detection, **paralyzed** her **wondrous** vigour of mind and frame,—when Varney entered.

French

arras: arras.
denouncing: dénonçant.
exasperated: exaspérâtes.
feebly: de façon faible, de manière faible.
fierceness: férocité, violence, ardeur.
gliding: vol à voile, glissement.
imminent: imminent.
lair: tanière, repaire.
paralyzed: paralysâtes, médusé.
parched: desséché.
peer: pair, affinitaire, homologue.
smitten: frappé.
speechless: muet, sans voix.
suddenness: soudaineté.
tarrying: restant, demeurant.
unforeseen: imprévu.
unspeakable: indicible, indescriptible, innommable.
wondrous: merveilleux, étonnant.
wrist: poignet, tourillon, carpe, axe de piston.

"They tell me she sleeps," he said, in **hoarse**, muttered accents, before he saw the **prostrate** form at his very feet. But Varney's step, Varney's voice, had **awakened** Lucretia's reason to consciousness and the sense of peril. Rising, though with effort, she related hurriedly what had passed.

"Fly, fly!" she gasped, as she concluded. "Fly, to **detain**, to **secrete**, this man somewhere for the next few hours. Silence him but till then; I have done the rest!" and her finger pointed to the fatal ring. Varney waited for no further words; he hurried out, and made at once to the stables: his **shrewdness** conjectured that Beck would carry his tale **elsewhere**. The groom was already gone (his fellows said) without a word, but towards the lodge that led to the Southampton road. Varney ordered the swiftest horse the stables held to be saddled, and said, as he sprang on his back,—

"I, too, must go towards Southampton. The poor young lady! I must prepare your master,—he is on his road back to us;" and the last word was scarce out of his lips as the sparks flew from the **flints** under the horse's **hoofs**, and he spurred from the yard.

As he rode at full speed through the park, the villain's mind sped more rapidly than the animal he bestrode,—sped from fear to hope, hope to assurance. Grant that the spy lived to tell his tale,—incoherent, **improbable** as the tale would be,—who would believe it? How easy to meet tale by tale! The man must own that he was **secreted** behind the tapestry,—wherefore but to **rob**? Detected by Madame Dalibard, he had coined this wretched **fable**. And the spy, too, could not live through the day; he bore Death with him as he rode, he fed its force by his speed, and the effects of the **venom** itself would be those of frenzy. Tush! his tale, at best, would seem but the **ravings** of **delirium**. Still, it was well to track him where he went,—delay him, if possible; and Varney's spurs plunged deep and deeper into the **bleeding flanks**: on desperately **scoured** the horse. He passed the lodge; he was on the road; a **chaise** and pair dashed by him; he heard not a voice **exclaim** "Varney!" he saw not the wondering face of John Ardworth; bending over the tossing **mane**, he was deaf, he was blind, to all without and around. A **milestone glides** by, another, and a third. Ha! his eyes can see

French

awakened: réveilla.
bleeding: saignant, hémorragie, purgeant, ressuage, dégorgement.
chaise: cabriolet, calèche.
delirium: délire, transport.
detain: détenir, retenir, détiens, retiens, réprimer.
elsewhere: ailleurs, autre part.
exclaim: exclamer, s'exclamer.
fable: fable.
flank: flanc, face de dépouille.
flint: silex, pierre à briquet, flint.
glide: glisser, planer, vol plané, coulé, patin.
hoarse: rauque, enroué.
hoof: sabot.
improbable: improbable, invraisemblable.
mane: crinière, tresser la crinière.
milestone: étape importante, borne.
prostrate: prosterné.
raving: délirant, divaguant.
rob: piller, ravir, voler, dévaliser.
scoured: frotta, décapèrent.
secrete: sécréter.
secreted: sécrétas.
shrewdness: perspicacité, sagacité.
venom: venin.

now. The object of his chase is before him,—he views distinctly, on the brow of **yon** hill, the horse and the rider, spurring fast, like himself. They descend the hill, horse and **horseman**, and are snatched from his sight. Up the steep strains the **pursuer**. He is at the summit. He sees the **fugitive** before him, almost within hearing. Beck has **slackened** his **steed**; he seems **swaying** to and fro in the saddle. Ho, ho! the **barbed** ring begins to work in his veins. Varney looks round,—not another soul is in sight; a deep wood skirts the road. Place and time seem to favour; Beck has reined in his horse,—he bends low over the saddle, as if about to fall. Varney utters a half-suppressed cry of triumph, shakes his reins, and spurs on, when suddenly—by the curve of the road, hid before—another chaise comes in sight, close where Beck had wearily halted.

The chaise stops; Varney pulls in, and draws aside to the **hedgerow**. Some one within the vehicle is speaking to the fugitive! May it not be St. John himself? To his rage and his terror, he sees Beck painfully **dismount** from his horse, sees him **totter** to the door of the chaise, sees a servant **leap** from the box and help him up the step, sees him enter. It must be Percival on his return,—Percival, to whom he tells that story of horror! Varney's brute-like courage **forsook** him; his heart was appalled. In one of those panics so common with that **boldness** which is but animal, his sole thought became that of escape. He turned his horse's head to the **fence**, forced his way desperately through the barrier, made into the wood, and sat there, cowering and listening, till in another minute he heard the wheels rattle on, and the horses **gallop** hard down the hill towards the park.

The autumn wind swept through the trees, it shook the branches of the lofty ash that **overhung** the Accursed One. What observer of Nature knows not that peculiar sound which the ash gives forth in the blast? Not the solemn groan of the oak, not the hollow murmur of the beech, but a shrill **wail**, a **shriek** as of a human voice in sharp anguish. Varney shuddered, as if he had heard the death-cry of his intended victim. Through **briers** and **thickets**, torn by the thorns, bruised by the boughs, he plunged deeper and deeper into the wood, gained at length the main path cut through it, found

French

barbed: barbelé, acéré.
boldness: audace, hardiesse.
brier: brier.
dismount: descends, mettre pied à terre, sors, sortent, démontent.
fence: barrière, clôture, faire de l'escrime, palissade, cloison de décrochage.
forsook: abandonnâtes, délaissai.
fugitive: fugitif, réfugié, couleur qui déteint, non solide à la lumière.

gallop: galoper.
hedgerow: haie.
horseman: cavalier, homme de chevaux.
leap: saut, bond, gambader, filon pauvre.
overhung: surplomba.
pursuer: poursuivant.
shriek: crier, hurler, cri perçant.
slackened: largua, ralentîtes, affaiblirent, desserrèrent.
steed: coursier.

swaying: roulis, balancement, dandinement, déplacement latéral, oscillation.
thicket: fourré, gaulis, bosquet.
totter: titubes, vacillez, chanceler.
wail: se lamenter, gémir.
yon: y, là.

himself in a **lane**, and rode on, **careless** whither, **till** he had reached a small town, about ten **miles** from Laughton, where he **resolved** to **wait** till his **nerves** had **recovered** their **tone**, and he could more calmly **calculate** the chances of safety.

French

calculate: calculer, compter, estimer, évaluer.
careless: négligent, distrait, étourdi, insouciant.
lane: voie, ruelle, couloir.
mile: mille, lieue.
nerve: nerf, toupet, courage, fortifier.
recovered: récupéra, recouvra.
resolved: résolu.
till: caisse, jusqu'à ce que, à.
tone: ton, tonalité, timbre, tonicité.

wait: attendre, servir.

CHAPTER XXVII

LUCRETIA REGAINS HER SON

It seemed as if now, when danger became most imminent and present, that that very danger served to restore to Lucretia Dalibard her faculties, which during the earlier day had been **steeped** in a kind of dreary **stupor**. The absolute necessity of playing out her **execrable** part with all suitable and **consistent hypocrisy**, **braced** her into iron. But the disguise she assumed was a **supernatural** effort, it stretched to **cracking** every fibre of the brain; it seemed almost to herself as if, her object once gained, either life or consciousness could hold out no more.

A **chaise** stopped at the porch; two gentlemen **descended**. The elder paused **irresolutely**, and at length, taking out a card, **inscribed** "Mr. Walter Ardworth," said, "If Madame Dalibard can be spoken to for a moment, will you give her this card?"

The **footman** hesitatingly stared at the card, and then invited the gentleman into the hall while he took up the message. Not long had the visitor to wait, **pacing** the dark oak floors and gazing on the faded **banners**, before the servant reappeared: Madame Dalibard would see him. He followed his guide up the stairs, while his young companion turned from the

---

French

banner: bannière, drapeau, pavillon, banderole, étendard.
braced: contreventé.
chaise: cabriolet, calèche.
consistent: cohérent, logique.
cracking: fissuration, craquage, concassage, fendillement.
descended: descendu, issu.
execrable: exécrable.
footman: valet de pied.
hypocrisy: hypocrisie.
inscribed: inscrit.
irresolutely: de façon indécise, de manière indécise.
pacing: gradation, entraînement, mesurer à l'enjambée, rythme, amble.
steeped: trempai.
stupor: stupeur, état de stupeur.
supernatural: surnaturel.

hall, and seated himself musingly on one of the benches on the deserted terrace.

Grasping the arms of her chair with both hands, her eyes fixed eagerly on his face, Lucretia Dalibard **awaited** the welcome visitor.

Prepared as he had been for change, Walter was startled by the **ghastly** alteration in Lucretia's features, increased as it was at that moment by all the emotions which raged within. He sank into the chair placed for him opposite Lucretia, and clearing his throat, said falteringly,—

"I **grieve** indeed, Madame, that my visit, intended to bring but joy, should chance thus **inopportunely**. The servant informed me as we came up the stairs that your niece was ill; and I sympathize with your natural anxiety,—Susan's only child, too; poor Susan!"

"Sir," said Lucretia, impatiently, "these moments are precious. Sir, sir, my son,—my son!" and her eyes glanced to the door. "You have brought with you a companion,—does he wait without? My son!"

"Madame, give me a moment's patience. I will be brief, and **compress** what in other moments might be a long narrative into a few sentences."

Rapidly then Walter Ardworth passed over the details, unnecessary now to repeat to the reader,—the injunctions of Braddell, the delivery of the child to the woman selected by his fellow-sectarian (who, it seemed, by John Ardworth's recent inquiries, was afterwards **expelled** the community, and who, there was reason to believe, had been the first **seducer** of the woman thus recommended). No clew to the child's parentage had been given to the woman with the sum intrusted for his maintenance, which sum had perhaps been the main cause of her reckless progress to infamy and ruin. The **narrator** passed lightly over the neglect and cruelty of the nurse, to her **abandonment** of the child when the money was exhausted. Fortunately she had **overlooked** the coral round its neck. By that coral, and by the initials V. B., which Ardworth had had the **precaution** to have burned into the child's wrist, the lost son had been discovered; the nurse herself (found in the person of Martha Skeggs, Lucretia's own servant) had been **confronted** with

French

abandonment: abandon, délaissement, abdication.
awaited: attendîmes.
compress: comprimer, condenser.
confronted: affrontèrent, confrontâtes.
expelled: expulsèrent.
ghastly: horrible, désagréable, repoussant, abominable, maussade, odieux.
grasping: avide, empoignant, étreignant, saisir.
grieve: affliger, chagriner, attrister, désoler.
inopportunely: de manière inopportune, de façon inopportune.
narrator: narrateur, récitant.
overlooked: négligé.
precaution: précaution.
seducer: séducteur.

the woman to whom she gave the child, and recognized at once. Nor had it been difficult to obtain from her the confession which completed the evidence.

"In this discovery," concluded Ardworth, "the person I employed met your own agent, and the last links in the chain they traced together. But to that person—to his **zeal** and intelligence—you owe the happiness I trust to give you. He **sympathized** with me the more that he knew you personally, felt for your sorrows, and had a **lingering** belief that you supposed him to be the child you yearned for. Madame, thank my son for the restoration of your own!"

Without sound, Lucretia had listened to these details, though her countenance changed fearfully as the narrator proceeded. But now she groaned aloud and in agony.

"Nay, Madame," said Ardworth, feelingly, and in some surprise, "surely the discovery of your son should create gladder emotions! Though, indeed, you will be prepared to find that the poor youth so reared wants education and **refinement**, I have heard enough to convince me that his dispositions are good and his heart grateful. Judge of this yourself; he is in these walls, he is—"

"Abandoned by a harlot,—reared by a **beggar**! My son!" interrupted Lucretia, in broken sentences. "Well, sir, have you **discharged** your task! Well have you replaced a mother!" Before Ardworth could reply, loud and rapid steps were heard in the corridor, and a voice, cracked, **indistinct**, but **vehement**. The door was thrown open, and, half-supported by Captain Greville, half **dragging** him along, his features **convulsed**, whether by pain or passion, the spy upon Lucretia's secrets, the **denouncer** of her crime, **tottered** to the threshold. Pointing to where she sat with his long, lean arm, Beck exclaimed, "Seize her! I 'cuse her, face to face, of the murder of her niece,—of—of I told you, sir—I told you—"

"Madame," said Captain Greville, "you stand charged by this witness with the most terrible of human crimes. I judge you not. Your niece, I **rejoice**

French

beggar: mendiant, gueux.
convulsed: convulsionna, bouleversé.
denouncer: dénonciateur.
discharged: déchargé.
dragging: traînant, entraînement d'image.
indistinct: confus, touffu, trouble, indistinct.
lingering: prolongé, traînant.
refinement: raffinement, délicatesse, affinage.
rejoice: réjouir, être joyeux.
sympathized: compatis, sympathisa.
tottered: vacillé, titubé, chancelèrent.
vehement: véhément, violent, passionné.
zeal: zèle, ferveur.

to bear, yet lives. Pray God that her death be not traced to those kindred hands!" Turning her eyes from one to the other with a wandering stare, Lucretia Dalibard remained silent. But there was still **scorn** on her lip, and **defiance** on her brow. At last she said slowly, and to Ardworth, —

"Where is my son? You say he is within these walls. Call him forth to protect his mother! Give me at least my son, — my son!"

Her last words were **drowned** by a fresh burst of fury from her denouncer. In all the coarsest **invective** his education could supply, in all the **hideous vulgarities** of his **untutored dialect**, in that uncurbed **licentiousness** of tone, look, and manner which passion, once aroused, gives to the **dregs** and **scum** of the **populace**, Beck poured forth his **frightful** charges, his frantic **execrations**. In vain Captain Greville **strove** to check him; in vain Walter Ardworth sought to draw him from the room. But while the poor wretch — maddening not more with the consciousness of the crime than with the excitement of the poison in his blood — thus **raved** and stormed, a terrible suspicion crossed Walter Ardworth; mechanically, — as his grasp was on the accuser's arm, — he **bared** the sleeve, and on the wrist were the dark-blue letters burned into the skin and bearing witness to his identity with the lost Vincent Braddell.

"Hold, hold!" he exclaimed then; "hold, unhappy man! — it is your mother whom you denounce!"

Lucretia sprang up erect; her eyes seemed starting from her head. She caught at the arm pointed towards her in **wrath** and **menace**, and there, amidst those letters that proclaimed her son, was the small **puncture**, surrounded by a livid circle, that **announced** her victim. In the same instant she discovered her child in the man who was calling down upon her head the **hatred** of Earth and the justice of Heaven, and knew herself his **murderess**!

She dropped the arm, and sank back on the chair; and whether the poison had now reached to the vitals, or whether so unwonted a passion in so frail a frame sufficed for the death-stroke, Beck himself, with a low,

---

French

announced: annonçai, affiché.
bared: barré.
defiance: défi.
dialect: dialecte.
dreg: résidu.
drowned: noyèrent, noyas, noyâtes, noyé.
execration: exécration.
frightful: affreux, effroyable, épouvantable.
hatred: haine.
hideous: hideux, horrible,
abominable, odieux, abject, repoussant, affreux.
invective: injure, invective.
licentiousness: licence.
menace: menacer, gronder.
murderess: meurtrière.
populace: peuple.
puncture: ponction, crevaison, perforation, piqûre.
raved: divaguai, déliré.
scorn: dédain, mépris.
scum: écume, mousse.
strove: combattirent.
untutored: non formé, peu instruit.
vulgarity: vulgarité.
wrath: colère, courroux.

suffocated cry, slid from the hand of Ardworth, and **tottering** a step or so, the blood **gushed** from his mouth over Lucretia's **robe**; his head drooped an **instant**, and, falling, **rested** first upon her **lap**, then struck heavily upon the floor. The two men **bent** over him and raised him in their arms; his eyes opened and closed, his throat rattled, and as he fell back into their arms a **corpse**, a laugh rose close at hand, — it rang through the walls, it was heard near and afar, above and below; not an ear in that house that heard it not. In that laugh **fled forever**, till the Judgment-day, from the **blackened ruins** of her lost soul, the reason of the murderess-mother.

French

bent: courbé, cambrai, penché, disposition.
blackened: noirci, mâchurâtes.
corpse: cadavre, corps.
fled: fui, fuit, fuis, fuirent, fuîtes, fuîmes, échappâmes.
forever: pour toujours, toujours.
gushed: jailli.
instant: instant, moment.
lap: clapoter, recouvrement, nappe, chevauchement, tour, giron, barboter.
rested: reposé.
robe: robe, peignoir.
ruin: ruine, abîmer, abaisser, ravager.
suffocated: suffoqua, étouffèrent.
tottering: chancelant, titubant, vacillant.

CHAPTER XXVIII

THE LOTS VANISH WITHIN THE URN

Varney's self-commune restored to him his constitutional audacity. He returned to Laughton towards the evening, and held a long conference with Greville. Fortunately for him, perhaps, and happily for all, Helen had lost all more dangerous **symptoms**; and the physician, who was in the house, saw in her state nothing not easily to be accounted for by natural causes. Percival had arrived, had seen Helen,—no wonder she was better! Both from him and from Helen, Madame Dalibard's fearful condition was for the present **concealed**. Ardworth's story, and the fact of Beck's identity with Vincent Braddell, were also **reserved** for a later occasion. The tale which Beck had poured into the ear of Greville (when, **recognizing** the St. John livery, the captain stopped his chaise to inquire if Percival were at the Hall, and when thrilled by the hideous **import** of his broken reply, that gentleman had caused him to enter the vehicle to explain himself further), Varney, with his wonted art and address, contrived to **strip** of all **probable semblance**. **Evidently** the poor lad had been already **delirious**; his story must be **deemed** the **nightmare** of his disordered reason. Varney insisted upon **surgical** examination as to the cause of his death. The **membranes** of the brain were found surcharged with blood, as in cases of great mental

---

French

concealed: cachas, dissimulèrent.
deemed: crurent, crûtes, crus, crûmes, cru, crut, réputé.
delirious: délirant.
evidently: évidemment, de façon évidente, de manière évidente.
import: importation, signifier.
membrane: membrane, paroi étanche, feuillet de parchemin, masque amont.
nightmare: cauchemar.
probable: probable, vraisemblable.
recognizing: reconnaissant, retrouvant.
reserved: réservé.
semblance: apparence, semblant.
strip: bande, se déshabiller, rayure, dépouiller, raie, feuillard, lame, déshabiller.
surgical: chirurgical.
symptom: symptôme, signe fonctionnel.

excitement; the slight **puncture** in the wrist, **ascribed** to the **prick** of a **rusty** nail, provoked no suspicion. If some doubts remained still in Greville's acute mind, he was not eager to express, still less to act upon them. Helen was declared to be out of danger; Percival was safe,—why **affix** by minute inquiry into the alleged guilt of Madame Dalibard (already so **awfully** affected by the death of her son and by the loss of her reason) so foul a **stain** on the honoured family of St. John? But Greville was naturally anxious to free the house as soon as possible both of Varney and that **ominous** Lucretia, whose **sojourn** under its roof seemed accursed. He therefore readily **assented** when Varney proposed, as his obvious and personal duty, to take charge of his mother-in-law, and remove her to London for immediate advice.

At the dead of the black-clouded night, no moon and no stars, the son of Olivier Dalibard bore away the form of the once-formidable Lucretia,—the form, for the mind was gone; that **teeming**, restless, and **fertile** intellect, which had carried along the projects with the preterhuman energies of the fiend, was hurled into night and chaos. Manacled and bound, for at times her **paroxysms** were terrible, and all partook of the **destructive** and **murderous** character which her faculties, when present, had betrayed, she was placed in the vehicle by the shrinking side of her accomplice.

Long before he arrived in London, Varney had got rid of his fearful companion. His chaise had stopped at the iron gates of a large building somewhat out of the main road, and the doors of the **madhouse** closed on Lucretia Dalibard.

Varney then hastened to Dover, with intention of flight into France; he was just about to step into the vessel, when he was tapped rudely on the shoulder, and a determined voice said, "Mr. Gabriel Varney, you are my prisoner!"

"For what? Some **paltry** debt?" said Varney, haughtily.

"For forgery on the Bank of England!"

French

affix: affixe, attacher, fixer, apposer.
ascribed: attribuèrent.
assented: assenties.
awfully: terriblement, affreusement, de façon horrible, de manière horrible.
destructive: destructif, ravageur.
fertile: fécond, fertile, fruitier.
madhouse: maison de fous.
murderous: meurtrier, homicide.
ominous: inquiétant, menaçant, sinistre.
paltry: misérable.
paroxysm: paroxysme.
prick: piqûre, bitte, zob.
puncture: ponction, crevaison, perforation, piqûre.
rusty: rouillé, rubigineux.
sojourn: séjour.
stain: tache, salir, souiller, colorant, teinture.
teeming: abondant, grouillant, coulée par le fond de la poche en lingotière.

Varney's hand plunged into his vest. The officer seized it in time, and **wrested** the **blade** from his grasp. Once arrested for an offence it was impossible to **disprove**, although the very smallest of which his conscience might charge him, Varney sank into the blackest despair. Though he had often boasted, not only to others, but to his own vain breast, of the easy courage with which, when life ceased to yield enjoyment, he could dismiss it by the act of his own will; though he had possessed himself of Lucretia's murderous ring, and death, if fearful, was therefore at his command,—self-destruction was the last thought that occurred to him; that **morbid excitability** of fancy which, whether in his art or in his deeds, had led him to strange delight in horror, now served but to haunt him with the images of death in those **ghastliest** shapes familiar to them who look only into the bottom of the charnel, and see but the rat and the worm and the **loathsome** agencies of corruption. It was not the despair of conscience that seized him, it was the **abject** clinging to life; not the remorse of the soul,—that still slept within him, too noble an **agency** for one so debased,—but the gross physical terror. As the fear of the tiger, once aroused, is more **paralyzing** than that of the deer, proportioned to the **savageness** of a disposition to which fear is a novelty, so the very **boldness** of Varney, coming only from the perfection of the nervous organization, and **unsupported** by one moral sentiment, once struck down, was **corrupted** into the vilest **cowardice**. With his audacity, his **shrewdness forsook** him. Advised by his lawyer to plead guilty, he obeyed, and the sentence of transportation for life gave him at first a feeling of reprieve; but when his imagination began to picture, in the darkness of his cell, all the true tortures of that penalty,—not so much, perhaps, to the **uneducated** peasant-felon, inured to toil, and familiarized with coarse companionship, as to one **pampered** like himself by all soft and half-womanly indulgences,—the **shaven** hair, the convict's dress, the rigorous **privation**, the drudging toil, the exile, seemed as grim as the grave. In the **dotage** of faculties **smitten** into drivelling, he wrote to the Home Office, **offering** to **disclose** secrets connected with crimes that had hitherto escaped or baffled justice, on condition that his sentence might be repealed, or

---

French

abject: abject, lâche, misérable, pauvre.
agency: agence, organisme de renseignement.
blade: lame, chaume, ailette, aube, pale.
boldness: audace, hardiesse.
corrupted: pervertis, corrompu, altéré.
cowardice: lâcheté, faiblesse.
disclose: divulguer, révéler, dévoiler.

disprove: réfuter.
dotage: gâtisme, sénilité.
excitability: excitabilité.
forsook: abandonnâtes, délaissai.
ghastliest: le plus horrible.
loathsome: détestable, répugnant.
morbid: morbide.
offering: offrande, proposition, sacrifice.
pampered: choyé, dorlotas.
paralyzing: paralysant, médusant.
privation: privation.

savageness: férocité, sauvagerie.
shaven: rasé.
shrewdness: perspicacité, sagacité.
smitten: frappé.
uneducated: inculte.
unsupported: boisage, non soutenu, sans support.
wrested: arrachâtes.

mitigated into the gentler forms of ordinary **transportation**. No answer was returned to him, but his letter **provoked** research. Circumstances connected with his uncle's death, and with various other dark passages in his life, **sealed** against him all hope of a more **merciful** sentence; and when some **acquaintances**, whom his art had made for him, and who, while **grieving** for his crime, saw in it some excuses (ignorant of his **feller** deeds), sought to **intercede** in his behalf, the reply of the Home Office was obvious: "He is a fortunate man to have been tried and condemned for his least offence." Not one **indulgence** that could distinguish him from the most execrable **ruffian** condemned to the same sentence was **conceded**.

The idea of the **gibbet** lost all its horror. Here was a gibbet for every hour. No hope,—no escape. Already that Future Doom which comprehends the "Forever" opened upon him black and **fathomless**. The hour-glass was broken up, the hand of the **timepiece** was arrested. The Beyond stretched before him without limit, without goal,—on into Annihilation or into Hell.

French

acquaintance: connaissance, relation, personne de connaissance, abord.
conceded: concédé.
fathomless: impénétrable, insondable.
feller: abatteuse, rabatteur.
gibbet: gibet.
grieving: affligeant, chagrinant, attristant.
indulgence: indulgence, tolérance.
intercede: intercéder.
merciful: indulgent, Clément, sensible, miséricordieux.
mitigated: mitigèrent, atténuèrent, adoucîmes.
provoked: provoqua, chiffonnées.
ruffian: apache, brute, voyou.
sealed: scellé, étanche, hermétique, fermé.
timepiece: montre, pendule moyenne, appareil horaire.
transportation: transport, moyen de transport.

EPILOGUE TO PART THE SECOND.

Stand, O Man! upon the hill-top in the **stillness** of the evening hour, and gaze, not with **joyous**, but with **contented** eyes, upon the beautiful world around thee. See where the mists, soft and dim, rise over the **green meadows**, through which the **rivulet** steals its way. See where, broadest and stillest, the wave **expands** to the full smile of the setting sun, and the **willow** that trembles on the **breeze**, and the oak that stands firm in the storm, are reflected back, peaceful both, from the clear glass of the **tides**. See where, begirt by the gold of the harvests, and backed by the **pomp** of a thousand groves, the roofs of the town bask, noiseless, in the calm glow of the sky. Not a sound from those abodes floats in **discord** to thine ear; only from the church-tower, **soaring** high above the rest, perhaps **faintly** heard through the stillness, swells the note of the holy bell. Along the **mead** low **skims** the swallow, — on the wave the silver **circlet**, breaking into **spray**, shows the sport of the fish. See the Earth, how **serene**, though all **eloquent** of activity and life! See the Heavens, how **benign**, though dark clouds, by yon **mountain**, blend the purple with the gold! Gaze contented, for Good is around thee, — not joyous, for Evil is the shadow of Good! Let thy soul **pierce** through the **veil** of the senses, and thy sight plunge deeper than the surface which gives delight to thine eye. Below the glass of that **river**, the **pike darts** on his prey; the circle in the wave, the soft **plash** amongst the reeds, are but

French

benign: bénin.
breeze: brise, souffle.
circlet: cercle.
contented: content, satisfait.
dart: dard, fléchette.
discord: discorde, désaccord.
eloquent: éloquent.
expands: développe, mousse.
faintly: de façon faible, de manière faible, faiblement.
green: vert, herbacé, inexpérimenté, cru, comprimé,

boulingrin, frais.
joyous: joyeux, heureux.
mead: hydromel.
meadow: pré, prairie, pâturage.
mountain: montagne, orophile, la montagne.
pierce: percer, perçons, transpercer.
pike: brochet, pique.
plash: clapoter, barboter.
pomp: pompe, splendeur.
river: fleuve, rivière, lézarde.
rivulet: ruisselet.

serene: serein, tranquille.
skim: écrémer, écumer.
soaring: essor.
spray: spray, pulvériser, embruns, atomiser, vaporisateur, arroser.
stillness: calme, tranquillité.
tide: marée.
veil: voile, dissimuler.
willow: saule.

signs of Destroyer and Victim. In the **ivy** round the oak by the margin, the **owl hungers** for the night, which shall give its **beak** and its **talons** living food for its young; and the spray of the willow trembles with the wing of the redbreast, whose bright eye sees the worm on the sod. Canst thou count too, O Man! all the cares, all the sins, that those noiseless **rooftops** conceal? With every curl of that smoke to the sky, a human thought soars as dark, a human hope melts as briefly. And the bell from the church-tower, that to thy ear gives but music, perhaps **knolls** for the dead. The **swallow** but chases the moth, and the cloud, that deepens the glory of the heaven and the sweet shadows on the earth, nurses but the thunder that shall **rend** the grove, and the storm that shall **devastate** the harvests. Not with fear, not with doubt, recognize, O Mortal, the presence of Evil in the world. [Not, indeed, that the evil here **narrated** is the ordinary evil of the world,—the lesson it **inculcates** would be lost if so construed,—but that the mystery of evil, whatever its degree, only **increases** the necessity of faith in the **vindication** of the **contrivance** which requires **infinity** for its range, and eternity for its **consummation**. It is in the existence of evil that man finds his duties, and his soul its progress.] Hush thy heart in the **humbleness** of awe, that its mirror may reflect as **serenely** the shadow as the light. Vainly, for its moral, dost thou gaze on the landscape, if thy soul puts no check on the dull delight of the senses. Two wings only raise thee to the summit of Truth, where the Cherub shall comfort the sorrow, where the Seraph shall **enlighten** the joy. Dark as ebon spreads the one wing, white as snow gleams the other,—mournful as thy reason when it descends into the deep; **exulting** as thy faith when it springs to the day-star.

 Beck sleeps in the churchyard of Laughton. He had lived to **frustrate** the monstrous design intended to benefit himself, and to become the instrument, while the victim, of the dread Eumenides. That done, his life passed with the crimes that had gathered around, out of the sight of mortals. Helen slowly regained her health in the atmosphere of love and happiness; and Lady Mary soon learned to forget the fault of the father in the virtues of the child. Married to Percival, Helen fulfilled the destinies of woman's genius, in

French

beak: bec.
consummation: consommation, perfection.
contrivance: invention, ingéniosité, dispositif.
devastate: dévaster, ravager, saccager.
enlighten: éclairer, illuminer.
exulting: exultant.
frustrate: frustrer, déjoue, décevoir.
humbleness: humilité.
hunger: faim, avoir faim, désir

increase: augmenter, accroissement, agrandir, grossir, s'accroître, redoubler, amplifier, croissance, hausse, majorer, étendre.
inculcate: inculquons.
infinity: infinité, foyer infini, valeur infinie.
ivy: lierre, vert lierre.
knoll: monticule.
narrated: racontèrent, contâtes.

owl: hibou, chouette, effraie.
rend: déchirer.
rooftop: toit.
serenely: de façon sereine, de manière sereine.
swallow: hirondelle, avaler, aronde, engloutir, gorgée, gober, déglutir.
talon: talon, griffe, serre.
vindication: justification, revendication, défense.

calling forth into action man's earnest duties. She breathed into Percival's warm, **beneficent** heart her own more steadfast and divine intelligence. Like him she grew ambitious, by her he became distinguished. While I write, fair children play under the cedars of Laughton. And the husband tells the daughters to resemble their mother; and the wife's highest praise to the boys is: "You have spoken truth, or done good, like your father."

John Ardworth has not paused in his career, nor **belied** the promise of his youth. Though the elder Ardworth, partly by his own **exertions**, partly by his second marriage with the daughter of the French merchant (through whose agency he had **corresponded** with Fielden), had **realized** a moderate fortune, it but sufficed for his own wants and for the children of his later nuptials, upon whom the bulk of it was settled. Hence, happily perhaps for himself and others, the easy circumstances of his father allowed to John Ardworth no **exemption** from labour. His success in the single episode from active life to literature did not **intoxicate** or **mislead** him. He knew that his real element was not in the field of letters, but in the world of men. Not undervaluing the noble destinies of the author, he felt that those destinies, if realized to the utmost, demanded powers other than his own, and that man is only true to his genius when the genius is at home in his career. He would not **renounce** for a brief **celebrity** distant and solid fame. He continued for a few years in patience and privation and confident self-reliance to **drudge** on, till the occupation for the intellect fed by restraint, and the learning accumulated by study, came and found the whole man **developed** and prepared. Then he rose rapidly from step to step; then, still **retaining** his high enthusiasm, he enlarged his sphere of action from the cold practice of law into those vast social improvements which law, rightly regarded, should lead and **vivify** and create. Then, and long before the twenty years he had imposed on his probation had **expired**, he gazed again upon the senate and the abbey, and saw the doors of the one open to his **resolute** tread, and anticipated the glorious **sepulchre** which heart and brain should win him in the other. John Ardworth has never married. When Percival rebukes him for his **celibacy**, his lip quivers slightly, and he **applies**

French

applies: applique, pratique, sollicite.
belied: démentîtes.
beneficent: bienfaisant.
celebrity: célébrité, star, vedette.
celibacy: célibat.
corresponded: correspondîmes.
developed: développai, perfectionnâtes, aménagèrent, contractèrent.
drudge: trimer, peiner, bête de somme.
exemption: exemption, dispense, exonération, franchise.
exertion: effort.
expired: expira, périmé, échut.
intoxicate: enivrer, griser.
mislead: égarer, tromper.
realized: réalisé, subi.
renounce: renoncer, abandonner, abjurer, résigner, renier.
resolute: résolu, déterminé.
retaining: retenant, contention.
sepulchre: sépulcre.
vivify: vivifier.

himself with more dogged earnestness to his studies or his career. But he never **complains** that his lot is lonely or his affections void. For him who **aspires**, and for him who loves, life may lead through the thorns, but it never stops in the desert.

On the minor **personages** involved in this history, there is little need to dwell. Mr. Fielden, thanks to St. John, has obtained a much better living in the rectory of Laughton, but has found new sources of pleasant trouble for himself in seeking to **drill** into the mind of Percival's eldest son the elements of Euclid, and the principles of Latin **syntax**.

We may feel satisfied that the Miverses will go on much the same while trade **enriches** without **refining**, and while, nevertheless, right feelings in the common paths of duty may unite charitable emotions with **graceless** language.

We may rest assured that the poor widow who had reared the lost son of Lucretia received from the **bounty** of Percival all that could comfort her for his death.

We have no need to track the dull crimes of Martha, or the quick, cunning vices of Grabman, to their inevitable goals, in the hospital or the prison, the **dunghill** or the gibbet.

Of the elder Ardworth our parting notice may be less brief. We first saw him in sanguine and generous youth, with higher principles and clearer insight into honour than William Mainwaring. We have seen him next a spendthrift and a fugitive, his principles **debased** and his honour **dimmed**. He presents to us no uncommon example of the corruption **engendered** by that vulgar self-indulgence which mortgages the **morrow** for the pleasures of to-day. No Deity **presides** where Prudence is absent. Man, a world in himself, requires for the development of his faculties patience, and for the balance of his actions, order. Even where he had deemed himself most **oppressively** made the martyr,—namely, in the profession of mere political opinions,—Walter Ardworth had but followed out into theory the restless, uncalculating impatience which had brought **adversity** on his manhood,

---

French

adversity: adversité, abaissement.
aspire: aspirer.
bounty: prime, générosité, libéralité.
complain: se plaindre, porter plainte, plaindre.
debased: abâtardis, avilîtes.
dimmed: estompé.
drill: foret, percer, perforatrice, coutil, mèche, fraise, drille.
dunghill: tas de fumier.
engendered: engendras.
enrich: enrichir, amender, étoffe, féconder, fertiliser.
graceless: inélégant, gauche.
morrow: lendemain.
oppressively: de manière étouffante, de façon étouffante.
personage: personnage.
presides: préside.
refining: raffinant, affinage, épurant.
syntax: syntaxe.

and, despite his constitutional cheerfulness, shadowed his age with remorse. The death of the child committed to his charge long (perhaps to the last) embittered his pride in the son whom, without merit of his own, Providence had spared to a brighter fate. But for the faults which had banished him his country, and the habits which had **seared** his sense of duty, could that child have been so abandoned, and have so **perished**?

It remains only to cast our glance over the punishments which **befell** the sensual villany of Varney, the intellectual corruption of his fell stepmother.

These two persons had made a very trade of those crimes to which man's law **awards** death. They had said in their hearts that they would dare the crime, but **elude** the penalty. By wonderful subtlety, craft, and **dexterity**, which reduced guilt to a science, Providence seemed, as in disdain of the vulgar instruments of common retribution, to concede to them that which they had **schemed** for,—escape from the **rope** and gibbet. Varney, saved from detection of his darker and more inexpiable crimes, **punished** only for the least one, retained what had seemed to him the master boon,—life. Safer still from the law, no mortal eye had plumbed the profound night of Lucretia's awful guilt. Murderess of husband and son, the blinded law bade her go **unscathed, unsuspected**. Direct, as from heaven, without a cloud, fell the **thunderbolt**. Is the life they have saved worth the **prizing**? Doth the **chalice**, unspilt on the ground, not return to the hand? Is the sudden pang of the **hangman** more fearful than the doom which they breathe and bear? Look, and judge.

Behold that dark **ship** on the waters! Its burdens are not of Ormus and Tyre. No **goodly merchandise** doth it **waft** over the wave, no blessing **cleaves** to its sails; freighted with terror and with guilt, with remorse and despair, or, more ghastly than either, the sullen apathy of souls hardened into stone, it carries the **dregs** and **offal** of the old world to **populate** the new. On a bench in that ship sit side by side two men, companions assigned to each other. Pale, **abject**, cowering, all the **bravery** rent from his garb, all the gay **insolence** vanished from his brow,—can that hollow-eyed, haggard wretch be the same man whose senses opened on every joy, whose nerves

French

abject: abject, lâche, misérable, pauvre.
award: adjuger, récompense, prix, jugement, décerner.
befell: arrivâmes.
bravery: bravoure, courage.
chalice: calice.
cleave: fendre, cliver, se fendre.
dexterity: dextérité, adresse.
dreg: résidu.
elude: éluder, éviter, déjouent.
goodly: de façon bonne, de manière bonne.
hangman: bourreau.
insolence: effronterie, insolence.
merchandise: marchandise, denrée, produit.
offal: abats, dépouille, déchets.
perished: péri, pérîtes.
populate: peupler, charger, garnissons.
prizing: pressage.
punished: punirent, punîtes.
rope: corde, la corde, filin.
schemed: comploté.
seared: saisîmes, endurcit, flétri, desséchas, brûlèrent.
ship: navire, bateau, expédier, vaisseau.
thunderbolt: chute de la foudre.
unscathed: indemne.
unsuspected: insoupçonné.
waft: bouffée.

mocked at every peril? But beside him, with a grin of vile glee on his features, all muscle and **brawn** in the form, all malice, at once spiteful and dull, in the heavy eye, sits his fit comrade, the Gravestealer! At the first glance each had recognized each, and the prophecy and the vision rushed back upon the daintier **convict**. If he seek to escape from him, the Gravestealer claims him as a prey; he **threatens** him with his eye as a slave; he kicks him with his **hoof** as they sit, and laughs at the writhings of the pain. Carry on your gaze from the ship, hear the cry from the **masthead**, see the land arise from the waste,—a land without hope. At first, despite the rigour of the Home Office, the education and intelligence of Varney have their price,—the sole crime for which he is convicted is not of the darkest. He escapes from that hideous comrade; he can teach as a schoolmaster,—let his brain work, not his hands. But the most **irredeemable** of convicts are ever those of nurture and birth and **culture** better than the ruffian rest. You may **enlighten** the clod, but the **meteor** still must feed on the **marsh**; and the pride and the vanity work where the crime itself seems to lose its occasion. Ever avid, ever grasping, he falls, step by step, in the foul sink, and the **colony** sees in Gabriel Varney its most **pestilent** rogue. Arch-convict amidst convicts, doubly lost amongst the damned, they banish him to the sternest of the **penal** settlements; they send him forth with the vilest to break stones upon the roads. **Shrivelled** and bowed and old prematurely, see that sharp face peering forth amongst that **gang**, scarcely human, see him **cringe** to the **lash** of the scornful **overseer**, see the pairs chained together, night and day! Ho, ho! his comrade hath found him again,—the Artist and the Gravestealer leashed together! Conceive that fancy so **nurtured** by habit, those tastes, so womanized by indulgence,—the one suggesting the very horrors that are not; the other **revolting** at all toil as a torture.

But intellect, not all gone, though hourly dying heavily down to the level of the brute, yet schemes for delivery and escape. Let the plot **ripen**, and the heart bound; break his chain, set him free, send him forth to the **wilderness**. Hark, the **whoop** of the wild men! See those things that **ape** our **species** dance and **gibber** round the famishing, hunted wretch. Hark, how he shrieks

French

ape: singe.
brawn: fromage de tête, hure.
colony: colonie, possession.
convict: détenu, bagnard, prisonnier, condamné.
cringe: reculer.
culture: culture, faire une culture, civilisation.
enlighten: éclairer, illuminer.
gang: bande, compagnie, clique, mariage.
gibber: baragouiner.
hoof: sabot.
irredeemable: irrachetable, incorrigible, non rachetable.
lash: fouetter, aiguilleter, dard, mèche, attacher.
marsh: marécage, marais, pelouse marécageuse.
masthead: tête de mat, adresse, ton de mât, bloc générique, générique.
meteor: météore.
mocked: bafouâmes.
nurtured: soutenue.
overseer: surveillant, contremaître, chef de salle.
penal: pénal, punissable, criminel.
pestilent: pestilentiel.
revolting: révoltant.
ripen: mûrir.
shrivelled: recroquevillé.
specie: monnaie, numéraire.
threatens: menace.
whoop: chant du coq, cri, reprise.
wilderness: désert, zone de nature protégée.

at the torture! How they tear and they pinch and they burn and they **rend** him! They, too, spare his life,—it is charmed. A Caliban amidst Calibans, they **heap** him with their burdens, and feed him on their **offal**. Let him live; he loved life for himself; he has **cheated** the gibbet,—*let him live*! Let him watch, let him once more escape; all **naked** and mangled, let him wander back to the huts of his gang. Lo, where he **kneels**, the foul tears streaming down, and cries aloud: "I have broken all your laws, I will tell you all my crimes; I ask but one sentence,—hang me up; let me die!" And from the gang groan many voices: "Hang us up; let us die!" The overseer turns on his heel, and Gabriel Varney again is chained to the laughing Gravestealer.

You enter those gates so **jealously** guarded, you pass, with a quick beat of the heart, by those groups on the lawn, though they are harmless; you follow your guide through those passages; where the open doors will permit, you see the **emperor brandish** his **sceptre** of straw, hear the speculator counting his millions, sigh where the maiden sits smiling the return of her shipwrecked lover, or gravely shake the head and hurry on where the **fanatic raves** his Apocalypse, and reigns in judgment on the world; you pass by strong gates into corridors gloomier and more remote. Nearer and nearer you hear the yell and the oath and **blaspheming** curse; you are in the heart of the **madhouse**, where they chain those at once cureless and dangerous,— who have but sense enough left them to **smite** and to **throttle** and to murder. Your guide opens that door, massive as a wall; you see (as we, who **narrate**, have seen her) Lucretia Dalibard,—a **grisly**, squalid, ferocious mockery of a human being, more appalling and more fallen than Dante ever **fabled** in his spectres, than Swift ever scoffed in his Yahoos! Only, where all other feature seems to have lost its stamp of humanity, still burns with unquenchable fever the red, **devouring** eye. That eye never seems to sleep, or in sleep, the lid never closes over it. As you shrink from its light, it seems to you as if the mind, that had lost **coherence** and harmony, still retained latent and **incommunicable** consciousness as its curse. For days, for weeks, that awful **maniac** will preserve **obstinate**, unbroken silence; but as the eye never closes, so the hands never rest,—they open and grasp, as if at some palpable

French

blaspheming: blasphémant.
brandish: brandir, agiter.
cheated: déçu, triché.
coherence: cohérence.
devouring: dévorant, engloutissant.
emperor: empereur.
fabled: légendaire.
fanatic: fanatique, exalté.
grisly: maussade, désagréable, horrible.
heap: tas, amas, entasser,

accumuler, foule, masse, troupe, bande, collection, ensemble, rassembler.
incommunicable: incommunicable.
jealously: de façon jalouse, de manière jalouse, jalousement.
kneel: s'agenouiller, agenouillement, se mettre à genoux.
madhouse: maison de fous.
maniac: maniaque, fou.
naked: nu, dénudé.

narrate: raconter, conter.
obstinate: obstiné, têtu, tenace, entêté.
offal: abats, dépouille, déchets.
rave: être fou, délirer.
rend: déchirer.
sceptre: sceptre.
smite: frapper.
throttle: étrangler, accélérateur, manette des gaz, papillon des gaz.

object on which they close, vicelike, as a bird's **talons** on its prey; sometimes they wander over that brow, where the **furrows** seem torn as the thunder **scars**, as if to wipe from it a stain, or charm from it a pang; sometimes they gather up the hem of that sordid robe, and seem, for hours together, striving to **rub** from it a soil. Then, out from prolonged silence, without cause or warning, will ring, **peal** after peal (till the frame, exhausted with the effort sinks senseless into stupor), the **frightful** laugh. But speech, **intelligible** and **coherent**, those lips rarely yield. There are times, indeed, when the attendants are persuaded that her mind in part returns to her; and those times experience has taught them to watch with peculiar caution. The crisis **evinces** itself by a change in the manner,—by a quick apprehension of all that is said; by a straining, anxious look at the dismal walls; by a soft, fawning **docility**; by murmured complaints of the chains that **fetter**; and (though, as we have said, but very rarely) by prayers, that seem rational, for greater ease and freedom.

In the earlier time of her dread **captivity**, perhaps when it was believed at the **asylum** that she was a patient of condition, with friends who cared for her state, and would liberally reward her cure, they in those moments relaxed her confinement, and sought the gentler remedies their art employs; but then invariably, and, it was said, with a cunning that **surpassed** all the proverbial **astuteness** of the mad, she turned this indulgence to the most deadly uses,—she crept to the **pallet** of some **adjacent** sufferer weaker than herself, and the **shrieks** that brought the attendants into the cell scarcely saved the intended victim from her hands. It seemed, in those **imperfectly lucid** intervals, as if the reason only returned to guide her to destroy,—only to **animate** the broken mechanism into the beast of prey.

Years have now passed since her entrance within those walls. He who placed her there never had returned. He had given a false name,—no clew to him was obtained; the gold he had left was but the quarter's pay. When Varney had been first **apprehended**, Percival requested the younger Ardworth to seek the **forger** in prison, and to question him as to Madame Dalibard; but Varney was then so apprehensive that, even if still **insane**, her

---

French

adjacent: adjacent, contigu, avoisinant, limitrophe, voisin.
animate: animer, encourager, vivifier.
apprehended: appréhendé, craignîtes.
astuteness: finesse, sagacité.
asylum: asile, refuge, abri.
captivity: captivité.
coherent: cohérent.
docility: docilité.
evinces: montre.
fetter: chaîne, enchaîner.
forger: faussaire, forgeur.
frightful: affreux, effroyable, épouvantable.
furrow: sillon, ride, raie.
imperfectly: imparfaitement, de façon imparfaite, de manière imparfaite.
insane: fou, insensé, aberrant, agité, aliéné.
intelligible: intelligible.
lucid: lucide, clair.
pallet: palette, soupape, tringle de clouage, petite planche dont se sert le colleur, ancre, levée, filet à dorer.
peal: tinter, sonner.
rub: frotter, récurer.
scar: cicatrice, balafre.
shriek: crier, hurler, cri perçant.
surpassed: dépassas, surpassai, maîtrisas.
talon: talon, griffe, serre.

very **ravings** might betray his share in her crimes, or still more, if she recovered, that the remembrance of her son's murder would **awaken** the **repentance** and the confession of crushed despair, that the wretch had judged it wiser to say that his accomplice was no more,—that her **insanity** had already terminated in death. The place of her confinement thus continued a secret locked in his own breast. **Egotist** to the last, she was henceforth dead to him,—why not to the world? Thus the partner of her crimes had cut off her sole resource, in the compassion of her unconscious kindred; thus the gates of the living world were shut to her evermore. Still, in a kind of compassion, or as an object of experiment,—as a subject to be dealt with **unscrupulously** in that living dissection-hall,—her grim **jailers** did not **grudge** her an asylum. But, year after year, the attendance was more **slovenly**, the **treatment** more harsh; and strange to say, while the features were scarcely **recognizable**, while the form **underwent** all the change which the shape suffers when mind deserts it, that **prodigious vitality** which belonged to the temperament still survived. No signs of decay are yet visible. Death, as if spurning the carcass, stands **inexorably** afar off. Baffler of man's law, thou, too, hast escaped with life! Not for thee is the sentence, "Blood for blood!" Thou livest, thou mayst pass the extremest boundaries of age. Live on, to wipe the blood from thy robe,—*live on*!

Not for the coarse object of creating an idle terror, not for the shock upon the nerves and the thrill of the grosser interest which the narrative of crime **creates**, has this book been **compiled** from the facts and materials afforded to the author. When the great German poet describes, in not the least noble of his **lyrics**, the sudden **apparition** of some "Monster Fate" in the circles of careless Joy, he **assigns** to him who teaches the world, through **parable** or song, the right to **invoke** the **spectre**. It is well to be awakened at times from the easy commonplace that surrounds our habitual life; to cast broad and steady and patient light on the darker secrets of the heart,—on the vaults and **caverns** of the social state over which we build the market-place and the palace. We recover from the dread and the awe and the half-incredulous wonder, to set closer watch upon our inner and hidden selves. In him who

French

apparition: apparition.
assigns: assigne, attribue, adjuge.
awaken: réveiller, éveiller.
cavern: caverne, antre.
compiled: compila, dressas.
creates: crée.
egotist: égotiste.
grudge: rancune.
inexorably: de façon inexorable, de manière inexorable, inexorablement.
insanity: folie, aliénation, démence,

aberration, affolement, insanité.
invoke: invoquer, appeler.
jailer: geôlier, gardien de prison.
lyric: lyrique, texte.
parable: parabole.
prodigious: prodigieux.
raving: délirant, divaguant.
recognizable: reconnaissable.
repentance: repentir.
slovenly: négligé.
spectre: spectre.
treatment: traitement, cure,

demande de règlement, plan général d'émission, scénario.
underwent: subîtes, subit.
unscrupulously: de manière sans scrupules, de façon sans scrupules.
vitality: vitalité, force vitale.

cultivates only the reason, and suffers the heart and the spirit to lie waste and dead, who schemes and constructs, and **revolves** round the **axle** of self, unwarmed by the affections, unpoised by the attraction of right, lies the **germ** Fate might ripen into the guilt of Olivier Dalibard. Let him who but lives through the senses, spreads the wings of the fancy in the **gaudy** glare of enjoyment **corrupted, avid** to seize, and impatient to toil, whose faculties are **curbed** but to the range of physical perception, whose very courage is but the strength of the nerves, who develops but the animal as he **stifles** the man, — let him gaze on the villany of Varney, and **startle** to see some **magnified** shadow of himself thrown dimly on the glass! Let those who, with powers to command and passions to wing the powers, would sweep without scruple from the aim to the end, who, trampling beneath their **footprint** of iron the humanities that bloom up in their path, would march to success with the proud stride of the **destroyer**, hear, in the laugh of yon **maniac** murderess, the glee of the fiend they have **wooed** to their own souls! Guard well, O Heir of Eternity, the portal of sin, — the thought! From the thought to the deed, the subtler thy brain and the bolder thy courage, the briefer and straighter is the way. Read these pages in disdain of self-commune, — they shall revolt thee, not instruct; read them, looking **steadfastly** within, — and how humble soever the art of the narrator, the facts he **narrates**, like all history, shall teach by example. Every human act, good or ill, is an angel to guide or to warn; and the deeds of the worst have messages from Heaven to the listening hearts of the best. Amidst the glens in the Apennine, in the lone wastes of Calabria, the sign of the cross marks the spot where a deed of violence has been done; on all that pass by the road, the symbol has varying effect: sometimes it startles the conscience, sometimes it invokes the devotion; the **robber** drops the blade, the priest counts the **rosary**. So is it with the record of crime; and in the witness of Guilt, Man is thrilled with the whisper of Religion.

> Our acts our angels are, or good or ill,
> The fatal shadows that walk by us still.

French

avid: avide.
axle: axe, essieu, arbre.
corrupted: pervertis, corrompu, altéré.
cultivates: cultive.
curbed: bridai.
destroyer: destroyer.
footprint: encombrement, empreinte de pas.
gaudy: voyant, criard.
germ: germe, microbe.
magnified: grossirent, magnifiâtes.
maniac: maniaque, fou.
narrates: raconte, conte.
revolve: tourner, ruminer.
robber: voleur, ravisseur.
rosary: rosaire, roseraie, chapelet.
startle: effarouches, surprenons, alarment.
steadfastly: de manière inébranlable, de façon inébranlable.
stifle: étouffer, grasset.
wooed: courtisâmes.

Fletcher.

GLOSSARY

abandon: abandonner, délaisser, quitter, renoncer, abdiquer, livrer, résigner
abandoned: abandonné, délaissa, immoral, malsain, abject
abandonment: abandon, délaissement, abdication
abasement: abaissement, humiliation
abashed: confus, décontenançai
abated: diminuèrent
abbey: abbaye
aberration: aberration, erreur
abetted: aidâmes, aidas, ému, aidé, troublâtes
abetting: troublant, secourant, émouvant, agitant, aidant
abhorred: abhorrâtes, exécras
abhorrent: odieux, hideux, horrible, abject, abominable
abhors: abhorre, exécre
abide: endurer, demeurer, persévérer, supporter, soutenir, attendre, subir, souffrir
abject: abject, lâche, misérable, pauvre
abjured: abjuras
abjuring: abjurant
abode: demeure, domicile, logis, gîte, habitation, localité, logement
abound: abonder, fourmiller, grouiller
abridge: abréger, abrèges, raccourcir, abaisser, diminuer, amoindrir, limiter
abridging: abrégeant
abroad: à l'étranger, dehors
abrupt: abrupt, brusque, raide, subit, soudain, escarpé, inattendu, à pic
abruptly: brusquement, abruptement, sèchement, de façon abrupte, de manière abrupte
absence: absence, manque, privation, défaut, vice, insuffisance

absent: absent
absolute: absolu, complet, inéluctable, immense, illimité, pur
absolutely: absolument, vraiment, en réalité, sûrement, sans faute, en vérité, en fait, de manière absolue, de façon absolue
absorb: absorber, amortir, disposer, assimiler
absorbed: absorbèrent, épongèrent, résorbé
absorbing: absorbant, passionnant, captivant
absorption: absorption, amortissement
abstain: s'abstenir, faire abstinence, se réserver, abstenir, m'abstiens, nous abstenons, t'abstiens, vous abstenez
abstaining: s'abstenant, abstenant
abstemious: sobre, frugal
abstinence: abstinence, voix refusée
abstract: abstrait, résumé, abrégé, déduire, retrancher, réduction de texte, ôter, conclure, extrait
abstracted: distrait, abstraits, abrégé
abstractedly: de façon distraite, de manière distraite
abstraction: abstraction, distraction, inattention
abstruse: mystérieux, abstrus
abundant: abondant, copieux
abused: abusa
abyss: abîme, abysse, gouffre
academic: académique, universitaire, étudiant, scolaire
accent: accent, souligner, emphase
accept: accepter, agréer, admettre, accueillir, recevoir, recueillir
acceptable: acceptable, satisfaisant
acceptation: acception
accepted: acceptâmes, agréé
access: accès, attaque, accéder, abord, entrée, impulsion, incitation, assaut

accession: adhésion, accession, présentation, inscription, acquisition
accident: accident, sinistre
accidentally: accidentellement, de manière accidentelle, par hasard, de façon accidentelle
accommodation: accommodation, logement, compromis, arrangement, habitation, construction, disposition, domicile, gîte, hébergement, logis
accompanied: accompagnâtes
accompanies: accompagne
accompaniment: accompagnement, escorte
accompany: accompagner
accompanying: accompagnant
accomplice: complice
accomplished: accomplîmes, réalisas, confectionnâmes, remplîtes, expérimenté, qualifié, compétent
accomplishment: accomplissement, réalisation, ouvrage
accordance: accord, conformité, convention, entente, concordance
according: selon, s'accorder
accosted: accosta, abordé
account: compte, rapport, client, relation, considérer, facture, penser que, être d'avis, motif, description, croire
accountant: comptable, agent comptable, expert comptable
accumulated: accumulâtes, entassai, s'amoncela, vous amoncelâtes, nous amoncelâmes, t'amoncelas, m'amoncelai
accumulating: accumulant, entassant, s'amoncelant
accuracy: exactitude, précision, justesse
accurate: précis, ponctuel, exact
accurately: de manière précise, de façon précise

accursed: maudit
accusation: accusation, plainte, dénonciation
accuse: accuser, dénoncer, incriminer, livrer
accused: accusé, inculpé, prévenu
accuser: accusateur
accusing: accusant
accustomed: accoutumé, se 'habitua, nous 'habituâmes, me 'habituai, te 'habituas, vous 'habituâtes, habituel
ache: douleur, mal, peine, soupirer, faire mal, aspirer
achieve: accomplir, atteindre, réaliser, remplir, parvenir, assurer, confectionner, poser, aboutir, faire, construire
acknowledge: reconnaître, croire, avouer, confesser
acknowledged: reconnus
acknowledging: reconnaissant
acknowledgment: accusé de réception, reconnaissance
acquaintance: connaissance, relation, personne de connaissance, abord
acquainted: renseignai, informé
acquiesce: se résigner, acquiescer
acquiesced: acquiesçâtes
acquired: acquîmes, appris
acquiring: acquérant
acquisition: acquisition, achat, prise en charge, emplette
acquitted: acquittai
acre: acre
acted: agi, agirent, agies
active: actif, agissant, laborieux
actively: activement, de façon active, de manière active
activity: activité, occupation, vigueur, besoin d'activité
actor: acteur, comédien
actual: réel, effectif, actuel
actuate: déclencher, remuer, mouvoir, mettre en action
actuated: déclenchai, actionné
acute: aigu, perçant, intense, sagace, piquant, coupant, aigre, rude, âcre, acéré, tranchant
acuteness: intensité, acuité
adaptability: adaptabilité, faculté d'adaptation
adaptation: adaptation, transformation
adapted: adapté
add: ajouter, additionner, joindre, adjoindre, rajouter
added: ajouta, additionnas, adjoignit

addition: addition, ajout, adjonction, rajout, appendice, extension
address: adresse, destination, interpeller, aborder, allocution, discours
addressed: adressé, accessibles
addresses: adresses
addressing: adressage
adept: adepte, expérimenté, maestro, maître
adequate: adéquat, compétent, convenable, suffisant
adhere: adhérer, adhères, correspondre, coller, concorder
adherent: adhérent, adepte
adieu: adieu
adjacent: adjacent, contigu, avoisinant, limitrophe, voisin
adjoined: about it
adjoining: adjacent, attenant, contigu, aboutissant
adjourned: ajourné
adjure: adjurer
administer: administrer, appliquer, gérer
administered: administrâmes
administration: administration, gouvernement
administrator: administrateur, gestionnaire
admirable: admirable, excellent
admirably: de façon admirable, de manière admirable, admirablement
admiral: amiral
admiration: admiration
admire: admirer
admired: admirâtes
admirer: admirateur
admiring: admirant
admiringly: de façon admirative, de manière admirative
admissible: recevable, admissible
admission: admission, entrée, aveu, confession, accueil, réception, abord, accès
admit: admettre, reconnaître, avouer, confesser, laisser entrer, permettre
admitted: admîmes, admirent
admitting: admettant
admixture: mélange, mixture, additif, adjuvant, dosage
admonition: sommation, avertissement, admonestation, observation, recommandation, remontrance
adolescent: adolescent
adopt: adopter, approuver, choisir
adopted: adoptas
adopting: adoptant

adorable: adorable, séduisant
adorer: adorateur
adorned: ornas, ornâmes, ornèrent, orné, para, parèrent, paré, parâtes
adroit: adroit, habile, actif, alerte, vif, vigilant
adulterated: falsifié, adultérai
adulteress: adultère, femme adultère
advance: avance, s'approcher, promouvoir, progrès, acompte, suggérer, proposer, accélérer, inspirer, hâter
advanced: avancé, poussé
advancing: avançant
advantage: avantage, intérêt
advantageously: de façon avantageuse, de manière avantageuse
adventure: aventure, spéculation hasardée, péripétie, entreprise maritime
adventurer: aventurier
adventures: aventures
adventurous: aventureux, périlleux
adversary: antagoniste, ennemi
adversity: adversité, abaissement
advertisement: annonce, publicité, réclame
advice: conseil, avis, renseignement
advisable: recommandé, judicieux, à propos
advise: conseiller, recommander
advised: conseillé, recommandai, avisée, informé
adviser: conseiller, annonceur
advocacy: plaidoyer, art de plaider
advocate: avocat, défenseur, préconiser
afar: loin
affable: affable, aimable, gentil, amène
affair: affaire, chose, cas
affect: affecter, influer, émouvoir, toucher, émeuvent, remuer, atteindre, concerner
affectation: affectation, minauderie, afféterie
affected: affecté, maniéré, artificiel, émus, influé, émut, émûmes, ému, émurent, émûtes, touché
affecting: affectant, attendrissant, émouvant, influant
affection: affection, amour
affectionate: affectueux, tendre, attaché, dévoué, amoureux
affectionately: affectueusement, de façon affectueuse, de manière affectueuse
affirmation: affirmation, promesse
affix: affixe, attacher, fixer, apposer
affixed: apposé

affixing: apposition
afflict: affliger, désoler, attrister
afflicted: affligeas, désolèrent
affliction: affliction, chagrin, désolation
afford: produire, permettre
afforded: produisîmes
affords: produit
affront: insulter, affront, offenser
afraid: timide, peureux, effrayé
afresh: de nouveau, encore
afternoon: relevée
afterward: après, plus tard
aged: âgé, vieilli, vieux
agency: agence, organisme de renseignement
agent: agent, représentant, mandataire, intermédiaire, ustensile, outil, instrument, commissionnaire, produit
aggrandizement: accroissement, agrandissement
aghast: stupéfait, atterré
agile: agile, alerte, vif, vigilant, actif
agitated: agitèrent, débattîtes, troubla, nerveux, remuas, émurent, émûmes, émus, émut, émûtes, inquiet
agitating: agitant, débattant, troublant, émouvant, remuant
agitation: agitation, bagarre, brassage, barouf
agonized: agonisâtes, tourmentâtes
agony: agonie, angoisse, abois
agree: consentir, être d'accord, s'accorder, donner son accord, s'harmoniser, admettre, approuver, accorder, accepter
agreeable: agréable, aimable
agreeably: agréablement, de façon agréable, de manière agréable
agreed: consenti, ça va, convenu, soit
agreement: accord, convention, pacte, concordance, entente, atmosphère, réglage, arrangement, contrat
agricultural: agricole, agronomique, agrarien
aha: ah
ahead: en avant, devant, auparavant, autrefois
aid: aide, secourir, assister, adjoint
aided: assisté
aiding: aider
ailing: souffrant
aim: but, viser, visons, peiner, dessein, avoir pour but, se démener, objectif
aiming: visant, pointage, peinant, visée

air: air, mélodie, aérer, air de musique, aria, ventiler
airy: désinvolte, aéré, bien aéré
ajar: entrouvert
akin: apparenté
alacrity: enthousiasme, avidité, empressement
alarm: alarme, alerte, sirène, timbre, réveil, stupéfaction, préoccuper, consterner, avertisseur, terreur, abattement
alarmed: alarmé
alarming: alarmant, consternant
alchemy: alchimie
alcove: alcôve, niche
alert: alerte, vif, vigilant, actif
alienated: aliénèrent
alike: semblable, pareil
aliment: aliment
alive: vivant, en vie
allay: apaisent
alleged: alléguâmes, présumé, prétendu
alley: allée, ruelle
alliance: alliance, coalition
allied: allié, apparenté
allotted: attribua
allow: permettre, laisser, autoriser, admettre, accorder
allowance: allocation, indemnité, tolérance, bonification, prestation, majoration
allowed: permîmes, autorisé, admis
allude: faire allusion, insinuer
alluded: insinuâtes
alluding: insinuant
allure: attrait, séduisez, attirez
allured: séduisîmes, attiré
allusion: allusion
ally: allié
almoner: aumônier
aloft: en haut, en l'air, vol
alone: seul
along: le long de, avec, d'après
aloof: distant
aloud: à haute voix, fort, haut
altar: autel
alteration: modification, transformation, altération, changement, retouche
altercation: altercation, dispute
altered: altérai, retoucha, modifié
altogether: tout, entièrement
alumni: anciens élèves
amateur: amateur, radioamateur
amaze: étonner, stupéfier, abasourdis
amazed: étonnèrent, abasourdi
amazement: étonnement, stupéfaction, abasourdissement
ambassador: ambassadeur

ambition: ambition, souhait, aspiration
ambitious: ambitieux
amiability: amabilité, gentillesse
amiable: aimable
amicably: de façon amicale, de manière amicale
amid: parmi, au milieu de
amidst: parmi, au milieu de
amongst: parmi, entre
amount: montant, somme, quantité, nombre, total
ample: ample, large, étendu
amply: amplement, de façon ample, de manière ample
amuse: amuser, divertir, faire rire
amused: amusèrent
amusement: distraction, amusement, détente, récréation, divertissement
amusing: amusant, drôle, plaisant
amusingly: de manière amusante, de façon amusante
analogy: analogie
analysis: analyse, ventilation, composition, dépouillement, étude
anathema: anathème
anatomist: anatomiste
anatomy: anatomie
ancestor: ancêtre, ascendant
ancestral: ancestral
ancestry: ascendance
anchor: ancre, mouiller, fixer, relâcher
ancient: antique, ancien
anecdote: anecdote
anew: de nouveau, encore
angel: ange
anger: colère, courroucer, emportement, irriter, mettre en colère, rage
angler: pêcheur à la ligne
angrily: de manière fâchée, de façon fâchée
angry: fâché, en colère, irrité, furieux
anguish: angoisse
angular: anguleux, osseux
animal: animal, bête
animate: animer, encourager, vivifier
animated: animé
animates: anime
animation: animation
ankle: cheville, la cheville
annexed: annexé
annihilate: anéantir, annihiler
annihilation: annihilation
announce: annoncer, publier, introduire
announced: annonçai, affiché

announcement: annonce, avis, renseignement
announcing: annonçant, affichant
annoyance: contrariété, peine, ennui, désolation
annuity: annuité, rente
anonymous: anonyme
answer: réponse, réplique
answered: répondis
answering: répondant
antagonist: antagoniste
antechamber: antichambre
anticipated: anticipa, prévu
antidote: antidote, contrepoison
antiquated: vieilli, désuet
antiquity: antiquité
anxiety: anxiété, inquiétude, angoisse
anxious: inquiet, soucieux, agité, anxieux, impatient
anxiously: de manière inquiète, de façon inquiète
anybody: quelqu'un, un, quiconque
anyhow: de toute façon, n'importe comment
anywhere: quelque part, n'importe où
apart: particulier, à part, séparément
apartment: appartement
apathetic: apathique, indifférent
apathy: apathie, abattement
ape: singe
aperture: ouverture, orifice, trou
apologist: apologiste
apologize: s'excuser, excusez
apoplectic: apoplectique
apoplexy: apoplexie
appall: consterner, épouvanter
appalled: consternai, épouvantâtes
appalling: épouvantable, consternant, effroyable
appalls: consterne, épouvante
apparent: évident, apparent
apparently: apparemment, évidemment, de façon apparente, de manière apparente
apparition: apparition
appeal: appel, recours, faire appel, pourvoi, attrait, charme
appear: apparaître, sembler, paraître, avoir l'air de, surgir, comparaître
appearance: aspect, apparence, comparution, allure, spectacle, air
appeared: apparus, comparus
appellation: nom, surnom
appertaining: appartenant
appetite: appétit, faim
apple: pomme, la pomme
application: application, demande, requête

applied: appliquèrent, pratiqué
applies: applique, pratique, sollicite
apply: appliquer, pratiquer
appoint: nommer, désigner, appointer
appointed: nommèrent, fixé, appointâmes, attitré
appointment: nomination, rencontre
apposite: juste, à propos, approprié, pertinent
appreciate: apprécier, estimer, aimer, aimons
appreciated: appréciâtes, aimé, aimâtes, aimas, aimèrent
appreciation: appréciation, estimation
appreciator: appréciateur, estimateur
apprehended: appréhendé, craignîtes
apprehends: appréhende, craint
apprehension: appréhension, arrestation, inquiétude
apprehensive: appréhensif, inquiet, craintif
apprenticeship: apprentissage, années d'apprentissage
apprise: informer, instruire
apprising: informant
approach: approche, aborder, s'avancer, méthode, s'approcher, voie d'abord, démarche
approached: approché, rapprocha
approaching: approchant, abordant, rapprochant, s'approcher
approbation: approbation, autorisation
appropriate: convenable, approprié, raisonnable, s'approprier, juste
appropriated: approprié
appropriating: appropriant
approve: approuver, donner son accord
approvingly: de façon approuvante, de manière approuvante
appurtenance: appartenance, dépendance locative, droit accessoire, accessoires
apron: tablier, aire de trafic, crampon
apropos: à propos, opportun
apt: doué, juste, apte, enclin, intelligent
arabesque: arabesque
arbour: tonnelle
arch: arc, cintre, voûte, arche, arcade
archive: archives

ardent: ardant, ardent
ardently: ardemment, de façon ardante, de manière ardante
ardour: ardeur
arduous: ardu, pénible
arena: arène, piste
argue: se disputer, argumenter, arraisonner
argument: argument, dispute, débat, discussion
argumentative: chamailleur, chicanier, argumentatif, raisonneur
arid: aride, ingrat
aright: juste
arise: naître, nais, se soulever, surgir, se lever
aristocracy: aristocratie
aristocrat: aristocrate
aristocratic: aristocratique
arm: bras, armer, branche, accoudoir
armchair: fauteuil, de salon, chaire à bras
armed: armé, armâmes, armai
armour: armure, blinder
army: armée
arose: naquit
aroused: réveillas, éveillé
arrange: arranger, disposer, ranger, régler, ordonner, accommoder, agencer, organiser
arranged: arrangé, disposâtes, rangea, ordonnas, accommoda, agencèrent
arrangement: disposition, arrangement, agencement, classement, aménagement, construction
arranging: arrangeant, disposant, rangeant, ordonnant, agençant, accommodant
arras: arras
arrayed: rangé
arrested: arrêté
arrival: arrivée, venue, ravitaillement, fourniture
arrive: arriver, atteindre, parvenir, réussir
arrived: arrivâtes
arriving: arrivant
arrogance: arrogance
arrogate: usurper, revendiquer à tort, s'arroger, s'attribuer
arrogating: usurpant
arrow: flèche, fiche
arsenal: arsenal, dépôt
art: art
artful: astucieux, rusé, malin
artfully: de façon astucieuse, de manière astucieuse
article: article, objet, chose

artist: artiste
artistic: artistique
artless: ingénu, sans art, naïf, naturel
ascend: monter, se soulever
ascended: montai
ascending: montant, ascendant
ascent: ascension, montée, phase propulsée, remontée
ascertain: constater, vérifier
ascertained: constatai
ascetic: ascétique, ascète
asceticism: ascétisme, ascèse
ascribed: attribuèrent
ascribing: attribuant
ash: cendre, frêne
ashamed: honteux
ashen: cendreux
aside: aparté, de côté, excepté
ask: demander, poser une question, prier
asking: demandant
aslant: obliquement
asleep: endormi
aspect: aspect, allure, spectacle, apparence, air, exposition, faciès
aspersion: aspersion
aspirant: aspirant
aspiration: aspiration, souhait, dépoussiérage
aspire: aspirer
aspiring: aspirant, futur
assailant: attaquant, assaillant
assailed: assaillis
assassin: assassin
assemblage: montage, réunion
assembled: monta, assembla
assembly: assemblée, montage, ensemble, accumulation, rassemblement
assent: assentiment, affirmation, consentement, avis conforme
assented: assenties
assertion: assertion, affirmation
asset: actif, bien, acquisition, atout, avoir, élément d'actif
assignation: attribution, affectation
assigned: assignâtes, attribuâmes, adjugeas
assigns: assigne, attribue, adjuge
assist: assister, aider, aidons, secourir
assisted: assista, aida, aidé, aidâtes, aidèrent
associate: associé, s'accoupler
associated: associé
association: association, fédération, société
assortment: assortiment
assume: assumer, prendre, supposer, présumer
assumed: assumâtes, supposé

assurance: assurance, garantie
assure: assurer, certifier, garantir
assured: assura, garantîtes
astonished: étonné, stupéfait, époustoufla
astonishing: étonnant, époustouflant, surprenant
astonishingly: de façon étonnante, de manière étonnante
astonishment: étonnement, surprise
astounded: confondit, stupéfièrent, étonné
astray: égaré
astronomer: astronome
astute: astucieux, avisé, sagace
astuteness: finesse, sagacité
asylum: asile, refuge, abri
ate: mangea, bouffèrent
atheist: athée
atmosphere: atmosphère, ambiance
atonement: expiation
atrocious: atroce, horrible, affreux
attache: attaché
attached: attachâtes, apposa
attachment: attachement, saisie, annexe, accessoire
attack: attaque, assaut, accès, agression
attacking: attaquant
attain: atteindre, parvenir, acquérir, remporter, aboutir
attained: atteint, parvîntes
attaining: atteignant, parvenant
attainment: réalisation, acquisition
attempt: tentative, essai, effort, requête, démarche, se démener, peiner, attentat
attempted: essayé, attentées
attempting: essayant, attentant
attend: être présent, soigner, assister, visiter
attendance: assistance, service, présence
attendant: surveillant, serviteur, gardien, préposé
attended: assisté, soignèrent
attends: assiste, soigne
attention: attention, prévenances
attentive: attentif
attentively: attentivement, de façon attentive, de manière attentive
attested: attesta
attic: grenier, mansarde
attire: vêtir, vêtement, habit, mise
attired: vêtis
attitude: attitude, assiette, orientation
attorney: mandataire, avocat, procureur
attract: attirer, allécher, allèches, solliciter, appâter

attracted: attirai, allécha, appâtèrent
attracting: attirant, alléchant, appâtant
attraction: attraction, appât
attractive: attrayant, attirant, alléchant, affriolant, attachant, séduisant
attracts: attire, allèche, appâte
attribute: attribut, imputer, privilège, propriété, caractère qualitatif
attributed: attribué
attributing: attribuant
attuned: accordâmes, adapté
auburn: châtain roux
audacious: audacieux, hardi
audacity: audace
audible: audible, appel d'automatique, perceptible
audibly: de manière audible, de façon audible
audience: audience, assistance
augment: augmenter, accroître, agrandir, amplifier, étendre, redoubler
aunt: tante
auspiciously: de manière propice, de façon propice
austere: austère, simple
austerely: de façon austère, de manière austère
austerity: austérité
author: auteur, écrivain
authority: autorité, pouvoir, instance
authorized: autorisai
authorizing: autorisant
authorship: paternité, origine d'une œuvre littéraire, profession d'auteur, qualité d'auteur
autograph: autographe, signer
autumn: automnal, arrière, saison
auxiliary: auxiliaire, sortie auxiliaire, subsidiaire
avail: profiter, avantage
avalanche: avalanche
avarice: avarice, cupidité
avenge: venger
avenger: vengeur
avenue: avenue, allée, boulevard
averse: opposé
aversion: aversion, antipathie
averted: détourné
averting: détournant
avid: avide
avoid: éviter, parer, esquiver, s'abstenir de
avoidance: évitement, action d'éviter, dérobade, évasion
avoided: évité, esquivas
avoiding: évitant, esquivant

avow: avouer, confesser
avowal: aveu, confession
avowed: déclaré, avouâmes
await: attendre
awaited: attendîmes
awake: éveillé, réveillé
awaken: réveiller, éveiller
awakened: réveilla
award: adjuger, récompense, prix, jugement, décerner
awarded: faveur
aware: conscient, averti
awe: crainte
awful: horrible, abominable, hideux, terrible, abject, odieux
awfully: terriblement, affreusement, de façon horrible, de manière horrible
awhile: pendant quelque temps
awkward: maladroit, gênant, embarrassant
awning: tente, auvent, marquise, bâche
axe: hache, cognée
axle: axe, essieu, arbre
babble: murmure confus, babiller, bavarder
babbling: babiller, bavardant
babe: bébé
bachelor: célibataire, garçon, bachelier
backbone: épine dorsale, réseau fédérateur, dorsale, colonne vertébrale
backed: chemisé, soutenu, doublage
backgammon: trictrac, jacquet
bad: mauvais, méchant, mal
baffling: chicanage, pose de chicanes
bag: sac, poche, ensacher
bailiff: huissier, bailli
balance: solde, balance, équilibre, bilan, reliquat, reste
balancing: équilibrage, balancement
balcony: balcon, le balcon
baldness: calvitie, platitude
ball: bal, balle, bille, pelote, sphère, globe, boule
balustrade: balustrade, rampe, accoudoir
band: bande, orchestre, tranche, fanfare, troupeau, ruban, zone
bandage: bandage, pansement, emmailloter
bane: fléau, peste
bang: coup, frange, boum
banged: frappé
banish: bannir, exilent
banished: exila, bannîtes
banishment: bannissement, exil

bank: banque, rive, bord, banc, berge, talus
banker: banquier, plateau pour gâcher, établi de maçon
bankrupt: failli, banqueroutier
banner: bannière, drapeau, pavillon, banderole, étendard
banquet: banquet, festin
banter: badinage, plaisanterie
baptism: baptême
bar: bar, barre, abreuvoir, lingot, mesure
barb: barbe, ardillon, bavure
barbarous: barbare
barbed: barbelé, acéré
bard: barde
bare: nu, dénudé, mettre à nu
bared: barré
bargain: marchander, négocier, bonne affaire, affaire, occasion
bark: écorce, aboyer, barque, coque, glapir
baronet: baronnet
baronial: baronnial
barred: barrâtes, exclu, forclos
barren: stérile, aride, infertile
barrier: barrière, bar, obstacle
barrister: avocat, défenseur
basement: cave, socle, soubassement
baseness: bassesse
bashfully: de façon timide, de manière timide
basket: panier, corbeille, nacelle
bastard: bâtard, métis, roche massive, salaud, enfant naturel
bated: rabattîmes, diminua
bath: bain, baignoire, cuvette
bathed: baignèrent
battered: en pâte à frire, battu, cabossé
battle: bataille, combat, lutte
battled: lutté
bauble: babiole, marotte
bawled: braillé
bazaar: bazar, foire, marché
beak: bec
beam: poutre, faisceau, rayon, bau, barrot, balancier, ensouple, madrier, rayonner
bear: ours, endurer, souffrir, produire, subir, mettre au monde, baissier, faire naître, porter, supporter
beard: barbe, blanc, talus de pied, soie, ombrage hachuré, la barbe, brosse, bec, hachures
beardless: imberbe
bearer: porteur, support, traverse
bearing: coussinet, relèvement, palier, roulement, support
beast: bête, animal, grosse fusée

beat: battement, frapper, heurter, temps, rythme
beaten: battu, abattue
beau: dandy, galant
beautiful: beau, belle, joli, très beau
beautifully: de façon belle, de manière belle
beauty: beauté
beaver: castor, flanelle
becalmed: encalminé
becomes: devient
becoming: devenant, convenable, raisonnable
becomingly: de façon convenable, de manière convenable
bed: lit, planche, couche, banc
bedding: literie, stratification, minerai homogénéisé
bedfellow: camarade de lit
bedroom: chambre à coucher
bedside: chevet
beech: hêtre, bois de hêtre
beef: bœuf, viande bovine
beefsteak: bifteck, tranche de bœuf
befall: arrives
befell: arrivâmes
beforehand: d'avance, au préalable
beg: mendier, demander, prier, solliciter, implorer, quémander, supplier
beget: engendrer
beggar: mendiant, gueux
beggary: mendicité
begged: mendiai, quémandèrent, supplièrent
begging: mendiant, suppliant, quémandant
begin: commencer, débuter, aborder
beginning: commençant, début, inauguration
begot: engendrâmes
begotten: engendré
begun: commencé, débuté
behalf: part
behaved: comporté
beheld: vit, remarquâtes, vu, vîmes, vis, vîtes, virent, aperçûtes
behold: voici, voilà, apercevoir, voir
belie: démentir
belied: démentîtes
belief: croyance, conviction, foi
believed: crurent, crut, crus, crûtes, cru, crûmes
believing: croyant
bell: cloche, sonnette
belly: ventre, panse, abdomen
belong: appartenir, faire partie de
belonged: appartenu
belonging: appartenant, coefficient d'appartenance

beloved: aimé, cher
below: sous, dessous, en bas
bench: banc, banquette, établi, gradin
bend: courber, fléchir, coude, incliner, ployer, plier, cintrer, virage, pencher, nœud, tournant
bending: pliage, flexion, courbure, cintrage
beneath: sous, dessous
benefactor: bienfaiteur
benefactress: bienfaitrice
beneficent: bienfaisant
benefit: avantage, bénéfice, prestation, intérêt, gain, allocation, profit, indemnité
benevolence: bienveillance
benevolent: bienveillant
benevolently: de façon bienveillante, de manière bienveillante
benighted: surpris par la nuit
benign: bénin
benignly: de manière Bénine, de façon Bénine
bent: courbé, cambrai, penché, disposition
bequeath: léguer, lègues
bequeathed: léguai
bequeathing: léguant
bequest: legs, promesse de don
bereavement: deuil, perte, endeuillement
bereft: dépossédas, privé
berth: couchette, poste à quai, accoster, zone d'arrêt, lit
beseech: implorer, solliciter, supplier, adjurer
beseechingly: de façon adjurante, de manière adjurante
beset: assaillir
besetting: assaillant
beside: près de, chez, tous près de, parmi, sur, au bord de, à côté de, à
besmeared: barbouillâtes
besotted: fou
bespeak: retenez, retiens, annonçons
bespeaks: annonce, retient
bespoke: fait sur mesure
bestial: bestial
bestow: accorder, octroyer
bestowed: accordas, me octroyai, nous octroyâmes, se octroya, te octroyas, vous octroyâtes
betoken: présager
betokened: présagèrent
betray: trahir, révéler
betrayal: trahison
betrayed: trahîtes
betrayer: traître
betraying: trahissant

betrothed: se fiancé, vous fiançâtes, nous fiançâmes, me fiançai, fiancé, te fianças
bettering: renforcement
beware: attention, prendre garde, se méfier
bewildered: effarâmes, éperdu
bewilderment: égarement, ahurissement, confusion
bewitches: ensorcelle, charme
beyond: plus loin, ensuite, après, outre
bid: offre, soumission, demander, enchère, prier, tentative de prise, mise dans les enchères, annonce
bide: attendent
bigger: plus grand
bigotry: bigoterie, sectarisme
bilious: bilieux
bilk: rouler, mystifier
bill: bec, addition, note, facture, billet, projet de loi, traite, ticket, effet, proposition de loi, lettre de change
bind: attacher, lier, relier, nouer
binding: bandeau, obligatoire, reliure, liaison, contraignant, fixation
biography: biographie
biped: bipède
bird: oiseau, volaille, poisson, objet volant, l'oiseau, type
birth: naissance, accouchement, mise bas
birthday: anniversaire
biscuit: biscuit, galette, gâteau sec
bit: morceau, bit, pièce, mors, fragment, pan, mordis, taillant, bout, embout
bite: mordre, morsure, bouchée, piquer
biting: mordant, âpre, morsure
bitter: amer, âcre, acerbe
bitterly: amèrement, de manière amère, de façon amère
bitterness: amertume, âcreté
blackened: noirci, mâchurâtes
blackguard: canaille, vaurien
blackness: noirceur, obscurité
blade: lame, chaume, ailette, aube, pale
blame: blâme, reprocher, gronder, sermonner, réprimander
blaming: blâmant
blanched: blanchis, étiolé, mondèrent
bland: doucereux, doux, fade
blasphemed: blasphéma
blasphemer: blasphémateur
blaspheming: blasphémant
blast: souffle, explosion, coup de mine, faire sauter

blasted: désolé, foudroyé, grenaille
blaze: flamme, feu
blazing: en flammes, flamboyer, griffage, éclatant, étincelant, enflammé
blazoned: blasonna
bleed: saigner, purger
bleeding: saignant, hémorragie, purgeant, ressuage, dégorgement
blend: mélanger, mêler, retourner, coupage
blended: mélangé
bless: bénir
blessed: bénirent, bénîmes, bienheureux
blessing: bénissant, bénédiction
blew: souffla
blighted: rouillé
blind: aveugle, store, éblouir
blinded: ébloui, aveuglèrent
blindly: de façon aveugle, aveuglément, de manière aveugle
blissful: bienheureux, heureux
blistered: cloqué
blithe: joyeux
blithely: de façon joyeuse, de manière joyeuse
bloated: gonflé, bouffi
blocked: bloqué
blood: sang, le sang
bloodless: exsangue, pâle
bloodshed: carnage, effusion de sang, massacre
bloodthirsty: sanguinaire, avide de sang
bloom: fleur, efflorescence, bloom, pruine, floraison, bleuissement
blooming: en fleur
blossom: fleur, floraison, affleurement oxydé
blot: tache, pâté
blow: coup, souffler, bataille
blubber: graisse de baleine, lard
blue: bleu, azur
bluff: bluffer, écore
bluish: bleuâtre
blundered: embrouillai
blundering: embrouillant, gaffe, maladroit
blunt: émoussé, épointer
bluntly: de façon émoussée, de manière émoussée
bluntness: état émoussé, manque de tranchant
blush: rougir, blush, opalescence
blushed: rougi
blushing: rougissant, voile d'un film, ternissement dû à l'eau, opalescence, louchissement, formation d'un voile
boa: boa

board: planche, carte, panneau, conseil, comité, pension, monter à bord, commission, aborder
boast: fanfaronner, vanter, se vanter, faire le malin
boasted: vanté
boasting: vantardise, fanfaronnade, taille de pierres
boat: bateau, barque, canot, embarcation, navire
bode: présagent
bodily: corporel, physique
boil: bouillir, furoncle
boiled: bouilli
boiling: bouillant, ébullition, cuisson
bold: gras, audacieux, épais, gros, hardi, intrépide
boldly: de façon grasse, de manière grasse, hardiment
boldness: audace, hardiesse
bolt: boulon, verrouiller, pêne, cheville
bomb: bombe
bond: obligation, lien, liaison, cautionnement, coller, lier, bon, titres, adhérence
bonded: garanti par une obligation, lié à la masse, sous douane, encollé, cautionné, couvert par une garantie
bone: os, désosser, arête
bony: osseux, plein d'os, maigre, décharné
bookcase: bibliothèque
boon: faveur, bienfait, chènevotte
boor: goujat, malotru, rustre, abruti
boorishly: rustrement
boot: botte, coffre, amorcer, tétine
booth: cabine, baraque
booty: butin
bordered: bordé
bordering: aboutissant, bordant, bourrage, garnissage
bore: ennuyer, forer, percer, alésage, rencontrer, lasser, fatiguer, vrille, toucher, calibre
born: né
borrow: emprunter, prêter, retenue
borrowed: emprunté
borrower: emprunteur
bosom: sein, poitrine
bottle: bouteille, embouteiller, flacon
bottom: fond, derrière, cul, bas, croupe, inférieur, dessous
bough: branche, rameau
bought: acheté
bouncing: rebondissement, bondissant
bound: bond, relié, limite, lié
boundary: limite, frontière, borne

boundless: sans bornes, illimité
bounty: prime, générosité, libéralité
bouquet: bouquet
bow: arc, proue, archet, s'incliner, saluer, avant
bowed: incliné, courbé, arqué
bower: tonnelle, ancre de bossoir
bowing: déformation en arc, bombage, cintrage
box: boîte, caisse, boxer, coffret, case, boite, loge, encadré, carton, buis, bac
boy: garçon, gosse, serviteur, gamin, domestique
boyhood: enfance, adolescence
boyish: puéril, de garçon, enfantin
brace: entretoise, croisillon, parenthèse, vilebrequin, étrésillon, bras, attache, accolade, tirant
braced: contreventé
bracket: parenthèse, support, crochet, potence, mettre entre parenthèses, fourchette, étagère, console, tasseau
braided: tresse de paille
brain: cerveau, encéphale
branch: branche, succursale, filiale, spécialité, rameau, domaine, bureau, embranchement, apophyse, ramification
brand: marque, positionner, tison, établir une image de marque, estampiller
brandish: brandir, agiter
brandy: cognac, brandy
brat: gosse, morveux
bravado: bravade
brave: courageux, vaillant, brave
bravery: bravoure, courage
brawn: fromage de tête, hure
brawny: musculeux
brazen: effronté
breach: brèche, infraction, trouée, violation
bread: pain, paner
breadth: largeur, travers
break: rompre, pause, briser, casser, rupture, interruption, violer, repos, fracture, trêve, coupure
breakfast: petit déjeuner, déjeuner, le petit déjeuner
breaking: rupture, floculation, brisement, broyage, fracture
breast: poitrine, sein, mamelle, front de taille
breath: souffle, haleine, respiration, le souffle
breathe: respirer, aspirer, exhaler, murmurer
breathed: respiré

breathing: respirant, pompage, souffle, pulsation, exploitation par jaillissement intermittent, reniflage
breathless: essoufflé, hors d'haleine, haletant
breech: culasse, fesse
breeding: reproduction, élevage, surgénération
breeze: brise, souffle
brethren: frères
brevity: brièveté, concision
bribe: corrompre, soudoyer
brick: brique, brik, la brique, maçonner
bricklayer: maçon, briqueteur
brickwork: briquetage, maçonnerie
bride: fiancée, mariée, accordée
bridge: pont, passerelle, traverse, chevalet, bridge, arête
brief: court, dossier, bref, sommaire, mémoire, passager
briefly: brièvement, de manière courte, de façon courte
brier: brier
brigand: brigand
bright: clair, lumineux, luisant, brillant, magnifique, vif, éclatant
brightened: avivas, éclaircîtes, blanchi
brightening: surbrillance, avivage, azurage, brillantage, éclaircissant, polissage
brighter: plus de lumière
brightly: de façon claire, de manière claire
brightness: luminosité, éclat, brillant
brilliancy: éclat, brillance, intensité d'image
brilliant: brillant, magnifique, luisant, génial, éclatant
brim: bord, lisière
bring: apporter, amener, amènent
bringing: apportant, amenant
brings: apporte, amène
brisk: vif, actif, alerte, vigilant
briskly: de façon vive, de manière vive, vivement
bristle: soie, poil, crin
broad: large, ample
broadened: élargi
broke: fauché, cassés de fabrication
broken: cassé, brisé, rompu
bronze: bronze, airain
brood: couvée, nichée, progéniture
brooding: élevage des poussins
broom: balai, genêt, le balai
brother: frère, frangin, le frère, confrère
brotherhood: fraternité, confrérie
brought: apporta, amenèrent

brow: sourcil, front
brown: brun, marron, faire dorer, rissoler, dorer
bruised: contusionné, coupure, meurtri
brush: brosse, pinceau, balai
brushed: brossa
brushing: brossage, peignage, fibrillation, thermobrossage, balayage, application au pinceau, affleurer, levée
brutal: maussade, brutal
brute: brute, ébruter, gros projecteur, sauvage
buckle: boucle, gondolement
bucolic: bucolique, pastoral
budded: bourgeonné
buff: polir, peau de buffle, feutre à polir, buffle
buffet: buffet, bar
build: construire, bâtir, maçonner, charpenter, poser, version, édifier
building: bâtiment, construction, édifice
built: construit, édifiés
bulk: vrac, grandeur, masse, ampleur, importance, volume, taille
bullied: brutalisâmes
bullock: boeuf, bouvillon
bullying: brutalisant, intimidation
bunch: botte, bouquet, paquet, tas
bundle: paquet, ballot, faisceau, liasse, botte, mille feuilles
bungler: bousilleur, maladroit, saboteur, gâcheur
buoyancy: flottabilité, fermeté, élasticité, poussée d'Archimède
burden: fardeau, charge, alourdir, grever, lit de fusion
bureau: bureau, office
burglar: cambrioleur, voleur
burial: enterrement, obsèques, ensevelissement, enfouissement
buried: enterra, inhumas, ensevelîmes
burlesque: parodier, burlesque
burly: robuste
burn: brûler, s'allumer
burned: brûlé
burning: brûlant, combustion, cuisson
burst: crever, salve, éclater, rafale, explosion, bouffée, choc d'ionisation
bursting: éclatement, ruptage
bushy: touffu, broussailleux
busily: activement, de façon occupée, de manière occupée
bussed: transporté
bust: buste

bustle: tournure, se démener, s'affairer
busy: occupé, actif, affairé
butler: maître d'hôtel, majordome
butterfly: papillon, le papillon, butterfly, oreilles
button: bouton, bourrelet, collier, insigne syndical, manette, mouche, touche, bosse
buttoned: boutonné
buttoning: boutonnage, pose des boutons
buy: acheter, achat, acquérir
bystander: spectateur
cab: cabine, taxi
cabin: cabine, cabane, hutte, chaumière
cabriolet: cabriolet
cadge: quémander, mendie
cafe: café
cage: cage, soupape à cage, tambour perforé, foulon grillagé, encager, couvercle protecteur, corbeille à matrices, case, camp
calamity: calamité, plaie, fléau
calculate: calculer, compter, estimer, évaluer
calculated: calculâtes, compta
calculating: calculant, comptant
calculation: calcul, note, addition
calendar: calendrier, analyse, liste chronologique de documents, régestes
calf: veau, mollet
call: appel, communication, nommer, visite, escale
calling: appelant, vocation, criant, prénommant
calm: calme, tranquille, quiet, repos, rassurer, abattre, paisible, accalmie
calmly: de façon calme, de manière calme
calmness: calme, repos
canary: Canari, indicateur, mouchard, serin
cancelled: annulé
candid: franc, impartial, sincère, candide
candle: bougie, chandelle, cierge
candlestick: chandelier, bougeoir
candour: candeur, franchise, sincérité
cane: canne, roseau, bâton, jonc, rotin
canine: canin
cannon: canon, rond
canopy: baldaquin, dais, verrière, couvert
cant: incliner, équarri, moulure biseautée, flache, canter, biseauter, tors, bille dédossée, argot, dévers

canvas: canevas, toile
cap: casquette, bonnet, toque, chapeau, calotte, capsule, capuchon, coiffe, bouchon, culot, plafond
capacious: vaste
capital: capital, fonds, chapiteau, majuscule
capitalist: capitaliste
caprice: caprice
capriciously: de façon capricieuse, de manière capricieuse
captain: capitaine, commandant
captivated: captivâtes
captivating: captivant, charmer
captivity: captivité
carcass: carcasse, gros œuvre
card: carte, fiche, carde
career: carrière, parcours
careful: prudent, soigneux, attentif
carefully: soigneusement, de façon prudente, de manière prudente
careless: négligent, distrait, étourdi, insouciant
carelessly: de façon négligente, négligemment, de manière négligente
carelessness: négligence, imprudence, insouciance
caressing: tendre, caressant
caressingly: de façon tendre, de manière tendre
careworn: rongé par les soucis
cargo: cargaison, chargement, fret, facultés
caricature: caricature
caring: soin, prise en charge globale
carnal: charnel, sexuel
carpenter: charpentier, menuisier
carpet: tapis, moquette
carpeting: moquette
carriage: wagon, chariot, voiture, affût
carried: portèrent, transportèrent
carry: porter, report, transporter, retenir
carrying: portant, transportant
cart: charrette, camionner
carve: ciseler, tailler, cisèle, buriner, découper
cased: retourné
casement: croisée, châssis, vantail
cashmere: cachemire
casket: cercueil, coffret, mettre en bière
cast: fondre, moule, couler, plâtre, distribution, acteurs
caste: caste
castle: château, tour
casual: désinvolte, accidentel, informel, occasionnel

casually: de façon désinvolte, de manière désinvolte
catastrophe: catastrophe, désastre
catch: attraper, prise, prenons, saisir, capturer, s'allumer, cliquet, atteindre, parvenir, frapper
catching: attrapant, prenant, capturant, accroche, frappant
catlike: félin
caught: attrapâtes, prit, prîmes, prirent, prîtes, pris, capturas, frappai
cause: cause, faire, rendre, procurer, situer, déterminer, entraîner des conséquences, occasionner, motif
caused: causé
causing: causant
caution: prudence, avertir, alerter, précaution, attention
cautious: prudent, circonspect
cautiously: avec précaution, de façon prudente, de manière prudente
cave: grotte, caverne, creux
cavern: caverne, antre
cavity: cavité, creux, caverne
cease: cesser, s'arrêter
ceased: cessé
ceaselessly: continuellement, de façon incessante, de manière incessante
ceasing: cessant
cedar: cèdre
ceiling: plafond, tillac, vaigrage, parquet
celebrated: célébra, fêtâtes, fêté, fêtas, fêtèrent
celebrity: célébrité, star, vedette
celerity: célérité
celestial: céleste
celibacy: célibat
cell: cellule, cachot, prison, compartiment, alvéole
cement: ciment, mastic, souder, liant, dissolution, conglutiner, coller, cémenter, adhésif, scellement
cemented: cimenté
censured: censuré
cent: cent
centred: centré
century: siècle
ceremony: cérémonie
certainly: certainement, sûrement, assurément, si, d'abord, de façon certaine, de manière certaine
certainty: certitude, assurance
chafe: frictionner, irriter, raguer, s'irriter, user
chagrin: chagrin, contrariété
chain: chaîne, enchaîner
chained: enchaîné
chair: chaise, siège, fauteuil
chaise: cabriolet, calèche
chalice: calice
chalk: craie, poudrer, pierre calcaire, partir en poudre blanche, marquer à la craie, fariner, chaux, calcaire, favori
chamber: chambre, salle, pièce, local
champion: champion
chance: hasard, chance, accidentel, occasion
chandelier: lustre
changed: changé
changing: changeant, modification
channel: canal, chenal, tube, voie, tuyau, chaîne, la Manche, conduit, rigole, radiocanal
chap: individu, gercer, type, gerçure
chapter: chapitre, section, direction
character: caractère, personnage, signe, nature, témoignage, tempérament
characteristic: caractéristique, typique, qualité, démographique
characterize: caractériser, décrire
characterized: caractérisai
characterizes: caractérise
characterizing: caractérisant
charge: charger, accusation, plainte, taxe, imputation, chef d'accusation
charged: chargé, saturé de fumée et de gaz, alimenté, défoncé, électrisé
chariot: char
charitable: indulgent, sensible
charity: charité, bienfaisance, aumône, compassion
charlatan: charlatan
charm: charme, amulette, ravir, breloque
charmed: charmé
charming: charmant, ravissant, gentil, mignon
charter: charte, affrètement
chase: chasser, pourchasser, pousser, faire avancer
chased: chassé, ciselé
chasing: ciselure, chassant, filetage au peigne
chasm: abîme, gouffre
chastened: châtièrent
chastised: châtia
chat: bavarder, causerie, babiller, conversation
chattel: biens meubles
cheap: bon marché, abordable
cheaply: de manière bon marchée, à bon marché, de façon bon marchée
cheated: déçu, triché
cheating: tricherie, escroquerie, fraude, tromperie
check: chèque, vérifier, contrôle, réprimer, surveiller, retenir, enrayer, bride, examiner, enregistrer, cocher
checked: quadrillé, à carreaux
checkered: tacheté de points en damier
cheek: joue, chape, la joue
cheer: acclamation, applaudir
cheerful: gai, joyeux
cheerfully: de manière gaie, de façon gaie
cheerfulness: gaieté, bonne humeur
cheerily: de façon gaie, de manière gaie
cheering: ovations
cheerless: morne
chemical: chimique, produit chimique
chemist: chimiste, pharmacien, apothicaire
chemistry: chimie, composition chimique, produit de traitement
cherished: chérîmes
chest: poitrine, coffre, caisse, sein, commode, bac, bahut
chide: réprimander, gronder
chief: chef, principal, dominant
chiefly: principalement, surtout, particulièrement, de façon chef, de manière chef
childhood: enfance
childish: enfantin, puéril
childishness: enfantillage
childless: sans enfant
childlike: enfantin
chill: froid, trempe, refroidir
chilled: frappé, refroidi
chilling: refroidissement brusque, chilling, trempe, givrage, réfrigération
chime: carillon, peigne
chimera: chimère
chimney: cheminée, évent
chin: menton, le menton, houppe du menton
chink: fente, crevasse, crique, fissure, lézarde, tapure
chintz: chintz
chipped: ébréché, écaillé, égrisé, émoussé
chivalrous: chevaleresque, galant
chivalry: chevalerie
choice: choix, réponse, sélection, option, assortiment, de choix, élection
choked: étouffé, étranglé, choké
choking: étranglement des gaz, obstruction, engorgement

choleric: cholérique, colérique
chop: hacher, côtelette, tailler, clapot, couper
choral: chorale
chord: corde, accord
chorus: chœur, chorale
chose: choisirent, optèrent, opta, optâmes
chosen: choisi, élu, opté
christened: baptisâmes
christening: baptême
chronic: chronique
chronicle: chronique
chuckle: glousser
churlish: grossier
churlishly: de façon grossière, de manière grossière
cicerone: cicérone
cigar: cigare
cinder: cendre, escarbille, scories
cipher: chiffre, zéro
circle: cercle, rond, encercler
circlet: cercle
circling: coupage circulaire
circuit: circuit, maille
circulated: circulé, dégorgeai
circumstance: circonstance, état de fait
citadel: citadelle
citizen: citoyen, habitant
civil: civil
civility: civilité
civilized: civilisé, poli, cultivé
claim: créance, revendication, réclamer, demande, requérir, exiger
claimed: réclamé, arrogeâmes
clamber: grimper
clambered: grimpâtes
clamorous: bruyant
clamour: clameur
clandestine: clandestin
clandestinely: de façon clandestine, de manière clandestine
clap: claquer, applaudir
clapped: claqua
clapping: claquage, physiothérapie respiratoire, applaudir
claret: vin de Bordeaux, bordeaux
clasp: agrafe, fermoir
classical: classique
clatter: cliquetis, bavarder, bruit
clause: clause, disposition, proposition, stipulation
clay: argile, colloïde minéral, glaise, terre glaise
clean: propre, pur, purifier, nettoyer, affiner, laver, ramoner, net
cleaned: purifièrent, nettoya
cleaning: nettoyage, purifiant, épuration, dégagement

cleanliness: propreté, netteté
cleanly: de façon propre, de manière propre, proprement
clearer: purgeur, nettoyeur
clearing: clairière, défrichement, dégagement, éclaircie
clearly: clairement, de façon claire, de manière claire, nettement
clearness: clarté, limpidité, netteté
cleave: fendre, cliver, se fendre
clenched: rivé
clergyman: prêtre, abbé, curé, ecclésiastique, pasteur
clergymen: ecclésiastique
clerk: commis, greffier
clever: habile, adroit, astucieux, rusé, malin, intelligent, artificieux
clew: point d'écoute
click: claquement, clic, déclic, cliquer
client: client, acheteur, acquéreur
climate: Climat
climb: grimper, gravir, monter
clinch: river, accrochage, coussin de jante, étalingure
cling: adhérez, vous cramponnez, te cramponnes, se cramponnent, s'accrocher, nous cramponnons, me crampone, adhères, cramponner
clinging: se cramponnant, adhérant, collant
cloak: manteau
clock: horloge, pendule, générateur de rythme
clod: boule, motte
clog: boucher, sabot, obstruer, entrave, raccommoder
close: fermer, proche, près, auprès, intime
closed: fermas, clos
closely: étroitement, attentivement
closeness: proximité, efficacité dans l'estimation, compacité
closer: clausoir, clé de voûte, dispositif de fermeture, piqueur
closet: armoire, placard
closing: fermant, clôture, enclenchement
cloth: tissu, étoffe, linge, toile, chiffon
clothe: vêtir, vêtent, vêts, vêtons, habiller, revêtir
cloud: nuage, brouiller, rendre trouble
clove: clou de girofle, fendîtes, clivâmes, girofle
clover: trèfle
club: club, trèfle
clumsiness: maladresse, gaucherie
clustered: en grappe
clutched: agriffa, saisi

coach: entraîneur, wagon, coach, autocar, voiture, répétiteur
coachman: cocher
coarse: grossier, vulgaire, rude, rustique, brut
coat: manteau, enduire, pardessus, capote, paletot, couche, napper, pelage, enrober
coax: cajoler, amadouer
coaxed: cajolai
coaxing: cajolerie, câlin
coffer: plafonnier encastré, coffre
coffin: cercueil, château, lacune
coherence: cohérence
coherent: cohérent
coil: bobine, serpentin, rouleau, enroulement
coiled: couronne
coin: pièce de monnaie, dresser, monnaie
coincidence: coïncidence
cold: froid, rhume
coldly: froidement, de façon froide, de manière froide
coldness: froideur
colic: colique
collar: col, collier, bague
collateral: collatéral, nantissement, garantie
collect: recueillir, rassembler, collectionner, ramasser, assembler, encaisser
collected: recueillîtes, rassemblâmes, collectionnèrent, ramassâmes
collection: collection, recueil, recouvrement, encaissement, ensemble, troupe, ramassage, quête, are, bande
college: collège, université
colonnade: colonnade
colony: colonie, possession
color: couleur, colorer
colossal: énorme, formidable, immense
colour: couleur, teinte, colorier
coloured: coloré
colouring: coloration, prétannage, teinture, encrage
colourless: incolore, sans couleur
column: colonne, pilier, rubrique, file, montant, chronique
coma: coma, comète
comb: peigne, crête, rayon
combination: combinaison, couplage, complexe, coalition, agrégat, assemblage
combined: combiné
comely: beau, avenant
comer: arrivant
comfort: confort, consoler, réconfort

comfortable: confortable, douillet, commode, à l'aise
comfortably: agréablement, confortablement, de façon confortable, de manière confortable
comforted: soulagé
comforter: aspirateur, soucette, consolateur
comforting: réconfortant, consolant
comic: comique, drôle
coming: venant, approche, venir, prochain, futur
command: commande, ordre, ordonner, enjoindre, sommer, instruction
commander: commandant, capitaine de frégate
commanding: commandant, dominant, ordonner
commemorated: commémorèrent
commence: commencer, débuter, aborder
commenced: commenças
commencement: début, commencement, inauguration
commencing: commençant
commensurate: proportionné
comment: commentaire, observation
commerce: commerce, négoce, affaires
commercial: commercial, annonce publicitaire, film publicitaire, message publicitaire, spot publicitaire, vocation
commiseration: commisération
commission: commission, groupe de travail, mandat
commit: commettre, engager, validation
committed: commîtes, engagé
commodious: spacieux
commodity: denrée, marchandise, produit, article
common: commun, ordinaire, vulgaire
commonly: de façon commune, de manière commune
commonplace: banal, trivial
commune: communauté
communicate: communiquer, transmettre
communicated: communiquâtes
communicates: communique
communicating: communiquant
communication: communication, renseignement
companion: compagnon, camarade, accompagnateur
companionship: compagnie, équipe, camaraderie

comparable: comparable
comparatively: comparativement, de façon comparative, de manière comparative
compare: comparer, conférer
compared: comparâmes
comparing: comparant
compartment: compartiment, spécialité, case, domaine
compassion: compassion, pitié, apitoiement
compassionate: compatissant
compel: obliger, imposer, contraindre, astreindre
compelled: obligeas, astreintes
compensated: compensa, récompensas
compensation: compensation, indemnisation, dédommagement, rémunération, réparation civile
competence: compétence, capacité, attributions
competitor: concurrent, compétiteur
compiled: compila, dressas
complacent: complaisant
complain: se plaindre, porter plainte, plaindre
complaint: réclamation, accusation
complaisance: complaisance
complement: complément
complete: complet, entier, remplir, finir, parfaire
completed: complété, achevé, terminé
complexion: teint, complexion
complexity: complexité, degré de complexité
compliance: conformité, souplesse, acquiescement, élasticité
complicated: compliquèrent, embrouillé, tarabiscoté
compliment: compliment, féliciter, flatterie
complimented: complimenté
compose: composer, écrire
composed: composa, tranquille, calme
composing: composant, montage
composition: composition, arrangement
composure: repos, calme, impassibilité
compound: composé, combiné, mot composé
comprehend: comprendre
comprehended: comprîmes
comprehending: comprenant
comprehension: compréhension
compress: comprimer, condenser
compressed: comprimé
compressing: comprimant

compression: compression, écrasement
compromise: compromis, transiger
compunction: componction, remords
comrade: camarade
conceal: cacher, dissimuler, celer, masquer
concealed: cachas, dissimulèrent
concealment: dissimulation, recel, réticence
conceals: cache, dissimule
concede: concéder
conceded: concédé
conceit: vanité, prétention
conceited: vaniteux, vain, frivole, suffisant
conceive: concevoir, conçois
conceived: conçurent
conceives: conçoit
concentrate: concentrer, aliment concentrée, se concentrer
concentration: concentration
conception: conception, élaboration
concern: souci, concerner, regarder, intéresser, soin, inquiétude, être en relation avec, importance, préoccupation
concerned: concerné, intéressé
concert: concert
concession: concession, acte de concession
conciliate: concilier, réconcilier
conciliated: concilié
conciliatory: conciliant
conclude: conclure, terminer
concluded: conclûmes, clôturé
concluding: concluant, final, clôturant
conclusion: conclusion, résultat
conclusive: concluant, décisif, convaincant
concord: accord, concorde
concurrence: accord, concordance, convention, entente
condemn: condamner, repousser
condemnation: condamnation
condemned: condamnèrent, réprouvèrent, dangereuse
condescend: condescendre, daignent
condescended: condescendîmes, daignâmes
condescends: condescend, daigne
condescension: condescendance
condition: condition, état, situation, manière d'être
condolence: condoléances
conduct: conduire, guider, mener, diriger, aboutir, procédé, régler
conducted: conduite, amenée, mené
confederate: confédéré

confer: conférer
conference: conférence, séance, association, colloque, congrès
conferred: conférâtes
confess: confesser, avouer, reconnaître
confessed: confessas, avoué
confessedly: de manière confessâmes
confession: confession, aveu
confidant: confident
confidante: confident
confide: confier
confided: confié
confidence: confiance, foi
confident: confiant, assuré
confidently: de manière confiante, de façon confiante
confiding: confiant
confine: limiter, confinent
confined: confiné, enfermé, accouchâmes
confinement: réclusion, internement, détention, emprisonnement
confirm: confirmer, ratifier
confirmed: confirmâtes
conflict: conflit, combat
conform: conformer, correspondre, concorder
conformity: conformité
confound: confondre, déconcerter
confounded: confondu, déconcertâmes
confronted: affrontèrent, confrontâtes
confused: confondîtes, embrouillèrent
confusedly: de manière confuse, de façon confuse
confusion: confusion, désordre, affolement
congenial: convenable, sympathique
congestion: congestion, encombrement, afflux de sang, embouteillage
congratulated: félicitèrent, congratulé, complimentèrent
congratulation: félicitation
congregation: congrégation, rassemblement
conjecture: conjecturer, prévoir, se douter de
conjugal: conjugal
conjured: conjura, escamotèrent
conjurer: conjurateur, illusionniste, prestidigitateur
connect: connecter, joindre, relier, réunir, brancher, allier, aboucher, attacher, raccorder, nouer, associer

connected: connecta, cohérent, raccordé, brancha, abouchâtes, allié, nouâmes, nouas, noué, nouèrent
connection: connexion, raccord, liaison, ligue, chaîne de connexion, rapport, branchement, relation, réunion, jonction, communication
connoisseur: connaisseur
conquer: conquérir, vaincre
conquered: conquîtes
conqueror: conquérant, vainqueur
conquest: conquête
conscience: conscience
conscientiously: de façon consciencieuse, de manière consciencieuse
conscious: conscient
consciousness: conscience, connaissance
consent: consentement, admettre, donner son accord, être d'accord, agrément
consented: consenti, acquiesçâmes
consequence: conséquence, répercussion, suite, aboutissement
conserved: préservé
consider: considérer, contempler, regarder, envisager
considerable: considérable, imposant, majeur
considerably: considérablement, de façon considérable, de manière considérable
consideration: considération, rémunération, provision, étude, délibération, cause, contrepartie
considered: considérâtes, envisagé
considering: considérant, envisageant, étant donné
considers: considère, envisage
consign: consigner, expédier
consigned: consigné
consigning: consignant
consist: consister, composition de traction, bulletin de composition, avis de composition, rame
consistent: cohérent, logique
consisting: consistant
consolation: consolation
console: consoler, pupitre de commande
consoled: consolé
conspicuous: visible, apparent
conspiracy: conspiration, complot, association de malfaiteurs
conspirator: conspirateur, comploteur
constant: constant, continuel, permanent, invariable, perpétuel

constantly: constamment, continuellement, de façon constante, de manière constante
consternation: abattement, consternation, stupéfaction, abasourdissement
constituency: circonscription, électeurs
constitute: constituer
constituted: constitué
constitutes: constitue
constituting: constituant
constitution: constitution, classement, loi fondamentale, statuts, structure d'une forêt
constitutional: constitutionnel
constitutionally: de façon constitutionnelle, de manière constitutionnelle
constrain: contraindre, forcez, forçons
constrained: contraint, forçâtes, gêné, forcé
constraint: contrainte, gêne, restriction
construct: bâtir, construire, poser
construes: analyse
consult: consulter
consulted: consultai
consulting: consultant
consume: consommer, dévorer
consuming: consommant
consummate: consommé
consummation: consommation, perfection
consumption: consommation, phtisie
contact: contact, s'aboucher avec
contagion: contagion
contagious: contagieux
contain: contenir, renfermer
contained: continrent, renfermas
containing: contenant, renfermant
contamination: contamination, interférence d'images, pollution, impureté, infection
contemplate: contempler, envisager, méditer
contemplated: contemplâtes
contemplating: contemplant
contemplation: contemplation, méditation, recueillement
contemplative: contemplatif
contemporaneously: de manière contemporaine, de façon contemporaine
contemporary: contemporain
contempt: mépris, désobéissance, dédain
contemptuous: dédaigneux, méprisant

contended: contestés, disputa, combattîmes
contending: contestant, combattant, disputant
content: contenu, satisfait
contented: content, satisfait
contest: concours, contester, disputer
contested: contesté
contiguous: contigu
contingency: contingence, éventualité, imprévu
continue: continuer, durer, durons, reconduire, maintenir, prolonger
continued: continuai, duras, durèrent, durâtes, duré
continuing: continuant, durant
continuous: continu, permanent
contour: contour, courbe de niveau
contracted: contracté
contracting: contractant, conclusion de marché, passage de contrat
contraction: contraction, retrait, endognathie, striction, étranglement, raccours, resserrement
contractor: entrepreneur, façonnier, maître des travaux, contrôleur délégué, prestataire
contradict: contredire, démentir
contradiction: contradiction
contradictory: contradictoire, opposé
contrary: opposé, contraire
contrast: contraste, mettre en contraste, opposition, antithèse, réglage du contraste
contrasted: contrasté
contributed: contribuâmes, te cotisas, se cotisé, vous cotisâtes, me cotisai, nous cotisâmes
contrivance: invention, ingéniosité, dispositif
contrive: inventer
contrived: inventâmes
convenience: convenance, commodité
convenient: commode, convenable, opportun
conveniently: de façon commode, de manière commode
conventional: classique, conventionnel, traditionnel
conversation: conversation, discussion, entretien
converse: converser, intervenir
conversed: conversé
conversing: conversant
conversion: conversion, transformation
convert: convertir, transformer

convey: transmettre, véhiculez, acheminent, communiquer
conveyance: moyen de transport, transport, acte de cession
conveyed: transmîtes, véhicula, acheminai
conveying: acheminant, transmettant, véhiculant
convict: détenu, bagnard, prisonnier, condamné
convicted: condamné
conviction: conviction, condamnation
convince: convaincre, persuader
convinced: convainquîtes
conviviality: convivialité
convulsed: convulsionna, bouleversé
convulsion: convulsion, bouleversement
convulsive: convulsif, spasmodique
convulsively: de façon convulsive, de manière convulsive
cool: refroidir, frais, froid
cooling: refroidissement, rafraîchissement
coolly: de façon refroidissante, froidement
copied: copié
copious: abondant, copieux
copper: cuivre, de cuivre, le cuivre
copse: taillis
copy: copier, exemplaire, reproduire, imiter
copying: copie, duplication
coquetry: coquetterie
coquette: coquette
coral: corail, de corail
cord: corde, câble, fil
cordial: cordial, chaleureux
cordiality: cordialité
cordially: cordialement, de manière cordiale, de façon cordiale
corduroy: velours côtelé, ondulations transversales
core: noyau, coeur, âme, centre, trognon, carotte, mandrin, tore
corked: bouché
corn: maïs, cor, grain, blé
corner: coin, accaparer, monopoliser, corner, angle
cornice: corniche, bandeau
coronation: couronnement
coronet: couronne
corpse: cadavre, corps
correct: corriger, rectifier, juste, exact, redresser
corrected: corrigé
correctness: exactitude, rectitude
correspond: correspondre
corresponded: correspondîmes

correspondence: correspondance
correspondent: correspondant, chroniqueur
corresponding: correspondant
corridor: couloir, corridor
corrupt: corrompu, pervertissons, altérer
corrupted: pervertis, corrompu, altéré
corrupter: corrupteur
corruptibility: corruptibilité
corruption: corruption
cost: coût, dépense, prix de revient
costly: coûteux, cher
cottage: cabanon, chaumière, petite maison
couch: canapé, divan, presse coucheuse
cough: toux, tousser
coughed: toussé
coughing: toussant, toux
counsel: conseil, avis, avocat, défenseur
counsellor: conseiller, guide
count: compter, comte, calculer, coup, chef d'accusation
counted: compté
countenance: encourager, figure, mine, visage
counter: compteur, guichet, voûte, contrefort
counterfeit: contrefaçon, faux
counterpoise: contrepoids, balancier
counting: comptage, dénombrement
countless: incalculable, innombrable
county: comté, circonscription électorale
couple: couple, accoupler, mari et femme, époux, apparier, atteler, embrayer
courage: courage, abattage
course: cours, route, plat, parcours, direction, leçon, piste, trivial, met, trajet, rangée
courted: briguées
courteous: courtois, poli
courtesy: courtoisie, affabilité, politesse
courtier: courtisan
courting: briguant
courtly: courtois
courtship: cour, balz
cousin: cousin
covered: couvert, revêtu, bâché, guipé
covering: revêtement, couverture, habillage, saillie, recouvrement, housse

covert: couvert, voilé, caché, implicite, invisible
covet: convoites
coveted: convoitèrent
covetous: avide
covetousness: avidité
coward: lâche, peureux, couard, poltron
cowardice: lâcheté, faiblesse
coyness: coquetterie
crack: fissure, craquer, fente, fêlure, crevasse, crack, crique, fêler, gercer, gerçure
cracked: fêlé, craqué, criqué, fendu, timbré, toqué, cassé
cracking: fissuration, craquage, concassage, fendillement
cradle: berceau, arceau, nacelle, cerceau
craft: métier, embarcation, engin, artisanat
crafty: astucieux, malin, rusé
crash: krach, fracas, s'écraser, accident
cravat: foulard, cravate
crave: sollicitons
craven: lâche, poltron
craving: désir ardent, envie, sollicitant
crawl: ramper, crawl
crawled: rampé
crawling: rampage, rétraction, refus à l'application, retrait, retirement d'émail, reptation
creak: grincer, craquer
creaked: grincé, craquai
creaking: grinçant, craquant
create: créer, créons, écrire, composer
created: créas, créâtes, créèrent, créé
creates: crée
creating: créant
creation: création, établissement, constitution
creator: créateur
creature: créature
credential: lettre de créance, recommandations, pouvoir
credible: croyable
credit: crédit, avoir, approvisionner, accréditif, honneur, unité, virer
creditable: honorable, estimable
credited: crédité
creditor: créancier, créditeur
credulity: crédulité
credulous: crédule
credulously: de façon crédule, de manière crédule
creed: credo, foi
creep: ramper, fluage, glissement, traîner

creeping: rampant, traînant, usure du presseur, reptation de talus, fluent, fluage, débordement de l'application, contraction, boursouflement du sol, cheminant, glissant
crept: rampé, cheminâmes, traîna, glissé
crest: crête, sommet
crevice: crevasse, fente, fissure
crew: équipage, personnel navigant
crib: berceau, lit d'enfant, copier, crèche, prise d'eau, mangeoire, encoffrement, cage, bûcher
cricket: grillon, cricket
cried: pleuré
crime: crime, délit, infraction
criminal: criminel, malfaiteur
cringe: reculer
cripple: estropié, paralyser
crippled: infirme, estropié
crisis: crise
critic: critique, censeur
critical: critique
criticism: critique
crooked: tordu, de travers
crop: récolte, jabot, rogner, couper, lot de gemmage
crossed: croisé, traversés, décussé, barré
crossing: croisement, traversée, intersection
crotchet: noire
crowd: foule, masse, amas, multitude, tas, cohue
crowded: bondé, encombré
crown: couronne, sommet, cime, sacrer, voûte
crowned: couronné
crowning: bombé longitudinal, capsulage, couronnement
crucible: creuset
cruel: cruel, atroce, méchant
cruelty: cruauté, sévices
crumbled: froissa, émietta
crumpet: crumpet
crumpled: froissé, chiffonné, fripé
crush: piler, écraser, briser, broyer, foule, réduire en miettes, fracasser, presse, aplatir
crushed: écrasé, broyé, accablé
crushing: écrasement, broyage, concassage
crust: croûte, abaisse
crutch: béquille, fourche, soutien
cry: pleurer, cri, vagir, crier
crypt: crypte
crystal: cristal, quartz
cuff: manchette, poignet, ballonnet, revers
culprit: coupable
cultivate: cultiver, fidéliser

cultivated: cultiva
cultivates: cultive
cultivation: culture, façons culturales, fidélisation
culture: culture, faire une culture, civilisation
cunning: rusé, malin, astucieux, ruse, artificieux, rouerie, sournois
cunningly: de façon rusée, de manière rusée
cup: tasse, coupe, godet
cupidity: cupidité
cupola: coupole, cubilot, dôme
curbed: bridai
cure: guérir, traitement, remédier, assainir, soigner, cure, cuisson, vulcanisation, durcissement d'un adhésif, prise
cured: guéri, maturé
curiosity: curiosité
curious: curieux, intéressant, singulier
curiously: de manière curieuse, avec curiosité, de façon curieuse
curl: boucle, friser, rotationnel, coiffer, faire tournoyer, battre, roulage, gode, fourche
curled: bouclé, frisé
curly: bouclé, frisé
current: courant, en cours
curse: maudire, malédiction, blasphémer
cursed: maudit
curt: brusque, sec
curtain: rideau, pont fixe, feston, courtine
curve: courbe, virage, cintre, se courber
curved: courbe, arqué, cintré, incurvé
cushion: coussin, gomme de liaison, amortir, matelas de vapeur dans un cylindre, élément d'émission élastique, carreau
custody: garde, détention
custom: coutume, habitude, usage
customary: habituel, accoutumé, coutumier
customer: client, abonné, acheteur, chaland
cut: couper, tailler, trancher, hacher, balafre, découper, tondre, faucher, réduction, entaille, incision
cutter: coupeur, tailleur, cotre
cycle: cycle, bicyclette, vélo, bécane, manœuvrer
cynic: cynique
cynicism: cynisme
dabbled: mouillâtes, barboté
dagger: poignard, dague

daily: quotidien, journellement, tous les jours, chaque jour
daintily: de façon délicate, de manière délicate
dainty: délicat, tendre, aimable
damask: damas
dame: demoiselle noble, dame
damn: damner, condamner
damned: damné, maudit
damning: damnant, condamner
damp: humide, amortir, mouiller
damsel: demoiselle
dance: danse, bal
danced: dansé
dancer: danseur
dancing: dansant, bouillement
dandy: chouette, dandy
danger: danger, péril
dangerous: dangereux, périlleux, redoutable
dangerously: de façon dangereuse, de manière dangereuse, dangereusement
dare: oser, ose, osez, aventurer, oses, osons, osent, défi
dared: osa, osèrent, osé, osâtes, osas, osâmes, osai, aventurèrent
daring: audace, hardi, osant, aventurant
dark: foncé, sombre, obscur, noir
darkened: fonça, foncé, assombris
darkening: fonçant, noircissement, assombrissant
darkly: de façon foncée, de manière foncée
darkness: obscurité, ténèbres
darling: chéri, favori, charmant
dart: dard, fléchette
dash: tiret, trait
date: date, datte, rencontre
daughter: fille, la fille
daunt: intimide, découragez
daunted: découragea, intimidai
dawn: aube, aurore, point du jour
daybreak: aube, aurore, point du jour
daydream: rêve, songer, rêvasser
daylight: lumière du jour, passage sous presse, ouverture entre plateaux d'une presse, intervalle, jour
daytime: journée
dazzle: aveugler, éblouissement
dazzling: éblouir, éclatant
dazzlingly: de façon éclatante, de manière éclatante
dead: mort, perdue, tension, stérile, sourd, sans tension, hors tension, inactif, fibres mortes par suite d'un raffinage excessif, claqué, peau de qualité inférieure
deadliest: le plus mortel

deadly: mortel, meurtrier, de façon morte, de manière morte
deaf: sourd
deal: distribuer, dispenser, traiter, affaire, transaction, bois blanc
dealing: négociation, tractation, traiter, transaction
dealt: opéré
dear: cher, coûteux
dearly: de manière chère, de façon chère
deathbed: lit de mort
debarred: exclut, interdit
debased: abâtardis, avilîtes
debate: débat, discussion
debating: débattant
debauch: faire la noce, bamboucher
debauchery: noce, débauche
debility: débilité, asthénie
debt: dette, créance, endettement
decanter: carafe, décanteuse, bassin décanteur
decay: abaissement, pourriture, déclin, désastre, décomposition, se délabrer, carie
decayed: délabra, caduc, infirme, vieux, carié, pourri
decease: décès, décéder
deceased: décédé, défunt
deceit: duperie, tromperie
deceitful: trompeur, dolosif, fourbe, mensonger
deceive: tromper, tricher, décevoir
deceived: trompâtes, déçu, trichâmes
deceiver: trompeur
deceives: trompe, triche
decent: convenable, décent, honnête
decide: décider, juge
decided: décidai, incontestable, résolu, jugèrent, jugeâtes, jugé
deciding: décidant, jugeant
decipher: déchiffrer, décrypte
deciphering: déchiffrant, décryptant
decision: décision, arrêt, résolution
declare: déclarer, proclamer
declared: déclarâtes
decline: déclin, diminuer, baisse, refuser, dépérir, régression
declined: déclina, dépéri
declining: déclinant, dépérissant
decorated: décora, agrémenté
decorous: bienséant
decorum: décorum, bienséance
decoy: attirer, leurre, appât
decreed: décrété
decrepitude: décrépitude
deducting: prélevant, défalquant, décomptant

deduction: déduction, décompte, défalcation, prélèvement
deed: acte, action
deem: croire, être d'avis, croyez, penser que, regarder
deemed: crurent, crûtes, crus, crûmes, cru, crut, réputé
deep: profond, foncé, fosse, grave, mouille
deepen: approfondir, foncer, rembrunissons, épaissir, devenir plus profond, creuser
deepened: approfondirent, rembrunîtes
deeper: plusieurs traductions selon le contexte
deepest: le plus profond
deeply: profondément, de façon profonde, de manière profonde
deer: cerf, chevreuil
default: par défaut, défaut
defeat: défaite, vaincre, abattre, surmonter
defeated: vaincu, battu
defeating: vainquant
defect: défaut, malfaçon, tare, imperfection, anomalie
defence: défense, mémoire en défense
defend: défendre, contester, protéger, soutenir
defer: différer, reporter
deference: déférence, ajournement
deferential: respectueux, déférent
deferred: différé
defiance: défi
deficiency: déficience, carence, insuffisance, manque, défaut
deficit: déficit, impasse, insuffisance, manque, pénurie, découvert
defied: provoqué, défié
defile: col, violer, défilé
defilement: souillure, profanation
defined: défini, précisèrent
defines: définit, précise
definite: définitif, ferme
defrauded: fraudai, escroqua
defray: paies, payer, remboursons, payons, défraie
defunct: défunt, décédé
defy: défier, provoquer
defying: défiant, provoquant
degradation: dégradation, déchéance, surcreusement
degrade: dégrader, avilir
degraded: dégrada, avilit
degrading: dégradant, avilissant
degree: degré, grade, titre, intitulé, diplôme, rang
deigned: daigné, condescendu
deigning: condescendant, daignant

deity: divinité, déité, dieu
dejected: abattu, déprimé, découragé
dejection: abattement, découragement, mélancolie
delay: retard, délai, différer, ajourner, renvoyer, reculer, suspendre, sursis
delayed: retardé, différé
delegated: délégué
deliberate: délibéré, intentionnel
deliberately: exprès, délibérément, de manière délibérée, de façon délibérée
deliberation: délibération
delicacy: friandise, délicatesse, finesse
delicate: délicat, tendre, fragile
delicately: de manière délicate, de façon délicate
delicious: délicieux, savoureux
delight: délice, enchanter, ravir, plaisir
delighted: enchanté, ravi
delightedly: de façon enchantée, de manière enchantée
delightful: délicieux, ravissant, superbe, charmant
delineation: tracé, délimitation, profil
delirious: délirant
delirium: délire, transport
deliver: livrer, fournir, délivrer
delivered: livrâtes, rendu destination, délivrai
delivering: livrant, délivrant
delivery: livraison, remise, transmission, accouchement, distribution, délivrance
dell: vallon
deluge: déluge, inondation
demand: demande, exiger, revendication, abattement, puissance
demanded: exigé
demarcation: démarcation, bornage
democracy: démocratie
demon: démon
demoniac: démoniaque
demurely: de manière modeste, de façon modeste
demureness: modestie
den: nid, repaire
denial: démenti, déni, refus, dénégation
denied: nié, nia, niai, niâmes, nias, niâtes, nièrent
denizen: habitant
denote: indiquer, dénoter
denoted: indiquâtes
denouement: dénouement
denounced: dénonças

denouncer: dénonciateur
denouncing: dénonçant
dense: dense, compact
denunciation: dénonciation
deny: nier, niez, nie, nient, nies, nions, renier, démentir
depart: partir, pars, s'en aller
departed: partîmes
departure: départ, disparition
depend: dépendre, compter sur
dependant: personne à charge
depended: dépendirent
dependent: dépendant, personne à charge, subordonné, charge de famille
depict: peindre, dépeindre, représenter, peignons
depicted: peignîmes, dépeignirent, peint
deplorable: déplorable, lamentable
deposed: destituai, déposâtes
deposing: déposant, destituant
deposit: déposer, dépôt, arrhes, gisement, consigne, acompte, cautionnement
deposited: déposé
depository: dépôt, établissement de dépôt, réceptacle de dépôt
deprecate: désapprouver
deprecates: désapprouve
deprived: privai, dépouilla
deprives: prive, dépouille
depth: profondeur, intensité, creux
depute: députes
deputed: députas
deranged: dérangé
derision: dérision
derived: dérivâtes
descend: descendre, baisser, s'abaisser
descendant: descendant
descended: descendu, issu
descending: descendant, décroissant
descent: descente, origine
describe: décrire, représenter, dépeindre
described: décrivirent
describes: décrit
description: description, signalement
desecrated: profané
desert: désert, abandonner, quitter, délaisser, livrer
deserted: déserté, abandonné
desertion: désertion, abandon de poste, défection, délaissement
deserving: méritant
design: dessin, conception, projet, plan, esquisse, modèle, élaborer, design, esthétique industrielle, stylique

designation: désignation, indication, libellé
designator: indicateur, code
designed: conçu
desirable: désirable, souhaitable
desire: désir, souhait, envie
desired: désiré
desk: pupitre, bureau
desolate: sombre, désolé, morne
desolation: désolation, dévastation, solitude
despair: désespoir
despatch: expédition, dépêche
desperate: désespéré, éperdu
desperately: de façon désespérée, de manière désespérée, désespérément
desperation: désespoir
despicable: méprisable, ignoble
despise: mépriser, dédaigner
despised: méprisèrent, dédaignâtes
despising: méprisant, dédaignant
despite: en dépit de, malgré
despoil: spolie
despoiled: spolié
despondency: découragement, abattement
despondent: découragé, abattu
despotism: despotisme
destination: destination
destined: destinas
destiny: destin, sort, fortune
destitute: dépourvu, indigent
destitution: indigence, misère
destroy: détruire, ravager, démolir, abaisser, abîmer
destroyed: détruisîmes, ravageai
destroyer: destroyer
destroying: détruisant, ravageant
destruction: destruction, ravage, annihilation
destructive: destructif, ravageur
desultory: décousu
detached: détaché
detachment: détachement, équipe, groupe, commando, séparation, décollement
detail: détail, particularité
detailed: détaillé
detain: détenir, retenir, détiens, retiens, réprimer
detained: détinrent, retîntes, retint, retenu, détîntes, détenu
detect: détecter, dépister
detected: détectâmes, dépisté
detection: détection, dépistage, découverte
detects: détecte, dépiste
determination: détermination, dosage, résolution
determined: déterminâtes, décidé
deterred: dissuadâtes

detest: détester, exécrez, abominez, haïr
detested: détestâtes, exécrâtes, abomina
deuce: égalité, deux
devastate: dévaster, ravager, saccager
devastated: dévastâmes, saccageâtes
develop: développer, évoluer, révéler, entraîner des conséquences, perfectionner
developed: développai, perfectionnâtes, aménagèrent, contractèrent
deviated: dévié, s'affolé, m'affolai, vous affolâtes, t'affolas, nous affolâmes
deviation: déviation, écart, déroutement
device: dispositif, appareil, périphérique, organe, engin
devil: diable, tourbillon, poêle à flamber, démon
devilish: diabolique, satané
devoid: dépourvu, dénué
devolved: incomba
devote: consacrer, dédier, adonner
devoted: dévoué, consacrâmes, affectueux, attaché
devoting: consacrant, adonnant, vouant
devotion: dévotion, piété
devour: dévorer, engloutissez
devoured: dévoré, engloutîmes
devouring: dévorant, engloutissant
devout: dévot, pieux
dew: rosée
dexter: dextre
dexterity: dextérité, adresse
dexterous: adroit, habile
dialect: dialecte
diamond: diamant, carreau
diapason: diapason
dictate: dicter, imposer
dictator: dictateur
die: mourir, meurs, décéder, décède, matrice, crever, puce
died: mourûmes, mort, décéda
differ: différer, être différent
differed: différâtes
difference: différence, divergence
differently: autrement, différemment, de façon différente, de manière différente
differing: différant
difficulty: difficulté, ennui, peine
diffuse: diffus, produire un halo, répandent
digest: digérer, condensé
digestion: digestion, lessivage, cuisson, scheidage

dignified: digne
dignity: dignité
dilate: dilater
dilated: dilatâtes
dim: faible, sombre, obscur, brouiller, rendre confus
diminished: diminuèrent, décrus
diminishing: diminuant, décroissant
dimly: de façon faible, de manière faible
dimmed: estompé
dimmer: gradateur, variateur
dimple: fossette, trace de coup, ride, alvéole, contraction latérale, cribler, dépression de l'émail, dermatomycose descaprins
din: vacarme, tapage
dine: dîner, dînons, souper
dined: dîné, dînèrent, dinâmes, dîna
dingy: terne
dining: dînant
dinner: dîner, déjeuner, souper
diplomacy: diplomatie
dire: terrible
direct: direct, diriger, guider, régler, droit
directed: dirigé
directing: direct, diriger
direction: direction, sens, orientation
directly: directement, debout, sans détour, de manière directe, de façon directe
directness: franchise
directs: dirige
disadvantage: inconvénient, désavantage
disadvantageous: désavantageux, défavorable, lésionnaire
disagree: être en désaccord
disagreement: désaccord, différend, mésentente
disappeared: disparûmes
disappointed: déçu, trompa, déçûtes
disappointment: déception, désolation, peine, désappointement
disarm: désarmer
disarmed: désarmai
disbelief: incrédulité
discard: écarter, jeter
discharge: décharge, congé, renvoyer, débit, écoulement, licencier, partir, quitus, suspendre, acquittement, rejet
discharged: déchargé
disciple: disciple
disciplinarian: disciplinaire

disclose: divulguer, révéler, dévoiler
disclosure: divulgation, révélation
discomfort: malaise, gêne
disconcerted: troublâtes, déroutâmes, déconcertèrent
discontent: mécontentement
discontented: mécontent
discontinuance: désistement, interruption, arrêt, cessation
discontinue: interrompre, discontinuer
discord: discorde, désaccord
discordant: discordant
discourteous: impoli, discourtois
discourteously: de façon impolie, de manière impoli
discourtesy: impolitesse
discover: découvrir, dépouiller
discovered: découvris, dépouilla
discoverer: découvreur, premier témoin
discovering: découvrant, dépouillant
discovery: découverte, trouvaille, communication préalable, invention
discreet: discret, prudent
discrepancy: écart, divergence, différence, désaccord, contradiction, anomalie
discretion: discrétion, prudence, précaution
discursive: discursif, décousu
discussing: discutant, débattant
discussion: discussion, entretien
disdain: dédain
disdainful: dédaigneux
disdainfully: de façon dédaigneuse, de manière dédaigneuse
diseased: malade
disembowel: éventre
disentangle: démêler, dénouer, débrouillez
disgrace: disgrâce, honte, déshonneur
disgraced: disgraciâmes
disguise: déguisement, travestir
disguised: déguisé
disguising: déguisant
disgust: dégoût, écoeurer
disheartened: décourageâtes
dishonesty: malhonnêteté, improbité
disinclined: peu disposé
disinherited: exhéréda, déshérité
disinterested: désintéressé, indifférent
disjointing: disjoignant
dislike: antipathie, détester, dédaigner

disliked: détestâtes
dislodge: déloger, détacher
dislodged: délogé
dismal: sombre, triste, morne, banal, désagréable, misérable, repoussant, pénible, pauvre, maussade, malheureux
dismay: consterner, stupéfier, abasourdir, atterrer
dismayed: atterrâmes, consterné
dismiss: renvoyer, licencier, débouter, suspendre, congédier
dismissed: licenciai, renvoyèrent, congédiâtes, déboutai
dismount: descends, mettre pied à terre, sors, sortent, démontent
disobedience: désobéissance
disobey: désobéir
disorder: désordre, trouble
disorderly: désordonné, en désordre
disown: renier, désavouer
disparagement: dénigrement, dépréciation
disparaging: dénigrant, désobligeant, vilipendant
disparity: disparité, inégalité
dispassionate: impartial
dispense: dispenser, délivrer un médicament, distribuer, exempter
dispensed: dispensé
displaced: déplaçâmes, dérégla, décalèrent
displayed: affichâmes, en affichage, montré
displease: déplaire, mécontentons, contrarier
displeased: mécontent, déplut
displeasing: déplaisant, mécontentant
displeasure: déplaisir, mécontentement
disposal: disposition, vente
dispose: disposer
disposed: disposé
disposition: disposition, don, talent, aptitude
disproportionally: de façon disproportionnée, de manière disproportionnée
disprove: réfuter
disproved: réfuta
dispute: dispute, se disputer, contester, différend, conflit, débattre
disputed: disputé, contesté
disputing: disputant
disquiet: déranger, perturber, rendre trouble, brouiller, inquiétude
disquieted: perturbâtes, dérangeâtes

disregard: négliger, méconnaissance, mépris
disrepute: déshonneur
disrobing: déshabillant
dissatisfied: mécontent
dissent: dissentiment, faire valoir sa dissidence, différer
dissenter: dissident
dissimulate: dissimuler
dissimulation: dissimulation
dissipated: dissipé, dispersai
dissipation: dissipation, noce
dissolute: dissolu, débauché
dissolution: dissolution
dissuaded: dissuadâtes
dissuading: dissuadant
distance: distance, éloignement
distant: lointain, distant, éloigné
distantly: de façon lointaine, de manière lointaine
distasteful: déplaisant, désagréable, répugnant
distinct: net, clair, limpide, distinct
distinction: distinction
distinctly: distinctement, de façon nette, de manière nette
distinctness: différenciation, distinction, netteté
distinguish: distinguer, dégager, identifier, reconnaître
distinguishable: distinguable
distinguished: distinguas, dégageâtes
distort: déformer, fausser, distordent, altérer
distorted: déformâtes, distordîmes, oblique, tordu
distract: distraire
distraction: distraction, récréation, amusement, détente
distress: détresse, attrister
distressed: affligé
distribute: distribuer, répartir, dispenser, diffuser
distrust: méfiance, se méfier, défiance
distrustful: méfiant, défiant
disturb: déranger, gêner, gênons, troubler, perturber
disturbance: perturbation, dérangement, trouble, désordre, émeute
disturbed: dérangeai, gêna, gênèrent, gêné, gênâtes
disturbing: dérangeant, gênant
dive: plonger, piqué
diverged: divergèrent
diversified: diversifié
diversion: distraction, déviation, amusement, détente, récréation, déroutement, détournement, diversion

divert: distraire, détourner, amuser, dérouter
diverted: distrait, détournai
divide: diviser, partager, disperser, séparer, répartir, trier, débiter, dissiper, trions
divided: divisa, partageâtes, séparas, trié, débitai, tria, trièrent, triâtes
divine: divin
diviner: devin
diving: plongée
divinity: divinité, théologie
division: division, partage, section
divorce: divorce
divorced: divorcé
divulged: divulgué
docile: docile
docility: docilité
doctor: docteur, médecin, toubib
doctrine: doctrine
document: document, acte, pièce, titre
doe: biche, hase, lapine, daine
doff: enlever, levée, lever
dog: chien, clébard, toc
dogged: obstiné
doggedly: de façon obstinée, de manière obstinée
domain: ensemble compact, propriété
domed: bombé, calotte
domestic: domestique, intérieur, aborigène, relatif à la maison, national
domicile: domicile
dominion: domination, fédéral, territoire, autorité
donation: don, donation
doom: ruine, condamner, destin
doomed: condamné
doorway: embrasure, baie de communication, entrée de porte, porte
dormant: dormant, en repos, en sommeil, endormi, inactif, insensible
dotage: gâtisme, sénilité
double: double, redoubler, sosie
doubled: doublé, en double ad
doublet: doublet, objectif dédoublable
doubling: doublant, renfort, cohabitation
doubly: de façon double, de manière double, doublement
doubt: doute
doubtful: incertain, douteux
doubtless: sans aucun doute
dower: douaire
downcast: abattu, abaissé, baissé
downfall: chute, débâcle, ruine

downstairs: dessous, en bas
downward: descendant, vers le bas
dowry: dot, don
doze: sommeiller, somnoler, remuer la terre avec un bulldozer, faire un petit somme
dozen: douzaine
dozily: de façon sommeillée
dozing: sommeillant
drab: terne, gris
dragging: traînant, entraînement d'image
dragonfly: libellule
drain: drainer, assécher, vidange, purge, faire écouler, égout, écoulement, évacuer, tuyau d'écoulement, vider
drained: drainé, assécha
dramatist: dramaturge
drank: burent
draper: finisseur de vêtements
drapery: draperie
draught: tirant d'eau, prise, profondeur d'enfoncement, esquisse, épure, dépouille, courant d'air, coup, appel d'air, plan, projet
draw: dessiner, puiser, tirer, appâter, solliciter, abaisser, allécher, tracer, match nul, tirage, traçons
drawer: tiroir, tireur, dessinateur
drawing: dessin, puisant, étirage, tirage, appâtant, traçant
drawn: dessiné, puisé, tracé, tiré, appâté
dread: crainte, redouter
dreaded: redouté
dreadful: terrible, affreux, épouvantable
dreading: option marchandises diverses
dream: rêve, songe
dreamed: rêvé
dreamer: rêveur, songeur
dreamy: rêveur
dreary: morne, triste, maussade, sombre, affreux, épouvantable, repoussant, mélancolique, horrible, foncé, désolé
dreg: résidu
dress: robe, habiller, vêtir, panser, s'habiller, revêtir, garnir, apprêter, dresser
dressed: habillé, vêtu
dresser: commode, habilleur
dried: séché, sec
drill: foret, percer, perforatrice, coutil, mèche, fraise, drille
drink: boisson, boire, consommation, s'enivrer
drinker: buveur

drinking: buvant, fait de boire
dripping: égouttement, bavure, dégoulinade, ruissellement, suintement
drive: conduire, pousser, prise, pourchasser, lecteur, faire avancer, piloter, actionner
driven: poussé, conduit, pourchassé, actionné, piloté
driving: poussant, conduisant, pourchassant, actionnant, pilotant
droll: drôle, comique
drooping: tombant, fanaison
drop: goutte, tomber, chute, faire tomber, abattre, s'amoindrir, s'abattre, laisser tomber, baisse, abandonner
dropping: largage, chute, déjections, dépôt de jeunes plants, dérivation des voies, goutte, rejet de la levure, touche en feinte
dropsy: hydropisie
drought: sécheresse, sècheresse
drove: conduisis, poussâmes, pourchassèrent, actionna, pilotèrent
drowned: noyèrent, noyas, noyâtes, noyé
drowning: noyant, noyer, submersion, la noyade, couvrant, asphyxie des racines
drowsily: de façon somnolente, de manière somnolente
drowsy: somnolent, assoupi, ensommeillé
drudge: trimer, peiner, bête de somme
drudgery: corvée
drug: drogue, médicament, stupéfiant, remède
drugget: droguet
drum: tambour, fût
drunk: ivre, bu, soûl
drunken: ivre
drunkenness: ivresse, ivrognerie
dry: sec, sécher, sèche
dryly: sèchement
dubious: douteux, suspect, véreux, discutable
dubiously: de manière douteuse, de façon douteuse
due: dû, exigible, droit, arrivé à échéance, normal
duel: duel
duke: duc
dull: terne, mat, obtus, abêtir, sot, bébête, ennuyeux, monotone
duly: dûment
dumb: muet
dun: brun foncé, isabelle, moisissure brune, relancer
dunce: cancre

dunghill: tas de fumier
dupe: internégatif, contretype
duped: dupé
duping: contretypage
dusk: crépuscule
dust: poussière, poudre, saupoudrer, épousseter
dusty: poussiéreux
dutiful: dévoué, consciencieux
duty: devoir, droit, service, taxe, obligation
dwell: demeurer, habiter, loger
dwelling: demeurant, habitation, domicile, logis, logeant, gîte
dying: mourant, décédant
dynasty: dynastie
eager: avide, désireux
eagerly: de façon avide, de manière avide
eagerness: avidité, empressement, ardeur, impatience
eagle: aigle
ear: oreille, épi
earl: comte
earlier: plus tôt, avant
earliest: le plus tôt
earn: gagner, remporter
earned: gagnâmes
earnest: sérieux, sincère, grave
earnestly: sérieusement, de façon sérieuse, de manière sérieuse
earnestness: sérieux, gravité
earning: gagnant, salaire
earthly: terrestre
ease: soulager, aise, aisance, facilité
easel: chevalet, établi
easily: facilement, aisément, de façon facile, de manière facile
east: est, orient
easy: facile
eat: manger, déjeuner, nourrir
eaten: mangé, bouffé
eating: mangeant, bouffant
eats: mange, bouffe
ebb: reflux, marée descendante, jusant
ebbing: baissant, jusant
ebony: ébène, ébénier
eccentric: excentrique, original
economical: économique
economy: économie, système économique
ecstasy: extase, ecstasie
ecstatic: extatique
edge: bord, rive, lisière, arête, tranche, affiler, carre, rebord
edged: déligné
educate: éduquer, instruire
educated: éduqua, cultivé
educational: éducatif, pédagogique
effeminate: efféminé
efficacious: efficace

efficiently: efficacement, de façon efficace, de manière efficace
effigy: effigie
effort: effort, peine, requête, démarche
egg: oeuf, graine, œuf de poisson, ovule
egotism: égotisme, égoïsme
egotist: égotiste
eight: huit
ejaculation: éjaculation
elaborate: élaborer, soigné, compliqué, développer, raffiné
elaborately: de manière élaborée, de façon élaborée
elapse: passer, s'écouler
elapsed: passé, écoulé
elastic: élastique, souple
elasticity: élasticité
elbow: coude, le coude
elder: sureau, aîné, ancien
elderly: de façon sureau, de manière sureau, âgé
eldest: aîné
elect: choisir, désigner, opter, adopter, élire, élu, élisent
election: élection, choix
electioneering: propagande électorale
elegance: élégance, chic, galanterie, grâce
elegant: élégant, excellent, chic, distingué
elegy: élégie
element: élément, bloc de plaques, ouvrage, organe, matière de base, foyer de cuisson, cartouche, crayon
elementary: élémentaire, primaire
elephant: éléphant
elevate: élever, hausser, élève
elevated: élevé, relevâtes, dressa, sublime, en élévation
elevating: élevant, relevant, dressant
elevator: ascenseur, élévateur, gouverne de profondeur
ell: aune
eloquence: éloquence
eloquent: éloquent
elsewhere: ailleurs, autre part
elucidation: élucidation, éclaircissement
elude: éluder, éviter, déjouent
eluded: éludas, déjouèrent
eluding: éludant, déjouant
emanates: émane
emancipate: émanciper
emancipated: émancipa
embarrassed: embarrassé, gêné
embarrassment: embarras, gêne
embassy: ambassade
embedded: enfonçai, incorporai, enrobas, inclus, imbriqué, intégré, encastras
embellished: embelli, enjolivas
ember: braise, tison
embitter: aigrir, acharnons
embittered: aigri, acharnées
emblem: emblème
emblematic: emblématique
embodied: incarnèrent
emboldened: enhardi
embrace: embrasser, prendre dans les bras, étreinte
embraced: embrassé
embracing: embrassant
embryo: embryon, foetus, germe, prégroupement
emendation: correction
emerald: émeraude
emerge: émerger, surgir, apparaître, paraître
emerged: émergeâtes, surgi
emerging: émergeant, surgissant
emigrant: émigrant
eminence: éminence
eminent: éminent, excellent, accompli
eminently: de façon éminente, de manière éminente, éminemment
emitted: émis, émit, émirent, émîmes, émîtes
emolument: émolument
emotion: émotion, attendrissement, sentiment
emperor: empereur
emphasis: emphase, accentuation
emphatically: énergiquement, de façon emphatique, de manière emphatique
empire: empire
employ: employer, embaucher, user de, se servir de, appliquer, engager
employed: employé
employee: employé, salarié, travailleur, ouvrier
employer: employeur, patron
employing: employant
employment: emploi, occupation, travail, embauche
emptied: vidé, vidâmes, vidèrent
empty: vide, vidanger
emptying: vidage, évacuation
emulation: émulation
enable: permettre, habiliter
enabled: permis, habilité, opérationnel
enamelled: émaillé
enamoured: épris
encased: enferma, emboîté, enrobé
enchanted: enchanté
enchanter: enchanteur, sorcier
enchantment: enchantement, ensorcellement
enclosed: enserras, inclus, clos, enclos
enclosure: enceinte, pièce jointe, clôture, enclos, enveloppe, encoffrement, annexe, boîtier
encounter: rencontre, abord
encountered: rencontrèrent
encountering: rencontrant
encourage: inciter, encourager, réconforter, stimuler
encouraging: encourageant, incitant, réconfortant
encouragingly: de façon encourageante, de manière encourageante
encroach: empiéter, usurper
encroached: empiétas
encumbered: encombré, obéra, grevé, être grevé d'un droit
encumbrance: encombrement, servitude
endangered: risquâmes, compromîtes, MIS en danger
ended: terminé, sortie, finirent
ending: fin, bout, finissant
endow: doter, dotons
endowment: dotation, fondation
endurance: endurance, résistance, autonomie
endure: supporter, endurer, souffrir, durer, durons, subir, tolérer, soutenir, continuer
enemy: ennemi, adversaire
energetic: énergique
energy: énergie
enervate: énerver, affaiblir, débiliter
enfeebled: débilita
enforce: mettre en vigueur, réalisez, imposez
enforced: imposèrent, réalisé, forcé
engaged: engageai, occupé
engagement: fiançailles, engagement, enclenchement, accordailles
engaging: engageant, accrochant, engrenant, enclenchant, attirant, embrayage
engender: engendrer, produire
engendered: engendras
engendering: engendrant
english: anglais, langue anglaise
engraving: gravure, tracé sur couche, ciseler, engravant
engrossed: grossoyâmes
engrossing: grossoyant, absorbant
enjoined: enjoignis
enjoy: jouir, être joyeux, savourer
enjoyed: jouirent, jouîtes

enjoying: jouissant, plaisant, savourant
enjoyment: jouissance, usufruit
enlarge: agrandir, accroître, augmenter, étendre, amplifier
enlarged: agrandi, prorogeâmes
enlighten: éclairer, illuminer
enlightened: éclairas
enlisted: enrôlai
ennui: ennui
enormous: énorme, immense, formidable
enraged: exaspéra, enragés, fâché
enrich: enrichir, amender, étoffe, féconder, fertiliser
enriched: enrichit, étoffé
enshrined: enchâssâtes
ensign: pavillon, enseigne, aspirant
enslaved: asservîtes
ensue: s'ensuivre, résultez
entail: comporter, entraîner
entangle: empêtrer, entortiller
entangled: empêtra, entortillé
entangling: empêtrant, entortillant
enter: entrer, introduire, inscrire, pénétrer
entered: entré, introduisit
entering: entrant, introduisant
enterprise: entreprise, initiative
enters: entre, introduit
entertain: distraire, régaler, divertir, se régalent, te régales, vous régalez, recevoir des visiteurs, abriter, nous régalons, me régale, amuser
entertained: distrait, divertîtes, vous régalâtes, te régalas, se régalèrent, nous régalâmes, me régalai
entertainment: divertissement, amusement, distraction
enthusiasm: enthousiasme
enthusiastic: enthousiaste
enticing: tentant, séduisant, entraînant, attirant, aguichant, affriolant, attrayant
entire: entier, total
entirely: entièrement, complètement, totalement, tout, de façon entière, de manière entière
entitle: intitules, titrons, autorisons
entitled: habilité, titrèrent, intitulé, autorisèrent
entrance: admission, porte, ravir, point d'entrée, façons de l'avant
entreat: implore, supplient
entreated: supplia, implorèrent
entreating: implorant, suppliant
entreaty: imploration, supplication

entry: entrée, inscription, présentation, article, écriture, introduction
entwined: entrelacèrent
envelope: enveloppe, ampoule
enveloped: enveloppa
enviable: enviable
envoy: envoyé, ambassadeur, émissaire, représentant
envy: envie, jalousie
epidemic: épidémie
epilepsy: épilepsie
episode: épisode
epistle: épître
epithet: épithète
epoch: époque, ère, période
equal: égal, pareil, conforme
equally: également, pareillement, de même, de façon égale
equip: équiper, outillez, armez, armons
equivocal: équivoque, douteux, incertain, ambigu
era: époque, ère
ere: avant
erect: fonder, ériger, droit, bâtir, construire, édifier
ermine: hermine
errand: commission, message, course
erring: errant, aberrant
erroneous: erroné, abusif
error: erreur, faute, méprise
erudite: érudit, savant
escape: échapper, s'échapper, évasion, fuite, enfuir, fuir
escaped: échappé, enfuirent
escaping: échappant, enfuyant
escutcheon: écusson, entrée de serrure
espalier: espalier, arbre en espalier
especial: exceptionnel, particulier, spécial
especially: surtout, principalement, tout d'abord, notamment, de façon spéciale, spécialement, particulièrement, de manière spéciale
essay: essai, thèse, composition
essence: essence
essential: essentiel, fondamental
essentially: essentiellement, de manière essentielle, de façon essentielle
established: établi, constatâtes
establishment: établissement, implantation
estate: domaine, propriété, bien, fonds, succession
esteem: estime, apprécier, considérer
esteemed: estimé

estimated: estimé, évaluai, taxa, taxâmes, taxèrent, taxé
estimation: estimation, évaluation, jugement
estranged: aliéné
eternal: éternel, perpétuel
eternally: éternellement, de façon éternelle, de manière éternelle
eternity: éternité
ethereal: éthéré
ethic: éthique
etiquette: étiquette, protocole, convenances
eulogy: panégyrique, éloge
evaporating: s'évaporant, évaporant
evasion: évasion, fraude
eve: veille, ève
evening: soir, égalisage
event: événement, occasion, fait, manifestation
eventful: mouvementé
everlasting: éternel, permanent, perpétuel, interminable, immortelle, infini, inusable
everlastingly: de façon éternelle, de manière éternelle
evermore: toujours
everything: tout, tous
everywhere: partout, en tous lieux
evident: évident, manifeste
evidently: évidemment, de façon évidente, de manière évidente
evil: mal, mauvais
evince: montres
evinced: montré
evinces: montre
evoked: évoquâtes
exact: exact, juste
exactly: exactement, justement, précisément, à l'heure, proprement, de façon exacte, de manière exacte
exaggerated: exagéré, outras
exaggerating: exagérant, outrant
exaggeration: exagération
examination: examen, vérification, inspection
examine: examiner, explorer, fouiller, reconnaître, rechercher, vérifier, inspecter
examined: examina, fouillas
examining: examinant, fouillant
example: exemple, ex, modèle
exasperated: exaspérâtes
exceed: dépasser, excéder, outrepasser, maîtriser, surmonter, dominer, excèdent
exceeded: dépassâtes, excédâtes, maîtrisâtes, outrepassé
exceeding: dépassant, excédant, maîtrisant, outrepassant

exceedingly: extrêmement, de façon excédante, de manière excédante
excellent: excellent, parfait, exquis
except: sauf, excepter, hormis, exempter, dispenser, en outre, exclure, à moins que
excepting: sauf, excepté
excesses: excès
excessively: de façon excessive, de manière excessive, excessivement
exchange: échange, central, change, commutateur, troquer, bourse
exchanged: échangées
exchanging: échangeant
excitability: excitabilité
excitable: excitable, impressionnable
excite: exciter, irriter, agacer, hérisser
excited: excitèrent, hérissèrent
excitement: excitation, agitation
excites: excite, hérisse
exciting: excitant, passionnant, captivant, palpitant, hérissant
exclaim: exclamer, s'exclamer
exclaimed: exclamâtes
exclaiming: exclamant
exclamation: exclamation
exclude: exclure, excepter, exempter, dispenser
exclusion: exclusion
exclusiveness: exclusivité
excusable: pardonnable, excusable
excuse: excuser, dispenser, pardonner
excused: excusé
excusing: excusant
execrable: exécrable
execration: exécration
execute: exécuter, effectuer, accomplir
executed: exécutâtes
executing: exécutant
execution: exécution, réalisation, poursuite par voie de saisie, passation, exercice, déroulement, achèvement
executioner: bourreau, exécuteur
executor: exécuteur
exemption: exemption, dispense, exonération, franchise
exercise: exercice, instruire, pratique, levée
exercised: exercé
exerted: pratiquas, t'efforças, s'efforça, nous efforçâmes, exerças, m'efforçai, vous efforçâtes, efforcés
exertion: effort
exhaust: échappement, épuiser, gaz d'échappement

exhausted: épuisé, exténué
exhaustion: épuisement, éreintement, essorage, procédé exhaustif, abattement
exhibit: exposer, exhiber, montrer, objet exposé
exhilarating: exhilarant, vivifiant
exhilaration: réjouissance
exhortation: sommation, observation, recommandation
exigency: exigence
exile: exiler, bannir
exiled: exilé
exist: exister, vivre, être
existed: exista
existence: existence
existing: existant, présent
exists: existe
exodus: exode
exorcising: exorcisant
exordium: exorde
expanded: expansé, développâmes
expanding: développant, croissance, expansion, mandrinage, moussant, renflement
expands: développe, mousse
expanse: étendue
expatiated: discoururent
expect: attendre, espérer
expectation: espérance, expectative
expected: attendit, prévu
expects: attend, espère
expediency: convenance, opportunisme
expedition: expédition
expel: expulser, renvoyer, repousser
expelled: expulsèrent
expended: dépensas
expense: dépense, frais
experienced: expérimenté, éprouvé
experiment: expérience, essai
expired: expira, périmé, échut
explain: expliquer, développer
explanation: explication, interprétation, libellé
expletive: explétif
exploring: explorant, recherchant, fouillant
expose: exposer, montrer, mettre à nu, insoler, affleurer, démasquer, dévoiler
exposed: exposé, irradié
expressed: exprimas, extériorisa, émise
expressing: exprimant, extériorisant
expression: expression, terme, locution, mine, air
expressive: expressif
expressly: expressément

exquisite: exquis, délicat
exquisitely: de manière exquise, de façon exquise
extended: étendîtes, prorogeai, allongé, débordant
extensive: étendu, extensif, ample, large, vaste
extensively: de manière étendue, largement, de façon étendue
extent: étendue, ampleur, domaine
exterior: extérieur, aspect, spectacle, vue
exterminator: exterminateur, désinsectiser, destructeur de nuisibles
external: externe, extérieur
extinct: éteint, disparu
extinguished: éteignîtes
extort: extorquer, soutire, arracher
extra: extra, figurant, supplémentaire
extract: extrait, arracher, retirer, soutirer, morceau choisi, cession, concentré
extraordinary: extraordinaire, formidable, prodigieux, singulier
extravagance: extravagance
extravagant: extravagant
extreme: extrême, cuir léger, hors tout
extremely: extrêmement, de façon extrême, de manière extrême
extremity: extrémité, queue
extricated: dégagèrent
extricating: dégageant
exuberant: exubérant
exult: exulter
exultation: exultation
exulted: exultai
exulting: exultant
eye: oeil, trou, chas, anneau
eyebrow: sourcil
eyed: embryonné
eyelid: paupière, déflecteur
fable: fable
fabled: légendaire
fabrication: fabrication, invention, première transformation
facade: façade
facile: facile
facilitate: faciliter, soulager
facility: facilité, moyen de transmission, installations, aménagements, organisme d'appui ou de soutien
faculty: faculté, corps professoral
fade: se faner, pâlir, déteindre, décolorer, fondu, flétrir, s'affaiblir
faded: pâlit, fané, pâlîmes, décolora, déteint

fading: évanouissement, fondu, pâlissant, fading, décoloration, déteignant, fluctuation
fail: échouer, avorter, rater, manquer, faillir
failed: faillies, échoué, manqué
failing: défaillant, échouer, faillant
failure: défaillance, échec, panne, manque, dérangement, banqueroute, avortement, insuccès, faillite, avarie, rupture
faint: s'évanouir, faible, défaillir
faintly: de façon faible, de manière faible, faiblement
faintness: malaise, faiblesse
fair: foire, juste, kermesse, blond, marché, équitable, moral, bazar, exposition, loyal, beau
fairing: carénage, coiffe
fairly: assez, relativement, de façon foire, de manière foire, équitablement
fairy: fée, lutin
fairyland: royaume des fées
faith: foi, confiance, croyance
faithful: fidèle, loyal, honnête, droit
faithfully: de façon fidèle, de manière fidèle, fidèlement, loyalement
falcon: faucon
fall: chute, tomber, baisse, choir, s'abattre, s'amoindrir, décrue, choyez, abats, pente
fallacious: trompeur, fallacieux
fallacy: erreur, fausseté
fallen: tombé, déchu, abattu, chu
falling: tombant, abattant, choyant, chute
false: faux, feint, perfide
falsehood: mensonge, supercherie
falseness: fausseté
falter: hésiter, vaciller, chanceler
faltered: hésitai, chancelâmes
falteringly: de manière hésitante, de façon hésitante
fame: renommée, gloire, réputation, célébrité
familiar: familier
familiarity: familiarité
familiarized: familiarisâtes
familiarly: familièrement, de façon familière, de manière familière
famous: célèbre, fameux, illustre, glorieux, renommé, réputé
fan: ventilateur, souffler sur, éventail
fanatic: fanatique, exalté
fancied: imaginaire
fancier: amateur
fanciful: fantaisiste, capricieux, imaginaire

fancy: imaginer, fantaisie, songer, rêver éveillé, aimer
fang: croc
fantastic: fantastique, formidable
fantasy: fantaisie, imagination
farce: farce
fare: aller, se porter, prix du billet
farewell: adieu
farm: ferme, affermer, domaine, prendre à bail, propriété, fonds, bien, bail, cultiver
farmer: agriculteur, fermier, paysan, cultivateur, laboureur, exploitant agricole, agrarien
farther: plus loin
farthest: le plus loin
fascinated: fascinai, passionnâmes, captivé
fascinating: fascinant, passionnant
fascination: fascination
fashion: mode, façon
fashionable: à la mode, dernier cri, moderne, actuel, dans le vent
fast: rapide, vite, jeûner, ferme, prompt, carême
fastened: attachâtes, verrouillai, liai, lié, lia, liâtes, lias, liâmes, lièrent
fastens: attache, verrouille, lie
fastidious: difficile
fat: gras, graisse, gros, épais
fatal: fatal, mortel
fate: sort, destinée, fatalité, fortune
fated: destiné, fatal
fatherless: sans père
fathom: brasse, sonder
fathomless: impénétrable, insondable
fatigue: fatigue, épuisement, usure
fault: défaut, panne, faute, faille, erreur
faultless: impeccable, irréprochable, parfait
favour: faveur, service, grâce, complaisance, favoriser
favourable: favorable, propice
favoured: favorisé
favourite: favori, préféré
fawn: faon, fauve
fear: peur, crainte, angoisse, redouter, appréhension, avoir peur
feared: craint
fearful: effrayant, affreux, craintif
fearfully: de manière effrayante, de façon effrayante
fearing: craignant
fearless: intrépide, courageux
fearlessly: de façon intrépide, de manière intrépide
fearlessness: intrépidité
feast: fête, banqueter, festin

feat: exploit
feature: trait, caractéristique, fonction, grand film
fed: alimentas, nourrîtes
fee: honoraires, droit, redevance, frais, cachet
feeble: faible, débile
feebleness: faiblesse, débilité
feebly: de façon faible, de manière faible
feed: alimenter, nourrir, manger, faire paître, déjeuner, avance, paître
feeding: alimentant, nourrissant, épaississement, affouragement
feeling: sentiment, palpant, ressentant, tâtant
feet: pieds, les pieds, faute de pied
feigning: feignant, simulant
felicity: félicité
fell: tombai, abattre, chut, chûtes, chus, churent, chûmes
feller: abatteuse, rabatteur
fellow: homme, individu, camarade, ensemble, mâle
fellowship: camaraderie, confrérie, titre universitaire, corporation, communion fraternelle, bourse universitaire, association, amitié
felon: criminel, panaris
feloniously: de manière criminelle, de façon criminelle
female: femelle, féminin, femme
feminine: féminin
femininely: de façon féminine, de manière féminine
fence: barrière, clôture, faire de l'escrime, palissade, cloison de décrochage
fenced: clôturé
fender: défense, aile, rehausse, rambarde de traînage
ferment: fermenter, humidifier
fern: fougère
ferocious: féroce, sauvage
ferocity: férocité
ferret: furet, véhicule de renseignement électronique, chasser au furet
fertile: fécond, fertile, fruitier
fertility: fertilité, fécondité
fervently: ardemment, de façon fervente, de manière fervente
festive: de fête
festivity: festivité, fête, réjouissance
fetch: apporter, amener, amènes, hente, aller chercher
fetter: chaîne, enchaîner
fettered: grevé
fever: fièvre, la fièvre
feverish: fiévreux, fébrile
few: peu, peu de

fibre: fibre, brin, nerf, filament, enveloppe cellulosique
fiction: fiction, œuvre d'imagination
fidelity: fidélité, exactitude, loyauté
fidgety: agité, remuant
field: champ, domaine, zone, trame, terrain, corps, gisement
fiend: démon, monstre, enragé
fiendish: diabolique
fierce: féroce, violent
fiercely: de façon féroce, de manière féroce
fierceness: férocité, violence, ardeur
fiery: ardent, fougueux
fifteen: quinze
fifty: cinquante
fight: combattre, lutter, batailler, luter
figure: figure, chiffre, compter, calculer, forme, silhouette
figured: figuré, chiffrées
filch: chipez
file: fichier, lime, dossier, file, classeur, rang, tour, collection à consulter, déposer, porte document
filial: filial
fill: remplir, obturer, plomber, compléter, charger, bourrer, remblai, emplir
filled: rempli, fourré
filthy: sale, dégoûtant, crasseux
final: finale, définitif, appel, dernier
finally: finalement, enfin, de façon finale, de manière finale
finch: pinson
finding: fondant, recherche d'une ligne appelante, trouvant
fine: amende, fin, excellent, beau, délicat, tendre, éminent, accompli, à merveille, contravention
finer: affineur
finesse: finesse, impasse
finest: le plus fin
finger: doigt, tâter
finish: terminer, finir, achever, achève, cesser, apprêter, fin, confectionner, arrivée
finished: termina, finîtes, finit, acheva, prêt
fire: feu, incendie, tirer, renvoyer, licencier, suspendre, partir, le feu
fired: traité par pointes de feu
fireplace: cheminée, foyer
firm: ferme, solide, firme, robuste, entreprise, stable
firmly: fermement, de façon ferme, de manière ferme
firmness: fermeté, résistance
fish: poisson, pêcher

fished: pêché
fishing: pêche, repêchage, sauvetage
fissure: fissure, fente, scissure, crevasse
fist: poing, main
fit: adapter, apoplexie, convenir, ajustement, crise, en bonne santé
fitful: irrégulier
fitted: ajusté
fitter: ajusteur, installateur, essayeur
fitting: convenable, ajustage, conforme, raccord, essayage, montage, posage, liquidation, ferrure, adaptation
fix: fixer, fixons, attacher, réparer, déterminer, refaire, restaurer, remédier, point, adapter, repère
fixed: fixe, fixèrent, fixa, fixâmes, fixé, réparèrent, remédia
fixedly: de façon fixe, de manière fixe
flag: drapeau, pavillon, indicateur, fanion, étendard, dalle, cavalier, banderole, écran opaque
flagging: balisage, distorsion en drapeau
flagrant: flagrant
flake: flocon, écaille, paillette, s'écailler, miette, doublure débouchante
flame: flamme, flinguer
flank: flanc, face de dépouille
flanked: flanqué
flare: fusée éclairante, vaciller, arrondi, lumière parasite, ondoyer, scintiller, torche, évasement, dévers
flash: flash, éclat, clignoter, bavure
flashing: clignotement, étincelable, solin, séchage à la vapeur, latensification, postlumination, tache, ébarbage, rappel sur supervision, doublage, brillant inégal
flashy: tapageur, voyant
flat: plat, appartement, aplati, bémol, uni, mat
flatter: flatter, aduler, amadouer
flattered: flatté, adulai, amadoua
flattering: flattant, adulant, amadouant
flatters: flatte, adule, amadoue
flattery: flatterie, adulation
fled: fui, fuit, fuis, fuirent, fuîtes, fuîmes, échappâmes
fleece: toison, tondre, polaire
fleeting: fugace, fugitif
flesh: chair, pulpe
flew: vola, volâmes, volèrent
flight: vol, fuite, volée, essor

flint: silex, pierre à briquet, flint
flirt: flirter, voltiger, conter fleurette
flirtation: flirt
flirting: flirt
flit: voltiger, flirter, conter fleurette
flitted: voltigé, flirtâmes
float: flotter, planer, nager, taloche
flock: troupeau, bourre, tontisse, flocon
flogged: fustigé, flagellé
floor: plancher, étage, sol, taux plancher, mur
florid: fleuri, florissant
flounce: volant
flourish: prospérer, rinceau, parafe, trait de plume, fleurir
flourishing: florissant, prospérant
flowed: coulé
flower: fleur, la fleur
flowing: écoulement, coulant, fluent
flown: volé
fluency: maîtrise, aisance, facilité
fluid: fluide, liquide, flot, coulant
flush: affleurant, rougeur
flutter: voltiger, scintillement, flottement, flirter, voleter, flutter, battement, conter fleurette, chevrotement, pleurage
fluttering: battement des gouvernes, flottant
fly: mouche, voler, volons, volant
foe: ennemi
fog: brouillard, voile, buée
foggy: brumeux, confus
foible: faible
fold: pli, plier, repli, plisser, pliure
folded: plié, plissé
folding: pliant, plissement
foliage: feuillage
folk: peuple, folklorique, gens
follow: suivre, suis, respecter, agir selon
followed: suivis, talonnâtes, ensuivues, vous ensuivîtes, t'ensuivis, s'ensuivit, m'ensuivis, nous ensuivîmes
follows: suit, talonne, ensuit, s'ensuit
folly: folie, sottise
fond: tendre, affectueux, indulgent
fondly: de manière tendre, de façon tendre, tendrement
fondness: affection, penchant, prédilection, tendresse
food: nourriture, aliment, pâture
fool: sot, imbécile, mystifier, idiot, duper, fou
foolhardiness: imprudence, témérité

foolish: sot, idiot, stupide, abracadabrant, insensé
foot: pied, patte, bordure, le pied
footboard: marchepied, pied de lit, planchette, petit dossier
foot-bridge: passerelle
footing: pied, semelle
footman: valet de pied
footprint: encombrement, empreinte de pas
footsore: aux pieds endoloris
footstep: pas, marche
footstool: tabouret
fop: dandy
foppish: dandy
forbade: interdit
forbear: s'abstenir
forbearing: patient
forbid: interdire, défendre, prohiber
forbidden: interdit, défendu
forbids: interdit
force: force, contraindre, imposer, obliger, violer, puissance, faire accepter
forced: forcé, forçâmes
forcible: de force, par force
forcibly: de façon de forcée, de manière forcée
forcing: forçage, forcer, forgeage, intensification de la valeur d'ajustage, pression, chauffage
fore: avant, à l'avant
foreboded: présagèrent
foreboding: pressentiment, présage
forefinger: index
forehead: front, chanfrein
foreign: étranger, extérieur
foreigner: étranger, inconnu
forelock: toupet, goujon d'arrêt, mèche
foreman: contremaître, chef d'équipe
forenoon: matinée
foresaw: prévis
foresee: prévoir, présager
foreseen: prévu
foreshadowed: présagèrent
foreshadowing: présageant
forestall: anticiper, devancer, empêcher, prévenir
forethought: prévoyance
forever: pour toujours, toujours
forewarning: préavis, prévenant, avertissant
forfeited: forfaits, perdu
forgave: pardonnâtes, excusâtes
forged: forgé, contrefait
forger: faussaire, forgeur
forgery: falsification, faux, contrefaçon
forget: oublier, désapprenons

forgetful: distrait, oublieux
forgetfulness: oubli, manque de mémoire
forgets: oublie, désapprend
forgetting: oubliant, désapprenant
forgive: pardonner, excuser
forgiven: pardonné, excusé
forgiveness: pardon, rémission
forgiving: pardonnant, excusant, indulgent
forgot: oubliâtes, désapprîtes
forgotten: oublié, désappris
forked: fourchu, bifurqué, en forme de fourche
forlorn: désespéré, délaissé, triste, abandonné
formal: formel, officiel
formalist: formaliste
formality: formalité
formally: de manière formelle, formellement, de façon formelle
formed: formé
former: ancien, précédent
formerly: autrefois, auparavant, devant, anciennement, jadis
formidable: formidable, extraordinaire, singulier, prodigieux, redoutable
forming: formation, profilage
forsake: abandonner, délaisser, quitter, livrer
forsook: abandonnâtes, délaissai
forsworn: abjuré
forth: en avant
forthcoming: prochain
fortitude: courage, force d'âme
fortnight: quinzaine
fortunate: heureux, chanceux
fortunately: heureusement, de manière heureuse, de façon heureuse
fortune: fortune, sort, destin
forty: quarante
forward: en avant, avancer
forwarded: achemina
fostering: encourager
foul: faute, fétide, engagé, salir
foundation: fondation, base, assise
foundling: enfant trouvé
fount: source, fonte, réservoir de lampe
fourteen: quatorze
fourth: quatrième, quart
fourthly: quatrièmement
fragile: fragile, délicat
fragment: fragment
fragrance: parfum, fragrance
fragrant: parfumé, aromatique, odorant
frail: fragile, frêle
frailty: fragilité, faiblesse

frame: cadre, trame, châssis, encadrer, image, charpente, membrure, carcasse, couple, bâti, photogramme
framework: cadre, charpente, armature, structure, ossature
franc: franc
frank: franc, affranchir
frankly: franchement, de façon franche, de manière franche
frankness: franchise
frantic: frénétique, effréné
frantically: de façon frénétique, de manière frénétique
fratricide: effet fratricide, fratricide
fraud: fraude, escroquerie, tromperie, imposture, dol, filouterie
fraudulently: de façon frauduleuse, de manière frauduleuse
fraught: chargé, plein
freed: libéré
freedom: liberté, la liberté, indépendance
freely: librement, de façon gratuite, de manière gratuite
freezing: congélation, gel, glacial, gelant, blocage
french: langue française, Français
frenzy: frénésie
frequent: fréquent, habituel
frequently: fréquemment, souvent, beaucoup, de façon fréquente, de manière fréquente
fresh: frais, nouveau
freshly: fraîchement, de façon fraiche, de manière frais
freshness: fraîcheur
fret: frette, mousser fortement, cloison, tracasser
friction: frottement, friction, désaccord
friend: ami, amie, copain, camarade, copine
friendless: sans amis
friendly: amical, aimable, gentil, affable, amène
friendship: amitié, camaraderie
frieze: frise, ratine, burat
fright: peur, effroi, anxiété, frayeur, terreur
frightened: effrayé, redouta
frightful: affreux, effroyable, épouvantable
frill: volant, froncer
fritter: beignet, gaspiller
frivolity: frivolité
frivolous: frivole, vain, vaniteux
frivolously: de manière frivole, de façon frivole
frock: robe, froc
frolicsome: malin, enjoué

front: front, devant, avant, face
fronting: façade, diffusion frontale
frown: froncement de sourcils, se renfrogner, sourciller
frowning: renfrogné
froze: gela, gelâmes, gelèrent
frozen: gelé, congelé
fruit: fruit, réponse parasite
fruitless: stérile, infructueux
frustrate: frustrer, déjoue, décevoir
frustrated: frustré, déjoua, déçu
frustrating: frustrant, déjouant
fugitive: fugitif, réfugié, couleur qui déteint, non solide à la lumière
fulfilment: réalisation, accomplissement
fuller: gravure de roulage
fully: entièrement, complètement, de façon pleine, de manière pleine, pleinement
fume: fumée, vapeur, odeur délétère, exhalaison
fun: amusement, plaisir, détente, distraction, récréation
fund: fonds, caisse
funeral: enterrement, obsèques, funérailles
furnished: fournîtes, meublâtes
furnishing: fournissant, meublant, ameublement
furniture: meubles, mobilier, les meubles, garniture, ameublement
furrow: sillon, ride, raie
furrowed: ridé, sillonné
furtive: furtif, sournois
fury: fureur, furie
fuse: fusible, mèche, cordeau, fusée
fusion: fusion
future: avenir, futur
gain: gain, gagner, profit, bénéfice, remporter, avantage, acquisition
gained: gagné
gainer: gagnant
gait: démarche, allure, marche
gaiter: guêtre, emplâtre
galaxy: galaxie, poivré
gall: bile, fiel, galle, amer
gallant: vaillant, brave, galant, courageux
gallantry: vaillance, galanterie, bravoure
gallery: galerie, tribune
gallop: galoper
gambler: joueur, parieur, spéculateur
gambling: jeu de hasard, pari
game: jeu, gibier, partie, match
gamester: joueur
gaming: jeu
gang: bande, compagnie, clique, mariage

gap: brèche, écart, lacune, interstice, espace inter électrode, créneau, trou, couloir, fente, jeu, goulet
gaper: badaud, mactre du Pacifique
garb: costume
garden: jardin, faire du jardinage
gardener: jardinier, ouvrier jardinier
garment: vêtement, habit
garnished: garni
garret: mansarde, grenier
garrulous: loquace, bavard
garter: jarretière
gate: porte, vanne, grille, barrière, gâchette, berceau, doigt, entrée
gather: rassembler, ramasser, réunir, recueillir, déduire, conclure, collectionner, assembler, fronce, grappiller, récolter
gathered: ramassée, rassemblé, cueilli
gathering: réunion, ramassage, rassemblement, cueillage, roulage
gaudy: voyant, criard
gaunt: morne, maigre, désert, désolé, sombre, maussade, mince, angulaire, décharné, mélancolique
gauze: gaze, mousseline, toile métallique, tamis
gawky: dégingandé, gauche, maladroit
gay: gai, joyeux, homosexuel, enjoué
gaze: regard
geese: oies
gem: gemme, pierre précieuse
gene: gène
genealogist: généalogiste
generalization: généralisation
generalize: généraliser
generally: généralement, en général, ordinairement, de manière générale, de façon générale
generation: génération, production
generosity: générosité, largesse
generous: généreux, abondant, copieux
genial: génien
genially: de manière génienne, de façon génienne
genius: génie
geniuses: génies
gent: monsieur
genteelly: de façon distinguée, de manière distinguée
gentility: distinction
gentle: doux, gentil, suave, sucré
gentleman: monsieur, gentilhomme
gentlemen: messieurs
gentleness: bonté, douceur

gently: doucement, gentiment, de façon douce, de manière douce
genuine: véritable, authentique, franc, sincère
genuinely: réellement, en réalité, de façon authentique, authentiquement, de manière authentique
germ: germe, microbe
gesticulation: gesticulation
gesture: geste, signe
gets: obtient
ghastliest: le plus horrible
ghastly: horrible, désagréable, repoussant, abominable, maussade, odieux
ghost: fantôme, apparition, image fantôme, revenant, spectre, hématie dépigmentée
giant: géant, colosse
gibber: baragouiner
gibbet: gibet
giddy: étourdi
gift: cadeau, don
gifted: doué, surdoué
gig: engagement d'un soir, machine d'extraction, guigue, gig
gigantic: gigantesque, énorme, formidable, colossal
gild: dorer, dorons
gilded: dorèrent, dora, dorâmes, doré
gilding: dorant, dorure
gilt: doré, jeune truie, cochette
gimlet: vrille, foret
gin: gin, mât de levage, rouet, égreneuse, chèvre, genièvre
gingerbread: pain d'épice
girl: fille, jeune fille, gosse, la fille
girlish: de petite fille, efféminé
girth: circonférence, sangle, tour, ceinture
giving: donnant, offrant, aboulant
glad: joyeux, content, heureux
gladden: réjouir
gladly: volontiers, avec plaisir, de façon joyeuse, de manière joyeuse
gladness: joie, allégresse
glance: coup d'œil, jeter un coup d'oeil, regard
glare: éblouissement, éclat, reflet
glaring: éblouissant, flagrant, éclatant
glazed: glacé, givré, lissé, vitré
gleam: lueur, luire
gleamed: luie, luis
gleaming: luisant
gleaned: glanai
gleaner: glaneur
gleaning: glanage, grappillage
glee: joie

gleefully: de façon joyeuse, de manière joyeusese
glide: glisser, planer, vol plané, coulé, patin
glided: glissa
gliding: vol à voile, glissement
glimmer: luire, briller, faible lueur
glimmering: éclat, miroitant
glimpse: entrevoir
glistened: scintillé
glitter: briller, scintillement
glittering: scintillant, éclat
gloat: jubiler, exulter
globule: globule
gloom: mélancolie, obscurité
gloomily: de façon sombre, de manière sombre
gloomy: sombre, morne
glorious: glorieux, fameux
glory: gloire, renommée, réputation
glossy: lustré, vernissé, luisant, glacée, éclatant, brillant
glove: gant, mitaine
glow: ardeur, incandescence, brûler, lueur, être en feu
glowing: incandescence, rougeoyant, feu avec incandescence, luire
glue: colle, adhésif
glutinous: glutineux
gnarled: noueux
gnaw: ronger
gnawed: rongea
gnawing: rongeant
goal: but, dessein, objectif
goblin: lutin, gnome
god: dieu, créateur
godfather: parrain
godlike: divin
godly: pieux, dévot
godsend: aubaine
godson: filleul
gold: or, l'or
golden: doré, en or, d'or
goldfinch: chardonneret
gone: allé, parti
goodly: de façon bonne, de manière bonne
gore: encorner, fuseau, godet
gorge: gorge, anglaise
gossip: cancaner, jaser, commérage, bavard
gout: goutte, bouchon, matière étrangère prise dans le tissage
govern: gouverner, régner, règne, surveiller, régir
governed: gouvernâmes, régnèrent
governess: gouvernante
gown: robe, toge
grace: grâce, charme
graceful: gracieux, élégant, mignon
graceless: inélégant, gauche
gracious: gracieux, courtois, gentil
graciously: de façon gracieuse, de manière gracieuse
graciousness: élégance, grâce
gradual: graduel, progressif
gradually: petit à petit, peu à peu, graduellement, de proche en proche, de façon graduelle, de manière graduelle
graft: greffe, garnir, corruption
grain: grain, bloc de poudre, fil, pépin, blé
grand: grandiose, magnifique
grandeur: noblesse, grandeur
grandfather: aïeul
grandmother: aïeule, mémé
granite: granit, de granit
grant: subvention, allocation, concéder
granted: alloua, accordé
grapple: grappin, attraper, saisir, capturer
grasp: saisir, agripper, empoigner, compréhension, prise, étreindre
grasped: saisi, empoignées
grasping: avide, empoignant, étreignant, saisir
grate: grille, râper, grincer, crisser
grateful: reconnaissant
gratefully: de manière reconnaissante, avec reconnaissance, de façon reconnaissante
gratification: satisfaction, plaisir
gratified: satisfîtes, gratifièrent, contentés
gratify: satisfaire, gratifient, contentons
gratifying: contentant, satisfaisant, gratifiant
gratitude: gratitude, reconnaissance, remerciement
gratuitously: de façon gratuite, de manière gratuite
grave: tombe, grave, sérieux
gravely: gravement, de façon tombe, de manière tombe
graver: burin, échoppe, gravoir, pointe à tracer
gravestone: pierre tombale
gravity: gravité, pesanteur
gray: gris, gray
grease: graisse, lubrifiant
greatly: de façon grande, de manière grande
greatness: grandeur
greed: avidité, avarice, cupidité
greediness: avidité
greedy: avide, glouton, gourmand, cupide, goulu
green: vert, herbacé, inexpérimenté, cru, comprimé, boulingrin, frais
greeted: saluai, accueillîtes
greeting: salutation, accueillant
greets: salue, accueille
grew: grandirent, crût, crûmes, crûs, crûrent
grief: peine, chagrin, désolation, abattement, douleur
grievance: grief, réclamation
grieve: affliger, chagriner, attrister, désoler
grieved: affligeâmes, chagrina, attristé
grieving: affligeant, chagrinant, attristant
grievingly: de façon chagrinante, de manière chagrinante
grim: macabre, menaçant, sinistre
grimy: crasseux, sale
grin: sourire, rictus
grinning: manque de pouvoir couvrant par opacité, pouvoir opacifiant insuffisant, clair, fendillement
grisly: maussade, désagréable, horrible
grist: blé à moudre, grand nombre
grit: gravier, poussière, grenaille, sable
groan: gémir, geindre
groom: palefrenier, marié, valet d'écurie, panser
groping: palpant, tâtant, tâtonnant
grossness: grossièreté
grotesque: ubuesque, grotesque
ground: terre, sol, fond, masse, échouer, motif
grounded: mis à la terre, interdit de vol
groundless: sans fondement
grouped: groupés
grove: bosquet, bois, ouvrage souterrain
grow: grandir, croître, cultiver, croissez, augmenter, devenir, s'accroître, redoubler
growing: grandissant, croissant
growl: grogner, râler, grondement
growled: grogné
growling: grondement, grognement
grown: crû, grandi
grows: grandit, croît
grudge: rancune
grumble: grogner, râler, grommeler, ronchonner
grumbling: grognon, rouspétance
grunt: grognement
guarantee: garantie, cautionner, assurer, aval
guard: garde, protéger, contrôleur, préserver, dispositif de protection, arrière, chef de train

guarded: protégé, gardé
guardian: tuteur, gardien, curateur
guardianship: curatelle, tutelle, garde
guarding: garde, placement des onglets, montage sur onglet, défense musculaire, dispositif de protection
guessed: deviné
guesses: devine
guessing: devinant
guest: hôte, invité, convive, client
guidance: guidage, tutorat, conseil, direction
guide: guide, diriger, conduire, mener, régler, aboutir
guided: guidé, dirigé
guile: astuce, fourberie
guillotine: guillotine, massicot
guilt: culpabilité
guiltless: innocent
guilty: coupable
guise: apparence
gulf: golfe, abîme, gouffre
gushed: jailli
gushing: jaillissement, giclage
gust: rafale, coup de vent
gusto: vigueur, délectation, plaisir
gutter: gouttière, caniveau, rigole, petits fonds, lézarde, rue, blanc de fond, logement de bavure, crochet de jante, dalot, goulotte
habit: habitude, coutume, port, usage
habitual: habituel
habitually: de façon habituelle, de manière habituelle, habituellement
habituated: te 'habituas, vous 'habituâtes, se 'habituèrent, nous 'habituâmes, me 'habituai
hack: hacher, tailler, rainette
haggard: hâve, blème, égaré, maigre
hailed: grêlé
hair: cheveux, poil
hall: salle, hall, couloir, vestibule
hallowing: sanctifiant
halt: arrêt, s'arrêter, halte
halting: arrêter, hésitant, immobilisation
hammock: hamac, groupe d'activités
handful: poignée
handkerchief: mouchoir, foulard
handsome: beau
handwriting: écriture, manuscrit
hang: pendre, suspendre, retomber, faisander, accrocher
hanging: pendaison, suspension, mise à la pente
hangman: bourreau

happen: arriver, avoir lieu, advenir, adviennent, devenir, se passer, intervenir
happened: arrivâmes, advinrent, advenu
happiest: le plus heureux
happily: heureusement, de façon heureuse, de manière heureuse
happiness: bonheur, félicité
happy: heureux, joyeux, content
harangue: harangue
harass: harceler, tracasse, troubler, déranger l'adversaire, tourmenter
harassed: harcelâtes, tracassâtes
harbour: port, héberger
hard: dur, pénible, difficile
hardened: durci, trempé, endurci
hardening: durcissant, trempant, endurcissant
hardly: à peine, péniblement, lourdement, difficilement, durement, de manière dure, de façon dure
hardness: crudité, degré du vide, difficulté, Dureté, compacité
hardy: robuste, courageux
hare: lièvre
harlot: prostituée
harm: nuire, préjudice, mal, tort, endommager
harmless: inoffensif, anodin, innocent
harmlessly: de façon inoffensive, de manière inoffensive
harmonious: harmonieux, mélodieux
harmonized: harmonisâtes
harmony: harmonie, concorde
harsh: vulgaire, rude, grossier, rustique, maussade, dur, acerbe, astringent, âpre
harshly: rudement, de façon vulgaire, de manière vulgaire
harshness: rudesse, dureté, sévérité
harvest: récolte, moisson, recueillir, vendange
haste: hâte, précipitation
hasten: hâter, hâtons
hastened: hâtâmes, hâté, hâtai, hâtèrent
hastening: hâtant, s'empressant, accourant, empressant
hastily: hâtivement, à la hâte, précipitamment, de façon précipitée, de manière précipitée
hasty: précipité, hâtif
hat: chapeau, le chapeau, bonnet, casque
hatch: écoutille, trappe, hachurer, couvée, panneau, éclosion
hate: haïr, haine, détester

hated: détesté, häirent, häimes, häi, haie
hateful: odieux, haïssable
hatred: haine
haughtily: de façon hautaine, de manière hautaine
haughtiness: arrogance, hauteur
haughty: hautain, arrogant
haunt: hanter, fréquenter
haunted: hanté, égaré
haunting: hanter
hawk: autour, colporter, faucon
hawker: colporteur, camelot, marchand ambulant
hazard: risque, danger, hasard, péril, aléa, aventurer, oser
hazardous: hasardeux, périlleux, dangereux
heal: guérir, assainir, cicatriser
healing: guérissant, curatif, assainissant, cicatrisation
healthful: salubre
healthiest: le plus sain
heap: tas, amas, entasser, accumuler, foule, masse, troupe, bande, collection, ensemble, rassembler
heaped: entassé
hear: entendre, ouïr, oyons, oient, écouter, ois, oyez
heard: entendirent, ouïs, ouï
hearing: entendant, audition, ouïe, oyant
hears: entend, oit
heart: coeur, le coeur
hearth: foyer, cheminée, sole
heartily: de façon cordiale, de manière cordiale, chaleureusement
heartiness: cordialité
hearty: cordial, chaleureux
heat: chaleur, chauffer, ardeur, charge de fusion, rut
heated: chauffé, échauffé
heathen: païen, barbare, sauvage
heaven: ciel, paradis
heavenly: céleste, divin, du ciel, merveilleux, paradisiaque
heavily: fortement, de manière lourde, lourdement, de façon lourde
heaviness: lourdeur, poids
heaving: pilonnement, gonflement
heavy: lourd, fort
hedgerow: haie
heed: attention
heedlessly: de façon insouciante, de manière insouciante
heel: talon, gîte
heifer: génisse
height: hauteur, altitude, taille

heighten: aggraver, amplifier, rehausser, augmenter
heightened: aggravai, rehaussâtes
heightening: aggravant, rehaussant
heir: héritier, légataire
held: tenu, tinrent
heliotrope: héliotrope, rouge hélio
hell: enfer, géhenne
helm: gouvernail, barre, timon
helpless: impuissant, abandonné, faible, délaissé
helplessness: impuissance, vulnérabilité, misère
helpmate: compagnon
hem: ourlet, bord, drapelet cousu
hence: par conséquent, donc, c'est pourquoi, d'où
henceforth: désormais, dorénavant, à l'avenir
heraldry: héraldique, science héraldique
herd: troupeau, bande, collection, ensemble, harde, are
hereafter: après, désormais, dorénavant
hereditary: héréditaire
herein: en ceci
heretofore: jusqu'ici
heritage: héritage, patrimoine
hero: héros
heroic: héroïque
herring: hareng
herself: même, se
hesitate: hésiter, barguigner
hesitated: hésita, barguignâmes
hesitating: hésitant, barguignant
hesitatingly: de façon hésitante, de manière hésitante
hesitation: hésitation
hid: cachai, masqua
hidden: caché, dissimulé, masqué
hideous: hideux, horrible, abominable, odieux, abject, repoussant, affreux
hideously: de façon hideuse, de manière hideuse
hiding: cachant, masquant, dissimulation
higher: plus haut
highest: le plus haut
highly: hautement, fortement, extrêmement, de façon haute, de manière haute
hilarity: hilarité
hill: colline, terrer, butter, coteau
hind: biche, suivant, de derrière
hindrance: obstacle, entrave
hinge: charnière, gond, articulation, paumelle
hint: insinuer, faire allusion, allusion, conseil
hinting: optimisation

hip: hanche, arête, fruit de l'églantier, cuisse
hippodrome: hippodrome
hire: louer, louons, embaucher, location
hired: louai, louèrent, loué, louâtes, embauché
hireling: stipendié, larbin
historian: historien
history: histoire, anamnèse, antécédents
hit: frapper, heurter, battre, coup, succès, atteindre, toucher, parvenir, saisir
hither: ici
hitherto: jusqu'ici
hoard: amas, thésaurisation, stocker, trésor
hoarse: rauque, enroué
hobbled: ambleur, entravé
hobby: hobby, violon d'Ingres, faucon hobereau
hold: tenir, maintien, prise, cale, retenir, contenir, pause, tenue, blocage
holding: entretien, tenue, maintien, attente
hole: trou, fossé, orifice, creux
holiday: jour férié, vacance, fête, blanc, congé, défaut d'enrobage, villégiature
hollow: creux, cavité, caver
hollowed: cavèrent, cavées, cava
hollowness: creux, son caverneux, cavité
holy: saint, sacré
homage: hommage
homeless: sans abri
homely: simple, sans charme
homily: homélie
honest: honnête, intègre, loyal, sincère
honestly: honnêtement, de façon honnête, de manière honnête
honesty: honnêteté
honeymoon: lune de miel, voyage de noces
honour: honneur, honorer
honourable: honorable, vénérable
honourably: de façon honorable, de manière honorable
hood: capot, capuchon, cagoule, hotte, couverture, apache, garniture frontale, chapeau
hoof: sabot
hookah: narguilé
hope: espoir, espérer, espères, souhaiter
hoped: espéra, souhaitâtes
hopeful: optimiste, plein d'espoir
hopeless: impossible, sans espoir, désespéré

hoping: espérant, souhaitant
horizon: horizon
horizontally: de façon horizontale, de manière horizontale
horrible: affreux, épouvantable, horrible, atroce, terrible, sinistre, odieux, désagréable, abominable, hideux, féroce
horribly: de façon affreuse, de manière affreuse
horrid: horrible, affreux, méchant
horror: horreur, aversion, dégoût, répulsion, abomination, atrocité
horse: cheval, le cheval
horseback: à cheval
horsehair: crin
horseman: cavalier, homme de chevaux
hospitable: hospitalier
hospital: hôpital, établissement hospitalier, hospitalier, infirmerie
hospitality: hospitalité, dépense de représentation, salon de réception
host: hôte, amphitryon, aubergiste, hostie, foule
hostile: ennemi, hostile
hostler: mécanicien de manœuvre
hot: chaud, épicé, brûlant, missile Hot
hotel: hôtel
hound: chien de chasse, talonner, traquer, jotteneau, capelage
hour: heure, l'heure
hourly: horaire, constant
household: ménage, famille
housekeeper: gouvernante, intendant de collectivité
houseleek: joubarbe
housemaid: femme de chambre, bonne
housewife: femme au foyer, ménagère
housework: travaux domestiques, ménage
hovel: taudis, masure
hovered: planas, voltigeai, flotté
hovering: planant, vol stationnaire, voltigeant, flottant
howl: hurler, mugir, gronder
hubbub: vacarme, brouhaha
hue: teinte, nuance, tonalité chromatique
huge: énorme, immense, gigantesque, formidable, vaste, colossal
hulk: ponton
hum: bourdonner, ronronner, ronflement, chantonner
human: humain
humanity: humanité
humanizing: humanisant
humankind: humanité

humble: humble, modeste
humbleness: humilité
humbly: humblement, de manière humble, de façon humble
humiliating: humiliant
humiliation: humiliation
humility: humilité, modestie
humming: bourdonnement, vrombissement
humorous: amusant, humoristique
humour: humour, humeur
hundred: cent
hung: pendu
hunger: faim, avoir faim, désir ardent
hungry: affamé, anémique
hunt: chasser, poursuivre
hunted: chassâtes
hunting: chasse, lacet, pompage
hurried: hâtif, pressé, dépêché
hurriedly: à la hâte, de façon hâtive, de manière hâtive, précipitamment
hurry: se dépêcher, hâte, presser, être urgent, dépêcher, se presser, se hâter
hurrying: dépêchant
hurt: blesser, offenser, vexer, nuire, faire mal, endommager, mal
husband: mari, époux
hush: silence, faire taire
husky: chien esquimau, husky
hut: hutte, cabane, chaumière, baraque
hypocrisy: hypocrisie
hypocrite: hypocrite
hypocritical: hypocrite
ice: glace, crème glacée
icy: glacé, verglacé
ideal: idéal
identity: identité
idiom: idiome, formation synaptique
idle: inactif, tourner au ralenti, ralenti, fainéant, inoccupé, paresseux, au repos
idleness: oisiveté, désœuvrement
idler: roue folle, oisif, paresseux, poulie de tension, fainéant, galet d'entraînement, rouleau, laveur
idly: de façon inactive, de manière inactive
idolatrous: idolâtre
ignoble: ignoble
ignominy: ignominie
ignorance: ignorance, méconnaissance
ignorant: ignorant
ill: malade, malsain, mal
illegally: illégalement, de façon illégale, de manière illégale

illegitimate: illégitime, bâtard, illogique
illiberal: intolérant
illness: maladie, infirmité
illogical: illogique
illuminating: illuminant, enluminant, coloriant, éclairant
illumination: éclairage, illumination, enluminure
illusion: illusion, imagination
illustrating: illustrant
illustrious: illustre, célèbre, fameux
image: image, figure
imagery: imagerie, cliché
imaginary: imaginaire, fantastique, fictif
imagination: imagination, fantaisie
imaginative: imaginatif
imagine: imaginer, se figurer, se représenter, s'imaginer
imagined: imagina
imbecility: imbécillité
imbibe: absorber, buvons, boire, bois, boivent, buvez
imbibed: absorbèrent, bus, but, bûmes, bu, bûtes, burent
imitate: imiter, copier, contrefaire
imitated: imitas, copia
imitating: imitant, copiant
immediate: immédiat
immediately: immédiatement, tout de suite, aussitôt, directement, sitôt, d'abord, de manière immédiate, de façon immédiate
immemorial: immémorial
immense: énorme, immense, formidable
imminence: imminence
imminent: imminent
immortal: immortel
immortality: immortalité
imp: lutin, diablotin
impaired: endommagèrent, diminuai, abîmèrent, altérèrent
impart: donner, communiquer
impartiality: impartialité
impartially: impartialement, de façon neutre, de manière neutre
impassioned: passionné
impassive: impassible
impatience: impatience
impatient: impatient
impatiently: de façon impatiente, de manière impatiente
impeded: empêchâmes
impediment: empêchement, entrave, obstacle
impending: imminent
impenetrable: impénétrable, imperméable
imperative: impératif

imperceptibly: de façon imperceptible, de manière imperceptible
imperfect: imparfait
imperfection: imperfection, défectuosité
imperfectly: imparfaitement, de façon imparfaite, de manière imparfaite
imperial: impérial
imperious: impérieux
imperiously: de façon impérieuse, de manière impérieuse
imperishable: impérissable
impertinence: impertinence, insolence
impertinent: hardi, impertinent
imperturbable: imperturbable
impetuous: impétueux, fougueux
impetuously: de façon impétueuse, de manière impétueuse
implacable: implacable
implanted: implantâmes
implement: instrument, outil, exécuter, implémenter
implicate: entortiller, empêtrer, impliquer
implicit: implicite, absolu
implicitly: implicitement, de façon implicite, de manière implicite
implied: impliquâtes, tacite
implies: implique
implore: implorer, conjurer
implored: implorai
imploring: implorant, conjurer, suppliant
imply: impliquer, signifier, suggérer
implying: impliquant
import: importation, signifier
importance: importance
importunity: importunité
impose: imposer, obliger, contraindre
imposed: imposa, contraignit
imposes: impose, contraint
imposing: imposant, contraignant
impossible: impossible
impostor: imposteur, charlatan
impotence: impuissance, impotence
impotent: impuissant, impotent
impoverish: appauvrir
impregnable: imprenable
impress: impressionner, clicher
impressed: impressionné
impression: impression, effet, empreinte, tirage
impressionable: impressionnable
impressive: impressionnant, grandiose, imposant
imprisonment: emprisonnement, incarcération

improbable: improbable, invraisemblable
improperly: de manière incorrecte, incorrectement, de façon incorrecte
improve: améliorer, amender, réformer, perfectionner, bonifier
improved: améliorâtes, amendai, réformé
improvement: amélioration, perfectionnement
imprudence: imprudence
imprudent: imprudent
imprudently: de façon imprudente, de manière imprudente, imprudemment
impudent: effronté, impudent
impugn: contester, attaquer
impulse: impulsion, incitation, pulsion
impunity: impunité
impure: impur
imputed: imputâmes
inability: incapacité, impuissance
inaction: inaction
inane: bête, inepte
inanimate: inanimé
inauspicious: peu propice
inborn: inné, naturel, congénital
incarnation: incarnation
incensed: courroucé
incessant: incessant
inch: pouce
incident: incident, événement, pollution accidentelle
incidentally: incidemment, de façon incidente, de manière incidente
incited: incitai, émûtes, émut, émus, ému, émurent, émûmes
inclination: inclinaison, propension, pendage, penchant, tendance, dévers, déclivité
inclined: enclin, incliné
incoherently: de manière incohérente, de façon incohérente
income: revenu, recette, produit, rente
incommunicable: incommunicable
incompatible: incompatible, inalliable, marchandises incompatibles
incomplete: incomplet, inachevé, imparfait, dépareillé
inconceivable: inconcevable, abracadabrant, inimaginable
inconstancy: inconstance, instabilité
incontestable: incontestable
incontinently: de façon incontinente, de manière incontinente

inconvenient: difficile, pénible, dur, inopportun, incommode, gênant
incorrigible: incorrigible
increase: augmenter, accroissement, agrandir, grossir, s'accroître, redoubler, amplifier, croissance, hausse, majorer, étendre
increased: augmenté
incredulous: incrédule
inculcate: inculquons
inculcating: inculquant
incur: encourir, subir, engager une dépense, contracter une dette
incurred: encouru, contractai
indebted: endetté, redevable
indeed: vraiment, certes, en vérité, si, réellement, en effet, en réalité, en fait, d'abord, voire, effectivement
indefatigable: infatigable, inlassable
indefinable: indéfinissable
indemnified: indemnisèrent
independence: indépendance, autonomie
independent: indépendant, impartial
indescribable: indescriptible
index: indice, index, tableau, liste, répertoire
indifference: indifférence
indifferent: indifférent, impartial
indifferently: de façon indifférente, de manière indifférente, indifféremment
indigestible: indigeste
indignant: indigné
indignantly: de façon indignée, de manière indignée
indignation: indignation
indirect: indirect, détourné
indirectly: indirectement, de façon indirecte, de manière indirecte
indiscretion: indiscrétion
indispensable: indispensable
indisposed: indisposé, souffrant
indistinct: confus, touffu, trouble, indistinct
indistinctly: de façon trouble, indistinctement, de manière trouble
individual: individu, particulier
individuality: individualité
individualized: individualisâtes
individualizes: individualise
indolent: indolent, peu évolutif
induce: induire, conclure, provoquer, persuader
induced: induit, bouton de vapeur, bilame

inducement: incitation, lieu, occasion
indulge: être indulgent, gâter
indulged: gâtas, gâtâtes, gâté, gâtèrent
indulgence: indulgence, tolérance
indurated: induré
industrious: laborieux, appliqué, assidu, industrieux, travailleur
industry: industrie, application
inebriation: enivrement, état d'ivresse
ineffable: ineffable
ineffably: de façon ineffable, de manière ineffable
inelegantly: de manière inélégante, de façon inélégante
inequality: inégalité, inéquation
inert: inerte, matière inerte, rendre incomburant
inevitable: inévitable, inéluctable
inexorable: inexorable
inexorably: de façon inexorable, de manière inexorable, inexorablement
inexperience: inexpérience, manque d'expérience
inexperienced: inexpérimenté
inexplicable: inexplicable
inexpressible: inexprimable, indicible
inexpressibly: de façon inexprimable, de manière inexprimable
inextricable: inextricable
inextricably: inextricablement, de façon inextricable, de manière inextricable
infallible: infaillible
infamy: infamie
infancy: enfance, minorité, petite enfance
infant: enfant, nourrisson, poupon
infatuated: infatué, entiché
infected: infectâtes, septique
inference: inférence, corollaire
inferior: inférieur, de second ordre, en indice inférieur, subordonné
infernal: infernal
infidelity: infidélité
infinite: infini, illimité
infinitesimally: de façon infinitésimale, de manière infinitésimale
infinity: infinité, foyer infini, valeur infinie
infirm: infirme, irrésolu
infirmity: infirmité
inflame: enflammer, s'enflammer
inflamed: enflammé
inflaming: enflammant
inflammable: inflammable

inflammatory: inflammatoire, séditieux, incendiaire
inflict: infliger, imposer
inflicted: infligé
inflicting: infligeant
influence: influence, empire
influenced: influencé
inform: informer, renseigner, faire part de
informed: informas, renseignas
infuse: infuser, injecter
ingenious: ingénieux, astucieux
ingeniously: de façon ingénieuse, de manière ingénieuse, ingénieusement
ingenuity: ingéniosité
ingenuous: ingénu, candide, naïf
inglorious: déshonorant
ingratitude: ingratitude
ingredient: ingrédient, composante, élément
inhabitant: habitant
inhabited: habitèrent
inhaled: inhala, humai, humé, humâtes, humèrent
inherit: hériter
inheritance: héritage, succession
inheritor: héritier
initial: initiale, parapher
initiated: initié
injected: injectai, réinjectas
injunction: injonction, avant dire droit, arrêt de la suspension
injure: abîmer, détériorer, blesser
injured: blessé, détériorâtes, abîmâtes, lésé
injuring: détériorant, abîmant, blessant
injury: blessure, lésion, préjudice, dégât
injustice: injustice, iniquité
ink: encre, couleur à semelles, pâte, tracé, colorer
inmate: détenu, interne, occupant, résident d'institution
inmost: le plus profond
inn: auberge, taverne, bar
innate: inné, naturel, congénital
inner: interne, intérieur
innkeeper: aubergiste, hôtelier
innocence: innocence, naïveté
innocent: innocent
innocently: de manière innocente, innocemment, de façon innocente
inopportunely: de manière inopportune, de façon inopportune
inquest: enquête
inquire: enquérir, m'enquiers, vous enquérez, t'enquiers, s'enquièrent, se renseigner, nous enquérons, demander

inquired: vous enquîtes, t'enquis, s'enquit, nous enquîmes, m'enquis
inquirer: demandeur
inquiring: interrogateur, s'enquérant
inquiringly: de façon interrogatrice, de manière interrogatrice
inquiry: enquête, demande de renseignements, interrogation, investigation
inquisitive: curieux, inquisiteur
inquisitor: inquisiteur
insalubrious: insalubre
insane: fou, insensé, aberrant, agité, aliéné
insanity: folie, aliénation, démence, aberration, affolement, insanité
insatiable: insatiable
inscribed: inscrit
inscription: inscription, exergue, légende
insect: insecte
insecurity: insécurité
insensible: insensible
insensibly: de façon insensible, de manière insensible
inseparable: inséparable, indivisible
insight: perspicacité, connaissance intuitive, intéroception, compréhension de soi, intuition
insignificance: insignifiance
insincerity: hypocrisie, manque de sincérité
insinuate: insinuer
insinuates: insinue
insipidity: insipidité
insisted: insistai, aheurté
insolence: effronterie, insolence
insolent: insolent, effronté
insolently: de façon insolente, de manière insolente
inspection: inspection, contrôle
inspector: inspecteur, contrôleur
inspire: inspirer, dicter, enthousiasmer
inspired: inspirâtes, s'enthousiasmé, vous enthousiasmâtes, nous enthousiasmâmes, m'enthousiasmai, t'enthousiasmas
installed: installâmes, emménagés
instance: exemple, instance
instant: instant, moment
instantaneously: de façon instantanée, de manière instantanée
instantly: aussitôt, directement, tout d'abord, d'abord, de façon instante, de manière instante, à l'instant

instead: plutôt, à la place, au contraire, au lieu de
instil: instiller
instilled: inculquas, insufflèrent
instinct: instinct, pulsion
instinctive: instinctif
instinctively: instinctivement, de façon instinctive, de manière instinctive
instruct: instruire, donner des instructions, enseigner
instructed: instruisis
instruction: instruction, enseignement
instrument: instrument, orchestrer, titre, acte instrumentaire, effet de commerce, appareil de mesure
insufficient: insuffisant
insult: insulte, offenser, injure, affront
insulting: insultant, offensant, agonissant, injurieux
insurance: assurance
insure: assurer, s'assurer
insured: assuras, maître de l'ouvrage
integrity: intégrité, honnêteté, probité
intellect: intellect, esprit, raison
intellectual: intellectuel
intellectually: intellectuellement, de façon intellectuelle, de manière intellectuelle
intelligence: intelligence, renseignement
intelligible: intelligible
intemperance: intempérance
intended: visé, visa, visâmes, visèrent, projetas, destiné
intense: intense, fort, aigu, vif, violent
intensely: de façon intense, de manière intense, intensément
intensity: intensité
intent: intention, alerte, résolu
intention: intention, dessein, propos
intently: attentivement, de façon intentionnelle, de manière intentionnelle
intercede: intercéder
intercepted: interceptai
intercession: intercession
interchange: échange, rupture de charge, compensation des données de factures, modification interchromosomique, point d'échange, relais
intercourse: rapport sexuel, relations
interested: intéressé

interesting: intéressant, curieux, singulier
interfered: interférâtes
interference: interférence, brouillage, ingérence, perturbation, immixtion, serrage
interferer: brouilleur
interfering: interférant, importun
interior: intérieur
interloper: intrus
intermarriage: mariage consanguin, intermariage
intermeddling: immixtion
intermission: pause, trêve, entracte, repos, intermittence
interpose: interposer
interpret: interpréter, traduire
interpretation: interprétation, décodage, définition
interrogatory: interrogateur
interrupt: interrompre
interrupted: interrompit
interruption: interruption, rupture, coupure
intersected: entrecoupâtes, intersecta, croisas
interval: intervalle, temps mort
intervened: intervînmes
interview: entrevue, interview
interwoven: entremêlé
intimacy: intimité
intimate: intime, pulsion intime
intimately: de façon intime, de manière intime, intimement
intolerable: intolérable, insupportable
intoxicate: enivrer, griser
intoxicated: ivre, enivras, intoxiqué
intoxication: ivresse, intoxication, ébriété, empoisonnement, griserie
intrigue: intriguer
introduce: présenter, introduire, offrir
introducing: introduisant, présentant
introduction: introduction, présentation
intruder: intrus, importun
intrusive: intrusif, importun
intuition: intuition
intuitive: intuitif
invade: envahir, invader
invaded: envahîtes, invadées
invader: envahisseur
invalid: invalide, non valable, périmé
invariable: invariable
invariably: invariablement, de façon invariable, de manière invariable
invective: injure, invective
invent: inventer

invention: invention, découverte
inventor: inventeur
inventory: inventaire, recensement, stocks
invest: investir, placer d'argent
invested: investîmes
investigation: enquête, examen, recherche, investigation, reconnaissance, instruction
investment: investissement, placement
invisible: invisible
invisibly: de façon invisible, de manière invisible, invisiblement
invitation: invitation
invite: inviter, conviez
invited: invitèrent, conviâtes
inviting: invitant, appétissant, attrayant, conviant
invoke: invoquer, appeler
involuntarily: de façon involontaire, de manière involontaire, involontairement
involuntary: involontaire
involve: impliquer, comprendre
involved: impliqué, compliqué
inward: intérieur, vers l'intérieur
ire: courroux
irksome: ennuyeux
iron: fer, fer à repasser, repasser
ironical: ironique
irony: ironie
irreconcilable: irréconciliable, inconciliable
irredeemable: irrachetable, incorrigible, non rachetable
irregular: irrégulier, non réglé
irregularity: irrégularité, inégalité
irregularly: irrégulièrement, de façon irrégulière, de manière irrégulière
irresistibly: irrésistiblement, de manière irrésistible, de façon irrésistible
irresolute: indécis, hésitant, irrésolu
irresolutely: de façon indécise, de manière indécise
irreverence: irrévérence
irrevocable: irrévocable
irrevocably: de façon irrévocable, de manière irrévocable
irritable: irritable, irascible
irritate: irriter, énerver, agacer
irritated: irrité, énervèrent, agacé
irritates: irrite, énerve
irritating: irritant, agaçant
irritation: irritation, agacement
isle: île, îlot
issue: émission, éditer, livraison, question, parution, problème, numéro, émettre, proclamer

issued: émis
isthmus: isthme
itch: démanger, prurit
item: article, item, individu, élément, entité, point, rubrique, poste
itinerant: itinérant, ambulant
ivy: lierre, vert lierre
jackal: chacal
jacket: veste, jaquette, chemise, enveloppe, blouson, pochette, gaine
jail: prison, geôle, emprisonner
jailer: geôlier, gardien de prison
jargon: jargon, charabia
jarring: battage, broutage d'un outil, discordant
jauntily: de façon désinvolte, de manière désinvolte
jay: geai
jealous: jaloux
jealously: de façon jalouse, de manière jalouse, jalousement
jealousy: jalousie, envie
jelly: gelée, gélation
jerk: secousse, saccade, suraccélération
jerkin: justaucorps, pourpoint
jest: badiner, plaisanter
jesting: plaisantant
jet: jais, jet, avion à réaction, gicleur
jetty: jetée, débarcadère, embarcadère
jewel: bijou, joyau
jilted: plaqua, délaissé
jingle: tinter, sonal
join: joindre, joignent, unir, relier, réunir, associer, accoupler, attacher, adhérer, nouer, raccorder
joined: joint, joignirent, relia, associas, accouplâmes, nouai, nouâmes, nouèrent, noué
joining: joignant, reliant, accouplant, associant, nouant, raccordement, rattachement
joint: articulation, commun, joint, raccord, pétard, interarmées, diaclase, charnière, mors
joke: plaisanterie, badiner, blague, farce
jolly: gai, enjoué, joyeux
jolt: secousse, cahoter
jostle: bousculer, jouer des coudes
jot: brin, noter
journal: journal, tourillon, quotidien, revue, livre journal, magazine, portée d'arbre
journey: voyage, trajet, parcours, périple
journeyman: compagnon, ouvrier qualifié
jovial: enjoué

joy: joie, allégresse
joyfully: de manière joyeuse, de façon joyeuse
joylessly: de manière triste, de façon triste
joyous: joyeux, heureux
joyously: de façon joyeuse, de manière joyeuse
jubilee: jubilé
judge: juge, magistrat assis, assesseur, arbitre, estimateur
judged: jugé
judging: jugement, taxation
judgment: arrêt, jugement
judicious: judicieux
junior: junior, cadet, débutant, jeune
jury: jury, jurés, commission d'arbitrage
justice: justice, équité
justified: justifié, dressé, cadrèrent
justify: justifier, dressez, cadrent, motiver
juvenile: juvénile, jeune, mineur
juvenility: juvénilité
keen: vif, aiguisé, vigilant, alerte, actif, affilé
keenly: de façon vive, de manière vive
keenness: finesse
keeping: gardant, élevant, remplissant
kennel: chenil, niche, ruisseau
kept: garda, élevèrent, remplit
kerchief: mouchoir, marmotte, carré
ketch: ketch
kettle: bouilloire, chaudron
key: clé, touche, clef, clavette, code, manipulateur
kick: coup de pied, recul, donner un coup de pied, botter
kicking: puits actif, coups de pied au ballon, bottant
kid: gosse, chevreau, gamin
kill: tuer, abattre, supprimer, rectifier
killing: meurtre, abattage
kin: parenté, famille
kindled: allumâtes, enflammé
kindly: complaisamment, de façon gentille, de manière gentille
kindness: amabilité, gentillesse, bonté, aménité
kindred: parenté, famille
king: roi, dame
kingdom: royaume, règne
kinsman: parent
kinsmen: parents
kinswoman: parente
kissed: baisée, embrassé
kisses: baise, bisous

kissing: embrasser, baisant
knapsack: havresac, sac tyrolien
knave: fripon, coquin
knee: genou, le genou, coude
kneel: s'agenouiller, agenouillement, se mettre à genoux
kneeling: baraquage, à genoux, agenouillé
knell: glas
knelt: agenouillé
knife: couteau, poignarder, le couteau
knight: chevalier, cavalier
knit: tricoter, mailler, prendre
knitted: tricoté
knock: frapper, coup, heurter, cogner
knocked: frappâmes
knocking: frappant, coups
knoll: monticule
knot: noeud, nouer, bécasseau maubèche, larme, nodule, nœud lâche
knowing: connaissant, entendu, sachant
knowingly: sciemment, de manière connaissante
knowledge: connaissance, savoir
knows: connaît, sait
laborious: laborieux, pénible
labourer: ouvrier, manoeuvre
labyrinth: labyrinthe, dédale
lace: dentelle, lacet
laced: triangulé, lacé
lack: manque, défaut, privation, insuffisance, vice
lacked: manqua
lackey: laquais, larbin
laconic: laconique
laconically: de façon laconique, de manière laconique, laconiquement
laconism: laconisme
lad: garçon, gosse
ladder: échelle, maille filée
laden: chargé
lady: dame, madame, demoiselle noble
laid: posèrent, posa, posâmes, posé, vergé, couchèrent, pondîmes
lair: tanière, repaire
lake: lac, laque
lamb: agneau, mettre bas
lameness: boiterie, impotence, boiterie ancienne intermittente, claudication, faiblesse
lament: lamentation, se lamenter, complainte
lamented: lamenté
lamp: lampe, ampoule
lamplight: lumière artificielle
lancet: lancette, ogive

land: terre, atterrir, pays, aborder, contrée, s'abattre
landlord: propriétaire, aubergiste, logeur
landmark: point de repère, repère
landscape: paysage, texte en largeur, format à l'italienne
lane: voie, ruelle, couloir
language: langue, libelle, parole
languid: langoureux, traînant, biseau, indolent
languidly: de façon languissante, de manière languissante
languor: langueur
lantern: lanterne, fanal
lap: clapoter, recouvrement, nappe, chevauchement, tour, giron, barboter
lapse: déchéance, défaillance, retomber
lapsed: dévolu par péremption, vieux, périmé, infirme, caduc, délabré
larger: plus grand
lark: alouette, blague
lash: fouetter, aiguilleter, dard, mèche, attacher
lassitude: lassitude
lasted: duré, durèrent, dura, durâmes
latch: loquet, verrou, clenche, bascule
late: tard, en retard
lately: dernièrement, de manière tarde, de façon tardive, récemment
lateness: retard
latent: latent, caché
latest: dernier
latter: dernier
laudable: louable
laugh: rire, rigoler
laughed: ries, rit, rirent, rie, ris
laughing: riant, rieur, rire
laughingly: de façon riante, de manière riante
laughter: rire
launched: lancé, lançai
laundress: blanchisseuse
laurel: laurier
lavish: généreux, prodigue
lawful: légal, légitime, licite
lawfully: de façon légale, de manière légale, légalement
lawn: pelouse, gazon, linon, batiste
lawyer: avocat, défenseur, juriste, homme de loi
lay: poser, posons, laïque, coucher, pondre, commettage
layer: couche, gisement, feuille de placage, assise, marcotte, strate
laying: pose, posant, ponte, pondant, couchant, levée

lazily: de façon paresseuse, de manière paresseuse, paresseusement
lead: plomb, mener, conduire, guider, mènes, menons, aboutir, avance, diriger, régler, mine
leader: guide, animateur, leader, conseiller, chef, amorce, dirigeant, commandant, meneur
leadership: direction, leadership, primauté
leading: conduisant, menant, guidant, aboutissant, plombage, principal, laissant
leaf: feuille, rallonge, vantail, pousse, lamelle, volant, aile
league: ligue, lieue
lean: maigre, appuyer, accoter, s'adosser, s'accoter, mince, adosser
leaned: adossés
leaning: penchant, tendance, appui, adossé
leap: saut, bond, gambader, filon pauvre
leaped: sauté
learn: apprendre, instruire
learned: apprit, cultivé, savant, érudit
learning: apprenant, érudition, savoir
learns: apprend
lease: bail, affermer, prendre à bail, location, louer, concession, encroix, contrat de location
least: moindre, le moins
leather: cuir, en cuir, relier en cuir
leave: partir, pars, abandonner, laisser, quitter, permission, congé, s'en aller, délaisser, livrer, sortir
leaving: partant, départ
lecture: conférence, exposé, cours magistral
led: menâmes, mena, conduit, mené, menèrent, guidâtes, about it, laissa
leer: regard mauvais, lorgner
leg: jambe, patte, gigot, branche, cuisse, pied, montant, étançon
legacy: legs, héritage
legal: légal, légitime, juridique
legally: de façon légale, de manière légale, légalement
legend: légende, marquage
legibly: de façon lisible, de manière lisible, lisiblement
legitimate: légitime, logique
leisure: loisir
leisurely: paisiblement, lentement, calme
lemonade: limonade, citronnade
lend: prêter, emprunter

length: longueur, traînée, portant, étendue, délai d'amortissement, durée de validité
lengthening: allongeant, rallongement, prolongation
leniently: de façon indulgente, de manière indulgente
lent: prêta, carême, empruntas
leopard: léopard
lessen: diminuer, amoindrir, abréger, abaisser
lesser: moindre
lesson: leçon, cours
lest: de peur que
lethargy: léthargie
letter: lettre, missive, la lettre, caractère
levity: légèreté
liability: responsabilité, passif, élément de passif
liable: responsable, assujetti, passible
libation: libation
libel: libelle, diffamation, calomnie écrite
liberal: libéral, généreux
liberality: libéralité, générosité
liberally: de manière libérale, libéralement, de façon libérale
liberty: liberté
librarian: bibliothécaire
license: licence, permis, autoriser
licentiousness: licence
licked: léché
lid: couvercle, capot, plaque de regard
lie: mensonge, mentir, être couché, gésir
lied: menti, gésie
lifeless: sans vie, inanimé
lifetime: vie, durée de vie
lift: ascenseur, lever, soulever, élever, portance, se soulever, sustentation
lifted: élevai, soulevé
lifting: levage, relevage, remontage, scarification, soulevé, prise, transfert, passerelle de chargement relevable, arrachage, levée du revêtement comme suite du revernissage, élevant
light: léger, lumière, clair, allumer, feu, faible, enflammer, rayonnement visible, lampe
lighted: allumé, éclairé, enflammé
lighten: alléger, éclaircir, allègent
lighter: briquet, allège, allumeur, péniche
lighting: éclairage, allumage
lightly: légèrement, de façon légre, de manière légre

lightness: clarté, légèreté, leucie, luminosité
lightning: éclair, foudre
liked: aimé
likeness: ressemblance, similitude, portrait
limb: membre, limbe, flanc
limit: limite, frontière
limited: limité, borné
limpid: limpide
lineage: lignage, descendance, souche
lineal: linéal, direct
lineament: linéament
lined: ligné, doublé
linen: lin, linge, toile
linger: traîner, s'attarder
lingered: traîné
lingering: prolongé, traînant
lingeringly: de façon prolongée, de manière prolongé
link: lien, liaison, maillon, chaînon, monter, lier, articulation, rapport, relation, biellette
linked: lié
linnet: linotte
lion: lion
lip: lèvre, bord
liquid: liquide, flot, fluide
list: liste, énumérer, répertoire, inventaire
listen: écouter, entendre, être en mode Réception
listened: écoutâtes
listener: auditeur, écouteur
listening: écoutant, interrogation
listless: apathique, indifférent
listlessly: de manière indifférente, de façon indifférente
listlessness: indifférence, alanguissement, indolence, langueur
literally: littéralement, de façon littérale, de manière littérale
literary: littéraire
literature: littérature, documentation
litigation: litige, contentieux
live: vivre, vis, vivent, vivons, habiter, demeurer, loger, vivant, actif, sous tension
lived: vécut, vécûmes, habitâmes, logeâmes, logé, logèrent
liveliest: le plus vif
livelihood: subsistance, vie
lively: animé, vif, spirituel, fin, mental, de manière vivre, plein d'entrain, de façon vivre
livery: livrée, couleurs d'une maison
livid: livide

living: vivant, habitant, en vie, logeant, bénéfice
load: charger, fardeau
loan: prêt, emprunt
loathed: abominâtes, haï, haïtes, haïrent, abhorrai, haïs, haïmes
loathing: abhorrant, abominant, haïssant, répugnance
loathsome: détestable, répugnant
locality: localité, lieu
lock: serrure, écluse, verrou, fermer
locked: bloqué, fermé
lodge: loge, héberger, gîte, pavillon, auberge, déposer
lodged: logé
lodger: locataire, pensionnaire
lodging: hébergement, logement, verse
loft: grenier, angle d'ouverture, coup bombé, empêchement libre, gonflant, lober, reconverti, séchoir à l'air
lofty: haut, élevé
log: journal, rondin, loch, log
logic: logique
logical: logique
loin: lombes, reins, longe
loitered: flânas
lolled: pendîmes
lolling: pendant
lone: solitaire, seul
loneliness: solitude, isolement
lonely: solitaire, seul, de façon solitaire, de manière solitaire, isolé
lonesome: seul, solitaire
longing: désir, envie, aspiration
loom: métier à tisser, manche, gaine isolante, lueur
loose: détaché, lâche
loosened: desserrâtes, se détendirent, nous détendîmes, te détendis, ameublîmes, me détendis, déliés, vous détendîtes
lop: taille, ébrancher, clapotis
lopping: élagage, taillant
lord: seigneur, monsieur
lordship: seigneurie
lore: lorum
lose: perdre, s'égarer, succomber, se perdre, paumez, être vaincu
loses: perd, paume
losing: perdant, paumant
losses: pertes, charges hors exploitation, résidus
lost: perdit, non vu
lot: lot, sort
loud: fort, sonore, bruyant, haut, criard
loudly: fort, à haute voix, bruyamment, de façon forte, de manière forte
lounger: fainéant

lovable: aimable
loved: aimé, chéri, aimèrent, aimai
loveliness: beauté
lover: amant, amoureux, maîtresse
loving: amoureux, aimant, aimer
lovingly: de façon amoureuse, de manière amoureuse
low: bas, basse, lâche, dépression, abject
lower: baisser, abaisser, inférieur
lowering: abaissement, baissant
lowest: le plus bas, déclive
lowly: de manière bas, modeste, de façon bas
loyal: loyal, dévoué, droit, fidèle, honnête
lucid: lucide, clair
luck: chance, fortune, sort, destinée
luckiest: le plus chanceux
luckily: heureusement, de façon chanceuse, de manière chanceuse
lucky: chanceux, heureux
lucrative: lucratif
ludicrous: grotesque, ridicule, risible
lukewarm: tiède
lull: bercer, accalmie
lumbering: lourd
lump: masse, bloc, morceau, boule, motte, pièce, fragment, gros morceau, grumeau, bosse, pan
lunatic: aliéné, fou
luncheon: déjeuner
lung: poumon
lure: leurre, attirer
lurid: aigu, acéré, âcre, rude, tranchant, piquant, coupant, aigre, perçant
lurk: se cacher, badauder
lurking: badaudage
lust: passion, volupté, convoitise, désir, luxure
lustily: de façon vigoureuse, de manière vigoureuse
lustre: lustre, éclat
lustreless: éclat, mat, terne
lusty: vigoureux, robuste
luxuriance: luxuriance, exubérance
luxuriant: luxuriant, exubérant
luxurious: luxueux, somptueux
luxury: luxe, richesse
lying: menteur, mensonge, gisant
lyric: lyrique, texte
machine: machine, usiner
mad: fou, aberrant, agité, enragé
maddened: exaspérâtes, rendu fou
maddening: à rendre fou, enrageant, exaspérant
maddens: exaspère
madhouse: maison de fous
madly: de manière folle, follement, de façon folle

magic: magie, enchantement, sorcellerie
magically: de façon magique, de manière magique
magistrate: magistrat
magnetic: magnétique, aimanté
magnificent: magnifique, grandiose
magnified: grossirent, magnifiâtes
mahogany: acajou
maid: femme de chambre, servante, domestique, bonne
maiden: brin, vierge
maidservant: domestique
mail: courrier, poste
mainly: principalement, surtout, de manière principale, en grande partie, de façon principale
maintain: maintenir, conserver, retenir, entretenir
maintained: maintîntes, conservai, entretenu
maintenance: entretien, maintenance, garde
majestic: majestueux, imposant
majestically: de façon majestueuse, de manière Majestueuse, majestueusement
majesty: majesté, seigneurie
malady: maladie
malcontent: mécontent
malice: méchanceté, malice, malveillance
malignant: malin, grave
malignity: malveillance, malignité
mall: mail, centre commercial
manage: administrer, diriger, gérer, gérons, gère, réussir
manageable: maniable, conciliant
managing: administrant, dirigeant, gérant
mane: crinière, tresser la crinière
manfully: de façon vaillante, de manière vaillante
manhood: virilité, âge d'homme
maniac: maniaque, fou
manifest: manifeste, évident
manifested: manifesté
manifold: multiple, manifold, divers, clarinette, tubulure, variété, distributeur
mankind: humanité, genre humain, l'humanité
manliness: virilité
manly: viril, mâle
manner: manière, façon
mannered: maniéré, affecté
manor: manoir
mansion: immeuble, château, mansion
mantelpiece: chambranle de cheminée, tablette

mantle: manteau, pèlerine
manufactured: fabriquâtes, manufacturâmes, ouvré
manuscript: manuscrit, restitution photogrammétrique, stéréominute, minute
map: carte, plan, mappe, application
mar: gâter, gâtons
marble: marbre, bille
marched: marché
marching: marcher
marge: marger
margin: marge, bord, couverture
mark: marque, estampiller, signe, cachet, mark, note, repère, témoignage, repérer, tracer, marc
marked: marqué
markedly: de façon marquée, de manière marquée, nettement
marquis: marquis
marriage: mariage, noces, alliance
married: marié, te marias, se marièrent, vous mariâtes, nous mariâmes, me mariai, épousas
marrow: moelle, courge
marry: marier, me marie, vous mariez, te maries, se marient, nous marions, épouser
marrying: se mariant, épousant
marsh: marécage, marais, pelouse marécageuse
mart: centre commercial, marché
martial: martial
martyr: martyr
martyrdom: martyre, supplice
marvel: merveille, s'étonner
masculine: masculin, mâle
mask: masque, cache
massive: massif, énorme
massively: de façon massive, de manière massive, massivement
massiveness: massiveté
master: maître, patron, maestro, apprendre à fond, capitaine, principal
mastered: gravé, maîtrisé
masterly: magistral
masterpiece: réussite exceptionnelle
mastery: maîtrise, prééminence
masthead: tête de mat, adresse, ton de mât, bloc générique, générique
match: allumette, apparier, match, s'entremettre, assortir, partie, égal, rencontre
matchless: incomparable, sans égal
mate: s'accoupler, compagnon, accoupler, camarade
material: matériau, tissu, étoffe, matière
materially: matériellement

maternal: maternel
mathematical: mathématique
mathematics: mathématiques
matrimonial: conjugal, matrimonial
matrimony: mariage
matron: matrone, directrice, mère de famille, surveillante
matted: maté, feutré
matter: matière, substance, affaire, cas, chose, question
mattress: matelas, clayonnage, entrelacs de protection
mature: mûr, adulte, fait, mûrir, font, faisons, mature, échoir
matured: mûrîtes, fit, fîtes, mûri, fis, fait, fîmes, firent
maturity: maturité, échéance
maudlin: larmoyant
mawkish: fade
maze: labyrinthe, dédale
mead: hydromel
meadow: pré, prairie, pâturage
meagre: maigre
meal: repas, farine
meaning: signification, sens, intention, importance, dessein, propos
meanness: mesquinerie, vilenie
meant: signifié
meanwhile: dans l'intervalle, en attendant, pendant ce temps
measure: mesure, taille, jauger
measured: mesuré
meat: viande, chair
mechanic: mécanicien, ouvrier mécanicien, garagiste
mechanical: mécanique, maquette, machinal
mechanically: de façon mécanique, de manière mécanique, mécaniquement
mechanism: mécanisme
meddle: mêlez, se mêler, mêlons
mediaeval: du moyen âge, médiéval
mediation: médiation, intermédiaire, entremise
medicinal: médicinal
medicine: médicament, médecine, remède
mediocrity: médiocrité
meditate: méditer, songer, réfléchir
meditated: méditâtes, songea
meditates: médite, songe
meditating: méditant, songeant
meditative: méditatif
meek: humble, doux
meekly: de façon humble, de manière humble
meekness: douceur de caractère, humilité
meet: rencontrer, réunir, se réunir

meeting: réunion, rencontrant, séance, croisement, assemblée
melancholy: mélancolie, sombre, abattement
melodious: mélodieux, harmonieux
melodrama: mélodrame
melody: mélodie, chant
melt: fondre, dégeler, faire fondre, fonte
melted: fondu, cuit
member: membre, adhérent, affilié, partisan
membrane: membrane, paroi étanche, feuillet de parchemin, masque amont
memoir: mémoire, livre mémorial
memorable: mémorable
memorandum: mémorandum, note, bordereau
memorial: mémorial, commémoratif, écrit mémorial, monument
memory: mémoire, souvenir
menace: menacer, gronder
menaced: menacé
menacing: menaçant, sinistre
menial: subalterne, de domestique, servile
mental: mental, intellectuel
mention: mentionner, citer
mentioned: mentionné
mercantile: mercantile, commercial
mercenary: mercenaire
merchandise: marchandise, denrée, produit
merchant: négociant, marchand, commerçant
merciful: indulgent, Clément, sensible, miséricordieux
mercifully: de façon indulgente, de manière indulgente
mercilessly: de façon impitoyable, de manière impitoyable
mercurial: mercuriel
mercy: pitié, miséricorde, compassion
mere: pur, seul, simple
merely: simplement, de façon pure, de manière pure
merged: fusionnèrent
merit: mérite, gloire
merited: mérité
merriest: le plus joyeux
merrily: joyeusement, de façon joyeuse, de manière joyeuse
merry: joyeux, gai
mesh: maille, engrener, treillis, s'engrener, prendre au filet, mesh, grillage
mesmerism: mesmérisme
message: message, renseignement
messenger: messager, coursier

met: rencontré
metaphorical: métaphorique
metaphysical: métaphysique
mete: infligez
meted: infligea
meteor: météore
method: méthode, modalité
methodical: méthodique, systématique
methodically: de manière systématique, de façon méthodique
mid: mi
middle: milieu, moyen, intermédiaire, centre
midnight: minuit
midst: milieu, millieux
mien: mine
mighty: puissant, considérable
mild: doux, suave, léger, faible, bénin
mile: mille, lieue
milestone: étape importante, borne
military: militaire
milk: lait, traire
milliner: modiste, chapelier
mincemeat: mincemeat
mindful: attentif, conscient
mine: mine, mienne
mingle: mélanger, mêler, mêlons, retourner
mingled: mélangeâtes, mêlé, mêlâtes, mêlas, mêlèrent
mingling: mêlant, mélangeant
miniature: miniature, maquette
minion: favori, mignonne
minor: mineur, secondaire, matière secondaire, enfant mineur
minuet: menuet
minute: minute, moment, la minute, instant
mire: mire, bourbier, boue
mirror: miroir, glace, rétroviseur
mirth: gaieté, allégresse
misanthropy: misanthropie
miscellaneous: divers
mischief: malice, tort, méfait, dégâts
misconduct: mauvaise conduite, inconduite
misdeed: méfait, délit
miser: avare, ladre
miserable: malheureux, misérable, pauvre, maussade, mauvais, méchant, vide, pénible, sombre, mal
miserably: de façon misérable, de manière misérable
misery: misère, tristesse
misfortune: malheur, infortune, malchance
misgiving: crainte, doute

misinterpret: mal interpréter
misjudge: mal juger, méjugez
mislead: égarer, tromper
misled: égara, trompé
misplaced: déplacé, égarâtes, en malposition
misrepresentation: fausse déclaration, information fausse ou trompeuse, déclaration inexacte, assertion inexacte, déformation
missed: manqué
misses: manque
mission: mission
missionary: missionnaire
missive: missive
mist: brume, brouillard, buée, voile
mistake: erreur, faute, méprise, se tromper
mistaken: abusif, trompé
mistress: maîtresse, madame
mistrust: méfiance, te méfies, se méfient, nous méfions, vous méfiez, me méfie, défiance
misty: brumeux, embué, vague, vaporeux
misunderstand: mal comprendre
misunderstood: mal compris, incompris
mitigate: mitiger, adoucir, atténuer
mitigated: mitigèrent, atténuèrent, adoucîmes
mix: mélanger, mêler, mixer, malaxer, retourner, gâcher, allier
mixed: mélangé, mixte, mêlé
mixing: mélange, malaxage, brassage, mixage
mixture: mélange, mixture
moaned: gémi, bêla, bêlèrent, bêlés
mob: foule, assaillir, bande
mobile: mobile, nomade
mock: bafouer, railler, se moquer de, faux
mocked: bafouâmes
mockery: moquerie, simulacre
mocking: bafouant, dérision
mockingly: de façon dérisionnelle, de manière dérisionnelle
mode: mode, manière
moderate: modéré, ralentir, raisonnable, abordable, retenir
modern: moderne
modest: modeste, modique, pudique
modestly: modestement, de manière modeste, de façon modeste
modesty: modestie, pudeur
moiety: groupe caractéristique, fragment
moistened: humidifia, humectâtes
mole: taupe, mole, môle, grain de beauté, tunnelier

mollified: apaisâtes
momentary: momentané
monarch: monarque
monitor: moniteur, appareil de surveillance, contrôler, surveiller
monomania: monomanie
monopolized: monopolisa, accaparâmes
monopolizing: monopolisant, accaparant
monosyllable: monosyllabe
monotonous: monotone
monster: monstre, clébard
monstrous: monstrueux, colossal
month: mois
monument: monument, borne cadastrale
mood: humeur, ambiance
moon: lune
moonlight: clair de lune
moped: vélomoteur, cyclomoteur, mobylette, pétrolette
moral: moral
moralist: moraliste
moralize: moraliser
morally: moralement, de manière morale, de façon morale
morbid: morbide
morbidly: de façon morbide, de manière morbide
moreover: en outre, d'ailleurs, en prime, et puis, de plus
morn: matin
morose: morose, maussade, sombre
moroseness: morosité
morrow: lendemain
mortal: mortel
mortality: mortalité
mortally: de façon mortelle, de manière mortelle
mortgage: hypothèque, lettre de gage, porteur de créance hypothécaire
mortified: mortifiai, humiliâmes
mossy: moussu
mostly: plupart, surtout
moth: mite, phalène
motherless: sans mère
motion: mouvement, motion, résolution, marche, requête
motionless: immobile, fixe, au repos
motive: motif, lieu, occasion, mobile
mould: modeler, moule, moisissure, fondre, forme, matrice, façonner
moulded: membres, moulé
mouldy: moisi, chanci
mound: monticule, butte
mount: monter, support, adapter, bague de raccordement

mountain: montagne, orophile, la montagne
mounted: monté, porté
mourn: regretter, vous lamentez, s'affliger, te lamentes, lamentez-vous, se lamentent, pleurer, me lamente, nous lamentons, être en deuil, porter le deuil
mourned: regretté, te lamentas, se lamenta, vous lamentâtes, me lamentai, nous lamentâmes
mourner: pleureuse, personne en deuil
mournful: morne, sombre, mélancolique, triste
mournfully: de façon sombre, de manière sombre
mourning: deuil, regrettant
mouth: bouche, embouchure, bec, gueule, ouverture, entrée, goulot
move: émouvoir, remuer, déplacer, mouvoir, se déplacer, coup, déménagement, affecter, bouger, proposer
moved: ému, émurent, remuèrent, mus, mouvé, émus, déplacé
movement: mouvement, déplacement
moving: émouvant, attendrissant, mobile, en mouvement, déménagement
mow: faucher, tas de balles
mowed: fauchas, tondîtes
mud: boue, vase, bourbe, limon
muffin: muffin
muffled: assourdirent, étouffé
mullion: meneau, montant central, cloison
multiform: multiforme
multitude: multitude, amas, foule, masse, tas
mumbled: marmonna, bredouillèrent, mâchonnèrent
murder: assassiner, meurtre, rectifier, crime de meurtre
murdered: assassiné
murderer: meurtrier, assassin
murderess: meurtrière
murderous: meurtrier, homicide
murmur: murmure, bruit
murmured: murmuré
murmuring: murmurer
muscle: muscle, le muscle
muscular: musculaire
muse: muse, songer, méditer, rêver
music: musique, partition
musical: musical, comédie musicale
musician: musicien
musing: méditer, rêverie
musingly: de façon rêveuse, de manière rêveuse
muslin: mousseline, toile écrue

mustache: moustache, la moustache
mute: muet, sourdine, commutateur de sourdine
mutely: de façon muete, de manière muette
mutilated: mutilé, détérioré, tronqué
mutinous: mutiné
muttered: barbotée
muttering: barbotant
mutual: réciproque, mutuel
myself: me
mysterious: mystérieux
mysteriously: de manière mystérieuse, de façon mystérieuse
mystery: mystère
mystic: mystique
nail: clou, ongle, river, pointe, cheville
naivete: naïveté
naked: nu, dénudé
nakedly: de façon nue, de manière nue
named: nommé
nameless: anonyme, inconnu
namely: à savoir
namesake: homonyme
naming: nomination, tests d'appellation, nommage, dénomination
nankeen: nankin
nape: nuque
narrate: raconter, conter
narrated: racontèrent, contâtes
narrates: raconte, conte
narrative: récit, relation, narratif
narrator: narrateur, récitant
narrow: étroit, rétrécir, serré, restreint, resserré, diminuer, défilé, borné, limité
narrowly: de façon étroite, étroitement, de manière étroite
narrowness: étroitesse, petitesse
nation: nation, peuple
native: autochtone, naturel, natif, inné, aborigène, indigène, natal
natural: naturel, marche, bécarre, au naturel, simple, inné
naturally: naturellement, bien sûr, de façon naturelle, de manière naturelle
nature: nature, caractère
nausea: nausée, écœurement, la nausée
naval: naval, douanier
nave: moyeu, nef
navy: marine
nay: non
near: près, proche, auprès, à
nearest: plus proche

nearly: presque, quasiment, de manière près, à peu près, de façon près
neat: net, propre
neatness: netteté
necessarily: nécessairement, forcément, de manière nécessaire, de façon nécessaire
necessary: nécessaire, indispensable, essentiel
necessitated: nécessitai
necessity: nécessité, besoin
neck: cou, col, goulot, collet, encolure
needed: nécessita
neediness: indigence
needing: nécessitant
needles: aiguilles
needlessly: de façon inutile, de manière inutile, inutilement
needy: indigent, vide, nécessiteux
neglect: négliger, dédaigner, coups partis avec éléments erronés
neglected: négligé
negro: nègre, noir
neighbour: voisin, semblable
neighbourhood: voisinage, quartier
neighbouring: adjacent, avoisinant
neither: ni, non plus, personne, nul
nephew: neveu
nerve: nerf, toupet, courage, fortifier
nervous: nerveux, intimidé, agité, excitable, inquiet
nest: nid, nicher, faire son nid
nestle: se nicher, se pelotonner
net: filet, réseau, net
network: réseau, filet
nevertheless: néanmoins, pourtant, cependant, tout de même, quand même
newcomer: novice, nouveau
newly: de façon nouvelle, de manière nouveau, récemment
newspaper: journal, gazette, quotidien
nicely: bien, de façon agréable, de manière agréable
niche: niche, microhabitat, lien écologique
nick: entaille, encoche, ébrécher
nickname: surnom, sobriquet
niece: nièce
niggardly: pingre, mesquin
nightingale: rossignol
nightmare: cauchemar
nine: neuf
ninny: nigaud
nipping: éclat, pilon, pinçage
nobility: noblesse
noble: noble, élevé
nobleman: noble, seigneur

nobly: noblement, de manière noble, de façon noble
nobody: personne, nul
nocturnal: nocturne
nod: signe de tête, somnoler, se balancer, incliner la tête, hochement, faire signe que oui
noise: bruit, tapage, souffle
noiseless: silencieux, antisouffle
noiselessly: de façon silencieuse, de manière silencieuse, silencieusement
noisiest: le plus bruyant
noisiness: bruyance, turbulence
noisy: bruyant, bruité, tapageur, tumultueux
nominal: nominal, symbolique, modique
none: aucun, personne, nul
noon: midi
noonday: midi
nor: ni
nose: nez, bec
nosegay: petit bouquet odorant
nostril: narine, naseau
notable: notable
notably: notamment, de façon notable, de manière notable
note: note, billet, nota, remarque, mention, ticket
noted: noté, annoté, célèbre
nothingness: néant, vide
notice: avis, remarquer, apercevoir, préavis, discerner, placard, saisir, renseignement, réflexion, percevoir, observation
noticeable: perceptible, évident
noticed: remarqué
notion: notion, idée
notoriety: notoriété
notorious: notoire, mal famé
notoriously: de façon notoire, de manière notoire
notwithstanding: malgré, nonobstant, néanmoins
nought: zéro
nous: nous
novel: roman, nouveau
novelist: romancier, nouvelliste
novelty: nouveauté, gadget, innovation
novice: débutant, novice
nowadays: actuellement, de nos jours, aujourd'hui
noxious: nocif, nuisible
numbed: engourdis
numbered: numéroté
numberless: innombrable
numbing: engourdissant
nun: nonne, religieuse
nurse: infirmière, soigner, nourrice, veiller sur, allaiter

nursery: pépinière, pouponnière, nourricerie, nursery, crèche, garderie
nursing: soins infirmiers, allaitement, sciences infirmières
nurture: nourriture, élever, entretenir, milieu
nurtured: soutenue
nutshell: coquille de noix
nymph: nymphe
oaf: balourd, mufle, dadais, lourdaud
oak: chêne, écorce
oat: avoine
oath: serment, juron
obedience: obéissance, soumission
obey: obéir, obtempérons
obeyed: obéis, obéîtes
obeying: obéissant, obtempérant
object: objet, chose
objection: objection, opposition, réclamation
obligated: obligé
obligation: obligation, engagement
oblige: obliger
obliged: obligea
obliquity: obliquité
obscure: obscur, cacher, assombrir, inconnu
obscurity: obscurité, ténèbres
observation: observation, remarque, réflexion
observe: observer, respecter, accomplir, réaliser, suivre, remplir, agir selon, assurer
observed: observâtes, respectèrent, remplîtes
observer: observateur, spectateur
observing: observant, respectant, remplissant
obsolete: obsolète, désuet, périmé
obstacle: obstacle, empêchement
obstinate: obstiné, têtu, tenace, entêté
obstinately: de façon obstinée, de manière obstinée, obstinément
obstruct: obstruer, barrer, entraver, bloquer, encombrer, faire obstruction, engorger
obstructing: obstruant, entravant
obtain: obtenir, obtiennent, acquérir, procurer
obtained: obtint, obtîntes, obtenu
obtaining: obtenant
obtuse: obtus, borné
obtuseness: stupidité
obviate: obvions
obvious: évident, manifeste, clair, apparent
occasion: occasion, lieu, fois
occasional: occasionnel, de circonstance, intermittent

occasionally: occasionnellement, de façon occasionnelle, de manière occasionnelle, de temps en temps
occupant: occupant, habitant, locataire
occupation: occupation, métier, profession, emploi
occupied: occupâtes
occupier: occupant
occupy: occuper, habiter, remplir
occupying: occupant
occur: arriver, avoir lieu, survenir, intervenir, se présenter
occurred: arriva, survins
occurrence: événement, cas, indice, occurrence, venue
occurs: arrive, survient
ocean: océan, mer
odd: bizarre, impair, singulier, étrange, drôle
odious: odieux
odorous: odorant
offal: abats, dépouille, déchets
offence: délit, infraction, offense, agacement
offend: offenser, insulter, pécher
offended: offensas, insultèrent
offender: offenseur, contrevenant
offending: offensant, insultant
offer: offre, proposition, présenter, sacrifier, faire offrande, consacrer
offered: offert, offrie
offering: offrande, proposition, sacrifice
officer: officier, fonctionnaire
official: officiel, fonctionnaire
offspring: descendant, progéniture, successeur
ogre: ogre
oil: huile, graisser, pétrole
older: âgé
omen: augure, présage
ominous: inquiétant, menaçant, sinistre
omnibus: omnibus, autobus
onward: en avant
oozed: suinta, exsudé
oozing: suintement, exsudant
opal: opale
opened: ouvert, ouvrîmes
opening: ouverture, ouvrant, orifice, début, déclenchement
openly: ouvertement, franchement, publiquement
openness: franchise, aspect découvert, degré relatif d'effilochage de la fibre d'amiante, ouverture
opera: opéra
operate: opérer, opère, fonctionner, actionner, exploiter, faire

fonctionner, diriger, agir, manœuvrer
operation: opération, exploitation, fonctionnement, manoeuvre
operator: opérateur, téléphoniste, entité exploitante
opinion: avis, opinion, vœu
opportunity: occasion, opportunité
oppose: opposer, se mettre en travers, rouspéter
opposed: opposé, rouspétâmes
opposing: opposant, rouspétant
opposite: opposé, en face de, contraire
opposition: opposition, résistance
oppressed: opprimé, serrâtes
oppressively: de manière étouffante, de façon étouffante
opprobrium: opprobre
optic: optique, moulure optique
option: option, alternative, choix, faculté
opulent: opulent
orb: orbe
orbit: orbite, mettre en orbite, graviter sur une orbite, satelliser
ordeal: désolation, épreuve
ordered: commandé, ordonné
orderly: ordonné, méthodique
ordinary: ordinaire
organ: organe, orgue
organization: organisation, implantation
origin: origine, provenance, source
original: original, inédit
originality: originalité
originally: de façon originale, de manière originale
ormolu: or moulu
ornamental: décoratif, ornemental
orphan: orphelin, bout de ligne
ostensibly: de manière prétendue, de façon prétendue
ostentatious: prétentieux, ostentatoire
otherwise: sinon, autrement
ottoman: ottoman, pouf
ought: devoir, doivent, doit, devez, dois
ours: nôtre
outcast: banni, rejeté, proscrit, exclu, exilé, paria
outer: extérieur, externe
outlaw: proscrit
outline: contour, silhouette, esquisse, profil, résumer, schéma, tracé, ébauche
outrage: outrage, scandale, attentat, infraction correctionnelle
outrageously: de façon scandaleuse, de manière scandaleuse

outshining: éclipsant, surpassant
outside: dehors, extérieur, en dehors de, à l'extérieur
outstretched: étendu, déployé, tendu
outward: sortie, vers l'extérieur
outwitted: dépista
overcast: couvert, surjetai, surfiler, fonças, fonce
overcome: triompher de, vaincre
overestimate: surestimer, majorer
overflow: déborder, déversoir, inonder, trop plein, surplus, dépassement de capacité
overflowed: débordé
overflowing: débordant, dégorgement
overhang: surplomber, débord, queue de vache, offre excédentaire, inclinaison de la ligne des dents, empilage en encorbellement, élancement, dépassement, saillie
overhanging: surplombant, déversé, débord, inclinaison
overhead: aérien, en haut, dessus, sur, temps système, frais généraux
overhear: entendre par hasard, surprendre
overheard: surprirent
overhearing: écoute indiscrète, surprenant
overhung: surplomba
overlook: omettre, négliger, avoir vue sur
overlooked: négligé
overpaid: surpayé
overrated: surtaxèrent, surfis, surévaluas
overreaching: zone étendue, révoquant
overseer: surveillant, contremaître, chef de salle
overstepped: dépassâtes
overthrown: renversé
overture: ouverture
overwhelmed: comblé, abreuva, accablai
owe: devoir, doivent, dois, devez, avoir une dette
owed: dûtes, dû, dûmes, durent, dus, dut
owes: doit
owing: devant, dû
owl: hibou, chouette, effraie
owned: possédé
owner: propriétaire, détenteur, possesseur, maître de la chose, titulaire, armateur
pace: pas, allure, faire les cent pas, rythme

pacing: gradation, entraînement, mesurer à l'enjambée, rythme, amble
pack: paquet, emballer, empaqueter, condenser, meute, tasser, compresse, bande, tas
packed: emballé, monté sous boîtier, tassé, bourré
packet: paquet, colis, entassement
packing: empaquetage, garniture, remplissage, bourrage, joint, colisage
padded: rembourré
page: page, paginer
pageant: reconstitution historique, réflecteur
paid: payai, payé, payèrent, payâtes
pain: douleur, mal, peine
painful: douloureux, pénible
painfully: de manière pénible, péniblement, de façon pénible
painstaking: assidu, soigneux
paint: peinture, couleur, dépeindre
painted: peint, peignirent, fardé
painter: peintre, tricoteuse double, artiste peintre, bosse, gouacheur
painting: peinture, tableau
pair: paire, couple, apparier
pal: camarade, copain
palace: palais, le palais
pale: pâle, blême
paleness: pâleur
palisade: palissade
pall: drap mortuaire, manteau
pallet: palette, soupape, tringle de clouage, petite planche dont se sert le colleur, ancre, levée, filet à dorer
pallid: pâle, blême
palm: palmier, paume
palpable: palpable
palpably: de façon palpable, de manière palpable
palsied: paralysé
paltry: misérable
pampered: choyé, dorlotas
pane: volet, vitre, carreau
panel: panneau, lambris, panel, tableau, jury
panelling: lambris, facettes, panneautage
pang: douleur
panic: panique, affolement
pantaloon: pantalon
panting: haletant, essoufflement, halètement, vibration
pantomime: pantomime, mime
paper: papier, document, tapisser, article, journal
par: pair, égalité
parable: parabole

parade: défilé, parade, pompe
paradise: paradis
paradox: paradoxe
paradoxical: paradoxal
paragraph: alinéa, paragraphe
paralysis: paralysie, immobilisation
paralytic: paralytique
paralyze: paralyser, méduser, pétrifier
paralyzed: paralysâtes, médusé
paralyzing: paralysant, médusant
paramour: amant
parapet: balustrade, parapet, rampe
parasite: parasite
parcel: paquet, colis, parcelle, lot
parched: desséché
pardon: pardon, excuser, grâce
pardonable: excusable, pardonnable
pardoned: pardonné
parent: parent, antériologue
parentage: naissance, filiation
parental: parental
parish: paroisse, commune
parishioner: paroissien
park: parc, garer, stationner, clairière pastorale, parquer, se garer
parliament: parlement
parliamentary: parlementaire
parlour: salon
parochial: paroissial
parody: parodie
paroxysm: paroxysme
parsimony: parcimonie, frugalité
parson: pasteur, curé, prêtre
parterre: parterre
partial: partiel
partially: en partie, partiellement, de façon partielle, de manière partielle
participate: participer, prendre part
participated: participai
particle: particule, grain
parting: raie, séparation
partly: en partie, partiellement
partner: associé, partenaire
partnership: association, partenariat, société en nom collectif
partook: prîmes, prirent, pris, prit, prîtes
partridge: perdrix
parvenu: parvenu, nouveau riche
passably: de façon passable, de manière passable
passage: passage, couloir, corridor, traversée, canal
passe: dépassé, fané
passed: passé
passenger: passager, voyageur

passing: passant, dépassement, écoulement
passion: passion, ardeur
passionate: passionné, brûlant
passionately: de façon passionnée, de manière passionnée
passionless: sans passion
passive: passif, inactif
passively: passivement, de façon passive, de manière passive
passport: passeport
pastor: pasteur, prêtre, curé, abbé
pastoral: pastoral
pasture: pâturage, pacage
pat: taper, caresse
patch: rapiécer, pièce, rustine, parcelle, réparer, correction, plaque, tache
patching: retouche, correction de programme, emploi partiel, placage, raccommodage, rapiéçage, redistribution en agrégats
patchwork: patchwork, mosaïque
paternal: paternel
path: chemin, sentier, trajectoire, piste
pathetic: pathétique, pitoyable
pathology: pathologie
pathos: pathétique
patience: patience, impatiens, balsamine
patient: patient, malade
patiently: de façon patiente, de manière patiente, patiemment
patriot: patriote
patron: protecteur, mécène, client
patronage: patronage, clientèle
patronize: patronner, protéger
patronymic: nom patronymique, patronyme
pattern: patron, modèle, schéma, motif, pattern, forme, configuration, dessin
pause: pause, repos, trêve
paved: pavé, pavai, pavâmes, pavèrent
pavement: pavé, trottoir, chaussée
paw: patte, pied, jambe
pawn: pion, soldat, emprunter sur gages, gage, mettre en gage
paying: payant, payer, rétribuant, salariant, soldant
peace: paix, tranquillité
peaceful: paisible, pacifique
peacock: paon, le paon
peal: tinter, sonner
pearly: nacré, perlé
peasant: paysan
peasantry: paysannerie
pebble: galet, gravillon naturel
peccant: coupable

peculation: péculat
peculiar: étrange, singulier, drôle, particulier
peculiarity: particularité, bizarrerie, singularité
peculiarly: de façon étrange, de manière étrange
pecuniary: financier, pécuniaire
peddling: colportage, commerce ambulant, vente à la chine
pedestal: socle, piédestal, décollement du niveau du noir
pedestrian: piéton, pédestre
pedigree: pedigree, ascendance
pediment: fronton, pédiment, glacis d'ablation
pedlar: colporteur, camelot
peep: pépier, gazouiller
peer: pair, affinitaire, homologue
peering: échange de trafic
pelisse: pelisse
pellucid: transparent
pen: stylo, plume, enclos
penal: pénal, punissable, criminel
penalty: pénalité, penalty, punition, amende
pencil: crayon, le crayon
pendant: pendentif, pantoire
penetrate: pénétrer, pénètres, entrer
penetrated: pénétra
penetrating: pénétrant, transfixiant, dégrippant, mordant
penetration: pénétration, densité téléphonique, saillie, croisement, collage noir, attaque de rupture, avancement
penitently: de façon pénitente, de manière pénitente
penny: sou, grain inférieur, penny
pension: pension, retraite
pensioner: pensionné, retraité, titulaire d'une pension
pensive: pensif, songeur
penury: indigence, pénurie
per: par, dans, à, parmi, pour, en, au milieu de, à raison de, afin de
perceive: apercevoir, percevoir, saisir, discerner, perçoivent, s'apercevoir, se rendre compte
perceived: aperçûmes, perçûtes, discernèrent
perceiving: apercevant, percevant, discernant
perceptible: perceptible, apercevable
perception: perception
perch: perche, jucher, se percher, porteuse, fixation oculaire, machine à raccoutrer
peremptorily: de façon péremptoire, de manière péremptoire

perfect: parfait, achevé, accompli
perfection: perfection, mise en état
perfidy: perfidie
perforated: perforâtes, poinçonnai, dentela, trouèrent, piqué
perforce: forcément, nécessairement
perform: réaliser, accomplir, faire, effectuer, exécuter, construire, poser, surgir, remplir, apparaître, paraître
performed: réalisé, accomplîmes, effectua, rempli, exécuté
performer: interprète, exécutant, artiste
perfume: parfum, le parfum
peril: danger, péril
perilous: périlleux
periodical: périodique, revue, gazette, journal
periodically: périodiquement, de façon périodique, de manière périodique
perish: périr, s'abîmer
perished: péri, pérîtes
perjured: parjuré, vous parjurâtes, te parjuras, se parjurèrent, nous parjurâmes, me parjurai
permanently: de manière permanente, de façon permanente
permission: autorisation, permission, licence
permit: permis, autoriser
permitted: permis
permitting: permettant
pernicious: pernicieux
perpetrated: perpétra
perpetration: perpétration
perpetual: perpétuel, éternel
perpetually: perpétuellement, de façon perpétuelle, de manière perpétuelle
perplex: embarrasse
perplexed: embarrassâtes, perplexe
perplexing: embarrassant
perplexity: perplexité, embarras
perseverance: persévérance, ténacité
persevering: persévérant
persist: persister, s'obstiner
persisted: persistèrent
personage: personnage
personal: personnel, propre
personally: personnellement, de façon personnelle, de manière personnelle
persuade: persuader, convaincre, inspirer
persuaded: persuada
persuading: persuadant
persuasion: persuasion, croyance
persuasive: persuasif, convaincant

pert: méthode du chemin critique, coquin
pertinacity: entêtement
pertly: de manière coquine, de façon coquine
perturbed: perturba, brouillèrent
pervaded: imprégnas
pervading: imprégnant
perverse: pervers
perversion: perversion
pervert: pervertir, fausser, dénaturer, dépraver
perverted: pervers
pestilence: peste
pestilent: pestilentiel
pet: animal de compagnie, dorloter, choyer, chouchou
petal: pétale
pettiness: petitesse, mesquinerie
petty: mesquin, petit
petulance: irritabilité
petulant: malin, maussade
petulantly: de façon maussade, de manière maussade
phantom: fantôme, apparition
pheasant: faisan
phenomenon: phénomène
phial: fiole, flacon
philosopher: philosophe
philosophical: philosophique
philosophically: de manière philosophique, de façon philosophique, philosophiquement
philosophy: philosophie
phlegm: flegme, expectoration
phrase: locution, phrase, groupe de mots
phraseology: phraséologie
phrenologist: phrénologiste
physical: physique
physically: physiquement, de façon physique, de manière physique
physician: médecin, docteur
physiognomy: physionomie
piano: piano
pick: cueillir, piquer, pioche, ramasser, pic, choisir
picked: cueillirent, piquâmes
picklock: crocheteur, rossignol
pickpocket: pickpocket, voleur à la tire
picture: image, figure, tableau, photo
picture-gallery: pinacothèque
picturesque: pittoresque
picturesquely: de manière pittoresque, pittoresquement, de façon pittoresque
piece: pièce, morceau, fragment, part, pan, contingent
pierce: percer, perçons, transpercer

pierced: perça, percèrent
piety: piété
pike: brochet, pique
pilaster: pilastre
pile: tas, amas, foule, pieu, pilotis, pile, multitude, hémorrhoïde, masse, empiler
piled: entassé
pillow: oreiller, coussin
pinch: pincer, serrer
pinched: pincé
pinching: pincement, croquage, pinçage
pint: pinte, chope, petite bouteille
pious: pieux
pipe: tuyau, tube, pipe, conduite, retassure
pistol: pistolet
pitched: abattu
pith: moelle
pitiable: pitoyable
pitiless: impitoyable
pity: pitié, plaindre, compassion, apitoiement, avoir pitié, mal, s'apitoyer
pitying: compatissant
placard: afficher, placard, coller, agglutiner
placed: placé, plaçai
placid: placide, serein, calme
plague: peste, fléau
plain: plaine, clair, uni, net, ordinaire, limpide, évident
plainly: de manière plaine, simplement, clairement
plaintive: plaintif
plan: plan, projet, dessein, organiser, intention, esquisser, propos
planet: planète
plank: planche, panneau
planning: planification, aménagement
plantation: plantation, futaie
planted: planté
planting: plantation, repeuplement, repiquage, encépagement, empoissonnement, peuplement
plash: clapoter, barboter
plate: plaque, assiette, plat, lame, cliché, met, planche
plausibility: plausibilité, vraisemblance
play: jouer, pièce de théâtre, jouons, jeu, représenter, passer
played: jouèrent, jouai, jouâmes, joué
playful: espiègle, ludique, badin
playfully: de manière espiègle, de façon espiègle
playfulness: enjouement
playing: jouant, jeu, jouer

plaything: jouet
plead: plaider, implorer
pleading: plaidant, excipant, implorant
pleasant: agréable, plaisant, charmant, sympathique
pleasantly: agréablement, de manière agréable, de façon agréable
please: s'il vous plaît, plaire, contenter, faire plaisir, satisfaire
pleased: content, satisfait, plu
pleases: plaît, plait
pleasing: plaisant, flatteur, satisfaisant
pleasurable: très agréable
pleasure: plaisir, jouissance
plebeian: plébéien
pledge: gage, nantissement, promettre, engagement
plenty: abondance, beaucoup
pliant: flexible, souple, docile
plied: manié
plod: chemines
plodded: cheminèrent
plot: intrigue, parcelle, tracer, terrain, conspiration, comploter, position visualisée
plotting: levé, traçant
plough: charrue, labourer
ploughed: labouré
pluck: cueillir, ramasser, plumer, fressure, courage
plucked: plumé
plumb: sonder, plomb
plumbing: plomberie, tuyauterie
plume: panache, traînée, souffle, plumet, faisceau de fumée, gaz d'échappement
plumed: empanaché
plunder: piller, ravir
plundered: pillé
plunderer: pillard
plunge: plonger, se jeter, se précipiter, risquer de grosses sommes, piquer du nez, inclinaison, chute, enfoncer
plunged: plongé
plunging: plonger, soyage
pocket: poche, empocher, case
pocketbook: livre de poche
pocketed: empochés
poem: poème, poésie
poet: poète
poetess: poétesse, femme poète
poetic: poétique
poetical: poétique
poetry: poésie
poignant: intense
pointed: pointu, aigu
pointing: pointage, repérage dans l'espace, jointement, collage de poils, braquant, appointage, précalibrage, piquage des nervures
poison: poison, venin, empoisonner, intoxiquer, substance toxique
poisoned: empoisonné, arséniqué
poisoner: empoisonneur
poisoning: empoisonnement, intoxication
poisonous: toxique, venimeux, vénéneux
poked: poussé
polemical: polémique
policeman: policier, agent de police
polished: poli
polite: poli, courtois
politely: poliment, de manière polie, de façon polie
politeness: politesse, galanterie
politic: politique
politician: politicien, homme politique
pollard: arbre étêté, têtard
pollute: polluer, contaminer
polluted: polluas, vicié
pollution: pollution, contamination
pomp: pompe, splendeur
pompous: pompeux
pond: étang, bassin, mare
ponder: peser, réfléchissent, pesons, pèses, considérons
pondering: réfléchissant, considérant, pesant
ponderous: lourd, pesant
poor: pauvre, mauvais, misérable, maigre, malheureux, méchant, mal, médiocre, faible
poorly: pauvrement, de façon pauvre, de manière pauvre
pop: dépiler, sauter, pop, petit coup de mine
populace: peuple
popular: populaire, célèbre
popularity: popularité, banalité
popularly: populairement, de façon populaire, de manière populaire
populate: peupler, charger, garnissons
population: population, peuplement
porch: porche, portique, véranda
port: port, bâbord, accès, lumière, orifice
portal: portail, tête de tunnel, entrée de tunnel
porter: porteur, bagagiste, concierge
portion: partie, portion
portly: corpulent
portmanteau: valise
portrait: portrait, effigie, format vertical
positive: positif, affirmatif, image positive, mère
positively: de façon positive, de manière positive
possessed: possédâtes
possession: possession, jouissance
possessor: propriétaire, possesseur, détenteur
possibly: de façon possible, de manière possible
post: poste, poteau, pieu, fonction, emploi, afficher, courrier, coller, office, agglutiner, service
poster: placard, mural, poster
posterity: postérité
posthumous: posthume, titre posthume
postmark: cachet de la poste, empreinte de timbre à date, marque postale, oblitération, timbrer
posture: posture, attitude, maintien
potato: pomme de terre, patate
potent: puissant, actif, fort
potion: potion
pounced: bondis
pound: livre, piler, broyer, fourrière, marteler, battre
pour: verser, servir, déverser, couler, affluer, fondre
poured: versé, en vrac
pouting: bouder, gode, tacaud
poverty: pauvreté, misère
powder: poudre, pulvériser
powdered: pulvérisé
powerful: puissant
powerfully: de façon puissante, de manière puissante
powerless: impuissant
practical: pratique, réel
practically: de façon pratique, de manière pratique, pratiquement
practice: pratique, exercice, appliquer, usage, cabinet, clientèle
practise: exercer, instruire, pratiquer
praise: glorifier, louange, louer, éloge
praised: loué
pray: prier, prions
prayed: prièrent, prié, priâtes, prias
prayer: prière, oraison
prays: prie
preach: prêcher
preaching: prêchant, sermon
precarious: précaire
precaution: précaution
precede: précéder, avancer
preceded: précédèrent, avançâmes
precedence: priorité, préséance

precept: précepte
preceptor: précepteur
precious: précieux, rare
precipitate: précipité, hâter, hâtif, irréfléchi
precise: précis, méticuleux
precisely: précisément, de façon précise, de manière précise
precision: précision, exactitude
preclude: empêchons, exclus
precluding: empêchant, excluant
precocious: précoce
predecessor: prédécesseur
predestined: prédestinâtes
predict: prédire, présager
predicted: prédirent, prévu
prediction: prédiction, prévision, prophétie
predilection: prédilection
predominant: prédominant, principal
preface: introduction, préface
preferred: préféra, privilégiâmes
preferring: préférant, privilégiant
prejudice: préjugé, léser
prejudicial: préjudiciable, nuisible
preliminary: préliminaire, partie liminaire, préalable
prelude: prélude
premature: prématuré, anticipé, avant terme, lavé, précoce
prematurely: de façon prématurée, de manière prématurée
premium: prime, récompense, prix, agio
preoccupied: préoccupèrent
preparation: préparation, rédaction, prise d'élan, établissement, élaboration, agréage
preparatory: préparatoire
prepare: préparer, apprêter
prepared: prépara, apprêtai, prêt
prepossess: préoccuper
prepossessing: avenant
prescription: ordonnance, prescription, recette
presence: présence, prestance, degré de présence
present: présent, cadeau, actuel, offrir, don
presented: présenté
presentiment: pressentiment
presenting: présentant
presently: actuellement, à présent
preserve: conserver, confire, préserver, maintenir, retenir, mettre en conserve, réserve
preserved: conservé
preside: présider
presided: présidai
presides: préside

presiding: présidant
pressed: appuyé, pressés, estampé à la presse
pressing: pressage, urgent, pièce forgée par pression, moulage, mise en balle, impression, formage à la presse, emboutissage, compression, chargement par introduction d'un bloc préformé, cas particulier d'emboutissage
pressingly: de manière pressage
pressure: pression, instance, impulsion, oppression, vive sollicitation
presume: présumer, supposer
presumed: présumas
presumption: présomption, supposition
presumptive: présomptif
presumptuous: présomptueux
presumptuously: présomptueusement, de façon présomptueuse, de manière présomptueuse
pretence: prétexte, simulacre
pretend: feindre, prétendre, feignent, simuler, se retrancher, faire semblant
pretended: feint, feignit, prétendu
pretending: feignant, prétendant
pretension: prétention, tension préalable
preternatural: surnaturel
preternaturally: de manière surnaturelle, de façon surnaturelle
pretext: prétexte
prettiest: le plus joli
pretty: joli, mignon, aimable, bath, assez
prevail: prévaloir, régner, prédominer
prevailed: prévalus
prevent: empêcher, prévenir
prevented: empêchâtes, prévins
previous: précédent, antérieur, préalable
previously: auparavant, précédemment, autrefois, devant, avant, de façon précédente, de manière précédente, préalablement
prey: proie
price: prix, cours
prick: piqûre, bitte, zob
pride: fierté, orgueil
priest: prêtre, curé, abbé
prim: collet monté, guindé
primary: primaire, principal
prime: amorcer, prime, apprêter
primer: amorce, apprêt, couche primaire
primeval: primitif

primitive: primitif
prince: prince
principal: principal, commettant, mandant, directeur, donneur d'ordre, dominant, capital
principally: principalement, surtout, de façon commettante
principle: principe, loi
print: imprimer, estampe, épreuve, gravure, caractères, tirer, empreinte, copie
printing: impression, tirage, gravure
prison: prison, geôle, maison centrale, pénitencier, établissement pénitentiaire
privacy: intimité, vie privée, secret, respect de la vie privée
private: privé, personnel, simple pompier, soldat, confidentiel
privation: privation
privilege: privilège, prérogative
privileged: privilégié
prize: prix, récompense
prizing: pressage
probable: probable, vraisemblable
probation: probation, liberté surveillée, période d'essai, stage
probe: sonde, enquête, scruter, palpeur, explorer
probed: sondé
proceed: procéder, avancer
proceeded: procédai, avançai
proceeding: procédant, avançant
procession: procession, cortège
proclaimed: proclamai
proclaiming: proclamant
procure: procurer, se procurer
procured: procuras
prodigal: prodigue
prodigious: prodigieux
prodigiously: de façon prodigieuse, de manière prodigieuse, prodigieusement
produce: produire, réaliser, fabriquer
produced: produisîmes, apparaissant p prés
profanation: profanation
professed: confessé, professai
professedly: de façon professée, de manière professé
profession: profession
professional: professionnel, spécialiste, membre d'une profession libérale, pro
profit: bénéfice, profit, gain, avantage
profitable: rentable, profitable, lucratif
profited: bénéficièrent
profiting: bénéficiant

profligacy: débauche
profligate: débauché, libertin
profound: profond
profoundly: profondément, de manière profonde, de façon profonde
profuse: abondant, profus, prodigue
profusion: profusion
prognostic: pronostique
progressive: progressif, évolutif
project: projet, plan
prolong: prolonger, étaler
prolonged: prolongeâtes
prominent: proéminent, marquant
promise: promettre, assurer
promised: promîmes
promising: promettant
promote: promouvoir, favorisent, encourager, monter en division supérieure, lancer
promoted: promu, favorisai
prompt: invite, ponctuel, prompt, mobile, sollicitation, souffler
prompting: assistance par programme souffleur, incitation, proposition, sollicitation de l'opérateur
promptly: ponctuellement, rapidement
prone: enclin
pronounce: prononcer
pronounced: prononcé
pronouncing: prononçant
proof: preuve, épreuve, témoignage, démonstration
prop: support, étai, appui, étançon, étayer
propensity: propension, prédisposition
proper: convenable, propre, exact, juste, approprié, adéquat
properly: convenablement, proprement, de manière convenable, comme il faut, correctement, de façon convenable
property: propriété, biens, domaine, qualité, possession, fonds, accessoire, patrimoine
prophecy: prophétie
propinquity: proximité
proportion: proportion, pourcentage, fréquence
proposal: proposition, offre
propose: proposer, soumettre, suggérer
proposed: proposèrent
proposition: proposition
prorogation: prorogation, clôture
proscribed: proscrivirent
prose: prose
prosecute: poursuivre

prospect: perspective, prospecter
prosperity: prospérité
prosperous: prospère
prostrate: prosterné
prostration: prostration
protect: protéger, abriter, garantir, sauvegarder, préserver, assurer
protected: protégé, préservas, sauvegardèrent, garantit, abritâtes
protection: protection, sauvegarde, garde
protector: protecteur, parafoudre, armement, dispositif de protection
protrude: dépasser
protruded: dépassèrent
proud: fier, altier, orgueilleux
proudly: fièrement, de façon fire, de manière fire
prove: prouver, démontrer
proved: prouvas, éprouvâmes
proven: prouvé
providence: providence, prévoyance
province: province, domaine, région
proving: prouvant, éprouvant
provocative: provocant
provoke: provoquer, irriter, agacer
provoked: provoqua, chiffonnées
provoking: provoquant, chiffonnant
provokingly: de façon provoquante, de manière provoquante
prowess: prouesse, exploit
proxy: procuration, mandataire, fondé de pouvoir, pouvoir
prudence: prudence, précaution
prudent: prudent, raisonnable
prying: fureteur, indiscret
publication: publication, parution
published: publia, édité
publisher: éditeur, propriétaire d'un journal, publication, diffuseur
puerile: puéril, enfantin
puffed: soufflé, bouffant
pull: tirer, tirons, traction, tirage, traîner, épreuve
pulled: tirèrent, tiré, tirâtes, tiras
pulmonary: pulmonaire
pulse: pouls, impulsion, pulsation
pun: calembour
punctilious: pointilleux
puncture: ponction, crevaison, perforation, piqûre
punish: punir
punished: punirent, punîtes
punishing: punissant
punishment: punition, peine, châtiment, sanction

punt: botté de dégagement, coup de pied de volée, fond, plate
puny: chétif
pupil: pupille, élève, écolier
puppy: chiot, caniche, jeune chien
purchase: achat, acheter, emplette, acquérir, palan
purchased: acheté
purchaser: acheteur, acquéreur
pure: pur, blanc, propre
purely: purement, de façon pure, de manière pure
purgatory: purgatoire
purify: purifier, épurer, assainir
purifying: purifiant, épurant
puritanical: puritain
puritanically: de façon puritaine, de manière puritaine
purity: pureté, propreté
purple: pourpre, violet
purport: signification, portée, prétendre
purpose: but, dessein, objet, intention
purpura: purpura
purse: sacoche, bourse, sac à main
pursed: fourreau
pursuance: exécution
pursue: poursuivre, continuer, rechercher
pursued: poursuivîtes
pursuer: poursuivant
pursuing: poursuivant
pursuit: poursuite, occupation, recherche
push: pousser, imposer, coup extérieur, charge incorrecte, biaiser, appuyer
pushed: poussé
pushing: poussant, dynamique
putting: mettant, lancement, rouler
puzzle: énigme, confondre, consterner, puzzle, stupéfier, troubler, abasourdir
puzzlement: perplexité
puzzler: Œdipe
puzzling: curieux, mystérieux
quadrille: quadrille
quaint: curieux, intéressant, singulier, étrange
qualify: qualifier, exprimer une réserve, être admis dans une profession, réussir à l'examen
quality: qualité, propriété
quarrel: querelle, dispute, se disputer, se quereller, noise
quarter: quartier, trimestre, le quart
quartered: quartier, en quartier
quartering: casernement, division par quartiers, inquartation, quartage

quarterly: trimestriel, revue trimestrielle, publication trimestrielle
quell: étouffer, suffoquer
quelled: étouffé
quench: étouffer, éteindre
querulous: quérulant, ronchon
query: requête, question
quest: recherche, quête
questioner: auteur de la question, questionneur, interrogateur
questioning: interrogateur, questionnant, sondage
quick: rapide, prompt, vite
quicken: hâte, accélérez, hâtons
quickened: hâtâtes, hâté, hâtas, accéléré, hâtèrent
quicker: plus vite
quickly: rapidement, vite, de façon rapide, de manière rapide
quickness: rapidité, vitesse
quiescent: quiescent, tranquille, passif, calme, repos
quiet: calme, tranquille, paisible, quiet, silencieux, abattre, rassurer, repos
quietly: paisiblement, tranquillement, de façon calme, de manière calme, calmement
quit: quitter, abandonner, démissionner, délaisser, re retirer, livrer
quits: quitte
quitted: quittèrent
quitting: quittant, sortie des employés
quiver: trembler, frisson, frémir
quivering: frisson, tremblant
quod: taule
quoted: cité, citèrent, citâmes, citai
race: course, race, s'élancer, se précipiter, raz, chemin de roulement
racer: coureur, aspe, couleuvre agile, racer
rack: crémaillère, grille, étagère, casier, râtelier, arack, armoire, bâti, chevalet, claie
racy: risqué, piquant, osé, plein de verve
radiant: rayonnant, radieux
raft: radeau, radier, rame, tapée
rag: chiffon, lambeau, torchon, guenille, haillon
ragamuffin: gueux
rage: fureur, rage, tempêter, furie
ragged: déchiqueté, déguenillé, dépenaillé, ébavuré, en haillons, en lambeaux, loqueteux
rail: rail, barre, rampe, rambarde, longeron
rain: pluie, pleuvoir, la pluie

raise: lever, élever, soulever, entonner, augmentation, relever, hausse, éduquer, majorer, dresser, ériger
raised: levé, levèrent, relief, levâmes, levai
raising: élevage, martelage, soulèvement, relèvement, relevage, percement d'un montage, montage, extraction, arborant, lainage, levant
rake: râteau, ringard, inclinaison, ratisser
rale: râle
rallied: rallia
rally: rallye, rassembler, amélioration, railler, échange
ramble: excursion, randonnée
ran: courûmes, coulèrent
rancour: rancune
range: portée, gamme, plage, étendue, fourneau de cuisine, base de lancement, distance, parcours, éventail, intervalle, domaine
ranged: étendu
ranging: télémétrie, contrôle de l'échelle, jalonnement, mesure de distance, parangonnage, recherche par rang
rank: rang, grade, file, tour
rap: rap, ébranler, rapper
rapid: rapide, prompt
rapidity: rapidité
rapidly: rapidement, de façon rapide, de manière rapide
rapscallion: vaurien
rapt: enthousiaste
rapture: ravissement
rare: rare, saignant
rarely: rarement, de manière rare, de façon rare
rarity: rareté
rascal: fripon, coquin, vaurien
rash: éruption, irréfléchi, rougeur, inconsidéré
rashly: de façon éruptive, de manière éruptive
rat: rat
rational: rationnel, raisonnable
rattle: cliquetis, claquer, crécelle, hochet
ravage: ravager, dévastation
rave: être fou, délirer
raved: divaguai, déliré
raven: corbeau, grand corbeau
ravening: vorace, rapace
raving: délirant, divaguant
ravishing: enchanteur, ravissant
raw: cru, brut, grossier, rustique, écru
ray: rayon, raie, bande, rayure, radio, rai

raze: rases, rasons
razed: rasa, rasâmes, rasé, rasèrent
reach: atteindre, parvenir, portée, remporter, aboutir, toucher, bief, étendue
reached: parvenu
reaction: réaction
reader: lecteur, chargé de cours, dispositif de lecture de bande, indicateur, livre de lecture, microlecteur, morceaux choisis, appareil de lecture
readily: aisément, de façon prête, de manière prête, facilement
readiness: disponibilité, empressement
reading: lecture, lisant
ready: prêt, disponible
reality: réalité
realize: réaliser, comprendre
realized: réalisé, subi
realizing: réalisant
realm: règne, royaume, puissance, domaine
reap: moissonner, faucher
reappearance: réapparition, résurgence
reappeared: reparûmes, réapparu
reaps: moissonne
rear: élever, arrière
rearing: élevage, éducation, encastage à crémaillère, cabrement
reason: raison, cause, motif
reasonable: raisonnable, modéré, prudent, abordable
reasoned: raisonné
reasoning: raisonnement
reassured: rassuré
rebel: rebelle, se révolter
rebellious: rebelle, révolté
rebuild: reconstruire, rechaper totalement, rebâtissez, réfection
rebuke: réprimander, gronder, reprocher, sermonner, repousser
recall: rappel, se rappeler, se souvenir, retenir, remémorer
recalled: rappelé
receding: fuyant, recédant, reculant
receipt: reçu, quittance, récépissé, réception, acquit, accusé de réception, ticket de caisse, recette
receive: recevoir, reçois, accueillir, admettre, agréer, recueillir, accepter, réception
received: reçûtes, reçurent, accueillis
receiving: recevant, accueillant, réception
recent: récent, frais
recently: récemment, dernièrement, de façon récente, de manière récente

reception: réception, accueil
recess: pause, alcôve, repos, niche, trêve, vacances
recital: récital, considérant
recite: réciter
recklessness: imprudence, témérité, insouciance
reckon: calculer, estimer
reckoned: calcula
reckoning: calculant, compte, estime
reclined: reposé
recognition: reconnaissance, identification, récognition
recognizable: reconnaissable
recognize: reconnaître, croire, retrouver
recognized: reconnu, retrouvâmes, admis
recognizes: reconnaît, retrouve
recognizing: reconnaissant, retrouvant
recoil: recul, ancre à recul, billot
recoiled: reculé
recollect: se rappeler, se souvenir, retenir, retiennent
recollection: souvenir, mémoire
recommencing: recommençant
recommend: recommander, conseiller
recommendation: recommandation, liste de présentation, préconisation, proposition
recommended: recommandai, préconisa
recommending: recommandant, préconisant
recompense: récompense
reconcile: réconcilier, raccommode, se réconcilier, concilier, rapprochez
reconciled: réconciliâtes, rapprochèrent, raccommodèrent
reconciles: réconcilie, raccommode, rapproche
reconstruct: reconstruire, rebâtissez
record: enregistrer, disque, record, rapport, document, relation, article, dossier, acte, compte rendu
recording: enregistrement, archivage
recourse: recours, garantie
recover: récupérer, recouvrer, guérir, regagner, retrouver, se remettre
recovered: récupéra, recouvra
recovering: récupérant, recouvrant
recovery: récupération, rétablissement, reprise, guérison, recouvrement, salut

recruit: recruter, enrôler, gagner, s'adjoindre des aides
rectitude: rectitude
rectory: presbytère
recumbent: étendu, alité, allongé, couché
recur: se reproduire, revenir, reviens, reparaissons
recurred: revenu, revînmes, revint, reparu
red: rouge
reddening: rougissant
redeem: racheter, rembourser
redeemable: rachetable, remboursable, amortissable
redeemed: rachetèrent, remboursé
redeeming: rachetant
redemption: rédemption, amortissement, rachat, remboursement
redirected: redirigeâmes, réorientèrent
redress: réparation, redresser
reduced: réduisîtes, modéra, comprimâtes, minora, amaigris, abaissai, amenuisa
reducing: réduisant, abaissant
reed: roseau, anche, peigne
reeling: bobinage, dévidage
refer: référer, réfère, déférer
referred: référé, déféré, adresser
referring: référant, déférant
refine: raffiner, épurer, affiner
refined: raffina, délicat, tendre, affiné, épuras
refinement: raffinement, délicatesse, affinage
refining: raffinant, affinage, épurant
reflect: refléter, réfléchir, renvoyer
reflected: refléta, réfléchîmes, renvoyèrent
reflection: réflexion, reflet
reflective: réfléchissante
reform: réformer, reformer, transformation, redresser
reformed: réformé, redressées
refresh: rafraîchir, actualiser
refreshed: rafraîchîmes, actualisas
refreshing: rafraîchissant, actualisant
refuge: refuge, abri, réserve, retraite
refund: remboursement, ristourne
refuse: refuser, rejeter, déchets, détritus, repousser, ordures
refused: refusé
regain: regagner, rattraper, recouvrer
regained: regagna, rattrapai
regard: considérer, estime, regarder, contempler, égard
regarded: considérâtes

regarding: considérant, concernant
regardless: inattentif, indifférent
regimen: régime
regiment: régiment, enrégimenter
region: région, contrée, district, zone
register: registre, enregistrer, recommander, inscrire, immatriculer, mettre en registre, liste
regret: regret, ménager
regular: régulier, cyclique, réglé, normal, standard, conforme, client habitué, habitué
regularity: régularité
regularly: régulièrement, souvent, fréquemment, beaucoup, de façon régulière, de manière régulière
regulate: régler, règles, régulariser
regulated: réglâtes, régulâmes
reign: règne, tenue, commandement, gouvernement
reigned: régné
reigning: régnant
rein: rêne, bride
reintroduction: réintroduction
reject: rejeter, refuser, repousser, rebuter
rejected: rejeté, rebutée, refusé
rejection: rejet, refus
rejoice: réjouir, être joyeux
rejoiced: réjouis
rejoinder: réplique
rejoined: rejoignit, répliquai, rallié
rekindled: raviva, rallumé
relate: raconter, conter, être en relation avec, concerner, relater
related: racontai, contèrent, apparenté, concerna
relation: relation, abord, rapport
relationship: relation, parenté, rapport
relative: parent, relatif
relax: relaxer, se relâcher, relâcher, se détendre
relaxation: relaxation, relâchement, décontraction, détente, assouplissement
relaxed: détendu, relaxâtes, relâchâtes
released: libéré, relâché
relentless: implacable, impitoyable
reliance: confiance
relic: relique, vestige
relief: soulagement, allégement, relief, relève, secours, détalonnage
relieve: soulager, relayer
relieved: soulagé, relayâmes, exonéré
religion: religion, confession, culte
religious: religieux, dévot

religiously: de façon religieuse, de manière religieuse
relinquished: abandonné, lâchai
reluctance: réluctance, répugnance
reluctant: peu disposé, réticent
reluctantly: à regret, de façon peu disposée, de manière peu disposée, à contrecœur
rely: comptez, fient, fiez, fions
remain: rester, demeurer
remainder: reste, débris, reliquat, culot
remainderman: héritier substitué, résiduaire, dernier bénéficiaire après distribution de tous les autres legs, appelé, titulaire d'un droit révisible
remained: restâtes
remaining: restant, qui reste, autre
remains: reste, vestige, débris
remark: remarque, observation, commentaire
remarkable: remarquable, saillant, insigne
remarkably: de façon remarquable, de manière remarquable, remarquablement
remarked: remarqué
remedy: remède, ressource, moyen, assainir, guérir
remember: se rappeler, se souvenir, retenir, rappeler, retiens
remembered: retint, rappelâmes, retîntes, retenu
remembrance: souvenir, mémoire
remind: rappeler
reminded: rappelèrent
reminding: rappelant
reminiscence: réminiscence
remodelled: remanié, remodelé
remonstrance: remontrance, protestation
remorse: remords
remorseful: plein de remords
remorseless: sans remords
remote: lointain, éloigné, distant, isolé, écarté
removal: enlèvement, déménagement, renvoi, révocation, piégeage, dépose
remove: supprimer, ôter, enlever, ôtez, ôtent, ôtes, ôte, ôtons, enlève, retirer, déplacer
removed: ôta, supprimai, ôtai, ôtâmes, ôtas, ôtâtes, ôté, ôtèrent, enlevâmes
rend: déchirer
render: rendre, plâtrez, reproduction, renformis, crépis, enduire, interpréter
rendered: rendis, plâtras, crépi

rendering: interprétation, enduit, rendu, crépi
rending: déchirant
renew: renouveler, reconduire
renewal: renouvellement, reconduction
renewed: renouvelèrent, reconduisit
renounce: renoncer, abandonner, abjurer, résigner, renier
renown: renommée, distinction, gloire, réputation
renowned: renommé, célèbre
rent: loyer, louer, location
rental: location, loyer
rented: loué, louèrent, accensa
reopened: réexaminai, rouvert
repaid: remboursa
repair: réparation, refaire, dépanner, restaurer, remédier, réformer, réfection, radouber, remettre en état
repaired: réparé
reparation: réparation
repay: rembourser, reprendre
repeat: répéter, répète, reprise, redire
repeated: répéta, redirent, redîtes
repeatedly: plusieurs fois, à plusieurs reprises, de façon répétée, de manière répétée
repel: repousser, refusons, refoulent
repelled: repoussas, refusé
repellent: épouvantable, horrible, affreux, répulsif
repelling: horrible, affreux, épouvantable, repoussant
repent: se repentir, regretter, repentir
repentance: repentir
repenting: regrettant, repentant
repetition: répétition, reprise
replace: remplacer, substituer, mettre en place de, replacer
replaced: remplaçâmes, substitua, replaçâmes
replacing: remplaçant, substituant, replaçant
reply: réponse, répliquer
reported: rapporté
repose: repos, se reposer, trêve
reposed: reposé
repossess: reprendre possession
represent: représenter, figurer
representation: représentation, figure
representative: représentant, député, délégué
represented: représenta, figuré
representing: représentant, figurant
repress: refouler, réprimer

reprieve: sursis, répit, grâce
reproach: reproche, gronder, réprimander, sermonner
reproaching: reprochant
reprobate: réprouver
reproduced: reproduisîmes
reproof: reproche
reprove: réprimander, reprocher, gronder, sermonner
reproving: réprimandant, reprochant, grondant, sermonnant
reptile: reptile
republican: républicain
repudiated: répudias, nié
repugnance: répugnance, aversion
repugnant: répugnant, inconciliable
reputable: honorable
reputation: réputation, prestige, renommée
repute: réputation, renommée
reputed: réputé
request: demande, prier, requête
requested: demandé
require: exiger, requérir, demander, réclamer, avoir besoin de
required: exigeas, requîtes, réclamé
requires: exige, requiert, réclame
requisite: requis, condition requise
requite: récompenser
rescue: sauver, secours, délivrance
resemble: ressembler, rejoindre
resembled: ressembla, rejoignîmes
resent: s'indigner de, ressentez
resented: ressenti
resentment: ressentiment, rancune, dépit
reserve: réserver, retenir, commander, demander
reserved: réservé
resided: résidâmes, demeurai
residence: résidence, domicile, habitation, demeure, logement, gîte, logis
residing: résidant, demeurant
residue: résidu, données résiduelles, reliquat, reste
resign: démissionner, résigner, abandonner, abdiquer, re retirer, renoncer
resignation: démission, résignation
resigned: démissionnèrent, résignâmes
resist: résister, épargne, enduit protecteur
resistance: résistance, défense
resisted: résistai
resisting: résistant, réimplantation
resolute: résolu, déterminé
resolutely: de façon résolue, de manière résolue, résolument
resolution: résolution, motion, pouvoir de résolution, définition

resolve: résoudre, décider
resolved: résolu
resolving: résolvant
resort: lieu de vacances, recours
resounded: résonnèrent, retentîtes
resource: ressource
respect: respect, égard
respectability: respectabilité, honorabilité
respectable: respectable, convenable
respectably: de manière respectable, de façon respectable
respected: respecté
respectful: respectueux
respectfully: de manière respectueuse, de façon respectueuse
respecting: respectant, en ce qui concerne
respite: répit, sursis
responds: répond, réplique
responsibility: responsabilité, concordance, correspondance
responsibly: de façon responsable, de manière responsable
rest: repos, se reposer, reste, débris, support, trêve, pause, appui, silence
rested: reposé
restless: remuant, agité
restlessly: de façon remuante, de manière remuante
restlessness: agitation, instabilité psychomotrice
restoration: restauration, rétablissement
restorative: fortifiant, restaurateur
restore: restaurer, rétablir, rénover, réparer
restored: restaurâmes, rétablit
restoring: restaurant, rétablissant
restrain: retenir, réprimer, retiennent, gouverner, surveiller, régner, restreindre
restraint: contrainte, mesure d'austérité, sollicitation, retenue, modération, maîtrise de soi, bridage, punition corporelle
resumed: reprîtes, recommençâtes
resuming: reprenant, recommençant
resurrection: résurrection
resuscitation: réanimation, ressuscitation
retain: retenir, retiennent, réprimer
retained: retînmes, retint, retenu
retaining: retenant, contention
retentive: fidèle
retire: se retirer, retirer
retired: retiré, retraité
retiring: retirant, sortant

retrace: retracer, reconstituer, retour du spot
retracing: reconstituer, retraçant
retreat: retraite, se retirer, décéder, recul, refuge
retreating: dépilage en rabattant
retribution: châtiment, récompense
retrieved: récupérai, rapportâmes, extrait
return: retour, revenir, rentrée, renvoyer, rendre, restituer, rappel, déclaration
returned: retourné, renvoyé
returning: renvoyant, retournant
reveal: révéler, révèle, publier, développer, déceler, jouée
revealed: révéla, décelas
revealing: révélant, décelant
revel: se divertir, s'amuser
revelation: révélation
reveller: fêtard, noceur
revenge: revanche, vengeance
revere: révérer, révères
reverence: révérence, vénération, respect
reverent: respectueux, révérend
reverently: de manière respectueuse, de façon respectueuse
reverie: rêverie
revert: revenir, reviens
revisit: revisitent
revive: ranimer, raviver, réanimer
revived: ranimai, revivifièrent, ravivèrent, réanima, aviva, ragaillardîmes
revoked: révoquâtes
revolt: révolte, se révolter
revolted: révolté
revolting: révoltant
revolution: révolution, tour, rotation
revolve: tourner, ruminer
revolved: tournai, ruminèrent
reward: récompenser, prime, rémunérer, salaire, sanction prémiale
rheumatic: rhumatismal
rheumatism: rhumatisme
rib: côte, nervure, membre
ribbon: ruban, feuille
rich: riche
richly: de façon riche, de manière riche, richement
richness: richesse, pouvoir couvrant
rickety: délabré, vieux, infirme, caduc, rachitique
rid: débarrasser, délivrer
riddle: énigme, puzzle, devinette, cribler

ride: chevaucher, monter à cheval, tour, aller, se déplacer
rider: cavalier, avenant, annexe, clause additionnelle, écuyer, acte additionnel
righteous: moral, juste, vertueux
rightful: légitime
rightly: correctement, de façon droite, de manière droite
rigid: rigide, raide
rigidity: rigidité, raideur
rigidly: rigidement, de façon rigide, de manière rigide
rigorous: rigoureux, sévère
rigour: austérité, rigueur
ring: anneau, bague, sonner, tinter, cercle, couronne, rondelle, cerne, ring, cycle, son
riot: émeute, baroufle, bagarre
riotous: séditieux, tapageur
ripen: mûrir
ripened: mûrîmes, mûrit
ripening: mûrissant, maturation
ripple: ondulation, ride
rise: monter, surgir, lever, sursauter, se soulever, se lever, hausse, augmenter, hauteur, s'élever, élévation
rising: élévation, lever, levée
risk: risque, aléa, aventurer, oser, péril
risked: risqué
rite: rite
rival: rival, concurrent
rivalry: rivalité, concurrence, antagonisme binoculaire
river: fleuve, rivière, lézarde
rivulet: ruisselet
roach: gardon, rousse, dévers, cafard
roast: griller, rôtir, torréfier
rob: piller, ravir, voler, dévaliser
robbed: pilla, ravi, ravîmes, dévalisa
robber: voleur, ravisseur
robbing: pillant, ravissant, dévalisant
robe: robe, peignoir
robin: rouge-gorge
robust: robuste, vigoureux
rock: roche, bercer, balancer, roc, basculer
rocking: balancement, basculant
rogue: gredin, canaille, fripon, polisson, escroc
roll: rouleau, petit pain, enrouler, tableau, cylindre
rolled: roulé, enroula, laminé
rolling: roulage, cylindrage, laminage
romance: romance, fabuler
romantic: romantique

romp: batifoler, folâtrer
roof: toit, voûte
roofless: sans toit
rooftop: toit
rook: tour, corbeau freux, freux
roost: perchoir, se jucher
root: racine, enraciner, s'enraciner, radical, origine
rooted: enraciné, raciné
rootedly: de façon enracinée, de manière enracinée
rope: corde, la corde, filin
rosary: rosaire, roseraie, chapelet
rose: rose, rosace
rosebud: débutante
rosy: rosé, rose
rot: pourrir, se gâter, rouir à l'excès, se pourrir, carie, clavelée, gâter
rough: brut, grossier, rude, rugueux, cru, rustique, maussade, rêche, râpeux
roughly: de façon brute, de manière brute, rudement
roundabout: alentour, carrefour giratoire, détourné, manège, autour
rounded: arrondi
rounder: bouleuse
rounding: arrondi, prédéroulage, dégradation d'angle, copeau arrondi, croupponnage, débrutage, brochage
roundness: rondeur, arrondi
rouse: exciter, stimuler, irriter, inciter, agacer, hérisser, réveiller
roused: irritâtes, excitèrent, stimulâtes
rousing: stimulant, excitant, irritant
rout: fraiser, mettre en déroute, détourer, déroute, débâcle, creuser les blancs d'un cliché
routine: routine, habituel
rove: rôdes, rôdons, vagabonde, mèche, boudinons
roved: rôdâtes, rôdé, rôdèrent, vagabonda, boudina, rôdai
roving: mèche, boudinage, rôdant, vagabondant, roving, rôder, affinage des mèches, bambrochage, itinérant
row: rangée, ramer, file, tour, ligne
royal: royal, cacatois, bleu roi
royalty: royauté, règne
rub: frotter, récurer
rubbed: frotté
rubbing: frottement, ponçage du feuil, dépolissage, broyage de minerai, estampe
rude: grossier, impoli, mal élevé
rudely: de façon grossière, de manière grossière
rueful: triste

ruff: chevalier combattant, combattant varié, fraise
ruffian: apache, brute, voyou
ruffle: hérisser, troubler, rider, ébouriffer, ruche
rugged: robuste, raboteux, accidenté
ruin: ruine, abîmer, abaisser, ravager
ruined: ruiné, foutu
ruining: ruinant
rule: règle, gouverner, régner, règne, surveiller, tenue, commandement, filet, régler
ruled: hachuré
ruler: règle, dominateur, souverain
ruling: réglage, dominant, décision
rumour: renommée, réputation, rumeur
rumpus: chahut, bagarre, boucan
runner: coureur, patin
running: courant, marche, coulant, fonctionnement
rupee: roupie
rural: rural, rustique
ruse: ruse, stratagème
rush: ruée, jonc, se dépêcher, épreuve, congestion, afflux de sang, urgent, précipiter, hâte
rushed: précipité
rust: rouille, se rouiller
rustic: rustique, villageois, paysan, campagnard, champêtre
rustling: bruissement, froissement
rusty: rouillé, rubigineux
ruthless: impitoyable, cruel
ruthlessly: de façon impitoyable, de manière impitoyable, impitoyablement
sable: zibeline, martre
sackcloth: toile à sac, treillis
sacred: sacré, saint
sacrifice: sacrifier, offrir, faire offrande, consacrer, immoler
sacrificed: sacrifié
sacrilegious: sacrilège
sad: triste, affligé, peiné, maussade, désolé, sombre
saddle: selle, col, ensellement
sadly: tristement, de façon triste, de manière triste
safe: sûr, en sûreté, sans danger, sauf, à l'abri
safeguard: sauvegarde, garantie
safely: de façon sûre, de manière sûre
safety: sécurité, sûreté
sagacious: sensé, intelligent, raisonnable
sagacity: sagacité
sage: sauge, sensé, raisonnable
sail: voile, naviguer

sailed: navigué
sailor: marin, matelot, navigateur
saint: saint
sake: saké
salable: vendable
sale: vente, solde, abattement
salient: saillant
salon: salon
saloon: bar, berline
salutary: salutaire
salutation: salut
salvation: salut
sanctified: sanctifia
sanction: sanction
sanctioned: sanctionné
sanctity: sainteté
sanctum: sanctuaire
sand: sable, arène
sang: chanta
sanguinary: sanguinaire
sanguine: sanguin, optimiste
sap: sève, suc, jus
sarcasm: sarcasme
sardonic: sardonique
sat: couva, s'assirent, t'assis, vous assîtes, nous assîmes, m'assis, assis
sated: assouvîmes, repu, saturé
satiety: satiété
satin: satin, de satin
satire: satire
satisfaction: satisfaction, contentement
satisfactorily: de façon satisfaisante, de manière satisfaisante
satisfactory: satisfaisant
satisfied: satisfait, contentâtes, rassasié
satisfy: satisfaire, contenter
saturnine: saturnin
saunter: flâner, se balader
sauntered: flânas
sauntering: flânant
savage: sauvage, attaquer férocement, barbare, brutal, féroce
savageness: férocité, sauvagerie
save: épargner, sauver, économiser, enregistrer, préserver
saved: épargna, sauvé, économisâmes, enregistrèrent
saving: épargnant, sauvant, économisant, enregistrant
saying: disant, adage, proverbe
scaffold: échafaud
scalding: brûlant, échaudage, roussissement, ébouillantage, bouillant
scaling: mise à l'échelle, écaillage, escalade
scamp: bâcler, polisson, vaurien, galopin, garnement

scan: balayage, scanner, analyser, échographie
scandal: scandale, agacement
scandalized: scandalisèrent
scanty: insuffisant, chiche
scar: cicatrice, balafre
scarce: insuffisant, rare
scarcely: à peine, de façon rare, de manière rare
scared: effrayé
scarf: foulard, écharpe, fichu
scarlet: écarlate, rouge écarlate
scattered: dispersa, répandis, disséminé, éparpillèrent
scene: scène, lieu
scent: odeur, fumet, parfum, senteur
scented: parfumé
scepticism: scepticisme
sceptre: sceptre
schedule: calendrier, tableau, horaire, programme, annexe, barème, liste, plan, ordonnancer
scheme: schéma, projet, plan
schemed: comploté
schemer: intrigant
scheming: intrigant, magouille, comploter
scholar: savant, écolier, érudit
scholastic: scolastique
schoolboy: écolier, collégien, élève
schooling: scolarisation, rassemblement en bancs, instruction, dressage
schoolmaster: instituteur, maître
science: science
scientific: scientifique
scoff: sarcasme
scold: réprimander, gronder, sommer, admonester, reprocher, exhorter, sermonner
scolding: réprimande, grondeur
scope: portée, champ d'application, étendue, cadre, compétence
scorch: roussir, brûler
scorched: échaudé
score: orchestrer, note, rayure, partition, marque, score, adapter, cote
scorn: dédain, mépris
scorned: dédaigné
scornful: dédaigneux, méprisant
scoured: frotta, décapèrent
scourge: fléau, plaie, fouet
scrambling: embrouillage, brouillant
scrap: ferraille, chiffon, lambeau, déchets, fragment, mettre au rebut, rebut, débris
scrape: gratter, racler, effacer en grattant
scraping: raclage, grattage

scratch: gratter, égratignure, griffer, éraflure, rayure, écorchure, raie, effacer en grattant, accroc, strie
scream: crier, cri, clameur, hurler
screen: écran, trame, paravent, filtre, grillage, blindage, crible
screened: trié, triâmes, trièrent, blindé, tria, tramé, simili
screwed: vissé, soûl
scribbling: droussage, précardage
scrubbing: lavage, débourbage, récurage, purification, nettoyage, épuration, frottement
scrubby: broussailleux, rabougri
scruple: scrupule
scrupulous: scrupuleux, méticuleux
scrupulously: de manière scrupuleuse, de façon scrupuleuse
scuffle: bagarre, combat, bataille, baroud, rixe, se bagarrer
sculptor: sculpteur
sculpture: sculpture, statuaire
scum: écume, mousse
sea: mer, marin
seal: sceau, phoque, sceller, cachet, plomber, joint, obturer
sealed: scellé, étanche, hermétique, fermé
seam: couture, joint, veine, filon, couche, paille
search: recherche, perquisition, chercher, fouille
searched: cherché
searching: recherche, chercher, fouille
seared: saisîmes, endurcit, flétri, desséchas, brûlèrent
season: saison, assaisonner
seasoned: assaisonné, épicé
seat: siège, assiette, banquette, selle, place
seated: assis
seating: places assises, portée, appui, assise
seclusion: solitude
secondary: secondaire, accessoire, auxiliaire
secondly: deuxièmement, de manière seconde, de façon seconde
secrecy: secret, discrétion
secret: secret, arcane
secretary: secrétaire
secrete: sécréter
secreted: sécrétas
secretly: secrètement, de façon secrte, de manière secrète, en secret
sect: secte
sectarian: sectaire
secure: fixer, sûr, fixons, en sûreté, attacher, à l'abri, obtenir, assurer

secured: fixa, fixèrent, fixé, fixâtes
securing: fixant, arrimage
sedan: berline, sedan
seducer: séducteur
seduction: séduction
seductive: séduisant, aguichant
sedulous: assidu
sedulously: de façon assidue, de manière assidue
seed: semence, graine, pépin, germe, ensemencer
seeing: voyant, sciant
seek: chercher, railler, recherche
seeker: chercheur, tête chercheuse
seeking: cherchant, raillant
seem: sembler, paraître
seeming: semblant, paraissant
seemingly: apparemment, de manière paraissante, de façon paraissante
seize: saisir, agripper, s'emparer de, gripper, attraper
seized: saisîtes, agrippâmes
seizing: saisissant, grippage, agrippant
seizure: saisie, prise, capture, apoplexie, confiscation, attaque
seldom: rarement
select: sélectionner, choisir
selected: sélectionna, choisi
selection: sélection, choix
self: même, soi
selfish: égoïste
sell: vendre, brader, écouler
semblance: apparence, semblant
senate: sénat
senator: sénateur, père conscrit
send: envoyer, adresser, expédier
senior: aîné, premier, personne âgée, chevronné, aimé, père
sensation: sensation, sentiment
senseless: insensé, stupide, sans connaissance, déraisonnable
sensibility: sensibilité
sensible: raisonnable, sensé, prudent
sensitive: sensible, délicat
sensitively: de façon sensible, de manière sensible
sensitiveness: sensibilité, susceptibilité
sensual: sensuel, voluptueux
sensualist: voluptueux, sensualiste
sent: envoyai, adressâmes
sentence: phrase, condamner, peine, sentence, verdict
sentenced: condamné
sentiment: sentiment
sentimental: sentimental
separate: séparer, particulier, disperser, diviser, dissiper, trier, débiter, indépendant

sepulchre: sépulcre
seraphic: séraphique
sere: série
serene: serein, tranquille
serenely: de façon sereine, de manière sereine
series: série, suite, collection
serious: sérieux, grave, important, considérable, majeur
seriously: sérieusement, de manière sérieuse, gravement, de façon sérieuse
seriousness: sérieux, gravité
serpent: serpent
servant: serviteur, domestique
serve: servir, sers, desservir, être de service
served: servîmes, desservîmes
servile: aplaventriste, servile
setter: piqueteur, setter, sertisseur, incubateur, gravure de cambrage, support d'enfournement, passeur
setting: réglage, calage, sertissage, cadre
settle: régler, règlent, s'abaisser, coloniser
settled: réglé, sédimenté, déposé, tassé, vida, vidâmes, vidé, vidèrent, colonisa, domicilié, arrangé
settlement: règlement, colonie, liquidation, tassement, possession, accord, établissement, arrangement
settling: réglant, tassement, affaissement, règlement
seven: sept
sevenfold: septuple
severally: individuellement ad
severance: disjonction, rupture
severe: sévère, austère, grave, rigoureux, difficile, dur
severed: disjoignîmes, rompîtes, coupa
severity: sévérité, austérité, rigueur, gravité
sew: coudre, cousons
sex: sexe, bagatelle
shabby: mesquin, miteux, usé
shade: ombre, nuance, teinte
shaded: ombragé, nuancé, dégradé
shading: ombrage, tache
shadow: ombre, prendre en filature
shadowy: ombragé, vague, indistinct
shady: ombragé, louche, véreux
shaggy: poilu, velu, hirsute
shake: secouer, ébranler, agiter, bardeau
shaken: secoué, ébranlé
shaking: secouant, ébranlant
shallow: peu profond, superficiel

shame: honte, pouah, vergogne
shameful: honteux, scandaleux
shank: tige, jambe, jarret, hampe, queue
shape: forme, façonner, modeler, profil
shaped: façonné, profilé
shapeless: informe, difforme
shaping: façonnage, taille de formation, profilage, rabotage à l'étau limeur, toupillage, formage, déformation, forçage, galbage
share: action, part, prendre part, portion, ration, diviser, débiter, contingent
shared: partagé, commun
sharing: partageant
sharp: aigu, acéré, coupant, tranchant, précisément, piquant, perçant, dièse, rude, justement, à l'heure
sharpen: affiler, affûter, acérer, appointer, acères
sharper: tricheur, escroc
sharply: de façon aigue, de manière aigue, nettement, brusquement
sharpness: acuité, netteté, finesse
shattered: brisa, fracassa
shaved: rasé, rasai, rasâmes, rasèrent, écroûté
shaven: rasé
shear: tondre, découper, cisaillement, couper avec des ciseaux
shed: hangar, verser, abri, baraque, kiosque, échoppe, stand, remise, foule, cabane
shedding: perte, relargage, formation de la foule, chute, déchaussement, foulée
sheepish: penaud
sheet: feuille, drap, plaque, écoute, tôle
shelter: abri, refuge, s'abriter, garantir, gîte, se mettre à l'abri, se retrancher, héberger
sheltered: abrité, protégé
shelve: enterrer, garnissez, ajourner
shepherd: berger, pasteur, pâtre, soigner
shet: toit éboulé
shield: bouclier, blindage, enseigne, écran de protection, protection, écusson, écu
shift: décalage, équipe, poste, déplacer, changement
shifting: déplacement, ripage, désarrimage
shilling: schilling
shine: briller, luire, être lumineux, éclat, lustre, reluire

shiner: point lustré, particule de charge transparente après calandrage, fil brillant
ship: navire, bateau, expédier, vaisseau
shock: choc, choquer, secouer, heurter, moyette
shocked: choqué
shocking: choquant, affreux, bouleversant, révoltant
shoe: chaussure, soulier, sabot, ferrer
shook: secouas, ébranlâtes
shooting: tirant, tir, tournage, fusillade, chasse, prise de vues
shop: boutique, magasin, atelier
shore: rive, bord, côte, rivage, accore, étai, étançon, étayer
short: court, manquant, tube court, petite longueur, insuffisant, cycliste, brusquement, bref, culotte
shorten: raccourcir, abréger, écourter, réduire
shorter: plus court
shortly: prochainement, bientôt, de façon courte, de manière courte
shot: tirèrent, tiré, tirâtes, tiras, tir, coup, grenaille, piqûre, injection
shoulder: épaule, accotement
shout: cri, crier, pousser des cris
shouted: crié, criai, criâmes
shoving: bourrelet
showed: montrèrent, manifesta, marquèrent
shower: douche, averse, se doucher, gerbe, prendre une douche, ondée
showing: montrant, manifestant, marquant, affichant, exposition
shown: montré, manifesté, marqué
showy: voyant, frimeur, prétentieux, tapageur
shrank: rétrécies
shred: lambeau, déchiqueter
shrew: mégère, musaraigne
shrewd: sagace, avisé, perspicace
shrewdly: de manière sagace, de façon sagace
shrewdness: perspicacité, sagacité
shriek: crier, hurler, cri perçant
shrill: aigu, perçant, strident, criard
shrink: rétrécir, se ratatiner
shrinking: rétrécissant, perte de volume, décatissage, contraction, retrait
shrivelled: recroquevillé
shrouded: enveloppé
shrub: arbuste, arbrisseau
shrug: hausser les épaules
shrunk: rétréci, retrait
shudder: frisson, frémissement

shuffling: réarrangement, entrelacement
shun: fuir, évite, fuyons, fuis, fuient, fuyez
shunned: évitèrent, fui, fuîtes, fuit, fuis, fuirent, fuîmes
shut: fermer, arrêter
shutter: obturateur, volet
shy: timide, ombrageux
shyly: timidement
shyness: timidité, embarras, réserve, sauvagerie
sick: malade, malsain
sicken: écoeurer, donner mal au coeur, blasons, rendre malade, tomber malade
sickened: écoeura, blasèrent
sickle: faucille, serpe
sickly: maladif, malsain, écoeurant, de manière malade, de façon malade
sickness: maladie
sidelong: de côté, oblique
siding: bardage, revêtement, voie de garage, embranchement, délignement, parement
siege: siège
sifting: tamisant, criblage
sigh: soupir
sight: vue, spectacle, visée, apparence, mire, air, aspect, apercevoir, allure
sign: signe, augure, témoignage, panneau, preuve, enseigne, écriteau, indication
signal: signal, transmettre des signalisations, témoignage, lampe de signalisation, attaquer, indiquer, feu, cavalier
signature: signature, indicatif musical, qualité, cahier, griffe, empreinte digitale, réponse
signed: signé
significant: significatif, appréciable, important, considérable
significantly: de façon significative, de manière significative, significativement
silence: silence, repos
silent: silencieux
silently: silencieusement, de façon silencieuse, de manière silencieuse
silk: soie, soyeux
silken: soyeux, de soie
silly: idiot, stupide, bête
silver: argent, hareng argenté
silvery: argenté
similar: semblable, pareil, similaire, analogue
similarity: similarité, ressemblance
simple: simple, pur
simplicity: simplicité, naïveté

simply: simplement, de façon simple, de manière simple
simulate: simuler
simulated: simulèrent
simulation: simulation
simultaneously: de façon simultanée, de manière simultanée
sin: péché, commettre une faute
sincere: sincère, honnête
sincerely: sincèrement, de façon sincère, de manière sincère
sincerity: sincérité, bonne foi
sinew: tendon
sinewy: tendineux
sinful: coupable, honteux
sing: chanter
singer: chanteur
singing: chantant, amorçage
single: célibataire, unique, seul, simple, individuel
singling: démariage, pli cassé
singly: de façon célibataire, de manière célibataire
sings: chante
singular: singulier
singularly: de façon singulière, de manière singulière, singulièrement
sinister: sinistre
sink: évier, forer, couler, lavabo, sombrer, rencontrer, puits, enfoncer, toucher, collecteur
sinking: affaissement, naufrage
sinner: pécheur
sir: monsieur
sister: soeur, la soeur
sisterly: de soeur
sit: être assis, couver, asseoir, m'assieds, nous asseyons, s'asseyent, siéger, t'assieds, vous asseyez, siéger
site: site, emplacement, endroit, chantier
sitting: couvant, séance, s'asseyant, service, sédentaire
situation: situation, condition, position
sixteen: seize
skeleton: squelette, ossature, charpente
sketch: esquisse, croquis, ébauche
sketching: traçage, esquisser
skilful: habile
skill: habileté, compétence, adresse
skim: écrémer, écumer
skin: peau, dépouiller, pelage, fourrure, poil d'animal, revêtement, éplucher, écorcher
skip: saut, skip, capitaine, benne
skirt: jupe, embase de blindage
skull: crâne, tête de mort
sky: ciel, le ciel

skylight: lucarne, tabatière, lanterneau, lumière du ciel
slack: mou, lâche
slackened: largua, ralentîtes, affaiblirent, desserrèrent
slang: argot
slap: gifle, claque, tape
slaughter: abattre, massacre, carnage, tuerie
slave: esclave, asservir
slay: tuer, tuons, tuez, tues, tue, tuent, abattre, rectifier
sleek: lisse, onctueux, filandre, film d'huile, ligne de ferrasse
sleeking: lissage
sleep: sommeil, dormir, dors, pioncer
sleeper: dormeur, traverse
sleeping: dormant, pionçant, roupillant, endormi
sleepless: sans sommeil
sleeve: manche, douille, bague, chemise, gaine
slender: mince, svelte, maigre
slept: dormîmes, roupillé, pioncé
slew: tuâmes, tuèrent, tuâtes, tuas, tua, tuai
sliced: tranché, en tranches
slide: diapositive, glissière, coulisse, lame
slight: léger, affront, insignifiant
slightly: légèrement, de manière légère, de façon légère
slim: mince, amincir, amaigrir, maigrir
slimy: visqueux, limoneux, vaseux
sling: écharpe, fronde, élingue, bretelle
slipped: glissé
slipper: pantoufle, mule, chausson
slipshod: négligé
slope: pente, côte, talus, inclinaison, versant, déclivité
sloping: talutage, déclive, en pente, incliné
slovenly: négligé
slow: lent, ralentir, lourd
slowly: lentement, de façon lente, de manière lente, doucement
slumber: dormir, sommeil
sly: rusé, malin, astucieux, artificieux
smaller: plus petit
smallest: le plus petit
smart: rusé, intelligent, malin, astucieux, artificieux, roublard, dégourdi, habile
smarting: cuisant
smile: sourire
smiled: souri
smiling: souriant

smilingly: de façon souriante, de manière souriante
smite: frapper
smitten: frappé
smoke: fumée, fumer, fumons
smooth: lisse, uni, plat, polir, égaliser, douce
smoothed: bords lisses
smoother: lisseuse
smoothing: amortissement, ajustement, modulation
smoothly: de façon lisse, de manière lisse, facilement
smote: frappa
smudged: maculé
smug: suffisant
snake: serpent, traînée, casse en long, multicâble, sardine
snap: mousqueton, claquement
snapped: pressionné
snare: piège, collet
snarl: enchevêtrement, grondement
snatch: arraché en flexion, saisir, fragment, chercher à attraper
snatched: saisi
snatching: arrachement
sneer: ricaner, tourner en ridicule, remarque moqueuse
sneered: ricané
sniff: renifler, flairer, respirer
snow: neige, blanche
snowy: neigeux, de neige
snubbed: amarré sur bitte
snuff: tabac à priser, effleurer, moucher
snuffbox: tabatière
snug: confortable, douillet, ergot, oreille de châssis
soar: monter en flèche, faire du vol à voile
soaring: essor
sob: sanglot, pleurer
sobbing: sanglotant
sober: sobre, dessoûler, modéré, sérieux
sociable: sociable
sociably: de façon sociable, socialement, de manière sociable
sod: gazon, motte
sofa: canapé, sofa
soft: doux, mou, tendre, moelleux, sucré, gentil, suave
soften: adoucir, amollir, attendrir, ramollir, te ramollis, se ramollissent, vous ramollissez, me ramollis, nous ramollissons
softened: amollîmes, adoucit, attendrit, se ramollit, me ramollis, nous ramollîmes, vous ramollîtes, te ramollis
softening: ramollissement, adoucissement, amollissant, attendrissant, assouplissement, se ramollissant
softens: adoucit, amollit, attendrit, se ramollit
softer: plus doux
softly: doucement, de façon douce, de manière douce
softness: douceur, mollesse
soil: sol, terre, souiller, salir, barbouiller
soiled: sale, souillé, sali
sojourn: séjour
sold: vendirent, bradées
soldier: soldat, militaire
sole: sole, semelle, seul, plante, pur
solely: seulement, de façon sole, de manière sole, uniquement
solemn: solennel, sérieux, grave
solemnity: solennité
solemnly: solennellement, de façon solennelle, de manière solennelle
solicitude: sollicitude
solid: solide, massif
solidity: solidité, coefficient de plénitude
soliloquy: soliloque, monologue
solitary: solitaire, seul, pur
solitude: solitude
sombre: sombre
somebody: quelqu'un, un
somehow: d'une façon ou d'une autre, de façon ou d'autre
somewhat: une certaine quantité, quelque peu, un peu
somewhere: quelque part
son: fils, fiston, le fils
song: chanson
soon: bientôt, tout à l'heure
soot: suie
soothe: abattre, rassurer, calmer, apaiser
soothed: rassurèrent, calmé, abattis
soothing: calmant, lénitif, rassurant, abattant, apaisant
sophism: sophisme
sordid: sordide, vil
sorrow: abattement, chagrin
sorry: désolé, navré, pardon
sought: cherchâtes, raillèrent
soul: âme, soul
sound: son, sonner, résonner, bruit, sain, sonder, solide, vibration acoustique, détroit, oscillation acoustique
sounded: sonna
sounding: sondage, sonore
soundly: de façon sensée ad, judicieusement, solidement
sour: aigre, acide, acerbe, s'aigrir, maussade, s'acidifier
source: source, origine, fontaine

southern: austral, du sud, méridional
sovereign: souverain
sow: semer, truie, coche, ensemencer
sown: ensemencées, semé, emblavé
space: espace, écartement, case, blanc, interligne, place, repos, spatial
spacious: spacieux, ample, étendu, large
spaniel: épagneul
spare: épargner, économiser, être indulgent, rechange, pièce de rechange
spark: étincelle, jaillir, trottinette des neiges, flammèche, ligne de feu, lueur
sparkle: étincelle, éclat, scintiller, pétiller, briller
sparkled: brillâmes
sparkling: brillant, étincelant, mousseux, pétillant
sparrow: moineau, passereau
spasm: spasme
spasmodic: spasmodique
spat: naissain
spawned: pondîmes
speak: parler, dire, obtenir la parole
speaker: orateur, conférencier, locuteur, enceinte, intervenant
speaking: parlant
speaks: parle
spear: lance, javelot
specially: spécialement, particulièrement, surtout, de manière spéciale, de façon spéciale
specie: monnaie, numéraire
specimen: spécimen, échantillon
spectacle: spectacle
spectator: spectateur
spectre: spectre
speculate: spéculer, boursicoter
speculation: spéculation
speculative: spéculatif
speculator: spéculateur
speech: discours, parole, langage, allocution, élocution
speechless: muet, sans voix
speed: vitesse, rapidité, allure, hâte
speedily: de façon rapide, de manière rapide, rapidement
spell: épeler, sortilège, charme
spellbound: envoûté
spelled: épela
spend: dépenser, passer, donner
spending: dépensant, passant
spendthrift: dépensier, gaspilleur, prodigue
spent: dépensa, passas, épuisé
sphere: sphère, boule, réservoir sphérique, théorie de la sphère

sphinx: sphinx
spider: araignée, croisillon
spile: épite, fausset, goulotte, tuyau d'alimentation des sillons
spinning: filage, rotation, repoussage
spinster: célibataire, femme célibataire, vieille fille
spire: flèche, spire, aiguille
spirit: esprit, vigueur
spirited: vif, animé, fougueux
spiritual: spirituel, ecclésiastique, religieux
spite: rancune, dépit
spiteful: malveillant, méchant, rancunier
spitefully: de façon rancunière, de manière rancunière
splash: clapoter, éclabousser, barboter, gicler
splendid: splendide, magnifique
splendour: splendeur, éclat, magnificence, pompe
spoil: abîmer, gâcher, gâter, détériorer, déblais
spoiled: gâté, abîmé, défectueux, invalidé
spoiler: déporteur, spoiler, déflecteur
spoiling: gâterie, abîmant
spoilt: gâté
spoke: parlâmes, rayon
spoken: parlé
spoliation: pillage
sponged: épongé
sponsor: parrain, commanditaire, promoteur, sponsor, mécène
spontaneous: spontané
sport: sport
sporting: sportif
sportive: sportif, folâtre
spot: tache, endroit, place, point, salir, lieu, destination, spot, souiller, localité, message publicitaire
spotless: sans tache, immaculé, impeccable
spouse: époux, conjoint
spray: spray, pulvériser, embruns, atomiser, vaporisateur, arroser
spread: enduire, étaler, étendre, écart, dispersion, propagation, se propager, se répandre, tartiner, diffusion
spreading: diffusion, enduisage, épandage
spring: ressort, source, fontaine, sauter, émaner, mouillère, sortir de
springing: naissance, sautage par mines pochées, gauchissement, détente mécanique, compensation,
bondir, agrandissement par explosion du fond d'un trou de mine, retombée
sprinkling: aspersion, arrosage
spruce: épicéa, impeccable, sapin
spur: éperon, inciter, embase de poteau, ergot
spurious: faux, fallacieux, parasite, simulé
spy: espion, épier
spying: espionnage, épiant
squalid: misérable, sordide
square: carré, place, équerre, droit, rectangle, esplanade, case, square
squareness: perpendicularité, équerrage, forme carrée
squint: loucher, strabisme, angle de strabisme
squire: chaperonner, châtelain
stability: stabilité, constance, permanence d'une couleur, résistibilité
stable: écurie, stable, étable, ferme
stage: étape, stade, phase, scène, tenue, station, niveau, étage, gare, mettre en scène, théâtre
staggered: disposé en quinconce
staid: sérieux, sobre
stain: tache, salir, souiller, colorant, teinture
stained: taché, souillé
stair: marche, escalier
staircase: escalier, cage d'escalier
stake: pieu, poteau, échalas, jalon, piquet, perche
stalk: tige, queue, chaume, faire les cent pas, rafle, pédoncule
stalwart: vigoureux, fidèle
stammered: bégayé
stammering: bégaiement, balbutiement
stamp: timbre, estampiller, tampon, poinçon, cachet, empreinte, emboutir, marque
stamped: affranchi, timbré
stand: stand, être debout, kiosque, support, échoppe, se dresser, peuplement, socle, pied, sursauter, position
standing: debout, permanent
staple: agrafe, parenthèse, crampon, fibre, cavalier de jonction
star: étoile, vedette, star, astral
starch: amidon, fécule, empeser, empois
starched: amidonné
stare: dévisager, regarder fixement, fixer
starless: sans étoiles
starlit: étoilé
starry: étoilé

started: démarré, commencé
starting: démarrage, commencement, début
startle: effarouches, surprenons, alarment
startled: surprîtes, effarouché, effrayé, alarmai
startling: surprenant, alarmant, ébouriffant, effarouchant, effrayant
starve: affamer, mourir de faim
starved: affamèrent
starving: affamant
stately: imposant, majestueux
statement: déclaration, constatation, instruction, énoncé
statesman: homme d'Etat
statesmanship: habileté politique, sens politique
station: station, gare, poste
statistic: statistique, fonction des observations
statistical: statistique
statue: statue
stature: stature, taille
stay: séjour, rester, étai, hauban, demeurer
stayed: restâtes, séjourna, haubané
staying: restant, chaînage, entretoisement, étayage, haubanant, séjournant
steadfast: ferme, inébranlable, constant
steadfastly: de manière inébranlable, de façon inébranlable
steadied: assujetti
steadiest: le plus régulier
steadily: de façon régulire, de manière régulire
steadiness: fermeté, régularité, stabilité
steady: régulier, stable
steadying: assujettissant
steal: voler, dérober, dépouiller, subtiliser, d'acier
stealing: vol, volant, voler
stealth: furtif
stealthily: de manière furtive, furtivement, de façon furtive
stealthy: furtif
steam: vapeur, buée, étuver
steaming: vaporisage, étuvage, fumant, injection de vapeur, procédé d'étuvage, stérilisation à la vapeur sous pression, traitement à la vapeur, ébouillantage
steed: coursier
steel: acier, aciérer
steep: raide, escarpé, à pic, abrupt, tremper

steeped: trempai
steeplechase: steeple
stem: tige, tronc, queue, étrave, racine, fût, jambe, rafle, radical, pied
step: pas, marche, étape, gradin, faire les cent pas, échelon, palier
stepped: échelonné
stepping: gradins, modification d'instruction, exploitation en gradins renversés, étagement, bois de marche, avance d'un ou de plusieurs pas, recul d'un ou de plusieurs pas
sterling: de bon aloi, sterling, de confiance
stern: poupe, arrière, sévère
sternly: de manière poupe, sévèrement
sternness: sévérité
stethoscope: stéthoscope, lunette de visée
steward: intendant, commissaire, économe, steward
stiff: rigide, raide
stiffness: raideur, inflexibilité, froideur, fermeté
stifle: étouffer, grasset
stifling: étouffant, suffoquant
stile: échalier, montant
stillness: calme, tranquillité
stimulant: stimulant, remontant
sting: piquer, aiguillon, piqûre, dard
stinging: piquant, piqûre, cuisant
stipend: traitement, appointements, bourse
stir: remuer, battre, émouvoir, affecter, faire tournoyer, vigueur, agiter, bouger
stirred: remué
stirring: agitation, mise en suspension par agitation, brassage, guinandage, malaxage
stock: stock, réserve, souche, action
stocking: bas, stockage, chaussette
stoic: stoïque
stoicism: stoïcisme
stole: étole, vola
stolen: volé
stolid: flegmatique, impassible
stomach: estomac, ventre, digérer
stone: pierre, lapider, calcul, noyau, dénoyauter, de pierre, caillou
stool: tabouret, banquette, escabeau, selles
stoop: s'incliner, pencher
stooping: penché, perchage, mirage raccourcissant verticalement l'image, baisse, dépilage
stop: arrêter, cesser, stopper, halte, interrompre, s'arrêter, station, butée, gare, faire cesser, taquet
stopped: arrêtèrent, cessa, stoppâmes, interrompîmes, bouché
stopper: bouchon, stoppeur, obturateur, prise de courant mâle
stopping: arrêtant, cessant, interrompant, stoppant, plombage, obturation
store: magasin, boutique, stocker, entreposer, mémoire, emmagasiner, ôter, enlever, réserve, dépôt, conserver
stored: entreposé, stockées
storm: tempête, orage, donner l'assaut
stormy: orageux, tempétueux, démonté, houleux
story: histoire, étage, récit, conte, relation, intrigue
stout: corpulent, fort, gros, stout
stoutly: de manière corpulente, de façon corpulente
straight: droit, direct, franc, tout droit, rectiligne, honnête, ligne droite
straightforward: simple, pur, franc
strain: tension, souche, fatigue, effort, tendre
strained: tendu, contraint, forcé
straining: filtrage, sollicitation, tendre, tension, colature, cadrage, raffinage du mélange
strange: étrange, singulier, drôle, bizarre
strangely: étrangement, de façon étrange, de manière étrange
strangeness: étrangeté, bizarrerie
stranger: étranger, inconnu
strapped: fauché, sanglé, câblé
stratagem: stratagème, ruse
straw: paille, chalumeau, chaume
stray: errant, écartons, formation géologique imprévue, égarer, champ de dispersion, animal errant, s'égarer
strayed: écartai
streaked: bigarrés, taché d'auréole
stream: ruisseau, courant, jet, fleuve, rivière, flot
streaming: effet de canalisation, lecture en transit, courant, continu, fuite, coulant
street: rue, pavé
strength: force, puissance, résistance mécanique
strengthen: fortifier, renforcer, raffermir
strengthened: fortifièrent, renforcé
strengthens: fortifie, renforce, affermit
stretch: tendre, étendre, étirer, s'étendre, allongement
stretched: tendu
stretching: étirement, câble de tension, extension des coutures, cintrage à plat, allongement, élasticité conférée, croquage
stricken: accablé, affligé, blessé
strict: sévère, austère, strict, rigoureux
stride: pas, faire les cent pas, enjambée, foulée
strife: conflit
strike: grève, frapper, heurter, forer, toucher, s'allumer, battre, saisir, rencontrer, atteindre, parvenir
striking: frappant, saisissant, reprise, radiation, impressionnant, éclatant, coup de talon, battage, assénant, amorçage d'un arc, développement de la couleur
stringing: déroulage, enfilage, enguirlandage, rangée de cordes, tamis
strip: bande, se déshabiller, rayure, dépouiller, raie, feuillard, lame, déshabiller
strive: s'efforcer, combats, se battre
striving: combattant
stroke: caresser, coup, course, trait, rayure, apoplexie, raie
stroll: promenade, se promener, flâner, faire un tour
strong: fort, puissant, vigoureux, solide, robuste
strongly: fortement, de façon forte, de manière forte
strove: combattirent
struck: frappé, assénée, raclé, démontage
struggle: lutter, combat, se débattre, bataille, luter
struggled: lutté
struggling: luttant
strut: entretoise, étrésillon, jambe de force, étai, support
stubborn: têtu, obstiné, entêté, tenace
stuck: collé, être embourbé
stud: goujon, clou, poteau, crampon, tige, montant
studded: clouté, pointes de diamant
student: étudiant, élève
studied: étudié, délibéré
studio: studio, atelier
studious: studieux
studying: étude

stuff: substance, fourrer, rembourrer, choses, affaires, trucs, bourrer, empailler, farcir, remplir
stuffed: bourré, farci
stumbled: trébuché, bronchai
stumbling: trébuchant, faux pas, bronchant
stung: piqué
stunned: étourdîmes, abasourdîmes, assommé, abruti
stunted: rabougri
stupid: stupide, sot, idiot, bébête, bête, abruti
stupidity: stupidité, ânerie, bêtise, connerie
stupor: stupeur, état de stupeur
sturdily: de façon robuste, de manière robuste
sturdy: robuste, fort
sty: étable, écurie, orgelet
style: style, mode
subdivided: subdivisèrent
subdivision: subdivision, lotissement, compartimentage
subdued: soumîmes, subjugua
subject: sujet, thème, composition, objet
subjoin: adjoindre
subjugated: soumîtes
sublime: sublimer
submission: soumission, dépôt
submissive: soumis, docile
submit: soumettre, abdiquer, se soumettre
submitted: soumîmes
submitting: soumettant
subordinate: subordonné, inférieur, subalterne
subordination: subordination
subscribe: s'abonner, souscrire
subscribed: souscrivîtes, signâtes, s'abonné, t'abonnas, nous abonnâmes, m'abonnai, abonnèrent, vous abonnâtes
subscribing: souscrivant, signant, abonnant, s'abonnant
subsequent: subséquent, postérieur, suivant
subsided: nous affaissâmes, t'affaissas, vous affaissâtes, s'affaissèrent, m'affaissai
subsistence: subsistance
substance: substance, fond
substantiated: justifié, prouvâtes
substitute: substituer, remplacer, succédané, mettre en place de
substratum: substrat
subterfuge: artifice, subterfuge
subtle: subtil, fin
subtlety: subtilité
subtly: de manière subtile, subtilement, de façon subtile

suburb: banlieue, faubourg
suburban: suburbain, de banlieue
succeed: réussir, arriver, succéder, parvenir, abouter
succeeded: réussis, succédâmes, about a
succeeding: réussissant, succédant, aboutant
successful: réussi, prospère, couronné de succès
succession: succession
successively: de façon successive, de manière successive, successivement
successor: successeur, descendant
succumb: succomber
sudden: subit, soudain
suddenly: soudainement, tout à coup, subitement, de manière subite, brusquement, de façon subite
suddenness: soudaineté
suffer: souffrir, subir, endurer
sufferance: tolérance, attente
suffered: souffrit, subîtes, subi
sufferer: victime, malade
suffering: souffrant, subissant
suffers: souffre, subit
suffice: suffire
sufficed: suffîmes
sufficient: suffisant
sufficiently: suffisamment, assez, passablement, plutôt, de façon suffisante, de manière suffisante
sufficing: suffisant
suffocated: suffoqua, étouffèrent
suggest: suggérer, proposer, indiquer, désigner, inspirer
suggested: suggéras
suggesting: suggérant
suggestion: suggestion, proposition
suit: costume, complet, convenir, procès, couleur
suitable: convenable, approprié, propice, raisonnable
suitably: de façon convenable, de manière convenable
suite: suite, clique, cortège, escorte
suitor: prétendant, soupirant
sullen: maussade, sombre, boudeur, morne, renfrogné
sullenly: de façon maussade, de manière maussade
sully: souiller
sum: somme, montant, addition
summer: été, estival
summit: sommet, cime, faîte, pointe, comble, summon, bout, haut
summoned: convoqués, appelé

summons: sommation, citation, appel, assignation, intimation, convocation, commandement
sun: soleil, ensoleillé
sunbeam: rayon de soleil
sundry: divers
sung: chanté
sunk: enfoncés, sombré
sunlight: lumière du soleil
sunlit: ensoleillé
sunny: ensoleillé, exposé au soleil
sunset: coucher du soleil, de temporarisation
sunshine: soleil, lumière du soleil
sup: souper, super
superabundance: surabondance
superabundant: surabondant
superb: superbe, magnifique, grandiose
supercilious: dédaigneux, hautain
superficial: superficiel
superfluous: superflu
superhuman: surhumain
superintendence: surveillance, contrôle, direction, personnel chargé de la conduite des travaux
superior: supérieur, suprême, surplombant, dominant
superiority: supériorité
superlatively: de façon superlative, de manière superlative
supernatural: surnaturel
superscription: inscription, suscription
superstition: superstition
superstitious: superstitieux
supper: souper, dîner
supplanted: supplantâtes
supple: souple
supplied: fourni
supply: fourniture, provision, approvisionnement, ravitaillement, alimentation, livrer, munir, réserve, pourvoir, de manière souple, de façon souple
supported: soutenu, appuyé
suppose: supposer, croire
supposed: supposâmes, prétendu
supposing: supposant
supposition: hypothèse, supposition
suppress: étouffer, réprimer, suffoquer, supprimer
suppressed: étouffé, réprimâmes
suppressing: étouffant, réprimant, supprimant
suppression: répression, suppression
supreme: suprême, souverain
sure: sûr, certain, assuré
surely: sûrement, certes, si, d'abord, de façon sûre, de manière sûre

surface: surface, superficie, comble, faîte, summon, haut, sommet
surged: enflées
surgeon: chirurgien
surgical: chirurgical
surlily: de façon maussade, de manière maussade
surly: maussade, bourru
surmise: conjecturer, supposer, prévoir, se douter de
surmised: conjecturé
surmount: surmonter
surmounted: surmontai
surname: nom de famille, nom
surpassed: dépassas, surpassai, maîtrisas
surpassing: surpassant, dépassant, maîtrisant
surprise: surprendre
surprised: surpris, étonné
surprising: surprenant, étonnant
surprisingly: de façon surprenante, de manière surprenante, étonnamment
surrender: abandon, se rendre, reddition
surrendered: rendu
surround: entourer, encercler
surrounded: entoura, environnâtes
surrounding: entourant, environnant
survey: enquête, étude, levé, inspection, sondage, arpenter, campagne d'évaluation
surveyed: levé, examiné
surveyor: arpenteur, géomètre
survive: survivre, subsister
survived: survécûmes
survives: survit
surviving: survivant, dernier mourant, rescapé
survivor: survivant, rescapé
susceptibility: susceptibilité, recevabilité, prédisposition, sensibilité
susceptible: sensible, susceptible
suspect: suspecter, soupçonner, se méfier
suspected: soupçonné
suspecting: soupçonnant
suspend: suspendre
suspended: suspendu, en suspens, flottant
suspense: suspens, en souffrance
suspicion: soupçon, méfiance, suspicion
suspicious: méfiant, soupçonneux, sinistre, suspect
suspiciously: de manière méfiante, de façon méfiante
suspiciousness: caractère suspect

sustain: maintenir, appuyer, soutenir, accoter, vous accotez, m'accote, nous accotons, s'accotent, t'accotes
sustaining: maintenant, appuyant, s'accotant
swallow: hirondelle, avaler, aronde, engloutir, gorgée, gober, déglutir
swam: nagea, nagèrent
swan: cygne
swarm: grouiller, essaim, fourmiller
sway: vaciller, balancement, oscillation, se balancer
swaying: roulis, balancement, dandinement, déplacement latéral, oscillation
swear: jurer, jurons, blasphémer, prêter serment
sweep: balayer, courbure, draguer
sweeper: balayeuse, arrière latéral, bétonneur, libero, verrouilleur, analyseur panoramique
sweeping: balayage, large
sweet: sucré, doux, suave, bonbon, friandise, gentil, dessert
sweetheart: amoureux, trésor
sweetly: de façon douce, de manière douce, doucement
sweetness: douceur, gentillesse, sucrosité, teneur en sucre
swell: gonfler, houle, enfler, s'enfler, se gonfler, grossir
swept: balayé
swerve: écart, zigzaguer, embardée
swift: rapide, prompt, martinet
swim: nager, baignade
swimming: nageant, natation, baignade
swine: porc, cochon
swing: balançoire, brandir, agiter, osciller, marge de découvert réciproque
swinging: balancement, pivotant, oscillation
swollen: gonflé, enflé
swoon: s'évanouir, se pâmer, pâmoison, évanouissement
sword: épée, sabre, glaive
swore: jura, jurâtes, jurèrent
sworn: juré, assermenté
swung: pivotai, balancé
syllable: syllabe
symbol: symbole, attribut, emblème, signe
symmetrical: symétrique
symmetry: symétrie
sympathize: compatir, sympathisez
sympathized: compatis, sympathisa
sympathizing: compatissant, sympathisant

sympathy: sympathie, compassion
symptom: symptôme, signe fonctionnel
synonym: synonyme
synonymous: synonyme
syntax: syntaxe
tablet: comprimé, tableau, liste
tacit: tacite
tacitly: de façon tacite, de manière tacite, tacitement
tact: tact, mesure
tactic: tactique
tail: queue, talon, pointe, pivot, piste, pile, pan, orgette, naissance du pivot, la queue, fouet
taint: entacher, infection
tainted: corrompu, vicié, pollué, infecté, entachées, avarié, altéré
tale: conte, récit, relation
talent: talent, don, aptitude
talisman: amulette, talisman
talk: parler, causerie, discuter, entretien
talked: parlèrent, bavardas
talking: parlant, bavardage
tall: haut, grand
talon: talon, griffe, serre
tame: apprivoisé, dresser, dompter, docile
tamed: apprivoisé
tangled: embrouillé
tantrum: crise de colère, colère
tap: robinet, taraud, forer, prise, taper, toucher, rencontrer
taper: cône, effiler, dépouille, conicité
tapestry: tapisserie
tapped: entaillé, taraudé
tarry: goudronneux, demeures, restons, bitumeux, s'attarder
tarrying: restant, demeurant
task: tâche, devoir
tassel: gland, houppe
taste: goût, saveur, déguster
tasted: goûté
tasteless: insipide, sans saveur, de mauvais goût, fade
tattered: déguenillé, en lambeaux
taught: enseigna, instruisîtes
taunt: sarcasme, railler
taunting: raillant
tavern: taverne
tawdry: clinquant
tawny: fauve
taxed: taxé
tea: thé, infusion, tisane
teach: enseigner, instruire, apprendre
teacher: enseignant, instituteur, maître, professeur
teacup: tasse à thé
tear: larme, déchirer, pleur

tearful: éploré, larmoyant
technicality: subtilité, détail de procédure, point de détail, terme technique
tedious: ennuyeux, fastidieux
teeming: abondant, grouillant, coulée par le fond de la poche en lingotière
teen: adolescent
teeth: dents, maillons
temerity: témérité
temper: humeur, tremper, durcir, tempérament, gâcher
temperament: tempérament, nature
temperance: modération, tempérance
temperate: sobre, tempéré, modéré
temple: temple, branche
temporary: temporaire, provisoire, intérimaire
tempt: tenter, séduire
temptation: tentation, séduction
tempted: tentai
tempter: tentateur
tempting: tentant, attrayant, séduisant
temptingly: de façon tentante, de manière tentante
tempts: tente
tenant: locataire, preneur, fermier, habiter comme locataire
tender: offre, tendre, adjudication, doux, annexe, suave, proposition, présenter, soumission, sucré, gentil
tenderly: tendrement
tenderness: tendresse, sensibilité à la palpation, câlinerie, endolorissement
tending: soins culturaux, surveillant, soignant
tenet: principe, doctrine
tent: tente, mèche
terminate: terminer, finir, cesser, résilier
terminated: terminèrent, résilias
terminating: terminant, d'arrivée, aboutissant, résiliant
terrace: terrasse, maisons en bande, rangée de maisons, gradin
terrible: terrible, affreux
terribly: terriblement, de façon terrible, de manière terrible
terrier: registre foncier, terrier
terrified: terrifié
terror: terreur, effroi
test: essai, test, examen, épreuve, contrôle, critère, expérimenter, éprouver
testament: testament
testamentary: testamentaire
testator: testateur

text: texte
thank: remercier, merci
thanked: remerciâtes
thankful: reconnaissant
thankfulness: gratitude, reconnaissance
thanking: remerciant
thanks: remercie, merci
theatre: théâtre
theatrical: théâtral, commercial
theatrically: de façon théâtrale, de manière théâtrale
thee: te, toi, vous
theft: vol, chapardage
theirs: leur
theme: thème, sujet, composition
thence: de là
theology: théologie
theory: théorie
thereof: de cela
therewith: avec cela
thick: épais, dense, gros
thickened: grossi, épaissis
thicket: fourré, gaulis, bosquet
thief: voleur, filou, cambrioleur, larron, échantillonneur, cathode auxiliaire, chapardeur, écran voleur de courant
thieve: vole, volons
thigh: cuisse
thimble: dé à coudre, dé, cosse, tulipe, chaussette, doigt de gant
thin: mince, maigre, fin
thinker: penseur, théoricien
thinking: pensant, rationnel
thinner: diluant, dissolvant, éclaircisseuse, démarieuse
thinness: maigreur, minceur
thinning: éclaircissage, amincissement
thirdly: troisièmement, en troisième lieu, tertio
thirst: soif, avoir soif
thirsty: assoiffé, altéré
thither: là
thorn: épine
thoroughfare: voie de communication
thoroughly: de façon minutieuse, de manière minutieuse
thou: tu, toi, vous
thoughtful: réfléchi, pensif
thoughtfully: de façon réfléchie, de manière réfléchie
thoughtless: irréfléchi, étourdi, inconsidéré
thousand: mille
thread: fil, filet, enfiler
threadbare: usé, tissu trop découvert
threaded: enfilé, visser, fileté
threat: menace

threaten: menacer, gronder
threatened: menaçâtes
threatening: menaçant, sinistre
threatens: menace
threshold: seuil, valeur de seuil, limite de circulation
threw: jetèrent, jeta, jetâmes
thrice: trois fois
thrift: économie, armeria commune, épargne
thrifty: économe, épargnant
thrill: frémissement, frisson, tressaillement
thrive: prospérer, pousser, se développer
thrives: prospère
throat: gorge, la gorge, gosier
throne: trône
throng: affluer, cohue, foule, multitude, se presser
throttle: étrangler, accélérateur, manette des gaz, papillon des gaz
throw: jeter, jet, projeter, lancer, course
throwing: lancement, tournassage, abattage directionnel, balle accompagnée, jet, jetant, moulinage
thrown: jeté, faillé, rappel publicitaire
thrust: poussée, force de propulsion, chevauchement, botte, réaction de la planche, butée
thrusting: persuasion
thunder: tonnerre, retenir
thunderbolt: chute de la foudre
thwart: contrecarrer, banc de nage
thwarting: déjouant, frustration, contrecarrant
thy: ton
thyme: thym
ticket: billet, ticket, le billet
tide: marée
tidy: ranger, ordonner, régler, soigné
tie: cravate, attacher, lien, nouer, relier, lier, tirant, liaison, traverse
tier: plan, étage, gradin, rangée
tiger: tigre
tight: strict, serré, tendu, étanche, étroit
tightened: serra, resserrâmes
tightening: serrant, resserrant
tightly: de façon stricte, de manière stricte
tigress: tigresse
tile: carreau, tuile, mosaïque, dalle
till: caisse, jusqu'à ce que, à
timepiece: montre, pendule moyenne, appareil horaire
timid: timide, peureux, craintif
timidity: timidité

timidly: timidement, de façon timide, de manière timide
timorous: craintif, timoré
timorously: de façon timorée, de manière timorée
tin: étain, tôle, étamer
tinder: amadou
tinged: teinté
tinkling: tintement
tip: pourboire, bout, pointe, sommet, cime, tuyau, conseil
tired: fatigué, las
tissue: tissu, écran, mouchoir en papier, papier mousseline, serpente
tithe: dîme, décime
title: titre, intitulé
toast: toast, griller, rôtir, pain grillé
toe: orteil, doigt du pied, bout
toil: labeur, travailler dur
toilet: toilette, cabinet
toilsome: pénible
token: jeton, témoignage, signe, marque, preuve, gage
tolerable: supportable, tolérable, passable
tolerably: de manière tolérable, de façon tolérable
tolled: sonné
tomb: tombe
tomorrow: demain
tone: ton, tonalité, timbre, tonicité
tongue: langue, tenon, timon, plaque de blocage, parole, lame d'aiguillage, la langue, emboîtement mâle, doigt guide, travelling latéral, barre de traction
tonic: tonique, remontant, fortifiant
tool: outil, instrument, produit, ustensile
top: sommet, haut, faîte, mutiler, summon, comble, supérieur, cime, tête, toupie, couvercle
topic: sujet, thème, topique, actualité, composition
topography: topographie, topique
torch: torche, lampe de poche, flambeau
torn: déchiré, lacéré
torpor: torpeur
torso: torse
tortuous: tortueux
torture: torture, supplice
tortured: torturé
total: total, additionner
totter: titubes, vacillez, chanceler
tottered: vacillé, titubé, chancelèrent
tottering: chancelant, titubant, vacillant
touch: toucher, contact
touched: touché
touching: attendrissant, touchant, émouvant
touchingly: de façon attendrissante, de manière attendrissante
touchy: susceptible, délicat
tower: tour, pylône
towering: mirage allongeant verticalement l'image, très haut
town: ville, cité, localité
toy: jouet, joujou
trace: trace, décalquer, calquer, empreinte, impression, retracer, piste, trait
traceable: traçable
tracing: recherche, calquage, tracé
track: piste, voie, route, trace, empreinte, impression, chenille, chemin de roulement, rail
tracked: chenillé
tracking: poursuite, cheminement
trade: commerce, métier, faire du commerce, négoce
trader: commerçant, marchand
tradesman: marchand, commerçant
tragedy: tragédie
tragic: tragique, dramatique
trailed: traîné
train: train, entraîner, rame, dresser, cortège, suite, former, escorte, clique
trained: diplômé, dressé
training: formation, entraînement, instruction, dressage
trait: trait, caractère
traitor: traître, criminel d'État
tramp: clochard, tramp, vagabond
trampled: piétiné
tranquil: tranquille, calme, paisible
tranquillity: tranquillité
tranquilly: de façon tranquille, de manière tranquille
transfer: transfert, mutation, cession, virement, dépasser, remuer, report, muter, passer, mutons, décalquer
transferred: transféré, muta, mutâmes, muté, mutèrent
transferring: transférant, mutant
transform: transformer, résoudre
transformation: transformation, métamorphose
transfuses: transfuse
transition: transition, pente concave, passage, mutation, conduite de transition
transmit: transmettre, envoyer, adresser
transmitted: transmit, adressa
transom: traverse, tableau, imposte
transparent: transparent, limpide
transport: transporter, reporter

transportation: transport, moyen de transport
transported: transporté
trap: piège, trappe, piéger, siphon
travel: voyage, course, aller, se déplacer, déplacement
travelled: voyagé
traveller: voyageur, curseur
travelling: itinérant, voyageant
traversed: traversé
treacherous: traître, déloyal
treachery: traîtrise, déloyauté
tread: piétiner, fouler aux pieds, semelle, marcher sur, giron, bande de roulement, faire les cent pas, chape
treading: côchage, marcher, piétinage
treason: trahison, haute trahison
treasure: trésor, cassette
treasury: trésorerie, fisc, ministère du Revenu
treat: traiter, soigner, régaler, guérir
treatise: traité
treatment: traitement, cure, demande de règlement, plan général d'émission, scénario
tree: arbre, arborescence
treetop: cime d'un arbre
tremble: trembler, frémir
trembled: tremblé
trembling: tremblant, frémissant
tremblingly: de façon tremblante, de manière tremblante
tremendous: énorme, terrible, prodigieux, immense, formidable, épouvantable, fantastique
tremor: tremblement
tremulous: timide, tremblotant
tremulously: de façon tremblotante, de manière tremblotante
trial: jugement, essai, épreuve, procès, désolation
tribe: peuplade
tribute: tribut, hommage
trick: artifice, truc, mystifier, ruse, tour, astuce
tricky: difficile, délicat, rusé
tried: essayé, éprouvé
trifle: bagatelle, babiole
trim: garnir, tailler, rogner, égaliser, décorer, ébarber, assiette
trimmed: taillé, paré, rogné
trinket: colifichet, bibelot
tripod: trépied, tripode
trite: banal
triumph: triomphe
triumphant: triomphant
triumphantly: de manière triomphante, triomphalement, de façon triomphante

trivial: insignifiant, banal
troop: troupe, bande
trophy: trophée
trot: trotter, aller au trot
troth: foi
trouble: gêner, problème, dérangement, panne, difficulté, trouble, ennui
troubled: inquiet, gêné, préoccupé, gênai, agité, gênâmes
troublesome: gênant, pénible
truce: trêve
true: vrai, véritable, réel, exact, qui a raison, juste
truly: vraiment, en vérité, réellement, en fait, en réalité, véritablement
trumpet: trompette, barrir
truncheon: matraque, souchet
trunk: tronc, malle, coffre, trompe, torse, jonction, tambour, circuit
trust: confiance, fiducie, trust, foi, se fier, fidéicommis
trustee: fiduciaire, curateur, fidéicommissaire, dépositaire, consignataire, administrateur
trustful: confiant
trustfully: de façon confiante, de manière confiante
trustworthy: sûr, digne de confiance, fiable
trusty: sûr, loyal
truth: vérité, définition
truthful: véridique, honnête
truthfully: véridiquement, de façon véridique, de manière véridique
trying: essayant, fastidieux, pénible
tucking: charge, serrage aux doigts, accrochage, tassement, bourrage
tug: remorqueur, tirer
tumbler: culbuteur, verre
tumbril: tombereau
tuned: accordé
turbulent: turbulent, agité
turf: gazon, engazonner, pelouse, turf
turn: tourner, changer, retourner, renverser, dévier, virage, spire, serrer, rangée, file, faire tourner
turned: tournèrent, retournâmes, changeas, déviâmes
turning: tournant, changeant, retournant, déviant, virage, rotation
turnpike: autoroute à péage, route à péage, barrière de péage
turret: tourelle, barillet, rotateur
tutor: tuteur, précepteur
twelve: douze
twenty: vingt
twice: deux fois, bis

twilight: crépuscule, pénombre, aube, scotopique
twin: jumeau, macle, cristal jumeau, biface, chambre double à deux lits
twinge: élancement
twinkled: scintillas, clignoté
twist: tordre, torsion
twit: taquiner, idiot
type: type, taper, dactylographier, modèle, espèce, genre, caractère
tyrannical: tyrannique
tyrannized: tyrannisai
tyranny: tyrannie
tyrant: tyran
ugliest: le plus laid
ugliness: laideur
ugly: laid, vilain, moche, mauvais
ulterior: ultérieur
ultimate: ultime
ultimately: finalement, enfin, de façon ultime, de manière ultime
umbrella: parapluie, pébroc
unable: incapable
unaccustomed: inaccoutumé, inhabituel
unambitiously: de manière sans ambition
unassisted: sans aide
unassuming: prétention, sans prétention
unavailing: inutile, inefficace
unawares: à l'improviste
unbecoming: inconvenant
unbelieving: incrédule
unbidden: spontanément
unblemished: sans tache
unbroken: intact, non cassé
unbuttoning: déboutonnant
unceremonious: brusque, sans façon
uncertain: incertain, aléatoire, vague
unchanged: inchangé, intact, stationnaire
uncharitable: peu charitable
unchecked: incontrôlé, non vérifié
unchristian: peu chrétien
uncle: oncle
uncomely: laid
uncommon: rare
uncompleted: inachevé
unconfirmed: non confirmé
uncongenial: antipathique
uncongeniality: incongénialité
unconscious: inconscient, évanoui, sans connaissance
unconsciously: de façon inconsciente, de manière inconsciente, inconsciemment
uncontrolled: incontrôlé
uncouth: grossier

uncultivated: inculte
undecided: indécis, hésitant, incertain
undeclared: non déclaré
undefinable: indéfinissable
undefined: indéfini, non défini, vague
undeniably: de façon indéniable, de manière indéniable, indéniablement
undergone: subi
undermine: miner, minons, saper, sapons
understand: comprendre, entendre
understanding: comprenant, abord, relation, entendement
understood: compris, entendu
undertake: entreprendre, se démener
undertaken: entrepris
undertook: entreprîmes
underwent: subîtes, subit
undisputed: incontesté
undisturbed: paisible, non détériorée, calme
undivided: indivis, non divisé
undone: défait, annulé
undoubtedly: sans doute, indubitablement, de façon indubitable, de manière indubitable
undressed: déshabillé, dévêtîmes
undue: indu
undulating: ondulant, ondoyant
unearthly: surnaturel, sinistre
uneasily: de façon inquiète, de manière inquiète
uneasiness: inquiétude, malaise
uneasy: agité, gêné, inquiet
uneducated: inculte
unerring: infaillible, sûr
unexpected: inattendu, imprévu, inespéré
unexpectedly: de façon inattendue, de manière inattendue, inopinément
unfamiliar: inconnu, peu familier
unfavourable: défavorable, désavantageux
unfeeling: insensible
unfinished: inachevé, incomplet
unfit: inapte, impropre, incapable de combattre, indigne
unflinching: décidé
unfolding: dépliant
unforeseen: imprévu
unfrequented: peu fréquenté
ungainly: dégingandé, disgracieux, gauche
ungracious: incivil
ungrateful: ingrat, disgracieux

unhappily: de façon malheureuse, de manière malheureuse
unhappiness: tristesse, chagrin, malheur
unhappy: malheureux, mécontent
unheeded: ignoré, inaperçu, négligé
unheeding: insouciant
unholy: profane
unimportant: mineur, insignifiant, négligeable, sans importance
uninfluential: sans influence
union: union, syndicat, raccord
unison: unisson, harmonie
unit: unité, élément, bloc, groupe
unite: unir, unissez, joindre, accoupler, apparier, unifier
united: unit, unîtes, uni, unîmes, unirent, unis, appariâmes
unites: unit, apparie, englobe
uniting: unissant, appariant
universal: universel, large plat
universe: univers
unjust: injuste, prévaricateur
unjustified: injustifié
unjustly: de façon injuste, de manière injuste
unkind: maussade, méchant, peu aimable
unknown: inconnu, ignoré
unless: à moins que, sauf
unlike: à la différence de, différent, dissemblable
unlimited: illimité, indéfini, sans bornes
unlocked: ouvrit, ouvert
unluckily: de façon malchanceuse, de manière malchanceuse
unmanageable: indocile, intraitable
unmannerly: mal élevé
unmarried: célibataire, double bande
unmerited: immérité
unmistakable: indubitable
unmixed: pur, sans mélange
unmoved: indifférent, insensible
unnatural: anormal, contre nature
unnecessary: inutile
unnoticed: inaperçu
unobserved: inobservé
unperceived: inaperçu
unpopular: impopulaire
unprejudiced: impartial, sans préjugés
unprepared: improvisé, non préparé
unprotected: non protégé
unpublished: inédit
unquestionable: incontestable, indiscutable
unquestionably: de façon incontestable, de manière incontestable
unquiet: inquiet
unreserved: non réservé
unrivalled: sans égal
unromantic: peu romantique
unsatisfactory: insatisfaisant, peu satisfaisant
unsatisfying: insuffisant
unscathed: indemne
unscrupulous: sans scrupules
unscrupulously: de manière sans scrupules, de façon sans scrupules
unseemly: inconvenant, malséant
unseen: inaperçu, invisible
unselfish: désintéressé, généreux
unselfishness: générosité, désintéressement
unsettle: perturbe
unsettled: perturbé, incertain, variable, instable
unsettling: perturbant
unshaken: inébranlable
unshaven: non rasé
unskilled: inexpérimenté, non qualifié
unsocial: antisocial
unsold: invendu
unsound: véreux, hasardeux, précaire, tiqueur
unsparing: prodigue, généreux
unspeakable: indicible, indescriptible, innommable
unstable: instable, incertain
unstained: sans tache
unsteady: instable, chancelant, inconstant
unsullied: sans tache
unsupported: boisage, non soutenu, sans support
unsuspected: insoupçonné
unthinkingly: de façon irréfléchie, de manière irréfléchie
untitled: sans titre
untold: jamais dévoilé
untouched: intact
untutored: non formé, peu instruit
unused: inutilisé, neuf
unusual: inhabituel, insolite
unusually: de manière inhabituelle, exceptionnellement, de façon inhabituelle
unutterable: inexprimable
unutterably: de manière inexprimable, de façon inexprimable
unwelcome: importun, fâcheux
unwell: indisposé, malade, souffrant
unwholesome: malsain, nocif, pernicieux
unwilling: peu disposé, rétif
unwittingly: involontairement, de façon involontaire, de manière involontaire
unwomanly: peu féminin
unwonted: insolite
unworthily: de manière indigne, de façon indigne
unworthy: indigne
unwritten: non écrit, verbal
upbraid: morigénez, réprimandons
upbraiding: morigénant, réprimandant
upheld: soutînmes
uphold: soutenir, maintenir
upper: supérieur, empeigne
uppermost: le plus haut, suprême, en dessus
upright: montant, droit, honnête, intègre, vertical, debout
uprightness: intégrité
uproarious: hilarant
upset: renverser, stupéfait, vexé, bouleverser
upsetting: bouleversant, déranger, forgeage par refoulement, matage, refoulage, vexant, aplatissement
upstart: parvenu, bascule, arriviste
upward: ascendant, vers le haut
urchin: galopin, gamin, hérisson, oursin, polisson
urge: inciter, presser, être urgent, exhorter, pousser
urged: exhorté
urgency: urgence, instance, vive sollicitation, impulsion
urgent: urgent, pressant, impérieux
urn: urne
usage: usage, coutume, utilisation
useful: utile, pratique
usher: placeur, huissier, portier
usual: habituel, ordinaire, général, usuel, accoutumé, courant
usually: ordinairement, habituellement, d'habitude, généralement, de façon habituelle, normalement, de manière habituelle
usurer: usurier
usurpation: usurpation
usurped: usurpèrent
utility: utilité, service public
utmost: extrême, le plus éloigné, maximum
utter: répandre, émettre, proférer, prononcer
utterance: expression, déclaration
uttering: prononcer
utterly: complètement, de façon répandre, de manière répandre, totalement
vacancy: vacance, poste vacant

vacant: vide, vague, vacant
vacantly: de façon vide, de manière vide
vagabond: vagabond, clochard, chemineau
vagary: caprice
vagrant: vagabond, clochard, chemineau
vague: vague, imprécis, flou
vaguely: vaguement, de manière vague, de façon vague
vain: vain, vaniteux, abortif, frivole
vainly: de manière vaniteuse, vainement, de façon vaniteuse
valet: valet
valetudinarian: valétudinaire
valid: valable, valide
valour: valeur, vaillance, courage
value: valeur, apprécier, mérite, évaluer
valued: estimé, précieux
vane: ailette, girouette, pale, aube, déflecteur de volet
vanish: disparaître
vanished: disparu
vanishes: disparaît
vanity: vanité, futilité
vanquish: vaincre
vanquished: vainquîtes
vantage: avantage
variance: variance, désaccord
variation: variation, déclinaison, fluctuation
varied: variâmes, divers
variety: variété, diversité
various: divers, varié, différents
varnished: verni
varying: variant, changeant
vassal: vassal
vast: étendu, large, vaste, ample
vault: voûte, chambre forte
vegetable: légume, végétal
vehemence: véhémence, ardeur
vehement: véhément, violent, passionné
vehemently: de façon véhémente, de manière véhémente
vehicle: véhicule, voiture, bagnole
veil: voile, dissimuler
veiled: voilé, caché
vein: veine, filon, nervure
velvet: velours, oodiniase, de velours, profit facile
venal: vénal
venerable: vénérable
vengeance: revanche, vengeance
vengeful: vindicatif
venial: véniel
venison: venaison, viande de cerf, cerf
venom: venin

vent: évent, conduit, décharger, cheminée
ventilator: aérateur, ventilateur
venture: risquer, aventurer, oser, entreprise, hasarder
ventured: osé
verdict: verdict, sentence, jugement
verge: accotement, bord
veriest: le plus très
verily: en vérité, vraiment
vermin: vermine, animaux nuisibles, ravageurs
versatility: versatilité, polyvalence
verse: vers, strophe
versed: versé
verve: brio, verve
vessel: navire, vaisseau, bateau, vase, pot, récipient, bac, baquet
vest: gilet, maillot de corps
vested: investi
vex: chagriner, vexer, vexons
vexing: chagrinant, vexant
vibrated: vibrèrent, trépidâmes
vicar: curé, pasteur
vicarage: presbytère
vice: vice, étau, vertu
vicinity: voisinage, environs, proximité
vicious: méchant, vicieux, perfide, malin
victim: victime
victorious: victorieux, vainqueur
victual: approvisionne
vigil: veille, vigile
vigilance: vigilance, état de veille
vigilant: vigilant, diligent
vigilantly: de façon vigilante, de manière vigilante
vigorous: vigoureux, énergique
vigorously: vigoureusement, de façon vigoureuse, de manière vigoureuse
vigour: force, vigueur, activité, énergie
vile: vil, abject, lâche, infâme
villa: villa, pavillon
village: village, localité
villager: villageois
vindicate: justifier, défendre
vindicating: justifiant
vindication: justification, revendication, défense
vindictive: vindicatif
vindictively: de façon vindicative, de manière vindicative
vine: vigne, plante grimpante
violated: violé, enfreignîtes, attentèrent
violates: viole, attente, enfreint
violation: violation, infraction
violence: violence
violent: violent, brutal

violently: violemment, de façon violente, de manière violente
violet: violet
viper: vipère, couleuvre
virgin: vierge, virginal
virtually: pratiquement, de façon virtuelle, de manière virtuelle
virtue: vertu
virtuous: vertueux
visage: visage
visible: visible, apparent, manifeste
visibly: visiblement, de façon visible, de manière visible
vision: vision, vue
visionary: visionnaire
visit: visite, aller voir
visited: visita
visiting: visitant
visitor: visiteur
vista: perspective, point de vue, vue
vital: vital
vitality: vitalité, force vitale
vitally: de façon vitale, de manière vitale
vivacity: vivacité, verve
vivid: vif, éclatant
vividly: de façon vive, de manière vive
vivify: vivifier
vocal: vocal
vocation: vocation
void: vide, manque, pore, interstice
volcano: volcan, artifice pour l'imitation des éruptions volcaniques
volume: volume, tome
voluntary: volontaire, bénévole
voluptuous: voluptueux, sensuel
vortex: tourbillon, vortex
vow: voeu, vouer, serment
voyage: voyage
vulgar: vulgaire, trivial
vulgarity: vulgarité
vulgarly: de façon vulgaire, de manière vulgaire, vulgairement
vulture: vautour
vying: rivalisant
wade: marcher dans l'eau, patauger
waft: bouffée
wag: remuer, farceur
wage: salaire, appointements, gaine, paie
wagon: chariot, wagon
wail: se lamenter, gémir
waist: taille, corset
waistcoat: gilet
wait: attendre, servir
waited: attendîtes
waiter: garçon, serveur
waiting: attendant, arrêt

wake: sillage, réveiller, se réveiller, s'éveiller, se lever
wakeful: éveillé
wakened: réveillèrent
waking: rester éveillé, réveiller
walk: marcher, promenade, se promener, démarche
walked: marcha, promena, déambula
walker: marcheur, promeneur, déambulateur
walking: marchant, promenade
wall: mur, paroi, cloison, muraille
wand: baguette, badine
wander: errer, errons, vaguer, rôder, voyager au loin, dérapage, vagabonder
wandered: errâmes, errèrent, erré, erras, vagué
wanderer: vagabond
wandering: errant, vaguant, vagabond, nomade
wanting: voulant, désirant
wanton: dévergondé, impudique, licencieux
wantonly: de façon dévergondée, de manière dévergondée
warble: gazouiller, bosse de varron, chanter, hululement, modulation de fréquence, varron
ward: quartier, salle, pupille, service
warden: directeur, gardien
wardrobe: penderie, armoire
ware: articles, marchandise
warm: chaud, cordial, chaleureux
warmed: bassinâmes, chauffâmes
warmer: plus chaud
warming: chauffant, bassinant, échauffement, réchauffant
warmly: chaudement, de façon chaude, de manière chaude
warmth: chaleur, cordialité
warn: avertir, alerter
warned: avertîmes, alertâmes
warning: avertissement, sommation, recommandation, alerte, avis
warrant: garantir, cautionner, assurer, mandat, warrant, bon de souscription
warranted: garanti, justifié
warrior: guerrier, militaire
wary: prudent
wash: laver, lavons, lavage, blanchissage
washy: délavé
waste: gaspiller, déchets, dissiper, perte, rebut, gâcher, prodiguer, déperdition
wasted: gaspilla, prodiguèrent, gâché

wasting: gaspillant, prodiguant, gâchant
watch: montre, regarder, horloge, veiller, être spectateur de, surveiller, pendule, garde, voir, observer, guetter
watchful: vigilant, attentif
watching: regarder
waterfall: cascade, chute d'eau
wave: onde, vague, brandir, agiter, onduler, lame
waved: ondulé
wayward: rebelle, rétif
weak: faible, mou, lâche, débile
weaken: affaiblir, atténuer, abattre, s'affaiblir
weakened: affaiblîmes, faiblîmes, fragilisé, amaigrîtes
weakness: faiblesse, débilité, impuissance, mollesse
wealth: richesse, fortune
wealthy: riche
weapon: arme
wear: usure, porter, avoir, user
wearily: de manière lasse, de façon lasse
weariness: fatigue, lassitude
weary: fatigué, las
weather: temps, doubler au vent, météo
weave: tisser, tramer, armure
weaving: tissage, entrecroisement
web: toile, web, âme
wed: marier, me marie, vous mariez, te maries, se marient, nous marions
wedded: se maria, vous mariâtes, te marias, nous mariâmes, me mariai, marié
wedge: cale, coin, clavette
wedlock: mariage
wee: faire pipi, tout petit
weed: sarcler, mauvaise herbe, désherber
weekly: hebdomadaire, chaque semaine
weep: pleurer, sourdons, suinter, larmoyez
weeping: pleurant, sourdant, larmoyant
weigh: peser, pèses, pesons
weighed: pesèrent, pesa, pesâmes, pesé
weight: pesanteur, masse, balance, charge, coefficient de pondération, graisse
weighty: important, lourd
welcome: bienvenue, accueillir, recevoir solennellement
welcomed: accueillis
welcoming: accueillant, hospitalier

wept: pleurâtes, sourdis, larmoyèrent
west: ouest, occident, à l'ouest, vers l'ouest
western: occidental, western
westward: vers l'ouest
wet: mouillé, humide
whatever: quoi que, n'importe quel, quel que, tout ce que
wheel: roue, volant, galet
wheeled: mobile, roues, sur roues, à roues
whelp: petit, savon de grande longueur, chienner, couteau pour voûte de four
whence: d'où
whenever: chaque fois que, toutes les fois que
whereas: tandis que, attendu que, durant, lors, pendant, alors que
wherefore: pourquoi
whereupon: après quoi, sur quoi
wherever: partout où, là où
whet: aiguiser, affûter, stimuler
whichever: celui que, n'importe quel
whim: caprice, lubie, manège à chevaux
whine: plainte, geindre, sifflement, se lamenter, gémissons, crie, geignez, crions
whining: criant, geignant, gémissant
whip: fouet, flageller, battre, faire tournoyer, cravache
whirl: faire tournoyer, tourbillon, battre
whirlpool: tourbillon, marmite, récepteur de moût tangentiel
whiskey: whisky
whisper: chuchoter, murmurer
whispered: chuchoté
whispering: chuchotement, murmure
whistled: sifflé
whistling: sifflement
whitened: blanchîmes
whiteness: blancheur, pâleur
whitewashed: blanchi, badigeonnèrent
whither: où
wholesome: sain, salubre
wholly: complètement, entièrement, totalement, tout
whom: qui, lequel, auquel, que
whoop: chant du coq, cri, reprise
whose: dont, de qui, duquel
wicked: mauvais, méchant
wickedness: méchanceté, atrocité, cruauté
wide: large, ample, étendu, vaste, grand

widow: veuve
widowhood: veuvage, viduité
width: largeur, ampleur, mesure de largeur
wielded: mania
wife: femme, épouse
wild: sauvage, effréné, fin de saison, frimé, irrégulier, violent
wilderness: désert, zone de nature protégée
wildly: de façon sauvage, de manière sauvage
wile: ruse
wilful: obstiné, têtu, entêté, délibéré, opiniâtre
wilfully: de façon obstinée, de manière obstinée
willing: volontaire, disposé, prêt
willingly: volontiers, de manière volontaire, de façon volontaire
willow: saule
wily: rusé, malin
win: gagner, remporter
wind: vent, enrouler, emmailloter, bobiner
winding: bobinage, enroulement, sinueux
window: fenêtre, guichet, hublot, créneau, la fenêtre
wine: vin, rouge vin
wing: aile, voilure
winging: arrimage en abord
wink: clin d'oeil, clignement, faire un clin d'oeil
winning: gagnant, remportant
winter: hiver
wipe: essuyer, effacer
wiped: essuyé, torchas
wiper: balai, frotteur
wiping: essuyant, torchant
wire: fil, câbler, toile, fil de fer, brin
wiry: raide, nerveux, tordu, vigoureux
wisdom: sagesse, intelligence
wise: sensé, raisonnable
wisely: sagement, de manière sensée, de façon sensée
wish: souhait, désir, vouloir, volonté, gré
wished: désira, souhaité
wishing: désirant
wistfully: de façon mélancolique, de manière mélancolique
wit: esprit, intelligence
witch: sorcière
withdraw: retirer, décéder, prélever
withdrawing: retirant
withdrawn: retiré
withdrew: retiras
wither: se faner, dessécher
withered: flétri, fané
withering: flétrissure, fanaison, desséchant
withheld: retint, retîntes, retenu
withholding: retenant, rétention, refus
witness: témoin, assister, être présent
witnessed: témoignai
witnesses: témoigne
wizard: sorcier, assistant, magicien, enchanteur
woe: hélas, aïe, malheur
wolf: loup, le loup, quinte du loup
won: gagnèrent, remportèrent
wonder: s'étonner, merveille, miracle, se demander
wondered: demandé
wonderful: merveilleux, formidable
wonderfully: merveilleusement, de façon merveilleuse, de manière merveilleuse
wondrous: merveilleux, étonnant
wont: coutume, accoutumé, habitude
wonted: habituel, accoutumé
woo: faire la cour, courtisez
wood: bois, au bois
woodland: bois, forêt claire, pays boisé, région boisée, terrain boisé, zone boisée
woodwork: menuiserie, boiseries
wooed: courtisâmes
wooer: prétendant
woof: trame, aboiement, aboyer, retraité bien nanti
wooing: courtisant
word: mot, parole, promesse
wordless: muet
workhouse: asile de pauvres
workman: ouvrier, homme d'équipe
worldly: mondain, terrestre
worm: ver, vis sans fin
worn: usé, porté, usagé
worse: pire, plus mauvais
worship: adorer, vénération
worshipper: adorateur
worst: pire, le plus mauvais
worth: valeur, mérite
worthily: de façon digne, de manière digne, dignement
worthless: nul, sans valeur
worthy: digne
wound: blessure, plaie
wounded: blessé
wounding: blessant
woven: tissé
wrap: envelopper, emballer
wrapped: enrobé
wrapping: emballage, encartage de deux cahiers, banderolage, mise en forme, enveloppement, enrobage, ruban de placage pour mise en forme, capage, cellophanage
wrath: colère, courroux
wreathed: tressai, tissé, nattâtes
wreck: épave, naufrage, accident, détruire
wrecked: démoli, naufragé
wrest: arrache
wrested: arrachâtes
wrestle: lutter, catcher, se débattre
wrestler: lutteur, catcheur
wrestling: lutte, catch
wretch: malheureux, scélérat
wretched: misérable, pauvre, pitoyable, infortuné, malheureux
wretchedness: misère
wring: tordre, essorez
wringing: tordant, torsion, essorant
wrinkle: ride, sillon, pli, plisser
wrinkled: ridé, moiré
wrist: poignet, tourillon, carpe, axe de piston
write: écrire, composer, rédiger
writer: auteur, écrivain, rédacteur
writhe: se débattre, se tordre
writhing: contorsions
writing: écrivant, inscription
writing-desk: secrétaire, commode à tablette pour écrire
writing-room: salon de correspondance
written: écrit, noté
wrong: faux, tort, abusif, incorrect, erroné, injustice, mal
wrote: écrivîmes, notâmes, notèrent, notas
wrought: forgé, travaillé
wrung: tordu, essoré
yard: cour, yard, chantier, dépôt, parc, vergue
yawn: bâillement
yawning: bâillement, béant
yearn: soupirer, aspirer, languir
yearned: soupiré, languîtes
yearning: soupirant, désir ardent, languissant
yell: clamer, hurler
yellow: jaune, froussard
yellowing: jaunissement
yellowish: jaunâtre
yeoman: secrétaire militaire
yesterday: hier
yield: rendement, céder, cédons, cèdes, abandonner, produire, reculer, abdiquer, récolte, rapporter, mise au mille
yielded: cédai, cédèrent, cédé, cédâtes

yielding: cédant, rendant, rapportant, produire, élastique, complaisant, coulissant
yon: y, là
yonder: là, y
yore: jadis
younger: plus jeune, puîné
youngest: le plus jeune
yours: vôtre, tien, votre, vous
yourself: vous
youth: jeunesse, ado
youthful: jeune, juvénile
youthfulness: fraîcheur, jeunesse, juvénilité
zeal: zèle, ferveur
zealot: fanatique, zélote
zealous: fervent, zélé
zero: zéro, division de calage, nul, mettre à zéro
zest: zeste, vigueur, enthousiasme

Printed in Great Britain
by Amazon